CLIO AWARDS

THE 43RD ANNUAL AWARDS COMPETITION

GLOUCESTER MASSACHUSETTS

ROCKPORT PUBLISHERS

CONTENTS

INTRODUCTION

Clio is proud to present the winners of its 2002 worldwide competition.

Clio is the largest and most celebrated festival of its kind. For forty-three years, we have sought to attract the best work from agencies and production houses all over the world. We have then submitted that work to a jury of leading professionals, who have distinguished themselves in their fields, who represent the very best of craft, and who take the responsibility of judging very seriously.

Clio does not instruct the jury, other than to encourage it to award ideas rather than mere execution. Clio supports an honest, democratic, and nonpolitical system of judging. Each piece is judged on its own merits. First, the jury votes a short list of the best work. From those finalists, the jury then determines which pieces, if any, are worthy of a statue. We present three statue levels: gold, silver, and bronze. And occasionally, the judges honor particularly outstanding work with a Grand Clio, our best of show.

To look at a Clio reel or to visit a Clio gallery is to see some of the world's most powerful ads. The winner's reel is sent to our representatives in thirty-nine countries—and those representatives seek to screen the reel for interested groups. Part of our effort is to acknowledge greatness, part to instruct students of the craft, and part to celebrate one of the most interesting and influential art forms in modern culture.

CHAIRMEN'S STATEMENTS

TELEVISION & RADIO CHAIRMAN

Awards serve a purpose. They separate the great work from the mediocre; the original from the copy; the brave from the meek. It's like the Olympics, where we find out who is the fastest, the strongest. Awards are a benchmark for the advertising industry, and the Clio is a benchmark for the awards industry. By being really tough to win, Clio spotlights and acknowledges only those that really make our profession something bigger than the simple business of selling ads.

MARCELLO SERPA
Executive Creative Director
AlmapBBDO
São Paulo, Brazil

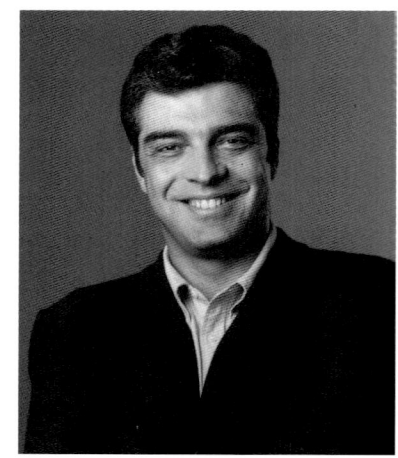

PRINT & POSTER CHAIRMAN

I love print because there is no place to hide—it is an utterly ruthless medium. If your idea isn't compelling, no amount of money or executional trickery is going to cover that up. Nothing is easier than to turn the page. From an award show judge's perspective, print is a level playing field in which small agencies and big agencies, modest clients and rich clients, start from the same place.

STEVE SIMPSON
Partner/Creative Director
Goodby, Silverstein & Partners
San Francisco, California

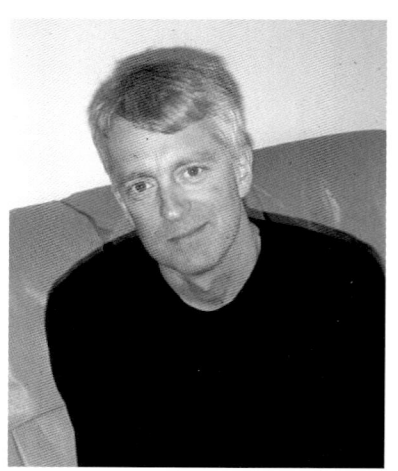

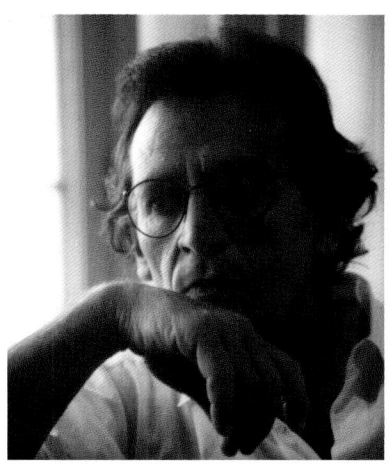

TECHNIQUE CHAIRMAN

The fact that competition brings together a body of work that will in-spire is, in itself, an inspiration—one that consistently rejuvenates and reinvents advertising.

LESLIE DEKTOR
Director
Dektor Film
Hollywood, California

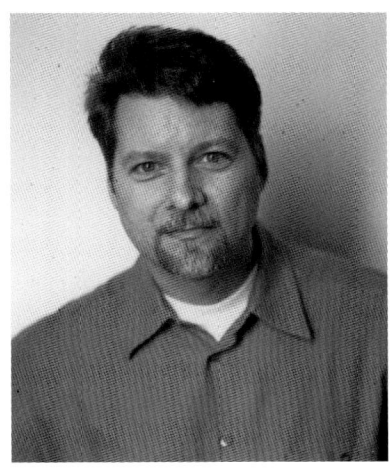

INTERNET CHAIRMAN

In the most brutal of economic climates, in the most challenging of years, we actually saw some of the most groundbreaking work. Though interactive has been through an absurdly dramatic ride on the pendulum of prominence, great interactive ideas still managed to be born. The work recognized in this year's Clios elevates the creative bar and signals that interactive will indeed survive. Darwin would be proud.

MATT FREEMAN
Chief Executive Officer, North America
Tribal DDB Worldwide
New York, New York

DESIGN CHAIRMAN

As design and its influence continue to grow, savvy marketers have seized the opportunity to apply the practice of design to overall busi-ness strategies and deep into all levels of corporate communications. As chair for this year's show, I am happy to help promote the finest work being done today. The winning work serves as even more evidence of what great design can do. Clio is known and respected around the world and brings a wider exposure than many awards shows. It provides an opportunity not only to showcase the best work to a world of savvy marketers, but it may also help persuade those less-than-savvy marketing types to get with it.

STEVE SANDSTROM
Creative Director
Steve Sandstrom Design
Portland, Oregon

2002 CLIO JURIES

EXECUTIVE JURY

TELEVISION & RADIO

CHAIRMAN

MARCELLO SERPA
Executive Creative Director
AlmapBBDO
São Paulo, Brazil

PIERRE BERVILLE
President
Callegari Berville Grey
Paris, France

ERIK HEISHOLT
Executive Creative Director
Leo Burnett
Oslo, Norway

THAM KHAI MENG
Regional Creative Director
Ogilvy & Mather Singapore
Singapore

ELSIE NANJI
Executive Creative Director
Ambience D'Arcy
Bombay, India

MARTIN PROSS
Executive Creative Director
Scholtz & Friends Berlin
Berlin, Germany

JOSE MARIA PUJOL
Creative/Founder
The Farm
Madrid, Spain

ANDREAS PUTZ
CEO/Creative Director
Jung von Matt/Donau Werbeagentur
GmbH
Vienna, Austria

RODRIGO FIGUEROA REYES
President/Executive Creative Director
DDB Argentina
Buenos Aires, Argentina

ED ROBINSON
Creative Group Head
Saatchi & Saatchi
London, England

SUMIKO SATO
Creative Director
Wieden & Kennedy
Tokyo, Japan

ERIC SILVER
Executive Creative Director
Cliff Freeman and Partners
New York, New York

MARTIN SPILLMAN
Executive Creative Director
Advico Young & Rubicam
Zurich-Gockhausen, Switzerland

JACK VAUGHAN
Principal Creative
The Principals
Sydney, Australia

PRINT & POSTER

CHAIRMAN

STEVE SIMPSON
Partner/Creative Director
Goodby, Silverstein & Partners
San Francisco, California

NICK BELL
Creative Director
Leo Burnett
London, England

PEDRO BIDARRA
Chief Creative Officer
BBDO Portugal—Agencia de
Publicidade, S.A.
Lisbon, Portugal

MICHAEL BOYCHUK
Associate Creative Director
WONGDOODY
Seattle, Washington

LAM KWEI CHEE
Executive Creative Director
Saatchi & Saatchi China
Beijing, China

MARK FISHER
Group Creative Director
Ogilvy & Mather, Rightford
Searle-tripp & Makin
Cape Town, South Africa

DAVID GUERRERO
Chairman/Executive Creative Director
BBDO/Guerrero Ortega
Manila, Philippines

ANTONIO HIDALGO
Vice President/Creative Services Director
Leo Burnett Mexico
Mexico City, Mexico

DAMIAN KEPEL
General Creative Director
Young & Rubicam
Buenos Aires, Argentina

DELLE KRAUSE
Executive Creative Director
Ogilvy & Mather
Frankfurt, Germany

JANET LYONS
Executive Vice President/
Senior Creative Director
BBDO New York
New York, New York

ANNA MARIA MONTEFUSCO
Creative Director
Inadv
Milan, Italy

EHR RAY
Creative Director
DM9 DDB
São Paulo, Brazil

JENEAL ROHRBACK
Creative Director
DDB NZ Ltd.
Auckland, New Zealand

TECHNIQUE JURY

CHAIRMAN

LESLIE DEKTOR
Director
Dektor Film
Hollywood, California

ANIMATION

SEAN BROUGHTON
Creative Director/Lead Flame Artist
Smoke & Mirrors
London, England

PIERRE BUFFIN
President
Buf Compagnie
Paris, France

NOEL CASTLEY-WRIGHT
Supervisor of Visual Effects Online
Company 3
Santa Monica, California

DENIS GAUTHIER
Senior CGI Artist
A52
Santa Monica, California

BOB KURTZ
Director
Kurtz & Friends
Burbank, California

JOHNNIE SEMERAD
President
Quite Man
New York, New York

ED ULBRICH
Senior VP Commercials
Digital Domain
Venice, California

STEPHEN VENNING
3D Operations Manager
The Mill
London, England

DIRECTION

FREDRIK BOND
Director
Harry Nash
London, England

LESLIE DEKTOR
Director
Dektor Film
Hollywood, California

KIM GELDENHUYS
Director
Egg
Cape Town, South Africa

LUDOVICK HOUPLAIN
Director
Partizan Midi Minuit
Paris, France

MAT HUMPHREY
Director
Film Graphics
Sydney, Australia

LOUIS NG
Director
Film Factory
Hong Kong, China

JOHN O'HAGAN
Director
Hungry Man
New York, New York

ERIC SAARINEN
Director/Cameraman/Partner
Plum Productions
Santa Monica, California

JAKE SCOTT
Director
RSA Films/Black Dog Films
London, England

FLORIA SIGISMONDI
Director
The Partners Film Company
Toronto, Canada

PETER SMILLIE
Director
Smillie Films
Venice, California

JEFF STARK
Director
Stark Films
London, England

EDITING

BOB CARR
Editor
Red Car
Chicago, Illinois

JOHNNY CHAN
Editor
Touches
Tokyo, Japan

ROGER HARRISON
President
Exit
Venice, California

RUSSELL ICKE
Editor/Partner
The Whitehouse
London, England

JJ LASK
Editor/Partner
P.S. 260
New York, New York

LIN POLITO
Film Editor
Version2
New York, New York

BOB SPECTOR
Editor
Bob 'n Sheila's Edit World
San Francisco, California

DREW THOMPSON
Senior Editor
Guillotine
Redfern, Australia

PAUL WATTS
Managing Director
The Quarry
London, England

MUSIC & SOUND DESIGN

JAVIER BLANCO
President/Composer
Taurus
Caracas, Venezuela

RICKY HO
Director/Composer
Yellow Box Studios
Singapore

REN KLYCE
Sound Designer
Mit Out Sound
Sausalito, California

ANDY MILBURN
President
tomandandy
New York, New York

JAMES O'BRIEN
President/Composer
Element
Santa Monica, California

SMITH&ELMS
Composers
Amber Music
London, England

CHRIS TAIT
Producer
Pirate Radio & Television
Toronto, Canada

WALTER WERZOWA
Owner/Composer
Musikvergnuegen
Hollywood, California

INTERNET ADVERTISING JURY

CHAIRMAN
MATT FREEMAN
Chief Executive Officer, North America
Tribal DDB Worldwide
New York, New York

MACH AROM
Creative Director
OgilvyInteractive
New York, New York

JONN BEHRMAN
President/Chief Operating Officer
Beyond Interactive
Ann Arbor, Michigan

DANIEL BONNER
Creative Director
AKQA
London, England

TANIA BREBERINA
Creative Director
Photomation Design & Communication
Richmond, Australia

MARTIN CEDERGREN
Art & Creative Director
Xnet.se Network
Stockholm, Sweden

BENJY CHOO
Creative Director
Kinetic Interactive
Singapore

YURI DOKTER
Managing Director
Pulse Interactive
Amsterdam, Netherlands

KATE EVERETT-THORP
President/Chief Executive Officer
Lot21
San Francisco, California

LEE FELDMAN
Chief Creative Officer
Blast Radius
Vancouver, Canada

GODEFROY JORDAN
Chief Executive Officer
B2L/BBDO
Issy Les Moulineaux, France

NICK KRULL
New Media Designer
OgilvyInteractive
Cape Town, South Africa

JOE McCAMBLEY
Chief Creative Officer
Digitas
Boston, Massachusetts

SVEN MENTEL
Creative Director
Elephant Seven
Hamburg, Germany

JOSH MUTCHNICK
Founder/Chief Creative Officer
DNA Studio
Beverly Hills, California

JONATHAN NELSON
Chief Executive Officer/Founder
Organic
San Francisco, California

TOM NICHOLSON
Chief Creative Officer/
Managing Director
Icon-Nicholson
New York, New York

ANTHONY PAPPAS
Vice President
Dimension Data
Reston, Virginia

PJ PEREIRA
Creative Director
AgenciaClick
São Paulo, Brazil

ITI SAKHARET
Creative Director
Deepend
New York, New York

FREDERIC SANZ
Creative Director
DoubleYou
Barcelona, Spain

CHRISTIAN SCHWARM
Creative Director
DORTEN GmbH
Stuttgart, Germany

RICK SHAUGHNESSY
Managing Partner, User Experience
Scient
Chicago, Illinois

MICHAEL VOLKMER
Managing Director/Creative Director
Scholz & Volkmer
Wiesbaden, Germany

MIKE YAPP
Creative Director
Freestyle Interactive
San Francisco, California

DESIGN JURY

CHAIRMAN
STEVE SANDSTROM
Creative Director
Steve Sandstrom Design
Portland, Oregon

STAN CHURCH
President/Executive Creative Director
Wallace Church Design
New York, New York

NIN GLAISTER
Creative Director
The Way Group
New York, New York

GARRICK HAMM
Creative Director
Williams Murray Hamm
London, England

DITI KATONA
Creative Director
Concrete Design
Toronto, Canada

KAT MCCORD
Creative Director
Citigate Corporate Branding
New York, New York

NEIL POWELL
President
Powell Design
New York, New York

BEST OF SHOW

THE 2002 CLIO JURIES AWARDED
GRAND CLIO STATUES TO WORK
IN INNOVATIVE MEDIA,
INTERNET ADVERTISING,
PRINT, AND RADIO.

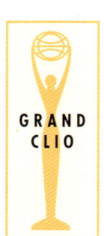

GRAND CLIO

CATEGORY
Campaign

ADVERTISER/PRODUCT
BMW of North America

TITLE
Ambush

TITLE
Star

TITLE
Powder Keg

TITLE
The Follow

TITLE
The Hire

ADVERTISING AGENCY
Fallon, Minneapolis

ACCOUNT EXECUTIVE
Ginny Grossman

CREATIVE DIRECTOR
David Lubars, Bruce Bildsten

COPYWRITER
Andrew Kevin Walker, Joe Sweet,
Wong Kar Wei, Guy Ritchie,
Alejandro Gonzalez Iñarritu,
David Carter, Guillermo Arriaga

ART DIRECTOR
David Carter, Martin Whis,
Joe Sweet, Tom Riddle

PRODUCTION COMPANY
Anonymous Content, Los Angeles

EDITING COMPANY
Spot Welders, Los Angeles; Jettone,
Hong Kong; Nomad Editing,
Santa Monica; Z Films, Mexico City

MUSIC COMPANY
Hi-Fi Productions, New York;
Universal Music Mexico,
Mexico City

SOUND DESIGN COMPANY
Mit Out Sound, Sausalito; Nomad
Editing, Santa Monica; Z Films,
Mexico City

SOUND DESIGNER
Ren Klyce

PRODUCER
Robyn Boardman, Aristides McGarry,
Rob Van de Weteringe Buys,
Tapas Blank

DIRECTOR
John Frankenheimer,
Wong Kar Wei, Guy Ritchie,
Alejandro Gonzalez Iñarritu

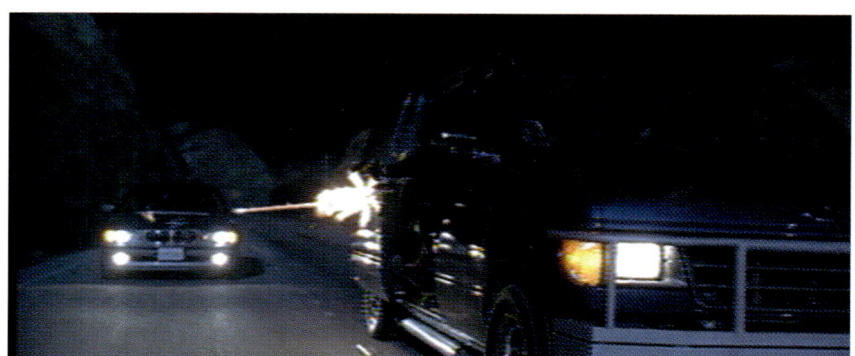

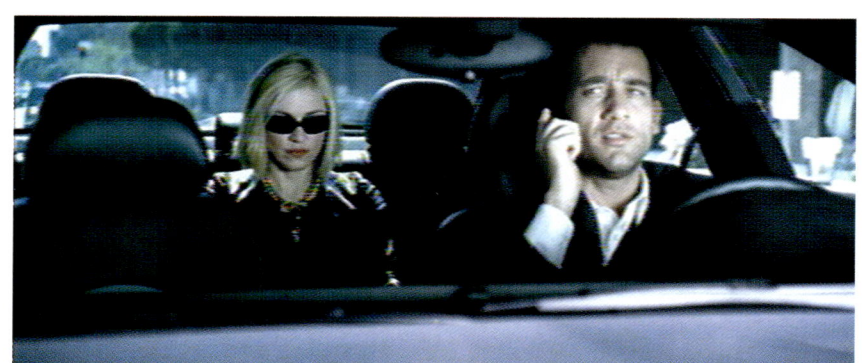

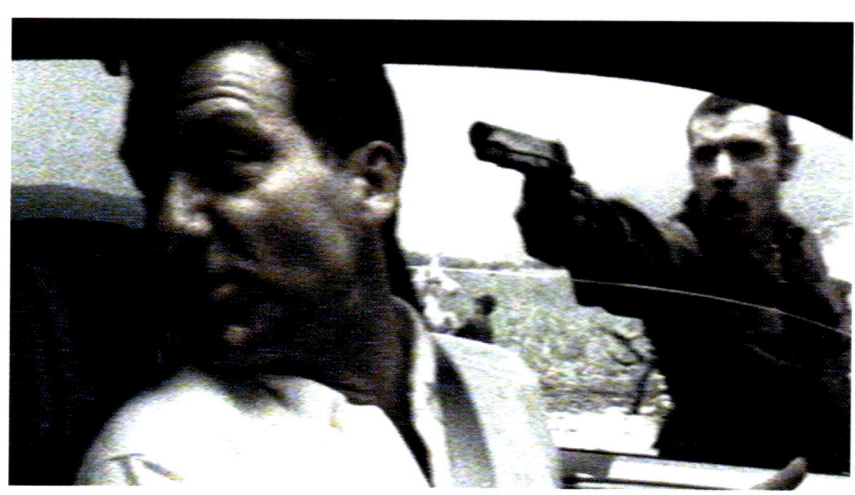

It began as an advertising brief, but advertising wasn't the answer. Traditional commercials could not impart what BMWs could really do, plus BMW customers increasingly were not watching television. They had, however, embraced the Internet in astounding numbers. The new idea was to create something so entertaining and so rewarding that people would actually seek it out. The question then became: Why not create an interactive experience more akin to home theater? What resulted

was BMW Films, a series of shorts directed by and starring A-list cinema talent. Each film revolved around a central character called The Driver, the world's best when it came to transporting people out of dangerous situations. The Driver's character traits—youthfulness, integrity, passion, willingness to take risks—reflected on both the brand and the audience. Each film featured The Driver using a BMW to complete his missions, showcasing BMW's true performance.

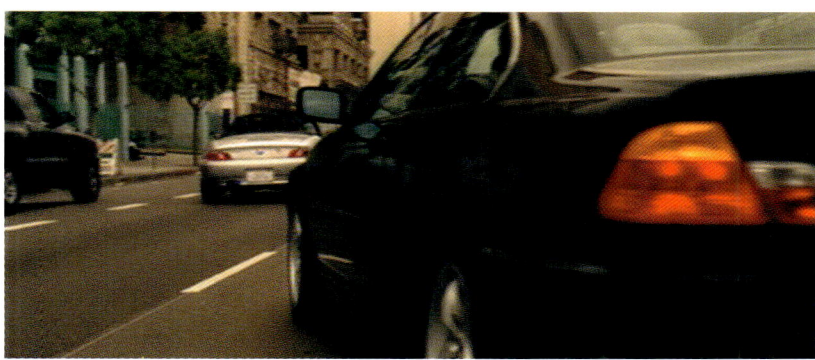

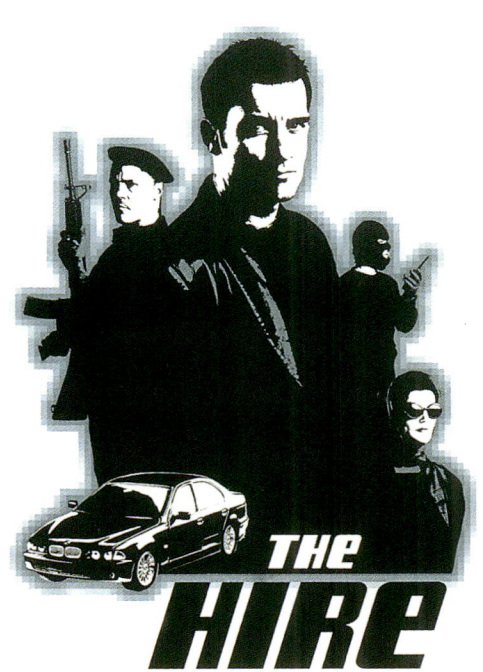

THE HIRE

'AMBUSH' DIRECTED BY JOHN FRANKENHEIMER / 'CHOSEN' DIRECTED BY ANG LEE / 'THE FOLLOW' DIRECTED BY WONG KAR-WAI
'STAR' DIRECTED BY GUY RITCHIE / 'POWDER KEG' DIRECTED BY ALEJANDRO GONZALEZ IÑARRITU
FROM BMW OF NORTH AMERICA IN ASSOCIATION WITH ANONYMOUS CONTENT AND EXECUTIVE PRODUCER DAVID FINCHER

A series of short films. Only at bmwfilms.com

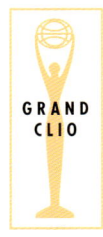

CATEGORY Campaign	**TITLE** Neck	**ADVERTISING AGENCY** BMP DDB, London	**PHOTOGRAPHER** Ben Stockley
ADVERTISER/PRODUCT Harvey Nichols Winter Sale	**TITLE** Stomach	**COPYWRITER** Adam Tucker	**TYPOGRAPHER** Kevin Clarke
	TITLE Shin	**ART DIRECTOR** Justin Tindall	

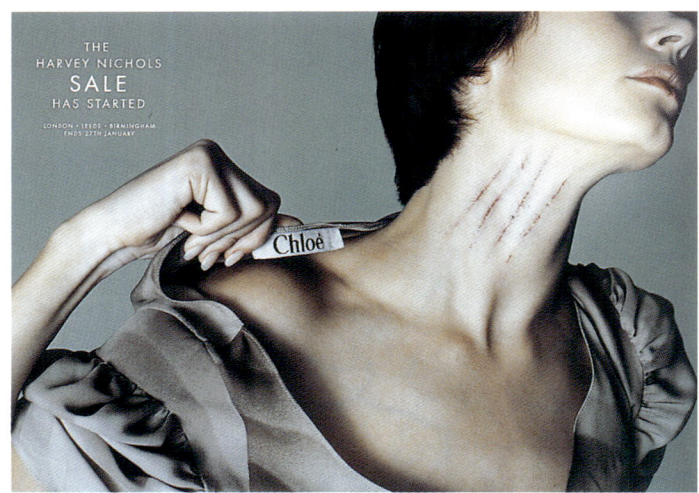

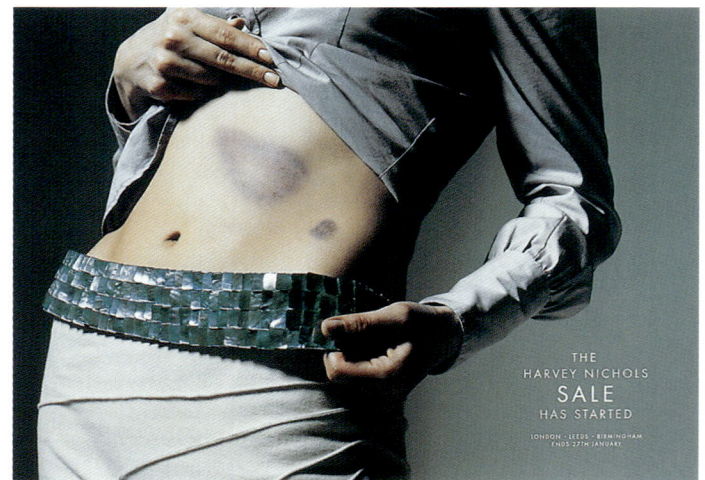

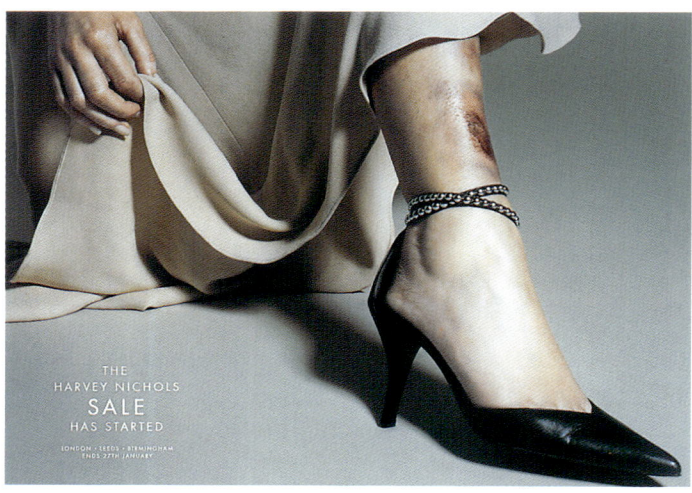

CATEGORY
Campaign

ADVERTISER/PRODUCT
Anheuser-Busch Inc./Bud Light

TITLE
Mr. Supermarket Free Sample Guy

TITLE
Mr. Horse-Drawn Carriage Driver

TITLE
Mr. Camouflage Suit Maker

ADVERTISING AGENCY
DDB, Chicago

PRODUCTION COMPANY
Chicago Recording Company,
Chicago

MUSIC COMPANY
Scandal Music, Chicago

GROUP CREATIVE DIRECTOR
John Immesoete

CREATIVE DIRECTOR
Bill Cimino, Mark Gross

COPYWRITER
John Immesoete

ADDITIONAL WRITING
Bill Cimino, Mark Gross,
Barry Burdiak, Bob Winter,
Pat Burke, Kitty Schulz

PRODUCER
Sam Pillsbury

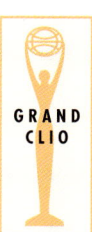

GRAND
CLIO

VO: Bud Light Presents…Real Men of Genius.

SINGER: *Real Men of Genius.*

VO: Today we salute you…Mr. Supermarket Free Sample Guy.

SINGER: *Mr. Supermarket Free Sample Guy!*

VO: Though man dreads few things more than a trip to the super-market, you offer us hope and sometimes a free mini-weenie.

SINGER: *Love that freebie weenie!*

VO: What exactly do you have? Aerosol cheese products, deep-fried morsels? Who cares? If it's on a toothpick and it's free, it could be plutonium and we'd eat it!

SINGER: *It's all good, baby!*

VO: For a guy wearing oven mitts and an apron, you're alright.

SINGER: *You're a star.*

VO: So crack open an ice cold Bud Light, titan of the toothpick.

SFX: Bottle cap opening.

VO: Because you put the free in freedom.

SINGER: *Let it be free…*

VO: Bud Light beer. Anheuser-Busch. St. Louis, Missouri.

VO: Bud Light Presents…Real. American. Heroes.

SINGER: *Real American Heroes.*

VO: Today we salute you…Mr. Camouflage Suit Maker.

SINGER: *Mr. Camouflage Suit Maker!*

VO: Your amazing skills of deception can trick a deer into thinking we're just a tree out for a walk, or a shrub having a cup of coffee.

SINGER: *Shrub having coffee!*

VO: Tirelessly you perfect your artistry. The squiggly black line. The blob. The slightly larger blob. All in spectacular shades of…green.

SINGER: *Green, green, green!*

VO: Thanks to you we look fabulous in or out of the forest—with a suit that can be easily accessorized with face paint and a few twigs.

SINGER: *Dressed to kill.*

VO: So crack open an ice cold Bud Light, Mr. Camouflage Suit Maker.

SFX: Bottle cap opening.

VO: Because when it comes to blending in, you really stand out.

SINGER: *Mr. Camouflage Suit Makerrrrrr.*

VO: Bud Light beer. Anheuser-Busch. St. Louis, Missouri.

VO: Bud Light Presents…Real Men of Genius.

SINGER: *Real Men of Genius.*

VO: Today we salute you…Mr. Horse-Drawn Carriage Driver.

SINGER: *Mr. Horse-Drawn Carriage Driver!*

VO: You start your day with a tip, tip!, and a cheerio!, which is odd because you're from Brooklyn.

SINGER: *Jolly Old Brooklyn!*

VO: While most people sit behind a desk, you proudly sit 2 feet behind a four-legged manure factory.

SINGER: *Oooh!*

VO: No one knows the guts it takes to ride the subway to work dressed as a foppish dandy from the eighteenth century.

SINGER: *Hey foppish dandy!*

VO: Blaring horns, profanity, vicious insults all met with a courtly tip of your stovepipe hat.

SINGER: *Cheerio!*

VO: So crack open an ice cold Bud Light, Buggy Boy.

SFX: Bottle cap opening.

VO: Because the way you say "giddy-up" makes us say "whoa."

SINGER: *Whoa! Whoa! Whoa!*

VO: Bud Light beer. Anheuser-Busch. St. Louis, Missouri.

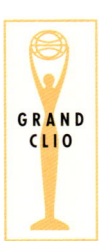

CATEGORY
Consumer-Targeted Site

ADVERTISER/PRODUCT
BMW Films

NAME OF SITE
BMW Films Campaign

ADVERTISING AGENCY
Fallon, Minneapolis

ACCOUNT EXECUTIVE
Ginny Grossman, Cori vanBrunt,
Marit Iverson, Lisa Lavigne,
Bryan Chang

CREATIVE DIRECTOR
David Lubars, Bruce Bildsten

COPYWRITER
Andrew Kevin Walker, Joe Sweet,
Wong Kar Wei, Guy Ritchie,
Alejandro Gonzalez Iñarritu,
David Carter, Guillermo Arriaga

ART DIRECTOR
David Carter, Martin Whis,
Joe Sweet, Tom Riddle

PRODUCTION COMPANY
Anonymous Content, Los Angeles

EDITING COMPANY
Spot Welders, Los Angeles;
Jettone, Hong Kong;
Nomad Editing, Santa Monica;
Z Films, Mexico City;
Good Edit, New York;
Assembly Line, Minneapolis

MUSIC COMPANY
Hi-Fi Productions, New York;
Universal Music Mexico, Mexico
City; Elements, Santa Monica

SOUND DESIGN COMPANY
Mit Out Sound, Sausalito;
Z Films, Mexico City

EXECUTIVE PRODUCER
David Fincher

PRODUCER
Robyn Boardman, Aristides McGarry,
Rob Van de Weteringe Buys,
Tapas Blank

DIRECTOR
John Frankenheimer,
Wong Kar Wei, Guy Ritchie,
Alejandro Gonzalez Iñarritu, Ang Lee

DIRECTOR OF PHOTOGRAPHY
Newton Thomas Sigel,
Harris Savides, Frederick Elmes,
Chris Soos, Bob Richardson

SOUND DESIGNER
Ren Klyce

DIRECTOR OF SUB-STORY
Ben Younger

DESIGNER
Mark Sandau, Brooke Posard

PROJECT MANAGER
Jennifer Bremer, Jobim Hume,
Valerie Threatt

MUTIMEDIA DEVELOPER
Mark Sandau, Christian Erickson,
Chris Wiggins, Chris Stocksmith,
Laurie Brown

DEVELOPER
George Hilal, Marc Gowland,
Josh Hagen, Chris Wiggins

TECHNICAL LEAD
Matt Heinrichs

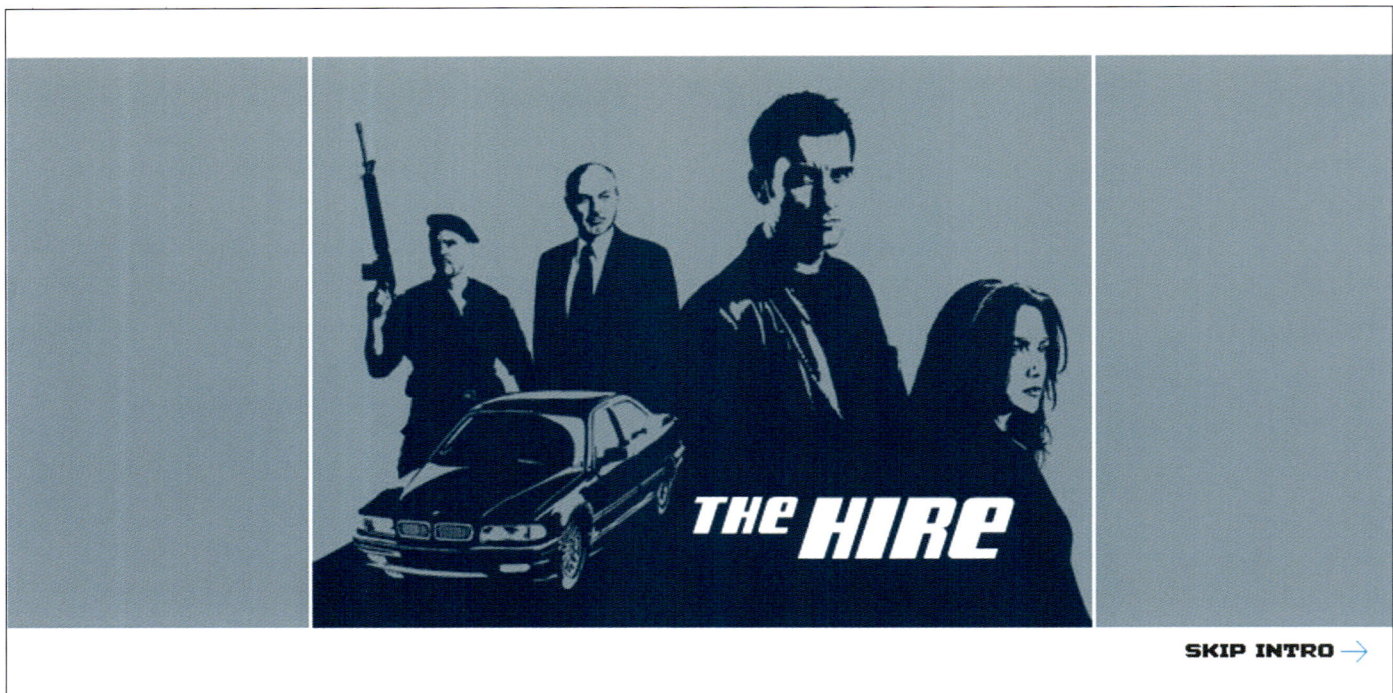

It began as an advertising brief, but advertising wasn't the answer. Traditional commercials could not impart what BMWs could really do, plus BMW customers increasingly were not watching television. They had, however, embraced the Internet in astounding numbers. The new idea was to create something so entertaining and so rewarding that people would actually seek it out. The question then became: Why not create an interactive experience more akin to home theater? What resulted was BMW Films, a series of shorts directed by and starring A-list cinema talent. Each film revolved around a central character called The Driver, the world's best when it came to transporting people out of dangerous situations. The Driver's character traits—youthfulness, integrity, passion, willingness to take risks—reflected on both the brand and the audience. Each film featured The Driver using a BMW to complete his missions, showcasing BMW's true performance.

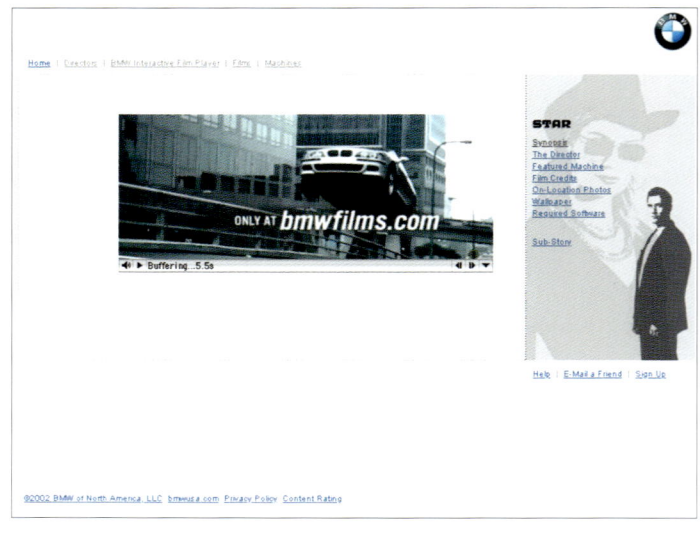

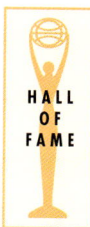

CATEGORY
Hall of Fame

ADVERTISER/PRODUCT
Energizer

TITLE
Launch/Tres Cafe/Nasatine

ADVERTISING AGENCY
Chiat/Day, Venice

PRODUCTION COMPANY
Coppos Films, Los Angeles

EDITING COMPANY
Simon Wachs, Hollywood

CREATIVE DIRECTOR
Lee Clow

COPYWRITER
Dick Sittig

ART DIRECTOR
Andy Dijak

PRODUCER
Elaine Hinton

DIRECTOR
Brent Thomas

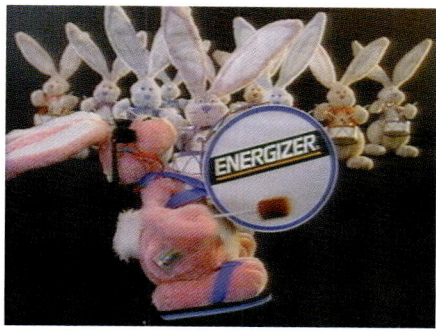

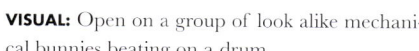

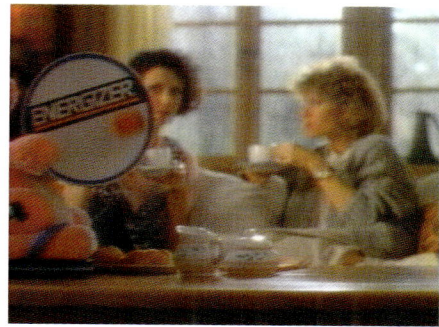

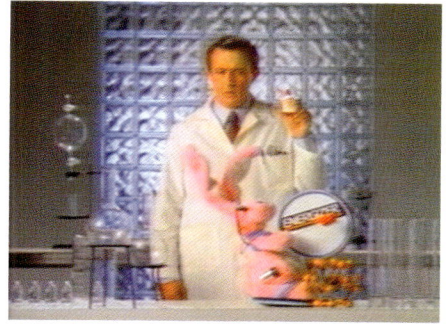

VISUAL: Open on a group of look alike mechanical bunnies beating on a drum.

SUPER: Simulated demonstration.

SFX: Methodical toy drum beats.

VO: Don't be fooled by commercials where one battery company's toy outlasts the other.

VISUAL: Enter the Energizer Bunny, who cuts across the screen in front of the lookalike bunnies.

SFX: Energizer Bunny drum beat.

VO: The fact is, Energizer was never invited to the playoffs because nothing outlasts the Energizer, they keep going and going…

VISUAL: Energizer Bunny exits the scene and goes into the back side of the set, showing camera equipment, craft services table, etc.

OFF-CAMERA VOICE: Someone stop the bunny!

SFX: Energizer Bunny drum beats and twirling of batons.

VO: And going and going…

VISUAL: Open on two women drinking coffee at a coffee table in the living room. Coffee table in front of them, window in back and book shelves around them.

SFX: The sound of rain.

WOMAN 1: Yummm, I love the sound of the rain.

WOMAN 2: And I love the taste of your fresh-brewed coffee.

WOMAN 1: Oh, thanks, but it's not fresh brewed—it's new Tres Café.

VISUAL: Enter Energizer Bunny, walking on the coffee table, knocking over the coffee pot and cups.

SFX: Crashing noises, cups and glass; Energizer Bunny drum beat.

VISUAL: Energizer Bunny walks through a scene displaying the Tres Café product and coffee beans.

VO: Like we said, nothing outlasts the Energizer, they keep going and going and going…

VISUAL: Open on a man sitting in a chair in his backyard with a little girl running up to him.

GIRL: Daddy, Daddy, smell my flowers.

VISUAL: Man touches his face near the nose.

MAN: Oh my sinuses.

VISUAL: Cut to a doctor in a lab coat in an office

DOCTOR: When sinus trouble strikes, reach for Nasatine. Only Nasatine has fast-acting Mucanal. Watch as…

VISUAL: Cut to a diagram on how to use the Nasatine (outline of a human face and the nasal passage with a bottle of Nasatine squirting into it).

VISUAL: Enter Energizer Bunny, which goes across the diagram, does a spin, and goes past the doctor off the screen.

SFX: Breaking glass, Energizer Bunny drum beat.

VO: Still going. Nothing outlasts the Energizer. They keep going and going and going…

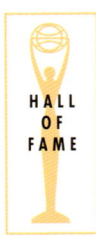

HALL OF FAME

CATEGORY Hall of Fame	**PRODUCTION COMPANY** Traktor, Stockholm & Los Angeles	**COPYWRITER** Linus Karlsson	**ACCOUNT MANAGER** Mia Kleist
ADVERTISER/PRODUCT Diesel	**MUSIC COMPANY** Jurgen Drews	**ART DIRECTOR** Joakim Jonason	**DIRECTOR OF PHOTOGRAPHY** Ed Lachman
TITLE 5 A.M. Mono Village	**ACCOUNT EXECUTIVE** Stefan Öström	**PRODUCER** Richard Ulfvengren	
ADVERTISING AGENCY Paradiset DDB, Stockholm	**CREATIVE DIRECTOR** Joakim Jonason	**DIRECTOR** Ulf Johansson, Pontus Löwenheim	

VISUAL: A scout leader with a trumpet blows the wake-up call.

SUPER: Diesel Jeans Presents: 5 A.M. Mono Village.

VISUAL: Boy scouts, dressed in camp shirts and jeans, emerge from their tents and begin to exercise.

VISUAL: The scout leader displays a picture of today's lesson to the boys: Mouth-to-Mouth Resuscitation.

SCOUT LEADER: Who wants to practice?

VISUAL: All the boys volunteer. One guy breaks through the group and wants to demonstrate the technique. The scout leader points out who is to be resuscitated: an older bearded scoutmaster. The boy puts his lips to the man's mouth and begins the demonstration. He fantasizes that he is with a beautiful young blond girl and they are riding horses together. The boy snaps back to reality and he is riding horses with the scoutmaster that he has resuscitated, through snowy mountains.

SUPER: For successful living

SINGER: and life will turn out to have more to offer than you could ever expect.

SUPER: Diesel Jeans and Work Wear.

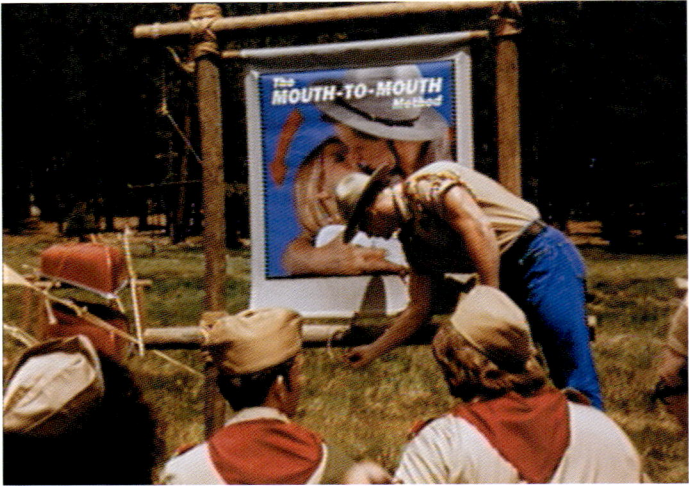

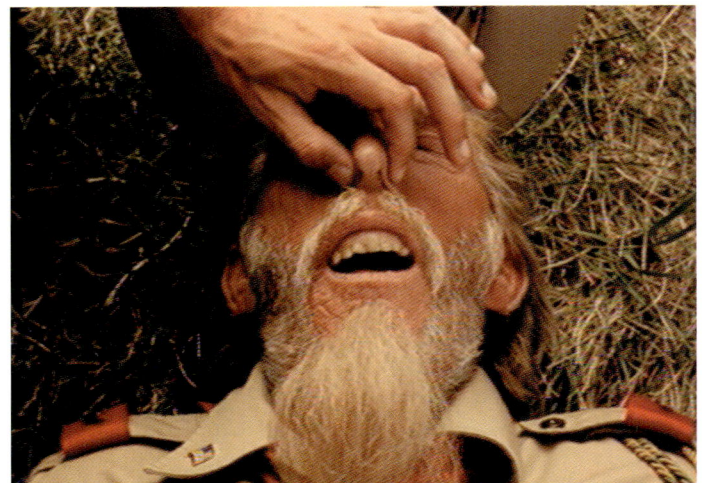

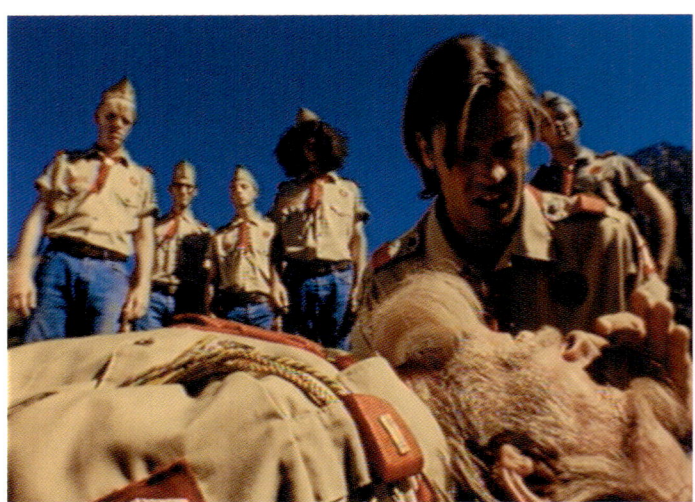

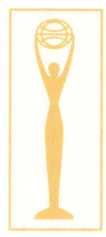

ADVERTISER OF THE YEAR

Nike
England, Netherlands, United States

AGENCY OF THE YEAR

Fallon
Minneapolis

PRODUCTION COMPANY OF THE YEAR

Harvest Productions
Santa Monica

AGENCY NETWORK OF THE YEAR

DDB Worldwide

LIFETIME ACHIEVEMENT AWARD
David Abbott
Cofounder,
Abbott Mead Vickers, London

Honoring the innovative and influential British creative director, who, for over two decades, has been a leader in London's creative revolution. With a generation of great work for Volvo, Guinness, and The Economist, among many others, Abbott's achievements are legendary.

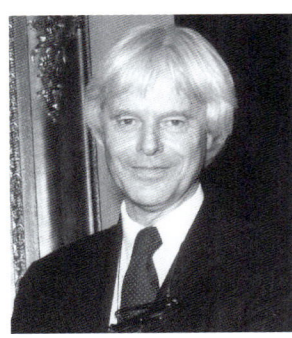

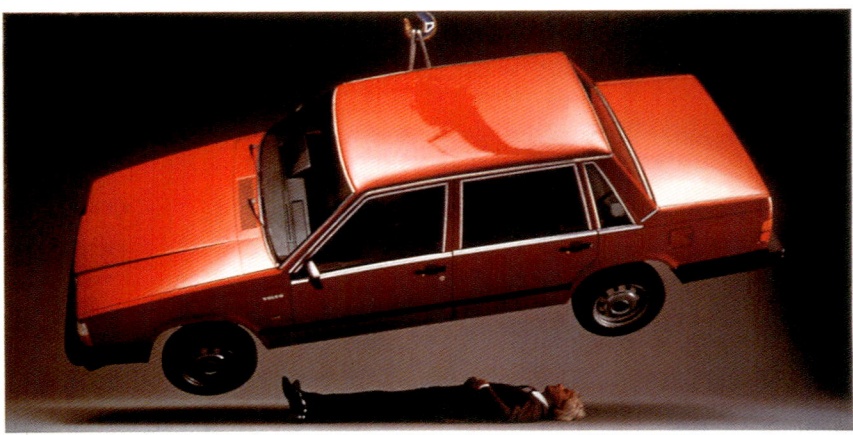

IF THE WELDING ISN'T STRONG ENOUGH, THE CAR WILL FALL ON THE WRITER.

THE NEW VOLVO 740. FROM £9249.

"Receiving a lifetime achievement award is an unnerving experience. Looking at a tape of people saying nice things about oneself is rather like being at your own memorial service.

Did you notice one or two of the witnesses on film were already talking about me in the past tense? Not that watching the tape was unpleasant. On the contrary, if I am to retain my current hat size, I shall have to remind myself of the perils of pride and take their kind comments with a grain of salt.

Personally, I believe my success was due to something that only John Hegarty picked up on the tape. He said that he had never seen me wear anything other than a suit. Not strictly true, but close enough. I was a teenager in the fifties and that was the era when your mother told you to put on a suit for a job interview. It was a mark of respect and seriousness. She always said, "You can't go wrong with a good suit." A piece of advice that ranks as the most influential I ever received, and is, without doubt, responsible for whatever success I had in advertising.

In the swinging sixties and flower-powered seventies, my somber suits and monotone ties tended to stick out. I was pushed forward by management

because I didn't scare the clients. They thought I looked like one of them, so no matter how wild the ads were that I presented, they tended to nod them through. T. S. Eliot, in his day a seriously revolutionary poet, dressed like a banker. I'm sure it helped him bamboozle a few publishers as my own serious garb hoodwinked unsuspecting marketing directors. So there it is in all its simplicity. You want a bright future? Wear a sober suit. (There'll be more career enhance advice like this as I go along, so you may want to keep a pen handy.)

I should also like to thank some others who helped me get here today. (I always find this tedious at the Oscars, but I promise to keep it short and I won't cry.) First, a tribute to my old friend and my art director at AMV for twenty-one years, Ron Brown. To Paul Hoppe, Arthur Wilson, Stanhope Shelton, David Ogilvy, John Withers, Bob Levenson, and Bill Bernbach, I give thanks for their teaching and inspiration.

At AMV, there were my partners Peter Mead and Adrian Vickers and countless others who fought the good fight alongside me. But most of all, my thanks go to Eve, my wife of forty years, and to my four children. I thank them for my life outside

the office; for my real life. It is easier to cope with suits who maul your ads by day when pajamas jump into your arms at night.

Advertising is a wonderfully engaging profession. I enjoyed my forty years in it immensely—but don't let it take over your life. When you walk away from it, as we all have to one day, it's good to have someone and somewhere to walk to. There's also another more immediate reason (for you) to have a life outside advertising. Our lives are the well from which we draw the experiences, truths, and intuitions that inform and direct our work. The fuller the life we had the bigger the pool of truths available to us. I have always been a writer who plunders his life for material.

Of course, in so doing, you run the risk of self-indulgence and sentimentality, but if you know your craft, you can avoid this danger. On sound tracks, swooning violin strings are to be avoided—as is the contrived choke in the voice. Use plain old gray words, not purple, and don't linger too long in the close-ups. In short, practice restraint. But don't, in your desire to avoid sentimentality, ignore sentiment. Most of the purchases we make are made for rational and emotional reasons—even something as everyday as bread. Would we get as much pleasure from croissants if they were called twisted rolls? I suspect not.

Over the past two days, we've heard a lot about how our industry is changing—how we have to regroup and adjust in the face of new media and new consumer dynamics. There's been a suggestion that the traditional skills of the advertising agency are redundant. I would like to add one additional thought to the debate—and it's this.

Crap sent 3000 miles at the touch of a button is still crap when it arrives.

The truth is, someone still has to fill these new air waves, these new screens, these new electronic pages with good work, and as the media proliferates, our clients will need the artistry and intuition of great communicators, not less but more.

What multichannel TV has shown us is that there isn't enough good stuff to go around? And what's so different about the new online opportunity to talk to our customers one to one? Hasn't the best

It's lonely at the top, but at least there's something to read.

The Economist

advertising always talked one to one? Isn't that what Bill Bernbach was preaching fifty years ago? And that aside, doesn't one-to-one communications take more talent, not less? Don't the divorce courts prove that?

Today, the fundamental challenge for advertising agencies is not how to reinvent themselves, but how to grow, attract, and retain creative talent. Because the narrower the consumer target, the more accurate your work has to be in its content, its tone, and its authenticity.

So how do you get and keep more than your fair share of creative talent? And I don't just mean writers or art directors. I could go on about this at considerable length—but I know the beach beckons, so here are just three headlines:

1. Good creative people want to work at places that do good creative work. It's obvious, but it's fundamental. It means that agency management must believe wholeheartedly in the primacy of great work—not just pay lip service to it. They must support it even if it causes them and their shareholders short-term pain. As Bill Bernbach once famously said, "A principle isn't a principle until it costs you money." Less famously, I used to repeat something the theater director Peter Brook once wrote: "Quality is always possible, and always under threat." So be rigorous about all aspects of your company—so that quality becomes second nature. Do nothing shoddy—better to say it's not ready than it will do. You can't pretend to be a creative agency—you're allowed the odd fall from grace, but make a habit of it and the word gets around and the good people go elsewhere.

2. Nothing grows in a chill wind. In my experience, the best writers and directors are self motivated and self policing. Even though you pay their wages they are essentially self employed. You don't need to create a harsh, competitive environment to get the best out of them—they have enough demons of their own driving them on. What they need from you, Mr. Management, is a secure, generous, stimulating setting where they can work hard to make you rich.

Do you remember the scene in *Kramer vs. Kramer* where the creative director takes the Dustin Hoffman character out to lunch and, over the platitudes du jour, fires him? Why? Because Mr. Kramer, whose wife has recently walked out on him, was finding it tricky coping with his job and the sole care of a five-year-old son. There were so many other things the boss could have done. Kramer needed help, not the push.

Running an agency *is* different. The people are bright and articulate, but experience has made them reluctant cynics. They don't want to be— the very ideas of coming in each day to create something new and exciting is the opposite of cynicism, it is a profoundly hopeful act—but life has shown them that too often agency bosses would rather make a buck than save a job.

There's a nineteenth-century chant that English children used to sing in the playground. "God bless the squire and his relations—and keep us in our proper stations." Them and us was no way to run a country; it's no way to run an agency.

3. Don't forget to play. In 1962, I went to work at my first agency. (Before that I had been in the advertising department at Kodak.) The agency was called Mather & Crowther and the creative director was a man called Stanhope Shelton. I remember he had an office without a desk and when you wrote something he liked he would send you a cheery word on salmon-colored notepaper. What I remember most about him, however, was a trip to the cinema. When Fellini's film *8½* came out, he bought tickets for everyone in the creative department, and on a working Tuesday afternoon we all went to the movies—on the company.

Doubtless we learned something about film technique that day, but what we remembered most was the fun of the trip and the audacity of the ideas. The headmaster had organized mass truancy! No wonder we loved him and worked hard for him.

Goofing-off time is necessary in an agency. We talk of **playing around** with words and pictures, and the phrase is not ill chosen. In our agency, there were always snooker tables, table tennis tables, summer parties, family days, Father Christmas, free breakfasts, and a bar in the evening. Did all this distract people from their work? Of course not; it made it fun, and by joining in we set a good example.

After all, who aspires to sit in the boss's chair if the boss's chair is never empty?"

David Abbott

May, 2002

TELEVISION & CINEMA

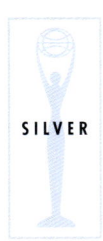

SILVER

CATEGORY	**PRODUCTION COMPANY**	**ANIMATION COMPANY**	**PRODUCER**
Apparel/Fashion	Gorgeous Enterprises, London	The Mill, London	Paul Rothwell
ADVERTISER/PRODUCT	**EDITING COMPANY**	**AGENCY PRODUCER**	**DIRECTOR**
Levi's Engineered Jeans	The Quarry, London	Andy Gulliman	Frank Budgen
TITLE	**MUSIC COMPANY**	**CREATIVE DIRECTOR**	**FLAME**
Twist	Pepe Duluxe	Russell Ramsay	Barnsley, Chris Knight, Jason Watts
ADVERTISING AGENCY	**SOUND DESIGN COMPANY**	**CREATIVE TEAM**	
Bartle Bogle Hegarty, London	Sound Tree Music	Tony McTeer, Mark Hunter	

VISUAL: A car, packed with teenagers, stops in front of a restaurant. The passengers begin to stretch their travel-weary limbs. One of the girls stretches her leg, twisting her foot around farther than normal. They all get out of the car and start stretching and dancing around. Some of the kids have the ability to twist their limbs beyond human capacity. This begins a choreographed series of body part twists: fingers, ankles, arms, heads, and the execution of various body spins. One guy attempts to use the men's bathroom and realizes it is locked. A girl emerges from the women's washroom, switches heads with him and he can now use the woman's bathroom. One of the girl's hands is pulled off and tossed from one kid to another like a baseball. As the pace of the game increases, many arms and legs are being untwisted from the bodies of their respective owners and tossed around. A young boy joins the fun and is running with his head twisted 180 degrees from normal. Eventually all the kids are back to normal. They climb into the car and drive away. A little dog picks up a stray hand and chases after the car.

SUPER: Levi's Engineered Jeans. Twisted to Fit.

VISUAL: A tiny male figurine, hanging from the car's rear-view mirror, is wearing miniature Levi's Engineered Jeans. We see his limbs twisting around with movement of the car.

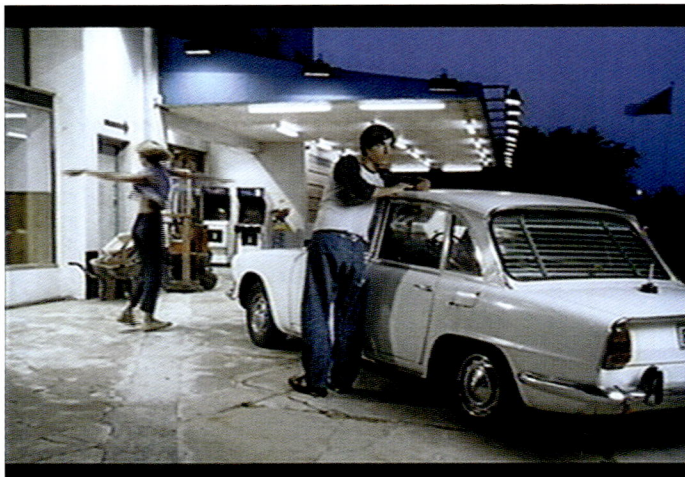

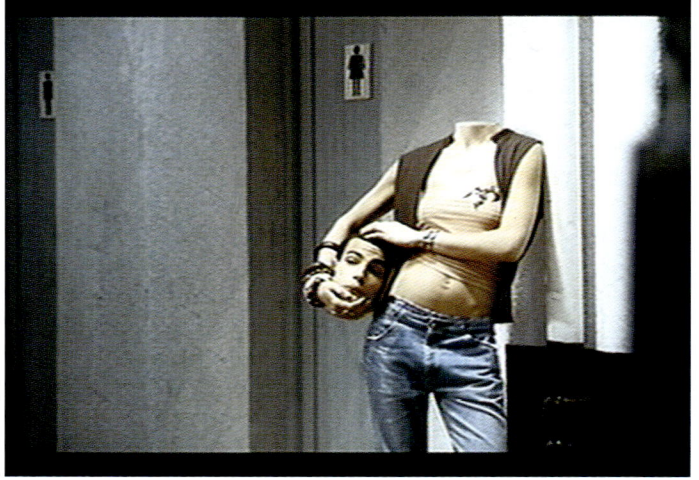

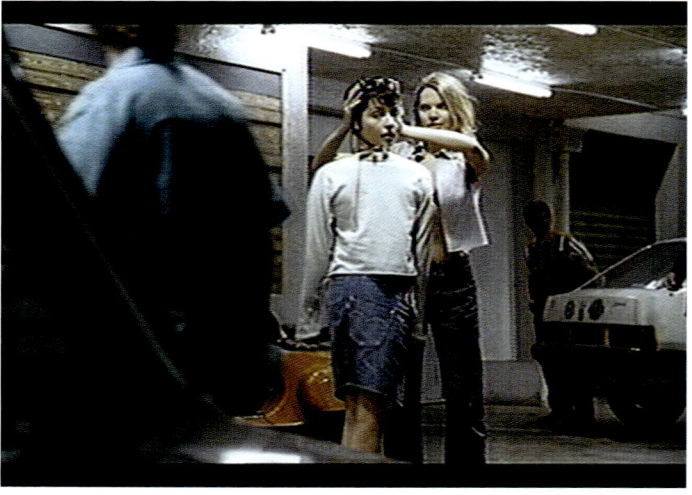

CATEGORY
Automotive

ADVERTISER/PRODUCT
Ninja ZX-12R

TITLE
The Road

ADVERTISING AGENCY
TBWA, Berlin

PRODUCTION COMPANY
Caspari Film, Düsseldorf

SOUND DESIGN COMPANY
U.F.O. Walter

CREATIVE DIRECTOR
Christoph Klingler

COPYWRITER
Helge Bloeck

ART DIRECTOR
Boris Schwiedrzik

PRODUCER
Anke Junghaehnel, Thomas Caspari

DIRECTOR
Oliver Julius

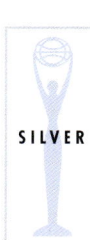

SILVER

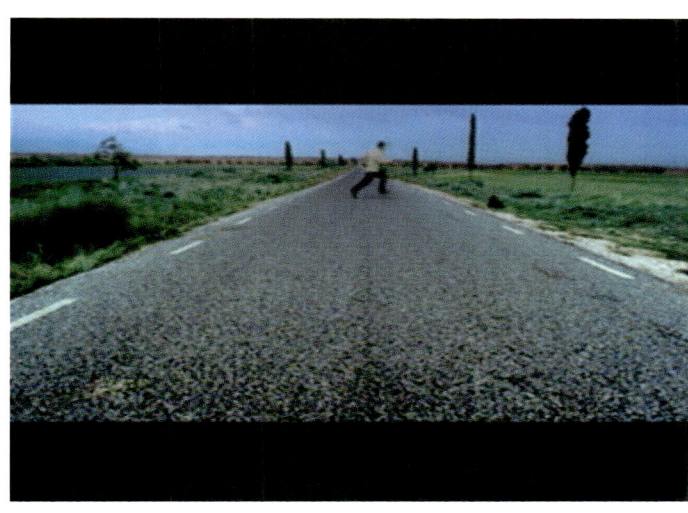

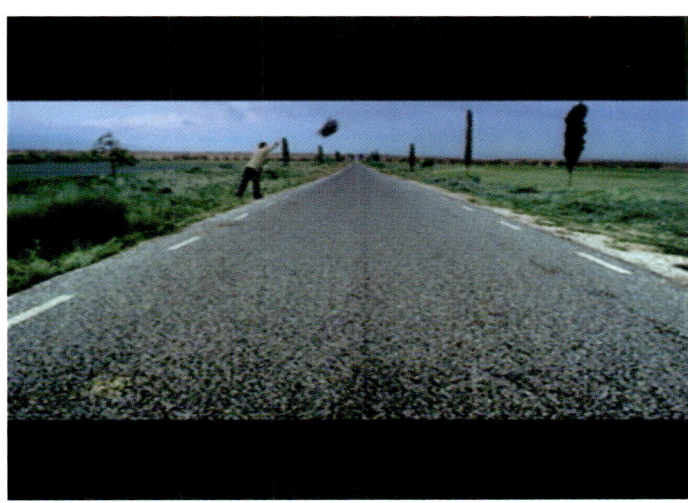

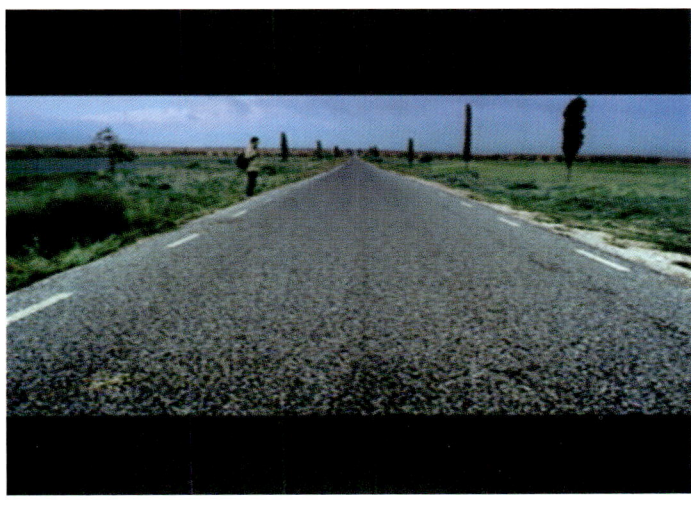

SYNOPSIS: A man approaches a quiet road in the middle of nowhere. You hear nothing, see nothing. He stops at the edge of the road, looks left, and then right. He seems apprehensive. He throws his rucksack to the other side of the road and prepares to run. Then he runs like crazy across the road. Is the man mad? No; but he knows the Ninja ZX-12 R, the fastest motorbike in the world.

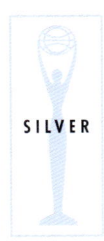

CATEGORY	Automotive
ADVERTISER/PRODUCT	Audi A3
TITLE	Babysitter

ADVERTISING AGENCY
Tandem Campmany Guasch DDB, Barcelona

PRODUCTION COMPANY
Lee Films International, Madrid; Microscope, Barcelona

CREATIVE DIRECTOR
Danny Ilario, Alberto Astorga

COPYWRITER
Nuria Argelich, Alberto Astorga

ART DIRECTOR
Fernando Codina, Danny Ilario

PRODUCER
Vicky Moñino

VISUAL: A man of about thirty-five sitting on a swing in a park. He looks toward the camera and begins to tell a story that has affected him strongly.

EDWARD: I had a babysitter. I'll never forget her.

VISUAL: Flashback to the house where Edward was born. From Edward's point of view, we see a strong and robust athlete. She undoes her dress and we see she has running gear on underneath.

EDWARD: She made me see the world in a different way.

VISUAL: Flashback to babysitter running through a park with a baby stroller, overtaking other joggers.

EDWARD VO: I remember those afternoons in the park.

EDWARD: That breeze on my face.

VISUAL: Babysitter doing long jump.

EDWARD VO: I liked it; I had fun.

VISUAL: Babysitter in relay race passing the baby as if he was the baton.

EDWARD: But she went. And everything seemed slow to me. I tried to get over it.

VISUAL: Audi A3 sitting in park.

EDWARD: But I still need to have that feeling.

SUPER: Audi S3. 210 CV. What's your reason?

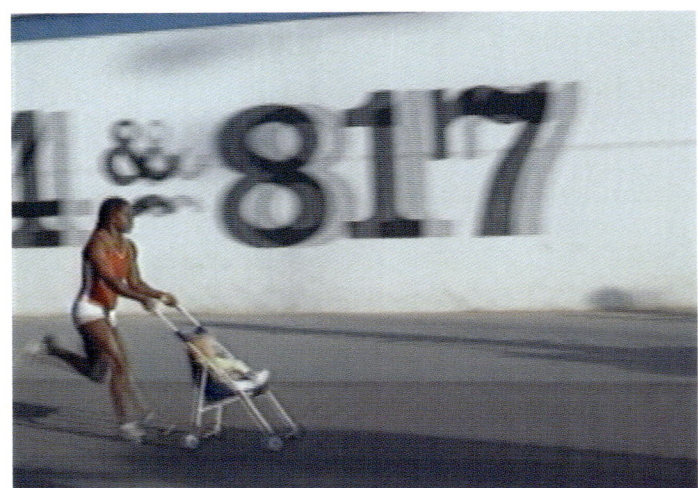

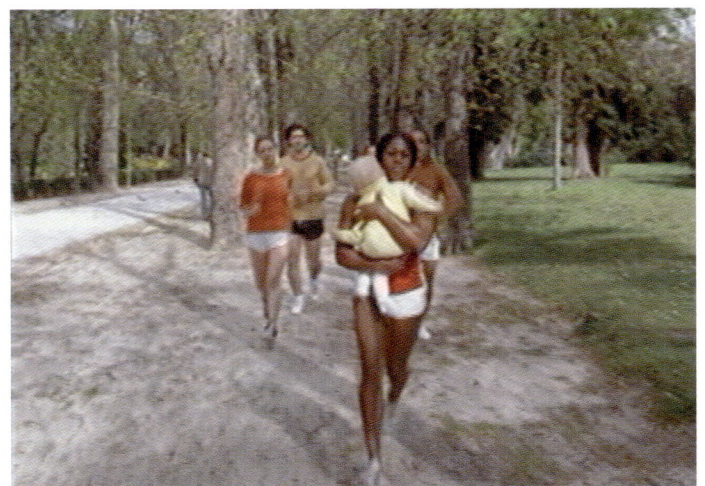

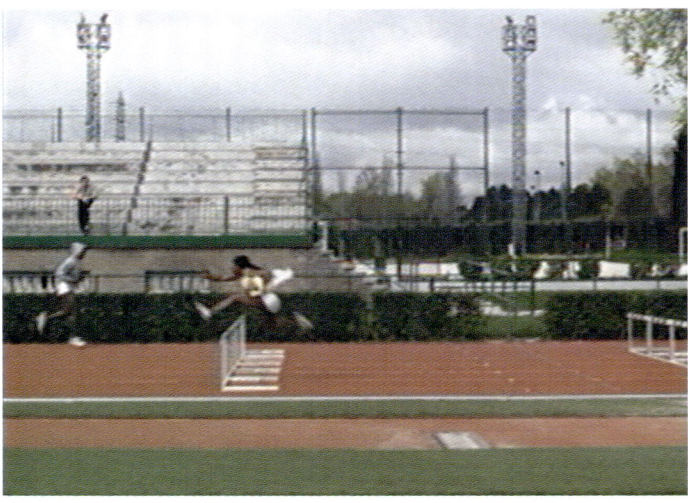

CATEGORY
Automotive

ADVERTISER/PRODUCT
Toyota Celica

TITLE
Dog

ADVERTISING AGENCY
Saatchi & Saatchi, Los Angeles

PRODUCTION COMPANY
Independent, Santa Monica

EDITING COMPANY
FilmCore, Santa Monica

MUSIC COMPANY
Ad Music, Santa Monica

ACCOUNT EXECUTIVE
Paul Imhoff

CREATIVE DIRECTOR
Steve Rabosky, Neal Foard,
Doug Van Andel

COPYWRITER
Sherry Hawkins

ART DIRECTOR
Verner Soler

PRODUCER
Elaine Adachi, Lindsay Skutch,
Susanne Preissler

DIRECTOR
Chris Smith

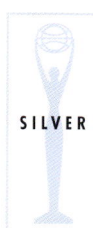

SILVER

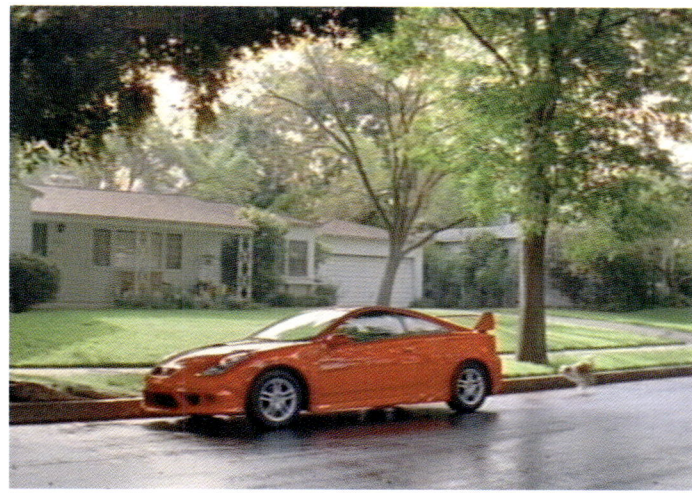

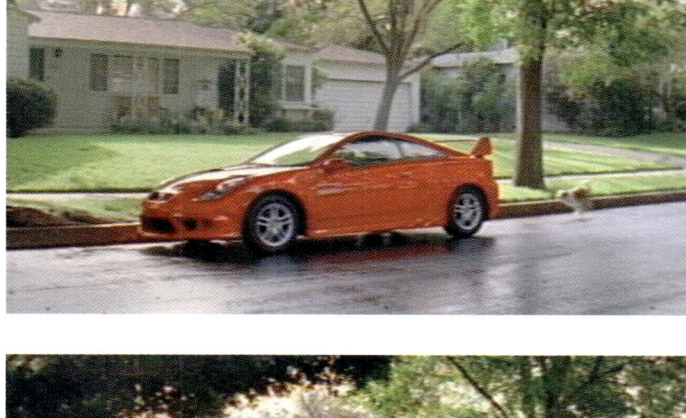

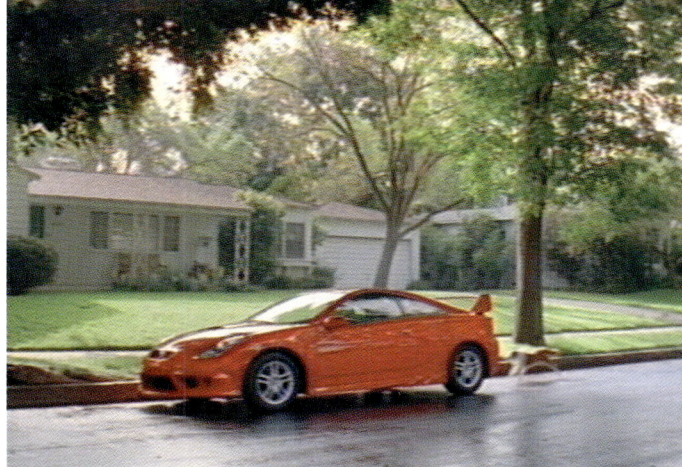

VISUAL: A red Celica is parked in a very quiet suburban neighborhood. After a few seconds, we see a barking dog running toward the rear of the car. As he approaches he shows absolutely no sign of slowing down. Finally, he hits the car.

SFX: Dog hitting car.

VISUAL: Car shakes slightly. The dog looks confused and slightly shaken. After a second he trots off.

SUPER: The Celica Action Package. Looks fast.

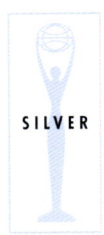

SILVER

CATEGORY
Automotive

ADVERTISER/PRODUCT
Audi Multitronic (Stepless Automatic
Transmission)

TITLE
The Fan

ADVERTISING AGENCY
Saatchi & Saatchi, Frankfurt

PRODUCTION COMPANY
Jo!Schmid, Berlin

EDITING COMPANY
VCC, Hamburg

ACCOUNT EXECUTIVE
H. Lutz, D. Suessenbach

CREATIVE DIRECTOR
Harald Wittig, Benjamin Lommel

COPYWRITER
Harald Wittig

ART DIRECTOR
Benjamin Lommel

PRODUCER
Michael Schmid

DIRECTOR
Martin Schmid

CHIEF CREATIVE OFFICER
Carsten Heintzsch

MUSIC PUBLISHER
EMI, Warner Chappel

SYNOPSIS: An obsessive music enthusiast who punishes his transmission to make a tiny doll on his dashboard dance to the tune of "King of the Road" by the King. His jalopy is well past its prime and the engine can't take this sort of abuse for long. But fate smiles on the likable fan and he soon finds himself settled in the passenger seat of a new Audi A4 equipped with the multitronic transmission. He soon pops in his cassette and places his doll on the dashboard. However, the doll doesn't want to dance even though the Audi is clearly picking up speed. It takes a friendly flick of a finger to get the doll started. Administered by the friendly Audi driver: That little jiggle gets the doll dancing, putting a smile back on the face of the "King of the Road."

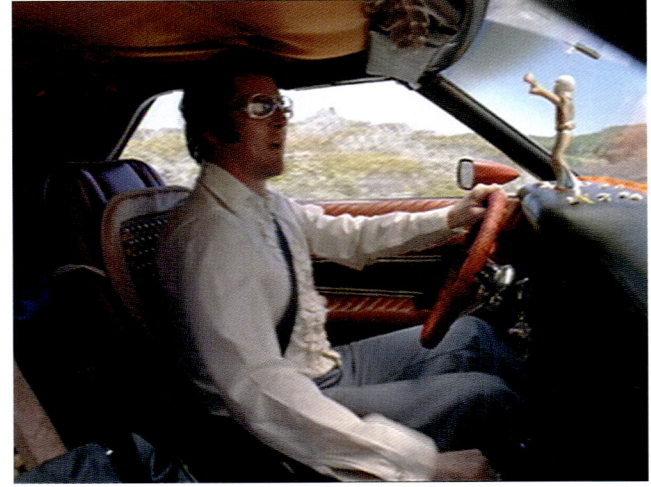

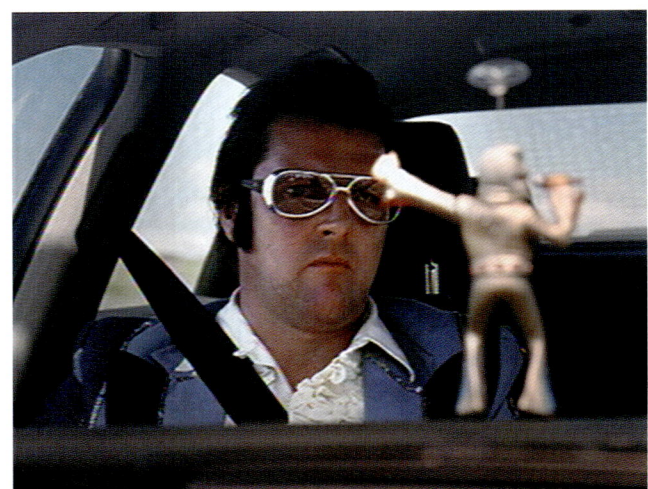

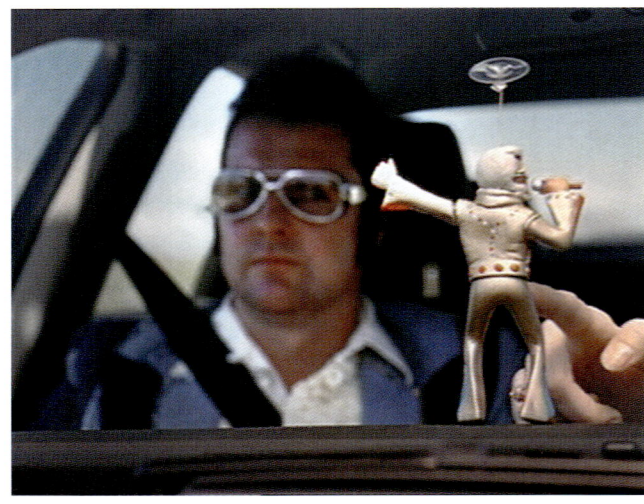

CATEGORY
Automotive

ADVERTISER/PRODUCT
Volkswagen of America

TITLE
Ransom

ADVERTISING AGENCY
ARNOLD Worldwide, Boston

PRODUCTION COMPANY
Crossroads

EDITING COMPANY
Bug Editorial

MUSIC COMPANY
Berman-Branco

AGENCY PRODUCER
Bill Goodell

CHIEF CREATIVE DIRECTOR
Ron Lawner

GROUP CREATIVE DIRECTOR
Alan Pafenbach

CREATIVE DIRECTOR
Alan Pafenbach

COPYWRITER
Dana Satterwhite

ART DIRECTOR
Tim Vaccarino

DIRECTOR
Nick Lewin

PRODUCER
Polly Johnson

CINEMATOGRAPHER
Georgio Scalli

EDITOR
Andre Betz

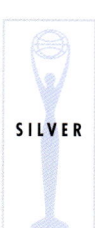

SILVER

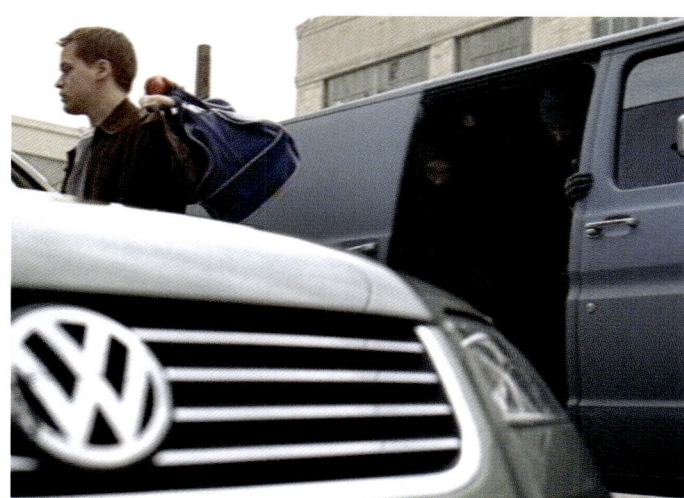

SYNOPSIS: A simple case of mistaken identity. A young Passat owner is kidnapped because his captors think that because he is driving a Passat he is a rich man and they can collect a lot of ransom money for him.

VISUAL: Man walking out to his parked Passat. He goes to unlock the car door when a big van pulls up. Two men reach out, pull him into the van, slide the door closed, and speed away.

SFX: Struggle noises.

VISUAL: A few seconds later, the van pulls up again, and returns the man to his car.

KIDNAPPER 1: Sorry about that.

KIDNAPPER 2: Our mistake.

KIDNAPPER 1: Sorry.

VO: The new Passat. It only looks like a million bucks.

SUPER: VW logo.

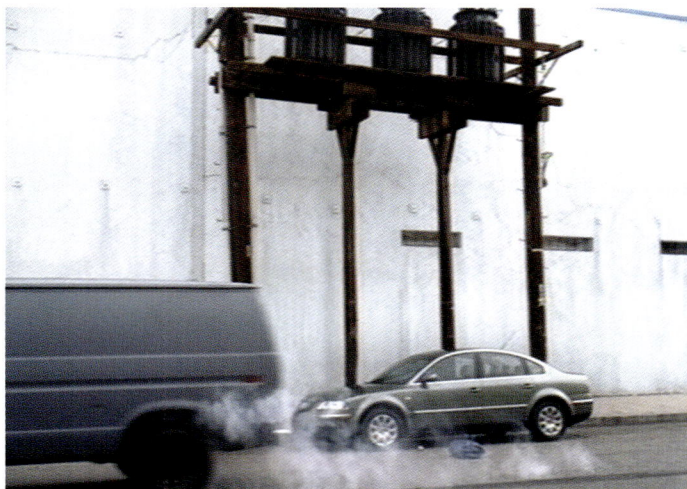

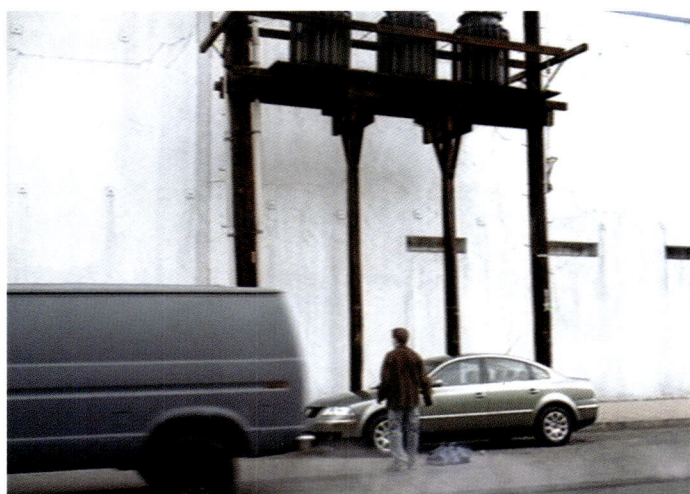

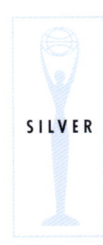

SILVER

CATEGORY Automotive	**PRODUCTION COMPANY** Arden Sutherland-Dodd, London	**CREATIVE DIRECTOR** Till Hohmann, Bernhard Lukas	**DIRECTOR** Paul Arden
ADVERTISER/PRODUCT BMW Munich/BMW C1 (Motorbike)	**MUSIC COMPANY** Karl Jenkins Music, London	**COPYWRITER** Till Hohmann, Bernhard Lukas	**AGENCY PRODUCER** Moritz Merkel
TITLE Magic Car	**ANIMATION COMPANY** Moving Picture Company, London	**ART DIRECTOR** Gudrun Muschalla	**EDITOR** Bryan Dyke
ADVERTISING AGENCY Jung von Matt/Isar, Munich	**ACCOUNT EXECUTIVE** Stephanie Fehrenbach, Elisabeth Baumgartner	**PRODUCER** Nick Sutherland-Dodd	**CAMERA** Nic Knowland

VISUAL: The headlights of a car as it drives along a coastal road at night.

SUPER: Safety passenger cell.

Seat belt system.

ABS.

Is that anything special?

VISUAL: Suddenly, the two headlights divide and it become obvious that the each light belongs to a BMW C1 motorcycle.

SUPER: On two wheels it is.

The BMW C1.

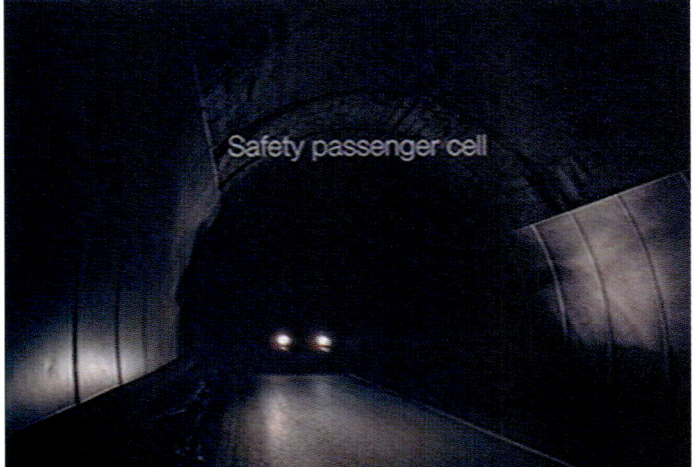

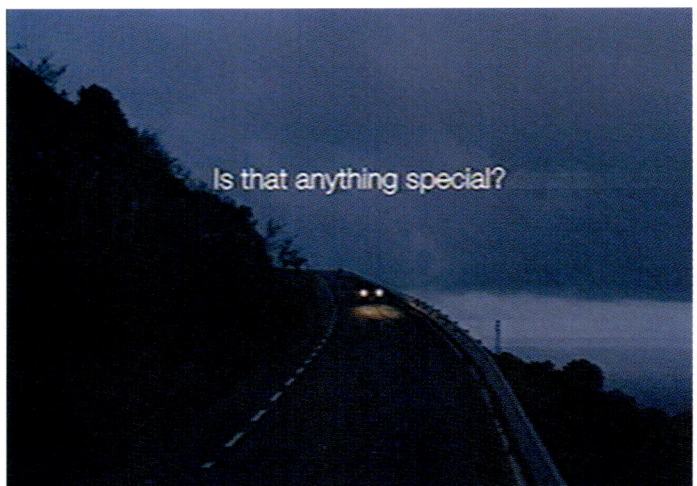

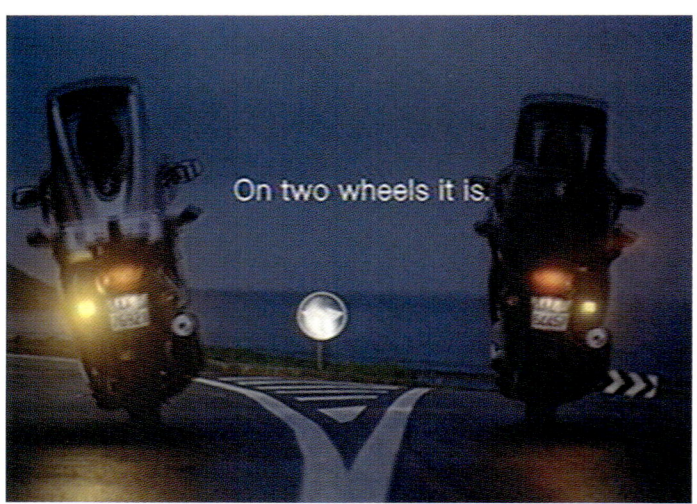

CATEGORY
Automotive

ADVERTISER/PRODUCT
Volkswagen Golf

TITLE
Cry

ADVERTISING AGENCY
BMP DDB, London

PRODUCTION COMPANY
Blink Productions, London

COPYWRITER
Jeremy Cragien

ART DIRECTOR
Joanna Wenley

CLIENT SUPERVISOR
Catherine Woolf

ACCOUNT SUPERVISOR
Jon Busk

AGENCY PRODUCER
Howard Spivey

PRODUCER
Johnny Frankel

DIRECTOR
Dominic Murphy

CINEMATOGRAPHER
Johnny Frankel

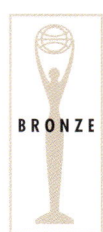

BRONZE

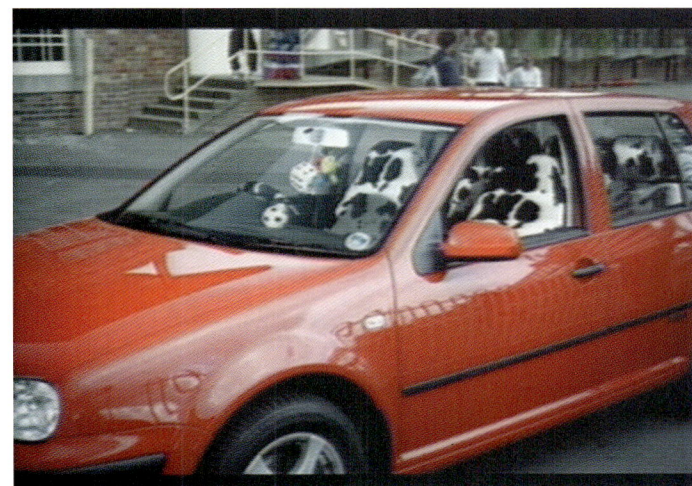

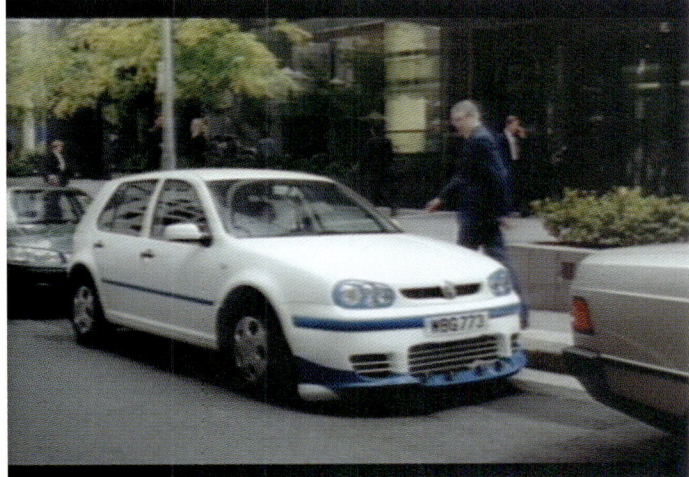

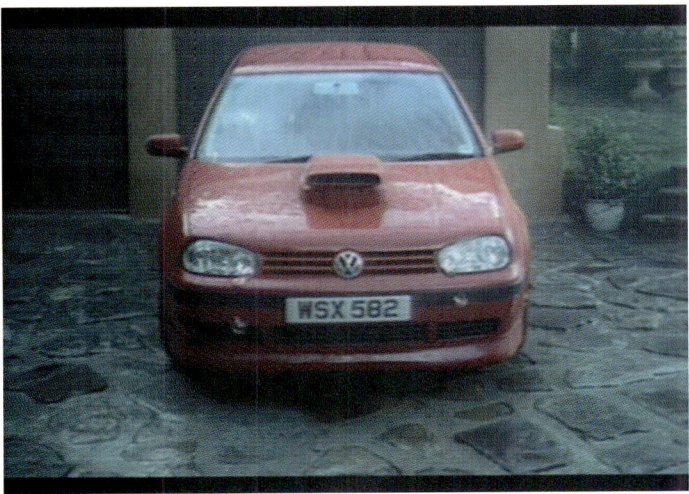

SYNOPSIS: A collection of Mark IV Golfs, which have had some "extras" added to them by their owners. The cars are shot to show off their beautiful lines and understated design, thus accentuating the contrast between them and the ridiculous "extras."

VISUAL: A Golf, with brightly colored flame transfers along the side of the car and a spoiler on the back. Interior of a Golf with cow-hide-covered steering wheel and seat covers, and a collection of furry dice hanging at the windshield. Golf parked on the side of the road with the sticker "DARREN ♥ ALISON" across the windshield. A comical-looking dog in the back window of a Golf. A white and blue Golf parked outside an office building. It has a full body kit with skirts, spoilers, etc. Golf on a cliff top. It has a Venetian blind on the back window and flags. A Golf with a personalized number plate that reads BIG BOY (BIG 80Y). Golf with a bull-bar on the front and rally spotlights on top. A yellow Golf with a big green whale tail spoiler. A Golf parked on a front driver in the pouring rain. On its hood is a raised bump with air intakes. The camera moves in on the headlamps. Rain appears to fill the headlamps like tears welling in an eye, until it overflows and falls to the ground.

SUPER: Some things are best left alone. Golf.

VW logo.

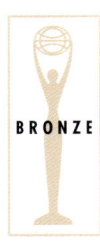

BRONZE

CATEGORY Automotive	**PRODUCTION COMPANY** Traktor, Los Angeles	**ACCOUNT EXECUTIVE** Gustav Aschan, Eva Carlheim-Müller	**PRODUCER** Traktor
ADVERTISER/PRODUCT Volvo S60	**EDITING COMPANY** Traktor, Los Angeles	**COPYWRITER** Filip Nilsson, Johan Olivero	**DIRECTOR** Traktor
TITLE Jogger	**ACCOUNT DIRECTOR** Olle Victorin	**ART DIRECTOR** Andreas Malm, Mikko Timonen, Anders Eklind	**MUSIC PUBLISHER** Universal Records
ADVERTISING AGENCY Forsman & Bodenfors, Gothenburg			

VISUAL: A woman in her thirties is driving through the city on a hot summer day; the traffic is very heavy. Suddenly she sees something in her rear-view mirror; a man in his forties is running behind her car. The woman looks puzzled. When she stops at a red light, the jogger stops as well and continues to run in place. The light changes; she drives off again and checks her rear-view mirror. The jogger is still following her. The woman looks worried. Again, she checks her mirror and sees that there are now two joggers behind her car. She looks really confused, checks the mirror and now finds three runners behind her car.

SUPER: A car that turns harmful ozone into oxygen while you drive.

The Volvo S60.

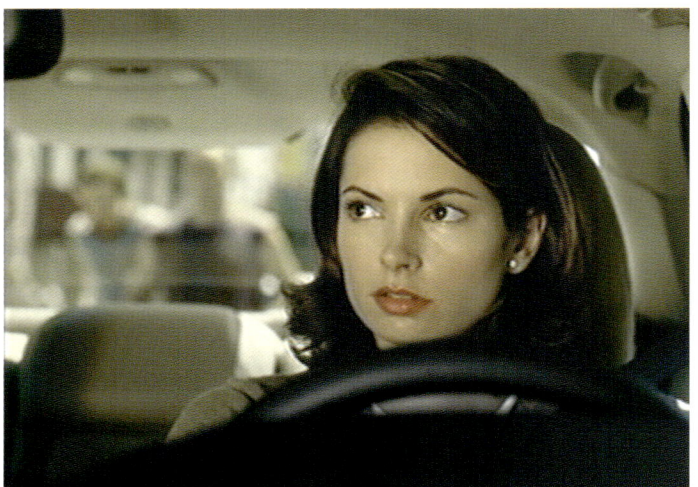

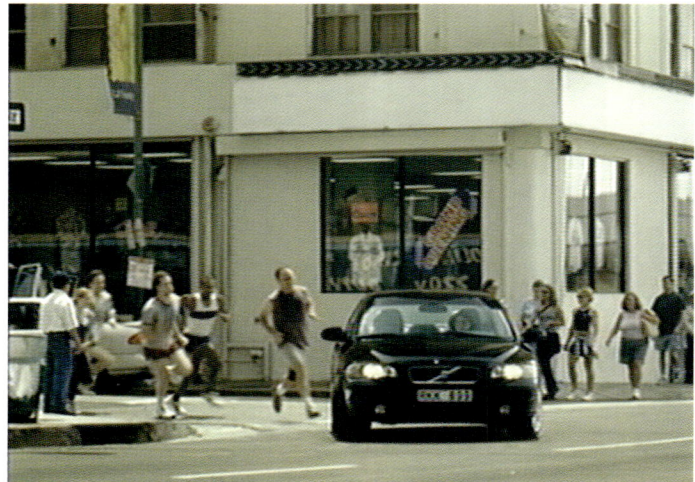

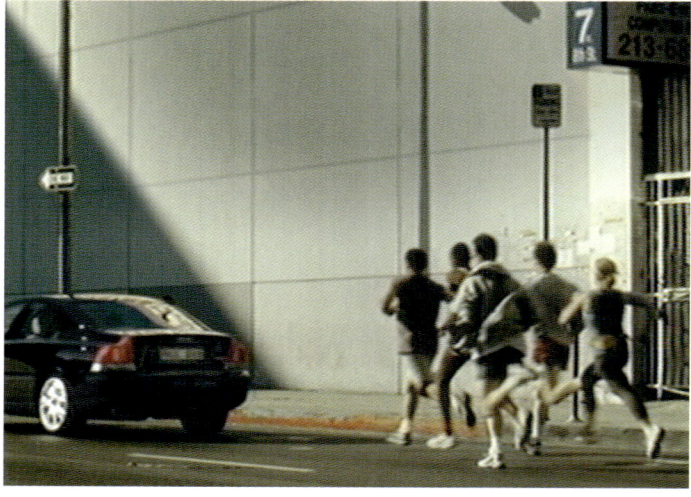

CATEGORY
Automotive

ADVERTISER/PRODUCT
Toyota Corolla

TITLE
School

ADVERTISING AGENCY
Saatchi & Saatchi, London

PRODUCTION COMPANY
Outsider, London

EDITING COMPANY
Final Cut, London

SOUND DESIGN COMPANY
Grand Central, London

AGENCY PRODUCER
Chris Moore

ACCOUNT EXECUTIVE
Jamie Copas

CREATIVE DIRECTOR
David Droga

COPYWRITER
Jo Stafford, Brett Salmons

ART DIRECTOR
Brett Salmons, Jo Stafford

PRODUCER
John Madsen

DIRECTOR
Dom & Nic

EDITOR
Struan Clay

SOUND DESIGNER
Raja Sehgal

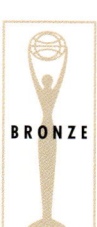

BRONZE

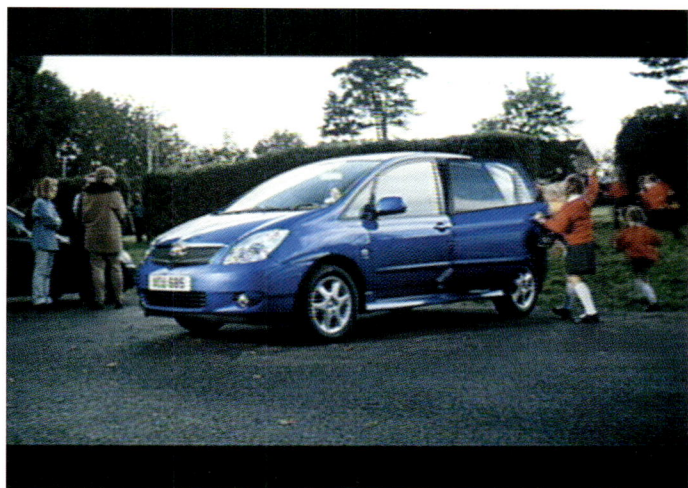

VISUAL: The entrance gate to a school. Parents' cars are parked outside waiting to collect their children.

SFX: School bell rings.

VISUAL: Children come streaming out and head toward the waiting cars.

VISUAL: One little girl climbs into a Corolla; there is a woman in the driver's seat.

GIRL: Mum.

WOMAN: Who are you?

GIRL (abruptly): Just shut up and drive.

SUPER: The new Corolla. A car to be proud of. Toyota logo.

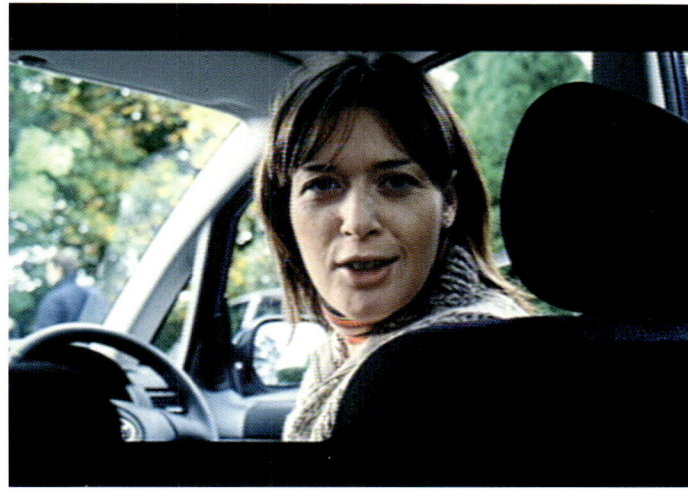

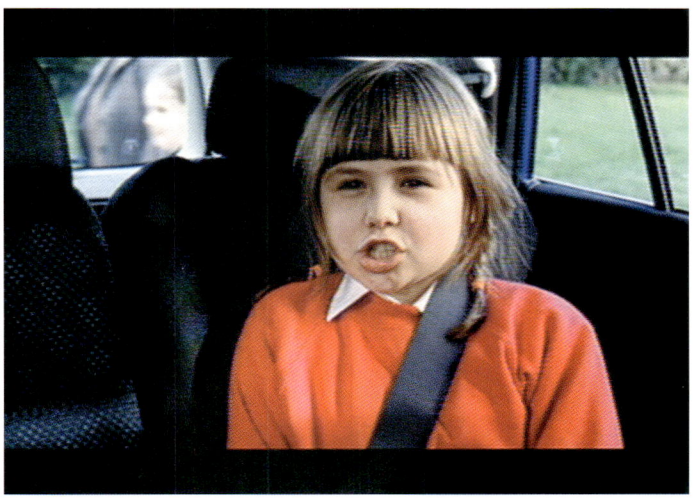

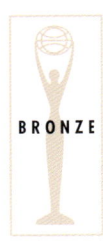

BRONZE

CATEGORY	**ADVERTISING AGENCY**	**MUSIC COMPANY**	**ART DIRECTOR**
Automotive	Result DDB, Amstelveen	Wim Vonk Sound, Amsterdam	Michael Janssen
ADVERTISER/PRODUCT	**PRODUCTION COMPANY**	**ACCOUNT EXECUTIVE**	**PRODUCER**
Volkswagen Polo	De Schiettent, Amsterdam	Ruby Lemm	Marloes van den Berg
TITLE	**EDITING COMPANY**	**COPYWRITER**	**DIRECTOR**
Hitchhiker	Jonno Griffith, Amsterdam	Bas Korsten	Sven Super

VISUAL: A confident-looking woman is driving down a forest road in her new Polo. She's humming to the music of her favorite CD. It's early evening and the weather is starting to get bad. She sees a lumberjack in his mid-thirties holding a big chainsaw, hitchhiking. She pulls over and lowers her window.

WOMAN: Hi, where are you going?

VISUAL: The man gestures with his hand.

WOMAN: OK, hop in. But do you mind sitting in the back?

VISUAL: She gestures toward a cake, which is taking in the front seat. The lumberjack gets into the rear seat. The woman continues humming to the music. The lumberjack is sitting in the rear seat with the chainsaw on his lap.

SUPER: You feel quite confident with the new Polo.

Volkswagen. Who else?

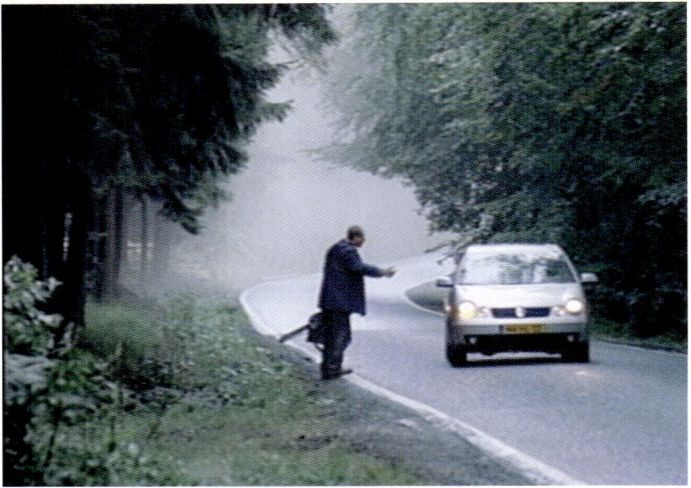

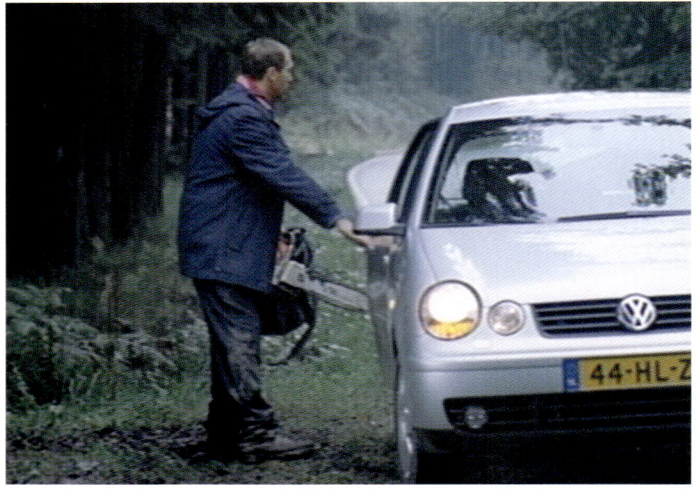

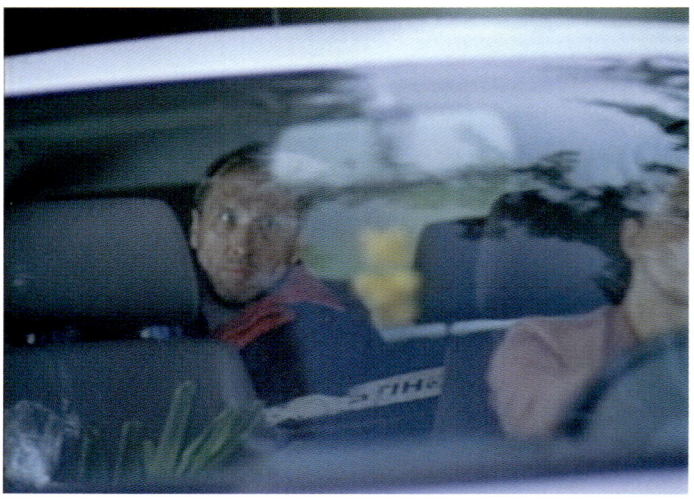

CATEGORY
Beverages/Alcoholic

ADVERTISER/PRODUCT
Guinness

TITLE
Dreamer

ADVERTISING AGENCY
Abbott Mead Vickers BBDO,
London

PRODUCTION COMPANY
Academy, London

EDITING COMPANY
Sam Sneade, London

MUSIC COMPANY
Soundtree Music, London

SOUND DESIGN COMPANY
Wave Studios, London

ANIMATION COMPANY
Computer Film Co., London

ACCOUNT EXECUTIVE
Clive Tanqueray

CREATIVE DIRECTOR
Peter Souter

COPYWRITER
Walter Campbell

ART DIRECTOR
Walter Campbell

PRODUCER
Yvonne Chalkley

DIRECTOR
Jonathan Glazer

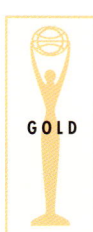
GOLD

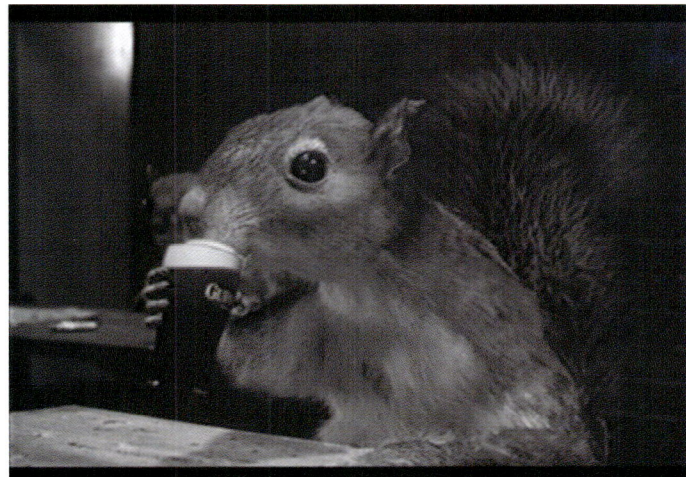

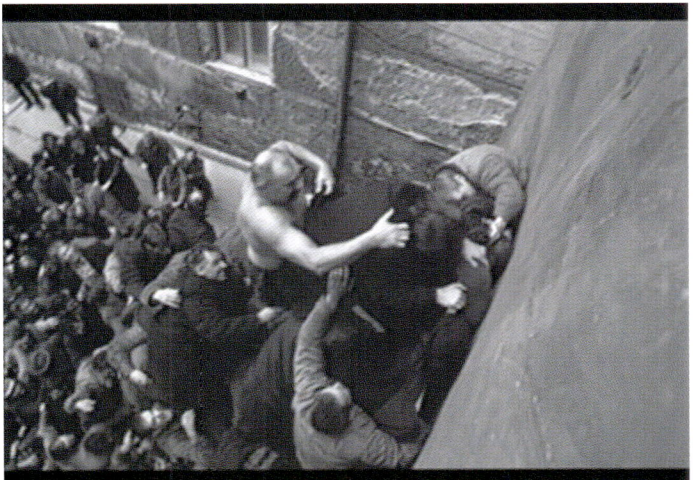

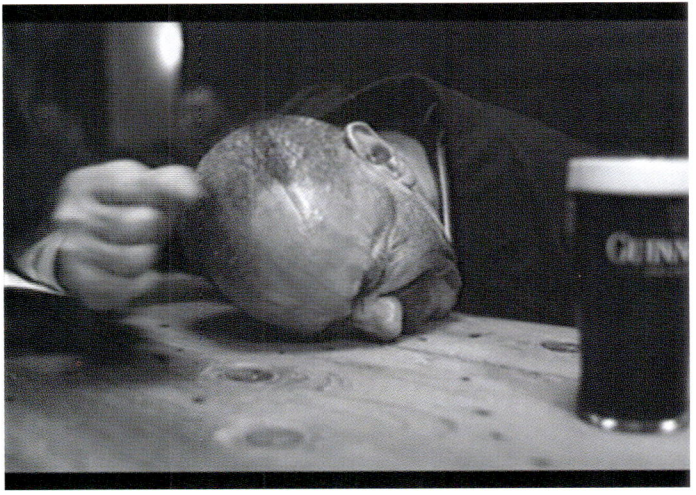

SYNOPSIS: It's the biggest event ever for the Dream Club, a group of four to five top dreamers. Quinn, one of the dreamers, is going for an absolutely brilliant dream: the meaning of life.

VISUAL: Quinn is sitting in a bar with the other Dream Club members.

VO: And then there's this guy…the champion of the Dream Club.

VISUAL: Quinn transitions into his dream. He is standing in a street, his head lowered, mirroring his posture in the bar.

BARTENDER: What are you drinking?

VISUAL: Quinn awakens from his dream and replies.

QUINN: The usual.

VISUAL: Quinn falls back asleep. As do the other Dream Club members. The pint he ordered is put on the bar.

VO: He drifts off with questions and wakes with answers.

VISUAL: Quinn opens his eyes and sees another sleeper seated opposite him. It's a squirrel. They squint at each other through sleepy eyes. The squirrel looks around and sees a bar full of squirrels playing darts and reading newspapers.

SQUIRREL: I've just had the weirdest dream.

VISUAL: The squirrel picks up the Guinness and starts to drink. Quinn is in his dream.

VO: It's a gift.

VISUAL: Quinn is running down the street. He is now in an open space. A massive curtain reaches up five or six stories high in front of him. A crowd is huddled round the curtain trying to see through it, but there is only one aperture for them to peek through. The people looking through the gap are laughing, fixated with what is on the other side.

VO: Tonight's dream: the big question…the one we all ask.

VISUAL: Quinn tries to get through the crowd but no one moves. He takes off his shirt and continues to make his way through the crowd. The people are laughing. A horse is rolling on his back laughing.

VO: What's the meaning of life?

VISUAL: Quinn makes his way through the crowd to the hole in the curtain. He begins picking people up and lifting them over his shoulder; as though weightless, they fly off into the distance, all the while laughing and full of fun. Quinn is in the bar and, then, on the street.

VO: Go on you rascal.

VISUAL: Two dogs are jumping up and laughing. Quinn reaches the aperture, puts his eye to the hole, and sees himself asleep. We're back in the bar. The other members of the Dream Club are watching over Quinn sleeping. He starts to laugh. The entire bar laughs; Quinn has discovered the meaning of life. The Dream Club has been joined by a huge crowd of other people all standing motionless. Everyone in the world is waiting for Quinn to wake and reveal his dream.

VO: This is the Dream Club. Ladies and Gentleman please charge your glasses.

SUPER: Good Things Come to Those Who Wait.

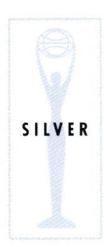

SILVER

CATEGORY Beverages/Alcoholic	**PRODUCTION COMPANY** Partizan, Santa Monica	**ACCOUNT EXECUTIVE** Shana Brooks	**PRODUCER** Ed Zazzera
ADVERTISER/PRODUCT Mike's Hard Lemonade	**EDITING COMPANY** Mackenzie Cutler, New York	**CREATIVE DIRECTOR** Eric Silver	**DIRECTOR** Traktor
TITLE Lumberjack	**SOUND DESIGN COMPANY** Mackenzie Cutler, New York	**COPYWRITER** William Gelner, Ian Reichenthal	
ADVERTISING AGENCY Cliff Freeman and Partners, New York	**ANIMATION COMPANY** Quiet Man, New York	**ART DIRECTOR** Guy Shelmerdine, Scott Vitrone	

VISUAL: Lumberjack chopping at a fallen tree with an axe. Someone yells his name.

FOREMAN VO: Hey, Ted!

VISUAL: The lumberjack looks up in the direction of the person yelling and accidentally chops off his foot. Close-up of his boot on the ground. The lumberjack gets up and brushes himself off. Only then does he realize that he chopped off his foot. The foreman enters the frame.

FOREMAN: Tough break, buddy.

VISUAL: The lumberjack looks down at his boot and hops to maintain his balance.

LUMBERJACK: Yeah, my wife just bought me them boots yesterday.

FOREMAN: Those are nice boots. Tell ya what: Let me buy you a tasty Mike's Hard Lemonade.

LUMBERJACK: Now you're talkin'.

VO: A hard day calls for a hard lemonade.

VISUAL: Interior of bar. A bunch of lumberjacks clink together bottles of Mike's Hard Lemonade in a toast. The foreman does the same but jokingly clinks his bottle with the man's boot instead of a Mike's. Everyone laughs at this, except the lumberjack who chopped off his foot.

VISUAL: A Mike's Hard Lemonade six-pack falls from above and lands on the bar.

VO: A hard day calls for a hard lemonade. Make it Mike's.

SUPER: Make it Mike's.

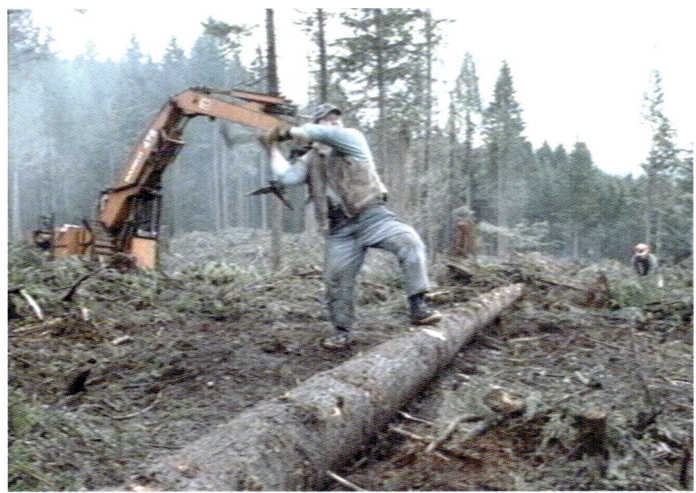

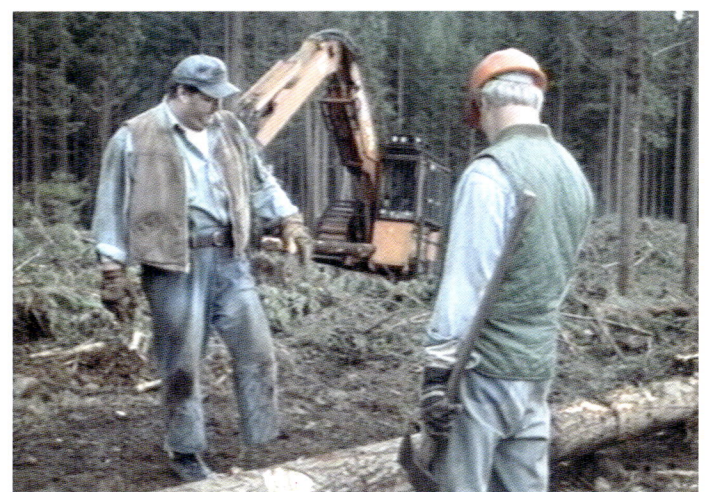

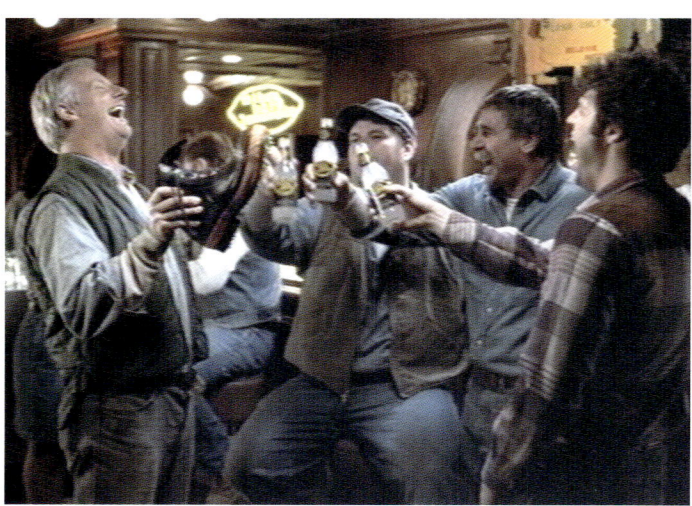

CATEGORY
Beverages/Alcoholic

ADVERTISER/PRODUCT
Anheuser-Busch Inc./Budweiser

TITLE
Mr. Really Bad Toupee Wearer

ADVERTISING AGENCY
DDB, Chicago

PRODUCTION COMPANY
Coppos Films, Los Angeles

EDITING COMPANY
Panic & Bob, Toronto

MUSIC COMPANY
Sandal Music, Chicago

CREATIVE DIRECTOR
Mark Gross, Bill Cimino,
Bob Winter

COPYWRITER
Bill Cimino

ART DIRECTOR
Mark Gross

PRODUCER
Greg Popp

DIRECTOR
Tom Schiller

GROUP CREATIVE DIRECTOR
John Immesoete

ANNOUNCER
Pete Stacker

VOCALIST
David Bickler

COMPOSER
Sandy Torano, Sam Struyk

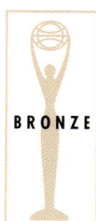

BRONZE

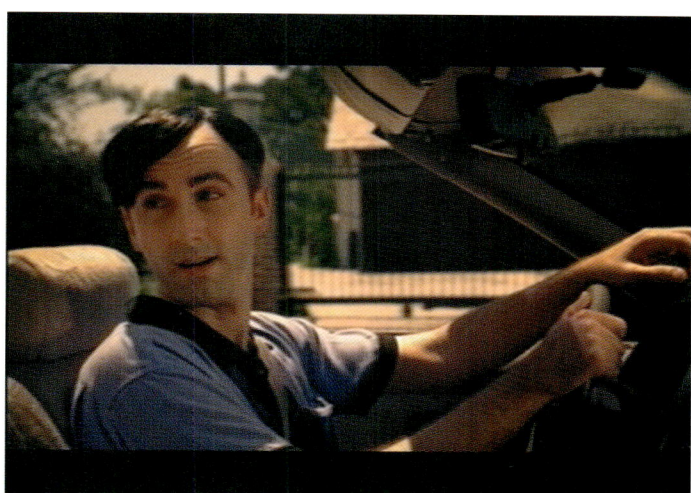

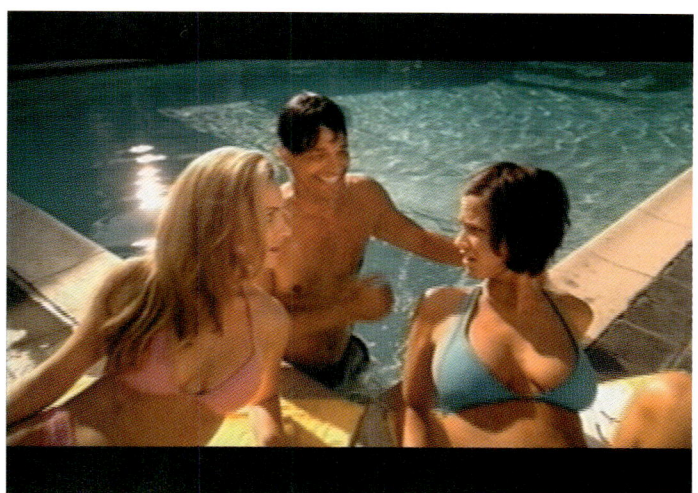

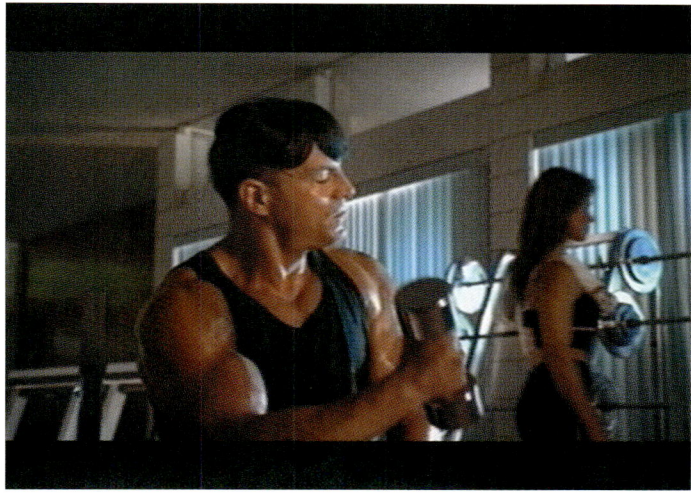

VISUAL: A singer in a recording studio and scenes of men involved in various activities, including jogging, driving, swimming, and weightlifting. Each guy is wearing a really bad toupee.

SUPER: Real Men of Genius.

VO: Budweiser presents, real men of genius.

SINGER: *Real men of genius…*

VO: Today we salute you…Mr. Really Bad Toupee Wearer.

SINGER: *Mr. Really Bad Toupee Wearer*

VO: More than any neon sign or exploding scoreboard ever could, your chrome-dome cover says, "Hey guys—look at me."

SINGER: *What could you be thinkin'?*

VO: You think it looks natural, but it couldn't look phonier if it had a chinstrap!

SINGER: *Couldn't fool a blind man…*

VO: Made of space age fibers, "it" can repel anything. Rain. Wind. Snow. And especially…young women.

SINGER: *I don't think so!*

VO: So crack open an ice-cold Budweiser, Mr. Stud in a Rug. Then crack open another for that thing on your head.

SINGER: *I don't think it's on straight…*

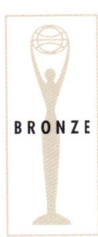

BRONZE

CATEGORY
Beverages/Alcoholic

ADVERTISER/PRODUCT
Anheuser-Busch Inc./Budweiser

TITLE
Mr. Pro Wrestling Wardrobe
Designer

ADVERTISING AGENCY
DDB, Chicago

PRODUCTION COMPANY
Coppos Films, Los Angeles

EDITING COMPANY
Panic & Bob, Toronto

MUSIC COMPANY
Scandal Music, Chicago

CREATIVE DIRECTOR
Mark Gross, Bill Cimino

COPYWRITER
Bill Cimino

ART DIRECTOR
Mark Gross

PRODUCER
Greg Popp

DIRECTOR
Tom Schiller

GROUP CREATIVE DIRECTOR
John Immesoete

ANNOUNCER
Pete Stacker

VOCALIST
David Bickler

COMPOSER
Sandy Torano, Sam Struyk

VISUAL: A singer in a recording studio and scenes of various wrestlers dressed outrageously, in pink or yellow spandex tights, capes, boots, masks, thongs, and feather boas.

SUPER: Real Men of Genius.

SINGER: *Real men of genius.*

VO: Today we salute you, Mr. Pro Wrestling Wardrobe Designer.

SINGER: *Mr. Pro Wrestling Wardrobe Designer.*

VO: While lesser designers would shy away from putting 300-pound men in spandex, you embrace it.

SINGER: *Yes you do.*

VO: Pushing fashion to its limits, literally, you pair tights with a cape, a leotard with a mask, leather boots with a thong.

SINGER: *Oww—lookin' good.*

VO: All understated ways of saying, "I'm going to rip your head off…and look fabulous doing it."

SINGER: *Ripping heads off.*

VO: So this Bud's for you, Mr. Pro Wrestling Wardrobe Guy.

SFX: Bottle cap opening.

VO: Because without you a man crushing another man's head in his arms would just look silly.

SINGER: *Mr. Pro Wresting Wardrobe Designer.*

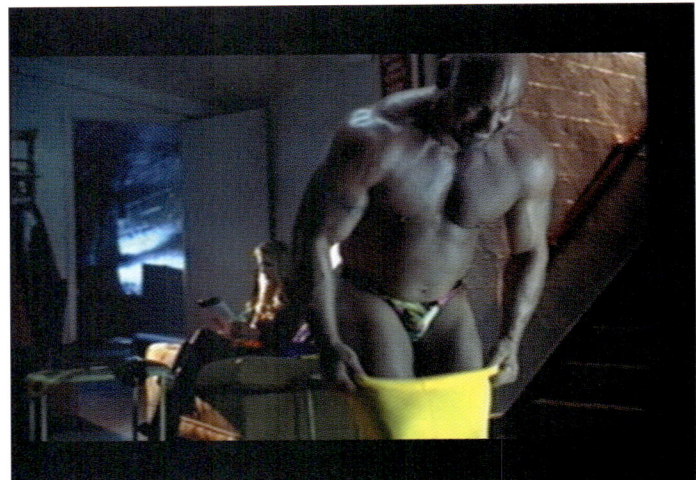

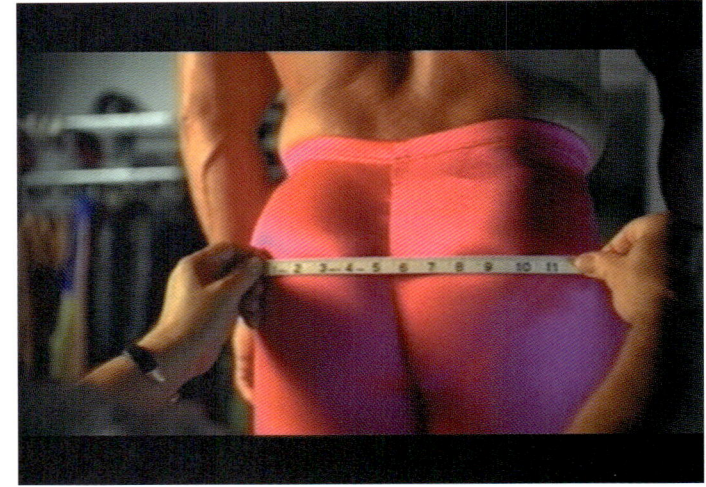

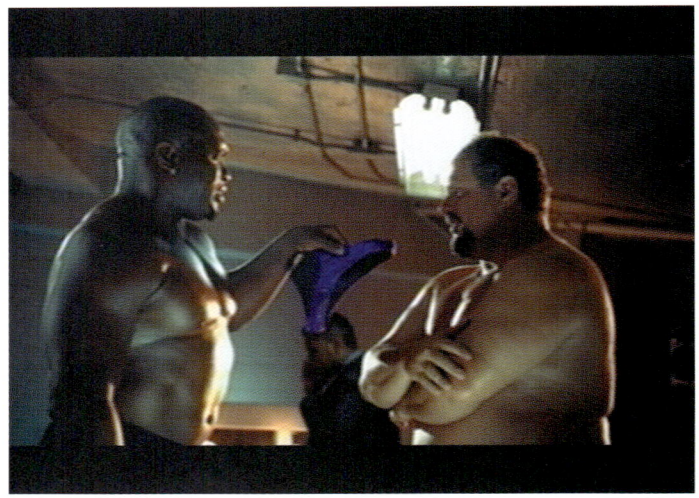

CATEGORY
Beverages/Alcoholic

ADVERTISER/PRODUCT
Anheuser-Busch Inc./Bud Light

TITLE
Sin & Sentimentality

ADVERTISING AGENCY
Downtown Partners, Toronto

PRODUCTION COMPANY
Avion, Toronto

MUSIC COMPANY
David Fleury Music, Toronto

ACCOUNT EXECUTIVE
Bob Shanks, Tim Binkley,
Kelley Bosley

CLIENT SUPERVISOR
Mike Calvery, John Verdon

CREATIVE DIRECTOR
Rich Pryce-Jones, David Chiavegato,
Dan Pawych

COPYWRITER
David Chiavegato

ART DIRECTOR
Rich Pryce-Jones

PRODUCER
Johnny Chambers

DIRECTOR
Martin Granger

EDITOR
David Hicks

SOUND DESIGNER
Dan Kuntz

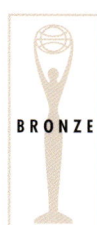

BRONZE

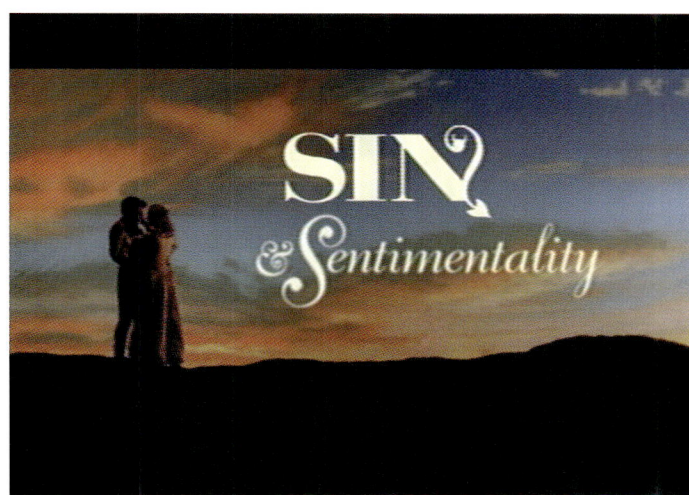

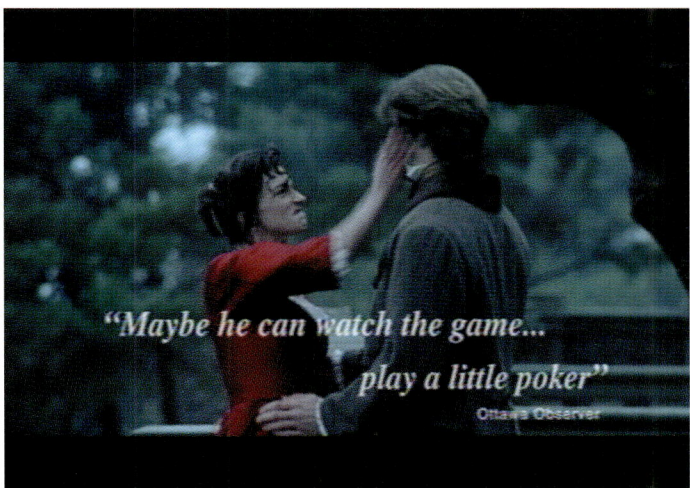

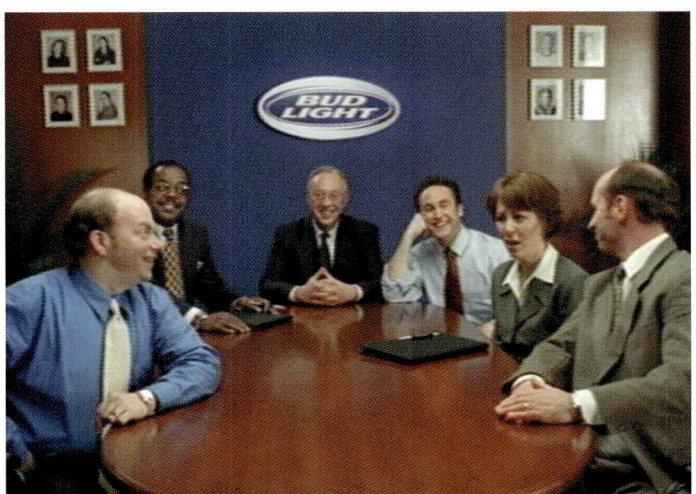

SYNOPSIS: A parody of a movie trailer for a period piece film.

VISUAL: In a variety of late nineteenth-century settings, women keep slapping men's faces.

VO: Coming soon to a theater near you. The world's first forty-eight-hour epic movie, made by women, for women.

SUPER: 48 hours long.

SUPER: Sin and Sentimentality.

VO: Sin and Sentimentality.

SUPER: One movie…all weekend long.

VO: One movie. All weekend long.

SUPER: "Definitely a ladies' weekend out."—*Vancouver Tribune*

VO: Definitely a ladies' weekend out. Vancouver Tribune.

WOMAN 1: Do you think I'm hot?

WOMAN 2: You're a regular Hotty Von Hottenheimer.

SUPER: "What will your husband do while you're gone?"
—*Montreal Chronicle*

VO: What will your husband do while you're gone? Montreal Chronicle.

WOMAN 1: Perhaps I'm nagging him too much.

SUPER: "I guess he'll have to hang out with his friends and drink beer."—*Calgary Spectrum*

VO: I guess he'll have to hang out with his friends and drink beer. Calgary Spectrum.

WOMAN 2: You may want to cut down on the nagging.

WOMAN 1: My nagging is getting in the way of my hotness.

SUPER: "Maybe he can watch the game…play a little poker."
—*Ottawa Observer*

VO: Maybe he can watch the game, play a little poker.
Ottawa Observer.

VO: Sin and Sentimentality. A Bud Light production.

VISUAL: It is revealed that the trailer is being screened by company executives in the Bud Light headquarters boardroom.

MALE EXECUTIVE: Not Bad, huh Linda?

FEMALE EXECUTIVE: Idiots!

VISUAL: Spokesman popping out of Bud Light bottle cap.

SPOKESMAN: This calls for a Bud Light.

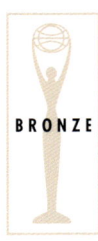

BRONZE

CATEGORY
Beverages/Alcoholic

ADVERTISER/PRODUCT
Heineken USA

TITLE
Birth of a Sign

ADVERTISING AGENCY
Lowe Lintas & Partners, New York

PRODUCTION COMPANY
harvest, Santa Monica;
Tate & Partners, Santa Monica

EDITING COMPANY
Mackenzie Cutler, New York

ACCOUNT EXECUTIVE
Michael Silver, Julie Mulholland

CREATIVE DIRECTOR
Lee Garfinkel

ART DIRECTOR
CJ Waldman

PRODUCER
Bob Nelson, Steve Ford

DIRECTOR
Baker Smith

EXECUTIVE PRODUCER
Bonnie Goldfarb, David Tate

VISUAL: It's the late 1960s, at a massive, Woodstock-type outdoor concert. Amid all the music and revelry, a hippie makes his way to a concession stand and holds up two fingers.

HIPPIE: Two Heinekens, please.

VENDOR: What did you say?

HIPPIE: Two Heinekens. Please.

VENDOR: Oh, two Heinekens.

VISUAL: The music is very loud and other people in the crowd think that the hippie has said "peace," not "please." They associate it with the two fingers the guy was holding up. Suddenly, hippies everywhere are going around holding two fingers up and saying "peace."

SUPER: July 16, 1969.

The Peace Sign Is Born.

VISUAL: The peace sign spreads like wildfire; everyone at the concert is now doing it.

SUPER: It's all about the beer. Heineken.

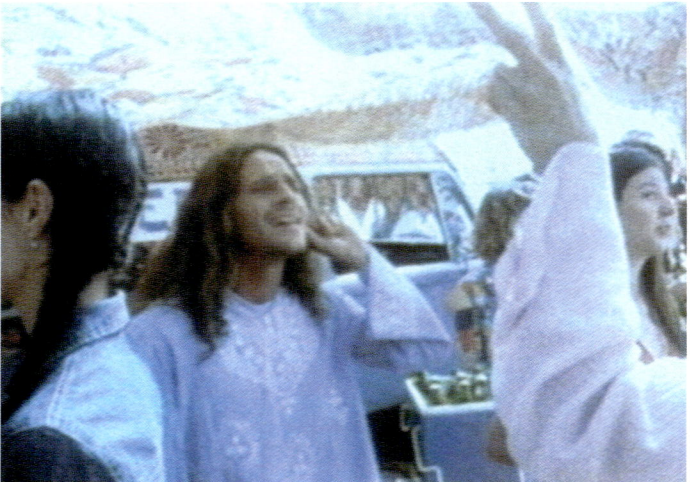

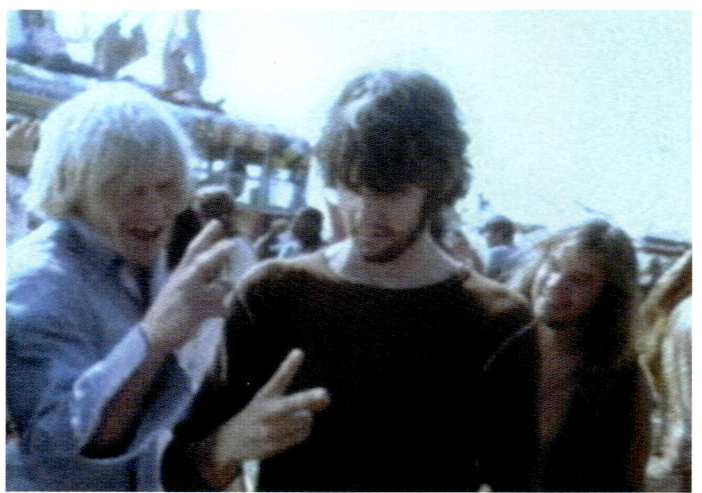

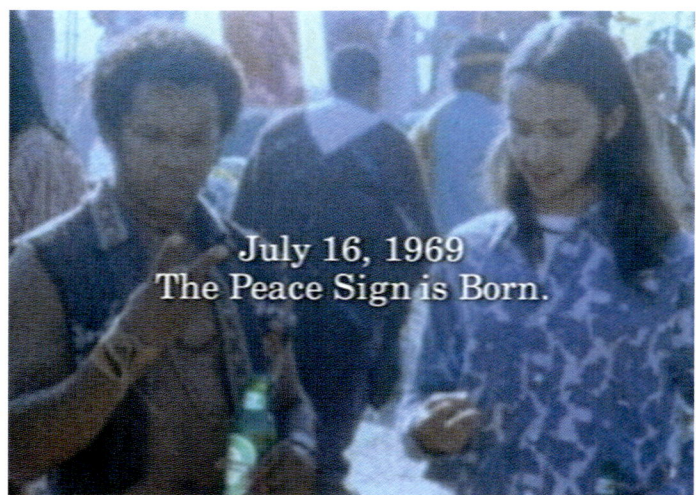

CATEGORY
Beverages/Nonalcoholic

ADVERTISER/PRODUCT
Pepsi

TITLE
Beckham

ADVERTISING AGENCY
AlmapBBDO, São Paulo

PRODUCTION COMPANY
@radical.media, New York

MUSIC COMPANY
DHMA, New York

CREATIVE DIRECTOR
Marcello Serpa

COPYWRITER
Alexandre Peralta, Cassio Zanatta

ART DIRECTOR
Giba Lages

PRODUCER
Brian Mitchell

DIRECTOR
Tarsem

MUSIC ARRANGER
David Horowitz

SILVER

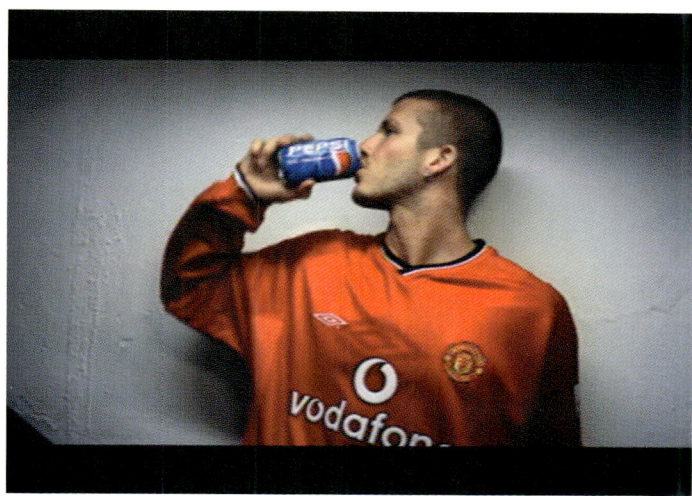

SYNOPSIS: World-famous football player David Beckham has been replaced in the game. He is walking down a stadium walkway, looking sad. He passes a boy drinking from a can of Pepsi, stops and asks for a sip. The boy hands him the can, Beckham drinks and hands the can back. The boy asks Beckham for the jersey he is wearing. He gives him the shirt and the boy uses it to wipe the top of his Pepsi can. The boy returns the jersey to Beckham who seems surprised and hurt.

SUPER: Ask for more.

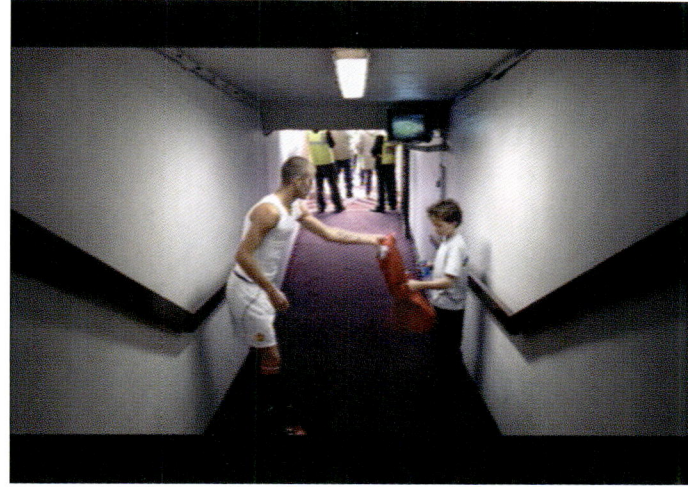

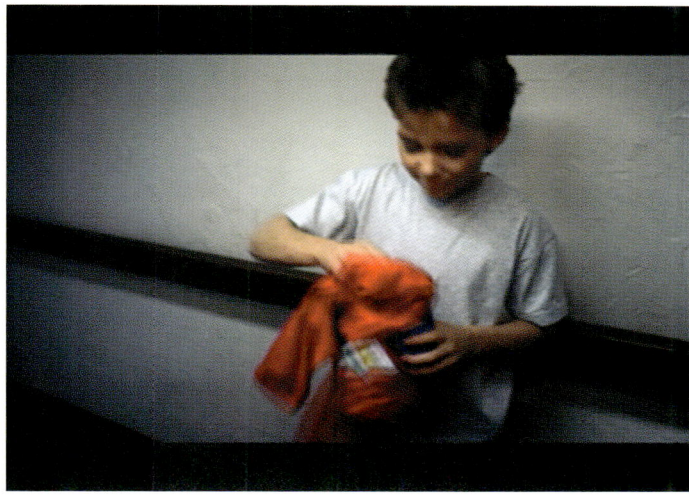

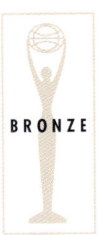

BRONZE

CATEGORY
Beverages/Nonalcoholic

ADVERTISER/PRODUCT
Café Pilão

TITLE
Cup

ADVERTISING AGENCY
AlmapBBDO, São Paulo

PRODUCTION COMPANY
Andreas Heiniger, São Paulo

MUSIC COMPANY
Play It Again, São Paulo

ACCOUNT EXECUTIVE
Wilson Pereira, Denise Nogueira

CREATIVE DIRECTOR
Marcello Serpa, Eugênio Mohallem

COPYWRITER
Roberto Pereira, Ricardo Chester

ART DIRECTOR
Luiz Sanches

PRODUCER
Egisto Betti

DIRECTOR
Anreas Heiniger

SYNOPSIS: Pilão is such a strong coffee that it doesn't lose its color, even when mixed with milk.

VISUAL: A cup of coffee is continually having milk poured into it yet remains black.

VISUAL: Pilão package.

SUPER: A Really Really Strong Coffee.

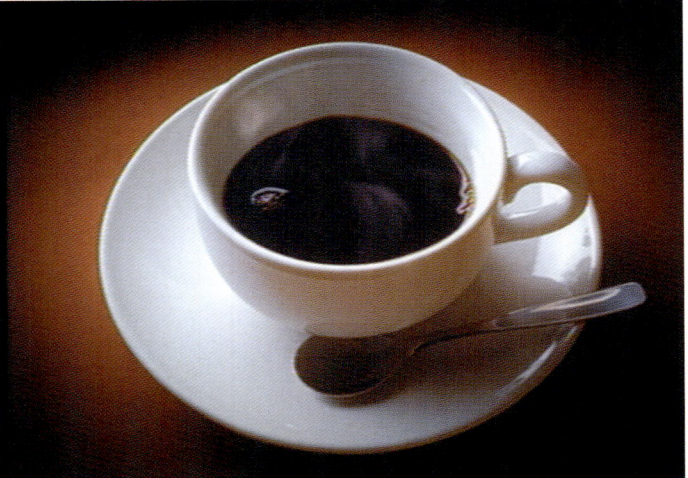

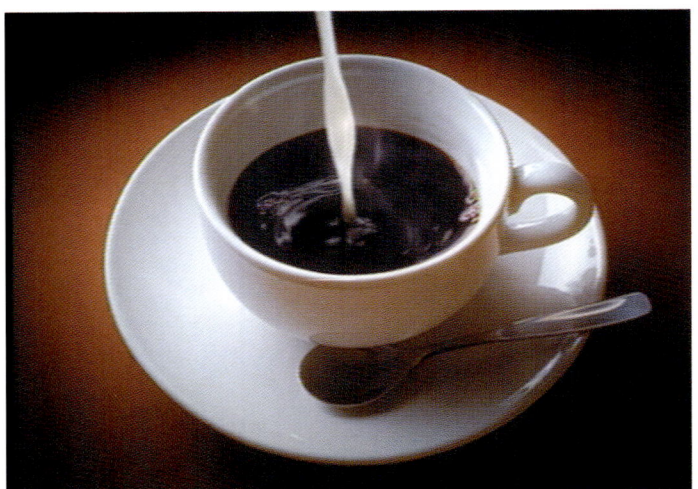

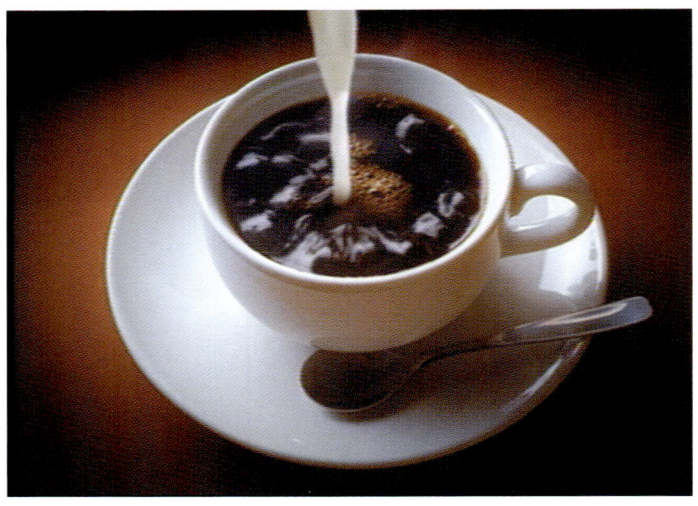

CATEGORY
Beverages/Nonalcoholic

ADVERTISER/PRODUCT
Bright Dairy

TITLE
Football

ADVERTISING AGENCY
D'Arcy, Shanghai

PRODUCTION/EDITING COMPANY
E&F Culture and Communication
Co., Shanghai

ACCOUNT EXECUTIVE
Yvonne Yin

CREATIVE DIRECTOR
Larry Ong

COPYWRITER
Gladys Meng

ART DIRECTOR
Larry Ong

PRODUCER
Yuan Ye

DIRECTOR
Yu Qing Lu

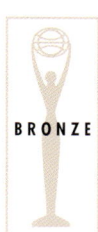

BRONZE

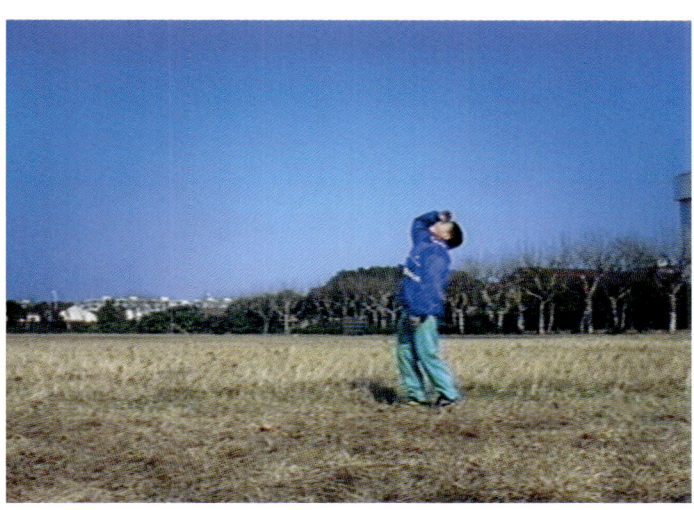

VISUAL: A boy stands alone on the playground, looking up into the sky. He seems to be looking for something and waiting for it to drop. After a while, a football falls into frame from the sky. He kicks the ball and it flies back into the sky at a very high speed. The boy is now enjoying a carton of Bright School milk.

SUPER: Want to be stronger? Drink Bright School milk.

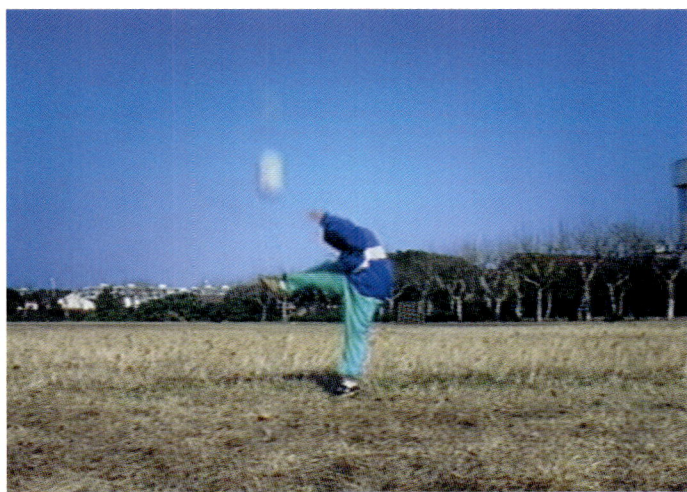

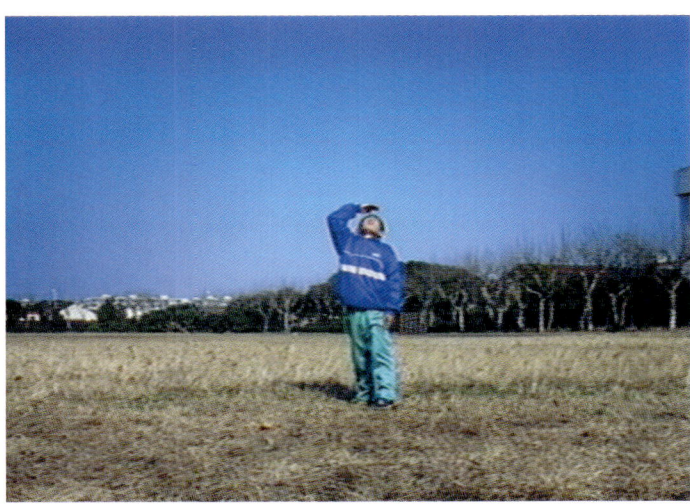

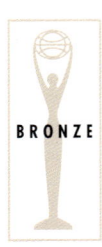

CATEGORY
Confections/Snacks

ADVERTISER/PRODUCT
Doritos 3Ds

TITLE
A Plug for 3Ds

ADVERTISING AGENCY
Clemenger BBDO, Sydney

PRODUCTION COMPANY
Great Southern Films, Sydney

SOUND DESIGN COMPANY
Pitchfork, Sydney

AGENCY PRODUCER
Jo Howlett, Rebekah Lawson

ACCOUNT EXECUTIVE
Jenny Scott, Ros Strong

CREATIVE DIRECTOR
Danny Searle

COPYWRITER
Jim Hall

ART DIRECTOR
Rohan Young

PRODUCER
Leanne Tonks

DIRECTOR
Vikki Blanche

DIRECTOR OF PHOTOGRAPHY
Graeme Woods

EDITOR
Mike Reeds

VISUAL: A fifteen-year-old boy is sitting on a bus, loudly crunching his Doritos 3Ds. A slightly older girl is sitting next to him and trying to read her book. The crunching is very distracting for her.

GIRL: Excuse me. Do you think I could have some?

VISUAL: The boy, thinking he could get lucky, gladly offers her the bag.

BOY: Yeah, sure!

VISUAL: She takes two Doritos 3Ds out of the bag and places a 3D in each of her ears as though they were earplugs. She happily goes back to reading her book and the boy looks dumbfounded.

VISUAL: Doritos 3D package shot.

SUPER: Cop an Earful.

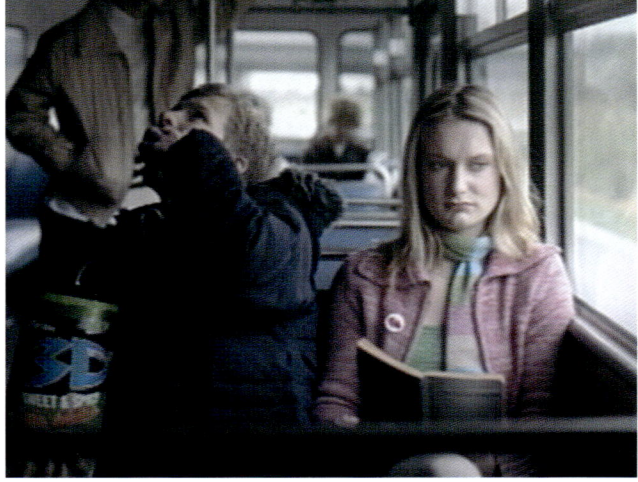

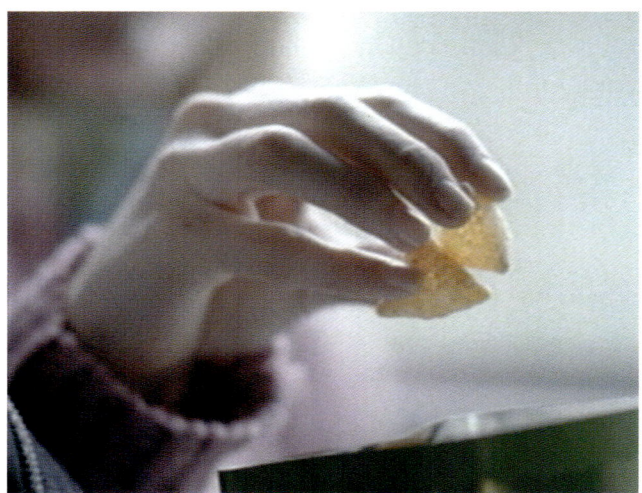

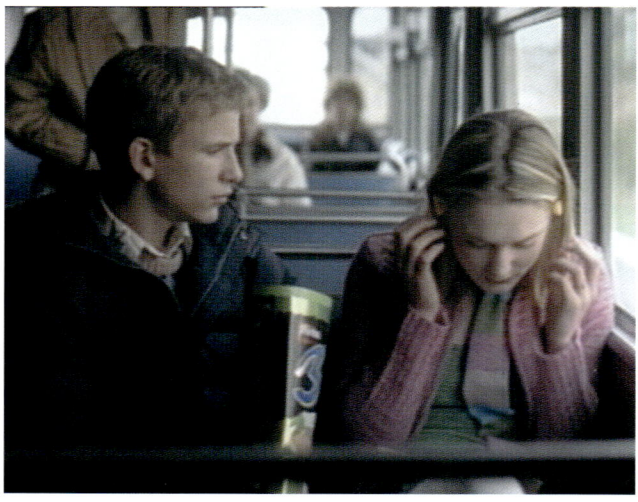

CATEGORY
Corporate/Institutional

ADVERTISER/PRODUCT
Telecom Argentina

TITLE
Yawn

ADVERTISING AGENCY
Agulla & Baccetti, Buenos Aires

PRODUCTION COMPANY
argentinacine, Buenos Aires

EDITING COMPANY
Post-Bionica, Buenos Aires

MUSIC COMPANY
Symphony, Buenos Aires

SOUND DESIGN COMPANY
Symphony, Buenos Aires

ACCOUNT EXECUTIVE
Mariano Mataloni

GENERAL CREATIVE DIRECTOR
Ramiro Agulla, Carlos Baccetti

CREATIVE DIRECTOR
Sebastian Wilhelm,
Maximiliano Anselmo

COPYWRITER
Christian Camean, Javier Mentasti

ART DIRECTOR
Juan Cabral, Santiago Chaumont

PRODUCER
Hernán Carnavale

DIRECTOR
Fabian Bielinsky

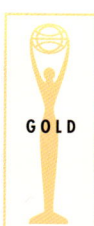

GOLD

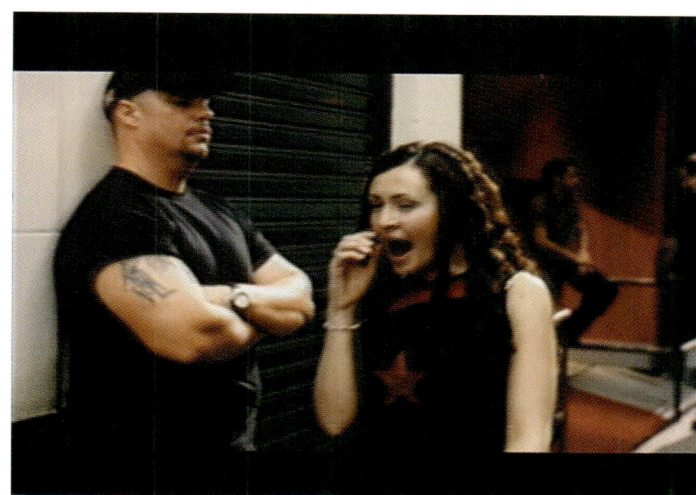

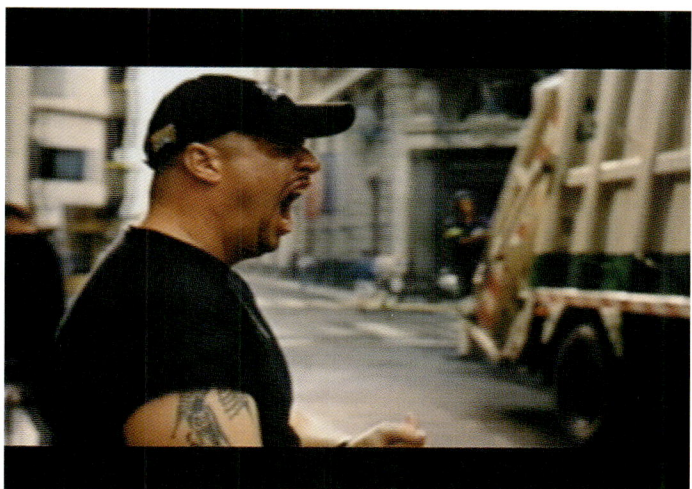

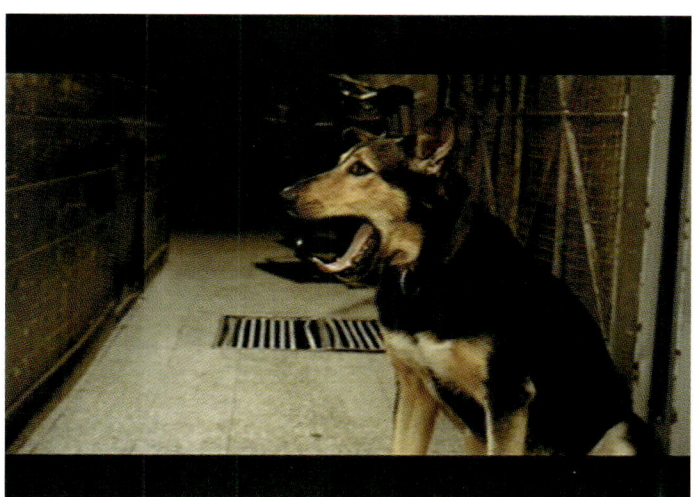

VISUAL: The commercial opens at a dance club entrance. We see a group of three girls leaving the club. One of them starts yawning and slightly covers her mouth with her hand. The club's bouncer sees her and he starts yawning. The camera travels, and we see a garbage truck passing in front of the employees, who starts yawning. There is an accident on the street. We see policemen and TV cameras. One of the policemen sees the man on the garbage truck and yawns. The cameras film him and broadcast his image on the air. A man who is jogging passes a home appliance store sees this image on TV and starts yawning. A dog sitting at the gate of an apartment building sees the jogger passing and yawns. The driver of a car passing by, who comes from a fancy-dress ball, sees the dog and starts yawning. The camera follows him to the gate of a house. The housekeeper sees him and starts yawning just as the original girl, who started the contagious yawn chain at the club's entrance, gets home. She waves at the house-keeper and starts yawning again.

SUPER: Communicate. It's simple. Telecom.

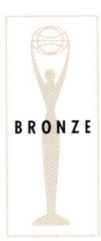

CATEGORY
Dot-Com Advertising

ADVERTISER/PRODUCT
MundoCelular.com/Web Site

TITLE
Mobile Phone Bill

ADVERTISING AGENCY
CraveroLanis Euro RSCG,
Buenos Aires

PRODUCTION COMPANY
Peluca Films, Buenos Aires

AGENCY PRODUCER
Carlos Volpe, Pablo Gagni

ACCOUNT EXECUTIVE
Elizabeth Ares

CLIENT SUPERVISOR
Javier Villarino

CREATIVE GROUP DIRECTOR
Juan Cravero, Dario Lanis

COPYWRITER
Martin Juarez, Dario Lanis,
Juan Cravero

ART DIRECTOR
Juan Cravero, Dario Lanis

DIRECTOR
Peluca

VISUAL: A man is sitting in a chair reading the newspaper. He notices that there is an envelope under the door of his apartment. He picks up the envelope and begins to read its contents, a bill. He looks uncomfortable. He throws himself against the door, and grabs his behind.

MAN: Screaming sounds.

VISUAL: He looks at the bill again, shoves it in his mouth, and walks off with great difficulty.

VISUAL: The same man sitting in front of his computer, trying to get comfortable in his chair. On the computer's monitor we see the logo for mundocelular.com.

VO: Enter mundocelular.com. Compare and choose the best.

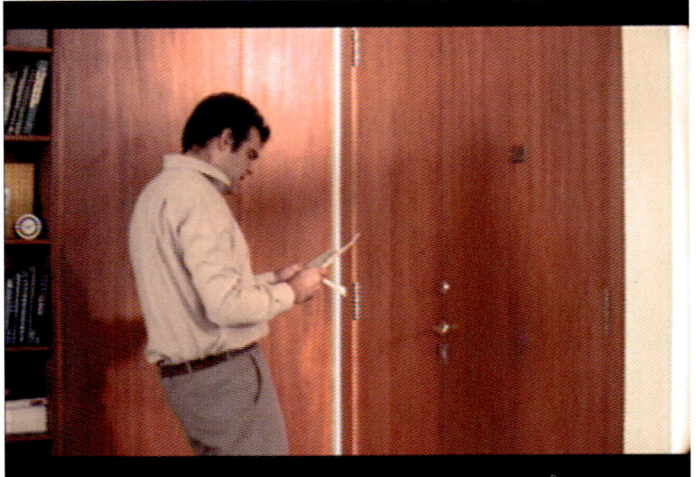

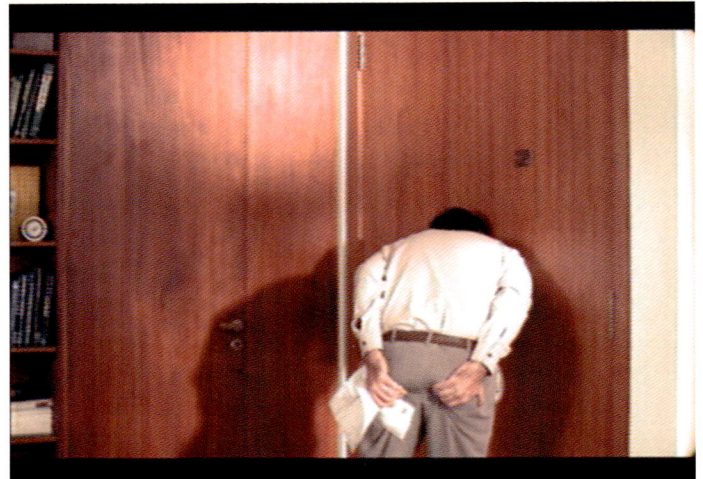

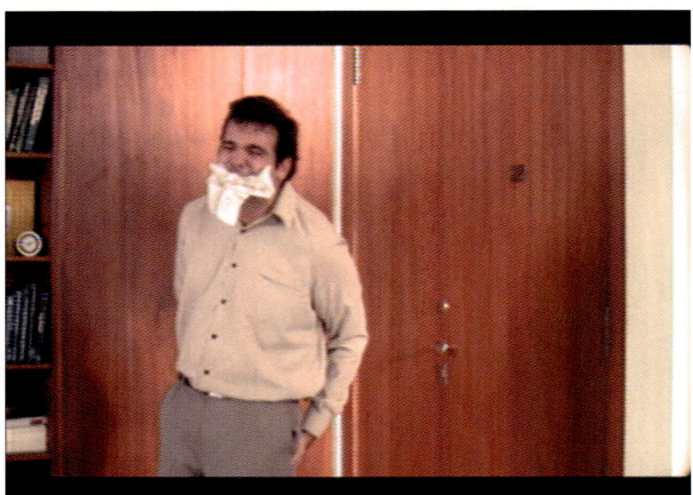

CATEGORY
Entertainment Promotion

ADVERTISER/PRODUCT
Moonlight Cinema

TITLE
Mozzie

ADVERTISING AGENCY
Whybin TBWA, Melbourne

PRODUCTION COMPANY
Complete Post, Melbourne

CREATIVE DIRECTOR
Scott Whybin

COPYWRITER
Rob Hibbert, Justine Gallagher

ART DIRECTOR
Justine Gallagher, Rob Hibbert

PRODUCER
Joanne Alach

EDITOR
Tim Parrington

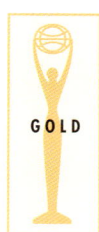

GOLD

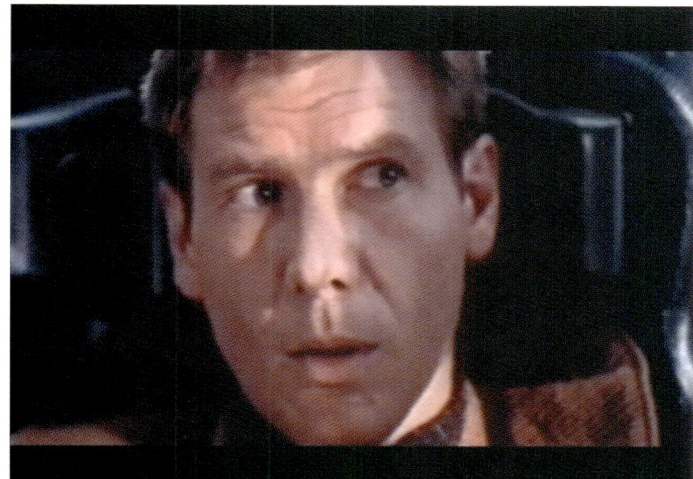

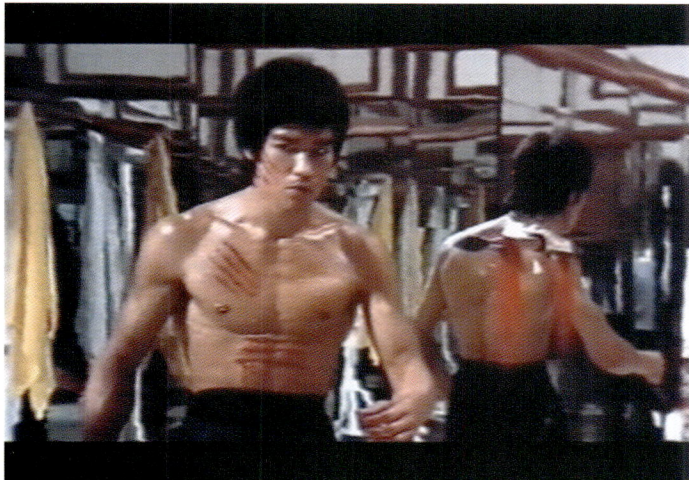

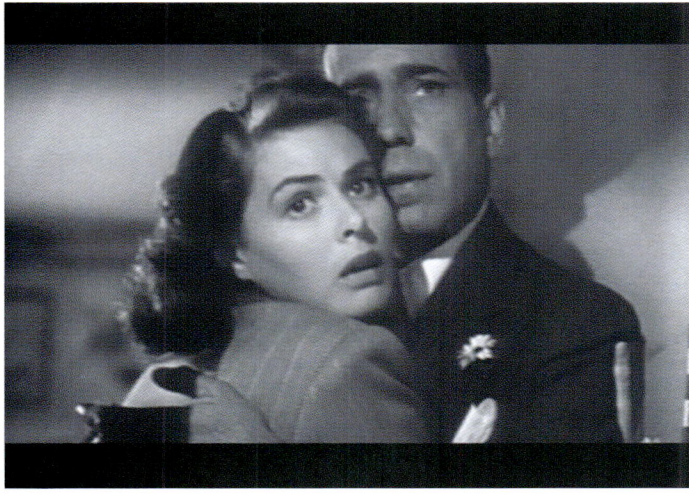

VISUAL: Harrison Ford in a scene from the film *Blade Runner*. He is looking around for something.

SFX: Mosquito buzzing.

VISUAL: Bruce Lee in a scene from the film *Enter the Dragon*. He too appears to be looking for something.

SFX: Mosquito buzzing.

VISUAL: Gregory Peck in a scene from the film *Roman Holiday*. Suddenly he awakens from sleeping.

SFX: Mosquito buzzing.

VISUAL: Steve McQueen in a scene from the film *Bullitt*. He is looking at a paper bag.

SFX: Mosquito buzzing.

SUPER: See your favourite films outdoors.

Moonlight Cinema logo.

VISUAL: Humphrey Bogart and Ingrid Bergman in a scene from the film *Casablanca*. They are kissing and then suddenly stop as if they are interrupted.

SFX: Mosquito buzzing.

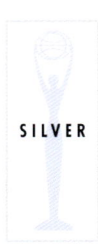

SILVER

CATEGORY
Entertainment Promotion

ADVERTISER/PRODUCT
São Paulo Museum of Art

TITLE
Faces

ADVERTISING AGENCY
DM9 DDB, São Paulo

PRODUCTION COMPANY
Vertical Filmes, São Paulo

MUSIC COMPANY
Voices, São Paulo

ACCOUNT EXECUTIVE
Vlademir Silva

CREATIVE DIRECTOR
Erh Ray, Jader Rossetto,
Pedro Cappeletti

COPYWRITER
Miguel Bemfica

ART DIRECTOR
Paulo Diehl

PRODUCER
Nivio de Souza

DIRECTOR
Carlos Manga Junior

VISUAL: A young man is making faces. He takes the hand of the friend next to him and passes it over his own face. The camera zooms back and reveals that his friend is blind. As the camera continues to zoom out, it is revealed that the two men are seated next to a cubist painting by Picasso. The man making faces is trying to get his blind friend to "see" the painting.

SUPER: Picasso at the São Paulo Museum of Art. No One Should Miss It.

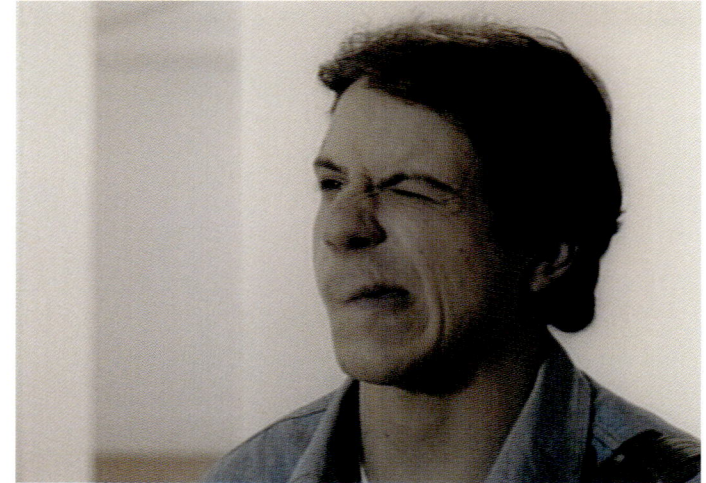

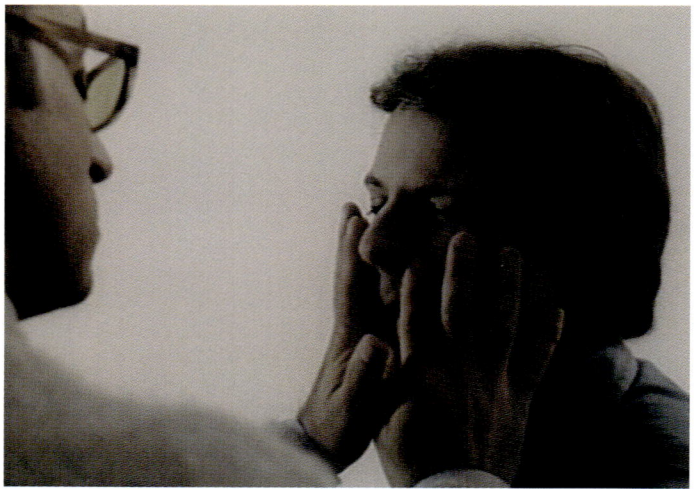

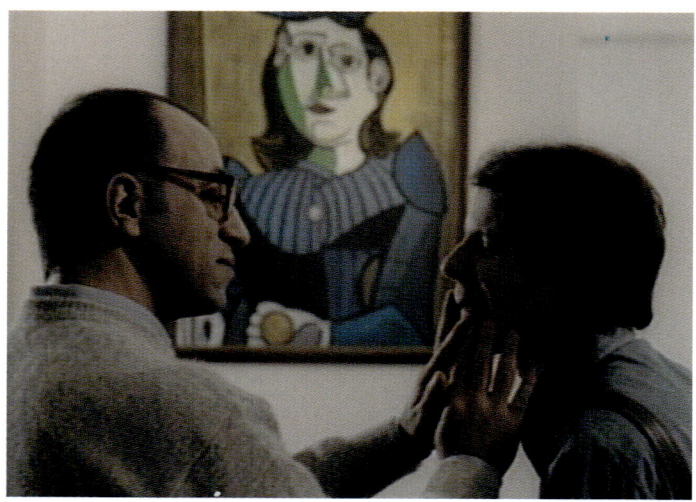

CATEGORY
Entertainment Promotion

ADVERTISER/PRODUCT
Walt Disney World

TITLE
Pillow Talk

ADVERTISING AGENCY
Leo Burnett USA, Chicago

PRODUCTION COMPANY
PYTKA, Venice

CREATIVE DIRECTOR
Ned Crowley, Jonathan Moore

COPYWRITER
Ned Crowley

ART DIRECTOR
Jonathan Moore

PRODUCER
Bob Harley

DIRECTOR
Joe Pytka

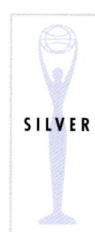

SILVER

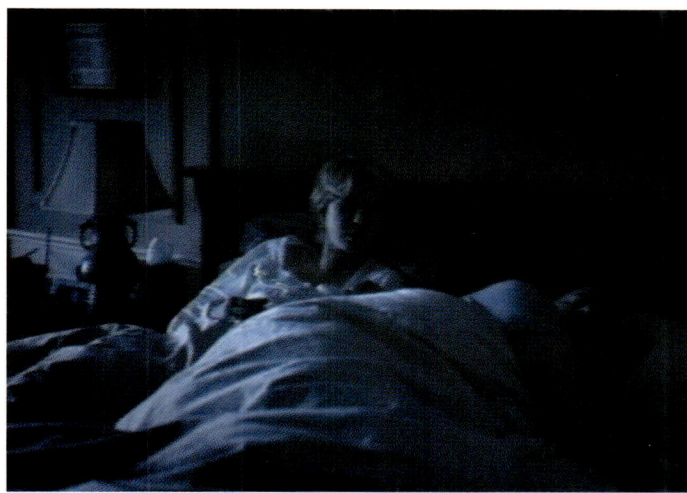

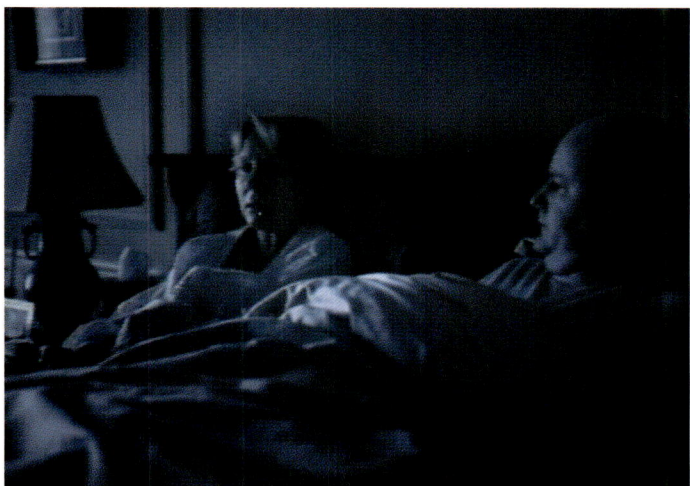

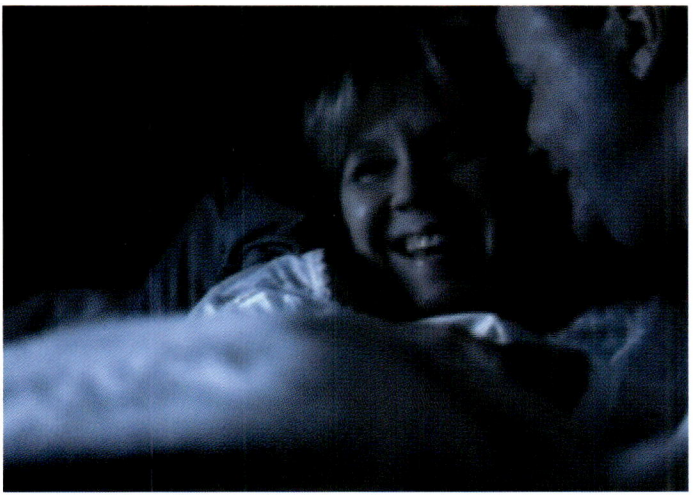

VISUAL: A woman and her husband are asleep in bed. She awakens.

WOMAN: Honey…

MAN: Huh?

WOMAN: Honey…

MAN: What…what's wrong?

WOMAN: Honey, I can't sleep.

MAN: What's the matter?

WOMAN: I don't know…I've been thinking about…you know, us.

MAN: Us? What about us?

WOMAN: I don't know…I, I worry we're drifting.

MAN: Okay…drifting. What about?

WOMAN: No, you know…apart. All we ever talk about any more is the bills and work and the kids and work.

MAN: I know, but that's just natural. It's just where we are in our lives. That's all.

WOMAN: And you never talk to me any more.

MAN (laughing): What do you mean I never talk to you? I'm talking to you right now.

WOMAN: No, I mean like you used to.

MAN: Oh, what do you mean?

WOMAN: You know, in that special way. You never talk to me in that special way like you used to.

MAN: Okay, Linda. I know, but…we were younger than. We were in college.

WOMAN: See, that's what I mean…we're drifting.

MAN: No, we're not drifting…just 'cause I don't talk to you in that special way.

SFX: Man takes a deep breath.

MAN (in Donald Duck voice): I love you.

SFX: Woman laughing.

MAN: I love you very, very much.

SFX: Woman giggles.

MAN continues talking in Donald Duck voice.

SFX: Woman laughing.

SUPER: Magic Happens. Disney.

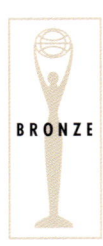

CATEGORY
Entertainment Promotion

ADVERTISER/PRODUCT
De Lotto

TITLE
Real Friends

ADVERTISING AGENCY
Result DDB, Amstelveen

PRODUCTION COMPANY
CZAR, Amsterdam

ACCOUNT EXECUTIVE
Julian Stevense, Nelly de Wit

AGENCY PRODUCER
Chantal Gulpers

CREATIVE DIRECTOR
Michael Jansen

COPYWRITER
Bas Korsten

ART DIRECTOR
Michael Jansen

PRODUCER
Sytske Rijkens

DIRECTOR
Bart Timmer

CONCEPT
Michael Jansen, Bas Korsten,
Joris Kuijpers, Dylan de Backer

EDITOR
Marc Bechtold

MUSIC
Alfred Klaasen

LIGHTING CAMERAMAN
Menno Westendorp

VISUAL: We see a man, Ruud, in bed with his wife. He's talking on the phone. A notepad is beside him on a table.

RUUD: Rob, it's me. I'm at the airport. Can you pick me up? Taxi…? OK, Rob, all I need to know.

VISUAL: Ruud crosses Rob's name off the list of names on the notepad.

VISUAL: Ruud is standing in the open doorway of a house. He is carrying a full duffel bag. In the doorway, we see the man of the house, dressed in pajamas. His wife is behind him, also ready for bed.

RUDD: Can I sleep on your couch for a month?

MAN: (caught off guard) A month…?

RUDD: OK, whatever.

VISUAL: Ruud and his friend Jos are at a pub. Ruud finishes his beer, takes Jos' full glass of beer and empties into his glass.

VO: Better find out now who your real friends are.

JOS: Do you mind?

VO: It'll be a lot more difficult when you're a millionaire.

SUPER: Lotto logo.

VO: Lotto. The biggest risk of becoming a millionaire.

VISUAL: The shower in the dressing room of a fitness club. Ruud is taking a bath with a sponge. He turns to another man in the showers, Herman, hands him the sponge and soap, and turns around. Rudd is expecting Herman to wash his back.

RUUD (loudly): Herman…?

VISUAL: Herman looks around, startled.

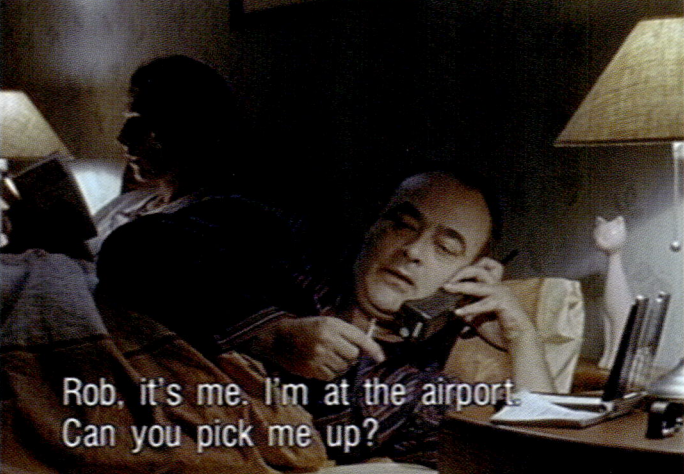

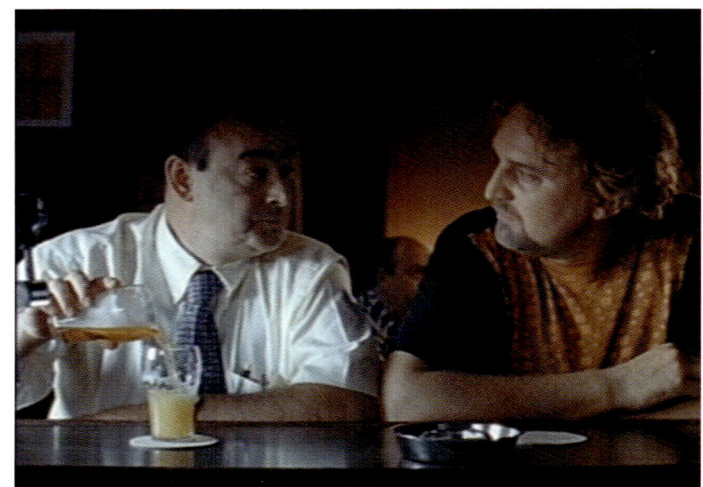

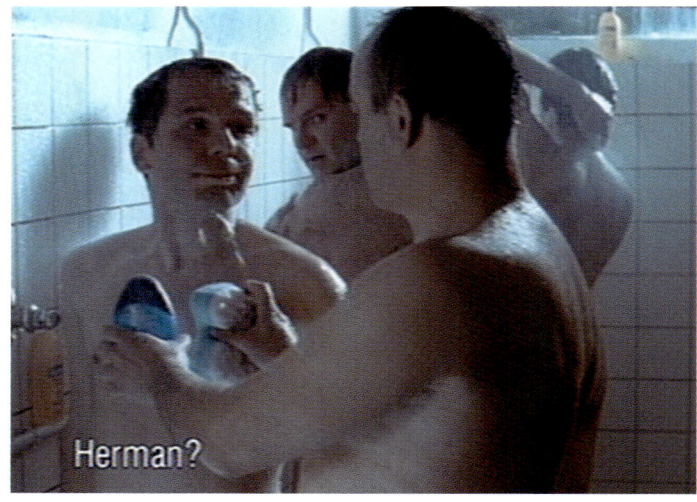

CATEGORY
Foods

ADVERTISER/PRODUCT
NutraSweet

TITLE
Fake

ADVERTISING AGENCY
Del Campo Nazca Saatchi &
Saatchi, Buenos Aires

PRODUCTION COMPANY
Wasabi, Buenos Aires

EDITING COMPANY
Metrovision, Buenos Aires

ACCOUNT EXECUTIVE
Roberto Fernández Monján

CREATIVE DIRECTOR
Pablo del Campo

COPYWRITER
Pablo Batlle

ART DIRECTOR
Hernán Jáuregui,
Iñaqui González del Solar

DIRECTOR
Diego Kaplan

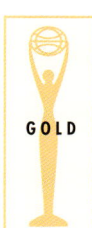

GOLD

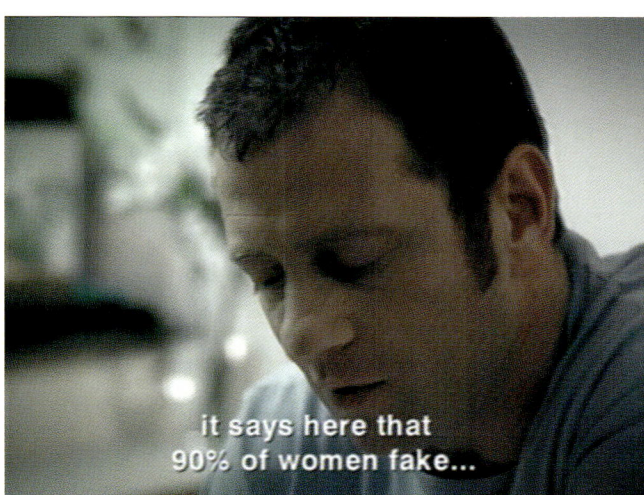

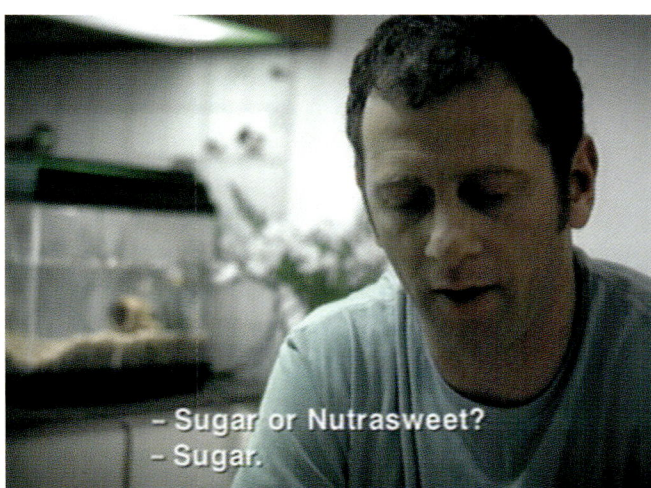

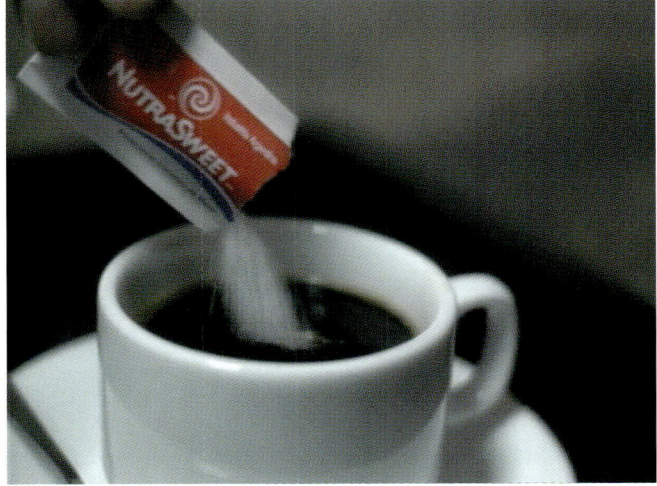

VISUAL: Open on a husband and wife in a kitchen setting. The husband is seated at a table, reading the newspaper.

HUSBAND: Darling, it says here that 90 percent of all women fake. Have you ever faked?

WIFE: No…You'd be able to tell.

VISUAL: They air kiss each other from several feet away. The wife pours the husband a cup of coffee.

WIFE (referring to sugar): One spoonful or two?

HUSBAND: Two.

VISUAL: The wife surreptitiously adds two packets of NutraSweet to the cup of coffee and gives it to the husband.

HUSBAND (tasting the coffee): Mmmmmm.

SUPER: NutraSweet. Tastes as good as sugar.

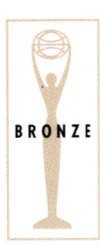

BRONZE

CATEGORY Health Care Services	**PRODUCTION COMPANY** Propaganda Films, New York	**ACCOUNT EXECUTIVE** Ted Gilvar, Patti Carson	**DIRECTOR** Tom Kuntz, Mike Maguire
ADVERTISER/PRODUCT Harvard Pilgrim Health Care	**EDITING COMPANY** Mad River Post, New York	**CREATIVE DIRECTOR** Gail Schoenbrunn	**EDITOR** Tom Scherma
TITLE Store	**MUSIC COMPANY** Hell's Kitchen, New York	**COPYWRITER** Eivind Veland	**CINEMATOGRAPHER** Jo Molitoris
ADVERTISING AGENCY Hill, Holliday, Connors, Cosmopulos, Boston	**AGENCY PRODUCER** Becky Malloy	**ART DIRECTOR** Doug Gould	**PRODUCER** Mark Fetterman

VISUAL: A salesclerk behind a counter in a clothing store. A customer walks up to her.

CUSTOMER: Hi!

SALESCLERK: Hi!

VISUAL: Customer is showing salesclerk a piece of clothing.

CUSTOMER: Do you have this in a medium?

SALESCLERK: Just a moment, please.

VISUAL: Instead of answering the customer's question, the salesclerk presses a button on her desk and "The Girl from Ipanema" starts playing—just like hold music you'd hear on the phone. The salesclerk stands there, smiling vacantly at the customer.

SFX: "The Girl from Ipanema" plays

VISUAL: The shopper is a perplexed by the salesclerk's behavior. The sales clerk presses a button again, and "The Girl from Ipanema" stops playing.

SALESCLERK: Your question is important to us. Thank you for waiting.

VISUAL: The store employee presses the button once more, and "The Girl from Ipanema" hold music starts playing again.

SFX: "The Girl from Ipanema" plays

SUPER: Life isn't this complicated. Why should your health plan be?

You ask a question. We answer it. On line or on the phone.

Harvard Pilgrim Health Care. Making great health care a little easier.

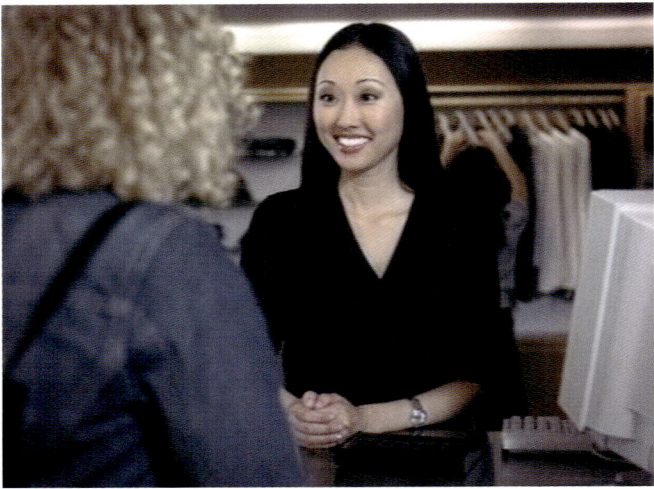

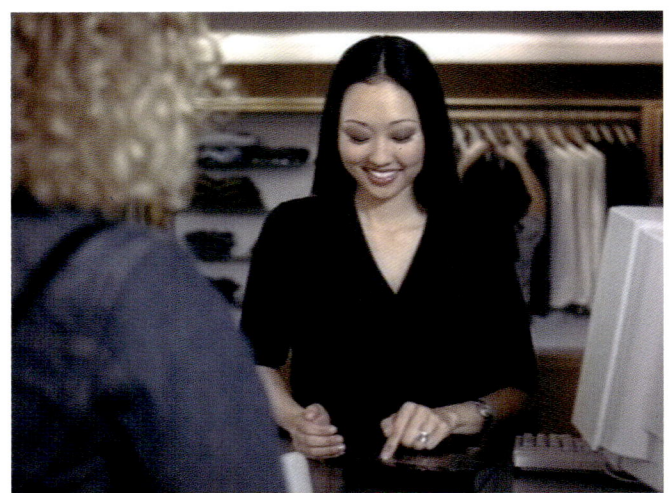

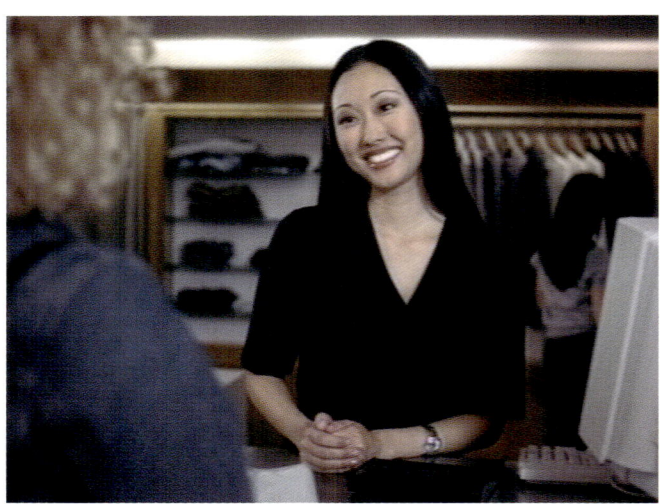

CATEGORY
Home Furnishings/Appliances

ADVERTISER/PRODUCT
Sampo Washing Machine

TITLE
Sheet

ADVERTISING AGENCY
J. Walter Thompson Taiwan, Taipei

PRODUCTION COMPANY
David Kung Films, Taipei

ACCOUNT EXECUTIVE
T.J. Wang, Chris Shen

CREATIVE DIRECTOR
Michael Dee, Amy Tseng

COPYWRITER
Shih-Yeh Lee

ART DIRECTOR
Tiffany Huang

PRODUCER
Yvonne Yeh

DIRECTOR
David Kung

MUSIC ARRANGER
Jr-Jian Ho

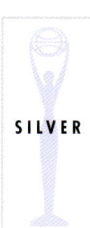

SILVER

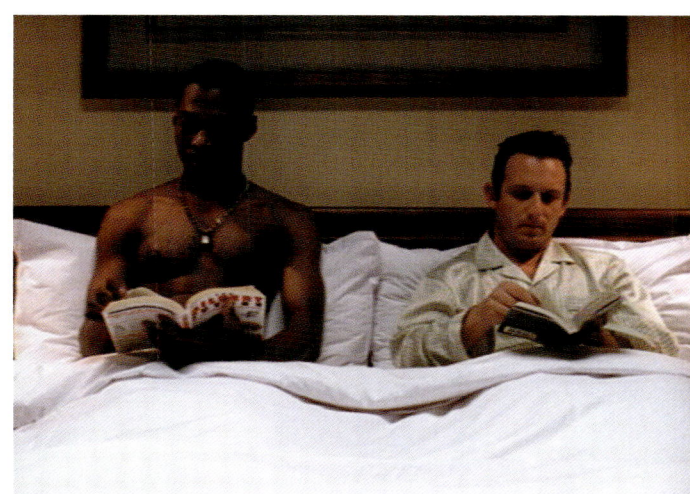

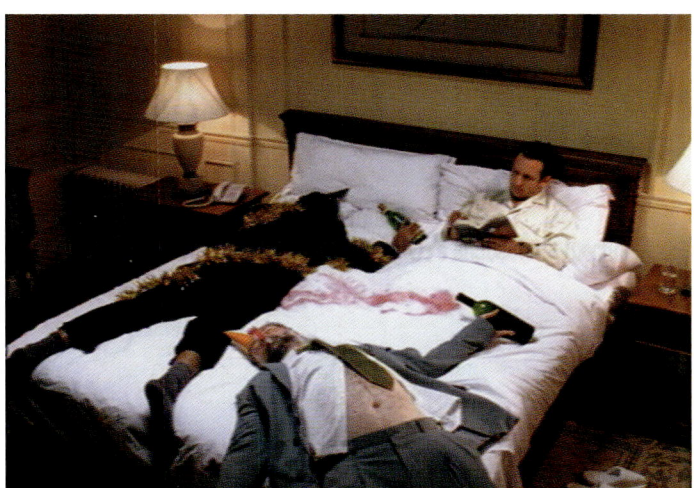

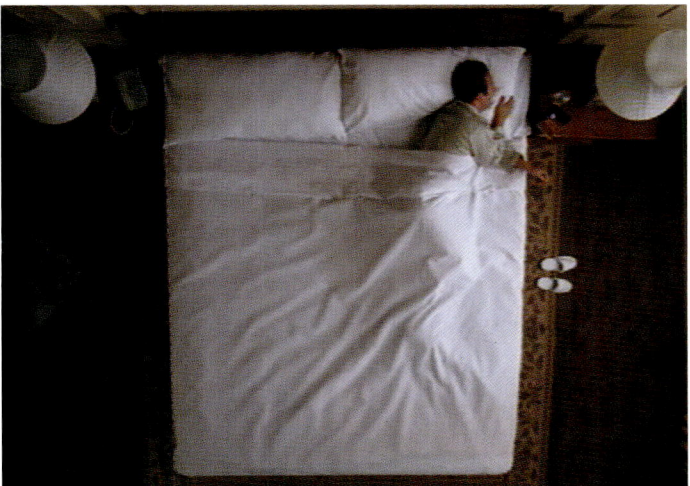

VISUAL: Man is lying by himself in a hotel bed, reading a book. As he lies there various people show up on the bed: A blonde woman and an Arab sheik, an African-American man, an Asian man clipping his toenails, a couple beneath the sheets, two dogs, two drunk men, and ten or fifteen people on a photo shoot. Eventually, all the above, animals, and people surround him.

SUPER: Do you really think you're the only one sleeping in that bed?

To be sure all their linens are absolutely clean, the top hotels in Europe and America use O3 for all their washing. Killing the bacteria.

In Taiwan, only Sampo washing machines offer O3's antibacterial function.

VISUAL: Once again, the man is by himself in the hotel bed reading a book.

SUPER: Kill the bacteria with O3; it's nicer to sleep alone.

VISUAL: Washing machine.

SUPER: Sampo O3, Washing Machine.

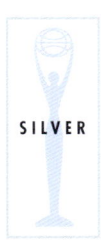

SILVER

CATEGORY
Home Furnishings/Appliances

ADVERTISER/PRODUCT
Sealy Mattress Company

TITLE
Boy

ADVERTISING AGENCY
Leo Burnett, Mexico City

PRODUCTION COMPANY
Garcia Bross y Asociados,
Mexico City

EDITING COMPANY
Garcia Bross y Asociados,
Mexico City

SOUND DESIGN COMPANY
Astro Estudio, Mexico City

ACCOUNT EXECUTIVE
Teresa Sordo

CREATIVE DIRECTOR
Tony Hidalgo

COPYWRITER
Tony Hidalgo, Simon Bross

ART DIRECTOR
Ruben Bross

PRODUCER
Federico Cárdenas

DIRECTOR
Simon Bross

MUSIC ARRANGER
Pedro Alberto Cárdenas

VISUAL: Open to a split screen: On the right side, a child's bed with a slate reading "Sealy" underneath. On the left side, a child's bed with a slate reading "Other" underneath. The spot opens with a young boy in pajamas energetically and repeatedly jumping up and down on the "Other" bed. He then bounces across the split screen onto the "Sealy" bed, and immediately collapses into sleep.

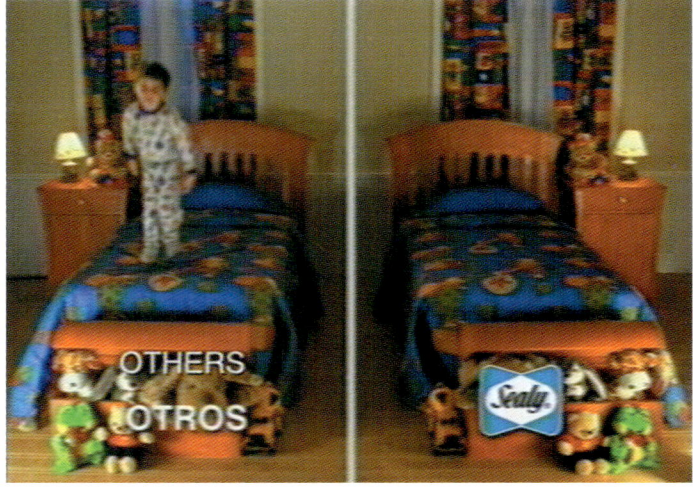

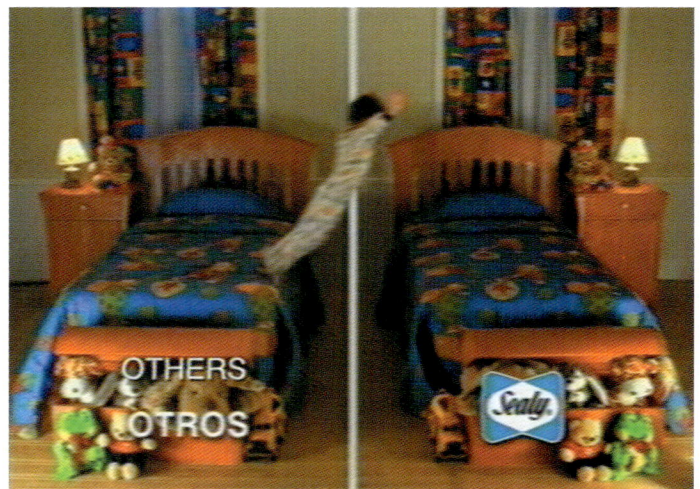

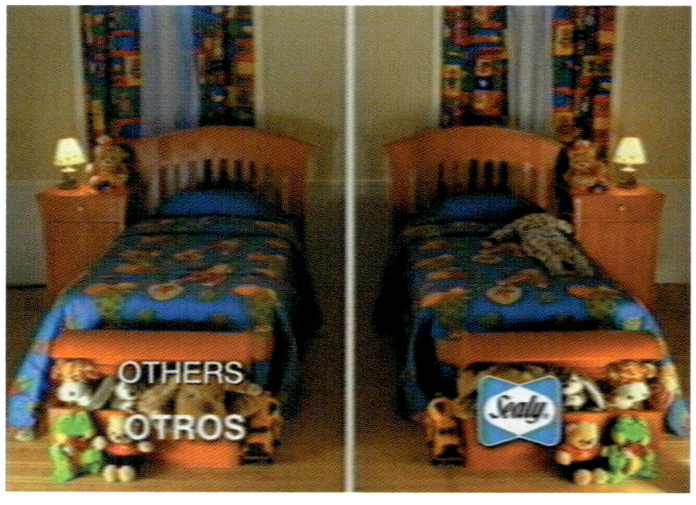

CATEGORY
Home Products

ADVERTISER/PRODUCT
Loctite

TITLE
Coin

ADVERTISING AGENCY
DDB Argentina, Buenos Aires

PRODUCTION COMPANY
Antidoto Films, Buenos Aires

EDITING COMPANY
VFX, Buenos Aires

MUSIC COMPANY
CCCI, Buenos Aires

SOUND DESIGN COMPANY
CCCI, Buenos Aires

ACCOUNT EXECUTIVE
Rolando Fernandez

CREATIVE DIRECTOR
Rodrigo Figueroa Reyes

COPYWRITER
Martin Jalfen

ART DIRECTOR
Julian Montesano

DIRECTOR
Julian Montesano

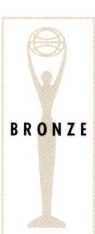

BRONZE

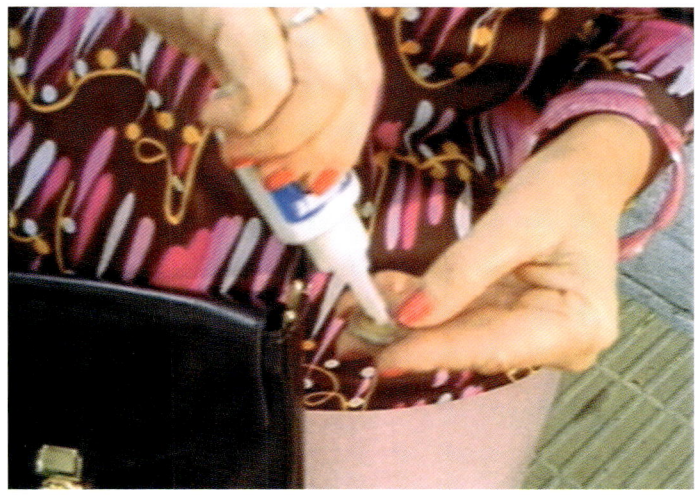

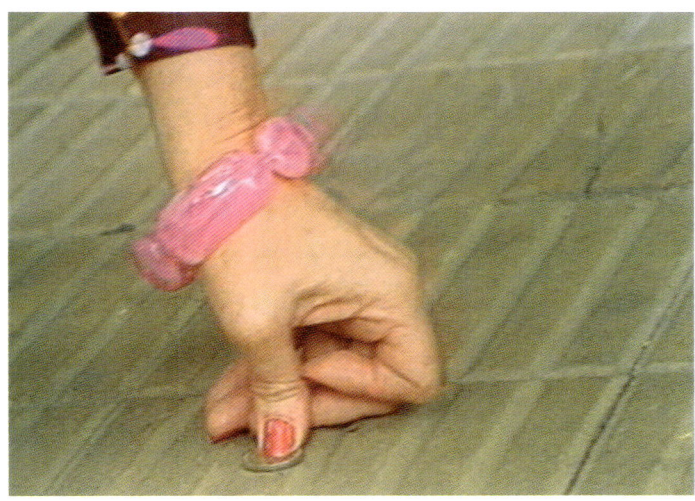

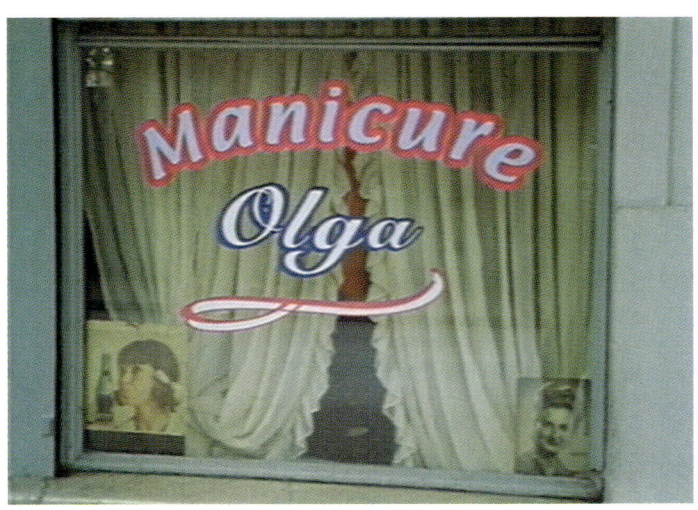

SYNOPSIS: A woman is walking down the street. She stops, takes a coin and Loctite glue from her purse, and glues the coin to the sidewalk. She opens the security gate on a storefront that is a manicure shop. She has glued the coin to the ground hoping that people will try and pick it up, break a fingernail, and then come into her shop to have it repaired.

SUPER: Loctite. The most effective short-term adhesive.

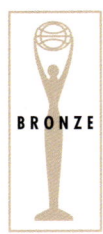

CATEGORY
Home Products

ADVERTISER/PRODUCT
Vizir Washing Powder

TITLE
Bird

ADVERTISING AGENCY
Leo Burnett, Warsaw

PRODUCTION COMPANY
Flying Colours, Prague

SOUND DESIGN COMPANY
Chimney Pot, Warsaw

ANIMATION COMPANY
Chimney Pot, Warsaw

AGENCY PRODUCER
Janusz Wlodarski, Piotr Owsianka

CREATIVE DIRECTOR
Darek Zatorski

COPYWRITER
Lech C. Król

ART DIRECTOR
Martin Winther

PRODUCER
Philip Waley

DIRECTOR
Darek Zatorski

ANIMATOR
Daniel Markowicz

VISUAL: A rural landscape covered in snow. A bird lands, but what he has perched on is not visible. When the bird flies away, it can be seen that he was sitting on a clothesline with white laundry hanging on it. The clothes are so white that they blend in with the snow and all that can be seen of them is their shadow.

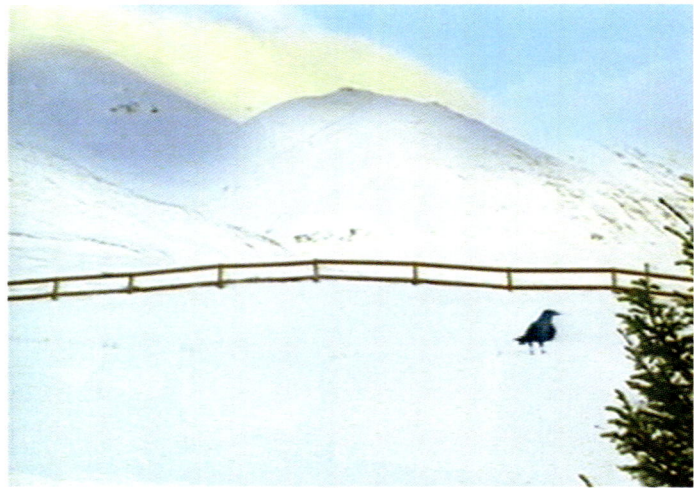

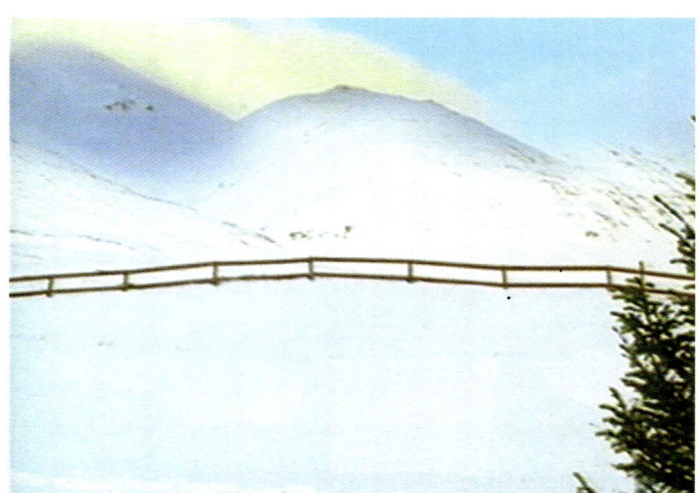

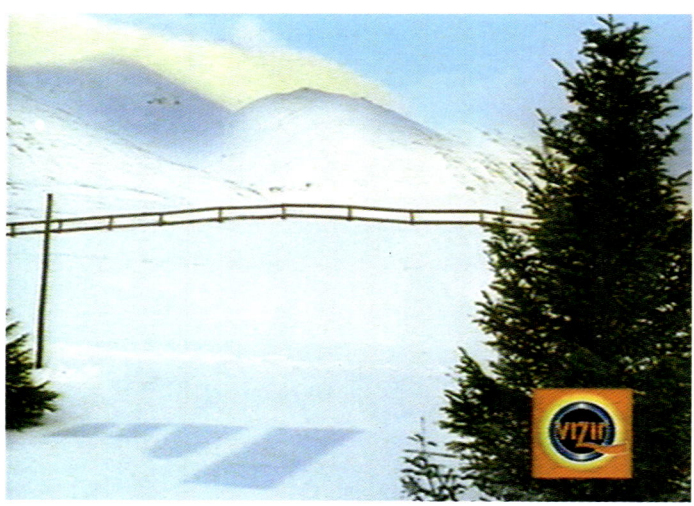

CATEGORY
Home Products

ADVERTISER/PRODUCT
Sylvania Lighting International

TITLE
Old Man

ADVERTISING AGENCY
Results Advertising, Bangkok

PRODUCTION COMPANY
Phenomena Film Production,
Bangkok

MUSIC COMPANY
Cine Digital, Bangkok

SOUND DESIGN COMPANY
Cine Digital, Bangkok

CREATIVE DIRECTOR
Jureeporn Thaidumrong

COPYWRITER
Jureeporn Thaidumrong

ART DIRECTOR
Joel Clement

PRODUCER
Yuthapong Varanukrohchoke

DIRECTOR
Thanonchai Sornsriwichai

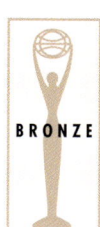

BRONZE

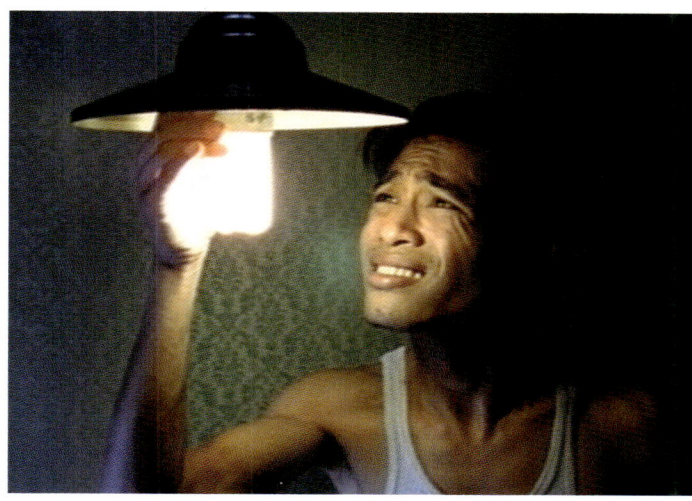

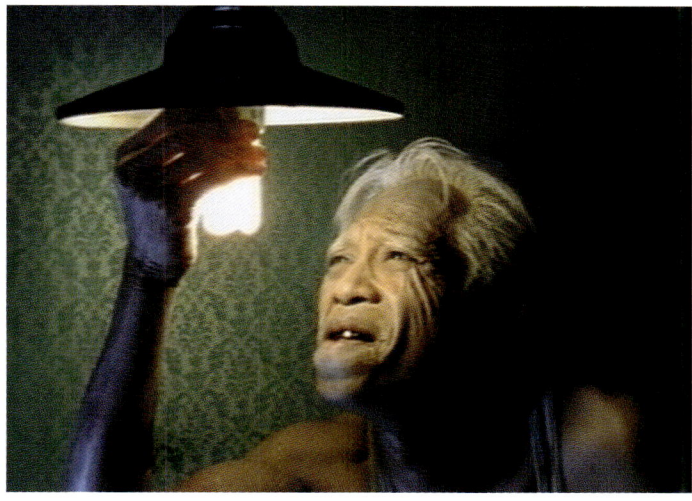

VISUAL: A young man is sitting in a barren room with one light burning. The lightbulb burns out. He opens a drawer and pulls out a package of Sylvania Long Lasting Bulbs, replaces the burned-out light, and sits down. The bulb goes out again; he goes into the drawer for a new bulb, replaces the old bulb and it is revealed that he is now a very old man.

SUPER: Sylvania. Long Life Bulb.

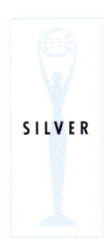

SILVER

CATEGORY Media Promotion	**PRODUCTION COMPANY** harvest, Santa Monica	**CREATIVE DIRECTOR** Chuck McBride	**EXECUTIVE PRODUCER** Bonnie Goldfarb
ADVERTISER/PRODUCT Fox Sports	**EDITING COMPANY** Lost Planet, Santa Monica	**COPYWRITER** Scott Wild, Eric King, Jeff Labbe	**LINE PRODUCER** Lauren Bayer
TITLE Nail Gun	**SOUND DESIGN COMPANY** Eleven, Santa Monica	**ART DIRECTOR** Eric King, Jeff Labbe	**SOUND DESIGNER** Jeff Payne
ADVERTISING AGENCY TBWA\Chiat\Day, San Francisco	**AGENCY PRODUCER** Betsy Beale	**DIRECTOR** Baker Smith	

VISUAL: A man in a garage is assembling a wooden shelf. He picks up his nail gun and pulls the trigger. Nothing happens. He pulls the trigger a half-dozen more times and still the gun does not respond. He places the tool on his workbench and, suddenly, it begins to wildly shoot off nails. Like an automatic weapon, the gun is firing nails everywhere. The man drops to the floor in defense. His wife enters the garage, sees what is happening, and also drops for cover. Some neighbors that are passing by are almost hit.

MAN: Get down, get down, get down.

VISUAL: The neighbors run for cover.

SUPER: Beware of things made in October.

VISUAL: A distracted factory worker is working on the assembly line for nail guns, while watching a baseball game on television. He is very involved in the game and does not notice that he is doing his work badly.

SUPER: Major League Baseball Playoffs Are Coming.

Fox baseball logo.

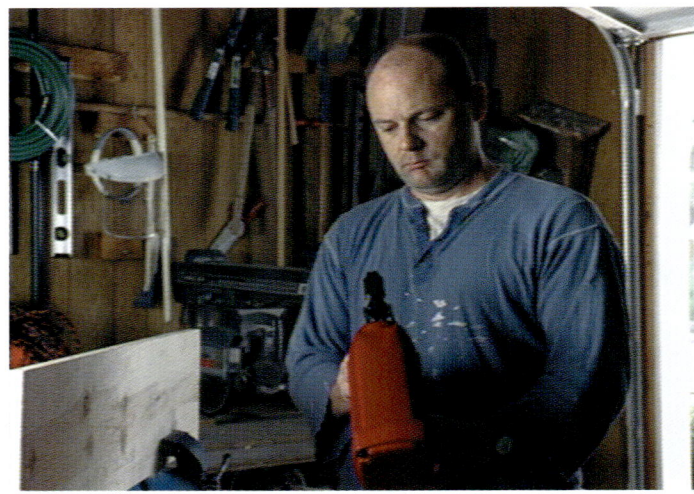

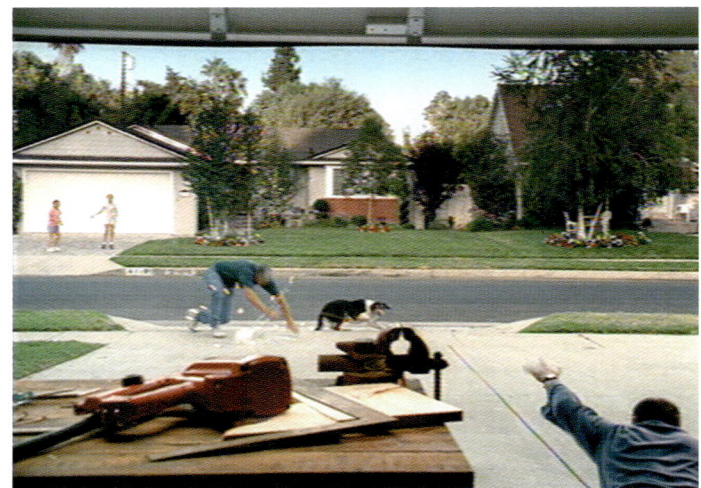

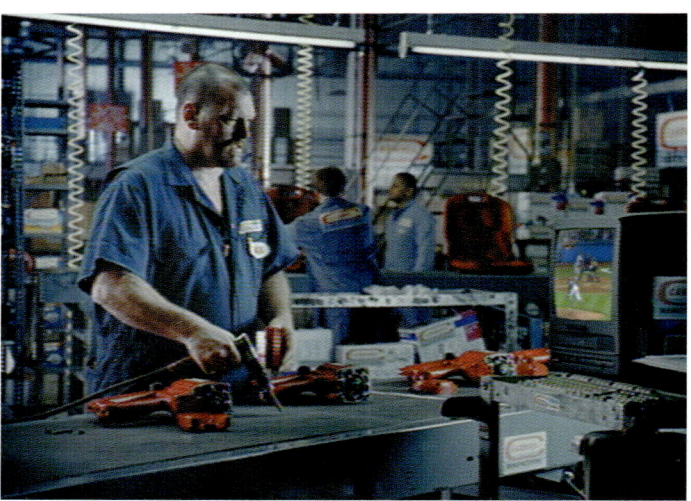

CATEGORY
Media Promotion

ADVERTISER/PRODUCT
The New Zealand Herald

TITLE
Fish & Chips

ADVERTISING AGENCY
M&C Saatchi, Auckland

PRODUCTION COMPANY
Republic Films, Auckland

POST AUDIO PRODUCTION COMPANY
Digital Post, Auckland

EDITING COMPANY
Original Cut, Auckland; Digital Sparks, Auckland

SOUND DESIGN COMPANY
Morris & Blood, Auckland

AGENCY PRODUCER
Tanya Haitoua-Cathro

ACCOUNT EXECUTIVE
Melanie Sloman, Rebecca Williams

CREATIVE DIRECTOR
Jason Ross

COPYWRITER
Giuliana de Felice

ART DIRECTOR
Murray Bransgrove

DIRECTOR
Simon Mark-Brown

PRODUCER
Andy Mauger, Neil Stichbury

EDITOR
Simon Clothier

CLIENT
Pip Elliott

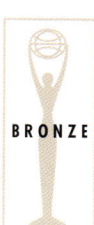

BRONZE

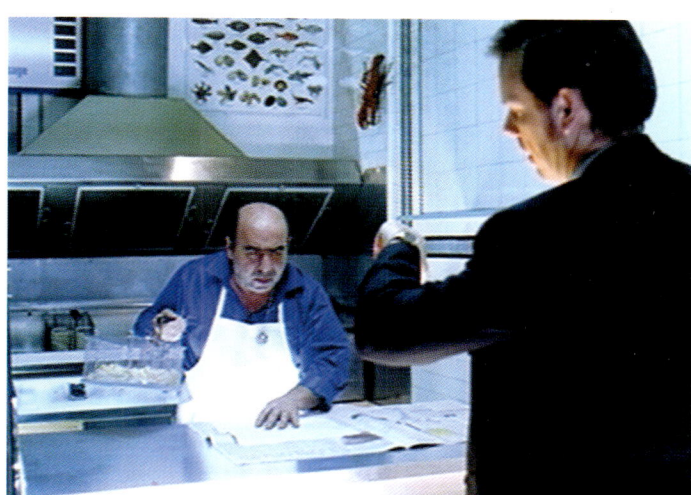

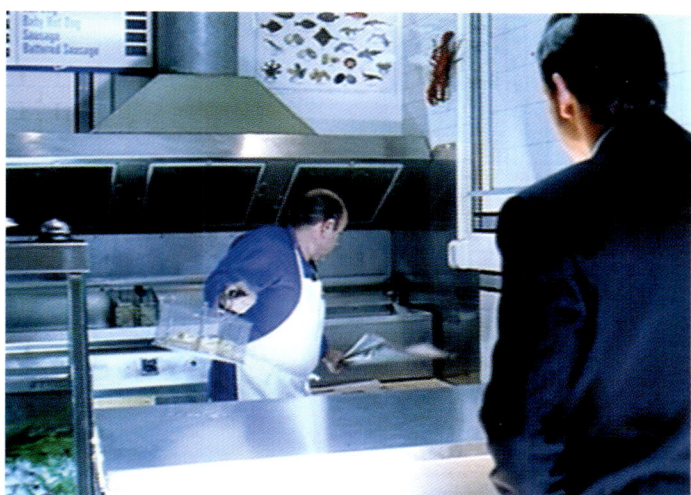

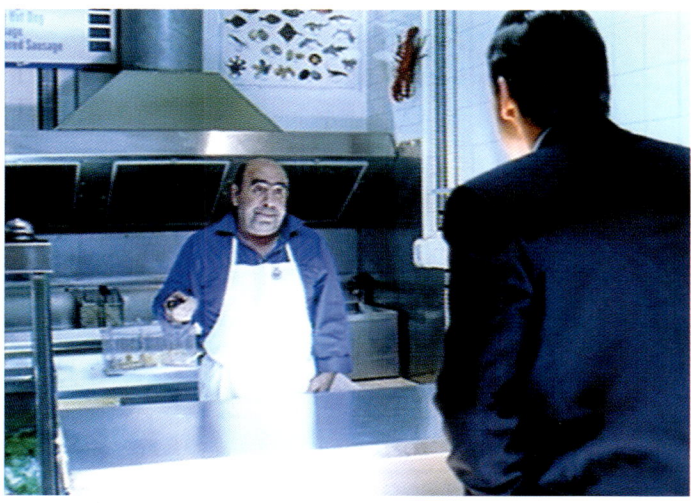

VISUAL: A guy in a suit is waiting for his order at a fish and chips shop. In one hand is his briefcase in the other, a copy of *The New Zealand Herald*. The cook lifts a fryer of chips out of the vat, gives it a couple of shakes, and turns to the counter, which has a newspaper spread on it. He stops himself from pouring the chips onto the paper as an article catches his attention. He decides to keep it and puts that section of the newspaper to one side. He gives the chips another shake and goes to tip them onto the next section of the paper, but again, an article catches his eye. He puts this section aside and, turning to the last section of the paper, sees another useful article. He puts this last part of the newspaper to the side and is left with a bare counter and a slightly puzzled customer.

Super: *The New Zealand Herald.*

There's a lot more to it.

www.nzherald.com.nz

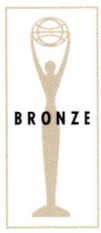

CATEGORY
Media Promotion

ADVERTISER/PRODUCT
Guardian Unlimited

TITLE
Rapper

ADVERTISING AGENCY
BMP DDB, London

AGENCY PRODUCER
Richard Chambers

COPYWRITER
Patrick McClelland

ART DIRECTOR
Grant Parker

DIRECTOR
Jamie Catto

PRODUCER
Jamie Catto

VISUAL: An aggressive-looking rapper with another young man standing behind him. The young man starts playing a record on a mixing turntable. The rapper raps.

RAPPER: I'm the inception of a counter cultural revolution. I expectorate axioms like they're pollution. Don't endeavor to vituperate me or I'll perambulate on your physiognomy. Get invidious of my rapacious capacity for coitus. If your skills aren't commensurate, get proptic with a vidious. I'm cryptic. I'm elliptic. In my vestibule I got a Rothko triptych. Is it any wonder the postpubescent glacial maidens come to me for their inculcation. I'm a pedagogue here for their libation.

YOUNG MAN: YO! DJ abrase those polymers. Let's get assiduous.

SUPER: Increase your vocabulary. A new interactive crossword everyday on line at Guardianunlimited.co.uk

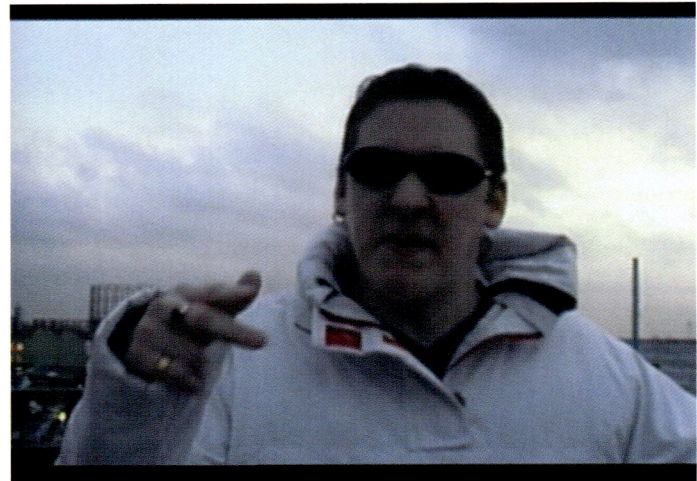

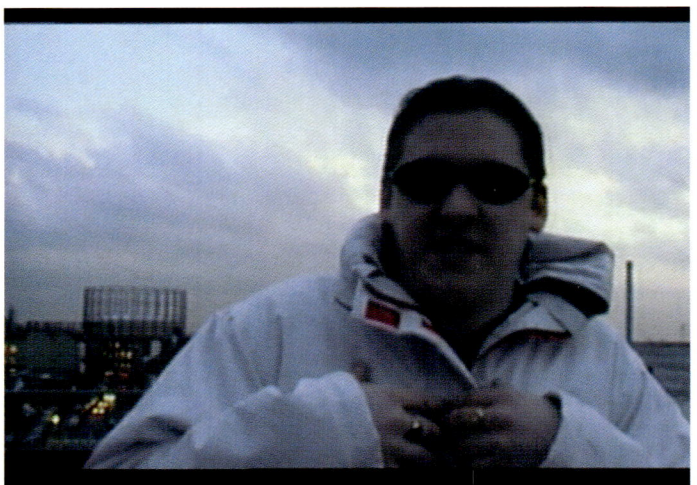

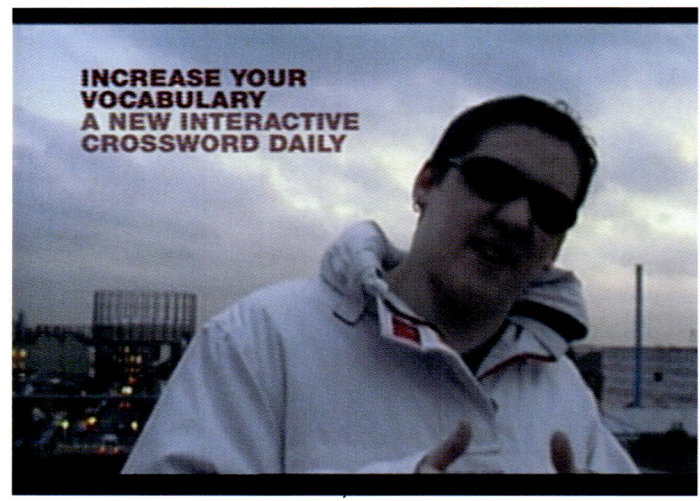

CATEGORY
Media Promotion

ADVERTISER/PRODUCT
Fox Sports

TITLE
Boat

ADVERTISING AGENCY
TBWA\Chiat\Day, San Francisco

PRODUCTION COMPANY
harvest, Santa Monica

EDITING COMPANY
Lost Planet, Santa Monica

SOUND DESIGN COMPANY
Eleven, Santa Monica

AGENCY PRODUCER
Betsy Beale

CREATIVE DIRECTOR
Chuck McBride

COPYWRITER
Scott Wild, Eric King, Jeff Labbe

ART DIRECTOR
Eric King, Jeff Labbe

DIRECTOR
Baker Smith

EXECUTIVE PRODUCER
Bonnie Goldfarb

LINE PRODUCER
Lauren Bayer

SOUND DESIGNER
Jeff Payne

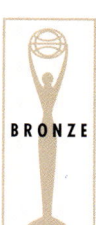

BRONZE

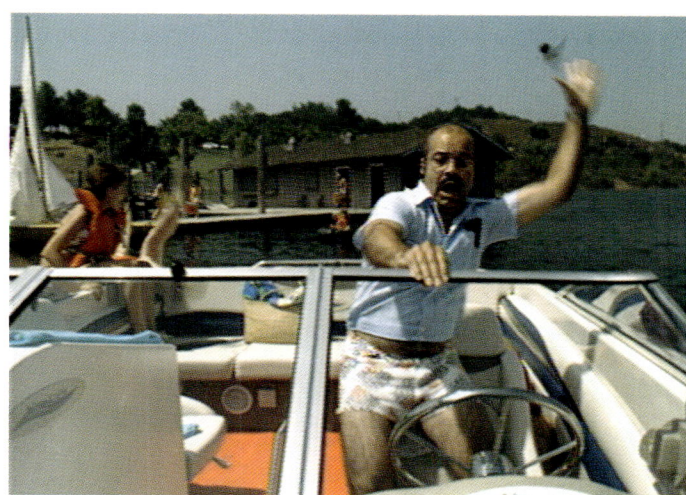

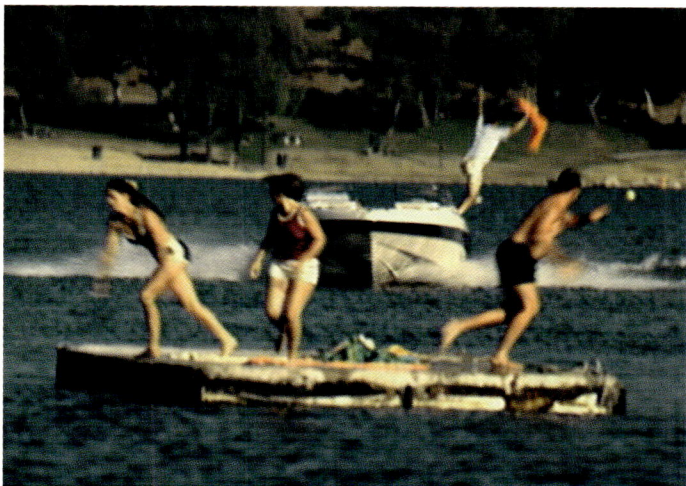

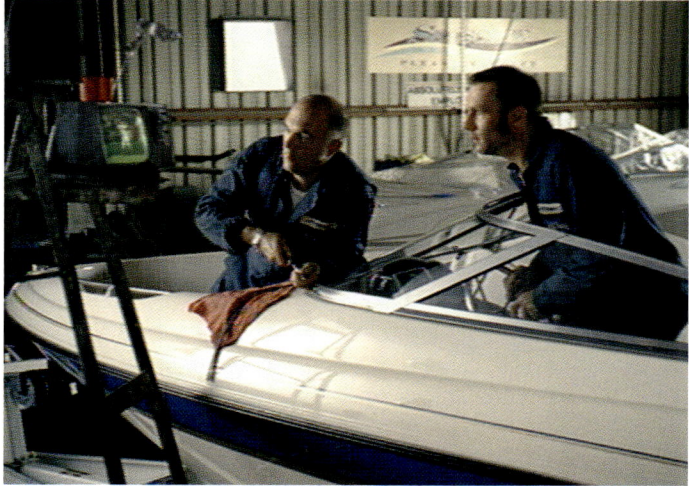

VISUAL: A man is at the steering wheel of an idle powerboat and his wife, holding a camera, and daughter are sitting on the rear edge of the boat.

WIFE: C'mon Dad, smile.

MAN: Here we go.

VISUAL: The man grabs for the throttle and yanks it. It breaks off.

The boat takes off and the man's wife and daughter are thrown into the water. The boat accelerates rapidly and the man grabs for the steering wheel. It breaks off and the vehicle is now headed for a raft full of sunbathers. They jump from the raft as the boat quickly approaches. The man then jumps from his out-of-control boat.

SUPER: Beware of things made in October.

VISUAL: Two distracted factory workers trying to attach a steering wheel to a boat they are assembling, while watching a baseball game on television. They are so involved in the game that they miss a few details in putting the boat together.

SUPER: Major League Baseball Playoffs Are Coming.

Fox baseball logo.

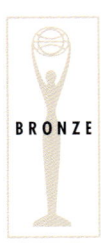

BRONZE

CATEGORY
Media Promotion

ADVERTISER/PRODUCT
Placar Football Magazine

TITLE
Prison

ADVERTISING AGENCY
Young & Rubicam Brasil, São Paulo

PRODUCTION COMPANY
Mauricio Oliveira Filmes, São Paulo

EDITING COMPANY
Equipe Mauricio Oliveira, São Paulo

MUSIC COMPANY
MCR, São Paulo

ACCOUNT EXECUTIVE
Celso Forster, Lais Marques

CREATIVE DIRECTOR
Tião Bernardi, Rita Corradi,
J.R. D'Elboux

COPYWRITER
Marcelo Sato

ART DIRECTOR
Pedro Pletitsch

PRODUCER
Estela Pardini

DIRECTOR
Mauricio Oliveira

VISUAL: The outside wall of a prison. A convict appears on top of the wall looking for something. He climbs down the outside wall using bed sheets that are knotted together and runs away, looking like he is escaping. After a few seconds he returns with a soccer ball and kicks it over the wall. We hear the roaring cheers of the convicts from inside the prison walls and the bustling sound of a game going on. The prisoner climbs back up the knotted bed sheets and goes back inside the prison grounds.

VO: Who loves soccer, can't live without *Placar*.

SUPER: *Placar* magazine. Every Friday for only R$1,99.

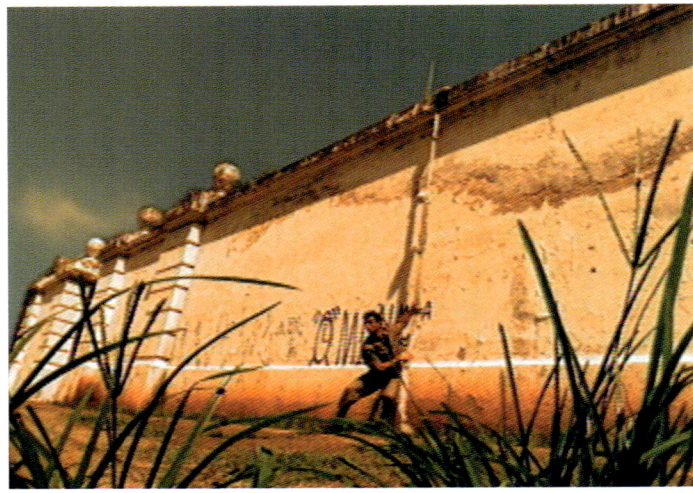

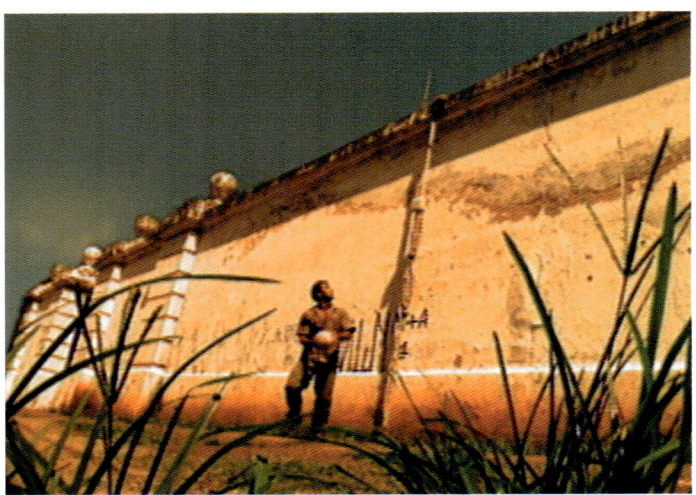

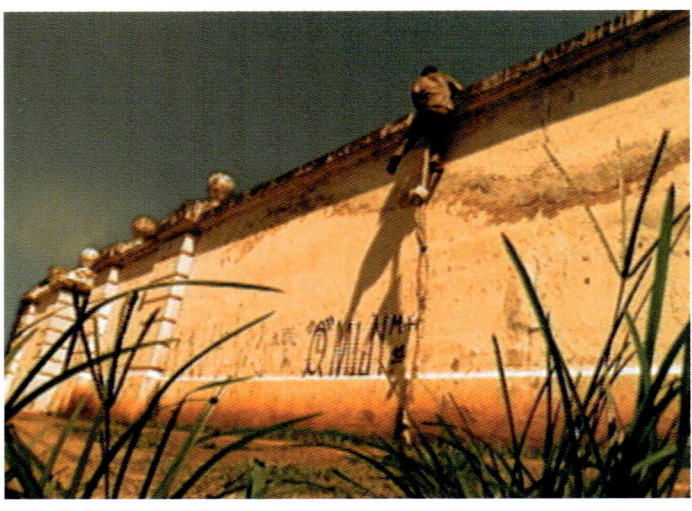

CATEGORY
Media Promotion

ADVERTISER/PRODUCT
ANJ (Brazilian Newspaper
Association)

TITLE
Personalities

ADVERTISING AGENCY
Young & Rubicam Brasil, São Paulo

PRODUCTION COMPANY
Dueto Filmes, São Paulo

MUSIC COMPANY
Dr. DD, Raw, São Paulo

ACCOUNT EXECUTIVE
Fernando Luz, Daniel Jotta

CREATIVE DIRECTOR
Tião Bernardi

COPYWRITER
Rita Corradi

ART DIRECTOR
J.R. D'Elboux

PRODUCER
Dueto Team

DIRECTOR
Maurício Guimarães, Luciano Zuffo

EDITOR
Alessandro Satori

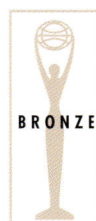

BRONZE

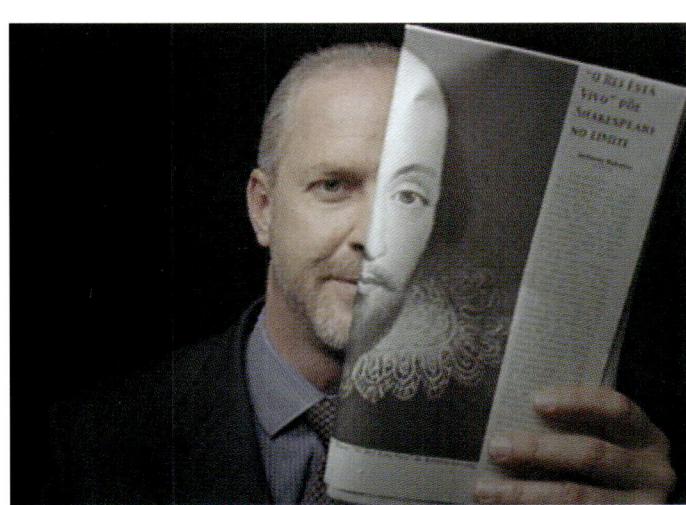

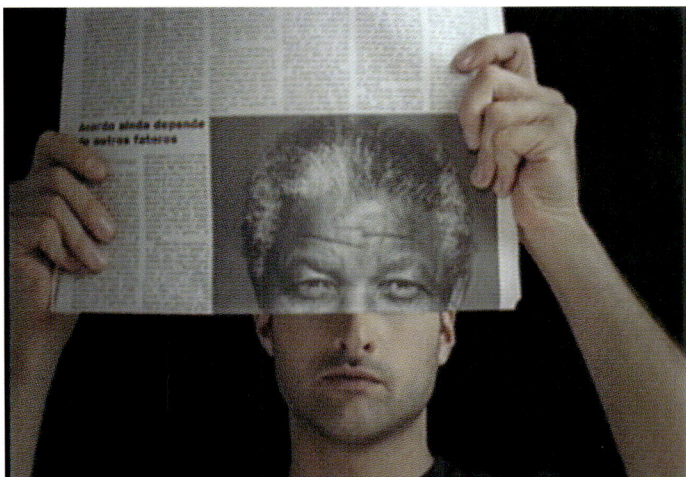

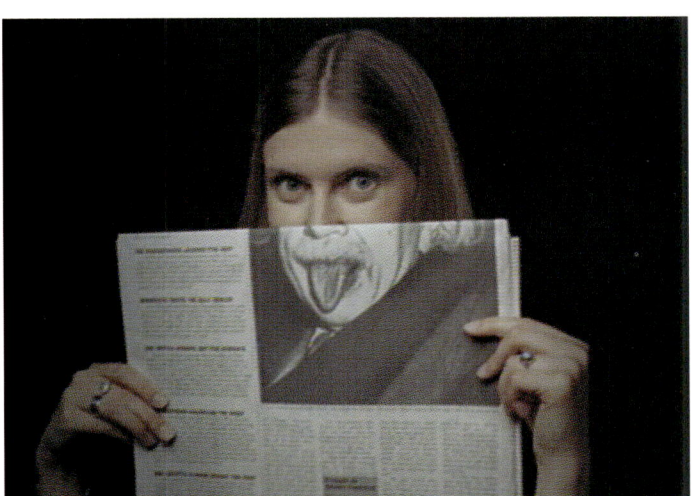

SYNOPSIS: A sequence of people are reading the newspaper. Each reader covers half of his or her face with the paper, on which is seen the photograph of a famous person. The two faces seemingly form one image.

VISUAL: Man 1 and photograph of Shakespeare.

VO: Every day you discover and learn from them. You are surprised by them.

VISUAL: Man 2 and photograph of Sigmund Freud.

VO: They make you think, change, evolve.

VISUAL: Man 3 and photograph of Nelson Mandela.

VO: They get you excited, angry.

VISUAL: Woman 1 and photograph of Mother Theresa.

VO: Happy, full of hope.

VISUAL: Man 4 and photograph of Salvador Dali.

VO: You might agree with them, or not. But you will never be indifferent.

SUPER: Newspapers. Making you a much more interesting person.

VISUAL: Woman 2 and photograph of Albert Einstein.

Super: ANJ

Brazilian Newspaper Association.

www.anj.org.br

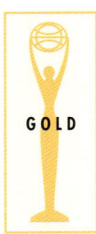

GOLD

CATEGORY
Public Service

ADVERTISER/PRODUCT
Médecins Sans Frontières
(Doctors without Borders)

TITLE
Frontières

ADVERTISING AGENCY
Advico Young & Rubicam,
Zurich-Gockhausen

PRODUCTION COMPANY
Propaganda Films, Los Angeles

MUSIC COMPANY
Machine Head, Venice

ACCOUNT EXECUTIVE
Isabella Bueeler

CREATIVE DIRECTOR
Martin Spillmann

COPYWRITER
Martin Spillmann, Juerg Brechbuehl

ART DIRECTOR
Martin Spillmann, Denis Schwarz

PRODUCER
Salli Shrewsbery

DIRECTOR
Marcel Langenegger

MUSIC ARRANGER
Chris Neilmann

VISUAL: A surgical procedure is taking place on a human body and the wounds that are being sutured end up forming the disputed borders of Kosovo, Albania, and Madedonia, the setting for much human tragedy during the war in the Balkans. Throughout, classical music is playing.

SFX: The sounds of war: explosions, gunshots, jet fighters, and screams

SUPER: Médecins sans Frontières.

Doctors without Borders.

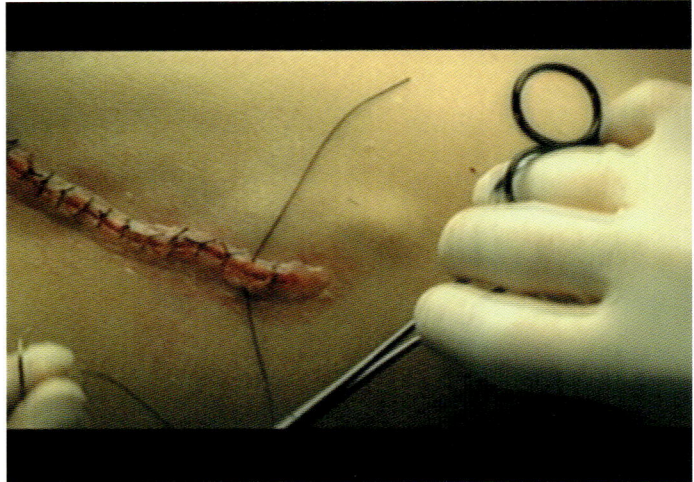

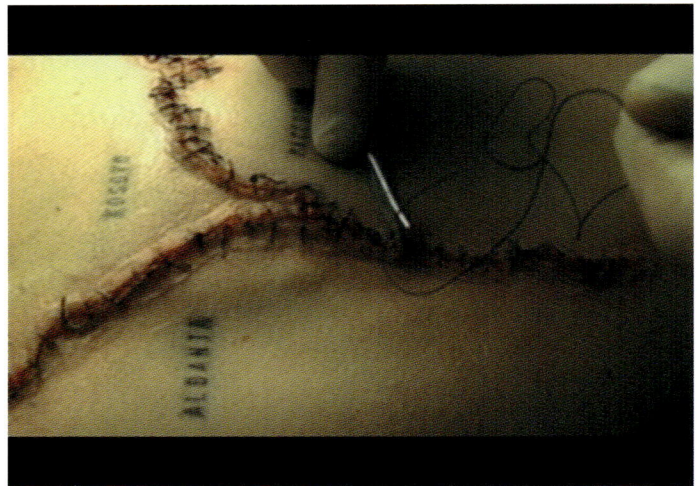

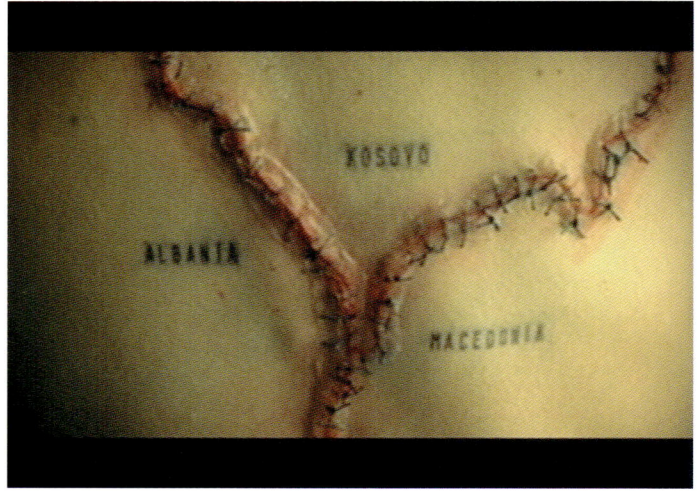

CATEGORY
Public Service

ADVERTISER/PRODUCT
Womankind Worldwide

TITLE
Women Abuse

ADVERTISING AGENCY
Rainey Kelly Campbell Roalf/
Young & Rubicam, London

PRODUCTION COMPANY
Thomas/Thomas, London &
New York

COPYWRITER
Mike Boles

ART DIRECTOR
Jerry Hollens

PRODUCER
Philippa Thomas

DIRECTOR
Kevin Thomas

EDITOR
Brian Dyke

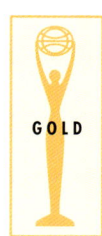

GOLD

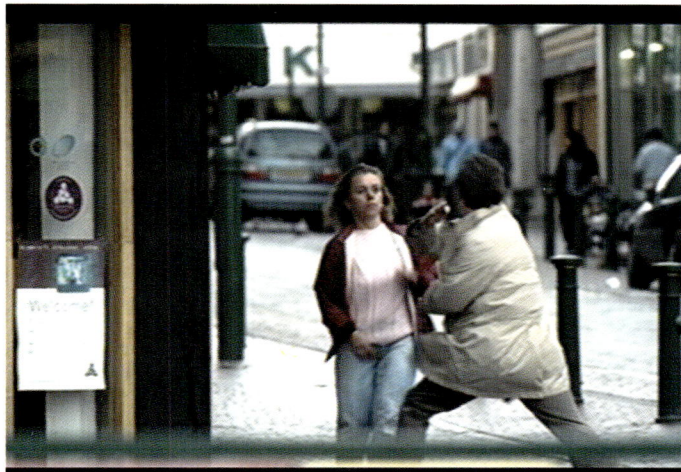

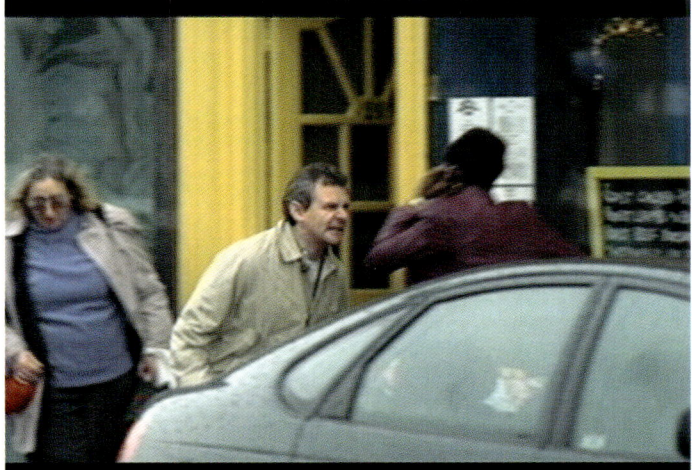

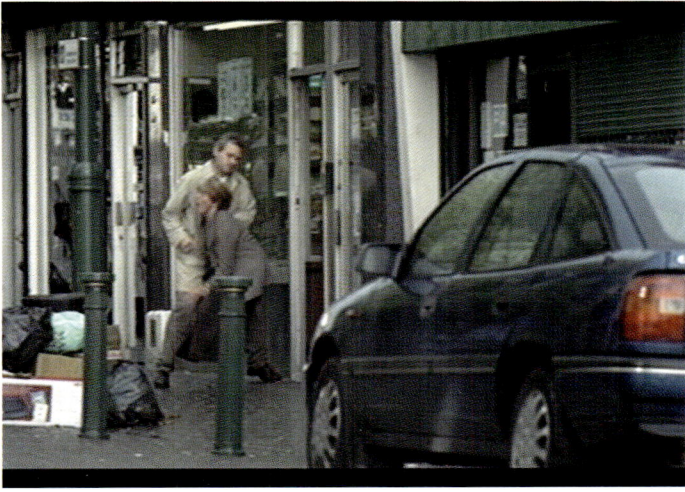

VISUAL: A well-dressed man is walking down a busy city street. As he walks, he is counting, to himself, each time he sees a new woman. The women are of various races, classes, and ethnicities.

MAN: One. Two. Three.

VISUAL: The fourth woman who passes is a nicely dressed, middle-class lady. He goes up to her and slaps her in the face. The woman is shocked but goes on walking. The man continues walking and counting.

MAN: One. Two. Three.

VISUAL: This time the fourth woman is a black lady.

MAN: Bitch!

VO: One in four women in the UK will suffer violent abuse by men.

VISUAL: The man continues walking and counting. This time the fourth woman is a girl in her mid-twenties. The man goes and hits her in the stomach. The woman doubles over in pain and the man continues on his walk.

VO: The only difference is, it's usually kept behind closed doors.

VISUAL: A white ribbon is displayed on someone's sweater.

VO: Domestic violence is wrong; wear a white ribbon.

SUPER: Womankind Worldwide logo. White Ribbon Day, November 25th.

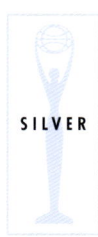

CATEGORY	**ADVERTISING AGENCY**	**ACCOUNT EXECUTIVE**	**ART DIRECTOR**
Public Service	Bartle Bogle Hegarty, New York	Julie Burke	Gianfranco Arena
ADVERTISER/PRODUCT	**PRODUCTION COMPANY**	**CREATIVE DIRECTOR**	**PRODUCER**
Feeding Children Better	PYTKA, Venice	Thomas Hayo	Mary Cheney, Leslie Vaughn
TITLE	**EDITING COMPANY**	**COPYWRITER**	**DIRECTOR**
Ketchup Soup	Go Robot!, New York	Peter Kain	Joe Pytka

VISUAL: A woman is at the counter of a fast-food restaurant looking somewhat embarrassed. She scoops a bunch of little ketchup packets and stuffs them into her purse. She repeats the same behavior at two other restaurants. She is now at her at home emptying the bags of the ketchup packets onto the kitchen counter. She pours water and squirts all the ketchup packs into a big pot. She gives it a final stir and takes the pot to the kitchen table where we see three little kids in front of their plates, looking somewhat desperate. She begins to serve what we now realize is some kind of soup. She attempts to spoon the ketchup soup into a little boy's mouth.

MOM: Open up a little bit.

LITTLE BOY: I don't want to eat it.

MOM: Come on—just one bite.

LITTLE BOY: I don't like it.

SUPER: 1 out of 5 children in the U.S. lives with hunger. The sooner you believe it, the sooner we can end it.

SUPER: Call 1-800 FEED KIDS.

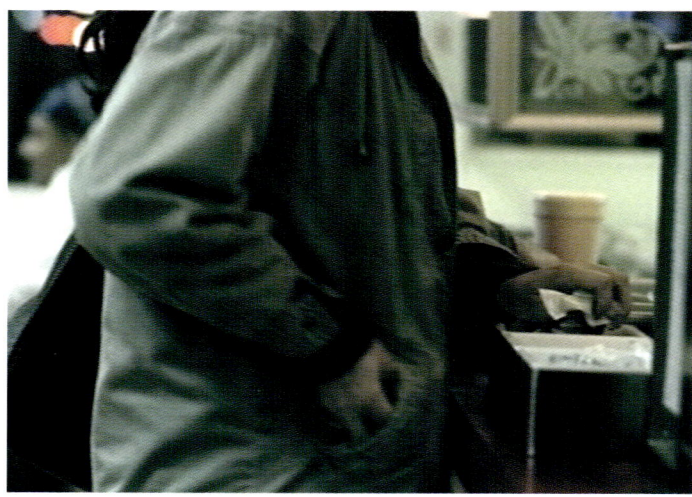

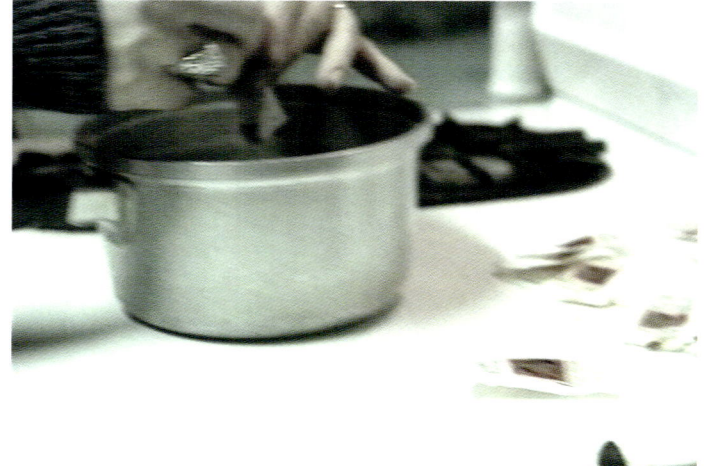

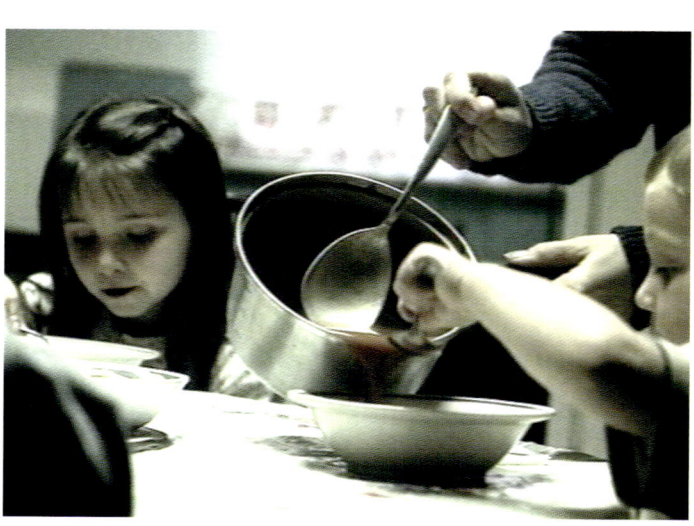

CATEGORY
Public Service

ADVERTISER/PRODUCT
Pedestrian Council of Australia

TITLE
Chopper Read—Killer

ADVERTISING AGENCY
Saatchi & Saatchi, Sydney

PRODUCTION COMPANY
Silverscreen, Sydney

EDITING COMPANY
Tait Gallery, Sydney

SOUND DESIGN COMPANY
Song Zu, Sydney

ACCOUNT EXECUTIVE
Mark Green

CREATIVE DIRECTOR
Malcolm Poynton

COPYWRITER
Jay Furby

ART DIRECTOR
Jay Furby

PRODUCER
Scott McBurnie

DIRECTOR
David Gaddie

EDITOR
Danny Tait

SOUND DESIGNER
Simon Lister

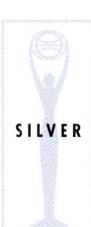

SILVER

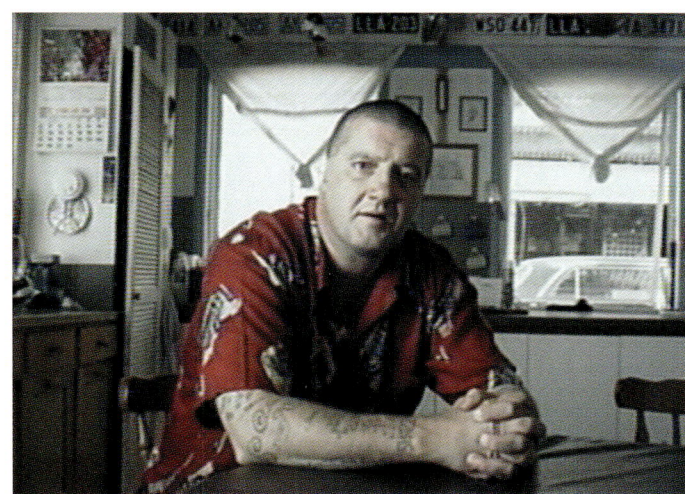

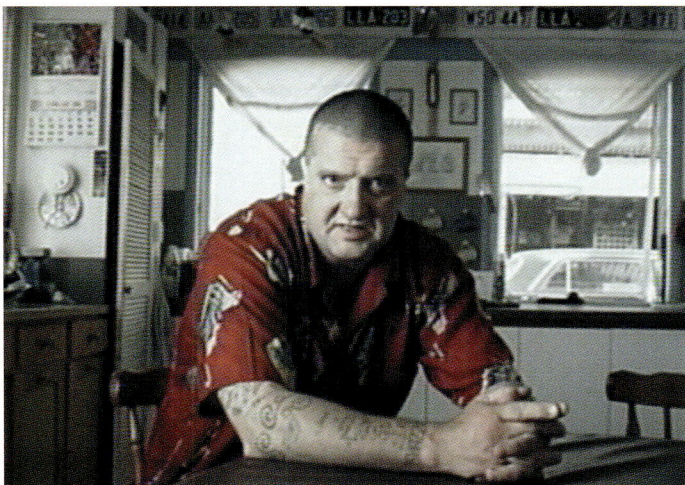

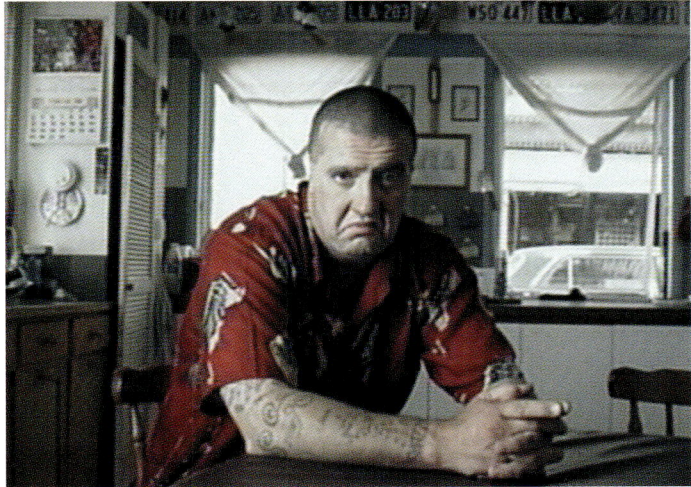

VISUAL: A tough-looking guy, Mark "Chopper" Read, is sitting at his kitchen table showing the scars on his body from injuries he received while he was in prison.

CHOPPER: A lot of you people might be very upset that I am doing this commercial. But I am advertising something I know a great deal about. And that's killing. I've shot people, I've baseball-batted them to death, I've iron-barred them to death, I've stabbed them to death, I've set fire to them. If you get into a car and you've been drinking too much and you kill somebody, then you're no different then me. That's all there is. You're a murdering maggot.

SUPER: A Killer Is a Killer. Don't Drink and Drive.

SUPER: Pedestrian Council of Australia logo.

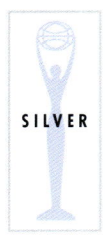

SILVER

CATEGORY Public Service	**ADVERTISING AGENCY** TBWA, Berlin	**CREATIVE DIRECTOR** Christoph Klingler	**PRODUCER** Tim Oberwelland, Fabian Massah
ADVERTISER/PRODUCT Behinderten-Sportverband Berlin e.V.	**PRODUCTION COMPANY** Centrifuge Film, Berlin	**COPYWRITER** Athanassios Stellatos	**DIRECTOR** Marc Malze
TITLE Josip	**SOUND DESIGN COMPANY** Stereo de Luxe, Berlin	**ART DIRECTOR** Philip Borchardt	**SOUND DESIGNER** Stephan Soltau

SYNOPSIS: A young man sees an athletic shoe in the window of a sporting goods store. The salesman takes notice of him as he tries on the shoe. Suddenly, the young man sprints off out of the store. The salesman takes off after him and a wild chase takes place through the city. Eventually the salesman gives up and it is revealed that the young runner is wearing the shoe on one foot and the other leg is an artificial limb.

SUPER: The Disabled Sports Association Would Like to Thank Adidas for Their Kind Support.

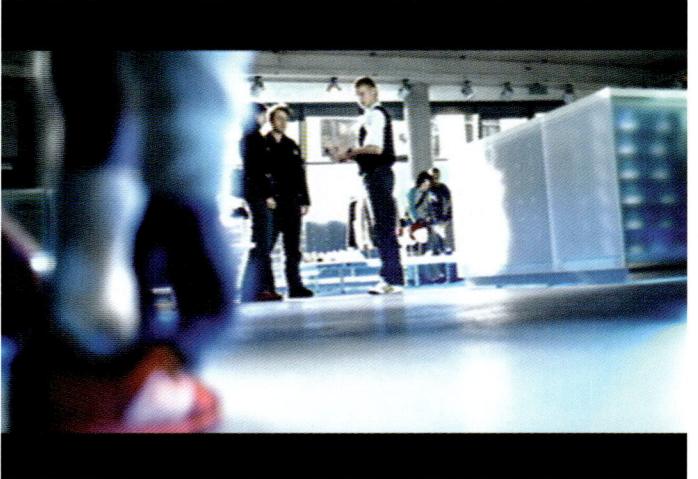

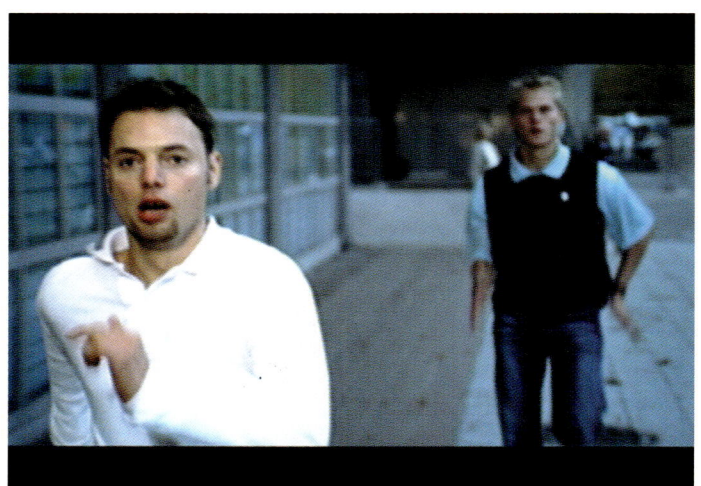

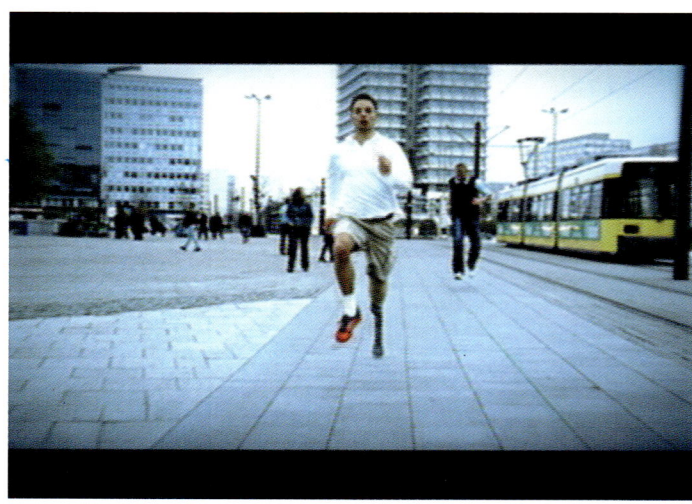

CATEGORY
Public Service

ADVERTISER/PRODUCT
DETR (Department of Transport)

TITLE
Kill Your Speed

ADVERTISING AGENCY
Abbott Mead Vickers BBDO, London

PRODUCTION COMPANY
Four Hundred Films, London

EDITING COMPANY
Four Hundred Films, London

SOUND DESIGN COMPANY
Wave, London

AGENCY PRODUCER
Francine Linsey

CREATIVE DIRECTOR
Peter Souter

COPYWRITER
Nick Worthington

ART DIRECTOR
Paul Brazier

PRODUCER
Adam Lyne

DIRECTOR
Stuart Douglas

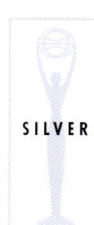

SILVER

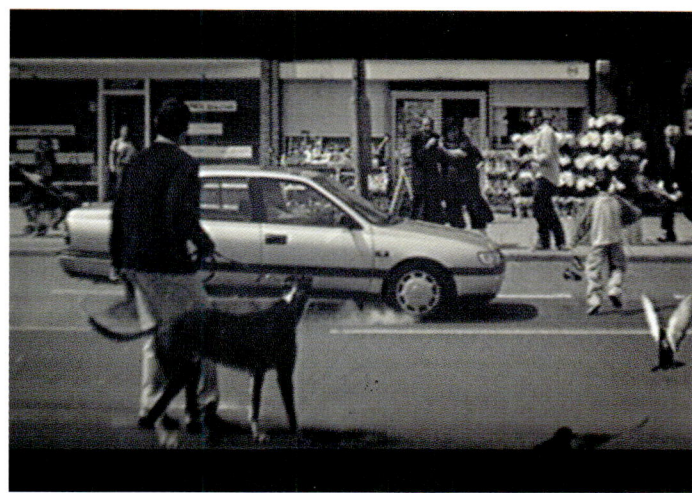

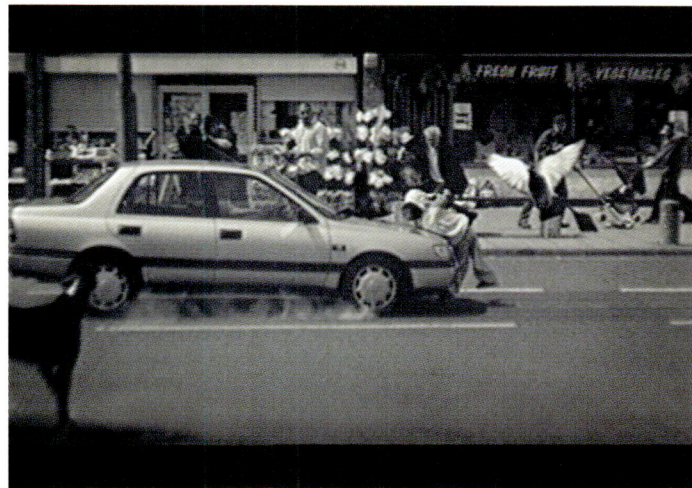

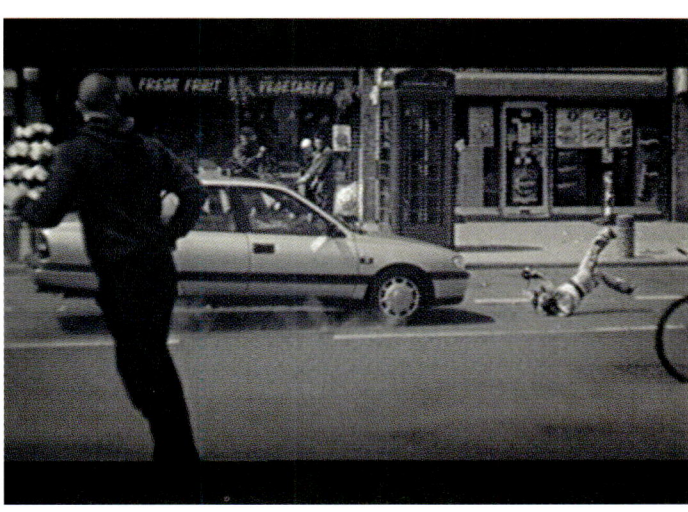

VISUAL: A car is traveling down an ordinary suburban street. It's filmed in extreme slow motion. The car begins to brake and smoke comes from the front tires.

VO: At just 5 miles per hour over the 30 mile per hour limit, how much further does it take to stop? 1 foot, 2 feet, 3 feet, 4 feet, 5 feet…16 feet, 17 feet…

VISUAL: The car hits a young boy crossing the road. The count continues until the car finally stops.

VO: Think. Slow Down.

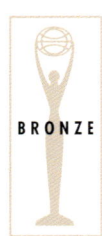

BRONZE

CATEGORY Public Service	**ADVERTISING AGENCY** AlmapBBDO, São Paulo	**CREATIVE DIRECTOR** Marcello Serpa, Eugênio Mohallem	**PRODUCER** Egisto Betti
ADVERTISER/PRODUCT Associação Instituto Sapientiae	**PRODUCTION COMPANY** Academia de Filmes, São Paulo	**COPYWRITER** Dulcidio Caldeira	**DIRECTOR** Tadeu Jungle
TITLE Selfish	**ACCOUNT EXECUTIVE** Fico Meirelles	**ART DIRECTOR** Luiz Sanches	

SYNOPSIS: A man explains the reasons why he will not donate sperm.

SUPER: Nature is wise. Selfish people never donate sperm.

SUPER: Help Complete a Family. Donate Sperm.

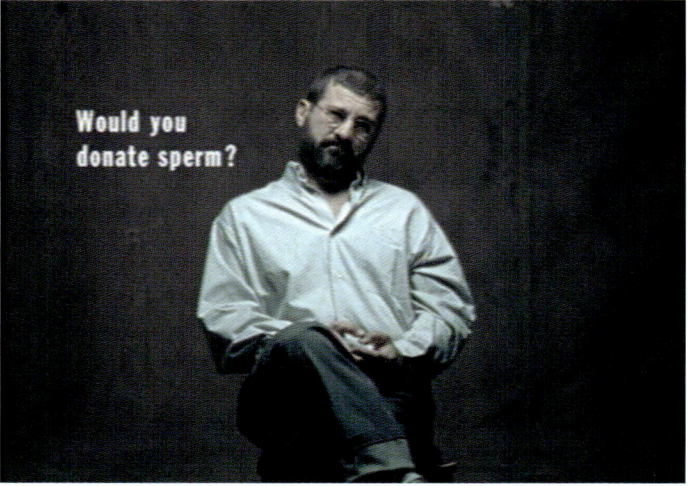

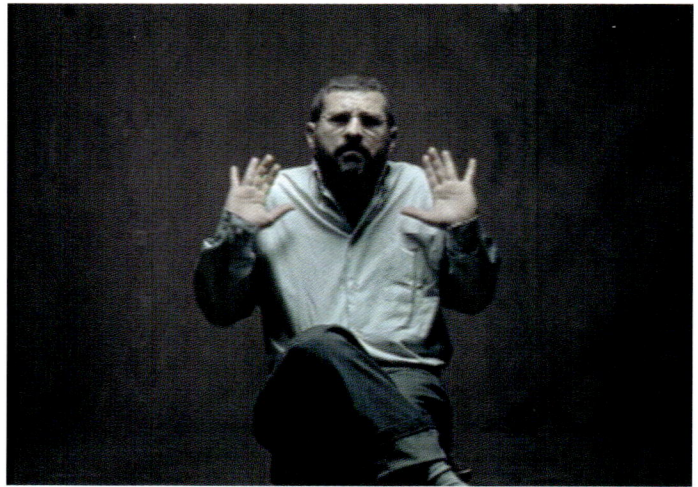

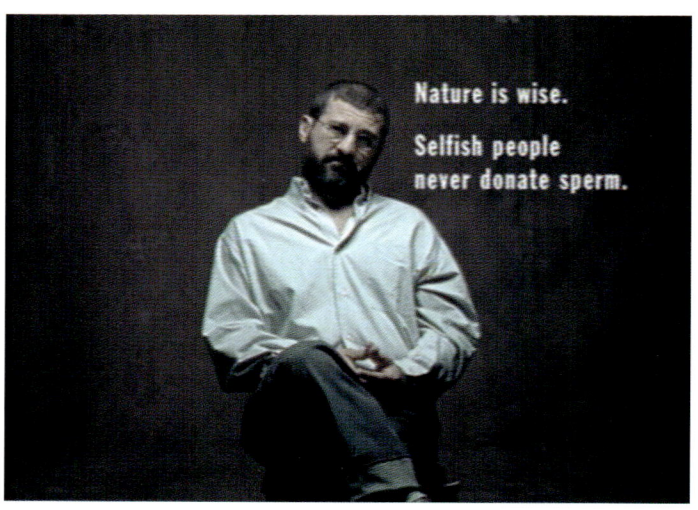

CATEGORY
Public Service

ADVERTISER/PRODUCT
Retina SA

TITLE
Braille

ADVERTISING AGENCY
Grey Worldwide, Johannesburg

PRODUCTION COMPANY
Visual Assault, Johannesburg

EDITING COMPANY
Videolab, Johannesburg

ACCOUNT EXECUTIVE
Jill McQuade

CREATIVE DIRECTOR
Alan Irvin

COPYWRITER
Haidee Nel

ART DIRECTOR
Alan Irvin

PRODUCER
Maja Mcintosh

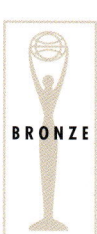

BRONZE

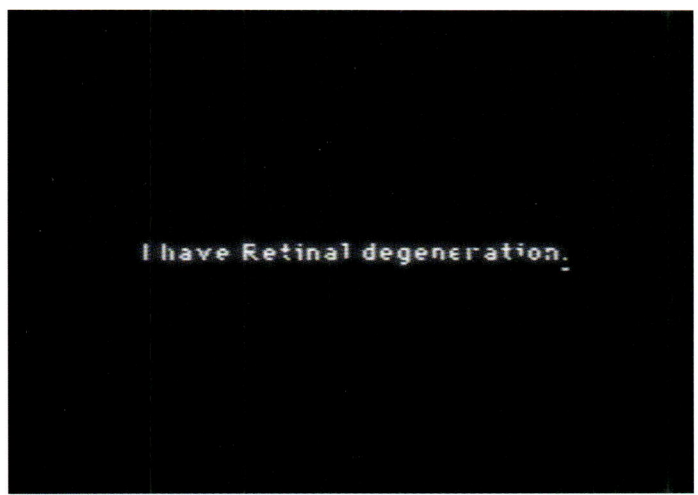

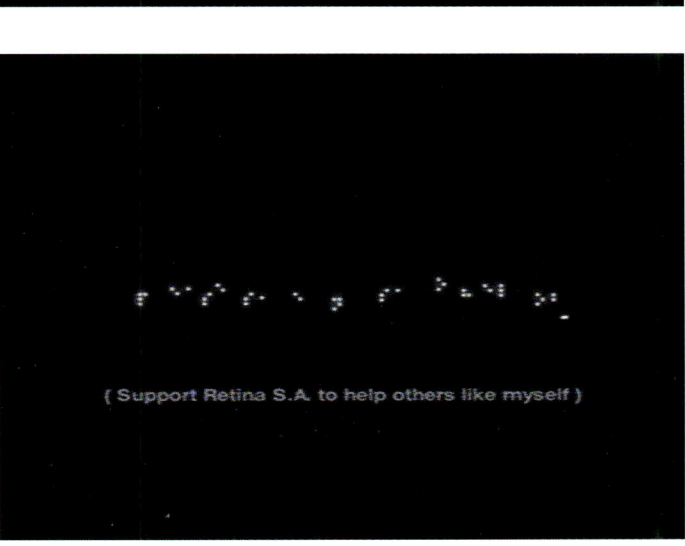

SYNOPSIS: On a black screen, the following words are being typed in white. As the page begins to fill up the letters break up into Braille.

VO: Hi, my name is Sara. I'm 19 years old. I grew up just like any other child until I started having problems with my eyes. I have retinal degeneration. Today, there's more Braille.

SUPER: Support Retina S.A. to help others like myself. Thank You.

SUPER: Retina logo.

SUPER: Fighting Blindness

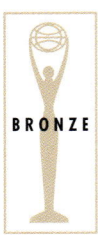

CATEGORY
Public Service

ADVERTISER/PRODUCT
Cancer Foundation—Target 15

TITLE
You Don't Want to Meet Us

ADVERTISING AGENCY
Marketforce, Perth

PRODUCTION COMPANY
Cyclops Films, Perth

EDITING COMPANY
First Light, Perth

SOUND DESIGN COMPANY
Double G, Perth

ACCOUNT EXECUTIVE
Karen Della Torre

CREATIVE DIRECTOR
Mike Edmonds

COPYWRITER
Adam Barker

ART DIRECTOR
Lori Canalini

PRODUCER
Debra Allday, Maggie Speak

DIRECTOR
Mark Powell

DIRECTOR OF PHOTOGRAPHY
Paul Cutter

VISUAL: Various medical staff are performing their procedures. They pause to introduce themselves to the camera.

MARTIN: Hi, I'm Martin. I'll be your consultant while you are having treatment for lung cancer.

MARK: Hi I'm Mark. I'll be your surgeon.

JOHN: Hi, I'm Dr. John. I'll be your radiation oncologist.

KIRSTY: Hi, I'm Kirsty. I'll be administering your chemotherapy.

SUE: I'm Sue. I'll be providing you with a wig when your hair starts to fall out.

BARBARA: Hello, I'm Barbara, your ward nurse.

DAVID: Hi I'm David, your chaplain. I'll be helping you come to terms with the possibility of dying.

SUPER: Nice people, but you don't want to meet them.

Keep smoking and you might.

VISUAL: Female medical attendant in a room with an empty bed. She is putting the patient's personal belongings into a box.

SFX: Low sound of radio; click; radio stops.

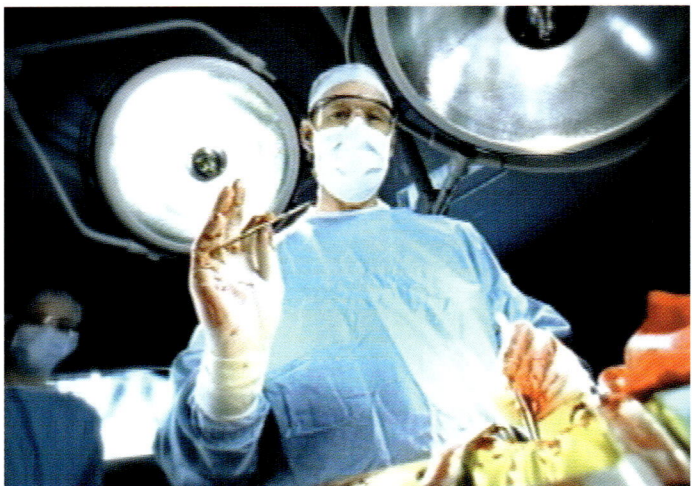

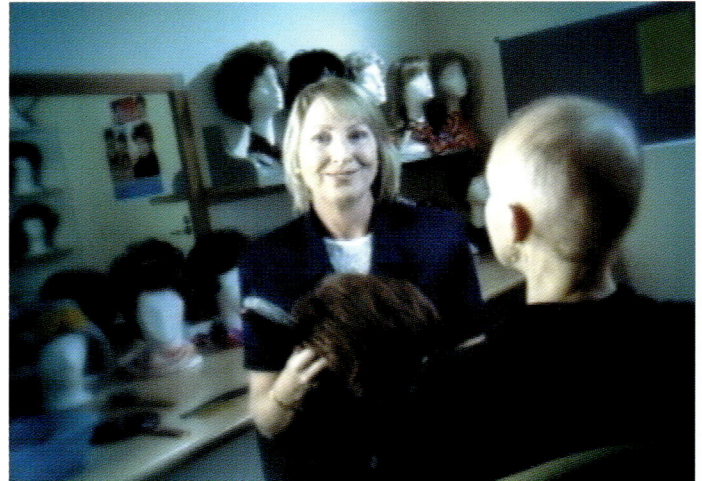

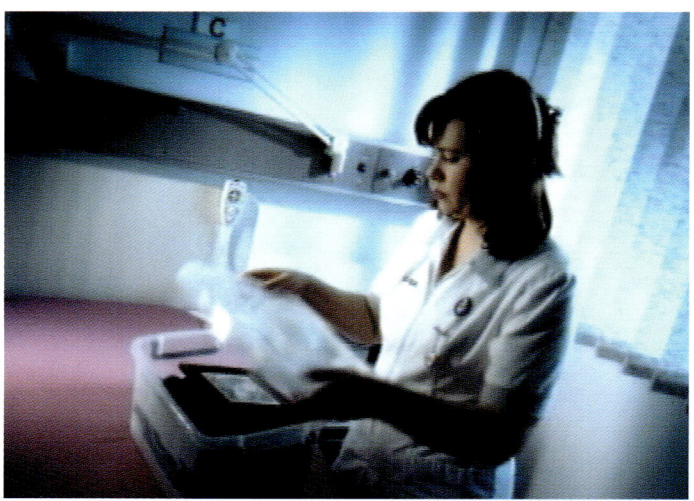

CATEGORY
Public Service

ADVERTISER/PRODUCT
Antisuicide Campaign

TITLE
Daughter

ADVERTISING AGENCY
Leo Burnett, São Paulo

PRODUCTION COMPANY
TV Zero, São Paulo

EDITING COMPANY
TV Zero, São Paulo

MUSIC COMPANY
Nova Onda, São Paulo

ACCOUNT EXECUTIVE
Renato Loes

CREATIVE DIRECTOR
Jose Henrique Borghi,
Bruno Prosperi

COPYWRITER
Renato Simoes

ART DIRECTOR
Bruno Prosperi, Andre Nassar

PRODUCER
Iracema Nogueira, Fernanda Moura

DIRECTOR
Roberto Berliner

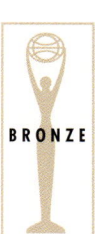

BRONZE

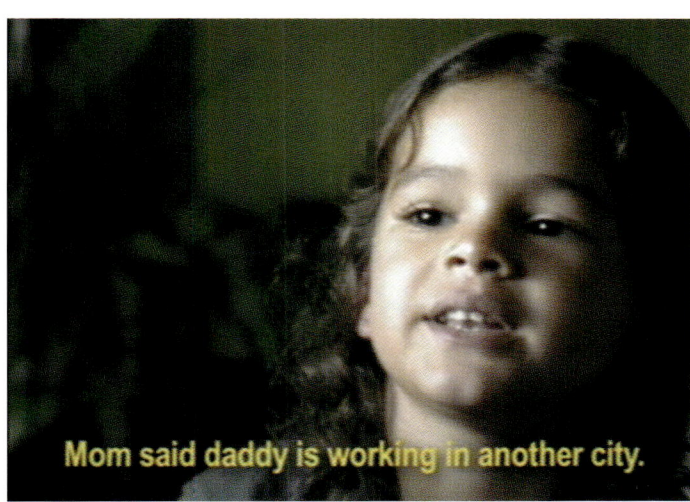

Mom said daddy is working in another city.

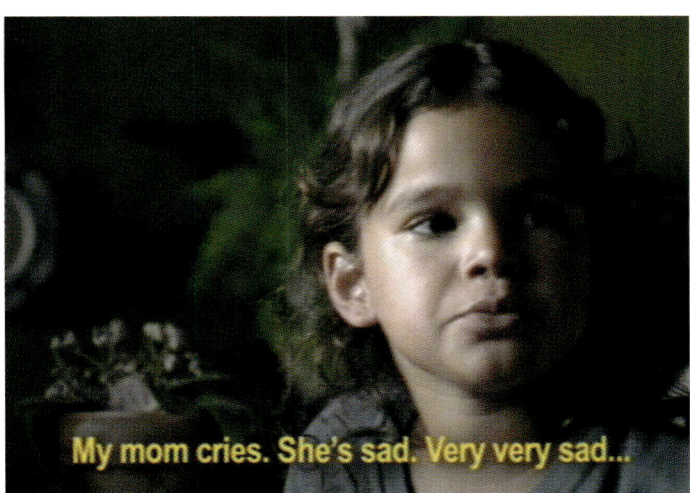

My mom cries. She's sad. Very very sad...

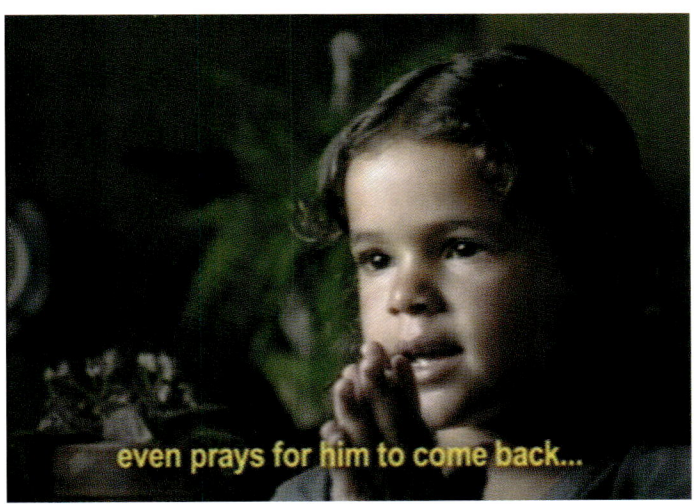

even prays for him to come back...

VISUAL: A five-year-old girl is talking about her life and family.

GIRL: My name is Bruna. I'm five years old. I live here with my dad and mom, but my dad is traveling. I have a parrot, too. When I woke up this morning, the parrot went like: Bruna! Bruna! My dad…My dad snores. (She laughs.) Sometimes he tickles my mother, but she doesn't like it.

Mom said Daddy is working in another city. I miss him, because he's far away from me.

SUPER: Her Father Committed Suicide 6 Months Ago.

GIRL: My mom cries. She's sad; very, very sad. Sometimes, she…even prays for him to come back.

SUPER: Your Life Doesn't Belong Just to You.

SUPER: A São Paulo Police Dept. Antisuicide Campaign.

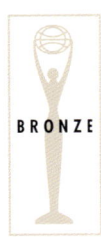

CATEGORY
Public Service

ADVERTISER/PRODUCT
UNHCR (United Nations High
Commissioner for Refugees)

TITLE
Sight

ADVERTISING AGENCY
Young & Rubicam, Buenos Aires

PRODUCTION COMPANY
Oruga Films, Buenos Aires

EDITING COMPANY
Dynamo Post, Buenos Aires

MUSIC COMPANY
Musica Aplicada, Buenos Aires

ACCOUNT EXECUTIVE
Giselle Boyer, Gonzalo Fasson

CREATIVE DIRECTOR
Damian Kepel

COPYWRITER
Pablo Capara

ART DIRECTOR
Javier Celentano

DIRECTOR
Javier Nir

SYNOPSIS: The commercial is shot as seen through the sight of a sniper's scope mounted on a shotgun. In a city at war, the scope scans some debris and stops because something is moving. It's a child feeding a goat. The scope follows the movements of the child, waiting for the right time to pull the trigger. The child stops moving and the scope settles on the center of the child's head. The sniper is ready to shoot. A telephone begins to ring. It rings three times. The sniper brings down the shotgun to answer the phone.

SUPER: A simple call can save a life.

Help the Refugees: 0605-111-0300

United Nations High Commissioner for Refugees.

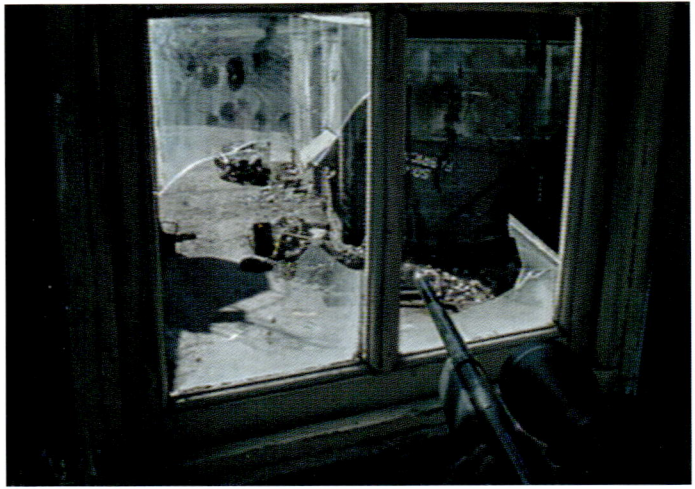

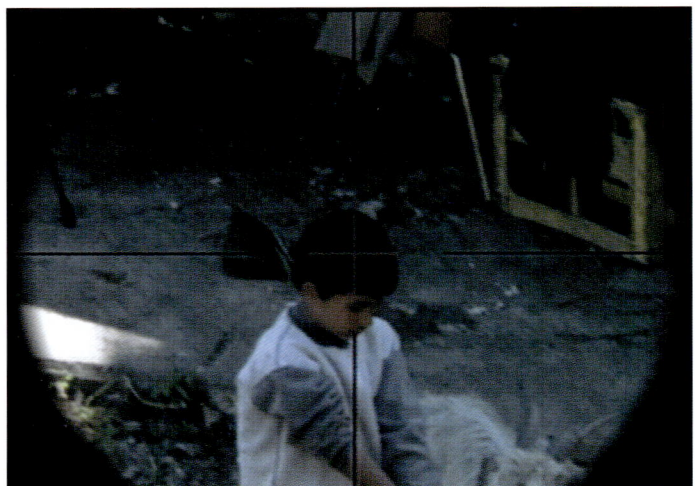

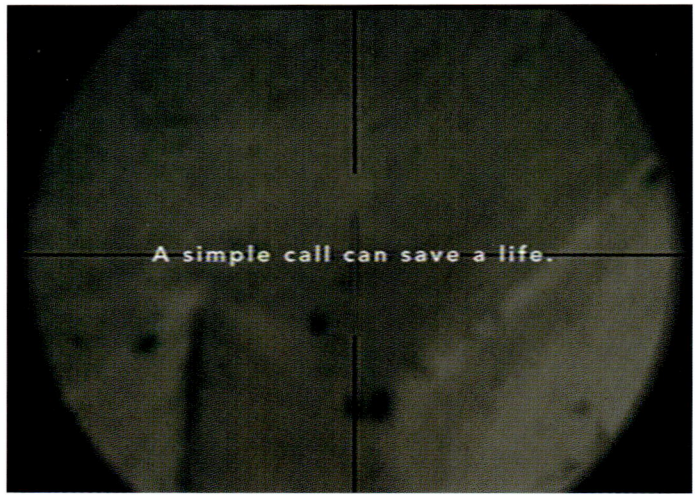

CATEGORY
Public Service

ADVERTISER/PRODUCT
Education/Japan Ad Council

TITLE
Imagination/Whale

ADVERTISING AGENCY
Dentsu, Tokyo

PRODUCTION COMPANY
Dentsu Tec Inc., Tokyo

CREATIVE DIRECTOR
Akira Kagami

COPYWRITER
Takuma Takasaki

PRODUCER
Hidehiko Kawasaki

DIRECTOR
Masahiro Takata

CAMERAMAN
Mamoru Suzuki

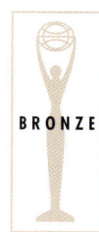

BRONZE

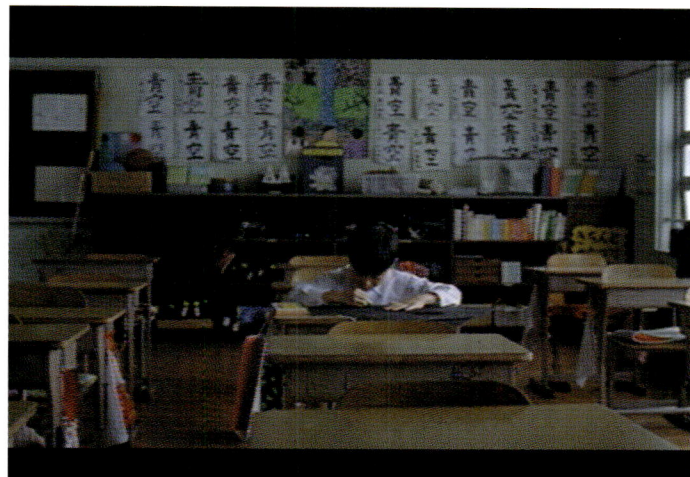

VISUAL: A classroom full of young students involved in drawing and painting. One schoolboy is making a picture that seems to be black and very abstract.

TEACHER: Today, draw anything comes up in your mind.

VISUAL: The schoolboy is working the same image at home and a doctor is speaking with him and his parents.

DOCTOR: What did you draw? Can you tell me?

VISUAL: The schoolboy is being evaluated by a team of doctors in a hospital and continues to draw his black abstract image. His teacher finally recognizes his drawing for what it is.

TEACHER: A whale.

SUPER: How can you encourage a child? Use your imagination.

Japan Ad Council.

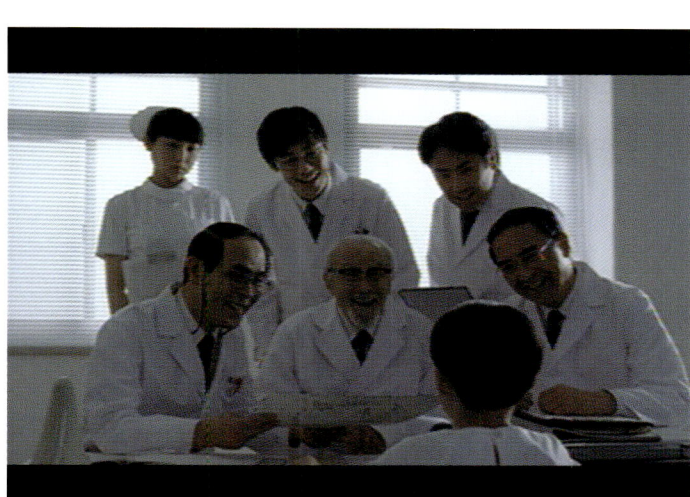

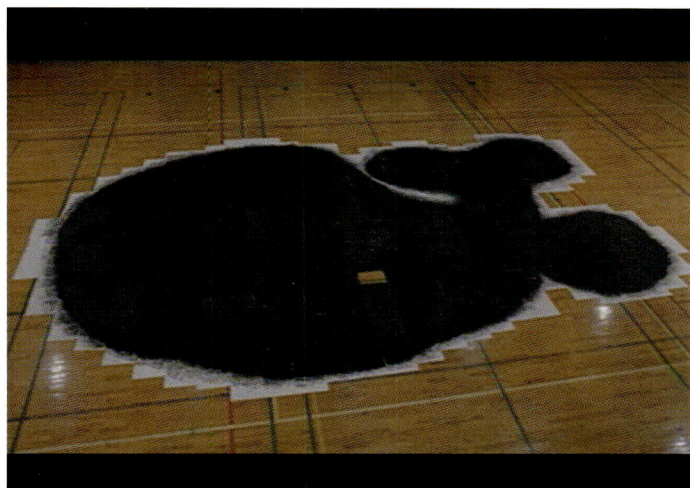

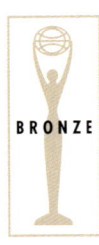

CATEGORY
Public Service

ADVERTISER/PRODUCT
Florida Department of Health

TITLE
Language Class (Swahili)

ADVERTISING AGENCY
Crispin Porter Bogusky, Miami

ACCOUNT EXECUTIVE
Lisa Armand

CREATIVE DIRECTOR
Alex Bogusky

COPYWRITER
Steve O'Connell

ART DIRECTOR
Ryan O'Rourke

DIRECTOR
Michelle Lazzarino

VISUAL: A classroom full of cowboys in full western gear: hats, leather chaps, and gloves. A woman teacher is addressing them.

COWBOYS: Come to Marlboro Country.

TEACHER: Ok, now in Swahili. Njoo pumzika na Marlboro.

COWBOYS: Njoo pumzika na Marlboro.

TEACHER: Njoo pumzika na Marlboro.

COWBOYS: Njoo pumzika na Marlboro.

SUPER: It's illegal to advertise tobacco without a warning label. Except in Africa.

When tobacco companies can't do something in the U.S., they just go someplace else.

COWBOYS: Njoo pumzika na Marlboro.

TEACHER: Very nice.

SUPER: truth.

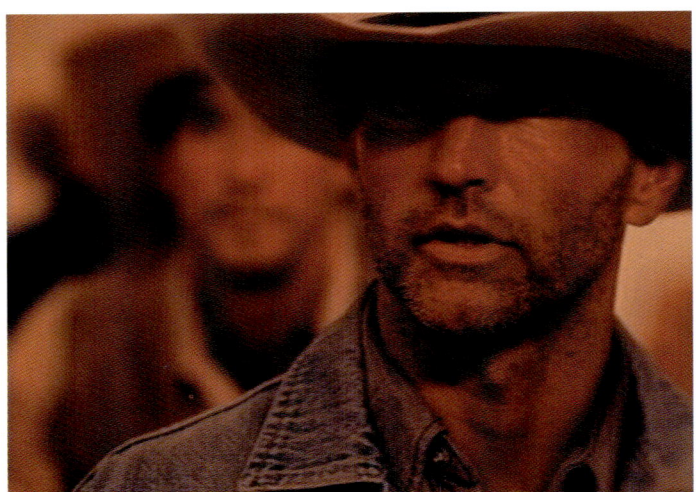

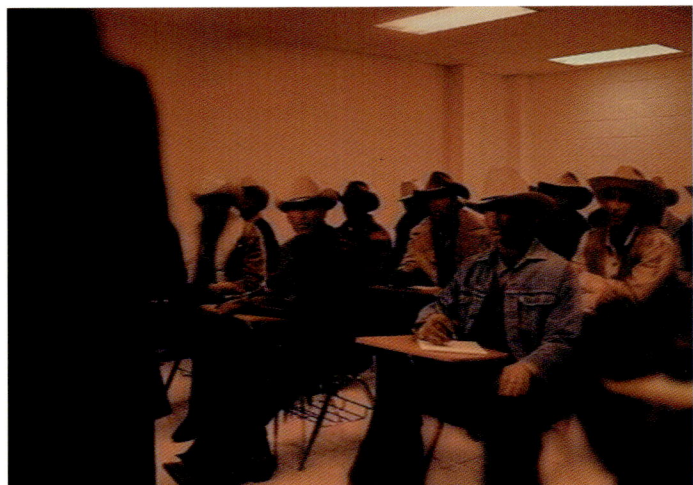

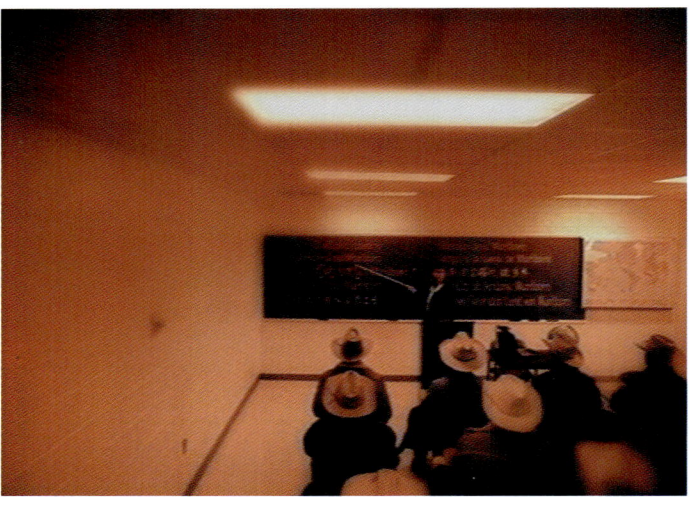

CATEGORY
Retail Stores

ADVERTISER/PRODUCT
The Great Indoors

TITLE
Hotel

ADVERTISING AGENCY
Young & Rubicam, Chicago

PRODUCTION COMPANY
Rock Fight

EDITING COMPANY
The Whitehouse, Chicago

MUSIC COMPANY
Chicago Recording Company, Chicago

CHIEF CREATIVE OFFICER
Mark Figliulo

CREATIVE DIRECTOR
Ken Erke

ART DIRECTOR/COPYWRITER
Blake Ebel, Ken Erke, Mark Figliulo

PRODUCER
Lee Goldberg

DIRECTOR
Pep Bosch

EDITOR
David Braxton, Stacy Levant

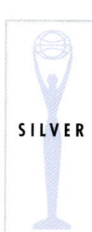

SILVER

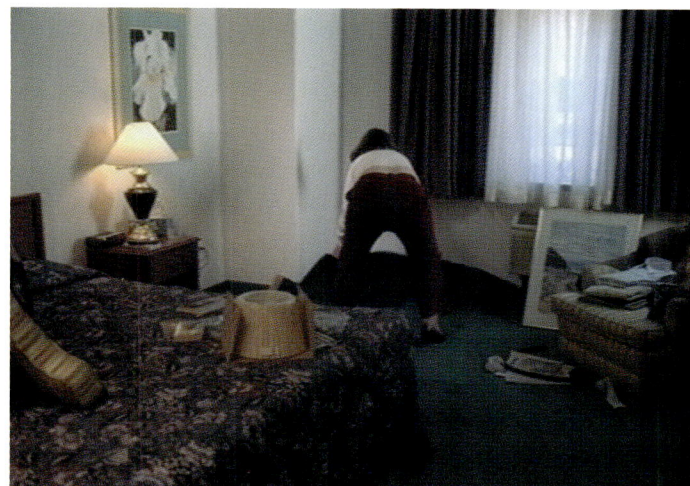

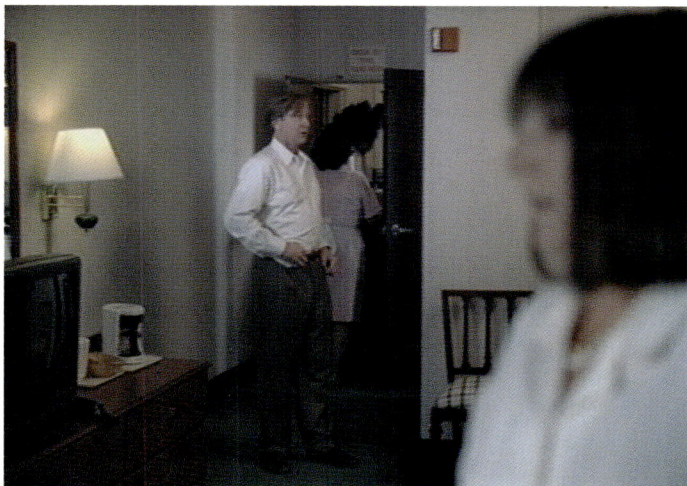

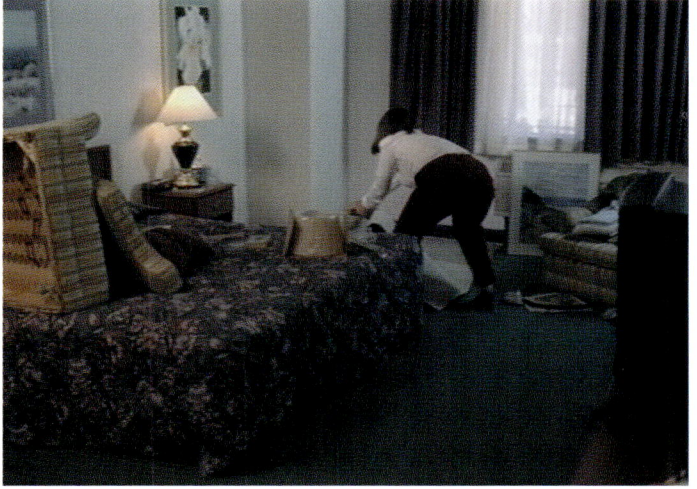

VISUAL: A man, the husband, walks out of the bathroom.

HUSBAND: Cheryl?

VISUAL: A woman, Cheryl, is ripping up the carpeting.

CHERYL: Right here, honey.

HUSBAND: What are you doing?

CHERYL: I was tired of this carpeting. And I'm thinking of changing the lighting while I'm at it.

VISUAL: A woman in a maid's uniform comes into the room.

MAID: Housekeeping, may I clean your room?

VISUAL: Cheryl continues to rip up the carpeting.

SUPER: There's a place for people like you.

VO: There's a place for people like you. The Great Indoors. The store for those who love to decorate, redecorate, and remodel.

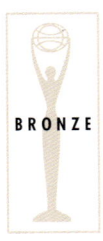

CATEGORY
Retail Stores

ADVERTISER/PRODUCT
Disco Supermarket

TITLE
Tribute

ADVERTISING AGENCY
Young & Rubicam, Buenos Aires

PRODUCTION COMPANY
La Doble A, Buenos Aires

EDITING COMPANY
Post-Bionica, Buenos Aires

ACCOUNT EXECUTIVE
Giselle Boyer, Gonzalo Fasson

GROUP CREATIVE DIRECTOR
Damian Kepel

COPYWRITER
Fernando Arrossi

ART DIRECTOR
Sebastian Olivieri

PRODUCER
Luis Pompeo, Juan Maidana

DIRECTOR
Esteban Sapir

MUSIC
Diego Frenkel

SUPER: Argentine women are the most beautiful women in the world.

VISUAL: Close-up of the flabby arm that belongs to an elderly woman who is kneading pasta. She is working in front of a large table set for the traditional Sunday family meal.

SUPER: The most beautiful women in the world.

VISUAL: The breast of a woman. She is stretching her arms to hold her baby and then begin to breast-feed it. Close-up of woman's face. She looks pale and drawn and has dark circles under her eyes. She's working late at night in front of a computer. She looks at her son's drawing that's stuck on to the computer; she smiles and keeps working.

SUPER: The most beautiful women in the world.

VISUAL: Close-up of a woman putting on lipstick in front of a mirror. She seems to be applying it very badly. She is getting dressed and putting on clown makeup for her daughter's birthday party. She walks to the front door of her house and opens it. There is a Disco's delivery boy who smiles and then helps her with the grocery bags.

SUPER: It is so good to help beautiful women every day.

Disco Supermarket logo.

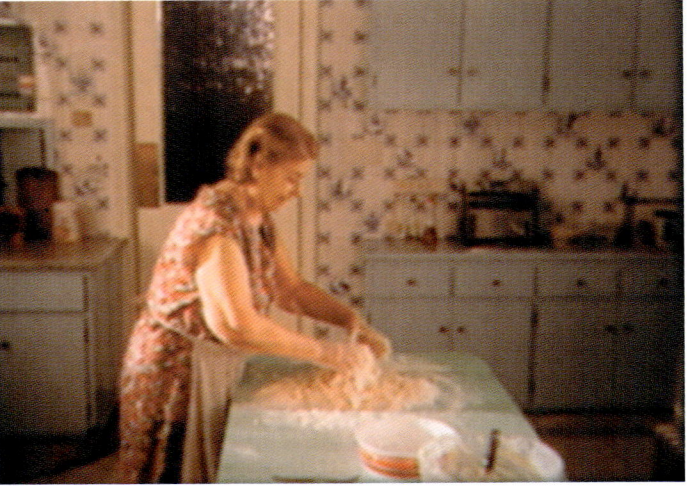

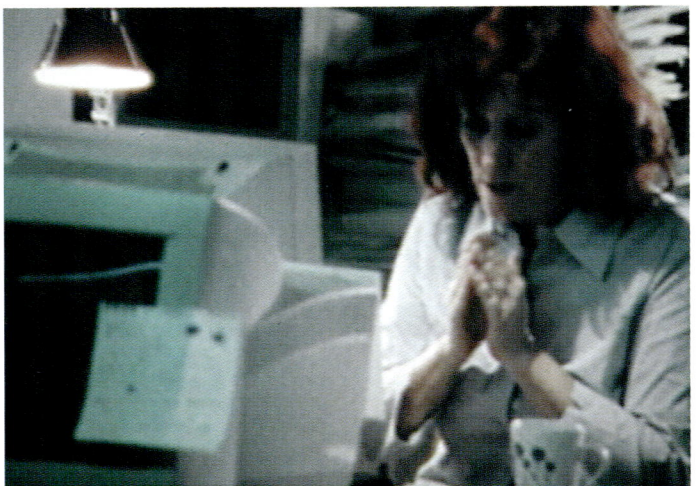

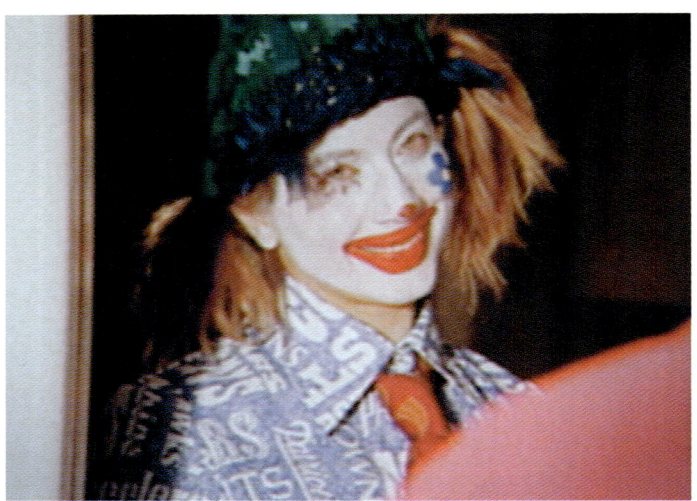

CATEGORY
Toiletries/Pharmaceuticals

ADVERTISER/PRODUCT
Neutrogena Skincare

TITLE
Glasses

ADVERTISING AGENCY
DM9 DDB, São Paulo

PRODUCTION COMPANY
Vertical Filmes, São Paulo

MUSIC COMPANY
Voices, São Paulo

ACCOUNT EXECUTIVE
Maria Antonia Teixeira

CREATIVE DIRECTOR
Erh Ray, Jader Rossetto,
Pedro Cappeletti

COPYWRITER
Marcelo Reis

ART DIRECTOR
Marcelo Kertesz

PRODUCER
Nivio de Souza

DIRECTOR
Caito Ortiz

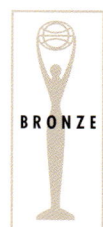

BRONZE

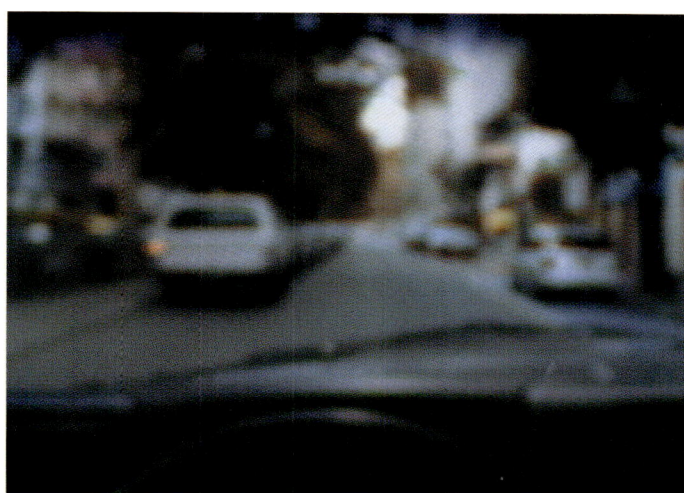

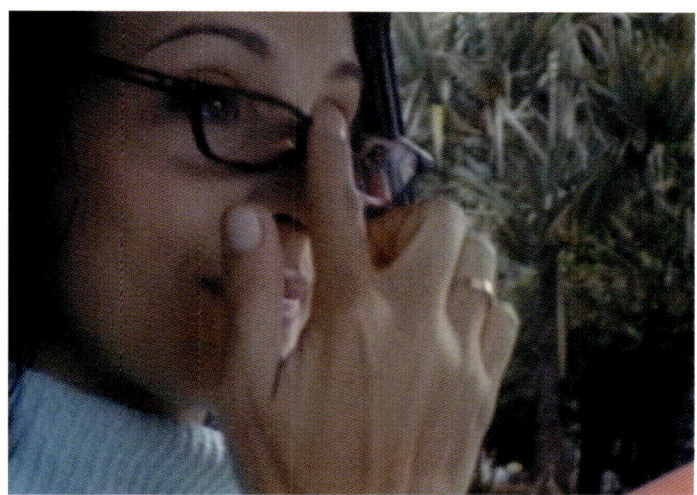

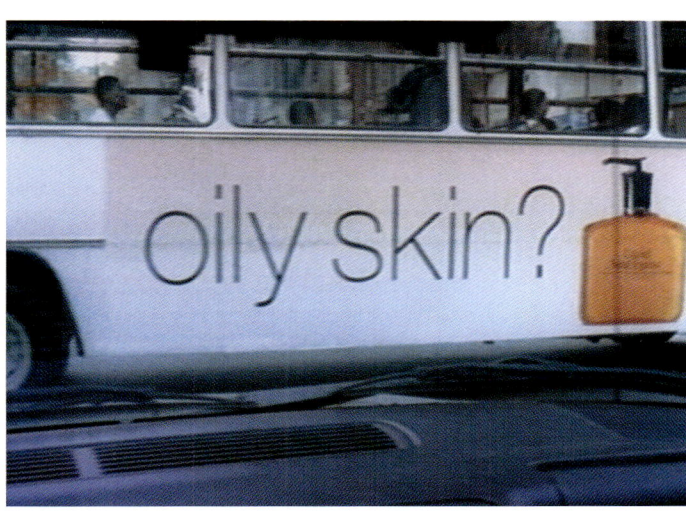

VISUAL: Driver's view through the windshield of a car in motion. The scene goes in and out of focus three times. A reverse shot shows the driver of the car pushing his glasses, which have slipped down his nose, back into place. A bus passes the car. The side of the bus is displaying a poster ad that says, "Oily skin?"

VO: Neutrogena.

Super: Neutrogena.

VO: Deep clean from Neutrogena. Removes oil from skin.

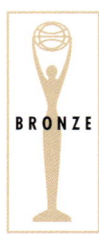

BRONZE

CATEGORY Toiletries/Pharmaceuticals	**PRODUCTION COMPANY** Keyline Films, Brussels	**ANIMATION COMPANY** Nozon, Brussels	**ART DIRECTOR** Alain Janssens
ADVERTISER/PRODUCT Humo/Fruit Flavoured Condoms	**EDITING COMPANY** Keyline Films, Brussels	**ACCOUNT EXECUTIVE** Veerle Devos	**PRODUCER** Marc van Buggenhout
TITLE The Wasp	**MUSIC COMPANY** Keyline Films, Brussels	**CREATIVE DIRECTOR** Jens Mortier	**DIRECTOR** Xavier Mairesse
ADVERTISING AGENCY Duval Guillaume, Brussels	**SOUND DESIGN COMPANY** Keyline Films, Brussels	**COPYWRITER** Jens Mortier	

VISUAL: A young woman is sitting at an outdoor café reading. A wasp keeps flying toward her; she shoos it away but it keeps returning.

SUPER: Fruit Flavoured Condoms. Free with this week's *Humo*.

VISUAL: A man at the same café experiences similar problems with an insect.

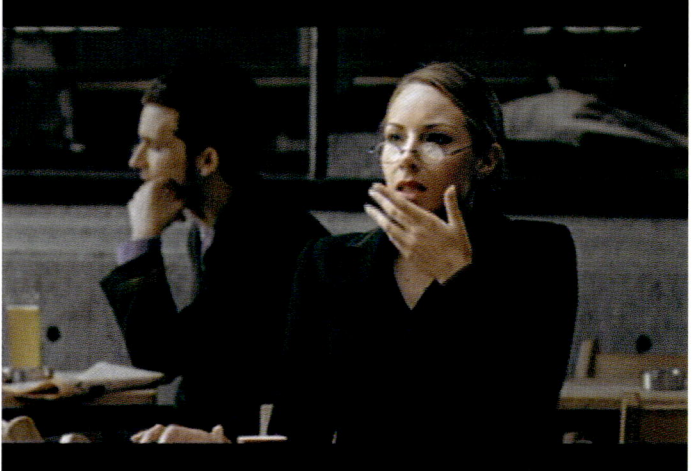

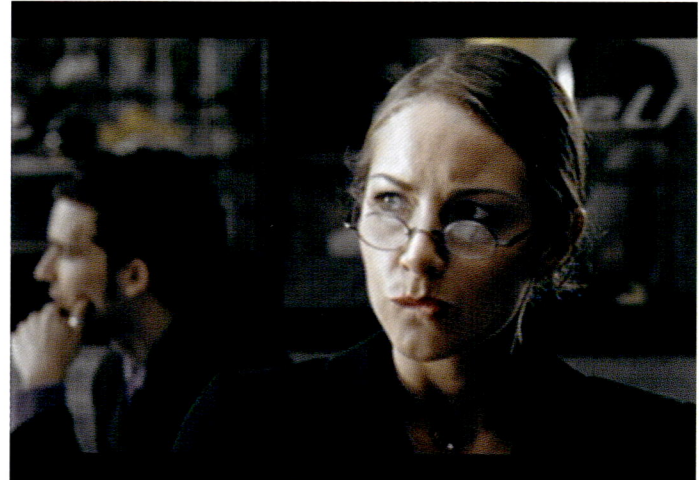

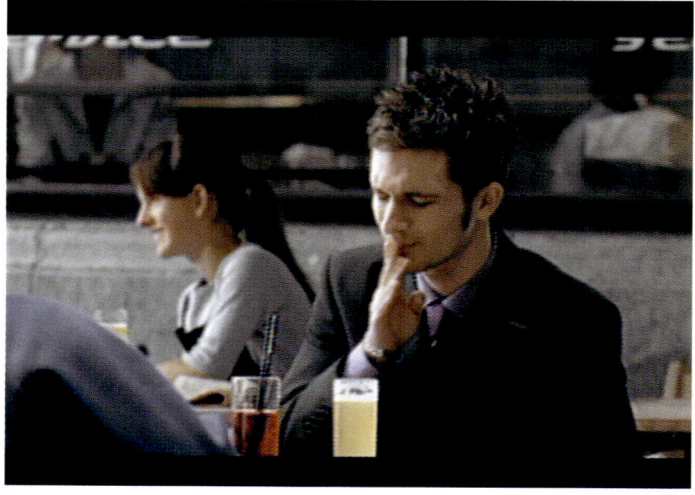

CATEGORY
Campaign

ADVERTISER/PRODUCT
Fox Sports

TITLE
Boat

TITLE
Leaf Blower

TITLE
Nail Gun

ADVERTISING AGENCY
TBWA\Chiat\Day, San Francisco

PRODUCTION COMPANY
harvest, Santa Monica

EDITING COMPANY
Lost Planet, Santa Monica

SOUND DESIGN COMPANY
Eleven, Santa Monica

AGENCY PRODUCER
Betsy Beale

CREATIVE DIRECTOR
Chuck McBride

COPYWRITER
Scott Wild, Eric King, Jeff Labbe

ART DIRECTOR
Eric King, Jeff Labbe

DIRECTOR
Baker Smith

EXECUTIVE PRODUCER
Bonnie Goldfarb

LINE PRODUCER
Lauren Bayer

SOUND DESIGNER
Jeff Payne

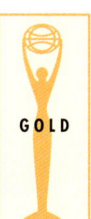

GOLD

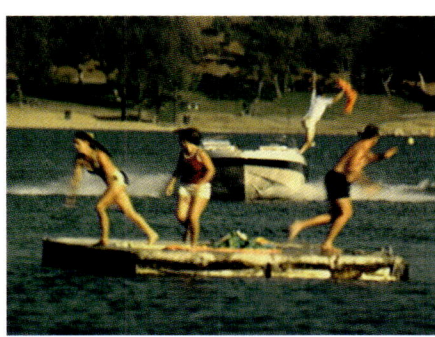

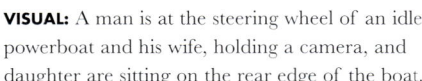

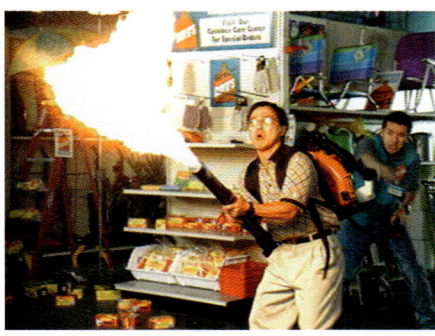

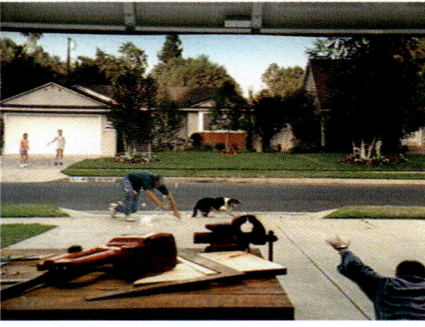

VISUAL: A man is at the steering wheel of an idle powerboat and his wife, holding a camera, and daughter are sitting on the rear edge of the boat.

WIFE: C'mon Dad, smile.

MAN: Here we go.

VISUAL: The man grabs for the throttle and yanks it. It breaks off.

The boat takes off and the man's wife and daughter are thrown into the water. The boat accelerates rapidly and the man grabs for the steering wheel. It breaks off and the vehicle is now headed for a raft full of sunbathers. They jump from the raft as the boat quickly approaches. The man then jumps from his out-of-control boat.

SUPER: Beware of things made in October.

VISUAL: Two distracted factory workers trying to attach a steering wheel to a boat they are assembling, while watching a baseball game on television. They are so involved in the game that they miss a few details in putting the boat together.

SUPER: Major League Baseball Playoffs Are Coming.

Fox baseball logo.

VISUAL: In the hardware section of a department store, a customer is testing out a leaf blower that is strapped to his back. A salesman approaches.

SALESMAN: Leaf blower is nice. Why don't you shut her down and we'll talk price.

VISUAL: The customer grabs the on/off switch. It breaks off in his hand. The leaf blower's power increases and begins to blow merchandise off the shelves. It then starts to blow flames and lights the salesman and much of the merchandise on fire.

SUPER: Beware of things made in October.

VISUAL: A distracted factory worker is working on the assembly line for leaf blowers, while watching a baseball game on television. He is very involved in the game and does not notice that he is attaching the gas tank incorrectly.

SUPER: Major League Baseball Playoffs Are Coming.

Fox baseball logo.

VISUAL: A man in a garage is assembling a wooden shelf. He picks up his nail gun and pulls the trigger. Nothing happens. He pulls the trigger a half-dozen more times and still the gun does not respond. He places the tool on his workbench and, suddenly, it begins to wildly shoot off nails. Like an automatic weapon, the gun is firing nails everywhere. The man drops to the floor in defense. His wife enters the garage, sees what is happening, and also drops for cover. Some neighbors that are passing by are almost hit.

MAN: Get down, get down, get down.

VISUAL: The neighbors run for cover.

SUPER: Beware of things made in October.

VISUAL: A distracted factory worker is working on the assembly line for nail guns, while watching a baseball game on television. He is very involved in the game and does not notice that he is doing his work badly.

SUPER: Major League Baseball Playoffs Are Coming.

Fox baseball logo.

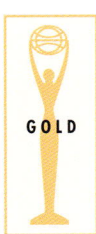

GOLD

CATEGORY
Campaign

ADVERTISER/PRODUCT
BMW of North America

TITLE
The Follow

TITLE
Star

TITLE
Powder Keg

ADVERTISING AGENCY
Fallon, Minneapolis

PRODUCTION COMPANY
Anonymous Content, Culver City

EDITING COMPANY
Jettone, Hong Kong; Nomad, Santa
Monica; Z Films, Mexico City

MUSIC COMPANY
Hi-Fi Productions, New York;
Universal Music Mexico,
Mexico City

SOUND DESIGN COMPANY
Nomad Editing, Santa Monica;
Z Films, Mexico City

ACCOUNT EXECUTIVE
Ginny Grossman

CREATIVE DIRECTOR
David Lubars, Bruce Bildsten

COPYWRITER
Andrew Kevin Walker, Joe Sweet,
Wong Kar Wei, Guy Ritchie,
Alejandro Gonzalez Iñarritu,
David Carter, Guillermo Arriaga

ART DIRECTOR
David Carter, Martin Whis,
Joe Sweet

PRODUCER
Rob Van de Weteringe Buys,
Aristides McGarry,
Robyn Boardman, Tapas Blank

DIRECTOR
Wong Kar Wei, Guy Ritchie,
Alejandro Gonzalez Iñarritu

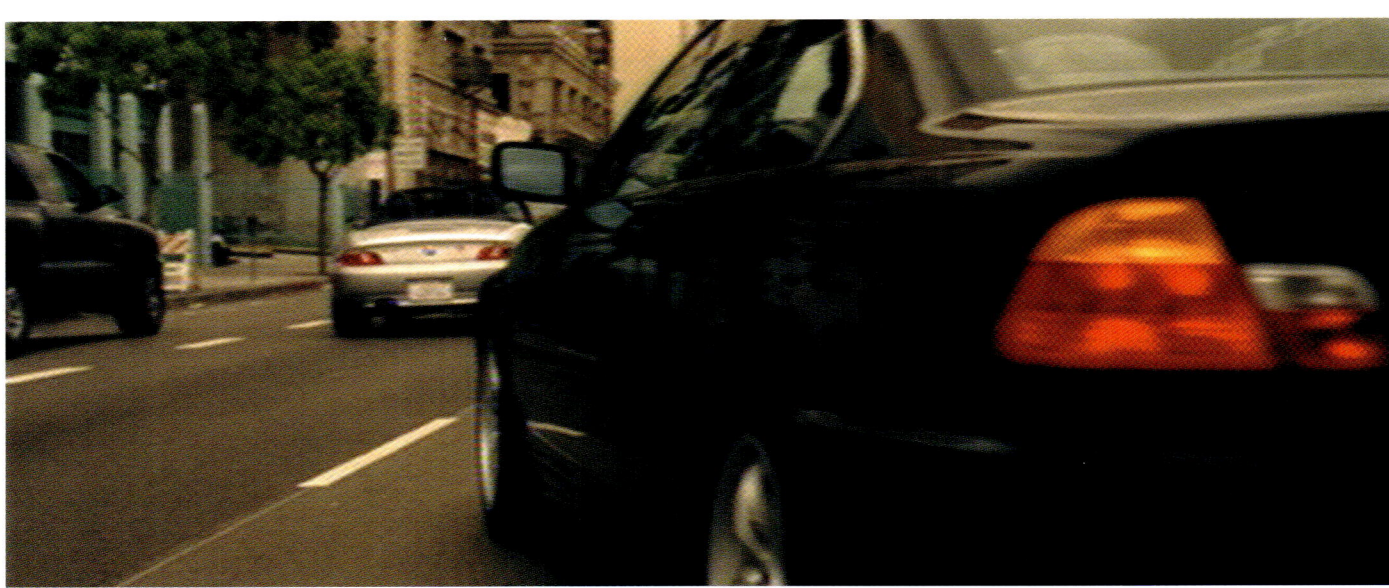

SYNOPSIS: A man, the Driver, is hired to follow a woman accused of cheating on her famous husband.

VISUAL: A BMW sedan is following a BMW Z3 roadster.

DRIVER VO: You vary your distance…you stay to the rear, to the right…never more than a few cars behind. It's all about patience…percentages…timing.

VISUAL: The Driver and manager sitting at a table.

MANAGER: I wouldn't be asking you…it's just I need somebody I can trust. He's on location all weekend, you know—this thing, this thing is driving him crazy! He's gotta know where she goes, who she sees…

DRIVER: There are people who do this.

MANAGER: C'mon, man…not very well, they don't. He's a movie star! C'mon.

VISUAL: Manager shows the driver a photo of the movie star's wife he is to follow.

VISUAL: Driver follows wife down various roads during the day and at night.

DRIVER VO: If you get too close, move into their blind spot. If you lose them, just keep moving—hope for the best. Out in the open, distance is subjective. You can let the target ride the horizon…so long as you know their patterns.

MANAGER (on telephone): I just want you to meet with him…a meeting! What's a meeting? It's not gonna cost you anything! He's at the top—no, he's at—he's at the top of his game. Look, he's in a meeting right now…he's in a meeting right now. He's got these interviews coming up afterwards…c'mon. I know they have an offer, but has the offer been accepted?

VISUAL: The Driver and movie star, inside dark room.

MOVIE STAR: You know, it's impossible to describe how painful infidelity is…I mean, it just, it just rips you apart at the seams.

DRIVER: Does she know you suspect her? Did you confront her?

MOVIE STAR: Do you have a wife?

DRIVER: Not any more.

MOVIE STAR: Well, I…I'm not gonna lose mine.

VISUAL: The Driver and manager in the cabin of an airplane.

MANAGER: He's one of those people who's so…beautiful in one way, and such a joke in another. I mean—"Mickey, Mickey, how could you do that to me, man?"—he can be like that. If you need any more, I'll get you some more. I really appreciate this.

VISUAL: The Driver is following the wife through the airport.

DRIVER: The waiting is the hard part. Your mind wanders, wondering what it would be like watching your own life from far away.

VO (P.A. announcement): This will serve as the final boarding announcement.

DRIVER: On foot is the same: distance, patterns, anticipation.

WIFE: Hello, is this flight going to Brazil?

TICKETER: No, no.

DRIVER: If the target doubles back, never react.

WIFE (on telephone): I'm fine, Mother. Really, I'm alright…but my flight is delayed…very late.

DRIVER: Whatever you do, don't get too close…never meet their eyes.

VISUAL: The driver is sitting in his car talking to the manager, who is outside the car's window. They are in a tunnel.

MANAGER: What is it? What's this?

DRIVER: I lost her.

MANAGER: Whaddaya mean, you lost her?

DRIVER: Don't ever call me again.

VISUAL: The Driver is on the road again.

DRIVER VO: There's always something waiting at the end of the road. If you're not willing to see what it is, you probably shouldn't be out there in the first place.

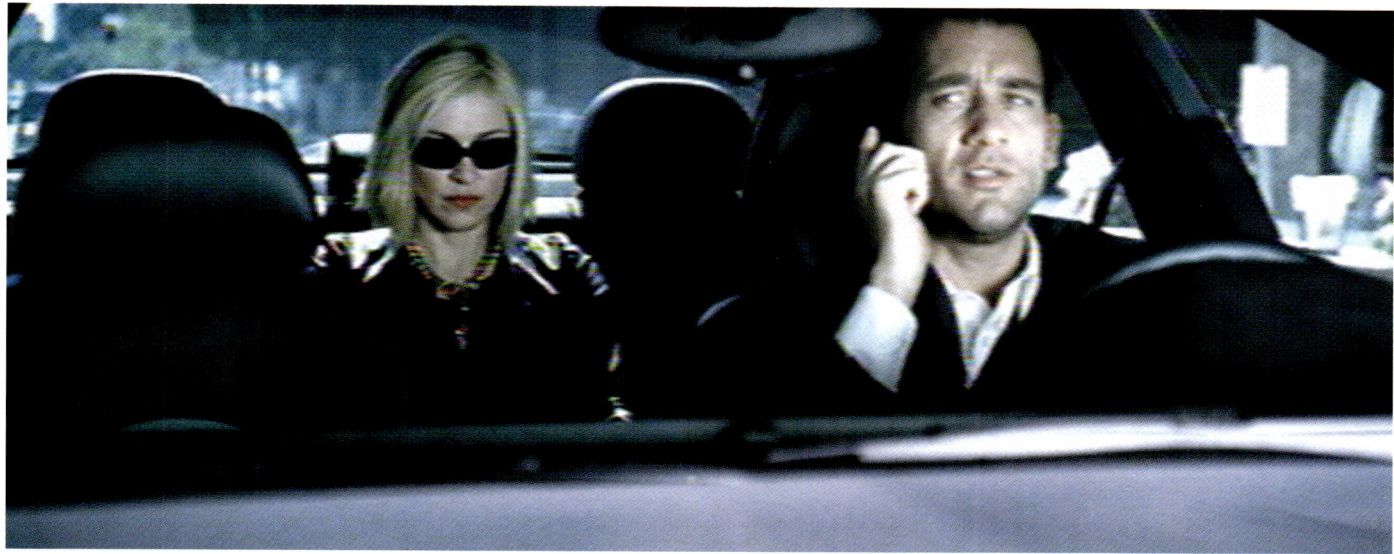

SYNOPSIS: The Driver must chauffer a hugely talented and successful rock star, with a serious attitude problem, to her concert venue.

VISUAL: The Driver's face seen through a windshield.

DRIVER: The first thing you notice physically about this lady is her eyes…bright blue eyes.

VISUAL: The star's eyes.

DRIVER: It's rare to actually see those eyes, 'cause they're usually covered up, but when you do, it's worth it. The next thing you notice is her hands.

VISUAL: The star's hands.

DRIVER: Strong, powerful, yet feminine, hands. But the real heart-stopper that this woman has in her galaxy of talents is her voice—her billion-dollar voice.

VISUAL: The star's lips.

DRIVER: She's a legend in her own lifetime.

VISUAL: Elevator doors open and the star steps out with her two bodyguards.

DRIVER VO: She's achieved giddy heights few have equaled, she's unrivalled in her world, and she's a complete c—

VISUAL: Inside a parking garage The star, her manager, Glen, and the entourage.

STAR: GLEN!

GLEN: Right here, darlin'! I'll be right back.

STAR: Glen, get over here.

GLEN: Hey, Glen is flying in. Glen is here—to say—you are the bomb!

STAR: Idiot! You are such a moron! This is not what I pay you for!

GLEN: All right.

DRIVER VO: Glen: her manager for seven years. No backbone on the man.

GLEN: Not a problem, sweetheart. We will work it out, okay?

DRIVER VO: But he gets paid enough not to have one.

STAR: Coffee. I want my coffee! It better not be cold.

GLEN: Piping, piping hot.

STAR: I am so over black.

GLEN: Get that for you. Okay.

VISUAL: The star gets into the rear seat of a BMW sedan.

STAR: Take the bus!

GLEN: Hey, hey.

STAR: This'll do. Take me to the venue.

DRIVER: I'm sorry, I'm booked for someone else.

STAR: Yeah, right. Just take me to the venue.

DRIVER: What venue?

STAR: I am gracing this armpit of a town for one night. If you also think I'm gonna know the name of the venue in El Armpitto, you're sadly mistaken. You are the driver. You are supposed to know.

BODYGUARD: We're going to the Palace.

STAR: We? Listen, my bone-from-the-neck-up driver friend, I suggest you put your foot down…and next time do your homework.

DRIVER: Okay. Fine.

VISUAL: Bodyguard attempts to get into the BMW.

STAR: What do you think you're doing?

BODYGUARD: Coming with you, ma'am.

STAR: Then get on the roof and hold on tight. Out! Out!

BODYGUARD: I'll follow behind.

STAR: Good idea, tough guy. What are you waiting for? Let's get out of here before he gets in the car. I don't want him following me!

DRIVER: Okay.

BODYGUARD: Don't lose them.

VISUAL: BMW sedan takes off out of the garage. The two bodyguards follow in a black SUV.

VISUAL: Inside BMW.

STAR: Why are we going so slow?

DRIVER: Excuse me?

STAR: Are you deaf as well as stupid? I said, "Why are we going so slow?" People are waiting for me.

DRIVER: Well, ma'am, I wouldn't like to put you in any danger.

STAR: Don't "ma'am" me, smarty-pants. It's a shame your driving isn't as smart as your mouth. I thought I told you I don't want that car following me. Huh? Not so smart as to answer that, are you, smarty-pants?

DRIVER: Would you excuse me for a second? Hello?

VISUAL: Driver on cell phone.

GLEN: Hey, is she doing okay?

DRIVER: Yeah, yeah, she's fine. I'll take care of her.

GLEN: No rush…show her the sights…give her everything I've paid you for—breakfast, lunch, and dinner.

DRIVER: She'll be there on time.

STAR: If you'd keep your eyes on the road instead of on me, we might be getting somewhere.

DRIVER: Let me see what I can do…sir. Just hold on tight, sir…I'll get you there safely. Looks like we've lost them, sir. Oh—let's try again! Well, we got you here…and in good time, too!

VISUAL: The BMW takes off for a high-speed ride. Swerving, accelerating, jumping, just missing a few cars that cross its path. The star is being tossed all over the rear of the car. The SUV attempts to follow.

VISUAL: The BMW pulls up to the concert hall, the driver slams on the brakes and the star is thrown out the car door on to the pavement. Her coffee has spilled and stained the crotch of her pants. Many photographers are waiting and snap pictures of this embarrassing situation.

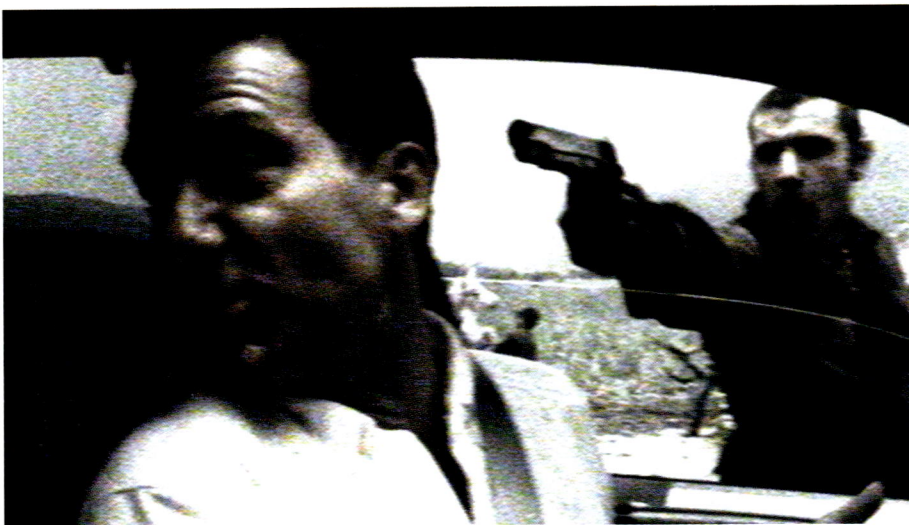

SYNOPSIS: Soldiers, fingers on triggers, patrol a coup-ravaged city in South America. Their mission: find a photojournalist who has taken a picture certain to enrage the world against their leader. The Driver must get the photojournalist and his film beyond the fiercely guarded border.

VISUAL: A truck full of peasants, men, women, and young men, drives through a cane field escorted by three trucks full of heavily armed paramilitaries. The lead truck comes to a halt and the paramilitaries get out.

LEADER: Get out.

VISUAL: The peasants get out of the truck. One of them carries a trumpet.

CHIEF: Play.

VISUAL: The man with the trumpet looks as if he doesn't understand. One of the paramilitaries pushes him.

PARAMILITARY: What, are you deaf?

VISUAL: The musician plays a sad melody. The paramilitaries force the peasants to line up with their hands behind their heads. A woman begs.

WOMAN: For the love of God, please don't hurt us.

VISUAL: The massacre of the peasants begins.

SFX: Camera shutter clicking; screams of paramilitary soldiers and peasants.

VISUAL: The paramilitaries laugh and finish their slaughter. The cane field is littered with bodies. One of the paramilitaries spots movement in the undergrowth.

SOLDIER: There, over there!

VISUAL: The person crawling through the undergrowth watches the massacre and is taking photographs of it.

SFX: Heavy breathing.

VISUAL: The paramilitaries stop firing their weapons and look to see if anyone is alive. The leader hurries them.

LEADER: That's it, let's go, let's go.

VISUAL: The paramilitaries load up on trucks and leave. The sight is full of dead peasants. We see part of a man's body, and a small Braille plaque covered in blood.

FADE OUT.

VISUAL: Inside of a house. Two peasants stare at the street through a small window. They watch some boys play basketball, and some soldiers looking out from barricades. A tense calm pervades the village.

VISUAL: Close-up of a woman's hands healing a punctured, bleeding abdomen. Their faces are not visible.

VISUAL: Inside of the house. One of the peasants spots a silver BMW X5 in the distance. He turns to a man.

PEASANT: Perico, here it comes.

VISUAL: Perico moves toward someone lying on a cot.

PERICO: They're here for you.

VISUAL: The man has trouble getting up. He is helped by a young woman. The man is Harvey Jacobs, a hard-faced American photojournalist. His beige shirt is blood-stained. An old woman enters the room.

OLD WOMAN: Hurry up and get this goddamn gringo out of here, or we'll be screwed too.

VISUAL: Harvey manages to get up. He grabs a leather briefcase and a camera and crosses the room slowly. He leaves the house, assisted by the woman and Perico. The driver opens the back door of an BMW X5 SUV. Harvey, obviously in pain, lies down on the car's rear seat and they take off.

VISUAL: Interior of the BMW X5. The truck moves through the town. Harvey makes an effort to sit up.

HARVEY: I've got to cross the border as soon as possible; I'm a sitting duck here.

DRIVER: Yeah, We have a doctor waiting for you there.

VISUAL: Harvey looks through the truck's window and sees children watching him through walls riddled with bullet holes. He also sees starving women carrying water, stray dogs. Some soldiers run across the street.

HARVEY: What are we doing with this country? All this so our happy yuppies can have their weekly lines of coke. What they don't know is that every gram they snort is spattered with a pint of blood.

VISUAL: The driver realizes a police van is following them down a parallel street. The X5 heads toward the highway; through the rear-view mirror, the driver verifies that they are being followed, but says nothing to Harvey, who hugs his stomach and looks at his bloody hand.

HARVEY: Do you know what gets me the most about being a war photographer? That I never had time to play with my kids.

DRIVER: How many do you have?

HARVEY: None.

VISUAL: They drive by a funeral procession. Over 150 people follow two adult and two children's coffins. In the background we can see the burnt earth; dead, bloated cows: the pestilence of death.

HARVEY: I've been in the worst hellholes, the worst slaughters…fifteen wars, man, fifteen…taking picture after picture after picture and sometimes wounded men would look me in the eyes and beg for me to help them and do you know what I would do? I'd take another picture…I never saved a life, not one good goddamned life.

DRIVER: Your photographs have helped a lot, Harvey.

HARVEY: Sure, to sell more newspapers. You don't know what I would give so that one, just one of my pictures would change things around here.

VISUAL: A military helicopter flies overhead. A police van tries to pass them, but the driver accelerates. The police come close to crashing into a military truck driving toward them. The driver looks at the helicopter through the windshield and then at his pursuers through the rearview mirror.

DRIVER: Can you duck a little?

VISUAL: Harvey ducks and in doing so his blood stains the upholstery.

HARVEY: Now I got your car dirty.

VISUAL: The police van tries to pass them, the X5 accelerates, and the police van almost smashes into a tractor.

VISUAL: Harvey looks terrible. He sits up and sees that they're being followed. He sees the countryside devastated by war.

DRIVER: Then, why are you a photographer?

HARVEY: Because of my mother. She taught me how to see, even though she's never seen any my photographs.

VISUAL: A police checkpoint. A group of policemen are working the checkpoint. Most are poorly dressed. Only a couple of the police chiefs wear shirts with the legend "Policia Departamental." Some of them play dominos in a corner. Others are playing with a donkey. A radio crackles. A police chief picks it up.

POLICE CHIEF: Checkpoint 4 here, checkpoint 4 here.

RADIO VO: An X5 is on its way, I repeat, an X5.

POLICE CHIEF: Roger.

VISUAL: The policeman orders a young man to put stones in the road. He carries them into place.

VISUAL: Interior of the BMW X5. They drive by a town graveyard. Harvey looks at it, then takes his camera, rewinds the film and pulls it out. He then takes out a couple rolls of film more from his shirt pocket. A helicopter circles overhead. The police van continues to follow them. Harvey hands the driver a few rolls of film.

HARVEY: Get this to John Elliot at the *Times*.

VISUAL: The driver pushes Harvey's hand back.

DRIVER: No, you'll give them to him.

VISUAL: Harvey shakes his head "no" and smiles. The driver takes the film.

DRIVER: What is it?

HARVEY: It's a Powder Keg.

DRIVER: The story?

HARVEY: The story.

VISUAL: Harvey takes the small Braille plaque and gives to the driver.

HARVEY: Find my mother and give her this, please.

VISUAL: The BMW nears the checkpoint, followed closely by the police van. The BMW slows down.

VISUAL: Inside the X5. The driver takes a card with the United States shield printed on it that says "Embajada Americana—Vehiculo Oficial (American Embassy—official vehicle)" and places it on the windshield. He lowers the window upon seeing two policemen approach on either side.

DRIVER (in bad Spanish): Buenas tardes.

POLICE CHIEF: Put your hands on the wheel and don't move.

VISUAL: The driver obeys.

POLICE CHIEF: Where are you going?

DRIVER: We're from the American embassy.

VISUAL: The chief sticks his hand in, takes the U.S. embassy card and throws it away.

POLICE CHIEF: I asked you where you were going.

SFX: Camera shutter.

VISUAL: The chief looks in and discovers Harvey, lying in a pool of blood, loading and shooting his empty camera repeatedly. The policeman pulls out his gun and points it at him.

POLICE CHIEF: Hey gringo, stop taking pictures.

VISUAL: Harvey pays no attention and continues to play with his camera. The police chief aims his gun at the driver's head.

POLICE CHIEF: Tell him to give me the camera.

DRIVER: It's not a problem, the camera doesn't have any film.

VISUAL: Harvey won't stop. The policeman cocks the pistol and aims.

POLICEMAN 1: Stop it or I'll shoot you, you son of a bitch.

DRIVER: Harvey, please stop.

VISUAL: Harvey will not stop. The policeman gets nervous and sticks his machine gun through the other window. The chief points his gun at the driver.

POLICEMAN 1: Either he stops, or I'll shoot you.

VISUAL: The driver smacks the pistol out of the chief's hand and it goes off. The bullet hits the other policeman, killing him. The driver slams his door into the chief, puts the X5 in reverse, and accelerates. They crash into the van behind them. They are surrounded by police shooting at them. They get back on the highway. At the border they find a group of soldiers signaling for them to stop. The X5 crashes through the barrier and drives across the border. The driver looks through the rear-view mirror at the chaos they have left behind.

DRIVER: We made it, we made it.

VISUAL: Harvey doesn't answer. He is curled up on the seat in a pool of blood. The car stops and the driver turns to look at Harvey.

DRIVER: Harvey, Harvey.

VISUAL: The driver pulls at Harvey and realizes that two bullets have gone through the seat and killed him. The driver exits the BMW and kicks it furiously.

FADE OUT

VISUAL: A BMW stops in front of a modest American house (Harvey's mother's house). The driver gets out carrying a newspaper in his hands. He knocks on the door. A blind old woman (Harvey's mother) opens it.

DRIVER: Good afternoon, Mrs. Jacobs?

OLD WOMAN: Yes, that's me.

DRIVER: Ma'am, I was with your son the last…I'm very sorry.

VISUAL: The driver is noticeably uncomfortable; he does not know what to say.

DRIVER: Your son won the Pulitzer…

OLD WOMAN (with slight irony): Yes, the Pulitzer…the Pulitzer…what matters is if his vision changed things.

DRIVER: He did ma'am, he surely did.

VISUAL: The driver takes the Braille plaque from his pants.

DRIVER: He asked me to give you this.

VISUAL: He gives it to her and she extends her hand to receive it. He sees the newspaper headlines: "25 people murdered in Nuevo Colón," and below: "Governor involved with paramilitary forces;" "United Nations condemns the attack." He is about to give her the newspaper but does not. The old woman is pensive. She begins to run her fingers over the plaque, reading the message in Braille. She holds in her tears and stares into emptiness as her eyes begin to glisten. From her distressed face shines a light, pained smile. The driver leaves the house.

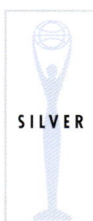

SILVER

CATEGORY
Campaign

ADVERTISER/PRODUCT
The Great Indoors

TITLE
Hotel

TITLE
Renovation

TITLE
Therapist

ADVERTISING AGENCY
Young & Rubicam, Chicago

PRODUCTION COMPANY
Rock Fight

EDITING COMPANY
The Whitehouse, Chicago

MUSIC COMPANY
Chicago Recording Company, Chicago

CHIEF CREATIVE OFFICER
Mark Figliulo

CREATIVE DIRECTOR
Ken Erke

COPYWRITER:
Blake Ebel, Ken Erke, Mark Figliulo

ART DIRECTOR
Blake Ebel, Ken Erke, Mark Figliulo

PRODUCER
Lee Goldberg

DIRECTOR
Pep Bosch

EDITOR
David Braxton, Stacy Levant

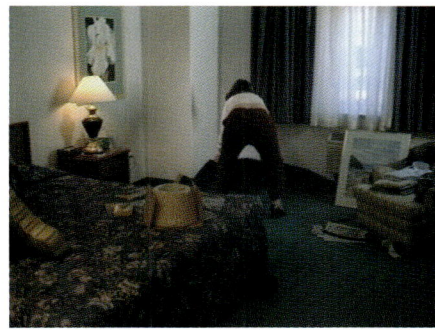

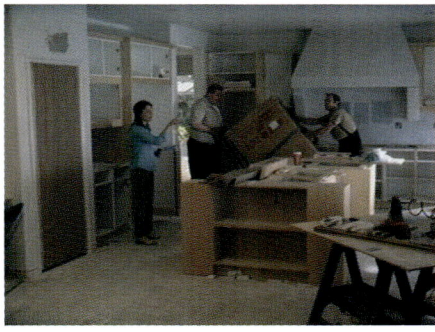

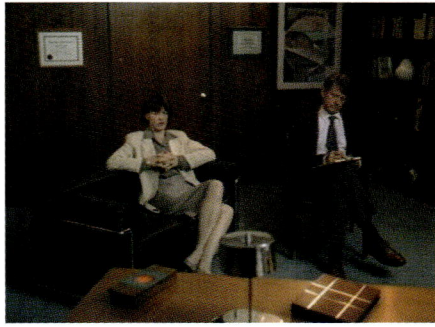

VISUAL: A man, the husband, walks out of the bathroom.

HUSBAND: Cheryl?

VISUAL: A woman, Cheryl, is ripping up the carpeting.

CHERYL: Right here, honey.

HUSBAND: What are you doing?

CHERYL: I was tired of this carpeting. And I'm thinking of changing the lighting while I'm at it.

VISUAL: A woman in a maid's uniform comes into the room.

MAID: Housekeeping, may I clean your room?

VISUAL: Cheryl continues to rip up the carpeting.

SUPER: There's a place for people like you.

VO: There's a place for people like you. The Great Indoors. The store for those who love to decorate, redecorate, and remodel.

VISUAL: Woman is standing in a kitchen measuring the length of a shelf. Two deliverymen enter pushing a large box.

WOMAN: Oh, there you guys are. Listen, I know that the double oven and fridge are supposed to go there and there. Oh, and I was thinking, I'd like to change the paint color to peony.

HUSBAND VO: Barbara, telephone.

VISUAL: The woman leaves the kitchen and walks outside and across the street to her home, where her husband is standing in front of the garage.

HUSBAND: What were you doing at the neighbor's?

WOMAN: Oh, nothing.

VISUAL: They walk into their house.

SUPER: There's a place for people like you.

VO: There's a place for people like you. The Great Indoors. The store for those who love to decorate, redecorate, and remodel.

VISUAL: A woman and her therapist are sitting in an office.

WOMAN: A group of people surround me, trying to convince me that if I tried to jump the river I wouldn't make it. I leaped, but instead of landing on the other side, I landed in the living room of the house I grew up in.

THERAPIST: This dream seems to make you uncomfortable.

WOMAN: Well, it's not the dream. It's just hard to relax when I know that this couch would look so much better over by that window.

SUPER: There's a place for people like you.

VO: There's a place for people like you. The Great Indoors. The store for those who love to decorate, redecorate, and remodel.

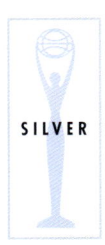

CATEGORY
Campaign

ADVERTISER/PRODUCT
Toyota Celica

TITLE
Motorcycle Cop

TITLE
Old Man

TITLE
Dog

ADVERTISING AGENCY
Saatchi & Saatchi, Los Angeles

PRODUCTION COMPANY
Independent, Santa Monica

EDITING COMPANY
FilmCore, Santa Monica

MUSIC COMPANY
Ad Music, Santa Monica

ACCOUNT EXECUTIVE
Paul Imhoff

CREATIVE DIRECTOR
Steve Rabosky, Neal Foard,
Doug Van Andel

COPYWRITER
Sherry Hawkins

ART DIRECTOR
Verner Soler

PRODUCER
Elaine Adachi, Lindsey Skutch,
Susanna Preissler

DIRECTOR
Chris Smith

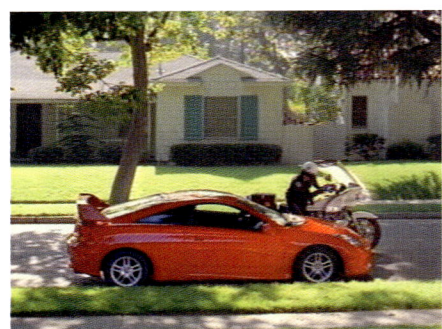

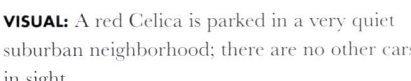

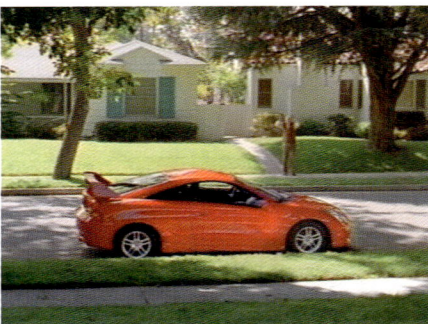

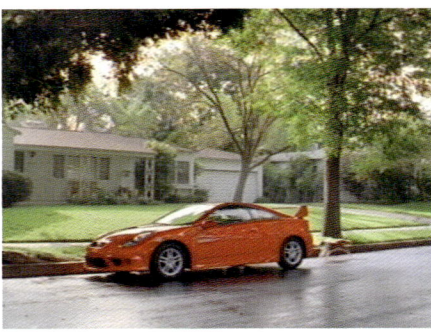

VISUAL: A red Celica is parked in a very quiet suburban neighborhood; there are no other cars in sight.

SFX: Police siren.

POLICEMAN VO: Red Celica, pull over.

VISUAL: A motorcycle policeman speeding past the Celica stops suddenly and then backs up. He realizes that the car wasn't actually moving. Embarrassed, he looks around to see if anyone caught his mistake, then drives off.

SUPER: The Celica Action Package. Looks fast.

VISUAL: A red Celica is parked in a very quiet suburban neighborhood; there are no other cars in sight. After a few seconds, we see an old man walking slowly down the other side of the street. He stops, looks over at the parked Celica, shakes his bony little fist in the direction of the car, and shouts.

OLD MAN: Slow down; this is a neighborhood! Punk.

VISUAL: The old man shakes his head and walk off.

SUPER: The Celica Action Package. Looks fast.

VISUAL: A red Celica is parked in a very quiet suburban neighborhood. After a few seconds, we see a barking dog running toward the rear of the car. As he approaches he shows absolutely no sign of slowing down. Finally, he hits the car.

SFX: Dog hitting car.

VISUAL: Car shakes slightly. The dog looks confused and slightly shaken. After a second, he trots off.

SUPER: The Celica Action Package. Looks fast.

CATEGORY
Campaign

ADVERTISER/PRODUCT
Interflora

TITLE
Formula 1

TITLE
Tool Shop

TITLE
Football Trophy

ADVERTISING AGENCY
Robert/Boisen & Like-Minded,
Copenhagen

PRODUCTION COMPANY
Bullet, Copenhagen

ACCOUNT EXECUTIVE
Dorte Tellerup

CREATIVE DIRECTOR
Michael Robert

COPYWRITER
Joachim Nielsen

ART DIRECTOR
Michael Robert

PRODUCER
Rikke Katborg

DIRECTOR
Kasper Wedendahl

CLIENT
Interflora, Lars Steen

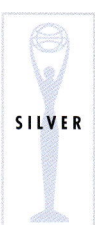

SILVER

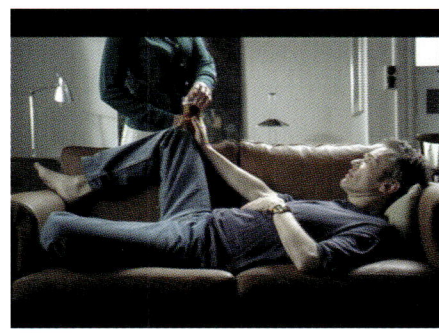

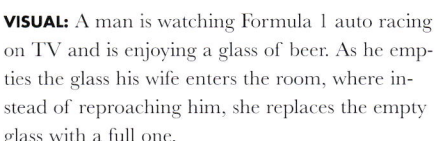

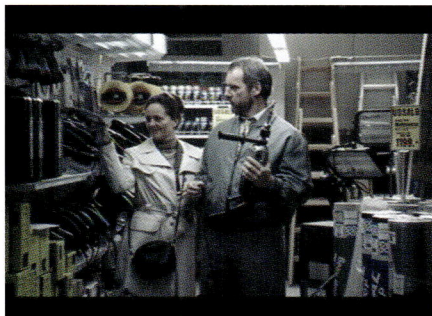

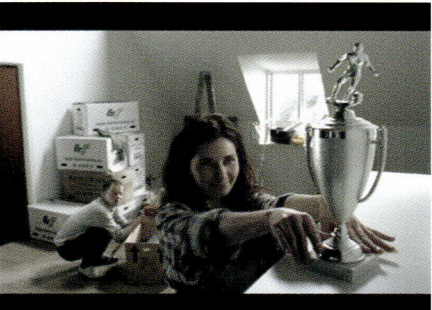

VISUAL: A man is watching Formula 1 auto racing on TV and is enjoying a glass of beer. As he empties the glass his wife enters the room, where instead of reproaching him, she replaces the empty glass with a full one.

SUPER: The power of flowers.

SUPER: Interflora.

VISUAL: A man at hardware store is standing and holding one small and one large electric drill in his hands. His wife surprises him by indicating that he should buy the large drill. She takes the small drill from his hand and places it back on the shelf.

SUPER: The power of flowers.

SUPER: Interflora.

VISUAL: A young couple is moving into a home together. The girl takes her boyfriend's football trophy from a box. The boyfriend expects her to get angry but instead she places the trophy on a shelf and smiles.

SUPER: The power of flowers.

SUPER: Interflora.

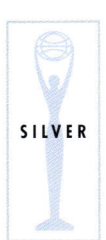

SILVER

CATEGORY
Campaign

ADVERTISER/PRODUCT
Office of the Mayor—
Project Miracle

TITLE
Philharmonic

TITLE
Yankee Stadium

TITLE
Skating

TITLE
Deli

TITLE
Turkey

ADVERTISING AGENCY
BBDO, New York

PRODUCTION COMPANY
PYTKA, Venice; Hungry Man,
New York

EDITING COMPANY
Crew Cuts, New York;
Mackenzie Cutler, New York

ACCOUNT EXECUTIVE
John Osborne

**CHAIRMAN/CHIEF
CREATIVE OFFICER**
Ted Sann

CREATIVE TEAM
Phil Dusenberry, Ted Sann,
Charlie Miesmer, Michael Patti,
Gerry Graf, David Johnson,
John Leu

COPYWRITER
Charlie Miesmer, Michael Patti

ART DIRECTOR
Gerry Graf, David Johnson, John Leu

PRODUCER
Regina Ebel, Alexandra Sterlin,
Lisa Petroni, Hyatt Choate,
Bob Emerson

DIRECTOR
Joe Pytka, Bryan Buckley,
Barry Levinson, Santiago Suarez

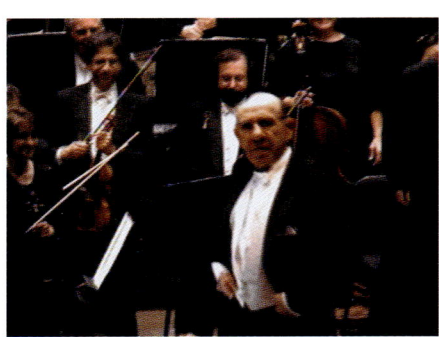

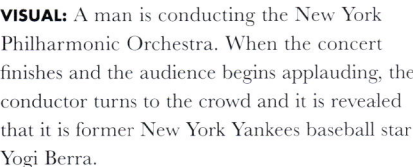

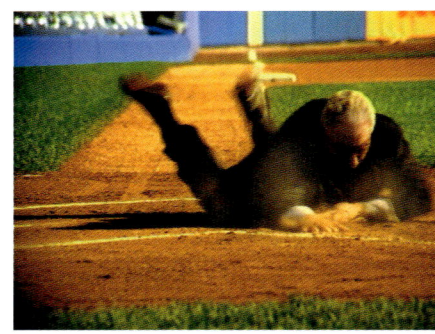

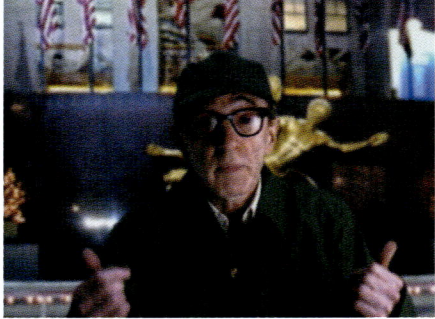

VISUAL: A man is conducting the New York Philharmonic Orchestra. When the concert finishes and the audience begins applauding, the conductor turns to the crowd and it is revealed that it is former New York Yankees baseball star Yogi Berra.

VO: Everyone has a New York dream. Be a part of it.

BERRA: Who in the heck is this guy, Phil Harmonic?

SUPER: Phil Harmonic. Didn't he play third for the Brooklyn Dodgers?

MAYOR RUDOLPH GIULIANI: The New York Miracle. Be a part of it.

SUPER: The New York Miracle. Be a part of it.

VISUAL: In an empty Yankees stadium, a man in a suit is pretending to swing his baseball bat and hit the ball. He then runs around the bases and slides into home plate. As he stands, it is revealed that he is former U.S. Secretary of State Henry Kissinger.

VO: Everyone has a New York dream. Come find yours.

KISSINGER: Derek who?

SECURITY GUARD: Hey, you. Get outta here!

MAYOR RUDOLPH GIULIANI: The New York Miracle. Be a part of it.

SUPER: The New York Miracle. Be a part of it.

VISUAL: A Man is ice-skating at Rockefeller Center, in New York City. He twists, jumps, and is obviously a very good skater. He stops and turns, and it is revealed that it's Woody Allen.

WOODY ALLEN: You're not gonna believe this. That was the first time I put skates on in my life.

VISUAL: Woody skates off.

VO: Everyone has a New York dream. Come find yours.

MAYOR RUDOLPH GULIANI: The New York Miracle. Be a part of it.

SUPER: The New York Miracle. Be a part of it.

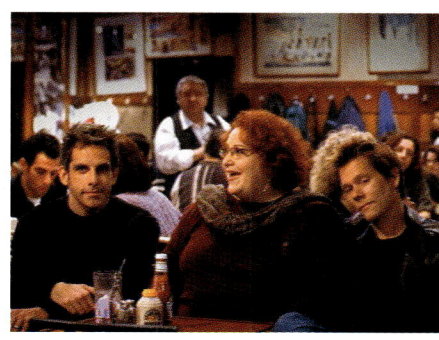

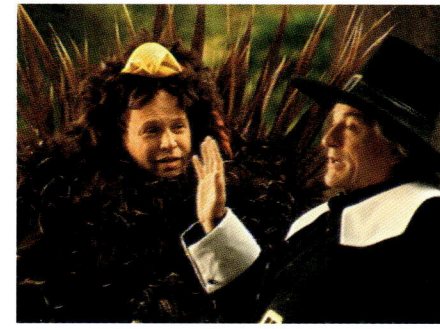

VISUAL: A woman is ordering lunch at the Stage Diner delicatessen in New York City.

WOMAN (looking at the menu): They all look so wonderful. How is the Ben Stiller?

WAITER: Ben Stiller, very popular.

WOMAN: Okay. I'll have the Ben Stiller.

WAITER: One Ben Stiller.

WOMAN: Oh, and could I get that with bacon?

WAITER: With Bacon. You got it. Hey Stiller!

VISUAL: Ben Stiller, at another table in the diner, stands up.

WAITER: Table 3, with bacon!

VISUAL: Kevin Bacon stands up and he and Stiller walk over to the woman's table.

VO: Everyone has a New York dream. Come find yours.

MAYOR RUDOLPH GIULIANI: The New York Miracle. Be a part of it.

SUPER: The New York Miracle. Be a part of it.

VISUAL: The woman is seated at her table with Bacon sitting on one side and Stiller on the other.

WOMAN: Waiter, can I have a doggie bag?

VISUAL: Actors Robert DeNiro and Billy Crystal are sitting on a bench in Central Park. Crystal is dressed like a turkey and DeNiro like a pilgrim.

DeNIRO: What's the matter?

CRYSTAL: You know what's the matter. I'm unhappy.

DeNIRO: You agreed to play the turkey.

CRYSTAL: Never agreed. Why would I agree to be the turkey?

DeNIRO: You know, it's not a big deal. All you do is—ya know, cluck-cluck, cluck-cluck, an' ya wave.

CRYSTAL: First of all we don't cluck, we gobble. Okay?

DeNIRO: I stand corrected.

CRYSTAL: Yeh. An' if it's, if it's not such a big deal, why don't you be the turkey?

DeNIRO: You want me to be the turkey?

CRYSTAL: Yeah, come on.

DeNIRO: You want me to be the turkey? I don't think so. You know turkey-isms that I don't know. Even the expression on your face is quintessential turkey.

VISUAL: Crystal and DeNiro walking in the park.

DeNIRO: I don't see myself as a turkey. Ya know, if it was an eagle I might consider it. An eagle is graceful.

VISUAL: DeNiro and Crystal sitting on a park bench.

DeNIRO: It flies, it soars. The only problem was the eagle wasn't very tasty. You're gonna be great.

CRYSTAL: What the hell are you talking about?

DeNIRO: I don't know.

VISUAL: Crystal and DeNiro walking in the park.

CRYSTAL: Boy, am I stuffed. You see what I did there?

DeNIRO: No.

CRYSTAL: I was in character.

DeNIRO: You see, that's the reason why you should be the turkey.

VISUAL: The Macy's Thanksgiving Day parade. Crystal and DeNiro are in their costumes riding on a float.

DeNIRO (waving): Maybe next year I'll think about it.

CRYSTAL: No, no, no. This is fun. (Waving). Cluck, cluck.

DeNIRO: What happened to gobble, gobble?

MAYOR RUDOLPH GIULIANI: The New York Miracle. Be a part of it.

SUPER: The New York Miracle. Be a part of it.

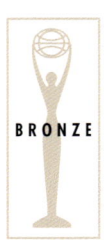

CATEGORY	**TITLE**
Campaign	Jerry
ADVERTISER/PRODUCT	**ADVERTISING AGENCY**
Anheuser-Busch Inc./Budweiser	DDB, Chicago
TITLE	**PRODUCTION COMPANY**
Phone Chain	Hungry Man, New York
TITLE	**EDITING COMPANY**
Card Night	Lookinglass, Chicago

GROUP CREATIVE DIRECTOR	**DIRECTOR**
John Immesoete	Allen Coulter
ASSOCIATE CREATIVE DIRECTOR	
Vinny Warren	
COPYWRITER	
Vinny Warren, Scott Smith	
PRODUCER	
Kent Kwiatt	

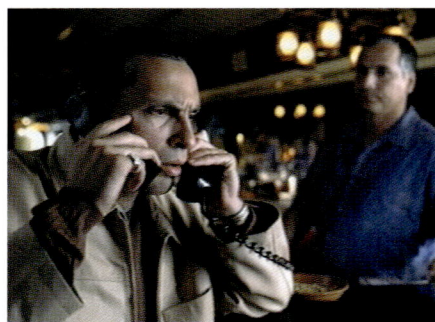

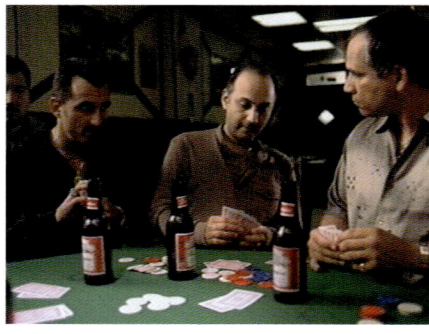

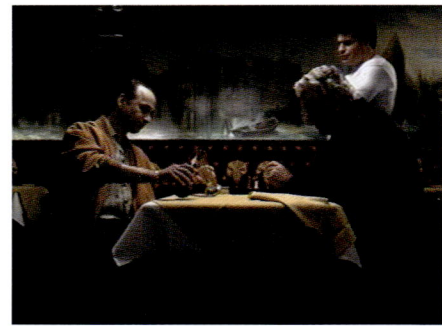

VISUAL: Ten men at various locations, a bar, street corner, golf course, and steam room, are on the phone with each other trying to determine if "dat ting" got taken care of.

MAN 1: How You Doin'?

MAN 2: How You Doin'?

MAN 3: Hello.

MAN 4: These guys take care of that ting, right?

MAN 5: Hey Mikey, we take care of that ting?

MAN 6: Mikey. You took care of dat ting right?

MAN 7: Yeah sure, come on please. Hey did you take care of dat ting yet?

MAN 8: Yeah.

MAN 9: You took care of dat ting right?

MAN 10: Yeah, hold on.

MAN 1: Yeah.

MAN 10: Jerry there?

MAN 2: Yeah.

MAN 10: You took care of dat ting right?

MAN 2: Mmmmm.

SUPER: True.

Budweiser logo.

VISUAL: Six men playing poker.

MAN 1: How you doin', Momma, How you doin'?

MAN 2: How you doin'?

MAN 3: How yoooou doin'?

MAN 4: How you doin', how you doin', how you doin'?

MAN 5: How you doin'?

MAN 6: How you doin'? What? Come on, let's play.

SUPER: True.

Budweiser logo.

VISUAL: Three men, Dominic, Jerry, and a bodyguard, at an empty restaurant.

DOMINIC: Jerry, Jerry, Jerry.

BODYGUARD: Jerry.

DOMINIC: Jerry, Jerry, Jerry, Jerry, Jerry, Jerry.

JERRY: Dominic.

BODYGUARD: Jerry.

DOMINIC: Jerry, Jerry, Jerry, Jerry, Jerry, Jerry, Jerry, Jerry,

SUPER: True.

Budweiser logo.

CATEGORY
Campaign

ADVERTISER/PRODUCT
Anheuser-Busch Inc./Bud Light

TITLE
Mr. Footlong Hotdog Inventor

TITLE
Mr. Really Bad Toupee Wearer

TITLE
Mr. Nudist Colony Activities Coordinator

ADVERTISING AGENCY
DDB, Chicago

PRODUCTION COMPANY
Propaganda, Hollywood; Coppos Films,
Los Angeles

EDITING COMPANY
School Editing, Toronto; Panic & Bob,
Toronto

MUSIC COMPANY
Scandal Music, Chicago

GROUP CREATIVE DIRECTOR
John Immesoete

CREATIVE DIRECTOR
Mark Gross, Bill Cimino

COPYWRITER
Bill Cimino

ART DIRECTOR
Mark Gross

PRODUCER
Greg Popp

DIRECTOR
Tom Kuntz, Mike McGuire,
Tom Schiller

COMPOSER
Sandy Torano, Sam Struyk

ANNOUNCER
Pete Stacker

VOCALIST
David Bickler

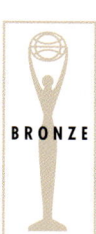

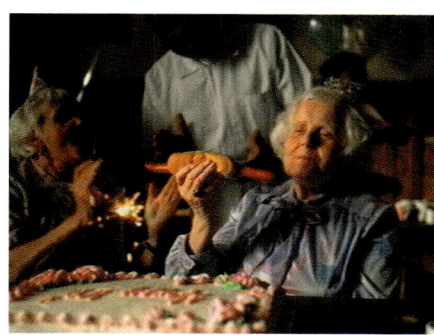

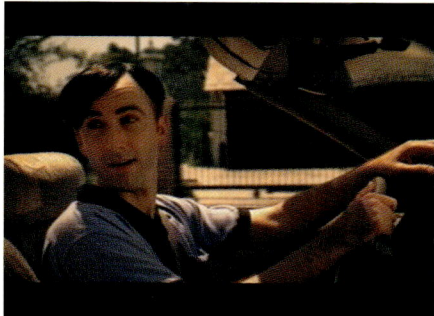

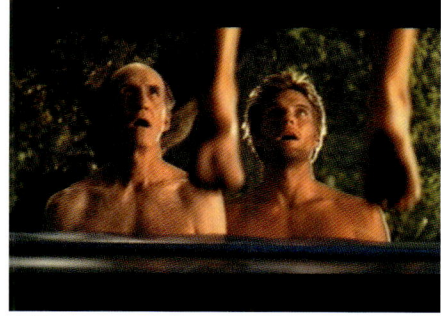

VISUAL: A singer in a recording studio, and shots of various people ordering and eating the hot dog: A businessman at a hot dog stand, two old women at a retirement home, an Asian couple at a carnival, two men barbequing. Also close-ups of a foot-long hot dog in a bun that is too small.

SUPER: Real American Heroes.

SINGER: *Real American heroes.*

VO: Budweiser salutes you, Mr. Foot-Long Hot Dog Inventor.

SINGER: *Mr. Foot-Long Hot Dog Inventor.*

VO: When conventional wisdom said no one could make a hot dog more than 6 inches, you dared to dream.

SINGER: *You dared to dream.*

VO: The crowd cheered your 10-inch wiener. "Wait," you said, "I can give you 2 more inches."

SINGER: *Yeah!*

VO: So this Bud's for you Mister…For giving us all…a bigger wiener.

SINGER: Thank you, Thank you, Thank you.

VISUAL: A singer in a recording studio and scenes of men involved in various activities: jogging, driving, swimming, and weightlifting. Each guy is wearing a really bad toupee.

SUPER: Real Men of Genius.

VO: Budweiser presents, real men of genius.

SINGER: *Real men of genius…*

VO: Today we salute you…Mr. Really Bad Toupee Wearer.

SINGER: *Mr. Really Bad Toupee Wearer.*

VO: More than any neon sign or exploding score-board ever could, your chrome-dome cover says, "Hey guys—look at me."

SINGER: *What could you be thinkin'?*

VO: You think it looks natural, but it couldn't look phonier if it had a chin strap!

SINGER: *Couldn't fool a blind man…*

VO: Made of space age fibers, "it" can repel anything. Rain. Wind. Snow. And especially… young women.

SINGER: *I don't think so!*

VO: So crack open an ice-cold Budweiser, Mr. Stud in a Rug. Then crack open another for that thing on your head.

SINGER: *I don't think it's on straight…*

VISUAL: A singer in a recording studio and scenes of naked people, involved in various activities at a nudist colony: folk singing, tossing a beach ball, canoeing, trampolining, and playing ping-pong.

SUPER: Real Men of Genius.

VO: Budweiser presents, real men of genius.

SINGER: *Real Men of Genius.*

VO: Today we salute you…Mr. Nudist Colony Activity Coordinator.

SINGER: *Mr. Nudist Colony Activity Coordinator!*

VO: Wearing nothing but a whistle and a clip-board, you're living the real American dream, getting paid to think up fun things to do naked.

SINGER: *Running free!*

VO: Sure, there's danger: vinyl chairs, sunburns, chafage. And lawn darts—completely out of the question.

SINGER: *Watch out, now!*

VO: Your keen instincts tell you to stick to activities that involve lots of bouncing and jiggling. And if that doesn't work, who cares, you're all naked.

SINGER: *It's your birthday!*

VO: So this Bud's for you, nudie boy. Because we all know when the going gets tough, the tough get naked.

SINGER: *Mr. Nudist Colony Activity Coordinator!*

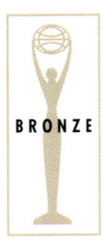

BRONZE

CATEGORY
Campaign

ADVERTISER/PRODUCT
Fanta

TITLE
What Are You?

TITLE
Fanta Beam

TITLE
The Weight Check

ADVERTISING AGENCY
Hakuhodo Creative Vox Inc.;
Hakuhodo Inc, Tokyo

PRODUCTION COMPANY
Aoi Advertising Promotion Inc,
Tokyo

EDITING COMPANY
Imagica Corporation, Tokyo

ACCOUNT EXECUTIVE
Takaaki Matsuo

CREATIVE DIRECTOR
Yasuaki Iwamoto

PRODUCER
Yasuhito Nakae

DIRECTOR
Shunichiro Miki

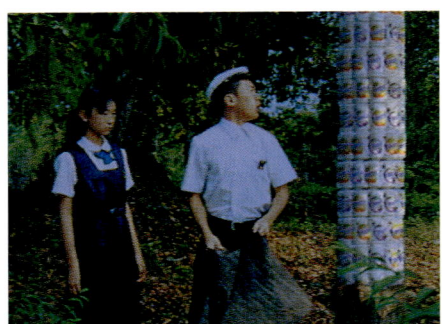

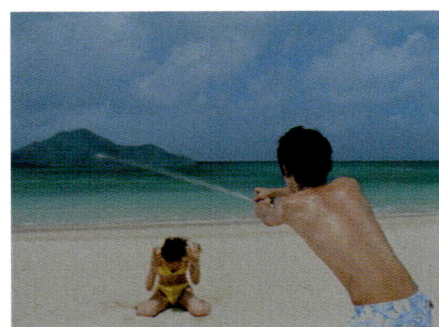

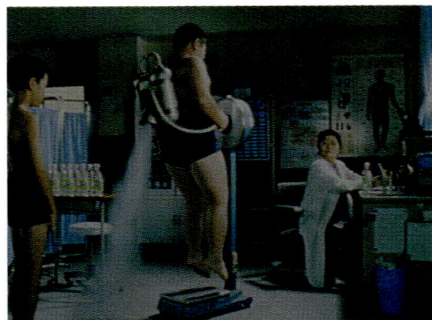

VISUAL: A schoolboy leads his favorite girl into the woods, they walk up to a tree, and he grabs it. All the tree's bark comes off, revealing that it is a tower made of Fanta soda.

VISUAL: Fanta soda bottles. Two girls wearing bathing suits pop out of plastic fruit.

SUPER: It's Fun Time. Fanta.

VO: It's fun time. Fanta.

VISUAL: A boy and girl are having fun at a beach. The boy shakes up a can of Fanta soda and points it at the girl, intending to spray her with it. Instead, the Fanta spray blows up an island in the distance.

VISUAL: Fanta soda bottles. Two girls wearing bathing suits pop out of plastic fruit.

SUPER: It's Fun Time. Fanta.

VO: It's fun time. Fanta.

VISUAL: Boys are lined up at an elementary school to have their weight checked by a nurse. A boy steps on the scale.

NURSE: 37 kilograms. Next, please.

VISUAL: An overweight boy steps on the scale wearing a rocket pack on his back. He turns on the rocket pack and levitates above the scale.

NURSE: 20 kilograms. Next, please.

VISUAL: Fanta soda bottles. Two girls wearing bathing suits pop out of plastic fruit.

SUPER: It's Diet Time. Fanta.

VO: It's diet time. Fanta.

CATEGORY
Campaign

ADVERTISER/PRODUCT
Mike's Hard Lemonade

TITLE
Lumberjack

TITLE
Construction

TITLE
Seaquarium

ADVERTISING AGENCY
Cliff Freeman and Partners,
New York

PRODUCTION COMPANY
Partizan, Santa Monica

EDITING COMPANY
Mackenzie Cutler, New York

SOUND DESIGN COMPANY
Mackenzie Cutler, New York

ANIMATION COMPANY
Quiet Man, New York

ACCOUNT EXECUTIVE
Shana Brooks

CREATIVE DIRECTOR
Eric Silver

COPYWRITER
William Gelner, Ian Reichenthal,
Garth Jennings

ART DIRECTOR
Guy Shelmerdine, Scott Vitrone

PRODUCER
Ed Zazzera

DIRECTOR
Traktor

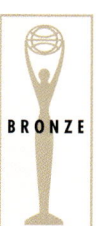

BRONZE

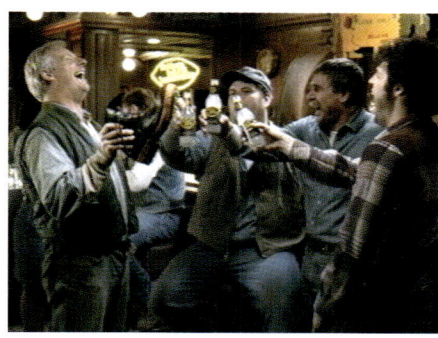

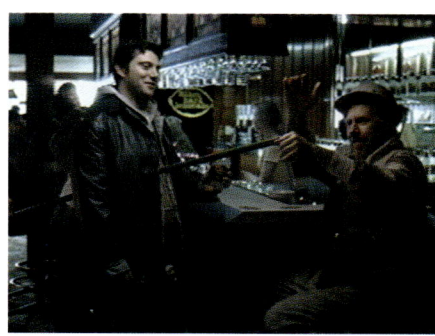

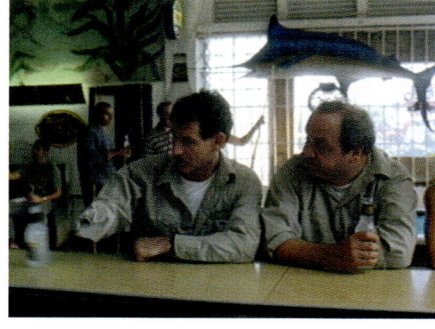

VISUAL: Lumberjack chopping at a fallen tree with an axe. Someone yells his name.

FOREMAN VO: Hey, Ted!

VISUAL: The lumberjack looks up in the direction of the person yelling and accidentally chops off his foot. Close-up of his boot lying on the ground. The lumberjack gets up and brushes himself off. Only then does he realize that he chopped off his foot. The foreman enters frame.

FOREMAN: Tough break, buddy.

VISUAL: The lumberjack looks down at his boot and hops to maintain his balance.

LUMBERJACK: Yeah, my wife just bought me them boots yesterday.

FOREMAN: Those are nice boots. Tell ya what: let me buy you a tasty Mike's Hard Lemonade.

LUMBERJACK: Now you're talkin'.

VO: A hard day calls for a hard lemonade.

VISUAL: Interior of a bar. A bunch of lumberjacks clink together bottles of Mike's Hard Lemonade in a toast. The foreman does the same but jokingly clinks his bottle with the man's boot instead of a Mike's. Everyone laughs at this, except the lumberjack who chopped off his foot.

VISUAL: A Mike's Hard Lemonade six-pack falls from above and lands on the bar.

VO: A hard day calls for a hard lemonade. Make it Mike's.

SUPER: Make it Mike's.

VISUAL: A construction worker is walking along a girder. He trips and falls three stories into a pile of rusty steel bars. He gets up and then notices that he has a long piece of rusty steel embedded through the center of his chest. He notices his injury and is disappointed. The construction site foreman walks up to him.

FOREMAN: Looks like you got a little nick there.

CONSTRUCTION WORKER: What? This? It's nothing.

FOREMAN: Maybe we should get it looked at.

CONSTRUCTION WORKER: Or *maybe* we should go get a delicious Mike's Hard Lemonade instead.

FOREMAN (laughs): You're on.

VISUAL: Interior of a bar. The construction worker and foreman are each holding a bottle of Mike's Hard Lemonade. The foreman uncaps his bottle of Mike's by using the piece of steel embedded in the construction worker's chest.

VISUAL: A Mike's Hard Lemonade six-pack falls from above and lands on the bar.

VO: A hard day calls for a hard lemonade. Make it Mike's.

SUPER: Make it Mike's.

VISUAL: Two maintenance workers at a sea aquarium are sweeping up around a large fish performance pool. One worker picks up a dead fish near his foot and reaches toward the pool. A huge killer whale leaps out of the water takes a piece of the fish and also bites off the worker's hand.

COWORKER: I've never seen him do that trick before. Does it sting?

WORKER: Nah; talk about your bad luck, though.

COWORKER: Well, let me get you a refreshing Mike's Hard Lemonade.

WORKER: I'd much appreciate it.

VO: A hard day calls for a hard lemonade.

VISUAL: The two men are sitting at the bar; two bottles of Mike's Hard Lemonade slide down the bar toward them. The coworker catches his bottle and, because he has no hand, the worker misses his and it goes crashing to the floor.

VISUAL: A Mike's Hard Lemonade six-pack falls from above and lands on the bar.

VO: Make it Mike's.

SUPER: Make it Mike's.

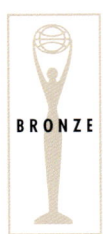

BRONZE

CATEGORY Campaign	**TITLE** Restaurant	**PRODUCTION COMPANY** Mican Film, Vienna	**COPYWRITER** Helge Bloeck, Christoph Klingler
ADVERTISER/PRODUCT Oesterreichischer Tierschutzverein	**TITLE** Shopping	**MUSIC COMPANY** Soundtrack	**PRODUCER** Ernst Mican
TITLE Unabashed	**ADVERTISING AGENCY** TBWA, Berlin	**CREATIVE DIRECTOR** Christoph Klingler	**DIRECTOR** David Ruehm

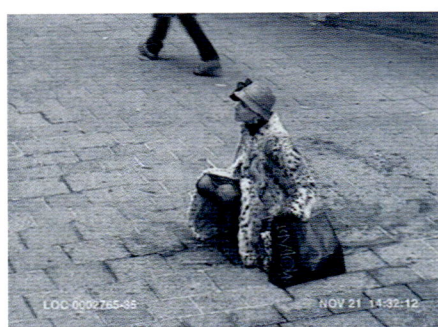 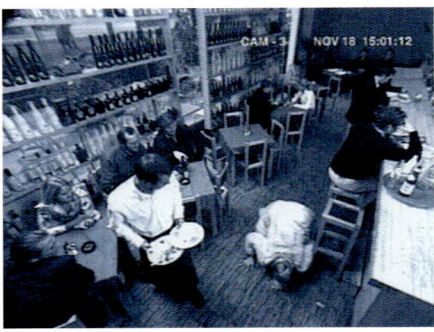 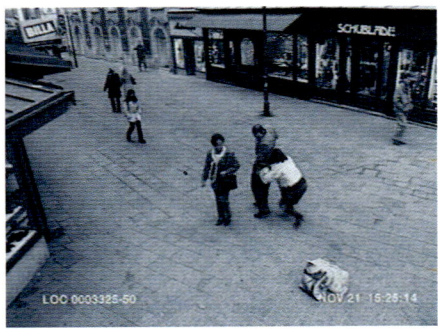

VISUAL (from the point of view of a surveillance camera): A woman in a long fur coat stops in the middle of busy shopping district. She places her shopping bags on either side of herself, squats down, and unabashedly begins to urinate from under her coat.

SUPER: Only animals wear fur.

VISUAL (from the point of view of a surveillance camera): A waiter in a restaurant is clearing a table of dirty plates. As he walks off, a woman in a fur coat enters the restaurant. She passes the waiter and knocks into him. Food from the plates falls to the floor. Suddenly, the woman drops to the floor and starts greedily scooping up the food and eating it.

SUPER: Only animals wear fur.

VISUAL (from the point of view of a surveillance camera): Two young women walking arm-in-arm in a busy shopping district. One is wearing a fur coat. The woman in the fur coat catches the eye of a man nearby. Abruptly, she drops her shopping bags and runs toward the man. She grabs hold of his waist, falls to the ground, and feverishly caresses and kisses his legs.

SUPER: Only animals wear fur.

CATEGORY
Campaign

ADVERTISER/PRODUCT
Dial

TITLE
Happy Dog

TITLE
Sauna

ADVERTISING AGENCY
GSD&M, Austin

PRODUCTION COMPANY
Ritts Hayden

EDITING COMPANY
Rock Paper Scissors

CREATIVE DIRECTOR
Rich Tlapek, Tom Gilmore

COPYWRITER
Carole Hurst, Rich Tlapek

ART DIRECTOR
Demian Fore, Tom Gilmore

PRODUCER
Khrisana Edwards

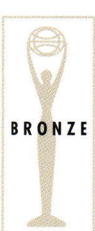

BRONZE

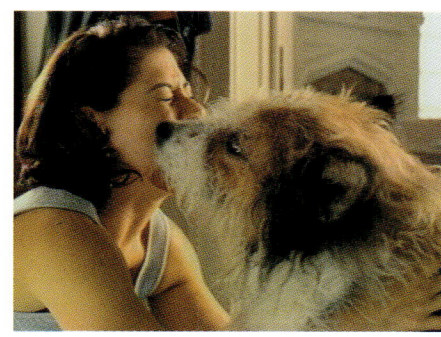

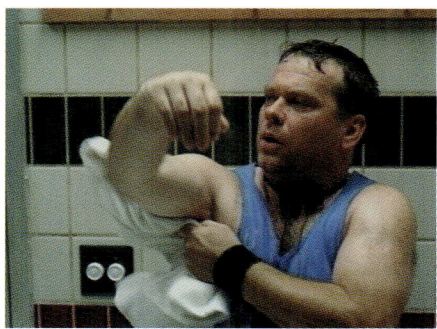

VISUAL: A big, lovable dog is drinking water from an open toilet. A mom and her son arrive home and the dog, hearing the front door open, goes racing down the stairs to greet them.

MOM: Hi, boy. How are you?

VISUAL: The dog begins to lick the woman's face greedily.

MOM: Ahhh. Emmm.

VISUAL: The dog continues to lick the woman's face.

VO: You're not as clean as you think.

SUPER: You're Not As Clean As You Think.

VISUAL: Bar of Dial soap.

VO: Aren't you glad you use Dial?

VISUAL: The doorway to a sauna with a towel hanging near it. A large, very sweaty man comes from exercising, takes the towel from the rack, and wipes the perspiration from his body. He hangs the towel back up and walks off. Another man emerges from the sauna and begins to use the same towel to wipe himself off.

VO: You're not as clean as you think.

SUPER: You're Not As Clean As You Think.

VISUAL: Bar of Dial soap.

VO: Aren't you glad you use Dial?

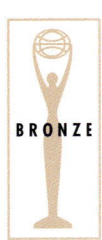

BRONZE

CATEGORY
Campaign

ADVERTISER/PRODUCT
Nashua Mobile

TITLE
Umpire

TITLE
Peek

TITLE
Sniff

ADVERTISING AGENCY
TBWA Hunt Lascaris, Johannesburg

PRODUCTION COMPANY
Accelerator Films, Johannesburg

EDITING COMPANY
Prime Cut, Johannesburg

SOUND DESIGN COMPANY
Sonovision, Johannesburg

ACCOUNT EXECUTIVE
Stephane Niemann

CREATIVE DIRECTOR
Sue Anderson

COPYWRITER
Sue Anderson, Chris Garbutt

ART DIRECTOR
Chris Garbutt, Paul Anderson, Paul Warner

PRODUCER
Juanita Strydom

DIRECTOR
David Gillard

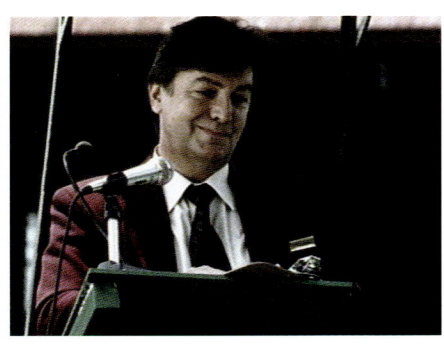

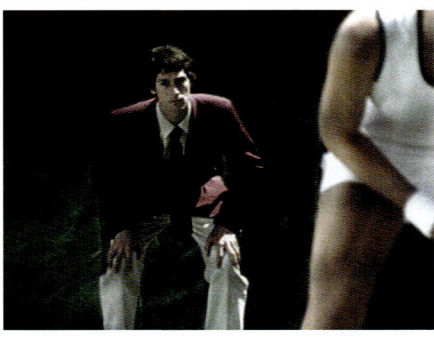

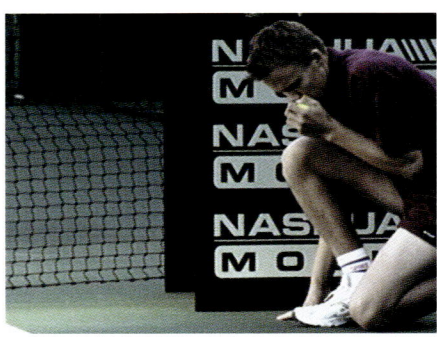

VISUAL: A tennis umpire is following a match.

UMPIRE: 40–Love.

VISUAL: Umpire smiles. He is charmed by Anna.

FEMALE VO: What, the ball was in.

UMPIRE: 30–15.

SUPER: Anna Kournikova's in South Africa.

Nashua Mobile Associate sponsor.

VISUAL: A linesman crouching, watching the match. He tilts his head and crouches more. He is trying to peer up a tennis player's skirt.

SUPER: Anna Kournikova's in South Africa.

Nashua Mobile Associate sponsor.

VISUAL: A geeky ball boy is crouching by the net; he darts off to retrieve a tennis ball. He returns to his position, sniffs the ball, and then looks around guiltily.

SUPER: Anna Kournikova's in South Africa.

Nashua Mobile Associate sponsor.

Campaign / **TELEVISION & CINEMA**

CATEGORY
Campaign

ADVERTISER/PRODUCT
Postbank/ValuePlus Mortgage

TITLE
Kitchen

TITLE
Bedroom

TITLE
Hoover

ADVERTISING AGENCY
S-W-H, Amsterdam

PRODUCTION COMPANY
hazazaH Film & Photography,
Amsterdam

EDITING COMPANY
Martyn Gould Productions Limited,
London

SOUND DESIGN COMPANY
Vonk Sound, Amsterdam

ACCOUNT EXECUTIVE
Mark Aink, Jennifer van der Schaaf

CREATIVE DIRECTOR
Lode Schaeffer, Erik Wünsch

COPYWRITER
Erik Wünsch

ART DIRECTOR
Lode Schaeffer

PRODUCER
Suzanne Huisman

DIRECTOR
Win van der Aar

EDITOR
Martyn Gould

SOUND DESIGNER
Marcel Walvisch

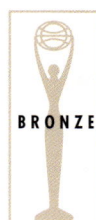

BRONZE

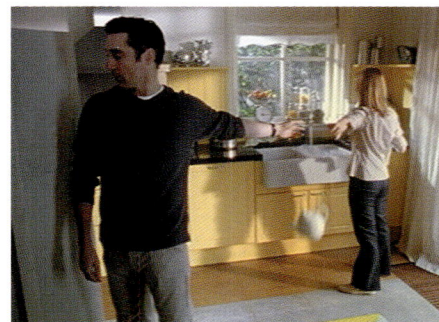

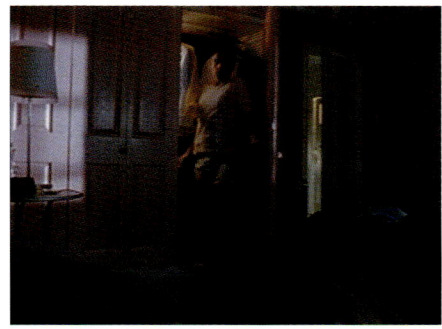

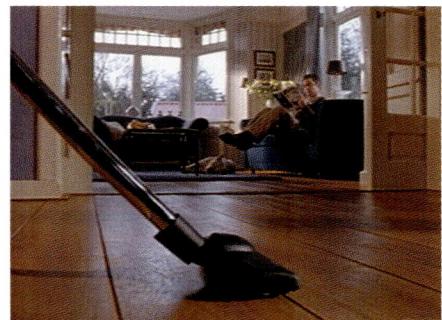

SYNOPSIS: With Postbank's ValuePlus mortgage, people can live in a larger, more expensive home, and keep their mortgage payments the same. Old habits can remain the same: The only thing to get accustomed to is more space in the new house.

VISUAL: A man and woman are washing the dishes after dinner. The woman finishes washing a cup and reaches her hand out to give it to the man. He turns around, without looking, and reaches for the cup. The woman thinks his hand has grabbed it and she lets go. The cup crashes to the floor.

SUPER: Same life. Bigger house.

It's possible with our new ValuePlus Mortgage.

Postbank makes it easy.

SYNOPSIS: With Postbank's ValuePlus mortgage, people can live in a larger, more expensive home, and keep their mortgage payments the same. Old habits can remain the same: The only thing to get accustomed to is more space in the new house.

VISUAL: A man and woman are sleeping.

SFX: An alarm goes off.

VISUAL: The man gets up, opens the closet door, walks in, and closes the door behind him. A few seconds later he opens the door, looks confused, and heads off toward the bathroom.

SUPER: Same life. Bigger house.

It's possible with our new ValuePlus Mortgage.

Postbank makes it easy.

SYNOPSIS: With Postbank's ValuePlus mortgage, people can live in a larger, more expensive home, and keep their mortgage payments the same. Old habits can remain the same: The only thing to get accustomed to is more space in the new house.

VISUAL: A man is sitting in a chair and reading the newspaper.

SFX: A vacuum cleaner starts up.

VISUAL: The man raises his feet from the floor as if the vacuum is under his feet.

SUPER: Same life. Bigger house.

It's possible with our new ValuePlus Mortgage.

Postbank makes it easy.

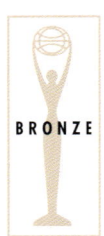

CATEGORY
Campaign

ADVERTISER/PRODUCT
Heineken USA

TITLE
Club/Scratch

TITLE
Lighter

TITLE
Birth of a Sign

ADVERTISING AGENCY
Lowe, New York

PRODUCTION COMPANY
Tate & Partners, Santa Monica;
@radical.media, New York

EDITING COMPANY
MacKenzie Cutler, New York

MUSIC COMPANY
Bang Music + Sound Design,
New York; Face the Music, Venice

ACCOUNT EXECUTIVE
Michael Silver, Julie Mulholland

AGENCY PRODUCER
Steven Ford, David Gerard

EXECUTIVE AGENCY PRODUCER:
Bob Nelson

CREATIVE DIRECTOR
Lee Garfinkel, Gary Goldsmith,
Dean Hacohen, C. J. Waldman

COPYWRITER
Lee Garfinkel, John Maxham,
C. J. Waldman

ART DIRECTOR
C. J. Waldman, Hank Kosinski

EXECUTIVE PRODUCER
Robert Fernandez, Jon Kamen

PRODUCER
Gregg Carlesimo

DIRECTOR
Baker Smith, Frank Todaro

DIRECTOR OF PHOTOGRAPHY
Adam Beckman

EDITOR
Dave Koza, Ian MacKenzie

COMPOSER
Wendell Hanes, Gil Talmi,
Chuck Kentis, David Palmer

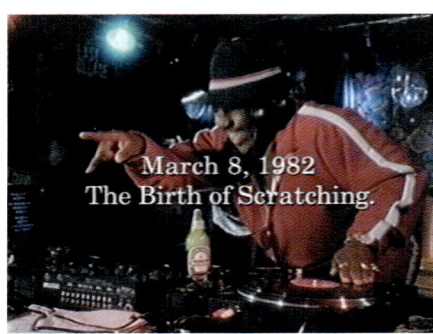

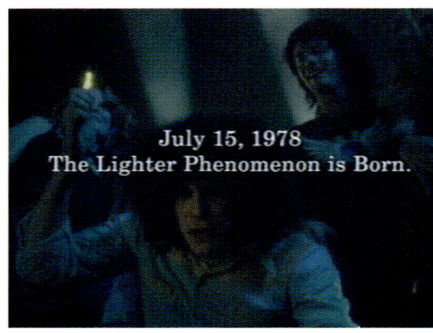

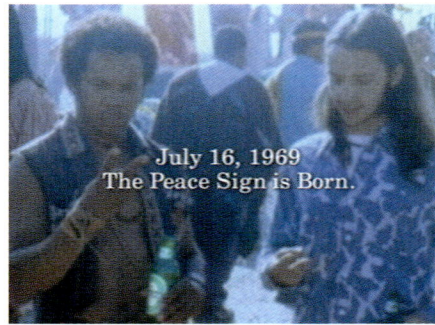

VISUAL: It's the early 1980s and a DJ is spinning records at a dance club. The music he's playing is not very good, and the people in the club are obviously not having a good time. Realizing that he needs to change the mood, the DJ reaches for a different record and knocks over a bottle of Heineken, spilling it on the record that is on the turntable. He tries to wipe the beer off the record and finds that it creates a strange scratching sound. The people in the club respond to this strange new sound and start dancing and having fun. The DJ points and winks at them like he knew what he was doing all along.

SUPER: March 8, 1982.

The Birth of Scratching.

VISUAL: The crowd continues to dance and party.

SUPER: It's all about the beer. Heineken.

VISUAL: It's the late 1970s at a huge rock concert. A hard-rock band has just finished a song, and the crowd goes wild. One guy puts his beer down on the floor so he can cheer for the band. The band begins another song; the guy remembers his beer and crouches down to pick it up. It's so dark he can't see a thing. He takes out his lighter to search for his beer. A friend standing next to him also takes out his lighter to assist in the search.

SUPER: July 15, 1978.

The Lighter Phenomenon Is Born.

VISUAL: The guy finally finds his beer and the two friends look up from the ground. To their amazement, they see lighters are lit throughout the entire arena.

SUPER: It's all about the beer. Heineken.

VISUAL: It's the late 1960s, at a massive, Woodstock-type outdoor concert. Amid all the music and revelry, a hippie makes his way to a concession stand and holds up two fingers.

HIPPIE: Two Heinekens, please.

VENDOR: What did you say?

HIPPIE: Two Heinekens. Please.

VENDOR: Oh, two Heinekens.

VISUAL: The music is very loud and other people in the crowd think that the hippie has said "peace," not "please." They associate it with the two fingers the guy was holding up. Suddenly, hippies everywhere are going around holding two fingers up and saying "peace."

SUPER: July 16, 1969.

The Peace Sign Is Born.

VISUAL: The peace sign spreads like wildfire; everyone at the concert is now doing it.

SUPER: It's all about the beer. Heineken.

CATEGORY
Campaign

ADVERTISER/PRODUCT
Quizno's

TITLE
Dart

TITLE
Cash

TITLE
Guillotine

ADVERTISING AGENCY
Cliff Freeman and Partners,
New York

PRODUCTION COMPANY
JGF, Los Angeles

EDITING COMPANY
Mad River Post, New York

SOUND DESIGN COMPANY
Machine Head, Venice

ACCOUNT EXECUTIVE
Kirsten Flanik, Jorge Hernandez

CHIEF CREATIVE OFFICER
Cliff Freeman

EXECUTIVE CREATIVE DIRECTOR
Arthur Bijur

CREATIVE DIRECTOR
Cliff Freeman, Arthur Bijur

COPYWRITER
Richard Bullock

ART DIRECTOR
Guy Shelmerdine, Taras Wayner

PRODUCER
Matt Bijarchi

DIRECTOR
Jeff Gorman

BRONZE

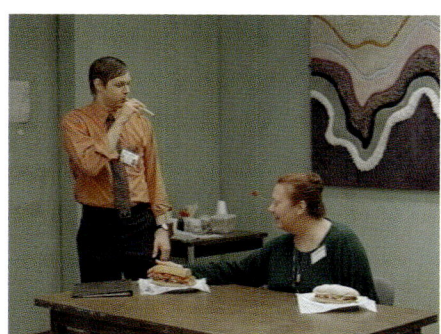 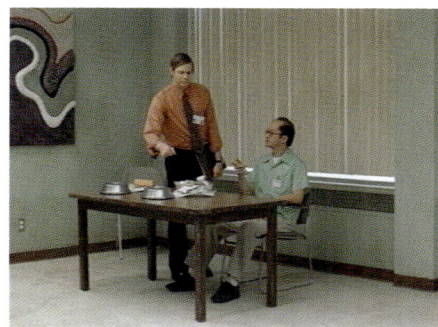 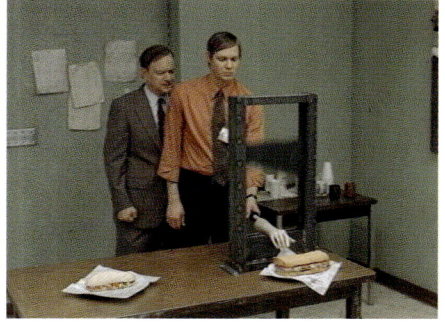

VISUAL: Sign on door: "Testing In Progress."

VISUAL: A researcher and test subject are in a test facility. The subject is sitting at a table on which there are two sub sandwiches: one from Quizno's, the other generic.

RESEARCHER: Which would you rather have, this untoasted sub, or this fresh, oven-toasted sub?

TEST SUBJECT: Ooh…toasted.

VISUAL: The test subject reaches for the Quizno's sub and the researcher takes out a bamboo straw and shoots a dart into her neck. She collapses into the untoasted sub. The researcher makes a notation on his clipboard.

RESEARCHER: Dives right into untoasted sub.

SUPER: Quizno's. Oven-toasted tastes better.

VISUAL: Sign on door: "Testing In Progress."

VISUAL: A researcher and test subject are in a test facility. The subject is sitting at a table on which there are two sub sandwiches: one from Quizno's, the other generic.

RESEARCHER: Which would you rather have, this fresh oven-toasted sub?

VISUAL: The researcher unwraps a tasty-looking Quizno's sub.

TESTER: Or this untoasted sub with lots of lettuce?

VISUAL: The researcher unwraps the pathetic-looking generic sub; it is sitting on a bed of dollar bills.

VISUAL: The researcher pushes the generic sub toward him and the test subject begins to rifle through the cash. The researcher makes a notation on his clipboard.

RESEARCHER: Ahh…likes the untoasted sub with the lettuce.

SUPER: Quizno's. Oven-toasted tastes better.

VISUAL: Sign on door: "Testing In Progress."

VISUAL: A researcher and nervous-looking corporate-type man are in a test facility. They are standing behind a table on which there is a small guillotine and two sub sandwiches: one from Quizno's, the other generic.

NERVOUS MAN: That Quizno's toasted sub looks better than ours. What happens if they choose it?

VISUAL: The researcher puts a mannequin's arm into the guillotine. The blade falls and chops off the hand.

RESEARCHER: They won't.

SUPER: Quizno's. Oven-toasted tastes better.

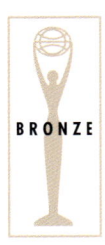

CATEGORY
Campaign

ADVERTISER/PRODUCT
Budget Rent-a-Car

TITLE
Chain Letter

TITLE
Personal Trainer

TITLE
Skating

ADVERTISING AGENCY
Cliff Freeman and Partners,
New York

PRODUCTION COMPANY
Partizan, Santa Monica;
Headquarters, Santa Monica

EDITING COMPANY
Mackenzie Cutler, New York

ANIMATION COMPANY
Quiet Man, New York

ACCOUNT EXECUTIVE
Brian Mulhern, Kim Trippett

CREATIVE DIRECTOR
Eric Silver

COPYWRITER
Steve Doppelt, William Gelner

ART DIRECTOR
Jason Gaboriau

PRODUCER
Kevin Diller, Brigette Whisnant

DIRECTOR
Traktor, Sean Mullens

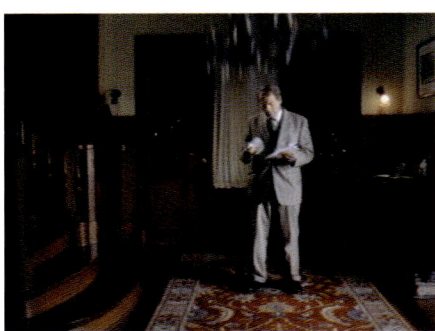

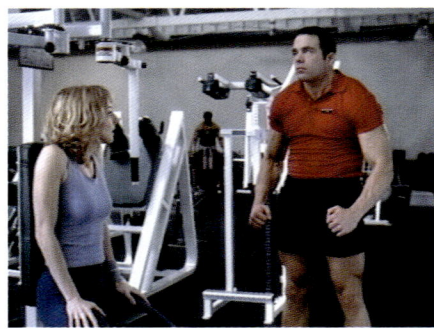

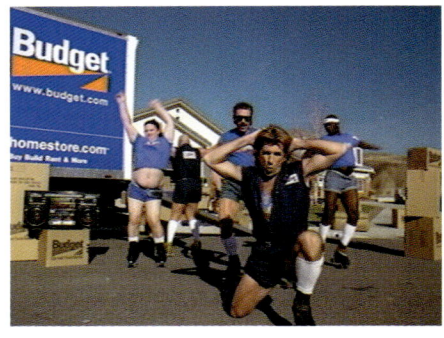

VISUAL: Five Budget employees are sitting around a conference table.

EMPLOYEE 1: Budget has all these cool cars.

EMPLOYEE 2: Jaguars (alt: Town Cars)…Rangers

EMPLOYEE 4: Mustang convertibles.

EMPLOYEE 1: Let's not forget the Explorer for only $39.99.

EMPLOYEE 3: Wow…how can we let everyone know about that?

EMPLOYEE 4: We'll send out a chain letter.

VISUAL: A man walks in the front door of his house with mail in his hand. He looks at the chain letter: "Ford Explorer for only $39.99. Pass this letter along to 7 friends or it's bad luck." He crumples up the letter and throws it out.

SFX: Lightbulb filament pops.

VISUAL: A chandelier falls from above and knocks the man to the ground.

VISUAL: Conference room.

EMPLOYEE 3: We don't need a chain letter.

SUPER: Rent the Ford Explorer for only $39.99.

VISUAL: Five Budget employees are sitting around a conference table.

EMPLOYEE 1: Perfect Drive is a great rewards program.

EMPLOYEE 2: Our customers can get everything from golf clubs to ski goggles after just four rentals.

EMPLOYEE 5: What else can we offer?

EMPLOYEE 1: Spa treatments.

EMPLOYEE 2: What if we also throw in a personal trainer?

VISUAL: In a gym, a very buff trainer is standing near an average-looking woman.

TRAINER: Hello. My name is Todd and I'll be your personal trainer.

VISUAL: The trainer makes a strange face and does an odd motion with his hips.

SFX: Crack.

VISUAL: The trainer reaches behind himself, pulls out a cracked walnut from between his buttocks and smiles. The woman nods.

VISUAL: Conference room.

EMPLOYEE 3: Personal trainers? Naaaaaaaaa.

SUPER: Earn cool rewards after just 4 rentals.

VISUAL: Five Budget employees are sitting around a conference table.

EMPLOYEE 1: Budget and Ryder TRS are working together to improve truck rental.

EMPLOYEE 2: Rates starting at $19.95.

EMPLOYEE 3: And a service where our movers help load and unload the truck.

EMPLOYEE 4: Can we make Load and Unload even better?

EMPLOYEE 5: Roller skates…to make the move even faster

VISUAL: Five furniture movers dressed in half-shirts, tight shorts, and roller skates, dancing to disco music.

VISUAL: Conference room.

EMPLOYEE 5: They don't need roller skates.

EMPLOYEE 2: No, not roller skates, but Load and Unload.

SUPER: Trucks starting at $19.95/Load and Unload service available

Budget and Ryder logos.

CATEGORY
Campaign

ADVERTISER/PRODUCT
Road Safety

TITLE
Fatigue

TITLE
Sleepiness

ADVERTISING AGENCY
FCB/Tapsa, Madrid

PRODUCTION COMPANY
Gardoqui Gold, Madrid

ACCOUNT EXECUTIVE
Ma Luz-Gardelegui, Paco Mendoza

CREATIVE DIRECTOR
Julian Zuazo

COPYWRITER
Luis Irache,
Manuel Perez de Camino

ART DIRECTOR
Ricardo Pastor, Antonio Botella

PRODUCER
Jesus Becedas, Javier Colvo,
Marisa Rodriguez

DIRECTOR
Marco de Aguilar

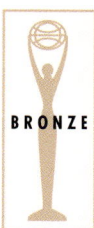
BRONZE

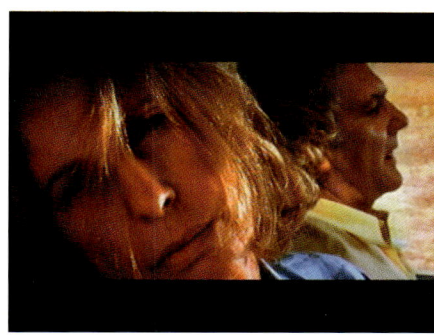

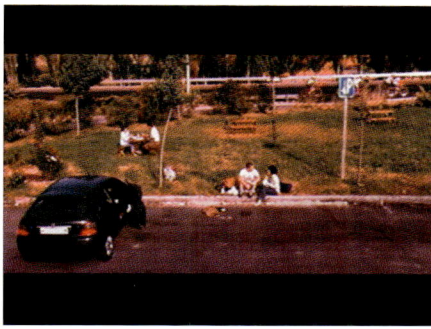

VISUAL: The interior of a car that is not moving. Inside the car is an older couple, their daughter, and baby granddaughter. There are various close-up shots of the car's occupants: a hand, bare foot, outstretched arm, man with his eyes closed. They appear to be dead.

VO: Sleepiness is one of the principal causes of road accidents.

VISUAL: The baby begins to cry.

BABY: Mommy.

VISUAL: The older couple and their daughter awaken and drive off.

VO: When symptoms start, stop and sleep.

SUPER: Take Care When Driving at Night.

Beware of Medicines. Eat Something Light.

SUPER: Department of Transport logo.

Only You Can Prevent It.

VISUAL: Various shots of what appears to be the aftermath of a car accident: The empty interior of the automobile; lying on the ground next to the car are a boot, a bare foot, an arm with a hand dangling off it, and an open bag with the contents spilled out

VO: Fatigue is one of the principal causes of road accidents.

VISUAL: Two young guys are having a rest and lunch by the side of the road.

SUPER: Take a Break Every 200 Kilometers.

If You Feel Tired, Don't Drive.

Stop at the First Sign of Tiredness.

SUPER: Department of Transport logo.

Only You Can Prevent It.

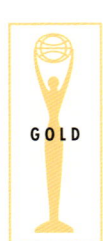

GOLD

CATEGORY
Animation—Computer

ADVERTISER/PRODUCT
Blockbuster

TITLE
Kung Fu

ADVERTISING AGENCY
Doner, Southfield

PRODUCTION COMPANY
Complete Pandemonium,
San Francisco

EDITING COMPANY
Bob 'n Sheila's Edit World,
San Francisco

MUSIC COMPANY
Blue Music and Sound Design,
Hollywood

SOUND DESIGN COMPANY
Soundelux DMG, Hollywood

ANIMATION COMPANY
Tippett Studios, Berkeley

SENIOR AGENCY PRODUCER
Josh Reynolds

CREATIVE DIRECTOR
John DeCerchio, John Parlato,
Don Fibich, Sheldon Cohn

COPYWRITER
Dan Margulis, Brian Hutson,
Mike Ceaser

ART DIRECTOR
Mark Cooke, Tom Gurisko,
Joel Friesch

PRODUCER
Clint Goldman

DIRECTOR
Steve "Spaz" Williams

EXECUTIVE PRODUCER
Clint Goldman

VISUAL EFFECTS
EXECUTIVE PRODUCER
Jules Roman

VISUAL EFFECTS SUPERVISOR
Frank Petzold, Scott Souter

VISUAL EFFECTS PRODUCER
Alonzo Ruvalcaba

LEAD CHARACTER ANIMATOR
Todd Labonte, Eric Reynolds

LIGHTING LEAD
Steve Reding

COMPOSITING LEAD
Jim McVay

VISUAL: Ray and Carl are in a pet shop window looking across the street into the window of a Blockbuster store. The store has a large poster ad on display that says: "Hot New Releases Guaranteed In Stock."

CARL: Ray, check this out. New releases guaranteed in stock.

RAY: That means they'll have my favorite kind of movie, Kung Fu.

VISUAL: Ray starts to do overdramatic Kung Fu moves. He grabs a carrot and, using it like a nunchaku, hits Carl.

CARL: Did you just whack me with a carrot?

VISUAL: Carl rolls his eyes, raises his paw, and snaps.

SFX: Finger snap.

VISUAL: A gang of ninja mice tumbles out of the shadows and surround Carl.

VISUAL: Ray, looking concerned, reacts to the group of ninja mice.

RAY: Ninja mice?

VISUAL: Exterior of Blockbuster store.

VO: At Blockbuster, the hottest new releases are guaranteed on DVD. So you'll always find your favorite movies.

VISUAL: Ray fighting with the ninja mice.

RAY: Off me, off me, you little varmints!

VISUAL: Glowing Blockbuster ticket

SUPER: Make It a Blockbuster Night.

VO: Make it a Blockbuster night.

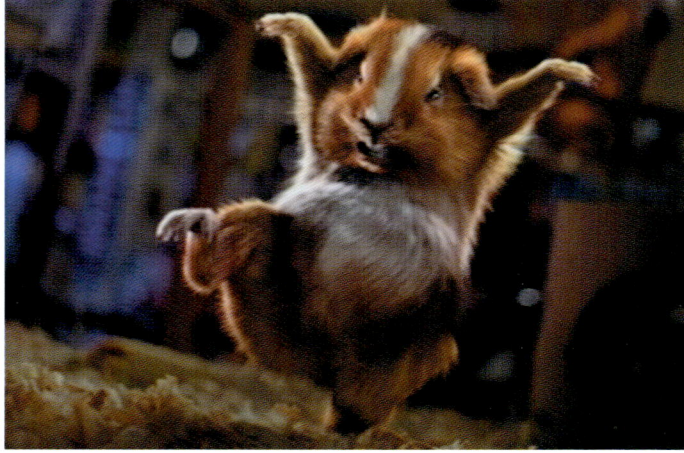

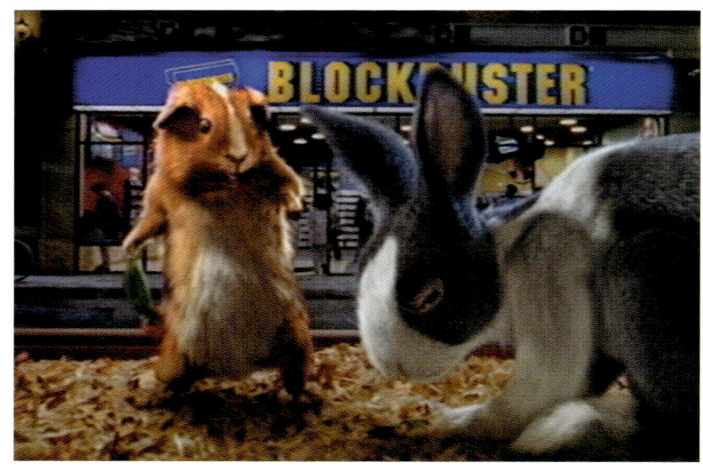

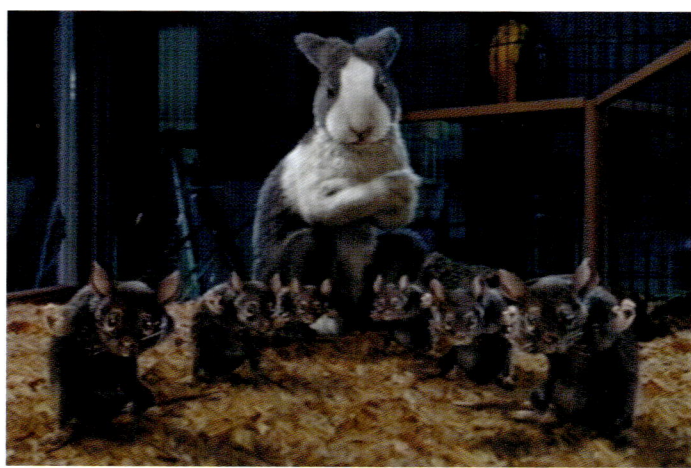

CATEGORY
Animation—Computer

ADVERTISER/PRODUCT
EDF (French Electricity Board)

TITLE
The Valley

ADVERTISING AGENCY
CLM/BBDO, Paris

PRODUCTION COMPANY
Partizan Midi-Minuit, Paris

MUSIC COMPANY
Barrera Prod, Paris

ANIMATION COMPANY
Buf, Paris

AGENCY PRODUCER
Pierre Marcus

ACCOUNT EXECUTIVE
Edouard Pacreau

CREATIVE DIRECTOR
Bernard Naville, Vincent Behaeghel

COPYWRITER
Bernard Naville

ART DIRECTOR
Vincent Behaeghel

PRODUCER
Georges Bergmann

DIRECTOR
Antoine Bardou-Jacquet

PROJECT MANAGER
Pierre Buffin, Olivier Gilbert

MAT PAINTING
Herve de Crecy, Jean Marie Vives,
Stephane Keller

3D
Jam

FLAME
Yves

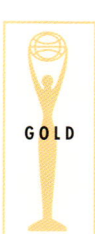

GOLD

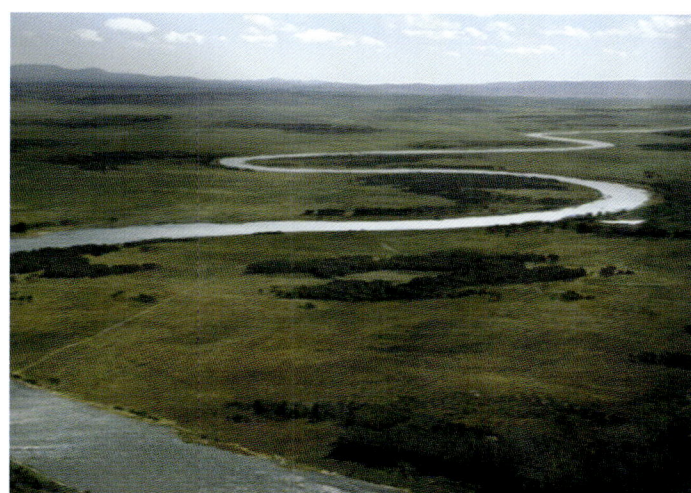

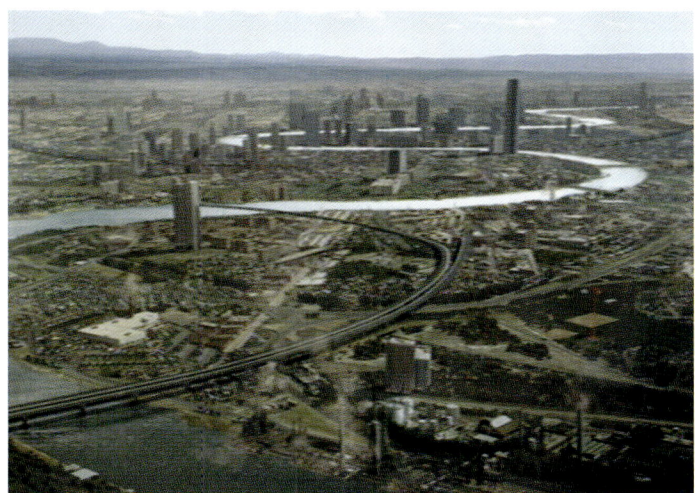

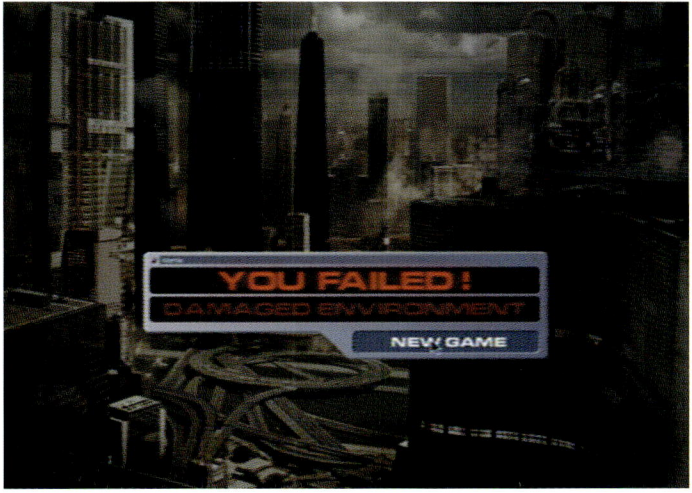

VISUAL: A charming mountain valley with a river flowing through it. A truck drives through the scene and a house begins to be built. A factory is built, more houses spring up and the valley is now a village. Many roads begin to cut through the valley, more factories appear, and the village is now a town. Large buildings and highways appear; skyscrapers, houses, roads, bridges, and expressway ramps fill the valley. The area has turned into a large city.

VISUAL: A computer instruction box displays the following message: "You failed—Damaged environment—New Game."

VO: Producing more power is a necessity; but so is preserving the environment.

VISUAL: A man is working on a computer. It is now obvious that the burgeoning city that was just built is on a computer monitor and is a game.

VO: Energy to make the world a better place.

SUPER: EDF logo. Energy to make the world a better place.

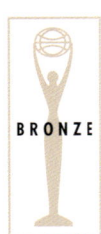

BRONZE

CATEGORY
Animation—Computer

ADVERTISER/PRODUCT
Blockbuster

TITLE
Prima Donna Ray

ADVERTISING AGENCY
Doner, Southfield

PRODUCTION COMPANY
Complete Pandemonium,
San Francisco

EDITING COMPANY
Bob 'n Sheila's Edit World,
San Francisco

MUSIC COMPANY
Blue Music and Sound Design,
Hollywood

SOUND DESIGN COMPANY
Soundelux DMG, Hollywood

ANIMATION COMPANY
Tippett Studios, Berkeley

AGENCY SENIOR PRODUCER
Josh Reynolds

CREATIVE DIRECTOR
John DeCerchio, John Parlato,
Don Fibich, Sheldon Cohn

COPYWRITER
Dan Margulis, Brian Hutson,
Mike Ceaser

ART DIRECTOR
Mark Cooke, Tom Gurisko

PRODUCER
Clint Goldman

DIRECTOR
Steve "Spaz" Williams

EXECUTIVE PRODUCER
Clint Goldman

**VISUAL EFFECTS
EXECUTIVE PRODUCER**
Jules Roman

VISUAL EFFECTS SUPERVISOR
Frank Petzold, Scott Souter

VISUAL EFFECTS PRODUCER
Alonzo Ruvalcaba

LEAD CHARACTER ANIMATOR
Todd Labonte, Eric Reynolds

LIGHTING LEAD
Steve Reding

COMPOSITING LEAD
Jim McVay

VISUAL: Ray and Carl are in a pet shop window looking across the street into the window of a Blockbuster store.

CARL: Hey Ray, look at all those movies, huh?

RAY: You think I could be a movie star, Carl?

CARL: Can you act?

RAY: Oh, I could act like a movie star.

VISUAL: Ray spits out water.

RAY: This isn't imported water!

VISUAL: Ray running on hamster wheel.

RAY: You call this a health spa?

VISUAL: Ray examining Carl's ears.

RAY: You know, my plastic surgeon can fix these.

VISUAL: Ray getting a massage from a mouse.

RAY: Yeah, that's good, yeah.

VISUAL: Ray at his food bowl. Holds up food pellets, looks disgusted and throws a fit.

RAY: These are brown; I specifically asked for green.

VISUAL: Exterior of Blockbuster store.

VO: At Blockbuster, the hottest new releases are guaranteed on DVD. So you'll always find your favorite stars.

VISUAL: Ray hiding in his hutch.

CARL: Ray, you can stop now.

RAY: Not until I get a bigger trailer.

VISUAL: Glowing Blockbuster ticket

SUPER: Make It a Blockbuster Night.

VO: Make it a Blockbuster night.

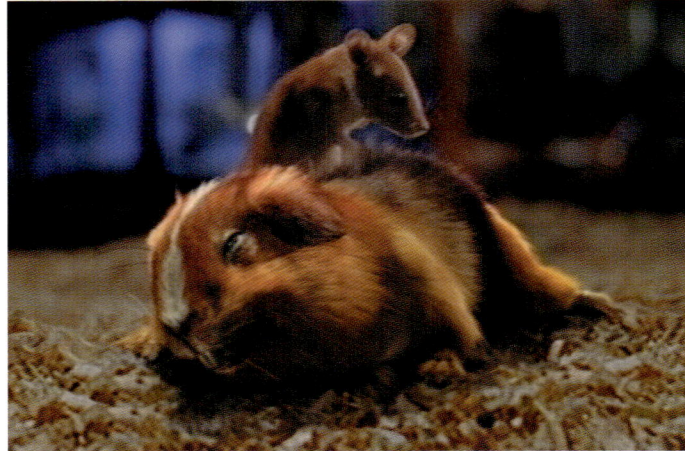

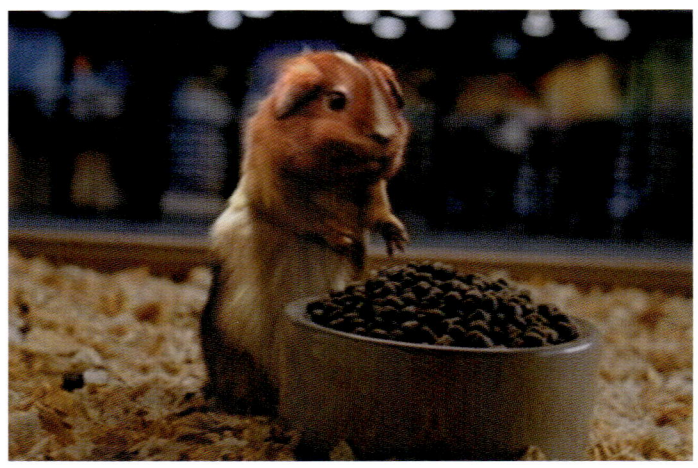

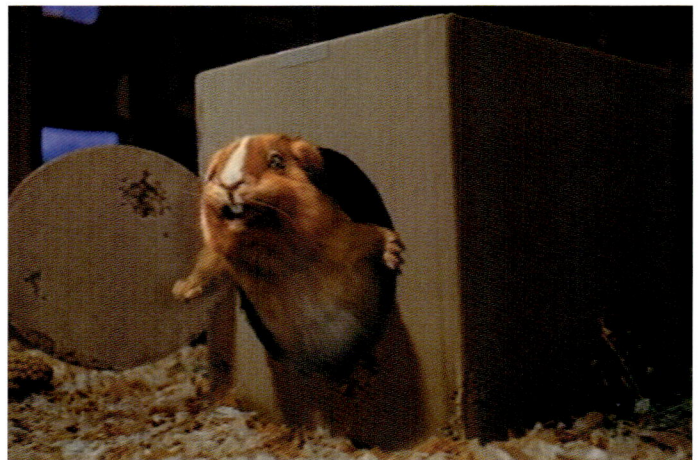

CATEGORY
Animation—Computer

ADVERTISER/PRODUCT
Blockbuster

TITLE
Gotta Dance

ADVERTISING AGENCY
Doner, Southfield

PRODUCTION COMPANY
Complete Pandemonium,
San Francisco

EDITING COMPANY
Bob 'n Sheila's Edit World,
San Francisco

MUSIC COMPANY
LANY Music, Santa Monica

SOUND DESIGN COMPANY
Soundelux DMG, Hollywood

ANIMATION COMPANY
Tippett Studios, Berkeley

SENIOR AGENCY PRODUCER
Josh Reynolds

CREATIVE DIRECTOR
John DeCerchio, John Parlato,
Don Fibich, Sheldon Cohn

COPYWRITER
Dan Margulis, Brian Hutson,
Mike Ceaser

ART DIRECTOR
Mark Cooke, Tom Gurisko,
Joel Friesch

PRODUCER
Clint Goldman

DIRECTOR
Steve "Spaz" Williams

EXECUTIVE PRODUCER
Clint Goldman

**VISUAL EFFECTS
EXECUTIVE PRODUCER**
Jules Roman

VISUAL EFFECTS SUPERVISOR
Frank Petzold, Scott Souter

VISUAL EFFECTS PRODUCER
Alonzo Ruvalcaba

LEAD CHARACTER ANIMATOR
Todd Labonte, Eric Reynolds

LIGHTING LEAD
Steve Reding

COMPOSITING LEAD
Jim McVay

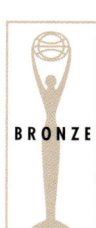

BRONZE

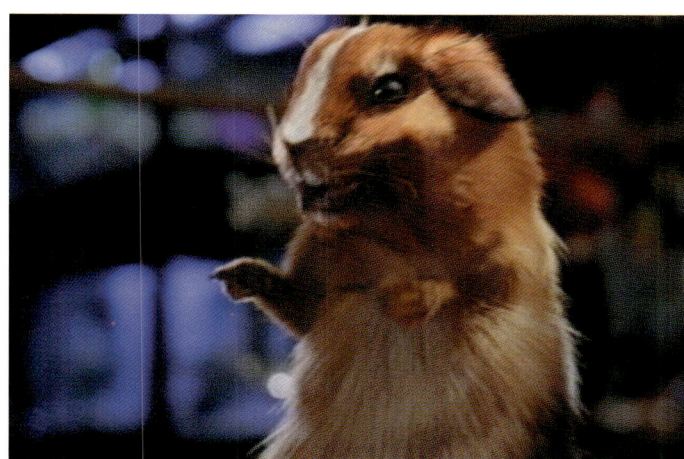

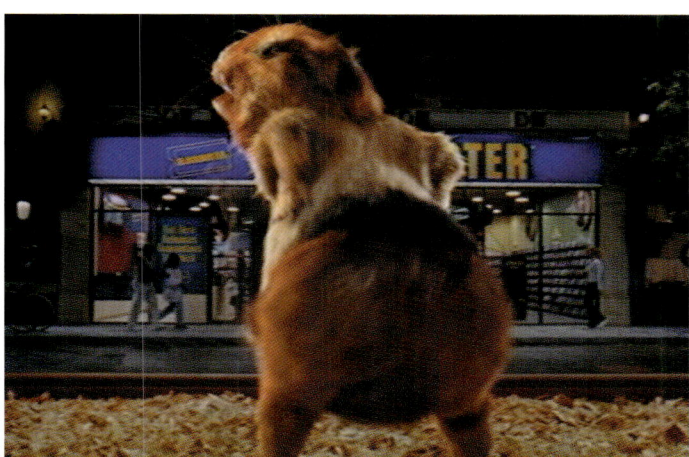

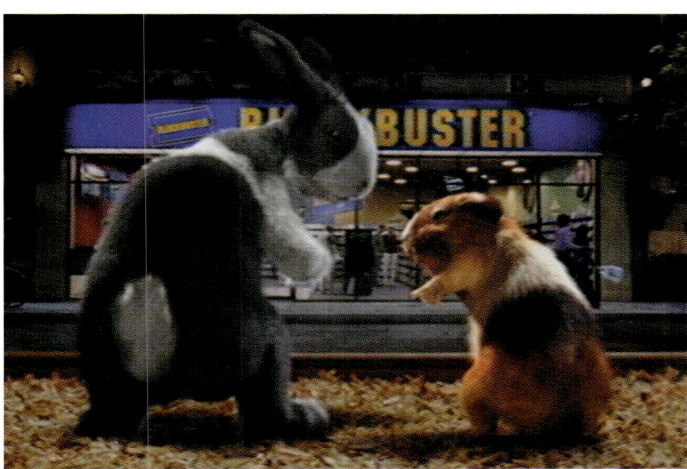

VISUAL: Ray and Carl are in a pet shop window looking across the street into the window of a Blockbuster store. Ray is doing dance moves from the movie *Flashdance*.

CARL: Hey Ray, Ray, look at this, wall-to-wall entertainment.

RAY: You want entertainment, Carl? I'll give you entertainment.

SFX: The song "Maniac" from *Flashdance* starts playing.

VISUAL: Ray continues to dance.

CARL: Oh boy.

RAY: Look, Carl, I'm a maniac, maniac.

CARL: No argument here!

RAY: Let's see their entertainment do this.

VISUAL: Ray wiggles his butt to the music.

CARL: Whoa, Ray, I don't want to see anything do that.

VISUAL: Exterior of Blockbuster store.

VO: At Blockbuster, the hottest new releases are guaranteed on DVD. So you'll always find the entertainment you want.

VISUAL: Glowing Blockbuster ticket

VISUAL: Ray wiggles his butt to the music. Carl starts to shake his butt.

RAY: That's it, Carl! Shake what your mama gave ya!

SUPER: Make It a Blockbuster Night.

VO: Make it a Blockbuster night.

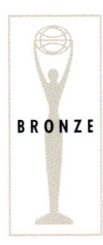

CATEGORY
Animation—Film

ADVERTISER/PRODUCT
AT&T

TITLE
I'm Okay

ADVERTISING AGENCY
Young & Rubicam, New York

PRODUCTION COMPANY
Acme Filmworks, Hollywood

MUSIC COMPANY
David Horowitz Music Associates,
New York

COPYWRITER
Kevin Fahey

ART DIRECTOR
Ann Lemon

PRODUCER
Mary Beth Sheridan

DIRECTOR
Michael Dudok De Wit

EXECUTIVE PRODUCER
Ron Diamond

**HEAD OF PRODUCTION/
SENIOR PRODUCER**
Peter Barg

SYNOPSIS: A father calls his daughter long distance.

FATHER: Hey sweetie. I got your e-mail.

DAUGHTER: Uh-huh.

FATHER: Where you said you were OK.

DAUGHTER: Uh-huh.

FATHER: So…was that "good" OK? Or "OK" OK?

DAUGHTER: No. I'm, Dad, you know, OK.

FATHER: Not so OK.

DAUGHTER: Unh-Unhm. But it's good to hear your voice.

VISUAL: Looking out the window of the daughter's apartment, the sun, and a few birds in flight.

SUPER: Nothing Else Has the Power of Your Voice.

AT&T Long Distance.

VISUAL: AT&T logo.

SUPER: Boundless.

Att.com

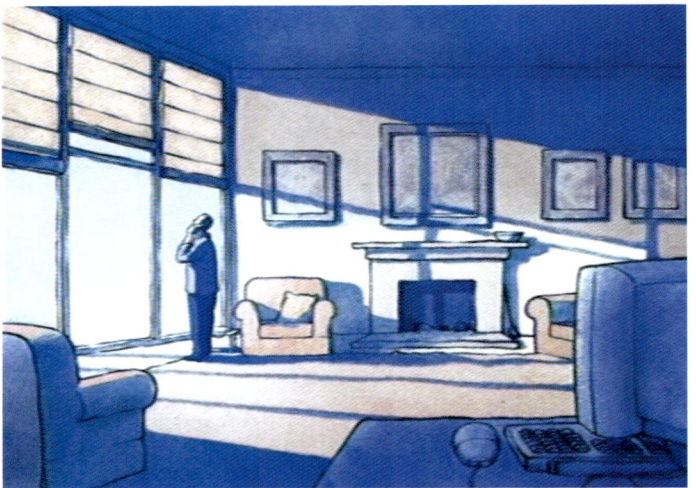

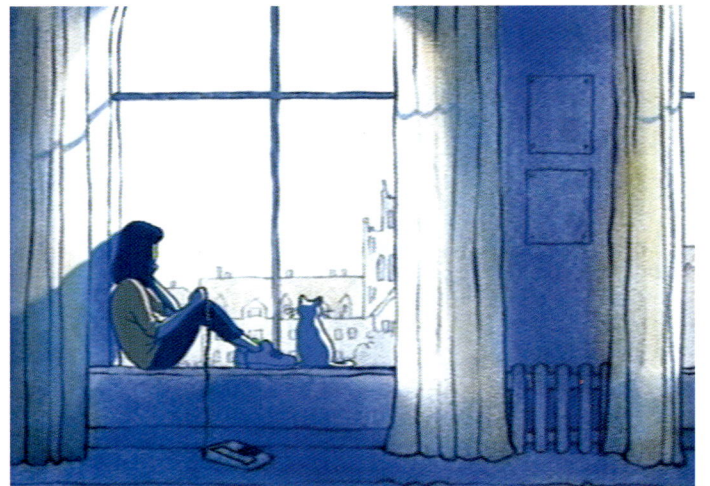

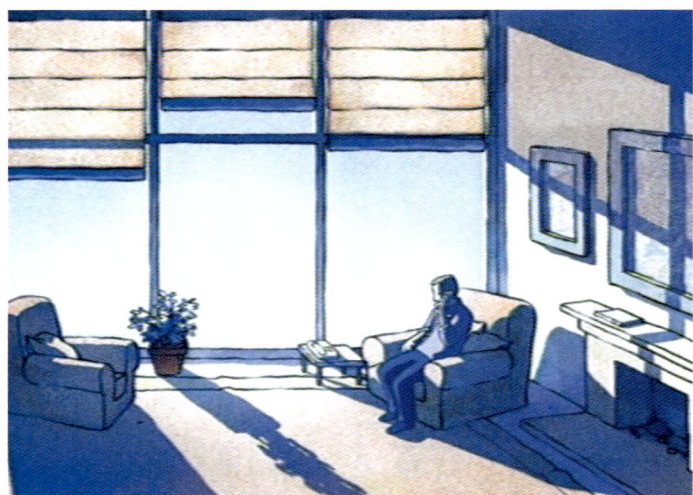

CATEGORY
Cinematography

ADVERTISER/PRODUCT
BMW of North America

TITLE
Powder Keg

ADVERTISING AGENCY
Fallon, Minneapolis

PRODUCTION COMPANY
Anonymous Content, Culver City

EDITING COMPANY
Z Films, Mexico City

MUSIC COMPANY
Universal Music Mexico,
Mexico City

SOUND DESIGN COMPANY
Z Films, Mexico City

ACCOUNT EXECUTIVE
Ginny Grossman

CREATIVE DIRECTOR
David Lubars, Bruce Bildsten

COPYWRITER
Alejandro Gonzalez Iñarritu,
David Carter, Guillermo Arriaga

ART DIRECTOR
Joe Sweet

PRODUCER
Robyn Boardman, Tapas Blank

DIRECTOR
Alejandro Gonzalez Iñarritu

DIRECTOR OF PHOTOGRAPHY
Bob Richardson

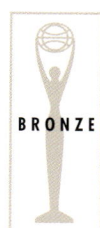

BRONZE

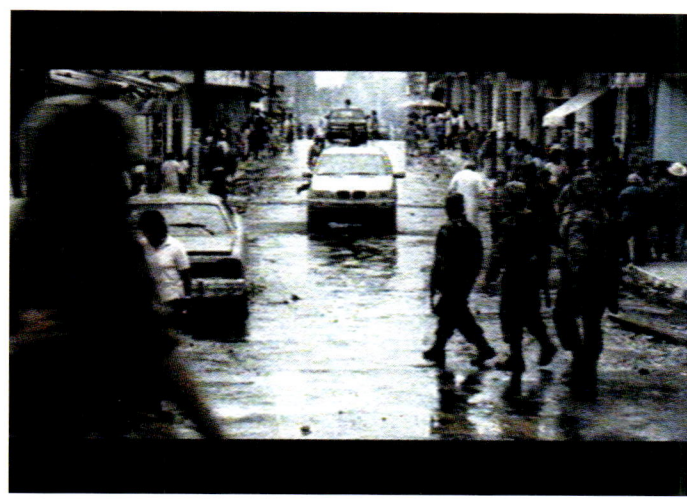

SYNOPSIS: Soldiers, fingers on triggers, patrol a coup-ravaged city in South America. Their mission: find a photojournalist who has taken a picture certain to enrage the world against their leader. The Driver must get the photojournalist and his film beyond the fiercely guarded border.

See page 86 for full script.

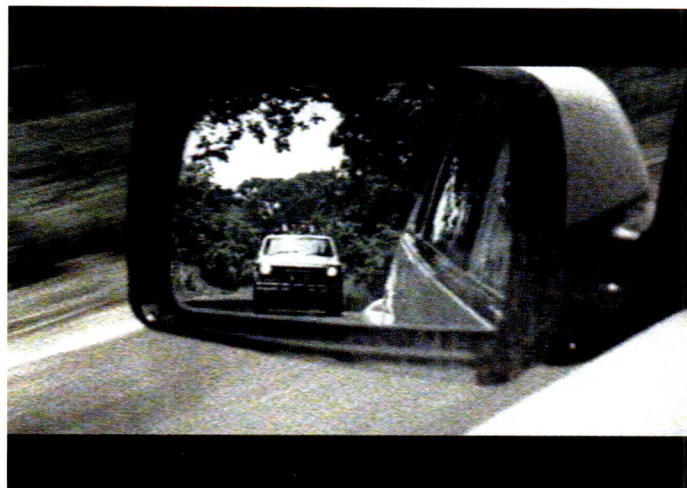

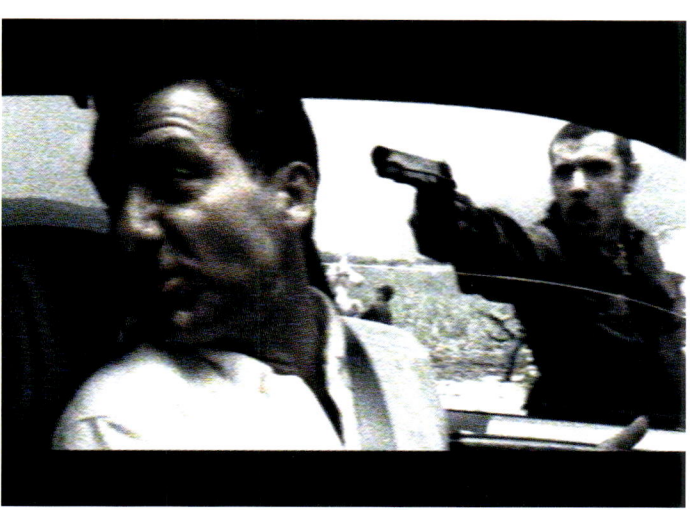

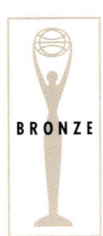

CATEGORY
Cinematography

ADVERTISER/PRODUCT
Pocari Sweat

TITLE
Tennis

ADVERTISING AGENCY
Asatsu-DK Inc./Makes, Tokyo

PRODUCTION COMPANY
Level 7 Productions, Hollywood

EDITING COMPANY
Chrome, Santa Monica

MUSIC COMPANY
Face The Music, Venice & New York

SOUND DESIGN COMPANY
Ear to Ear, Santa Monica

ANIMATION COMPANY
Digital Domain, Venice

EXECUTIVE AGENCY PRODUCER
Hisashi Nakano

AGENCY PRODUCER
Saburo Masuda

ACCOUNT EXECUTIVE
Hisashi Nakano

CREATIVE DIRECTOR
Joel Peissig, Shinichiro Nakaso

COPYWRITER
Michael Folino, Michael Horsham

DIRECTOR
Joel Peissig

EXECUTIVE PRODUCER
Larry Serraino, Chris van Howten

PRODUCER
Joel Peissig

EDITOR
Lance Pereira

CINEMATOGRAPHER
Claudio Miranda

CAMERA OPERATOR
Pete Romano

VISUAL EFFECTS PRODUCER
Stephanie Gilgar

VISUAL EFFECTS SUPERVISOR
Leslie Ekker

VISUAL EFFECTS COORDINATOR
Cyndi Ochs

COMPOSITOR
Mark Larranaga, Christine Lo,
Darren Poe

TECHNICAL DIRECTOR
Jonah Hall

FX ANIMATOR SUPERVISOR
Nikos Kalaitzidis

FX ANIMATOR - HOUDINI
Archil Gogoladze

DATA INTEGRATION
Tim Conway (Lead), Nancy Adams,
Jason Doss, David Niednagel,
Chris Simmons

MODELER—MAYA
Vernon Wilbert

ROTOSCOPE
Lou Pecora, Byron Werner

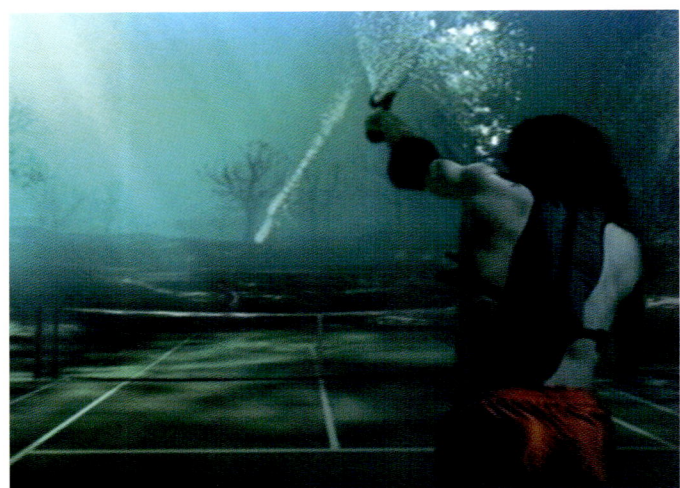

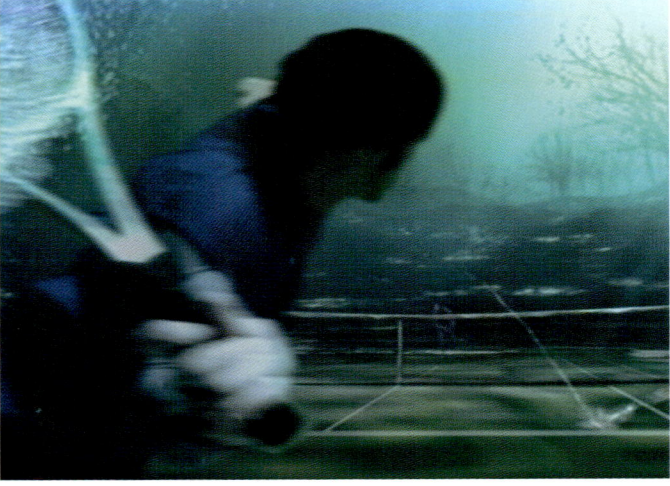

VISUAL: Two players engage in a very competitive game of tennis that is being played underwater.

SUPER: Pocari Sweat. Part of You.

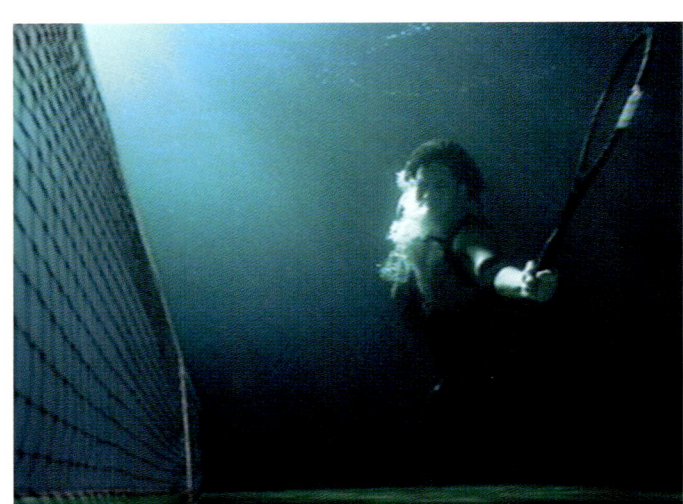

CATEGORY
Direction

ADVERTISER/PRODUCT
Budweiser

TITLE
Letting Go

ADVERTISING AGENCY
DDB, Chicago

PRODUCTION COMPANY
Propaganda Films, New York

EDITING COMPANY
Final Cut, New York

GROUP CREATIVE DIRECTOR
John Immesoete

ASSOCIATE CREATIVE DIRECTOR
Dick Tracy

COPYWRITER
Geoff McCartney

ART DIRECTOR
Dick Tracy

DIRECTOR
Tom Kuntz, Mike McGuire

PRODUCER
Greg Popp

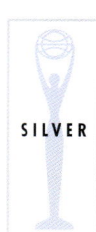

SILVER

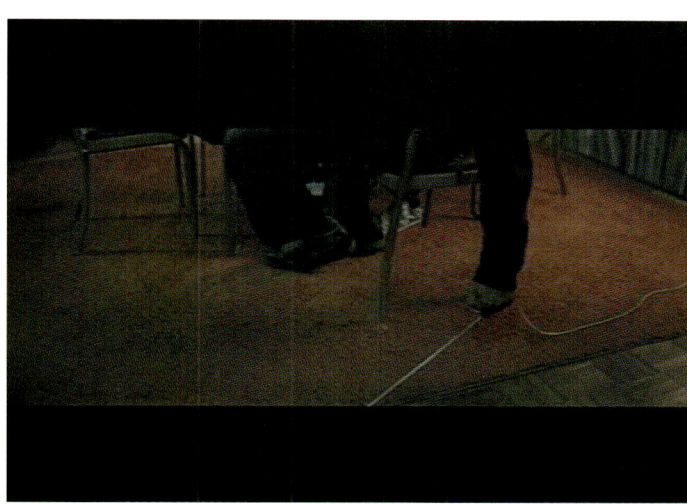

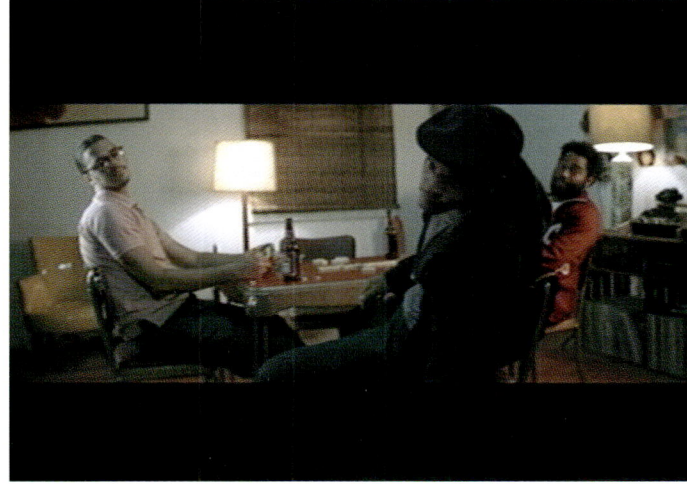

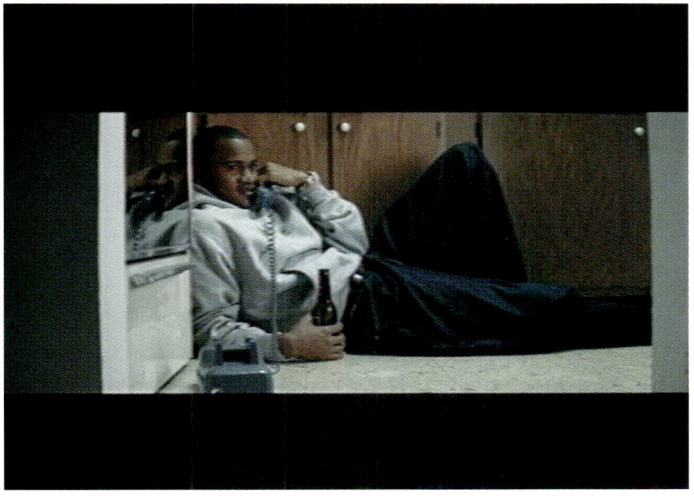

VISUAL: A man is on the phone talking to his girlfriend. His friends are sitting around a table in the background.

MAN: Nooo, I don't want to go yet. Come on. Okay, you hang up first then. Mmm, Okay. I count to three and then we hang up, okay. One, two. Okay, okay, okay I'll do it; I'll do it for yeah.

VISUAL: One of his friends is disgusted by the conversation and yanks the phone cord out of the wall.

SUPER: Budweiser True logo

www.budweiser.com.

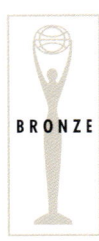

CATEGORY
Direction

ADVERTISER/PRODUCT
LTSA—Urban Speed

TITLE
Consequences

ADVERTISING AGENCY
Clemenger BBDO, Wellington

PRODUCTION COMPANY
Film Graphics, Sydney

EDITING COMPANY
Paul Maxwell, Wellington

SOUND DESIGN COMPANY
Song Zu, Sydney

AGENCY PRODUCER
Marty Collins

ACCOUNT MANAGER
Sarah Spencer

CREATIVE DIRECTOR
Philip Andrew

COPYWRITER
Nigel Corbett

ART DIRECTOR
Philip Andrew

PRODUCER
Marge McInnes

DIRECTOR
Mat Humphrey

VISUAL: A man in his late twenties is sitting on a bus holding a small cardboard box.

VISUAL: He is now in a work environment with a colleague.

COLLEAGUE: Not your fault, eh?

MAN: Yeah, see ya.

VISUAL: He leaves the office. All his coworkers avoid making eye contact with him.

VISUAL: Again he is on the bus.

VISUAL: He is driving a sports car with an attractive female passenger. They flirt and laugh.

GIRL: Do you always drive this fast?

MAN: This isn't fast.

SFX: Screeching brakes.

VISUAL: He is on the bus next to a mother and her young son.

VISUAL: The speedometer of his car: It reads 65 km/h. He is driving down the street and there are people picking up their kids from school. He puts the car in a higher gear, accelerates, and then slams on the brakes. He has hit the rear bumper of an SUV. He is angry. He gets out of his car slams the door, inspects the damage to his car, and approaches the driver of the SUV.

MAN: I think we've done a lot more damage to my car than yours.

WOMAN (repeatedly): Oh my god, Oh my god.

MAN: Its OK, it's OK, it's all covered by insurance.

VISUAL: The woman stares ahead then brings her hands to her face in shock. A four-year-old boy is standing in front of the SUV. He is unharmed. The man circles around in front of her car and sees an arm and a leg protruding from beneath the SUV. It is the boy's mother.

BOY: Mommy?

MAN: Call an ambulance.

WOMAN VO: Do something.

VISUAL: The man stands helpless, horrified.

BOY: Mommy?

SUPER: The Faster You Go, the Bigger the Mess.

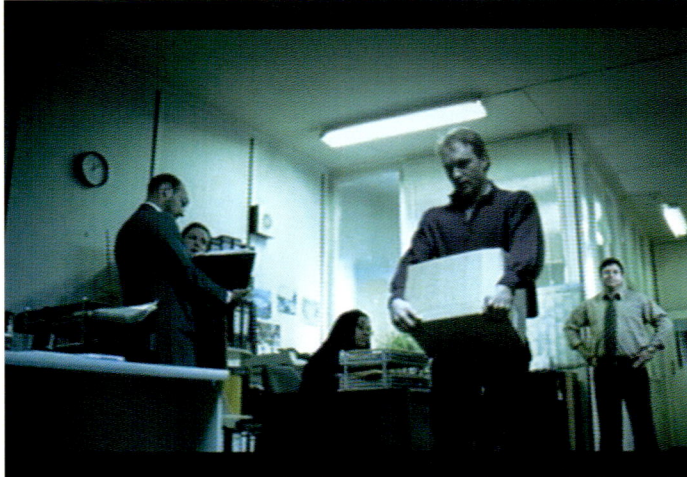

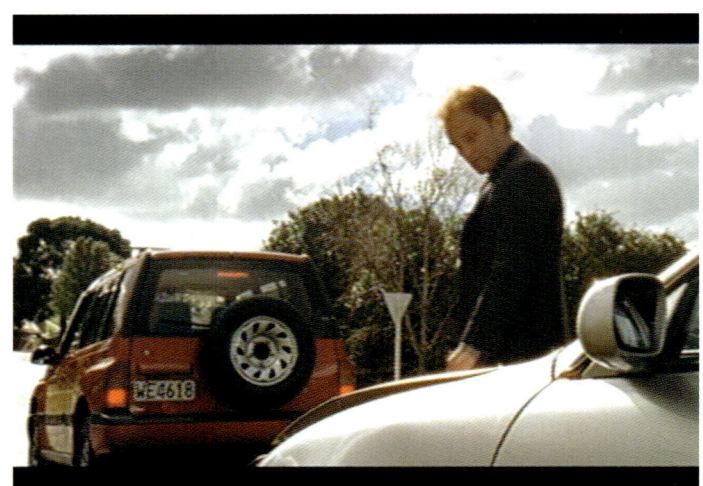

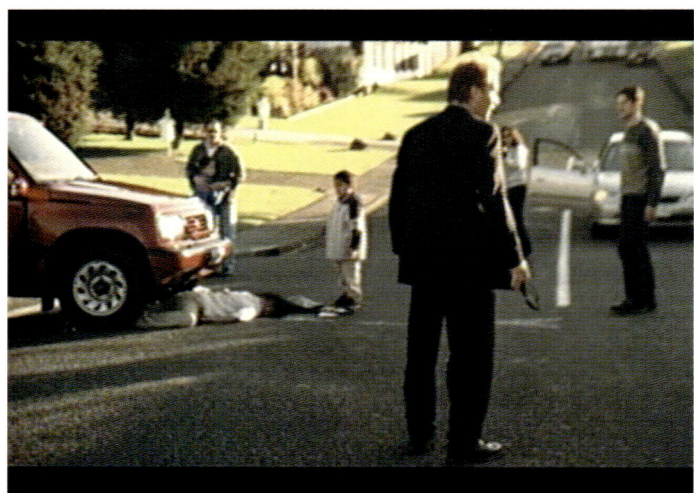

CATEGORY
Editing

ADVERTISER/PRODUCT
Nike

TITLE
Freestyle

ADVERTISING AGENCY
Wieden & Kennedy, Portland

PRODUCTION COMPANY
HSI, Los Angeles

EDITING COMPANY
Rock Paper Scissors, Los Angeles

SOUND DESIGN COMPANY
Endless Noise, Los Angeles

CREATIVE DIRECTOR
Hal Curtis

ART DIRECTOR
Jim Elchman

PRODUCER
Vic Palumbo

DIRECTOR
Paul Hunter

EDITOR
Adam Pertofsky

SOUND DESIGNER
Jeff Elmassian

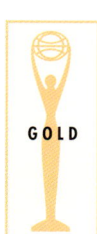

GOLD

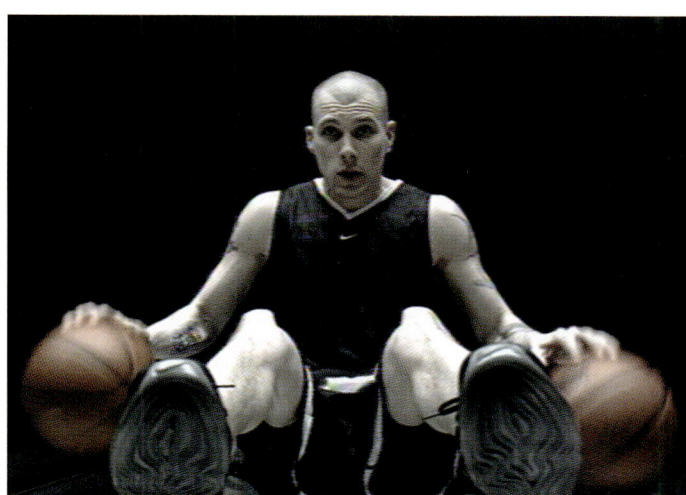

SYNOPSIS: Various NBA stars and street basketball players create a music track by dribbling, handling, and passing a basketball. The sound of their athletic shoes squeaking on the wooden floor adds an additional element to the music. The sound fades out and one player performs a slam dunk.

SUPER: Nike logo.

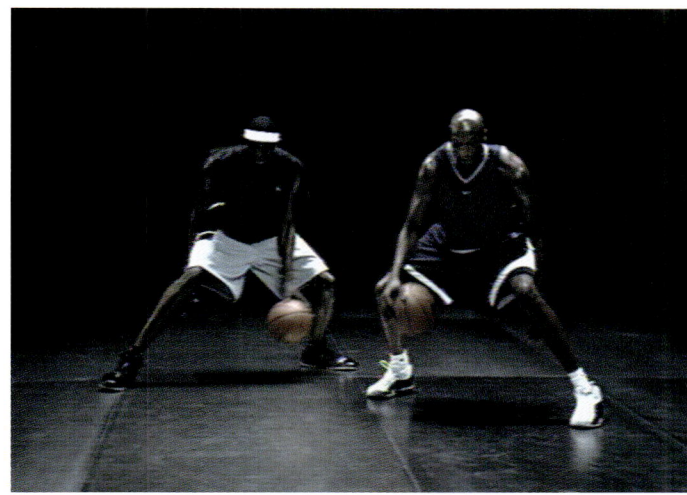

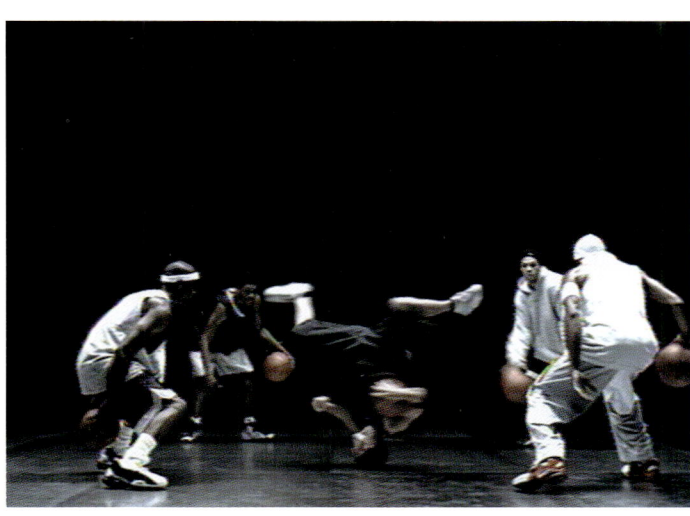

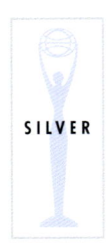

SILVER

CATEGORY Editing	**EDITING COMPANY** The Whitehouse, International	**COPYWRITER** Mike Byrne, Kash Sree	**EDITOR** Russel Icke
ADVERTISER/PRODUCT Nike	**MUSIC COMPANY** Elias Arts, Santa Monica	**ART DIRECTOR** Andy Fackrell, Monica Taylor	**ASSISTANT EDITOR** Gareth McEwan
TITLE Tag	**SOUND DESIGN COMPANY** Pop Sound, Santa Monica	**EXECUTIVE PRODUCER** Sue Dawson	**SOUND DESIGNER** Loren Silber
ADVERTISING AGENCY Wieden & Kennedy, Portland	**ACCOUNT EXECUTIVE** Biron Oshiro	**PRODUCER** Andrew Loevenguth	
PRODUCTION COMPANY Anonymous, Culver City	**CREATIVE DIRECTOR** Dan Wieden, Hal Curtis	**DIRECTOR** Frank Budgen	

SYNOPSIS: A man walks down the street with his coffee and newspaper; he is tagged and the game begins. He desperately and fervently chases the other players around the city: through streets, in and out of buildings, and, eventually, he bolts down the subway stairs. The subway train's doors close, and our hero seems to have lost. Hope is restored when the subway riders gesture to the tagged man letting him know that he is not alone on the platform and the game can continue. The chase begins again and the entire city is now a playground.

SUPER: Play.

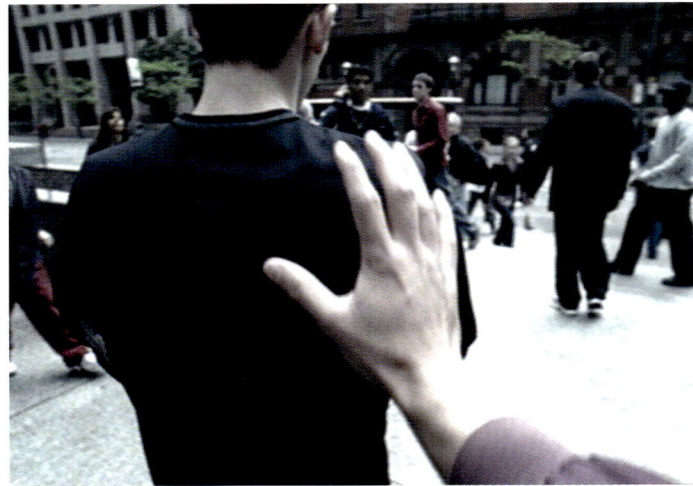

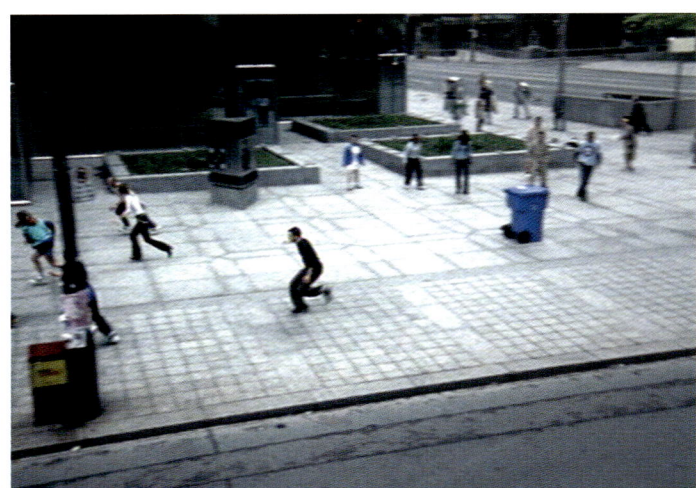

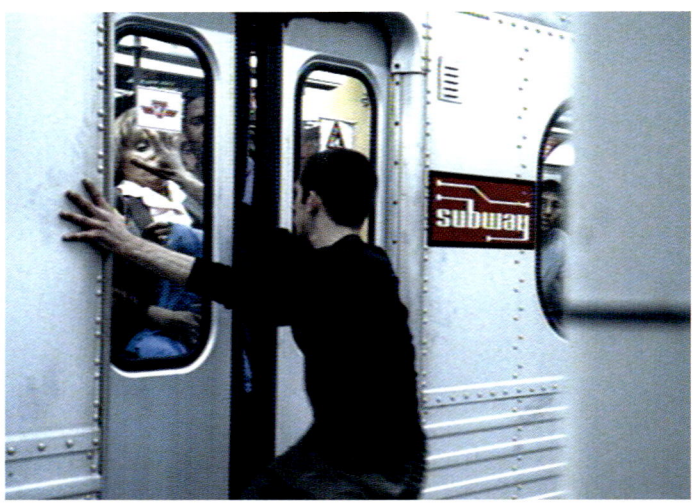

CATEGORY
Editing

ADVERTISER/PRODUCT
Visa

TITLE
Dining Out

ADVERTISING AGENCY
BBDO/Guerrero Ortega, Manila

PRODUCTION COMPANY
@radical.media, Sydney

EDITING COMPANY
Guillotine P/L, Sydney

MUSIC COMPANY
Song Zu, Sydney

SOUND DESIGN COMPANY
Song Zu, Sydney

ANIMATION COMPANY
Fin Design, Sydney

CREATIVE DIRECTOR
David Guerrero

ART DIRECTOR
David Guerrero

COPYWRITER
David Guerrero

EXECUTIVE PRODUCER
Gerry Gentemann

PRODUCER
Bruce Davidson, Julianne Shelton

DIRECTOR
Bruce Hunt

EDITOR
Drew Thompson

COMPOSER
Mark Rivett

SOUND DESIGNER
Simon Kane

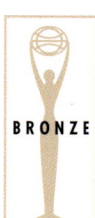

BRONZE

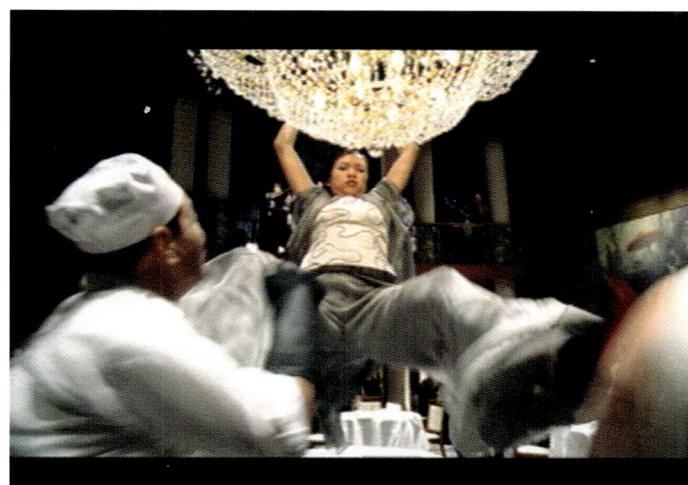

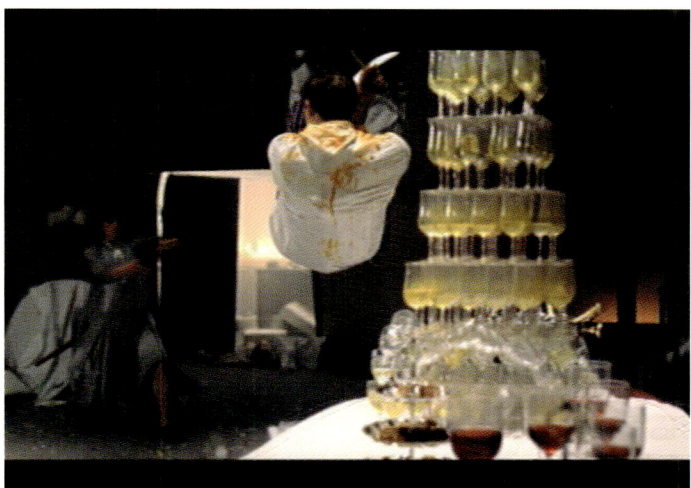

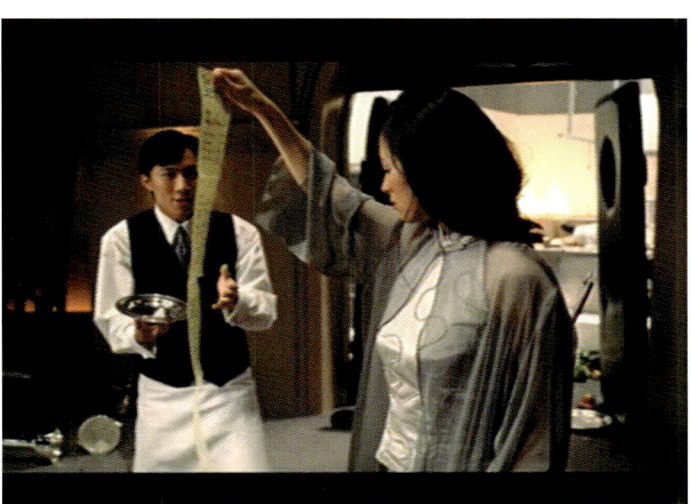

VISUAL: In a restaurant kitchen, a chef tastes the soup before serving it.

CHEF: Magnifique!

VISUAL: The waiter sets the soup on the table of a female customer. She tastes the soup.

CUSTOMER: The soup is too salty.

VISUAL: The chef hears her, storms out of the kitchen and confronts the diner.

CHEF: It is not too salty!

VISUAL: The chef motions to his kitchen staff to attack the customer. A classic martial-arts-style battle takes place during which the restaurant gets destroyed.

SUPER: Dining out?

WAITER: No charge for the soup.

VISUAL: Waiter unfolds a restaurant bill that is 20 feet long.

WAITER: But this is for the extras.

VISUAL: The woman flings her Visa Gold card into a silver tray.

VISUAL: Visa card.

SUPER: All It Takes.

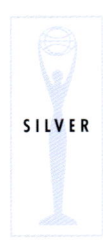

SILVER

CATEGORY Music—Adaptation	**PRODUCTION COMPANY** Gorgeous Enterprises, London	**CREATIVE DIRECTOR** Dan Wieden, Hal Curtis	**DIRECTOR** Frank Budgen
ADVERTISER/PRODUCT Nike	**EDITING COMPANY** The Whitehouse, Santa Monica	**COPYWRITER** Mike Byrne, Kash Sree	**ARRANGER** Jimmy Haun
TITLE Shade Runner	**MUSIC COMPANY** Elias Arts, Santa Monica	**ART DIRECTOR** Monica Taylor, Andy Fackrell	**MUSIC CREATIVE DIRECTOR** David Gold
ADVERTISING AGENCY Wieden & Kennedy, Portland	**ACCOUNT EXECUTIVE** Byron Oshiro	**PRODUCER** Andrew Loevenguth	**MUSIC PRODUCER** Dayna Turcott

SYNOPSIS: A female jogger is running through the city streets on a very sunny day, constantly in search of shade. She runs under a sky-bridge, an awning, beside a truck, and next to some construction equipment. Eventually, she rests against a shaded brick wall. The music track is an adaptation of "You Are My Sunshine."

SUPER: Shade Running.

Nike logo/Play.

nike.com/play.

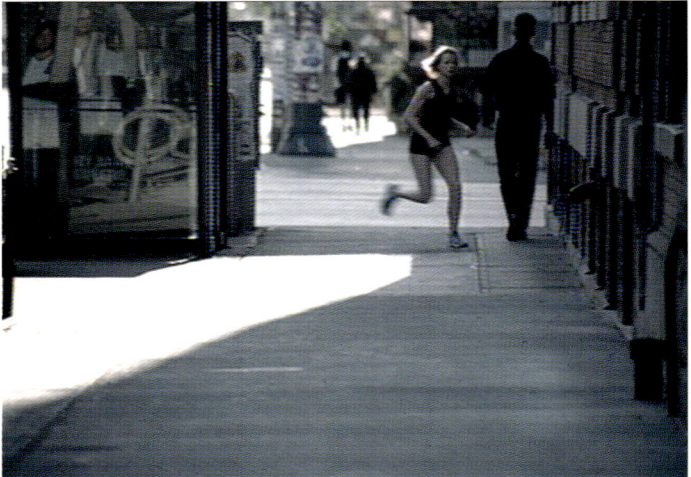

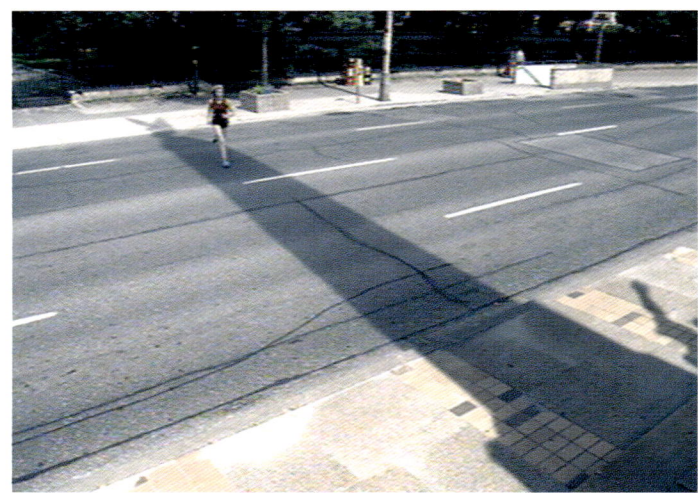

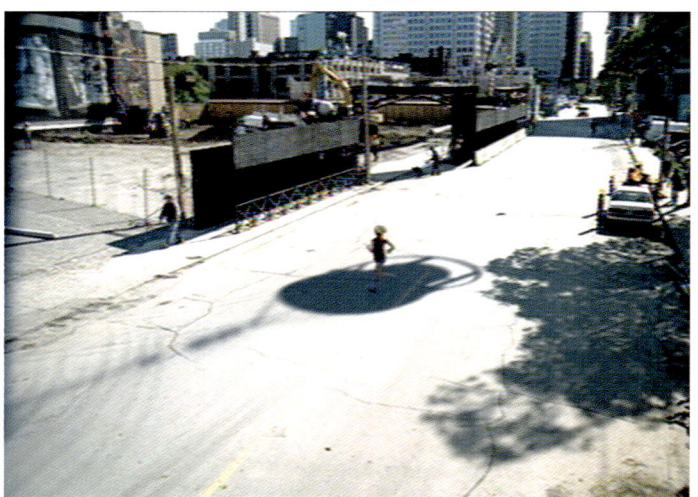

CATEGORY Music—Adaptation	**PRODUCTION COMPANY** Rawi Macartney Cole, London	**ANIMATION COMPANY** Clear, London	**ART DIRECTOR** David Lyle, Julie Anne Bailie
ADVERTISER/PRODUCT Road Safety—Seat belts	**EDITING COMPANY** Final Cut, London	**ACCOUNT EXECUTIVE** John, Brolly, Robert Lyle	**PRODUCER** Julie Anne Bailie, Ruck Strauss
TITLE Damage	**MUSIC COMPANY** Amber Music, London	**CREATIVE DIRECTOR** David Lyle, Julie Anne Bailie	**DIRECTOR** Syd Macartney
ADVERTISING AGENCY McCann-Erickson Belfast, Belfast	**SOUND DESIGN COMPANY** The Tape Gallery, London	**COPYWRITER** David Lyle, Julie Anne Bailie	

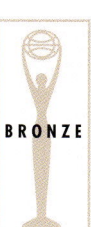

BRONZE

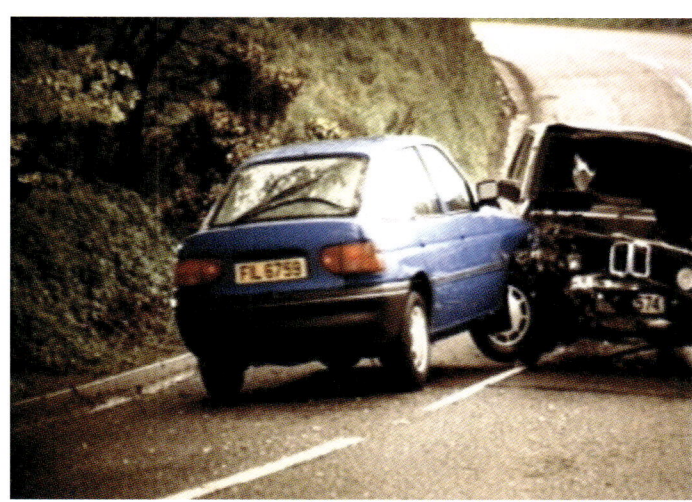

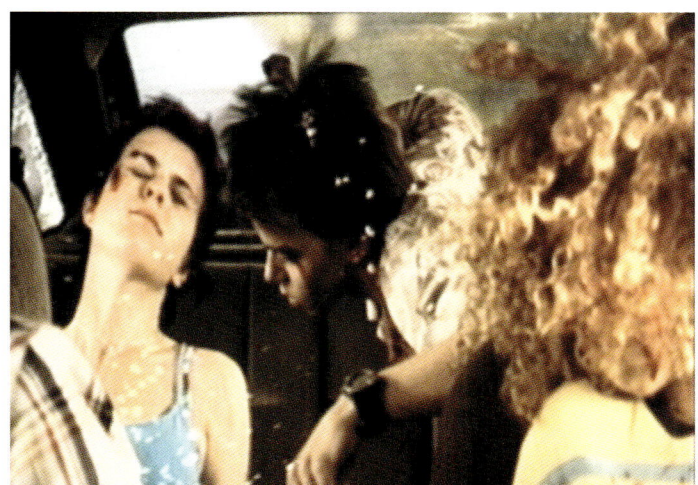

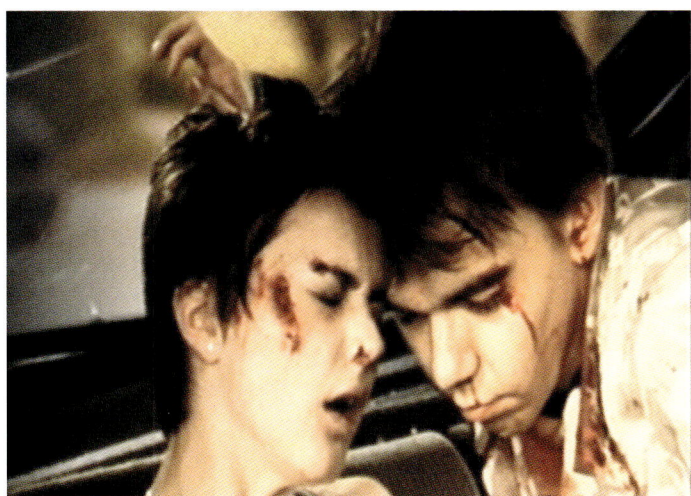

SYNOPSIS: A road safety commercial using an adaptation of Samantha Mumba's "Body to Body" and the Captain & Tennille's "Do That to Me One More Time" mixed over the "Body to Body" rhythm track.

VISUAL: A teenage couple are snuggling and having fun on a park bench. A car pulls up and their friends signal them to join them for a ride.

VO: This is Michael. Today he is going to hit his girlfriend so hard she ends up with permanent brain damage.

VISUAL: The two couples are riding in the car having a great time. They hit another car and are eventually hit by a second vehicle. All four of them are tossed around the car and injured quite badly. The police arrive on the scene.

POLICE OFFICER: Three dead in this vehicle. The girl is critical. They say the guy without the seat belt did the damage.

VISUAL: The aftermath of the crash scene, with police and paramedics wandering around. The girl is on a stretcher and there are three full body bags in an ambulance.

VO: No seat belt, no excuse.

SUPER: No Seat Belt. No Excuse.

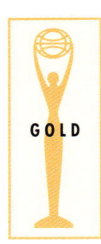

GOLD

CATEGORY
Music—Original

ADVERTISER/PRODUCT
Sony Wega

TITLE
Kite

ADVERTISING AGENCY
Young & Rubicam, New York

PRODUCTION COMPANY
Joy Films, London;
Chelsea Films, New York

EDITING COMPANY
Final Cut, New York, London

MUSIC COMPANY
Amber Music, New York

SOUND DESIGN COMPANY
Amber Music, New York

CREATIVE DIRECTOR
Ross Southerland

COPYWRITER
David McMillan

ART DIRECTOR
Paul Sofsel

PRODUCER
Rosanne Haine, Josh Rabinowitz

DIRECTOR
Mehdi Newzian

COMPOSER
Robert Miller

SOUND DESIGNER
Ross Gregory

VISUAL: A boy walks into a curiosity shop named "Joy, Mirth, and Merriment," full of oddities and nostalgic games. There is a kindly looking shopkeeper working behind the counter. The boy drops a ball of string; it rolls to the back of the store and underneath a red curtain. He picks up the string and follows it through the curtain. He now finds himself in a field with thousands of static red pinwheels. Everything in this fantasyland appears lifeless. He now notices the shopkeeper standing next to a Sony Wega television. The shopkeeper presses a button on the television's remote and a windmill on the screen begins turning. Now the thousands of pinwheels begin to turn. The grass begins to move, and the wind carries through the trees and across a vast field. Vertical red banners, mounted on the wall of a castle, spring to life with the power of the wind. Suddenly, a kite takes off. The boy runs, excitedly, through the field of spinning pinwheels.

VO: With Wega, you don't watch TV, you feel it. In a place called Sony.

SUPER: Sony Wega logo.

Dream On.

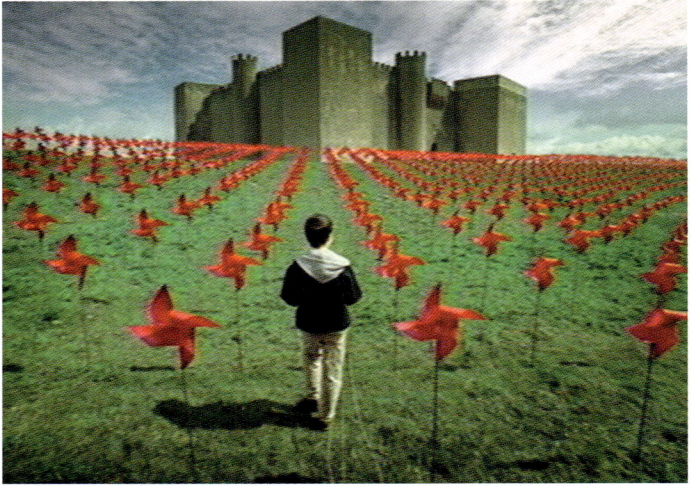

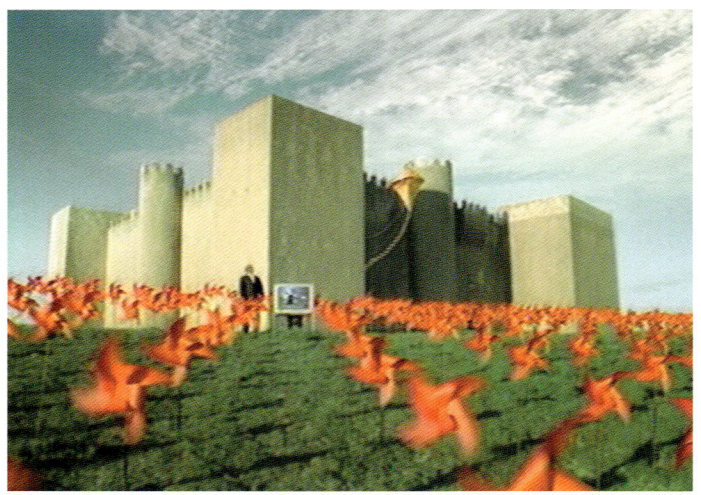

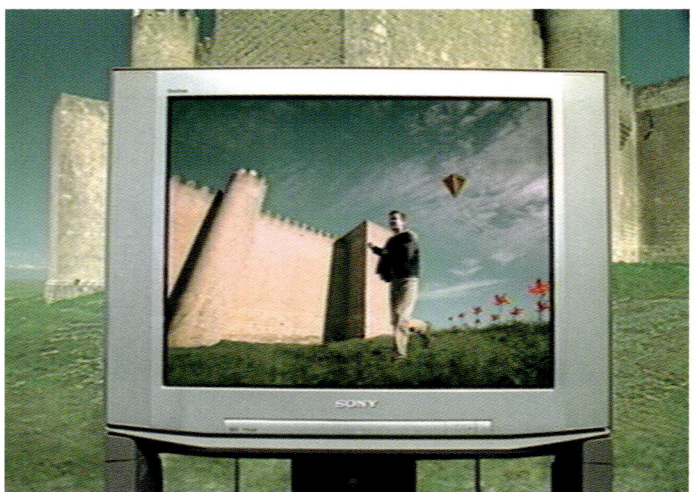

CATEGORY
Music—Original

ADVERTISER/PRODUCT
Nike

TITLE
Freestyle

ADVERTISING AGENCY
Wieden & Kennedy, Portland

PRODUCTION COMPANY
HSI Productions, Inc, Culver City

EDITING COMPANY
Rock Paper Scissors, Los Angeles

MUSIC COMPANY
Afrika Bambaataa, New York;
Endless Noise, Los Angeles;
Breakthru Productions, New York

SOUND DESIGN COMPANY
Endless Noise, Los Angeles

ANIMATION COMPANY
A-52, Los Angeles

ACCOUNT EXECUTIVE
Lee Davis

CREATIVE DIRECTOR
Jim Riswold, Hal Curtis

COPYWRITER
Jimmy Smith

ART DIRECTOR
Hal Curtis

PRODUCER
Vic Palumbo

DIRECTOR
Paul Hunter

MUSIC COMPOSER/PRODUCER
Afrika Bambaataa, Jeff Elmassian,
Steven "Boogie" Brown

EDITOR
Adam Pertofsky

SOUND DESIGNER
Jeff Elmassian

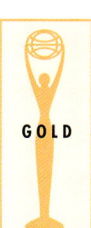

GOLD

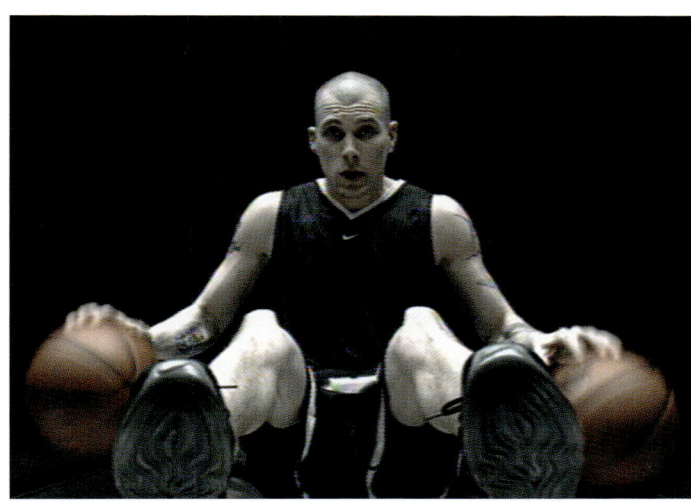

SYNOPSIS: Various NBA stars and street basketball players create a music track by dribbling, handling, and passing a basketball. The sound of their athletic shoes squeaking on the wooden floor adds an additional element to the music. The sound fades out and one player performs a slam dunk.

SUPER: Nike logo.

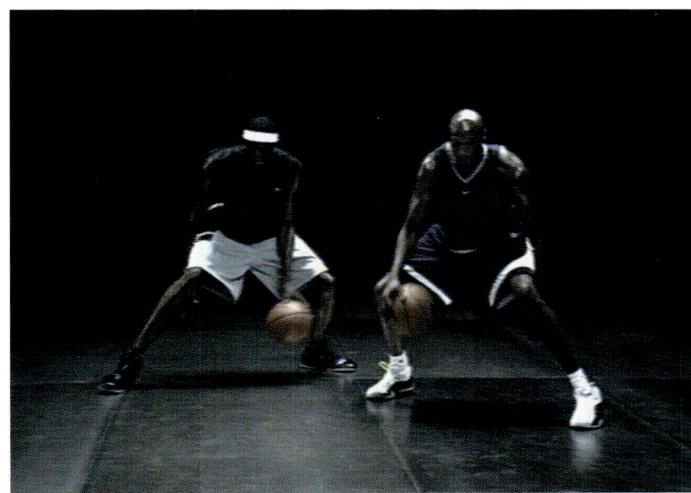

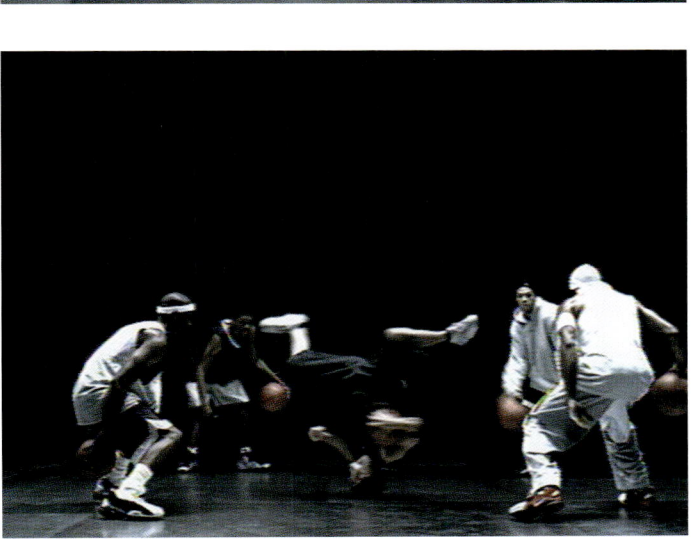

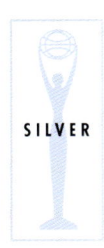

CATEGORY
Music—Original

ADVERTISER/PRODUCT
Mercedes-Benz

TITLE
Coffee Shop

ADVERTISING AGENCY
Merkley Newman Harty, New York

PRODUCTION COMPANY
Morton Jankel Zander, New York

MUSIC COMPANY
Fluid, New York

COPYWRITER
Scott Zacaroli

ART DIRECTOR
Tom Sullivan

PRODUCER
Sara Eolin

DIRECTOR
Jonathan David

COMPOSER
Andrew Sherman, David Shapiro,
Steve Walsh

VISUAL: A man is sitting in a coffee shop reading the newspaper. Time passes and the waitress continues to fills his cup with fresh coffee. She offers, he nods; she offers, he nods. This continues for a while and, eventually, the man looks a little wired.

SUPER: Two things that are free in New York.

VISUAL: The man asks for another coffee. His hand and the cup and saucer are quite jittery.

SUPER: Refills on coffee.

VISUAL: The man knocks over his cup. He is now outside the restaurant in front of an E-class Mercedes. He waves to the waitress and she waves back.

SUPER: And scheduled maintenance on your Mercedes-Benz.

Mercedes-Benz Tri-State Dealers.

We understand. We live here too.

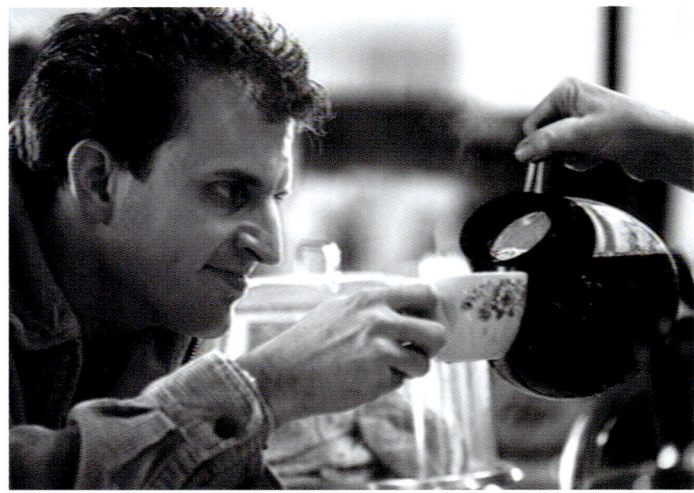

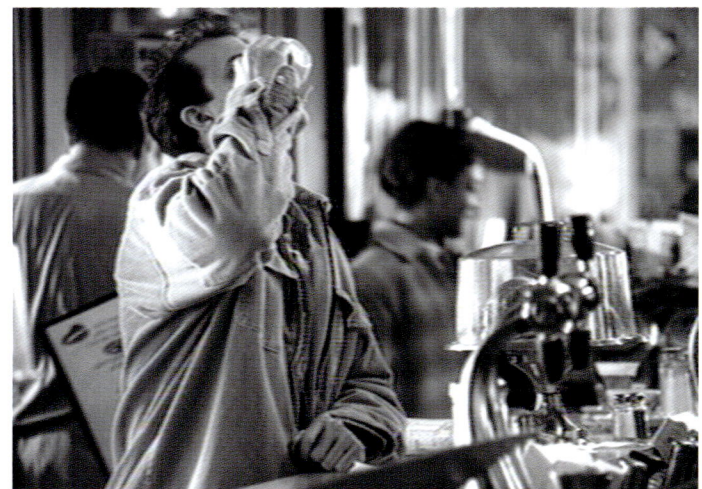

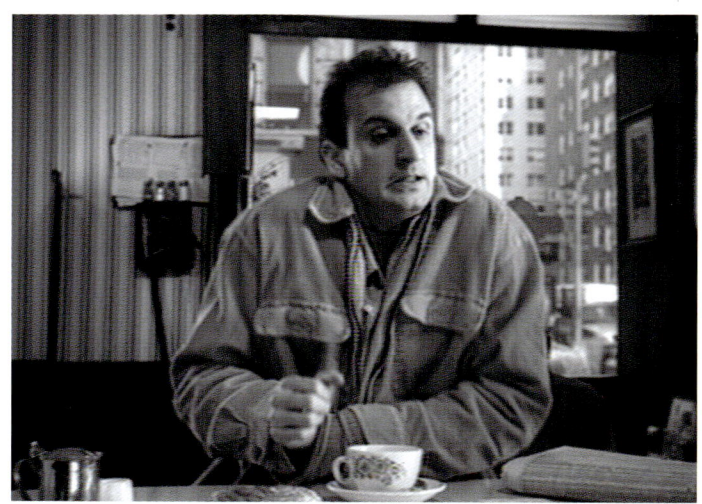

CATEGORY
Music—Original

ADVERTISER/PRODUCT
Mercedes-Benz

TITLE
Better

ADVERTISING AGENCY
Merkley Newman Harty, New York

PRODUCTION COMPANY
Morton Jankel Zander, Los Angeles

EDITING COMPANY
Jump Edit, New York

MUSIC COMPANY
Amber Music, New York & London

SOUND DESIGN COMPANY
Amber Music, New York & London

CREATIVE DIRECTOR
Randy Saitta, Andy Hirsch

PRODUCER
Chris Ott

DIRECTOR
Victor Garcia

COMPOSER
Mike Hewer

SILVER

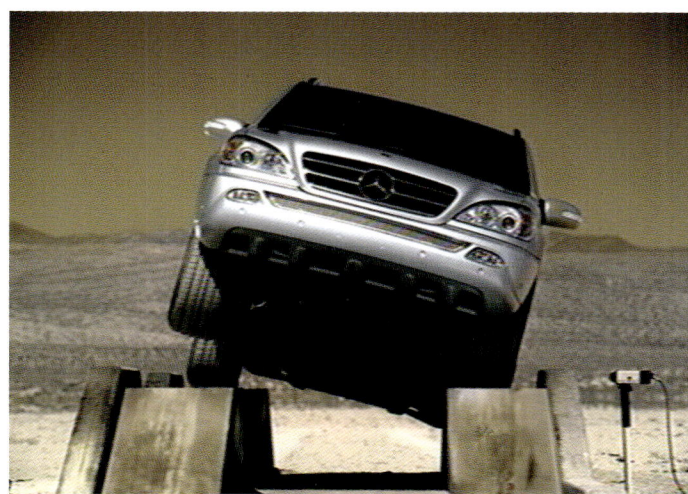

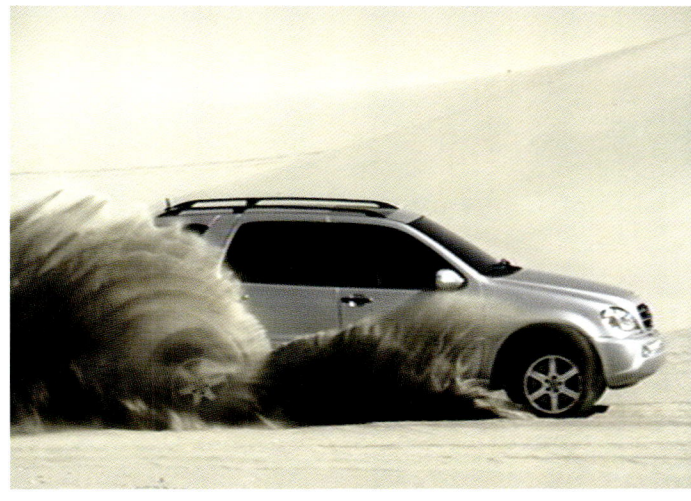

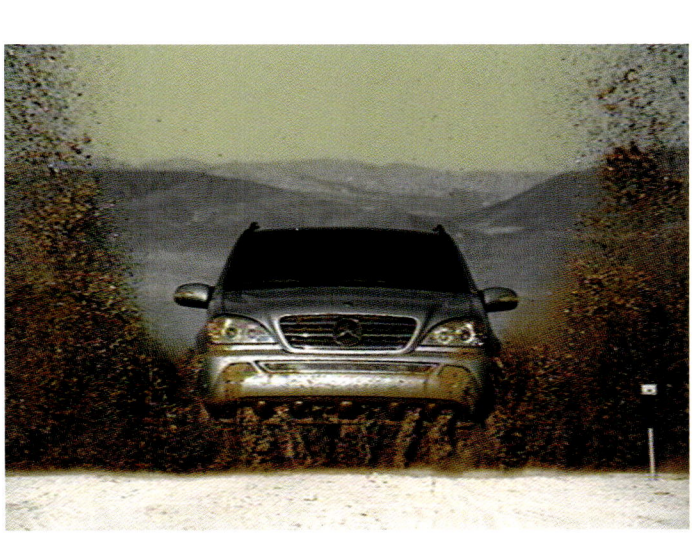

VISUAL: Various shots of the Mercedes ML320 SUV being designed by engineers, assembled in the factory, and road tested in the desert.

VO: We didn't just build a better SUV. We built a better Mercedes. Introducing the redesigned 2002 M-Class.

SUPER: The M-Class starts at $36,965 with free scheduled maintenance.

Mercedes-Benz logo.

mbusa.com

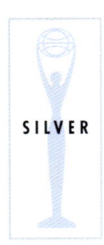

SILVER

CATEGORY
Music—Original

ADVERTISER/PRODUCT
Visa

TITLE
Dining Out

ADVERTISING AGENCY
BBDO/Guerrero Ortega, Manila

PRODUCTION COMPANY
@radical.media, Sydney

EDITING COMPANY
Guillotine P/L, Sydney

MUSIC COMPANY
Song Zu, Sydney

SOUND DESIGN COMPANY
Song Zu, Sydney

ANIMATION COMPANY
Fin Design, Sydney

CREATIVE DIRECTOR
David Guerrero

ART DIRECTOR
David Guerrero

COPYWRITER
David Guerrero

EXECUTIVE PRODUCER
Gerry Gentemann

PRODUCER
Bruce Davidson, Julianne Shelton

DIRECTOR
Bruce Hunt

EDITOR
Drew Thompson

COMPOSER
Mark Rivett

SOUND DESIGNER
Simon Kane

VISUAL: In a restaurant kitchen, a chef tastes the soup before serving it.

CHEF: Magnifique!

VISUAL: The waiter sets the soup on the table of a female customer. She tastes the soup.

CUSTOMER: The soup is too salty.

VISUAL: The chef hears her, storms out of the kitchen and confronts the diner.

CHEF: It is not too salty!

VISUAL: The chef motions to his kitchen staff to attack the customer. A classic martial-arts-style battle takes place during which the restaurant gets destroyed.

SUPER: Dining out?

WAITER: No charge for the soup.

VISUAL: Waiter unfolds a restaurant bill that is 20 feet long.

WAITER: But this is for the extras.

VISUAL: The woman flings her Visa Gold card into a silver tray.

VISUAL: Visa card.

SUPER: All It Takes.

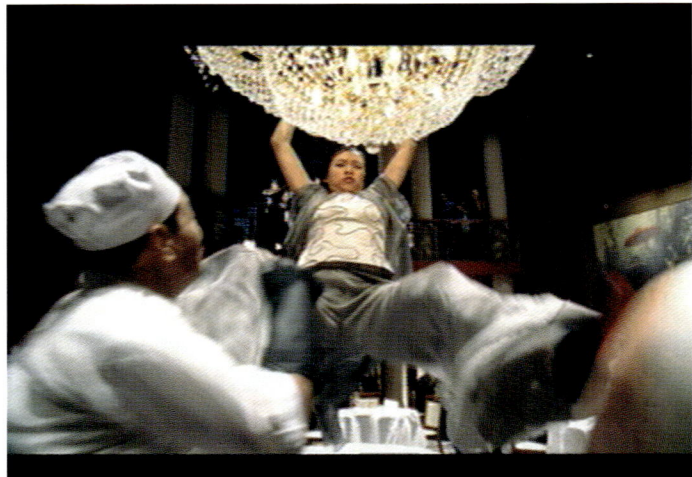

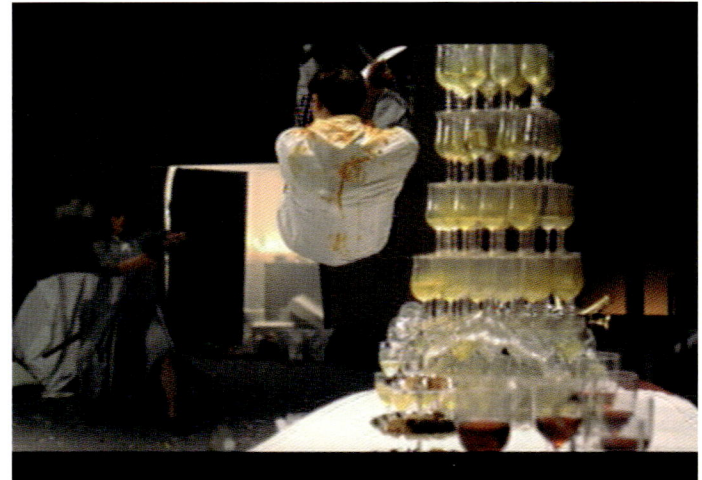

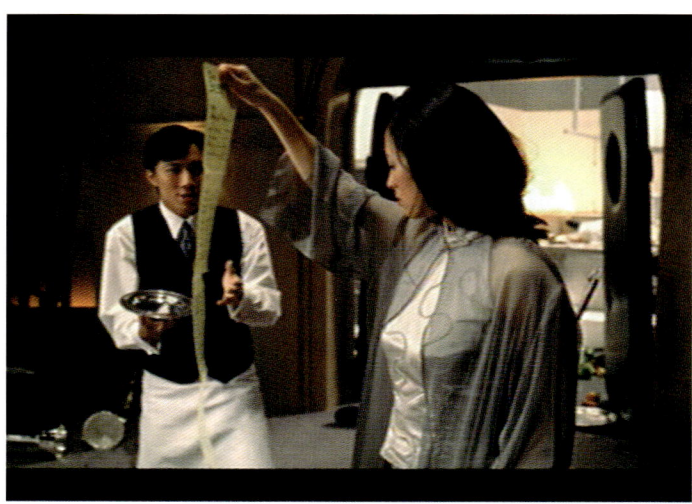

CATEGORY
Music—Original

ADVERTISER/PRODUCT
Smart/Micro Compact Car

TITLE
Show Cars

ADVERTISING AGENCY
Springer & Jacoby, Hamburg

PRODUCTION COMPANY
Lichtspielhaus, München

ANIMATION COMPANY
Chris Faber, ARRI

ACCOUNT EXECUTIVE
Tanja Achenbach

CREATIVE DIRECTOR
Amir Kassaei, Florian Grimm,
Antje Hedde

COPYWRITER
Daniel Grether

ART DIRECTOR
Frank Aldorf

PRODUCER
Tobias Bösing

DIRECTOR
Andreas Link

COMPOSER/SOUND DESIGNER
Volker Kretschmer

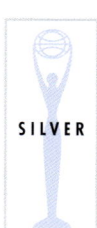

SILVER

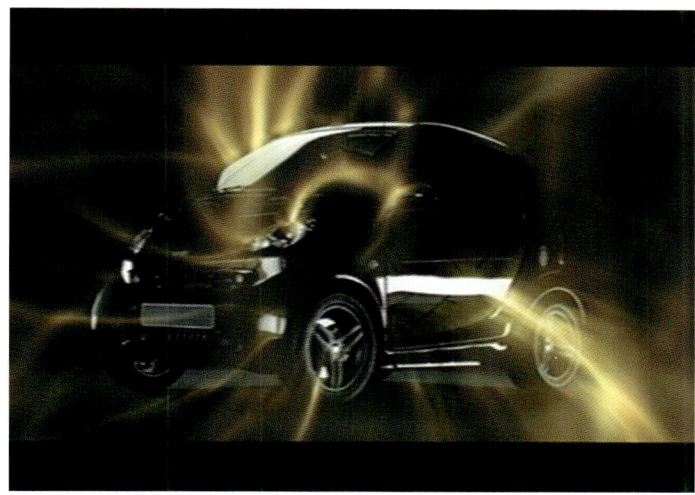

SYNOPSIS: Four different Smart cars are introduced using innovative graphics and a different piece of original music for each car.

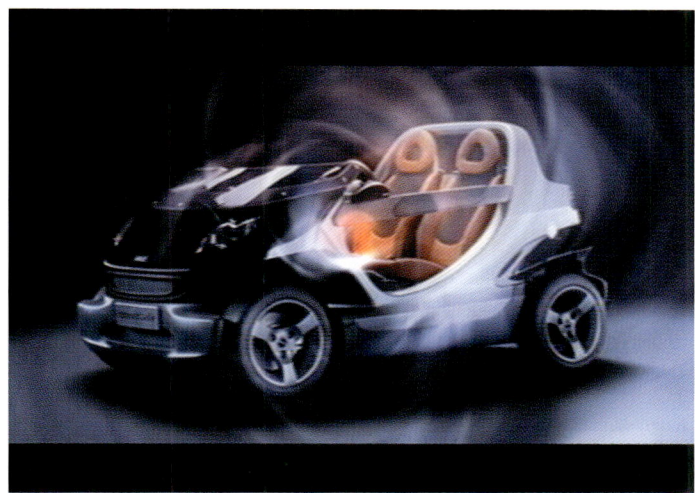

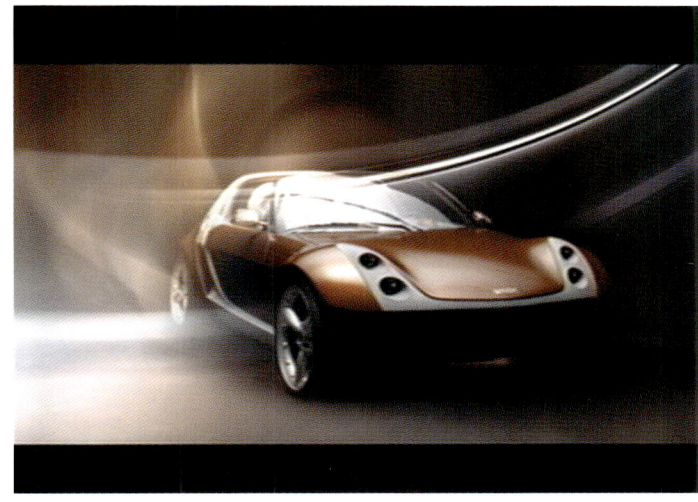

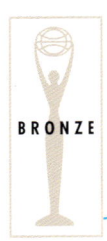

BRONZE

CATEGORY
Music—Original

ADVERTISER/PRODUCT
Smart/Micro Compact Car

TITLE
Ambience

ADVERTISING AGENCY
Springer & Jacoby, Hamburg

PRODUCTION COMPANY
Lichtspielhaus, München

ANIMATION COMPANY
Chris Faber, ARRI

ACCOUNT EXECUTIVE
Tanja Achenbach

CREATIVE DIRECTOR
Amir Kassaei, Florian Grimm,
Antje Hedde

COPYWRITER
Daniel Grether

ART DIRECTOR
Frank Aldorf

PRODUCER
Tobias Bösing

DIRECTOR
Andreas Link

COMPOSER/SOUND DESIGNER
Volker Kretschmer

SYNOPSIS: Using music and visual elements, Smart questions various conventions of automobile design and manufacturing.

FRAME ONE: How environmentally friendly should your car be?

FRAME TWO: How safe should your car be?

FRAME THREE: How intelligent should your car be?

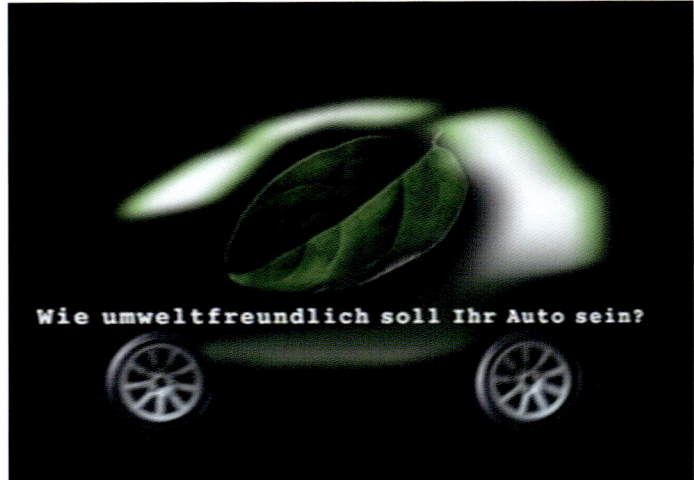

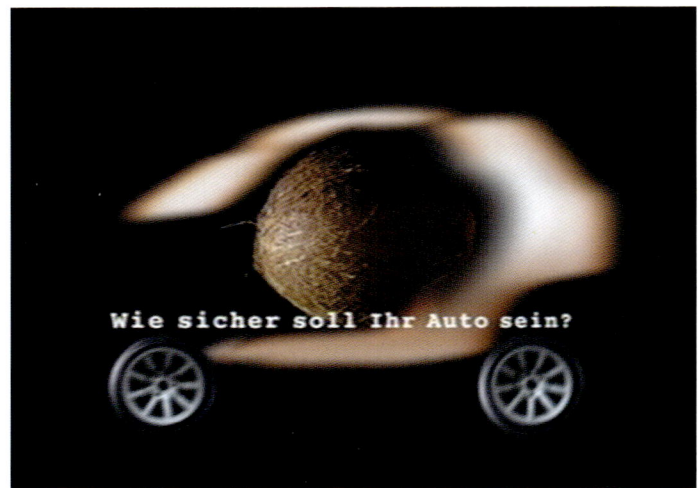

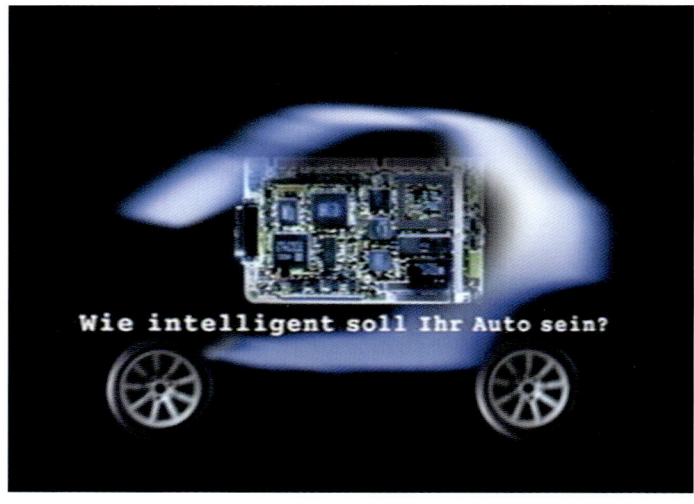

CATEGORY
Music—Original

ADVERTISER/PRODUCT
Jaguar

TITLE
Brag

ADVERTISING AGENCY
Young & Rubicam, New York

PRODUCTION COMPANY
Anonymous Content, Culver City

EDITING COMPANY
V2, New York

MUSIC COMPANY
Sacred Noise, New York

SOUND DESIGN COMPANY
Sacred Noise, New York

EXECUTIVE CREATIVE DIRECTOR
Ross Sutherland

COPYWRITER
Jill Applebaum

ART DIRECTOR
Marwan Khuri

EXECUTIVE PRODUCER (Y&R)
Robin Dobson

EXECUTIVE MUSIC PRODUCER (Y&R)
Peter Greco

ASSISTANT PRODUCER (Y&R)
Jeremy Fox

DIRECTOR OF BROADCAST PRODUCTION (Y&R)
Ken Yagoda

EXECUTIVE PRODUCER (ANONYMOUS CONTENT)
Andy Traines, Matthew Jones

LINE PRODUCER (ANONYMOUS CONTENT)
Rob McKinney

EXECUTIVE PRODUCER (SACRED NOISE)
Jeff Rosner

PRODUCER (SACRED NOISE)
Marit Burch

DIRECTOR
Andrew Douglas

EDITOR
Lin Polito

COMPOSER
Michael Montes

SOUND DESIGNER
Michael Montes

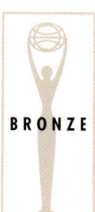

BRONZE

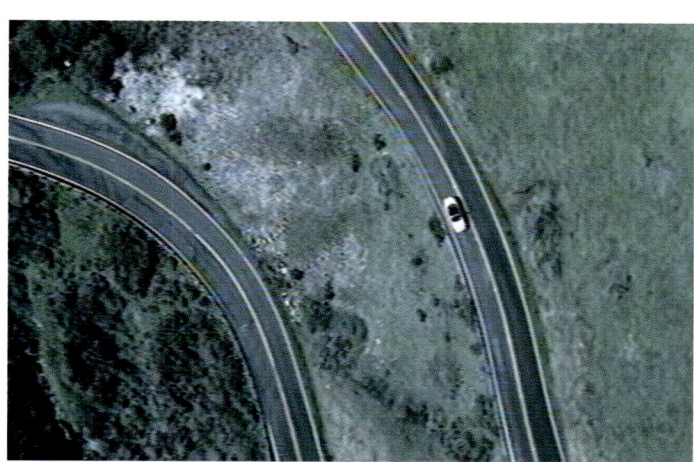

VISUAL: Various shots of a Jaguar driving down a winding road.

SUPER: For those who hate to brag.

SUPER: A car that does the dirty work for you.

VISUAL: Jaguar logo.

SUPER: Jaguar. The art of performance.

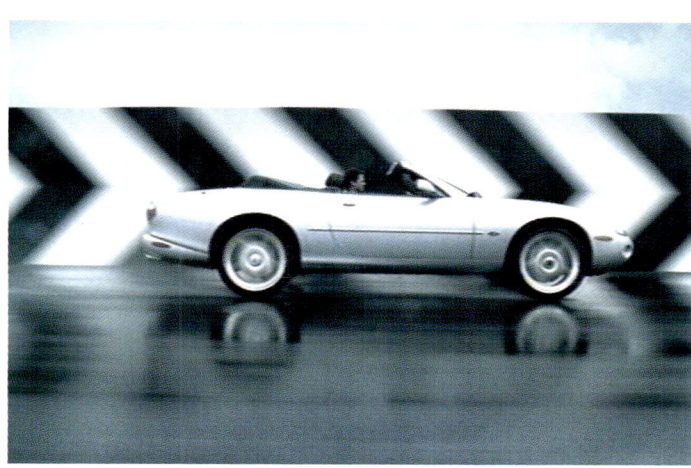

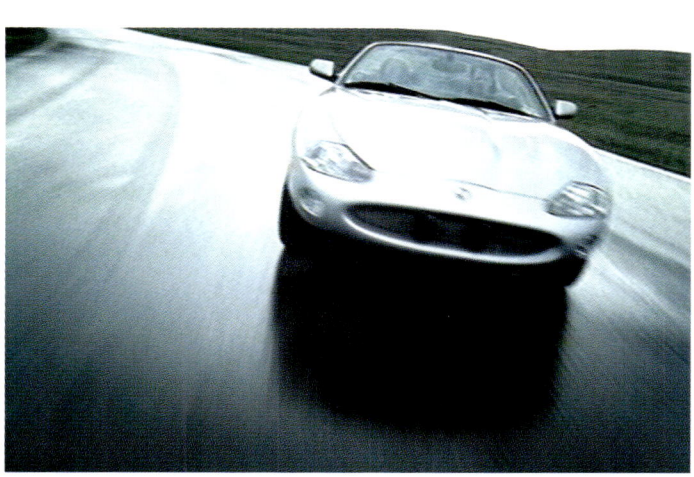

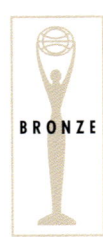

CATEGORY
Music—Original

ADVERTISER/PRODUCT
Audi

TITLE
Gasoline

ADVERTISING AGENCY
McKinney Silver, Raleigh

EDITING COMPANY
MacKenzie Cutler, New York

MUSIC COMPANY
Elias Arts, New York

ACCOUNT EXECUTIVE
Rod Brown

CREATIVE DIRECTOR
David Baldwin

COPYWRITER
Jon Wagner

ART DIRECTOR
Gerardo Blumenkrantz

PRODUCER
Cathy Jenkins

EDITOR
Gavin Cutler

MUSIC COMPOSER
Todd Schietroma

MUSIC CREATIVE DIRECTOR
Alex Lasarenko

COMPOSER
Andy Solomon

VISUAL: Various shots of an Audi A4 driving through the countryside. The supers are interspersed throughout the commercial.

SUPER 1: Is it possible

SUPER 2: that gasoline

SUPER 3: is an aphrodisiac?

SUPER 4: Form. Performance.

SUPER 5: Audi logo. The A4.

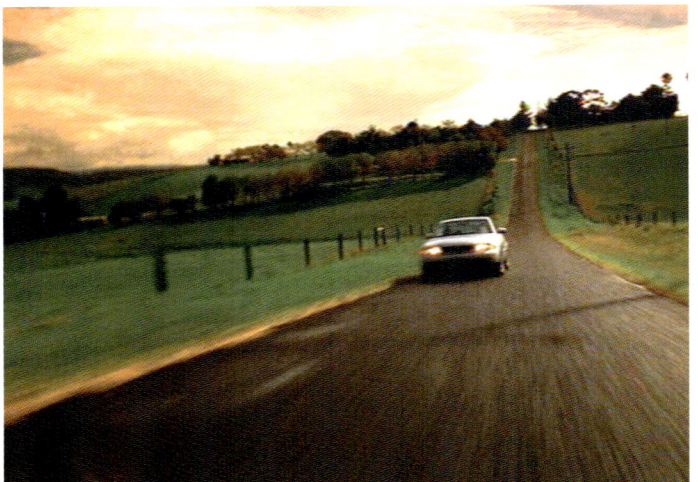

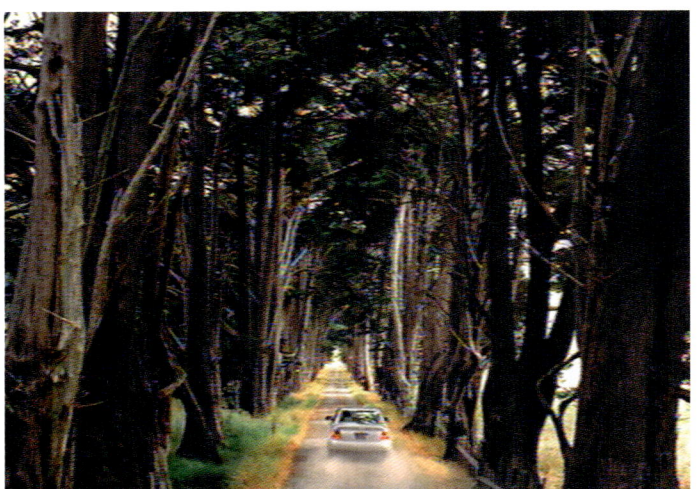

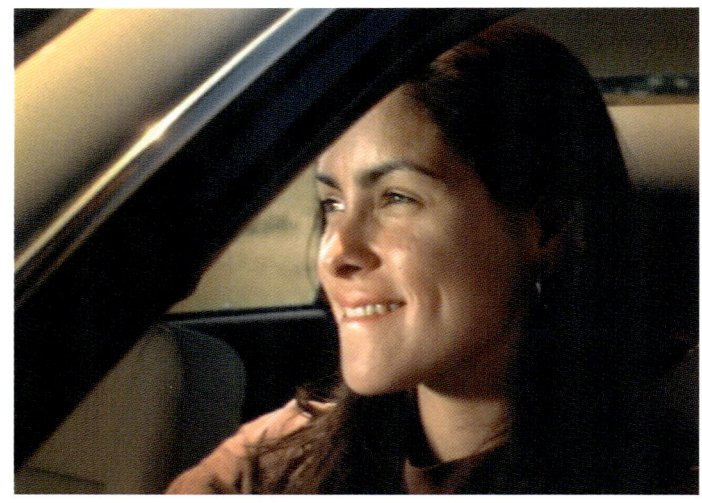

CATEGORY
Music—Original

ADVERTISER/PRODUCT
Nike—Sponsorship of the Amakhosi

TITLE
Kid

ADVERTISING AGENCY
The Jupiter Drawing Room
(South Africa)

PRODUCTION COMPANY
Velocity, Johannesburg

EDITING COMPANY
City Cuts, Johannesburg

MUSIC COMPANY
MCM Productions, Johannesburg

SOUND DESIGN COMPANY
Nicky Campass, Johannesburg

ACCOUNT EXECUTIVE
Chiquita King

CREATIVE DIRECTOR
Graham Warsop

COPYWRITER
Gavin Williams

ART DIRECTOR
Michael Bond

PRODUCER
Hazel Neuhaus

DIRECTOR
Keith Rose

COMPOSER
Nicky Campos

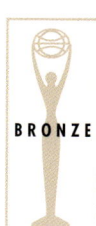

BRONZE

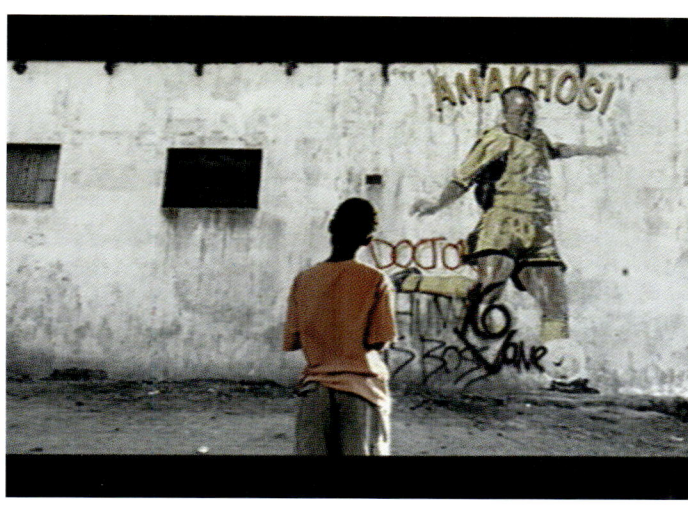

SYNOPSIS: A kid carrying a soccer ball walks through an African city and the lyrics of the commercial raplike song comment on what he sees: Kids playing, a mother and child, a group of protesters and street violence. Eventually, he comes upon the wall of a building on which a footballer and the word *Amakhosi*, the name of a popular national soccer team, are painted. The kid walks into a large room that is filled with people watching Amakhosi on television and cheering wildly.

SUPER: Nike logo. Amakhosi.

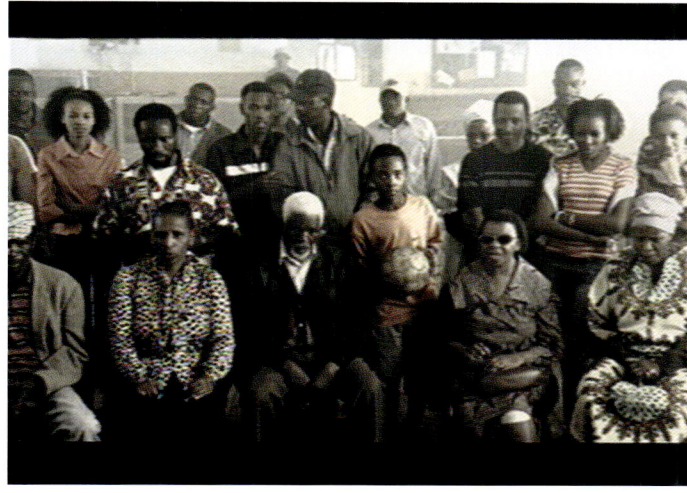

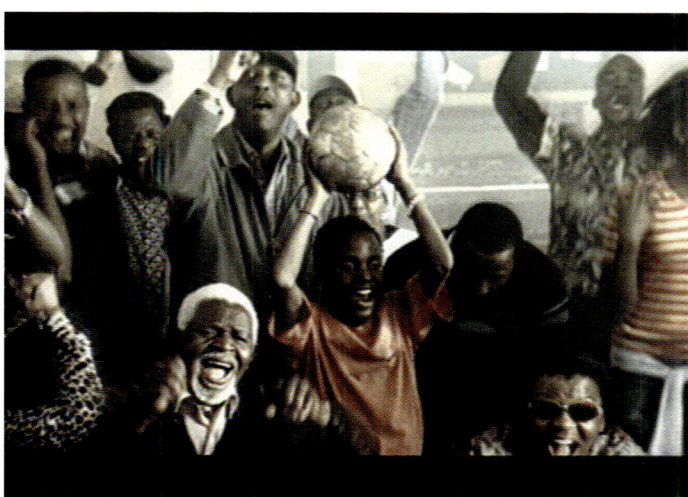

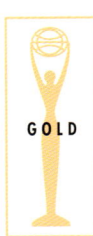

CATEGORY
Sound Design

ADVERTISER/PRODUCT
BMW of North America

TITLE
Ambush

ADVERTISING AGENCY
Fallon, Minneapolis

PRODUCTION COMPANY
Anonymous Content, Culver City

EDITING COMPANY
Spot Welders, Los Angeles

SOUND DESIGN COMPANY
Mit Out Sound, Sausalito

ACCOUNT EXECUTIVE
Ginny Grossman

CREATIVE DIRECTOR
David Lubars, Bruce Bildsten

COPYWRITER
Andrew Kevin Walker, Joe Sweet

ART DIRECTOR
David Carter

PRODUCER
Robyn Boardman, Aristides McGarry

DIRECTOR
John Frankenheimer

SOUND DESIGN
Ren Klyce

VISUAL: A BMW 740i and a van are driving down a highway at night. The van swerves near the car, the van's door slides open and a number of masked men with guns shine a flashlight into the BMW's window. Inside the car are a driver and a passenger in the rear seat.

DRIVER: Who are they?

PASSENGER: I don't know. What is he doing?

VISUAL: The gunman signals the BMW driver to turn on his radio. The driver complies. The gunman puts a walkie-talkie to his mouth and begins to speak. There is a close-up of the BMW's radio, out of which comes the gunman's voice.

MASKED GUNMAN: Listen carefully. This is going to happen very quickly. If you deviate from my instructions, we will open fire. Your passenger is carrying 2 million dollars in stolen uncut diamonds.

VISUAL: The BMW and van continue driving down the highway together.

DRIVER: True?

MASKED GUNMAN: Go ahead, ask him.

PASSENGER: The deal was, "no questions asked."

MASKED GUNMAN: Now, I will count backwards from ten, and then you will slow your vehicle.

DRIVER: Is it true?

MASKED GUNMAN: And we will escort you to the side of the road.

PASSENGER: Don't do it! Don't, please!

MASKED GUNMAN: Nod your head if you understand me.

DRIVER: I'm not getting killed for your merchandise.

PASSENGER: Listen to me!

DRIVER: We're going to give them what they want.

MASKED GUNMAN: Ten.

PASSENGER: You don't go through customs with 2 million in diamonds.

MASKED GUNMAN: Nine.

PASSENGER: In your suitcase!

MASKED GUNMAN: Eight.

PASSENGER: I swallowed them.

MASKED GUNMAN: Seven.

PASSENGER: The diamonds are inside of me.

MASKED GUNMAN: Six.

PASSENGER: They will cut me wide open!

MASKED GUNMAN: Five.

PASSENGER: Please.

MASKED GUNMAN: Four.

PASSENGER: Don't stop.

MASKED GUNMAN: Three.

PASSENGER: If you stop, you might as well kill me yourself!

MASKED GUNMAN: Two…one.

PASSENGER: Please.

MASKED GUNMAN: Slow down.

PASSENGER: No no no no no no no no no.

MASKED GUNMAN: Slow down now.

DRIVER: Buckle up.

VISUAL: The driver slams his foot down on the gas pedal and the BMW takes off with the van in pursuit. A wild chase begins with gunmen constantly shooting at the BMW, and both vehicles having to avoid hitting other cars on the highway. The BMW swerves and just misses hitting a semi truck.

PASSENGER: Ahh!

DRIVER: Are you still alive?

PASSENGER: Yeah.

VISUAL: The BMW crashes through wooden barriers and onto a road construction site. The van follows.

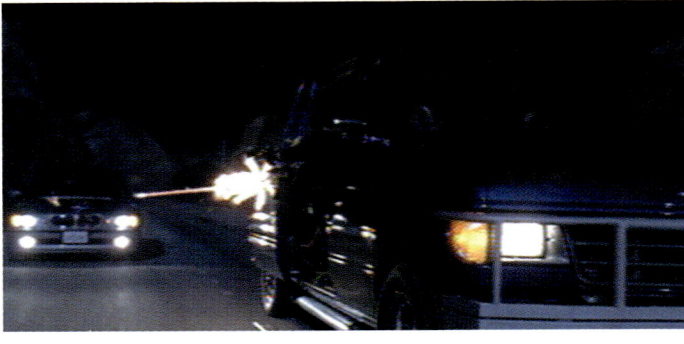

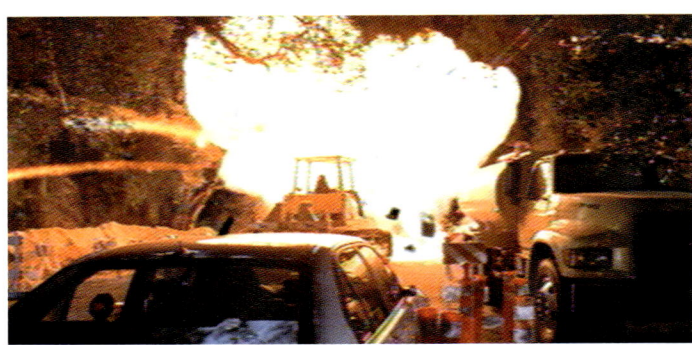

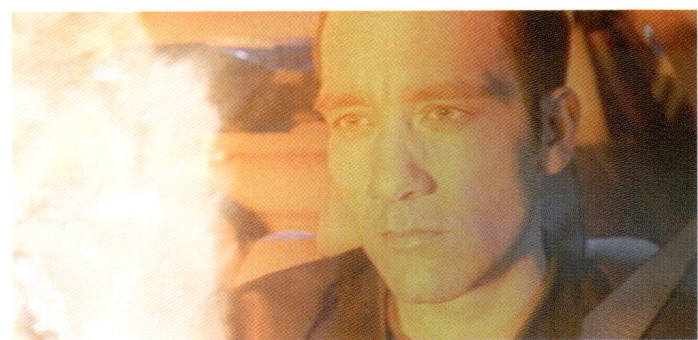

ROAD WORKER: What, are you crazy? What are you doing?

VISUAL: The BMW continues driving through the construction sight with the van in pursuit. The car's driver loses the van, pulls over behind a large dump truck, stops the car, and turns off the engine and headlights.

PASSENGER: Ah! What are you doing?

DRIVER: Shh.

VISUAL: The van full of gunmen heads toward the BMW. They are driving with their head-lights off and do not see the many construction vehicles ahead. They crash into a front-loader and the van explodes. The driver and passenger react and then drive on.

PASSENGER: Oh my God. Oh my God.

DRIVER: We'll call in to Highway Patrol from the next town…it's more than they would've done for us.

VISUAL: It is the next morning. The BMW pulls up to the curb of a busy urban street and stops. The passenger gets out of the car and goes around to the driver's window,

PASSENGER: Thank you.

DRIVER: Tell me…what you said about having swallowed the diamonds. Was it true?

VISUAL: The passenger laughs and walks off. The BMW pulls away and drives off.

CATEGORY
Sound Design

ADVERTISER/PRODUCT
Pepsi

TITLE
Foosball

ADVERTISING AGENCY
BBDO, New York

PRODUCTION COMPANY
@radical.media, Santa Monica

EDITING COMPANY
The Whitehouse, Los Angeles

SOUND DESIGN COMPANY
Elias Arts, New York; M62, London

AGENCY PRODUCER
Brian Mitchell

AGENCY MUSIC PRODUCER
Loren Parkins

ACCOUNT EXECUTIVE
Sandy Goebel, Larent Garnier

WORLDWIDE CREATIVE DIRECTOR
Phil Dusenberry

GROUP CREATIVE DIRECTOR
Jordan Allen, Sue Levine

MUSIC CREATIVE DIRECTOR
Alex Lasarenko

ART DIRECTOR
Sue Levine

COPYWRITER
Jordan Allen

SOUND DESIGN PRODUCER
Keith Haluska

DIRECTOR
Tarsem

SOUND DESIGNER
Kerry Smith, Michael Cook

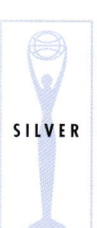

SILVER

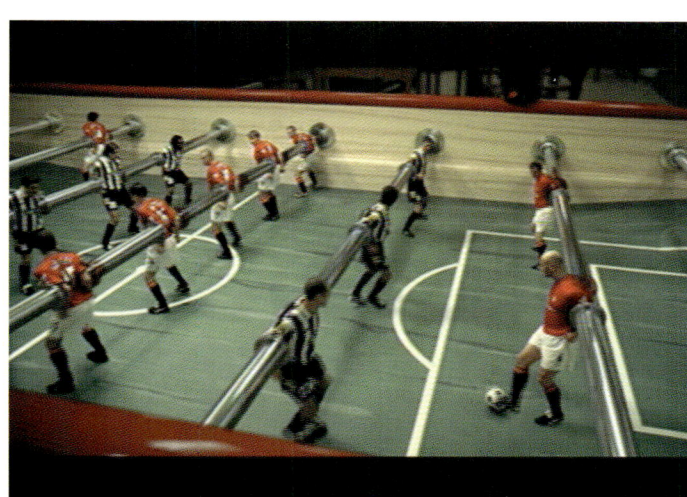

SYNOPSIS: In an empty home-recreation room, there is a foosball table whose inanimate players, one team representing Manchester United and the other, Juventus, suddenly come alive and play an intense game of football. There is a Pepsi bottle sitting on the edge of the table.

DAVID BECKHAM (Manchester United): You thinkin' what I'm thinkin'?

EDGAR DAVIDS (Juventus): Winner takes the Pepsi?

DAVID BECKHAM: Sure.

VISUAL: The game begins. Yorke (Manchester United) ricochets the ball off the Pepsi bottle and into the Pepsi net.

YORKE: Sco-o-o-re!

JUVENTUS PLAYERS: You cheated.

VISUAL: Two boys enter a now quiet rec room.

BOY 1: There it is.

VISUAL: The boy grabs the Pepsi and takes a drink. They start to leave the room.

ROY KEANE (Manchester United): Hey! Get back here! We won that!

BOY 2: Did you hear something?

FOOTBALLER VO: Hey mate! That's our Pepsi!

BOY 1: No.

VISUAL: The two boys leave the room.

FOOTBALLERS (grumbling): Big idiots.

SUPER: Pepsi logo.

Ask for More.

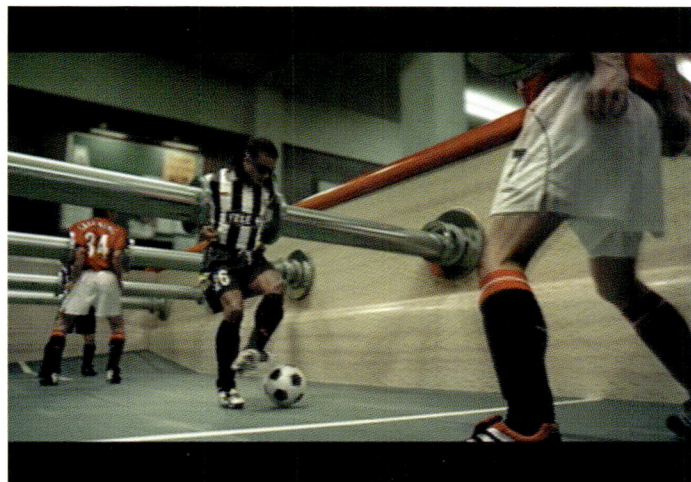

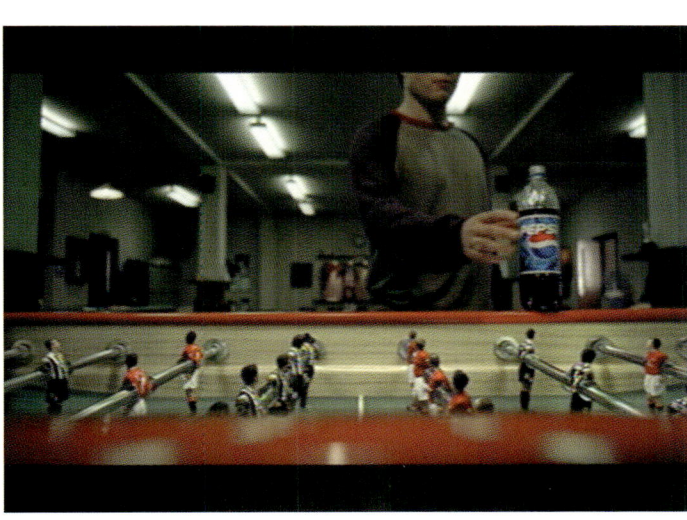

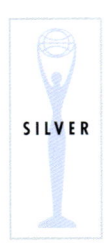

CATEGORY Sound Design	**EDITING COMPANY** Guillotine P/L, Sydney	**ART DIRECTOR** David Guerrero	**EDITOR** Drew Thompson
ADVERTISER/PRODUCT Visa	**MUSIC COMPANY** Song Zu, Sydney	**COPYWRITER** David Guerrero	**COMPOSER** Mark Rivett
TITLE Dining Out	**SOUND DESIGN COMPANY** Song Zu, Sydney	**EXECUTIVE PRODUCER** Gerry Gentemann	**SOUND DESIGNER** Simon Kane
ADVERTISING AGENCY BBDO/Guerrero Ortega, Manila	**ANIMATION COMPANY** Fin Design, Sydney	**PRODUCER** Bruce Davidson, Julianne Shelton	
PRODUCTION COMPANY @radical.media, Sydney	**CREATIVE DIRECTOR** David Guerrero	**DIRECTOR** Bruce Hunt	

VISUAL: In a restaurant kitchen, a chef tastes the soup before serving it.

CHEF: Magnifique!

VISUAL: The waiter sets the soup on the table of a female customer. She tastes the soup.

CUSTOMER: The soup is too salty.

VISUAL: The chef hears her, storms out of the kitchen and confronts the diner.

CHEF: It is not too salty!

VISUAL: The chef motions to his kitchen staff to attack the customer. A classic martial-arts-style battle takes place during which the restaurant gets destroyed.

SUPER: Dining out?

WAITER: No charge for the soup.

VISUAL: Waiter unfolds a restaurant bill that is 20 feet long.

WAITER: But this is for the extras.

VISUAL: The woman flings her Visa Gold card into a silver tray.

VISUAL: Visa card.

SUPER: All It Takes.

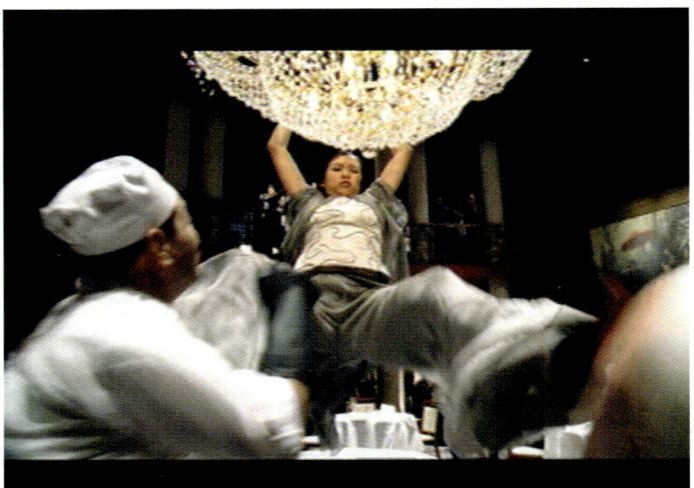

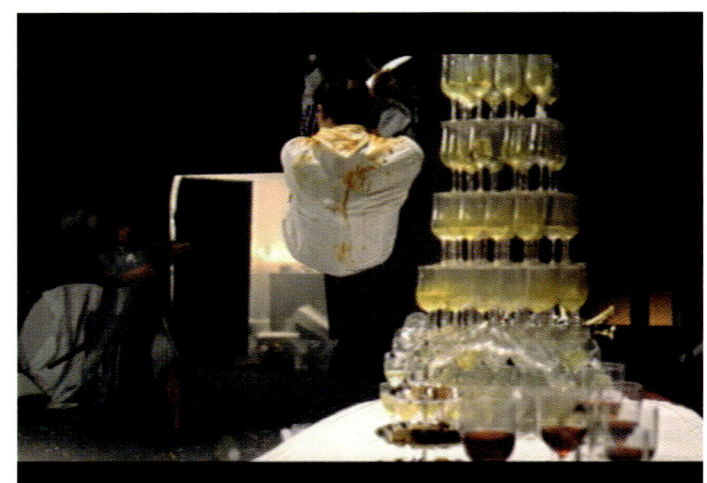

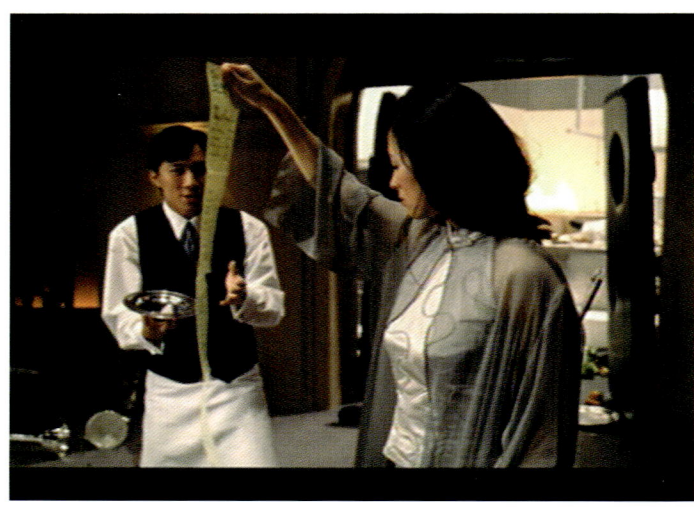

CATEGORY
Sound Design

ADVERTISER/PRODUCT
BMW of North America

TITLE
Powder Keg

ADVERTISING AGENCY
Fallon, Minneapolis

PRODUCTION COMPANY
Anonymous Content, Culver City

EDITING COMPANY
Z Films, Mexico City

MUSIC COMPANY
Universal Music Mexico,
Mexico City

SOUND DESIGN COMPANY
Z Films, Mexico City

ACCOUNT EXECUTIVE
Ginny Grossman

CREATIVE DIRECTOR
David Lubars, Bruce Bildsten

COPYWRITER
Alejandro Gonzalez Iñarritu,
David Carter, Guillermo Arriaga

ART DIRECTOR
Joe Sweet

PRODUCER
Robyn Boardman, Tapas Blank

DIRECTOR
Alejandro Gonzalez Iñarritu

DIRECTOR OF PHOTOGRAPHY
Bob Richardson

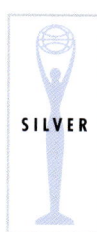

SILVER

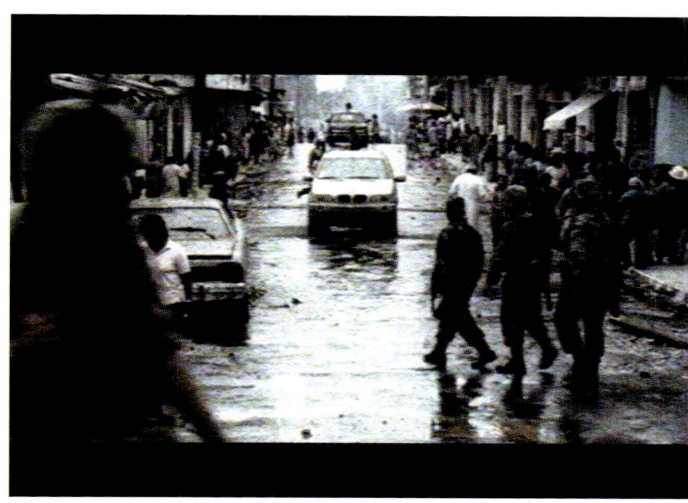

SYNOPSIS: Soldiers, fingers on triggers, patrol a coup-ravaged city in South America. Their mission: find a photojournalist who has taken a picture certain to enrage the world against their leader. The Driver must get the photojournalist and his film beyond the fiercely guarded border.

See page 86 for full script.

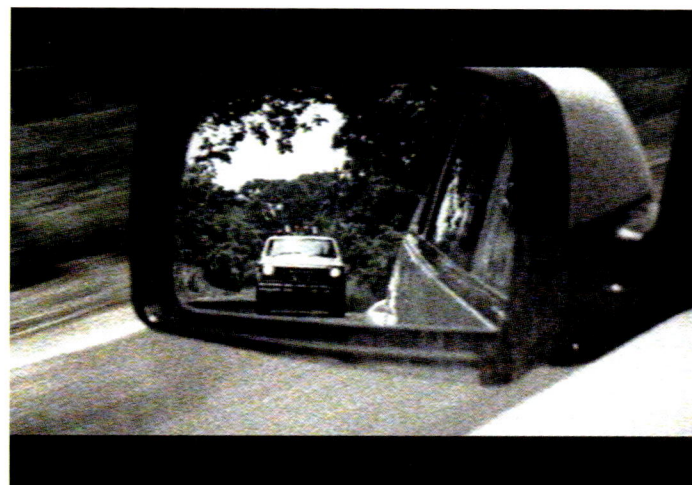

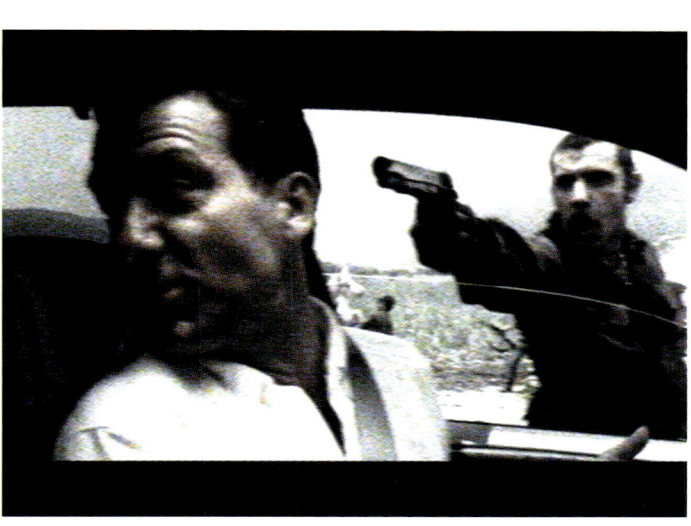

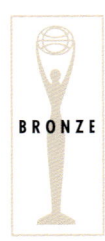

CATEGORY
Sound Design

ADVERTISER/PRODUCT
Nike

TITLE
Freestyle

ADVERTISING AGENCY
Wieden & Kennedy, Portland

PRODUCTION COMPANY
HSI Productions, Inc., Culver City

EDITING COMPANY
Rock Paper Scissors, Los Angeles

MUSIC COMPANY
Afrika Bambaataa, New York;
Endless Noise, Los Angeles;
Breakthru Productions, New York

SOUND DESIGN COMPANY
Endless Noise, Los Angeles

ANIMATION COMPANY
A-52, Los Angeles

ACCOUNT EXECUTIVE
Lee Davis

CREATIVE DIRECTOR
Jim Riswold, Hal Curtis

COPYWRITER
Jimmy Smith

ART DIRECTOR
Hal Curtis

PRODUCER
Vic Palumbo

DIRECTOR
Paul Hunter

MUSIC COMPOSER/PRODUCER
Afrika Bambaataa, Jeff Elmassian,
Steven "Boogie" Brown

EDITOR
Adam Pertofsky

SOUND DESIGNER
Jeff Elmassian

SYNOPSIS: Various NBA stars and street basketball players create a music track by dribbling, handling, and passing a basketball. The sound of their athletic shoes squeaking on the wooden floor adds an additional element to the music. The sound fades out and one player performs a slam dunk.

SUPER: Nike logo.

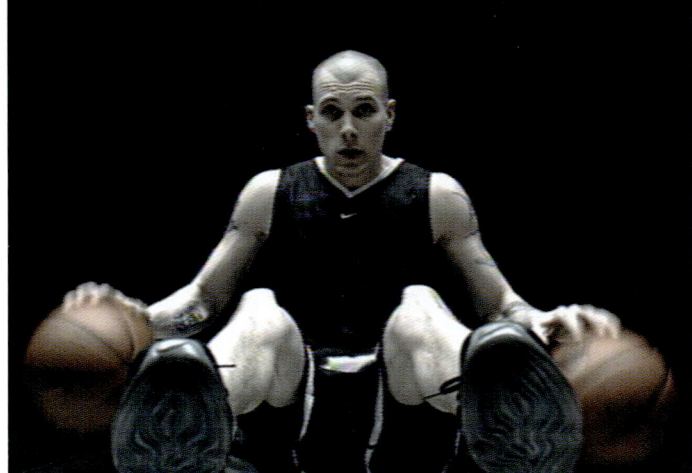

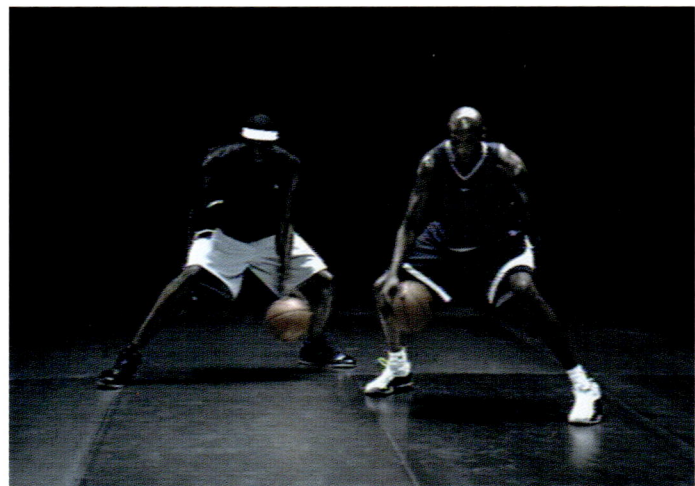

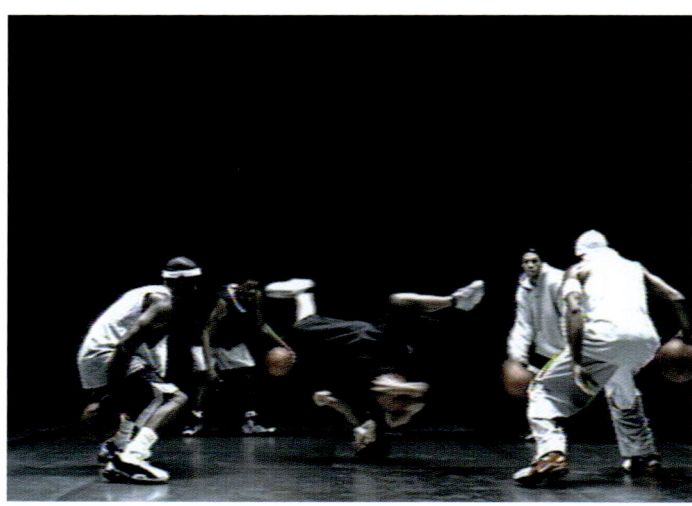

CATEGORY
Sound Design

ADVERTISER/PRODUCT
Land Baden Wuerttemberg

TITLE
Natalie Lumpp

ADVERTISING AGENCY
Scholz & Friends, Berlin

PRODUCTION COMPANY
Glass Films, Berlin

ACCOUNT EXECUTIVE
Stefanie Wurst, Christine Winter

CREATIVE DIRECTOR
Martin Pross

COPYWRITER
Ingo Hoentschke

ART DIRECTOR
Julia Schmidt

PRODUCER
Anke Specht, Claudia Knipping

SOUND DESIGNER
Cristian Aeby

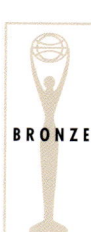

BRONZE

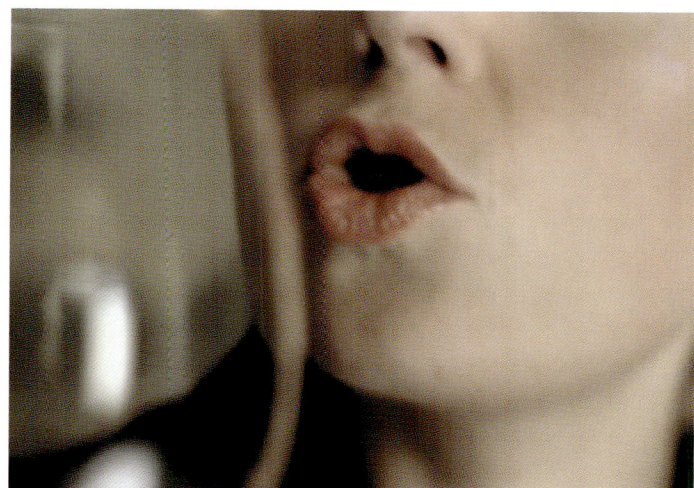

SYNOPSIS: Natalie Lumpp, a German wine connoisseur, is sampling various glasses of wine. The sounds of her tasting—gargling, spitting, gobbling noises—allude to the strange dialect spoken in the region of Baden-Wuerttemberg.

SUPER: Natalie Lumpp. Germany's Leading Wine Expert. Baden-Baden.

SUPER: Baden-Wuerttemberg. The German Southwest.

SUPER: We are perfect. If you ignore our accent.

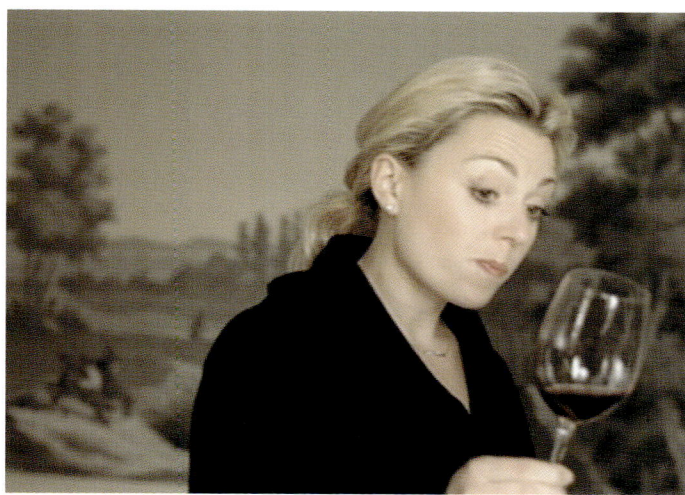

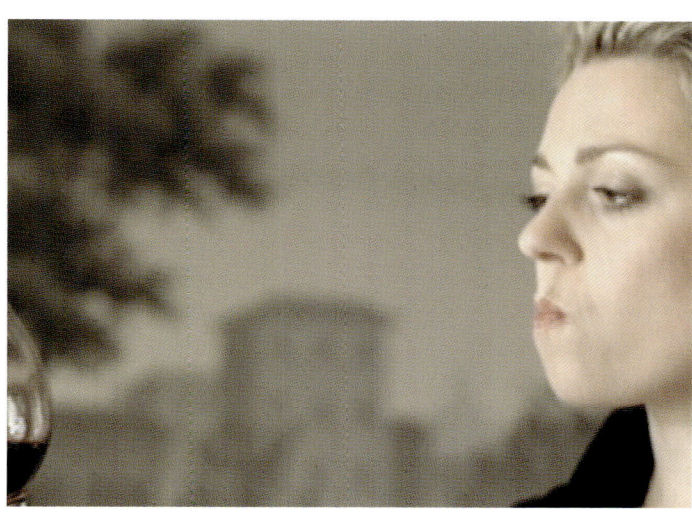

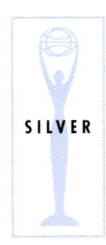

SILVER

CATEGORY
Visual Effects

ADVERTISER/PRODUCT
EDF (French Electricity Board)

TITLE
The Valley

ADVERTISING AGENCY
CLM/BBDO, Paris

PRODUCTION COMPANY
Partizan Midi-Minuit, Paris

MUSIC COMPANY
Barrera Prod, Paris

ANIMATION COMPANY
Buf, Paris

ACCOUNT EXECUTIVE
Edouard Pacreau

CREATIVE DIRECTOR
Bernard Naville, Vincent Behaeghel

COPYWRITER
Bernard Naville

ART DIRECTOR
Vincent Behaeghel

PRODUCER
Georges Bergmann

DIRECTOR
Antoine Bardou-Jacquet

AGENCY PRODUCER
Pierre Marcus

PROJECT MANAGER
Pierre Buffin, Olivier Gilbert

MAT PAINTING
Herve de Crecy, Jean Marie Vives, Stephane Keller

FLAME
Yves

3D
Jam

VISUAL: A charming mountain valley with a river flowing through it. A truck drives through the scene and a house begins to be built. A factory is built, more houses spring up, and the valley is now a village. Many roads begin to cut through the valley, more factories appear, and the village is now a town. Large buildings and highways appear; skyscrapers, houses, roads, bridges, and expressway ramps fill the valley. The area has turned into a large city.

VISUAL: A computer instruction box displays the following message: You failed—Damaged environment—New Game.

VO: Producing more power is a necessity, but so is preserving the environment.

VISUAL: A man is working on a computer. It is now obvious that the burgeoning city that was just built is on a computer monitor and is a game.

VO: Energy to make the world a better place.

SUPER: EDF logo. Energy to make the world a better place.

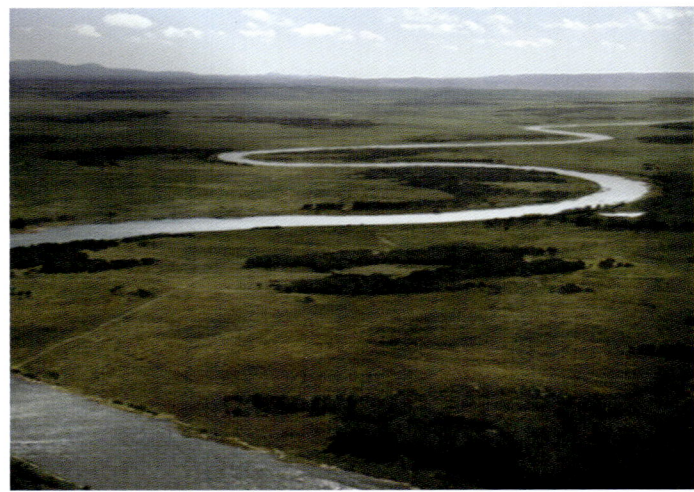

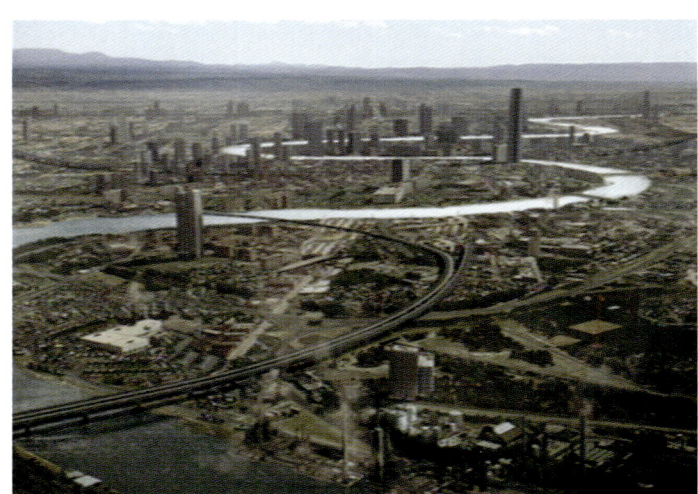

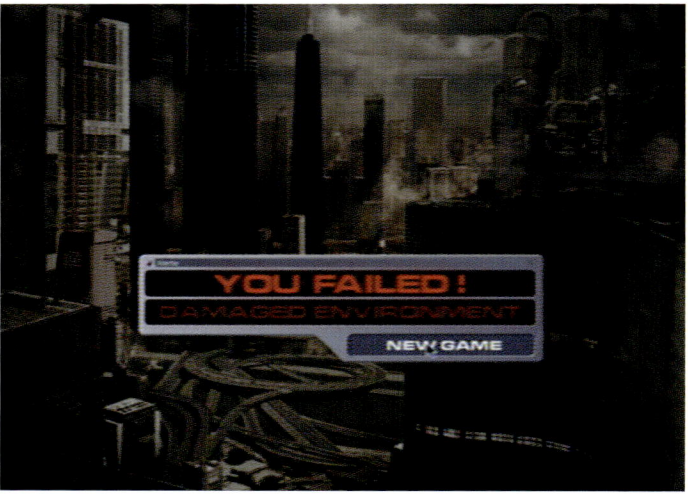

CATEGORY
Visual Effects

ADVERTISER/PRODUCT
Levi's Engineered Jeans

TITLE
Twist

ADVERTISING AGENCY
BBH, London

PRODUCTION COMPANY
Gorgeous Enterprises, London

EDITING COMPANY
The Quarry, London

MUSIC COMPANY
Pepe Duluxe

SOUND DESIGN COMPANY
Sound Tree Music

ANIMATION COMPANY
The Mill, London

AGENCY PRODUCER
Andy Gulliman

CREATIVE DIRECTOR
Russell Ramsay

CREATIVE TEAM
Tony McTeer, Mark Hunter

DIRECTOR
Frank Budgen

PRODUCER
Paul Rothwell

FLAME
Barnsley, Chris Knight, Jason Watts

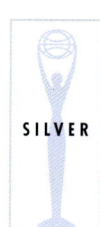

SILVER

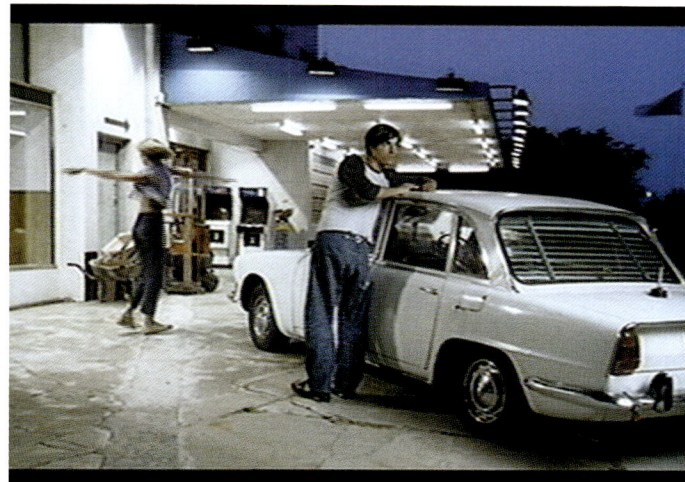

VISUAL: A car, packed with teenagers, stops in front of a restaurant. The passengers begin to stretch their travel-weary limbs. One of the girls stretches her leg, twisting her foot around farther than normal. They all get out of the car and start stretching and dancing around. Some of the kids have the ability to twist their limbs beyond human capacity. This begins a choreographed series of body part twists: fingers, ankles, arms, heads, and the execution of various body spins. One guy attempts to use the men's bathroom and realizes it is locked. A girl emerges from the women's washroom, switches heads with him, and he can now use the women's bathroom. One of the girls' hands is pulled off and tossed from one kid to another like a baseball. As the pace of game increases, many arms and legs are being untwisted from the bodies of their respective owners and tossed around. A young boy joins the fun and is running with his head twisted 180 degrees from normal. Eventually all the kids are back to normal. They climb into the car and drive away. A little dog picks up a stray hand and chases after the car.

SUPER: Levi's Engineered Jeans. Twisted to Fit.

VISUAL: A tiny male figurine, hanging from the car's rear-view mirror, is wearing miniature Levi's Engineered Jeans. We see his limbs twisting around with movement of the car.

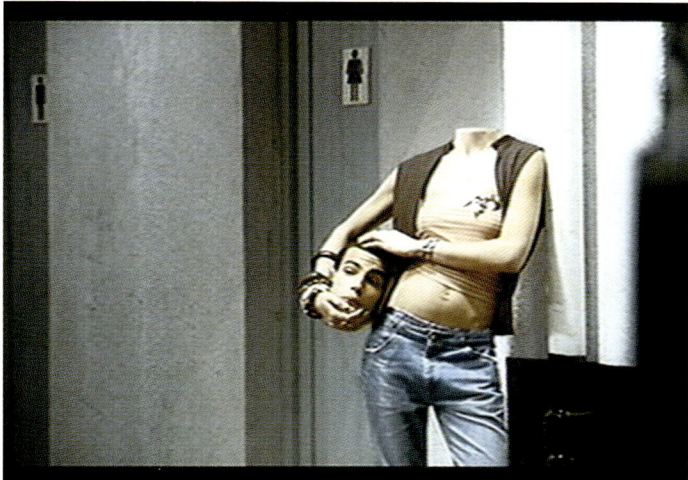

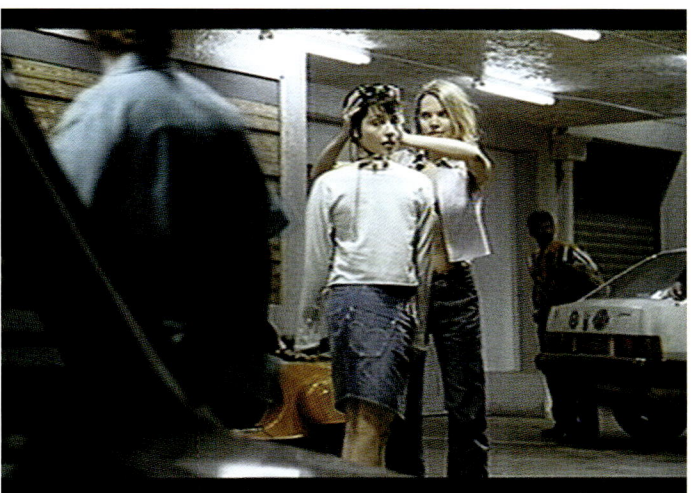

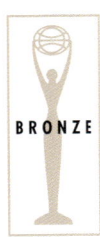

CATEGORY
Visual Effects

ADVERTISER/PRODUCT
Blockbuster

TITLE
Kung Fu

ADVERTISING AGENCY
Doner, Southfield

PRODUCTION COMPANY
Complete Pandemonium,
San Francisco

EDITING COMPANY
Bob 'n Sheila's Edit World,
San Francisco

MUSIC COMPANY
Blue Music and Sound Design,
Hollywood

SOUND DESIGN COMPANY
Soundelux DMG, Hollywood

ANIMATION COMPANY
Tippett Studios, Berkeley

SENIOR AGENCY PRODUCER
Josh Reynolds

CREATIVE DIRECTOR
John DeCerchio, John Parlato,
Don Fibich, Sheldon Cohn

COPYWRITER
Dan Margulis, Brian Hutson,
Mike Ceaser

ART DIRECTOR
Mark Cooke, Tom Gurisko,
Joel Friesch

DIRECTOR
Steve "Spaz" Williams

EXECUTIVE PRODUCER
Clint Goldman

VISUAL EFFECTS SUPERVISOR
Frank Petzold, Scott Souter

VISUAL EFFECTS PRODUCER
Alonzo Ruvalcaba

LEAD CHARACTER ANIMATOR
Todd Labonte, Eric Reynolds

LIGHTING LEAD
Steve Reding

COMPOSITING LEAD
Jim McVay

**VISUAL EFFECTS
EXECUTIVE PRODUCER**
Jules Roman·

VISUAL: Ray and Carl are in a pet shop window looking across the street into the window of a Blockbuster store. The store has a large poster ad on display that says: "Hot New Releases Guaranteed In Stock."

CARL: Ray, check this out. New releases guaranteed in stock.

RAY: That means they'll have my favorite kind of movie, Kung Fu.

VISUAL: Ray starts to do overdramatic Kung Fu moves. He grabs a carrot and, using it like a nunchaku, hits Carl.

CARL: Did you just whack me with a carrot?

VISUAL: Carl rolls his eyes, raises his paw, and snaps.

SFX: Finger snap.

VISUAL: A gang of ninja mice tumbles out of the shadows and surround Carl.

VISUAL: Ray, looking concerned, reacts to the group of ninja mice.

RAY: Ninja mice?

VISUAL: Exterior of Blockbuster store.

VO: At Blockbuster, the hottest new releases are guaranteed on DVD. So you'll always find your favorite movies.

VISUAL: Ray fighting with the ninja mice.

RAY: Off me, off me, you little varmints!

VISUAL: Glowing Blockbuster ticket

SUPER: Make It a Blockbuster Night.

VO: Make it a Blockbuster night.

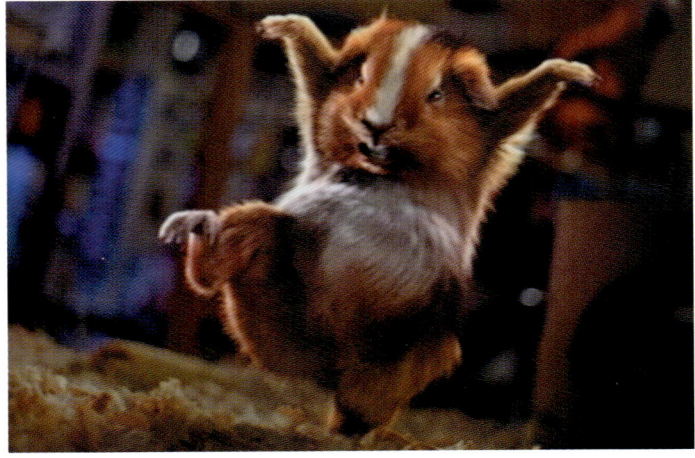

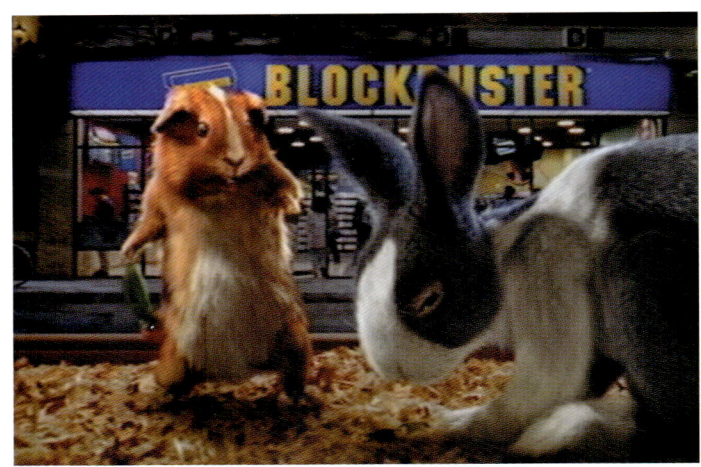

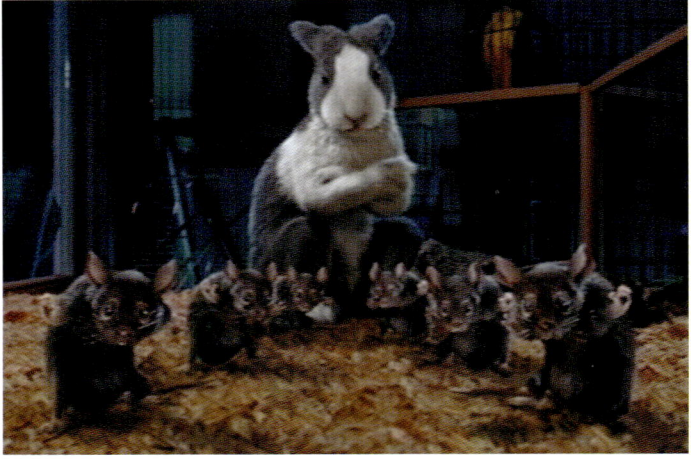

CATEGORY
Visual Effects

ADVERTISER/PRODUCT
Pocari Sweat

TITLE
Tennis

ADVERTISING AGENCY
Asatsu-DK Inc./Makes, Tokyo

PRODUCTION COMPANY
Level 7 Productions, Hollywood

EDITING COMPANY
Chrome, Santa Monica

MUSIC COMPANY
Face The Music, Venice & New York

SOUND DESIGN COMPANY
Ear to Ear, Santa Monica

ANIMATION COMPANY
Digital Domain, Venice

EXECUTIVE AGENCY PRODUCER
Hisashi Nakano

AGENCY PRODUCER
Saburo Masuda

ACCOUNT EXECUTIVE
Hisashi Nakano

CREATIVE DIRECTOR
Joel Peissig, Shinichiro Nakaso

COPYWRITER
Michael Folino, Michael Horsham

DIRECTOR
Joel Peissig

EXECUTIVE PRODUCER
Larry Serraino, Chris van Howten

PRODUCER
Joel Peissig

EDITOR
Lance Pereira

CINEMATOGRAPHER
Claudio Miranda

CAMERA OPERATOR
Pete Romano

VISUAL EFFECTS PRODUCER
Stephanie Gilgar

VISUAL EFFECTS SUPERVISOR
Leslie Ekker

VISUAL EFFECTS COORDINATOR
Cyndi Ochs

COMPOSITOR
Mark Larranaga, Christine Lo,
Darren Poe

TECHNICAL DIRECTOR
Jonah Hall

FX ANIMATOR SUPERVISOR
Nikos Kalaitzidis

FX ANIMATOR—HOUDINI
Archil Gogoladze

DATA INTEGRATION
Tim Conway (Lead), Nancy Adams,
Jason Doss, David Niednagel,
Chris Simmons

MODELER—MAYA
Vernon Wilbert

ROTOSCOPE
Lou Pecora, Byron Werner

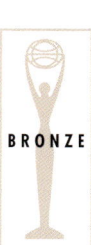

BRONZE

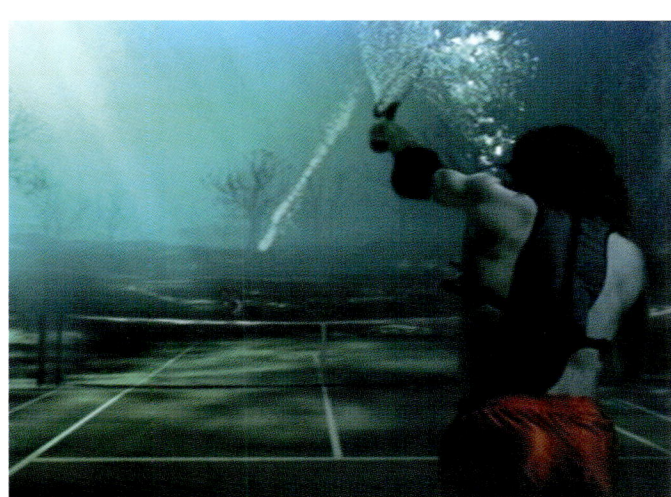
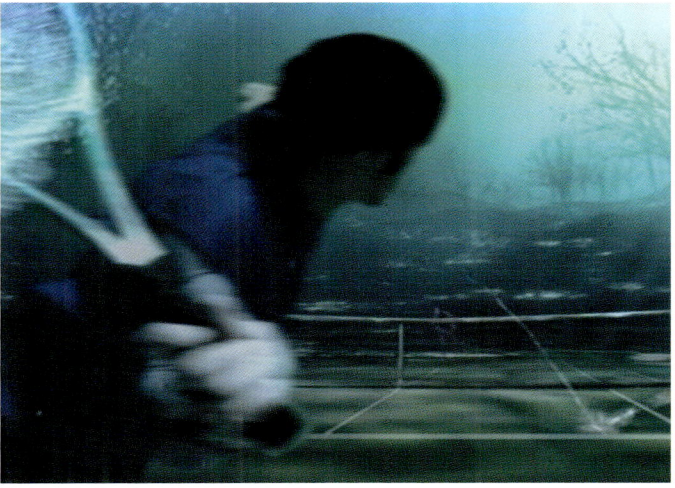

VISUAL: Two players engage in a very competitive game of tennis that is being played underwater.

SUPER: Pocari Sweat. Part of You.

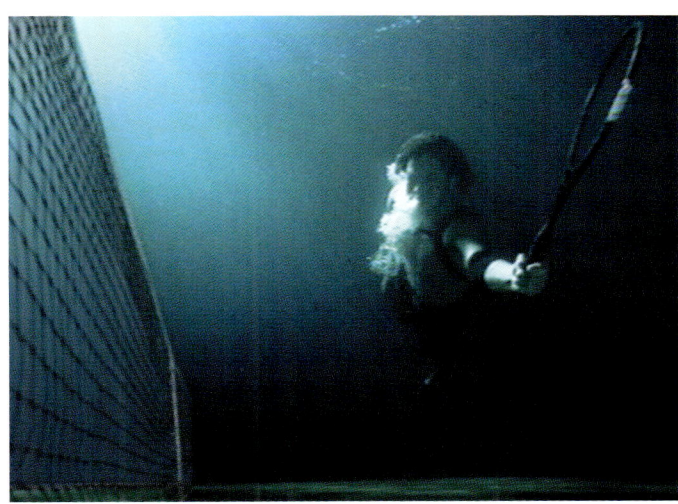

RADIO

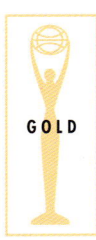

CATEGORY
Beverages/Alcoholic

ADVERTISER/PRODUCT
Anheuser-Busch Inc./Bud Light

TITLE
Mr. Supermarket Free Sample Guy

ADVERTISING AGENCY
DDB, Chicago

PRODUCTION COMPANY
Chicago Recording Company,
Chicago

MUSIC COMPANY
Scandal Music, Chicago

GROUP CREATIVE DIRECTOR
John Immesoete

CREATIVE DIRECTOR
Bill Cimino, Mark Gross

COPYWRITER
John Immesoete

ADDITIONAL WRITING
Bill Cimino, Mark Gross,
Barry Burdiak, Bob Winter,
Pat Burke, Kitty Schulz

PRODUCER
Sam Pillsbury

VO: Bud Light Presents…Real men of genius.

SINGER: *Real men of genius*

VO: Today we salute you…Mr. Supermarket Free Sample Guy.

SINGER: *Mr. Supermarket Free Sample Guy!*

VO: Though man dreads few things more than a trip to the supermarket, you offer us hope and sometimes a free mini-weenie.

SINGER: *Love that freebie weenie!*

VO: What exactly do you have? Aerosol cheese products, deep-fried morsels? Who cares? If it's on a toothpick and it's free, it could be plutonium and we'd eat it!

SINGER: *It's all good, baby!*

VO: For a guy wearing oven mitts and an apron, you're alright.

SINGER: *You're a star.*

VO: So crack open an ice-cold Bud Light, titan of the toothpick.

SFX: Bottle cap opening

VO: Because you put the free in freedom.

SINGER: *Let it be free…*

VO: Bud Light beer. Anheuser-Busch. St. Louis Missouri.

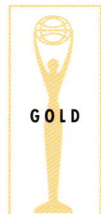

CATEGORY
Beverages/Alcoholic

ADVERTISER/PRODUCT
Anheuser-Busch Inc./Bud Light

TITLE
Mr. Horse-Drawn Carriage Driver

ADVERTISING AGENCY
DDB, Chicago

PRODUCTION COMPANY
Chicago Recording Company,
Chicago

MUSIC COMPANY
Scandal Music, Chicago

GROUP CREATIVE DIRECTOR
John Immesoete

CREATIVE DIRECTOR
Bill Cimino, Mark Gross

COPYWRITER
John Immesoete

ADDITIONAL WRITING
Pat Burke, Kitty Schulz, Bill Cimino,
Mark Gross, Barry Burdiak,
Bob Winter

PRODUCER
Sam Pillsbury

VO: Bud Light Presents…Real men of genius.

SINGER: *Real men of genius.*

VO: Today we salute you…Mr. Horse-Drawn Carriage Driver.

SINGER: *Mr. Horse-Drawn Carriage Driver!*

VO: You start your day with a tip, tip!, and a cheerio!, which is odd because you're from Brooklyn.

SINGER: *Jolly Old Brooklyn!*

VO: While most people sit behind a desk, you proudly sit two feet behind a four-legged manure factory.

SINGER: *Oooh!*

VO: No one knows the guts it takes to ride the subway to work dressed as a foppish dandy from the eighteenth century.

SINGER: *Hey foppish dandy!*

VO: Blaring horns, profanity, vicious insults all met with a courtly tip of your stovepipe hat.

SINGER: *Cheerio!*

VO: So crack open an ice-cold Bud Light, Buggy Boy.

SFX: Bottle cap opening.

VO: Because the way you say "giddy-up" makes us say "whoa."

SINGER: *Whoa! Whoa! Whoa!*

VO: Bud Light beer. Anheuser-Busch. St. Louis Missouri.

CATEGORY
Beverages/Alcoholic

ADVERTISER/PRODUCT
Anheuser-Busch Inc./Bud Light

TITLE
Mr. Camouflage Suit Maker

ADVERTISING AGENCY
DDB, Chicago

PRODUCTION COMPANY
Chicago Recording Company, Chicago

MUSIC COMPANY
Scandal Music, Chicago

GROUP CREATIVE DIRECTOR
John Immesoete

CREATIVE DIRECTOR
Bill Cimino, Mark Gross

COPYWRITER
John Immesoete

ADDITIONAL WRITING
Bill Cimino, Mark Gross,
Barry Burdiak, Bob Winter,
Pat Burke, Kitty Schulz

PRODUCER
Sam Pillsbury

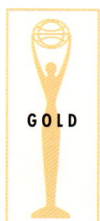

GOLD

VO: Bud Light Presents…Real American heroes.

SINGER: *Real American heroes.*

VO: Today we salute you…Mr. Camouflage Suit Maker.

SINGER: *Mr. Camouflage Suit Maker!*

VO: Your amazing skills of deception can trick a deer into thinking we're just a tree out for a walk, or a shrub having a cup of coffee.

SINGER: *Shrub having coffee!*

VO: Tirelessly, you perfect your artistry. The squiggly black line. The blob. The slightly larger blob. All in spectacular shades of…green.

SINGER: *green, green, green!*

VO: Thanks to you we look fabulous in or out of the forest—with a suit that can be easily accessorized with face paint and a few twigs.

SINGER: *Dressed to kill.*

VO: So crack open an ice-cold Bud Light, Mr. Camouflage Suit Maker.

SFX: Bottle cap opening.

VO: Because when it comes to blending in, you really stand out.

SINGER: *Mr. Camouflage Suit Makerrrrrr.*

VO: Bud Light beer. Anheuser-Busch. St. Louis Missouri.

CATEGORY
Beverages/Alcoholic

ADVERTISER/PRODUCT
Anheuser-Busch Inc./Bud Light

TITLE
Mr. Company Computer Guy

ADVERTISING AGENCY
DDB, Chicago

PRODUCTION COMPANY
Chicago Recording Company, Chicago

MUSIC COMPANY
Scandal Music, Chicago

GROUP CREATIVE DIRECTOR
John Immesoete

CREATIVE DIRECTOR
Bill Cimino, Mark Gross

COPYWRITER
John Immesoete

ADDITIONAL WRITING
Bill Cimino, Mark Gross,
Barry Burdiak, Bob Winter,
Pat Burke, Kitty Schulz

PRODUCER
Sam Pillsbury

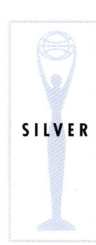

SILVER

VO: Bud Light Presents…Real American heroes.

SINGER: *Real American heroes.*

VO: Today we salute you…Mr. Company Computer Guy.

SINGER: *Mr. Company Computer Guy!*

VO: Though we "worker bees" scarcely know our modems from our scrotums, you are there to guide us.

SINGER: *Modems and scrotums!*

VO: When we screw up the "boot up," you are there. Without you, computers would mega-bite.

SINGER: *Megabyte!*

VO: The countless hours we spend surfing the Internet and accidentally stumbling upon porn sites would instead be spent…working.

SINGER: *Working for the man!*

VO: So crack open an ice-cold Bud Light, Mr. Company Computer Guy.

SFX: Bottle cap opening.

VO: For it's you who keeps our "log ons"…log on…and our hard drives hard.

SINGER: *You've got to see this porn site.*

VO: Bud Light beer. Anheuser-Busch. St. Louis Missouri.

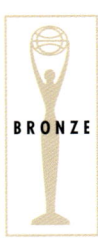

CATEGORY
Beverages/Alcoholic

ADVERTISER/PRODUCT
Anheuser-Busch Inc./Budweiser

TITLE
Mr. Wedding Band Guitar Player

ADVERTISING AGENCY
DDB, Chicago

PRODUCTION STUDIO
Chicago Recording Company,
Chicago

MUSIC COMPANY
Scandal Music, Chicago

GROUP CREATIVE DIRECTOR
John Immesoete

CREATIVE DIRECTOR
Bill Cimino, Mark Gross

COPYWRITER
John Immesoete

ADDITIONAL WRITING
Barry Burdiak, Bob Winter,
Bill Cimino, Mark Gross, Pat Burke

PRODUCER
Sam Pillsbury

VO: Bud Light Presents…Real American heroes.

SINGER: *Real American heroes.*

VO: Today we salute you…Mr. Wedding Band Guitar Player.

SINGER: *Mr. Wedding Band Guitar Player!*

VO: Any guitar player can rock a packed stadium, but it takes real talent to keep the Washinsky reception going all night long.

SINGER: *Mazel tov!*

VO: Perched on the stage in your undersized tuxedo, you tirelessly churn out tunes from the 50s, 60s, 70s, 80s, and 90s.

SINGER: Keep on rockin'!

VO: Sound check? You don't need no stinkin' sound check.

SINGER: *No!*

VO: And even though you've never had groupies, you have bagged the occasional bridesmaid.

SINGER: *Never forget you!*

VO: So crack open an ice-cold Bud Light, guitar guy.

SFX: Bottle cap opening.

VO: Because every wedding you go to, you're the real best man.

VO: Bud Light beer. Anheuser-Busch, St. Louis Missouri.

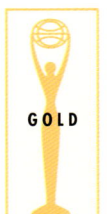

CATEGORY
Entertainment Promotion

ADVERTISER/PRODUCT
Kansas City Blues & Jazz Festival

TITLE
No Kenny G

ADVERTISING AGENCY
David Marks Marketing &
Advertising, Leawood

PRODUCTION COMPANY
Wheeler Audio, Kansas City

CREATIVE DIRECTOR
David Marks

COPYWRITER
David Marks

PRODUCER
David Marks

ENGINEER
Jim Wheeler

TALENT
Skip Quimby

VO: Your attention please: Kenny G will not be appearing at this year's Kansas City Blues & Jazz Festival. Even though Kenny G was never scheduled to appear at this year's Kansas City Blues & Jazz Festival, we want to make it absolutely clear that Kenny G would not be appearing at the Kansas City Blues & Jazz Festival, even if Kenny G underwrote the entire cost of the event (although he is certainly welcome to do that). Frankly, if every blues and/or jazz musician on the face of the earth were to mysteriously vanish, Kenny G would still not be appearing at this year's Kansas City Blues and Jazz Festival. But, you may ask, what if Kenny G were somehow to seize control of the military? Under this scenario, Kenny G would still not appear with Ramsey Lewis, Arturo Sandoval, and nearly fifty other authentic blues and jazz greats at this year's Kansas City Blues and Jazz Festival. Finally, on a personal note, if you are Kenny G, under no circumstance will you be appearing at the 11th Annual Kansas City Blues & Jazz Festival, July 20th through the 22nd at Penn Valley Park.

For tickets call 1-800-530-KCMO.

CATEGORY
Entertainment Promotion

ADVERTISER/PRODUCT
Georgia Lottery

TITLE
14 Chances

ADVERTISING AGENCY
Austin Kelley, Atlanta

PRODUCTION STUDIO
Doppler Studios, Atlanta

ACCOUNT EXECUTIVE
Lou Ann Russell

CREATIVE DIRECTOR
Jim Spruell

COPYWRITER
John Spalding, Dan Miranda

PRODUCER
Kevin Wilson

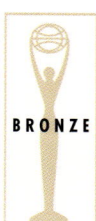

BRONZE

SFX: Phone ringing

WOMAN: Hello.

MAN: Uh hi, this is Bob, from the pay phone. Wanna go out with me?

WOMAN: No.

MAN: Wanna go out with me?

WOMAN: No.

MAN: Wanna go out with me?

WOMAN: No.

MAN: Wanna go out with me?

WOMAN: No.

MAN: Wanna see a movie?

WOMAN: No.

MAN: A play?

WOMAN: No.

MAN: A hockey game?

WOMAN: No.

MAN: Wanna go skating?

WOMAN: No.

MAN: Biking?

WOMAN: No.

MAN: Jogging?

WOMAN: No.

MAN: Wanna get dinner?

WOMAN: No.

MAN: Lunch?

WOMAN: No.

MAN: Coffee?

WOMAN: No.

MAN: Turned me down thirteen times. Aw, what the heck. Want to go out with me?

WOMAN: Sure.

MAN: Really?

VO: See how great it is when you've got fourteen chances? With Monte Carlo, the new $5 instant game from the Georgia lottery, you could win up to fourteen times on each ticket. Fourteen times! So, play Monte Carlo today, with a top prize of $125,000.

SFX: Phone ringing.

MAN: Hey, Bob again. Want to come over to my place?

WOMAN: No.

MAN: Want to come over to my place?

WOMAN: No.

MAN: Want to come over to my place?

WOMAN: No.

MAN: Want to come over to my place?

WOMAN: No.

VO: And don't forget to play the new $1 instant game, Pay Me. Instant games from the Georgia lottery. They're instant fun.

MAN: Want to come over to my place?

WOMAN: No.

MAN: Nice comforter…

WOMAN: N…O.

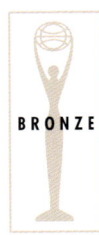

BRONZE

CATEGORY	**ADVERTISING AGENCY**	**CREATIVE DIRECTOR**
Media Promotion	FCB, Johannesburg	Eoin Welsh
ADVERTISER/PRODUCT	**PRODUCTION STUDIO**	**COPYWRITER**
True Love Magazine/Feb. 2001 Issue	Sonovision, Johannesburg	Anneline Strydom
TITLE	**ACCOUNT EXECUTIVE**	**PRODUCER**
Maybe Maybe	Annelize Stroebel	Tessa Weakley

THEMBI: Oh Steven, aaah that's soooo good…Oh, don't stop, that feels so good…Oh Steven—Aaah…maybe…oh…maybe…maybe…maybe—maybe—maybe…aaah…(more urgently)…MAYBE! MAYBE! MAYBE! (screams)…Aaah, MAYBEEEEEEE!

VO: Why you shouldn't say "yes" too soon. Sex on the first date—in the February issue of *True Love*. Also, Generations' Archie and Zoleka talk to us exclusively on their troubled marriage. True Love. On sale now. It's all a woman needs.

SFX: Voices.

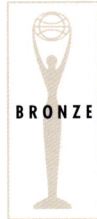

BRONZE

CATEGORY	**ADVERTISING AGENCY**	**COPYWRITER**
Personal Items	BBDO, Düsseldorf	Bill Marbach
ADVERTISER/PRODUCT	**PRODUCTION STUDIO**	
Knirps Umbrella	Studio Funk, Düsseldorf	
TITLE	**MUSIC COMPANY**	
Raindrops	Tobias Grumbach, Düsseldorf	

MUSIC: "Raindrops Keep Fallin' on My Head"

SFX: Umbrella opening.

VO: Knirps. The original umbrella.

CATEGORY
Public Service

TITLE
Ketchup Soup

CREATIVE DIRECTOR
Thomas Hayo

PRODUCER
Mary Cheney

ADVERTISER/PRODUCT
Feeding Children Better

ADVERTISING AGENCY
Bartle Bogle Hegarty, New York

COPYWRITER
Peter Kain

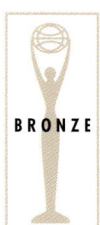

VO: The sun is setting. The air's getting chilly. Children are running home. The smell of good food abounds. It's dinnertime in America. And you know what that means—it's time for ketchup soup. When you've got hungry mouths to feed, take boiling water, add half a cup of ketchup, and presto. You've got ketchup soup. The essence of tomato, vinegar, and water, and a hot meal for the whole family. And tonight, it's being served all across America. Ketchup soup. 'Cause when kids are hungry enough, they'll eat anything. Unfortunately, ketchup soup is more popular than you'd think. Right now, 1 out of 5 American children is living with hunger, as their parents struggle to make ends meet. Please call 1-800-FEED KIDS and find out how you can fight child hunger. The sooner you believe it, the sooner we can end it. Brought to you by the Ad Council, America's Second Harvest, and Feeding Children Better.

CATEGORY
Public Service

ADVERTISING AGENCY
Paradiset DDB, Stockholm

ACCOUNT MANAGER
Marie Nodbrink

DIRECTOR
Patrik Larsson

ADVERTISER/PRODUCT
The Church of Sweden

PRODUCTION STUDIO
Forsberg & Co, Stockholm

PLANNER
Marie Malm

PRODUCER
Lotta Kjellman

TITLE
The Breasts

ACCOUNT EXECUTIVE
Helena Westin

COPYWRITER
Anders Lidzell

SOUND
Fredrik Eliasson

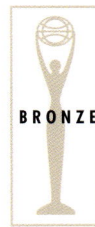

WOMAN: It's always the same thing at work, I'm mostly quiet, and if I have an opinion for once, then it's as if I'm not heard or don't even exist. I'm truly sad about this and I've been looking for a way to gather strength in peace and quiet. Then it hit me, I'm going to have my boobs done.

VO: Are you searching in the right place? Church of Sweden.

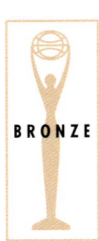

BRONZE

CATEGORY
Retail Stores

ADVERTISER/PRODUCT
Hollywood Video

TITLE
Sixty-Second Theater/Shrek

ADVERTISING AGENCY
Cliff Freeman and Partners,
New York

PRODUCTION STUDIO
Kamen Entertainment Group,
New York

SOUND DESIGN COMPANY
Kamen Entertainment Group,
New York

ACCOUNT EXECUTIVE
Shana Brooks

CREATIVE DIRECTOR
Arthur Bijur

COPYWRITER
Ari Weiss, Aaron Adler

PRODUCER
Katherine Cheng

VO: Hollywood Video presents *60 Second Theater*, where we try (unsuccessfully) to pack a 2-hour Hollywood production into 60 seconds. Today's presentation…*Shrek*.

SFX: Trumpets.

FARQUAAD: Shrek, you must rescue a princess for me.

SHREK: Where is she, your highness?

FARQUAAD: In the lair of a vicious fire-breathing dragon.

SHREK: Why don't you rescue her?

FARQUAAD: What part of vicious fire-breathing dragon didn't you understand?

SHREK: The first part, it's a little ambiguous…

FARQUAAD: Just get going!

SFX: Horse galloping and whinnying

SHREK: I'm here to rescue you, fair princess. (Thinking) Wow, she's pretty.

PRINCESS: Why, thank you, fair ogre. (Thinking) Wow, he's ugly.

SHREK: It's getting dark, we'd better camp.

PRINCESS: I'll sleep in this cave.

SHREK: I'll sleep outside.

BOTH (calling out): Goodnight.

SFX: Crickets, campfire.

SHREK: The princess could never fall in love with an ugly beast like me.

PRINCESS (echo SFX): I think I'm falling in love with that ugly beast…I must tell him the truth about me.

SFX: Rooster crow.

PRINCESS: Shrek, there's something I have to tell you.

SHREK: What is it?

PRINCESS: I'm…ugly.

SHREK: Nobody looks good in the morning.

PRINCESS: No, I mean I'm really ugly.

SHREK: Oh, that's just bed head.

PRINCESS: Kiss me, you'll see.

SFX: Kiss. Aaah!

SFX: Magical tingling.

PRINCESS: What do you think?

SHREK: Well, we're going to have ugly babies. *[or (shouting) Don't call me, I'll call you!]*

VO: If this doesn't satisfy your urge to see *Shrek* (and we can't say we blame you) then rent it today at Hollywood Video. Where *every* rental is yours for *five days*, and where *Shrek* is *guaranteed* to be in stock or next time it's *free*. Hollywood Video. Celebrity voices impersonated.

CATEGORY	**TITLE**	**PRODUCTION COMPANY**	**COPYWRITER**
Campaign	F.B.I.	B+S Studios, Cape Town	Alistair King
ADVERTISER/PRODUCT	**TITLE**	**ACCOUNT EXECUTIVE**	**PRODUCER**
20twenty	Oxford	Lesley Thomas	Alexis Roberts
TITLE	**ADVERTISING AGENCY**	**CREATIVE DIRECTOR**	**SOUND ENGINEER**
Guinness Book of Records	King James, Cape Town	Alistair King	Graham Merril

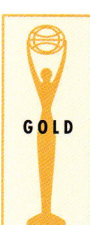

GOLD

SFX: Phone ringing and answered.

FEMALE 1: Good afternoon, Guinness world records.

MALE 1: Hi, um, I'd like to speak to someone about a new entry, please.

FEMALE 1: OK, one moment please.

FEMALE 2: Guinness world records, how can I help?

MALE 1: Umm, I'd like to know what records have been set in the banking field?

FEMALE 2: The banking field? OK, do you have anything in particular in mind?

MALE 1: Well, what happened was this morning I applied for a line of credit with 20twenty and it was approved within seconds. And I figured that must be some kind of a record.

FEMALE 2 (after a pause): Right. We don't actually have a record for this.

MALE 1: You don't have a category? Because I think you should because it was absolutely amazing. I mean, my friends have never seen anything like it. I just applied and…whoosh…within seconds I had approval. Um, I just thought that you should know that.

FEMALE 2: Ah, we don't have anything like this.

MALE 1: Alright. Thank you very much for your help.

FEMALE 2: OK, thank you.

MALE 1: Bye-bye.

FEMALE 2: Bye-bye.

VO: Introducing 20twenty, the revolutionary, new twenty-first-century bank that will change the way you view banking. Visit www.20twenty.com. It's the new word for banking.

SFX: Phone rings and is answered.

FEMALE 1: FBI; good morning.

MALE 2: Good morning, can I speak to an investigator please?

FEMALE 1: Sure.

SFX: Phone rings.

FEMALE 2 (inaudible): …agent.

MALE 1: Hi, is that an FBI agent?

FEMALE 2: Yes, can I help you?

MALE 1: Yes, I wonder if you can. I've heard that the FBI knows everything about everything. And um, I've forgotten my access code to my new 20one account on 20twenty. So I was hoping you'd be able to tell me what it is.

FEMALE 2 (laughing to herself): Oh, I'm sorry, we don't know that.

MALE 1: Are you sure?

FEMALE 2: Yes.

MALE 1: OK, thank you.

FEMALE 2: OK.

SFX: Phone is put down.

VO: Introducing 20twenty. The revolutionary new twenty-first-century bank that's 100 percent safe and secure. Visit www.20twenty.com. It's the new word for banking.

SFX: Phone ringing.

FEMALE 1: Oxford University Press.

MALE 1: Um, I'd like to speak to someone about a new word for the dictionary, please.

SFX: Call is put through.

FEMALE 2: Hello, dictionary department.

MALE1: Hello, hi, I wonder if you can help me. I'd like to query whether it's possible to have a word deleted from the Oxford dictionary?

FEMALE 2: Deleted from? No, we don't delete words from the complete *Oxford English Dictionary.*

MALE 1: Absolutely not?

FEMALE 2: No, it's a matter of historical record.

MALE 1: OK, the thing is, I feel the word bank simply isn't relevant anymore. I think we need a new, fresh, up-to-date word for that. And I think that should be 20twenty.

FEMALE 2 (big breath): Well, we only put things in when we have quite a large body of evidence to show that they are in actual use.

MALE 1: Oh, well, everyone is using 20twenty so that shouldn't be a problem. Thank you very much for your help, ma'am.

FEMALE 2: Right.

VO: Introducing 20twenty. The revolutionary new twenty-first-century bank that's taking banking to a new level. www.20twenty.com. It's the new word for banking.

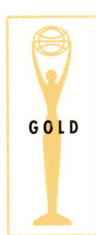

GOLD

CATEGORY
Campaign

ADVERTISER/PRODUCT
Anheuser-Busch Inc./Bud Light

TITLE
Mr. Supermarket Free Sample Guy

TITLE
Mr. Horse-Drawn Carriage Driver

TITLE
Mr. Camouflage Suit Maker

ADVERTISING AGENCY
DDB, Chicago

PRODUCTION COMPANY
Chicago Recording Company, Chicago

MUSIC COMPANY
Scandal Music, Chicago

GROUP CREATIVE DIRECTOR
John Immesoete

CREATIVE DIRECTOR
Bill Cimino, Mark Gross

COPYWRITER
John Immesoete

ADDITIONAL WRITING
Bill Cimino, Mark Gross, Barry Burdiak, Bob Winter, Pat Burke, Kitty Schulz

PRODUCER
Sam Pillsbury

VO: Bud Light Presents…Real men of genius.

SINGER: *Real men of genius.*

VO: Today we salute you…Mr. Supermarket Free Sample Guy.

SINGER: *Mr. Supermarket Free Sample Guy!*

VO: Though man dreads few things more than a trip to the supermarket, you offer us hope and sometimes a free mini-weenie.

SINGER: *Love that freebie weenie!*

VO: What exactly do you have? Aerosol cheese products, deep-fried morsels? Who cares? If it's on a toothpick and it's free, it could be plutonium and we'd eat it!

SINGER: *It's all good, baby!*

VO: For a guy wearing oven mitts and an apron, you're alright.

SINGER: *You're a star.*

VO: So crack open an ice-cold Bud Light, titan of the toothpick.

SFX: Bottle cap opening.

VO: Because you put the free in freedom.

SINGER: *Let it be free…*

VO: Bud Light beer. Anheuser-Busch. St. Louis Missouri.

VO: Bud Light Presents…Real men of genius.

SINGER: *Real men of genius.*

VO: Today we salute you…Mr. Horse-Drawn Carriage Driver.

SINGER: *Mr. Horse-Drawn Carriage Driver!*

VO: You start your day with a tip, tip!, and a cheerio!, which is odd because you're from Brooklyn.

SINGER: *Jolly Old Brooklyn!*

VO: While most people sit behind a desk, you proudly sit two feet behind a four-legged manure factory.

SINGER: *Oooh!*

VO: No one knows the guts it takes to ride the subway to work dressed as a foppish dandy from the eighteenth century.

SINGER: *Hey foppish dandy!*

VO: Blaring horns, profanity, vicious insults all met with a courtly tip of your stovepipe hat.

SINGER: *Cheerio!*

VO: So crack open an ice-cold Bud Light, Buggy Boy.

SFX: Bottle cap opening.

VO: Because the way you say "giddy-up" makes us say "whoa."

SINGER: *Whoa! Whoa! Whoa!*

VO: Bud Light beer. Anheuser-Busch. St. Louis Missouri.

VO: Bud Light Presents…Real American heroes.

SINGER: *Real American heroes.*

VO: Today we salute you…Mr. Camouflage Suit Maker.

SINGER: *Mr. Camouflage Suit Maker!*

VO: Your amazing skills of deception can trick a deer into thinking we're just a tree out for a walk, or a shrub having a cup of coffee.

SINGER: *Shrub having coffee!*

VO: Tirelessly, you perfect your artistry. The squiggly black line. The blob. The slightly larger blob. All in spectacular shades of…green.

SINGER: *green, green, green!*

VO: Thanks to you we look fabulous in or out of the forest—with a suit that can be easily accessorized with face paint and a few twigs.

SINGER: *Dressed to kill.*

VO: So crack open an ice-cold Bud Light, Mr. Camouflage Suit Maker.

SFX: Bottle cap opening.

VO: Because when it comes to blending in, you really stand out.

SINGER: *Mr. Camouflage Suit Makerrrrr.*

VO: Bud Light beer. Anheuser-Busch. St. Louis Missouri.

CATEGORY
Campaign

ADVERTISER/PRODUCT
American Legacy Foundation/
Infect Truth

TITLE
Flavor Suggestions

TITLE
Dog Walker

TITLE
Hearse

ADVERTISING AGENCY
ARNOLD Worldwide, Boston;
Crispin Porter Bogusky, Miami

AGENCY PRODUCER
Ben Raynes, Karen Kenney

ACCOUNT EXECUTIVE
Azurae Chambers

CHIEF CREATIVE DIRECTOR
Ron Lawner

GROUP CREATIVE DIRECTOR
Pete Favat, Alex Bogusky

CREATIVE DIRECTOR
Roger Baldacci

COPYWRITER
Roger Baldacci, Mike Martin,
Rich Mackin

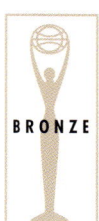

BRONZE

Per the request of the client, the transcriptions for these spots are not
for publication.

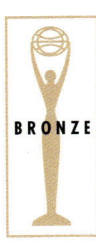

BRONZE

CATEGORY
Campaign

ADVERTISER/PRODUCT
Anheuser-Busch Inc./Budweiser

TITLE
Frank Can't Dance

TITLE
The New Catch Phrase

TITLE
The Ferret's Thong

ADVERTISING AGENCY
Goodby, Silverstein & Partners,
San Francisco

PRODUCTION STUDIO
Crescendo!, San Francisco;
ServiDigital, New York

ACCOUNT EXECUTIVE
Stan Fiorito, Brian Coate

CREATIVE DIRECTOR
Jeffrey Goodby, Rich Silverstein

COPYWRITER
Steve Dildarian

PRODUCER
Jennie Lindstrom

LOUIE: Hey, Frankie?

FRANK: Yeah, Louie.

LOUIE: You know what we're doing this weekend?

FRANK: Pondering our sad existence?

LOUIE: No. We're going clubbing.

FRANK: Clubbing?

LOUIE: Yeah, that's how you meet women. You buy 'em a Budweiser, then show them your moves on the dance floor.

FRANK: I don't have any moves.

LOUIE: Well you got to get some. Come on, practice.

FRANK: Where?

LOUIE: Come on, no one's watching.

SFX: Club music playing on a radio.

FRANK: What's that?

LOUIE: Come on, Frankie.

FRANK: Alright, alright, how's this?

LOUIE: How's what?

FRANK: This.

LOUIE: Frankie, that's your eyelid. You got to move more than that.

FRANK: Alright, okay, I'm getting warmed up.

LOUIE: Come on, shake your booty.

FRANK: Like this?

LOUIE: No, that's your elbow. Come on Frankie, shake your booty!

FRANK: That is my booty.

LOUIE: No shake that thing there.

FRANK: Okay, alright, hold on, watch this one. Who, who, who, who.

LOUIE: Oh my goodness, this is embarrassing.

FRANK: Alright, turn off the music, then.

SFX: Music out

LOUIE: No, no I didn't mean that, I didn't mean that. All I meant is that you have to practice.

FRANK: Listen, I don't have to dance to meet women. I do fine with my own technique.

LOUIE: No, no, I'm not going to sleep until I see that booty move. UP!

SFX: Music in

FRANK: Alright. Who, who.

LOUIE: There you go!

FRANK: Who, who.

LOUIE: There it is.

FRANK: Who, who.

LOUIE: Ahhh, ahh!

FRANK: Who, who.

LOUIE: Oh, yeah!

VO: Anheuser-Busch, St. Louis, Missouri.

LOUIE: Hey, Frank.

FRANK: Yeah, Louie.

LOUIE: I've got the new Budweiser catch phrase for summer 2001.

FRANK: What are you talking about?

LOUIE: Well, first they said, "Whassup."

FRANK: Yeah, that was good.

LOUIE: Yeah, but then they posed the question, "What are you doing?"

FRANK: Ah, that was catchy.

LOUIE: Ah, but then they creatively morphed to, "How are you doing?"

FRANK: And a great morph it was.

LOUIE: Okay so now, all summer long, the new Budweiser catch phrase will be…

FRANK: Yeah?

LOUIE: "Hi."

FRANK: "Hi?"

LOUIE: The simplicity is profound.

FRANK: Simplicity—that's it?

LOUIE: It says nothing while saying everything.

FRANK: It says nothing, period.

LOUIE: Yeah well, Budweiser loves it.

FRANK: Really?

LOUIE: They're making T-shirts, blimps; they have talking beer mugs.

FRANK: Yeah, what do they say?

LOUIE: "Hi."

FRANK: Oh, how creative.

LOUIE: And it sounds better with repetition.

FRANK: Yeah, I'm sure.

LOUIE: Hi. Hi. Hi. Hi. Hi—

FRANK: Yeah stop it, that's annoying. Louie, stop. Louie?

LOUIE: Frankie?

FRANK: Louie?

LOUIE: Frankie?

FRANK: What?

LOUIE: Hi.

FRANK: Stop, Louie.

LOUIE: Hi.

FRANK: Not all summer with this.

LOUIE: Hi.

VO: Anheuser-Busch, St. Louis, Missouri.

LOUIE: Oh, this is exciting, Frank.

FRANK: Yeah, it is, Louie.

LOUIE: Three guys heading to the beach.

FRANK: It's gonna be good.

LOUIE: Just kicking back with some ice cold Buds, watching the girls walk by.

FRANK: Nothing wrong with that. Hey, here comes the ferret.

FERRET: Squeak.

LOUIE: I am going to be sick.

FRANK: Whoa.

LOUIE: Oh, that is gross.

FRANK: No, no.

LOUIE: Is that what I think it is?

FRANK: Yeah, the ferret's wearing a thong.

LOUIE: Hey ferret, no one wants to see that.

FERRET: Squeak.

LOUIE: No, no debate; ditch the slingshot.

FRANK: Please.

FERRET: Squeak.

LOUIE: What did he say?

FRANK: He said where he comes from, thongs are a badge of man-dom.

LOUIE: Yeah well, I thought he was from the swamp. Where's he from?

FRANK: No, he's from a small Mediterranean island where the men are men, and they're not afraid to flaunt it.

LOUIE: What? How do you know this?

FRANK: I have no idea.

LOUIE: This is like a nightmare. Hey bikini boy, go change. You're not wearing that to the beach.

FERRET: Squeak.

LOUIE: What'd he say?

FRANK: He said you're just jealous because you don't have a body like his.

LOUIE: A body like his? He's a ferret. I am a buff lizard.

FRANK: Yeah, but you know the old saying.

LOUIE: What saying?

FRANK: Short, hairy guys get all the babes.

LOUIE: Oh right, of course; short, hairy guys. Everyone gets the babes except Louie.

FRANK: Yep.

LOUIE: Ditch that stupid thong.

Anheuser-Busch, St. Louis, Missouri.

DESIGN

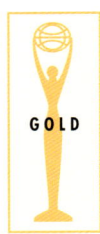

GOLD

CATEGORY
Annual Reports

ADVERTISER/PRODUCT
Silicon Valley Bank 2000
Annual Report

DESIGN COMPANY
Cahan & Associates, San Francisco

ACCOUNT EXECUTIVE
Katie Kniestedt

CREATIVE DIRECTOR
Bill Cahan

COPYWRITER
Thom Elkjer

ART DIRECTOR
Bill Cahan, Michael Braley

PRODUCTION MANAGER
Kelly St. John-Ongpin

DESIGNER
Michael Braley

PHOTOGRAPHER
Jock McDonald, Graham MacIndoe

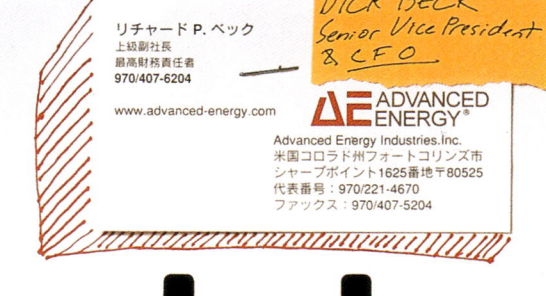

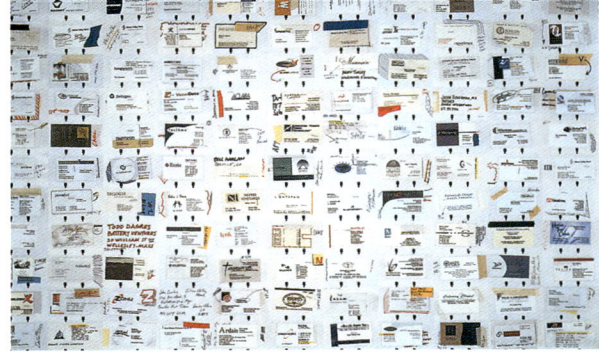

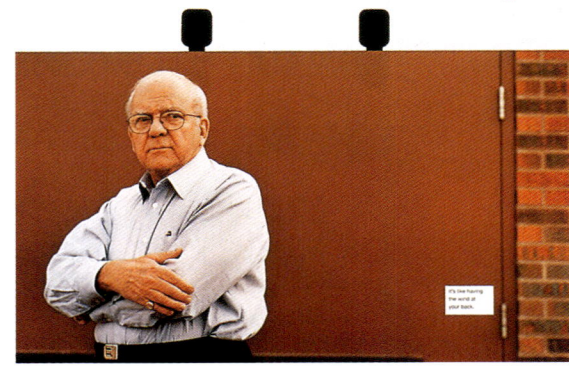

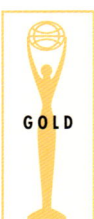

GOLD

CATEGORY
Annual Reports

ADVERTISER/PRODUCT
Maxygen 2000 Annual Report

DESIGN COMPANY
Cahan & Associates, San Francisco

ACCOUNT EXECUTIVE
Natalie Linden

CREATIVE DIRECTOR
Bill Cahan

COPYWRITER
Maxygen

ART DIRECTOR
Bill Cahan

PRODUCTION MANAGER
Gabriella Rossi

DESIGNER
Gary Williams

PHOTOGRAPHER
Ann Giordano, Esther Henderson,
Ray Manley, Robert Markow,
John Sann

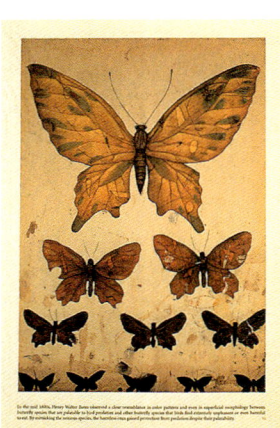

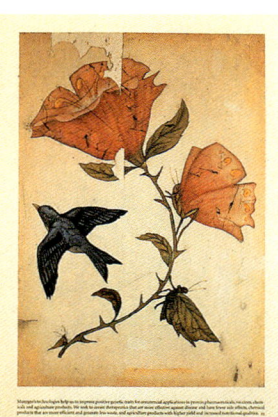

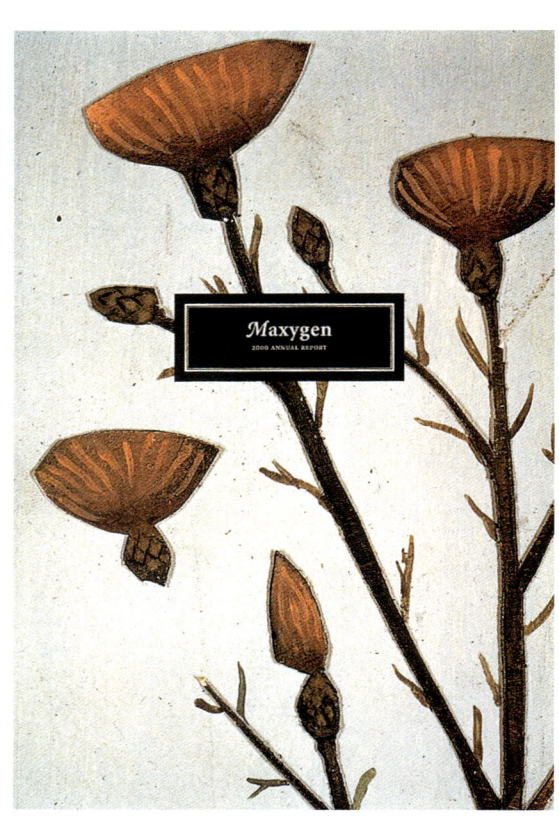

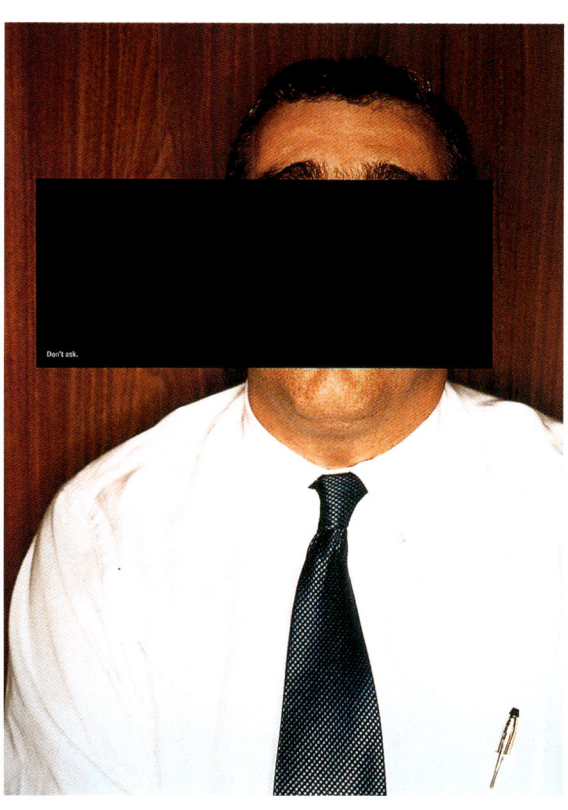

CATEGORY
Annual Reports

ADVERTISER/PRODUCT
Gartner 2000 Annual Report

DESIGN COMPANY
Cahan & Associates, San Francisco

ACCOUNT EXECUTIVE
Bella Banbury

CREATIVE DIRECTOR
Bill Cahan

COPYWRITER
Tony Leighton

ART DIRECTOR
Bill Cahan, Kevin Roberson

PRODUCTION MANAGER
Gabriella Rossi

DESIGNER
Kevin Roberson

PHOTOGRAPHER
Lars Tunbjork, Steven Ahlgren,
Catherine Ledner

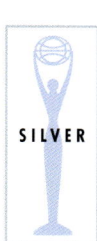

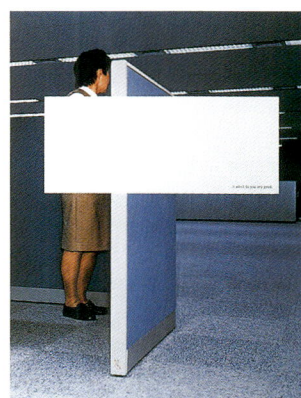

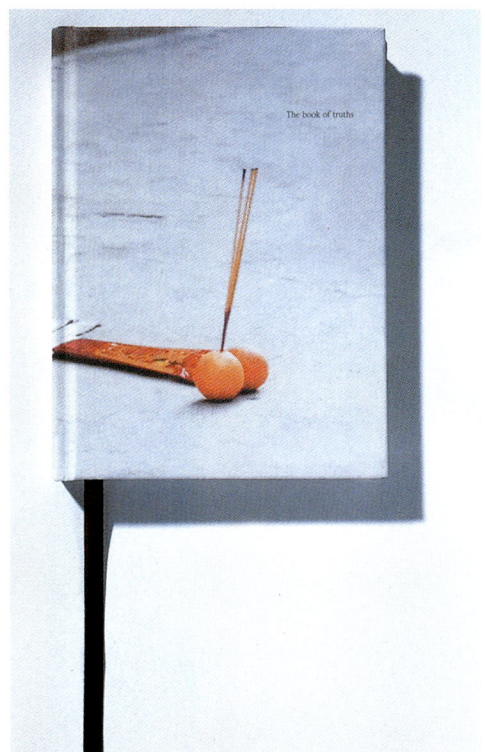

CATEGORY
Brochures-Product/Service

ADVERTISER/PRODUCT
GF Smith & Sons Paper Company

TITLE
Verus—The Book of Truths

DESIGN COMPANY
Elmwood, Leeds

DESIGNER
Alan Ainsly

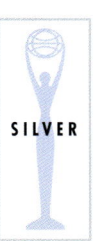

DESIGN

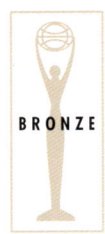

CATEGORY
Brochures-Product/Service

ADVERTISER/PRODUCT
Nike—Book of Lies

ADVERTISING AGENCY
Wieden + Kennedy, Amsterdam

DESIGN COMPANY
Wieden + Kennedy, Amsterdam

ACCOUNT EXECUTIVE
Julia Porter, Becky Barwick

CREATIVE DIRECTOR
Glenn Cole, Paul Shearer

COPYWRITER
Jessica Lehrer

ART DIRECTOR
Judith Francisco

DESIGNER
Judith Francisco

PHOTOGRAPHER
Anette Aurell

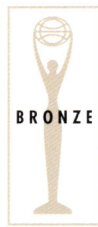

CATEGORY
Brochures—Product/Service

ADVERTISER/PRODUCT
Waggener Edstrom Book

DESIGN COMPANY
Sandstrom Design, Portland

CREATIVE DIRECTOR
Steve Sandstrom, Peter Wegner

COPYWRITER
Peter Wegner

ART DIRECTOR
Steve Sandstrom

PRODUCTION MANAGER
Kelly Culp

DESIGNER
Steve Sandstrom

PHOTOGRAPHER
Garry Winogrand, Chris Mueller,
John Bohls

PRODUCTION DESIGNER
Starlee Matz, John Bohls

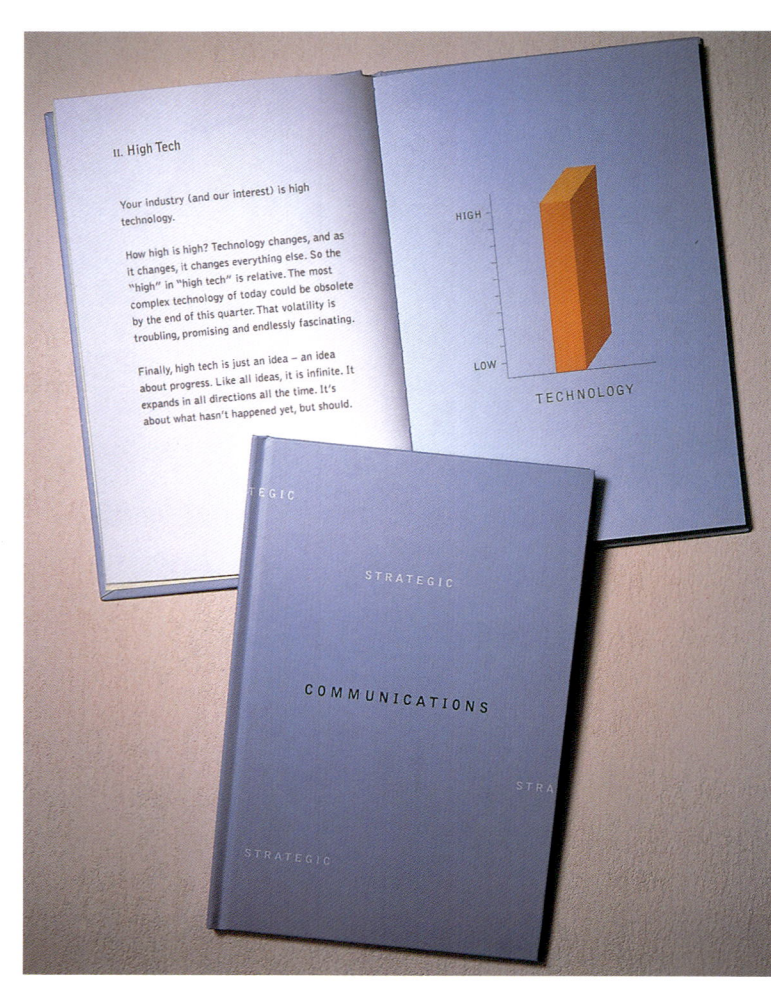

CATEGORY
Corporate Identity

ADVERTISER/PRODUCT
Hovis Bakery

ADVERTISING AGENCY
Williams Murray Hamm, London

DESIGN COMPANY
Williams Murray Hamm, London

MANUFACTURER
British Bakeries, London

ACCOUNT EXECUTIVE
Kellie Chapple

CREATIVE DIRECTOR
Garrick Hamm

ART DIRECTOR
Stewart Devlin

DESIGNER
Stewart Devlin

PHOTOGRAPHER
Jess Kopple

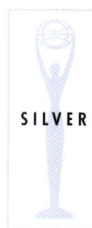

SILVER

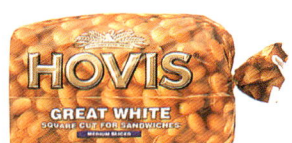
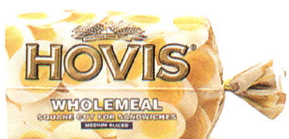
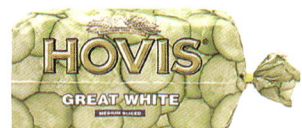
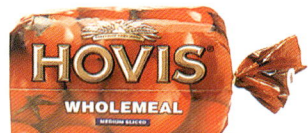
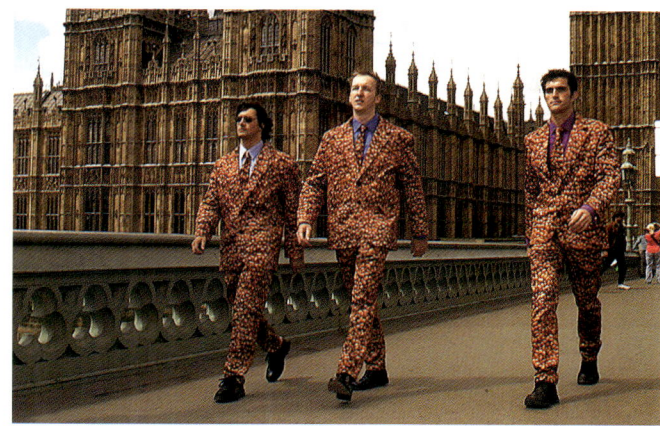
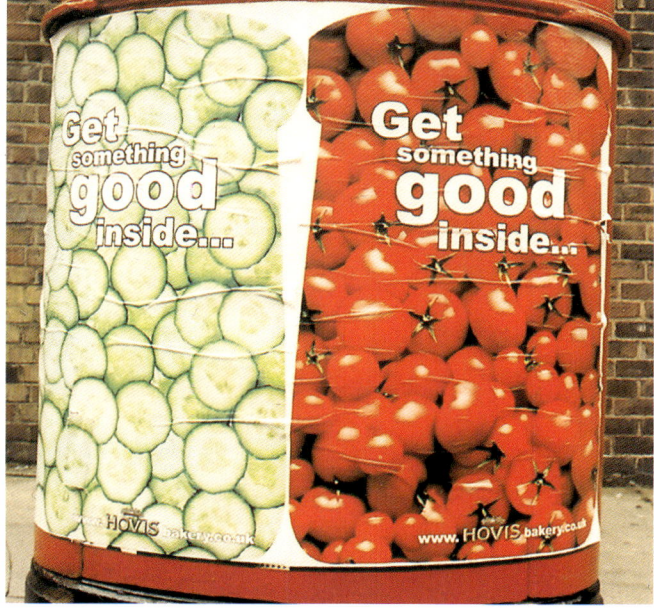
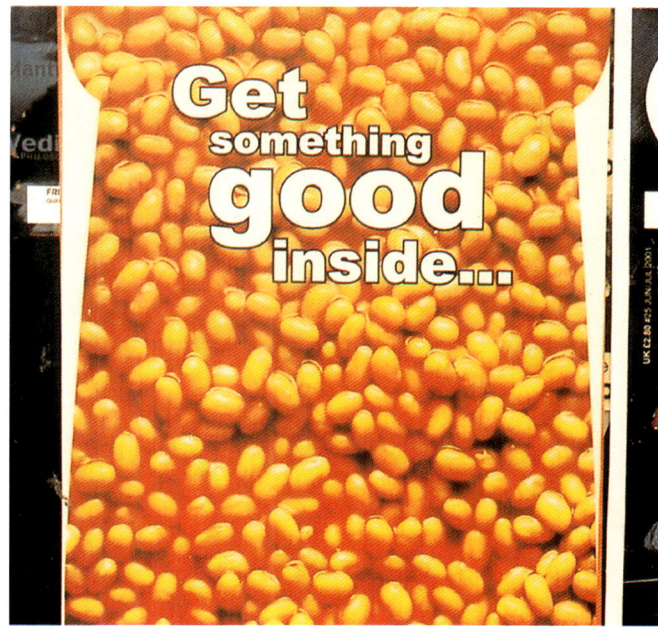
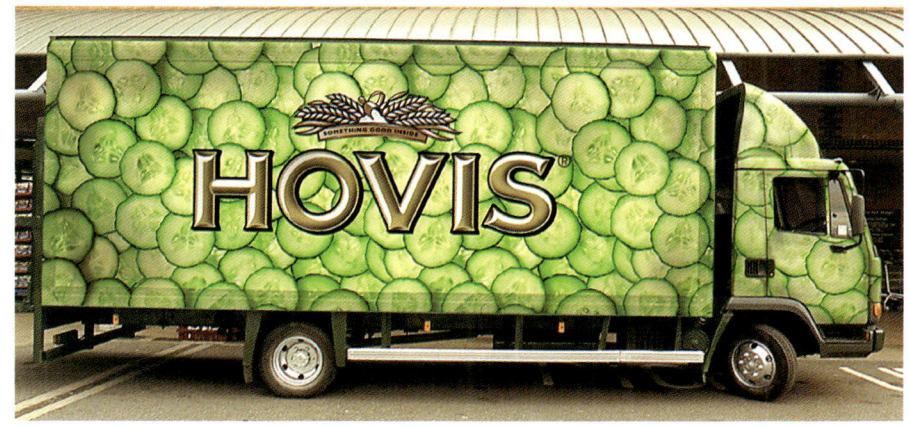

DESIGN

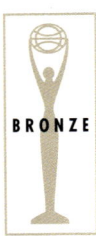

BRONZE

CATEGORY
Corporate Identity

ADVERTISER/PRODUCT
Claire—Radio Producer

ADVERTISING AGENCY
Saatchi & Saatchi Eye Design,
Cape Town

DESIGN COMPANY
Eye Design, Cape Town

MANUFACTURER
Spectra Printers, Cape Town

ACCOUNT EXECUTIVE
Cheryl-Anne Doveton

CREATIVE DIRECTOR
Vanessa Pearson

COPYWRITER
Razia Essack

ART DIRECTOR
Isaac February

PRODUCTION MANAGER
Isaac February

DESIGNER
Gavin Bloys

Business Card 30"

FVO:	*(Warm but confident delivery.*
	Background music under throughout.)
	Hi there. It's me Claire from **Claire inc**. The producer in Radio & Music Producer. The specialist in African Production Specialist. And the flippin' as in flippin' hot person for the job.
SFX:	*(Sound of telephone ringing.)*
FVO:	Give me a buzz on 083 260 2131 or clairebell1@hotmail.com
ANNCR:	Claire inc. Anything but background noise.

Note: Same text on all pieces.

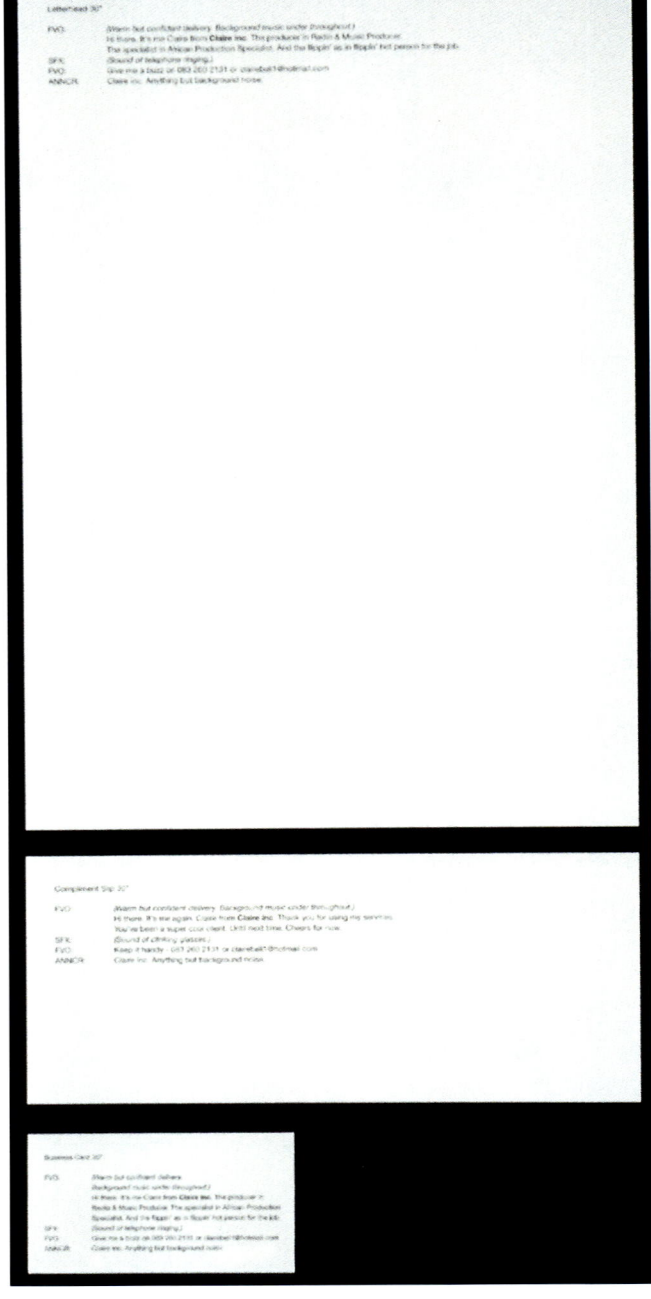

CATEGORY
Corporate Identity

ADVERTISER/PRODUCT
Munkedal Corporate Identity

ADVERTISING AGENCY
Happy Forsman & Bodenfors,
Gothenburg

MANUFACTURER
Munkedals AB, Munkedal

ACCOUNT EXECUTIVE
Yngve Nygren

CREATIVE DIRECTOR
Anders Kornestedt

ART DIRECTOR
Andreas Kittel

PRODUCTION MANAGER
Jessica Thorén

PHOTOGRAPHER
Branko Photographer

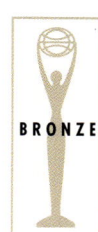

BRONZE

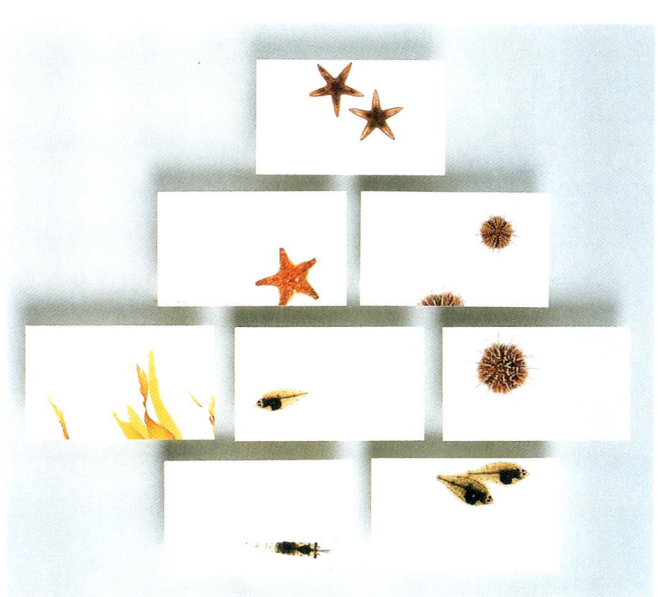

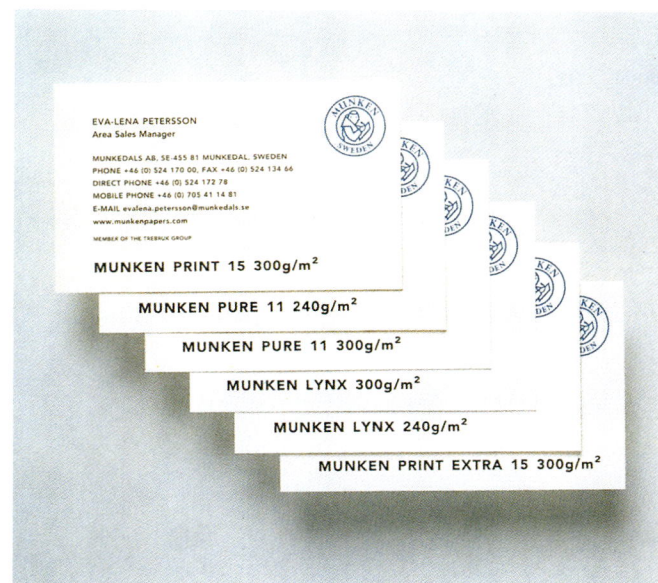

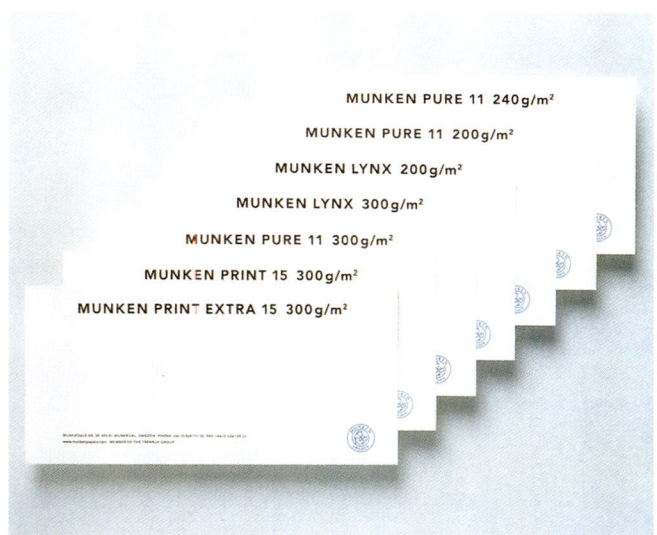

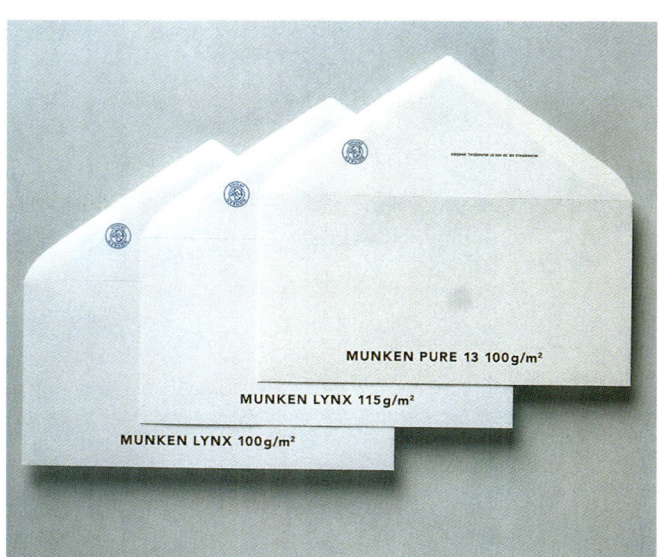

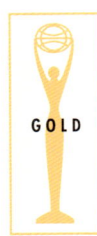

GOLD

CATEGORY
Environmental Design

ADVERTISER/PRODUCT
Toys 'R' Us

ARCHITECT
Gensler Architecture, Design &
Planning Worldwide, New York

**CONCEPT, THEMING &
RETAIL DESIGN**
J. Newbold Associates, New York

LIGHTING DESIGNER
Focus Lighting, New York

**AUDIOVISUAL/TECHNOLOGY
DESIGNER**
Show and Tell Productions,
New York

CONSTRUCTION MANAGER
F.J. Sciame Construction Co.,
New York

**VERTICAL TRANSPORT
CONSULTANTS**
VDA, Livingston

TECHNICAL LIGHTING ADVISER
Hillman DiBernardo, New York

MEP ENGINEER
FMC Associates, New York

**STRUCTURAL ENGINEER AND
CURTAIN WALL CONSULTANT**
Gilsanz, Murray, Steficek LLP,
New York

ACOUSTIC CONSULTANT
Cerami & Associates, New York

CODE
Jerome S. Gillman, New York

**SCROLLER PRINTER &
INSTILLATION**
Vomela Graphics, St. Paul

SCROLLING SYSTEM FABRICATOR
Diazit Company, Youngsville

**SCROLLING SYTEM
CONTROL FABRICATOR**
LSI Controls, Waynesboro

CURTAIN WALL FABRICATOR
W&W Glass Systems, Nanuet

SIGNAGE
Sign Project Management,
Shoreham

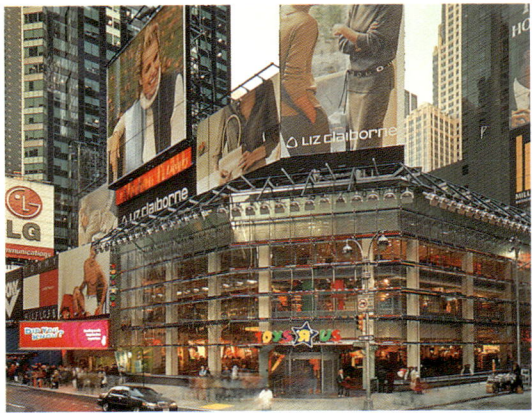
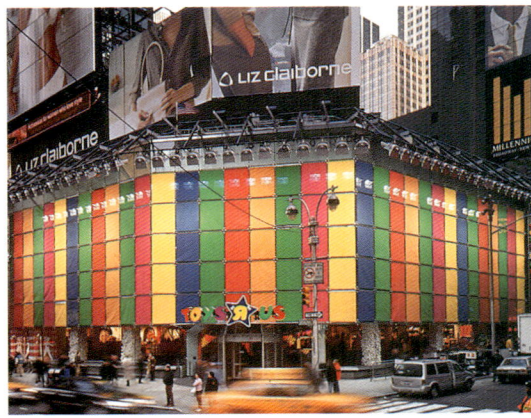
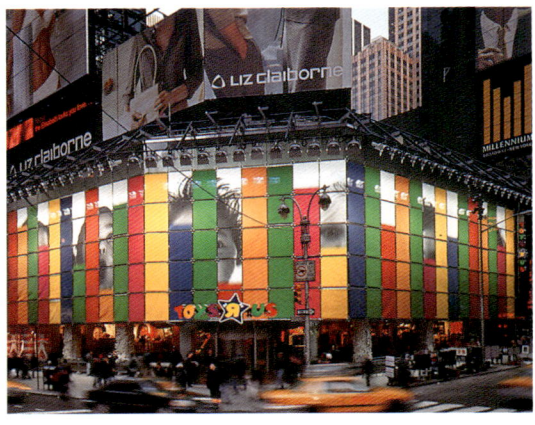
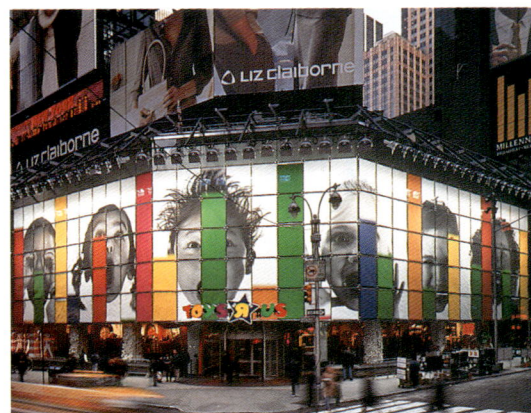
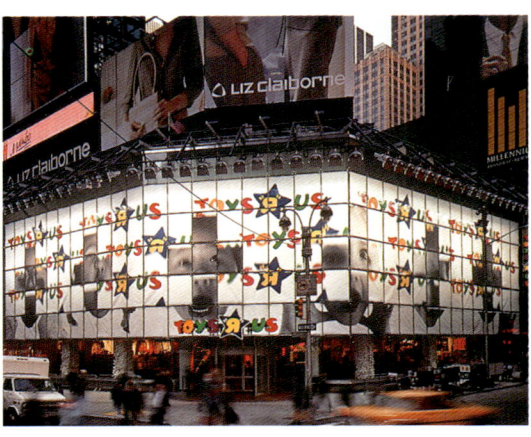
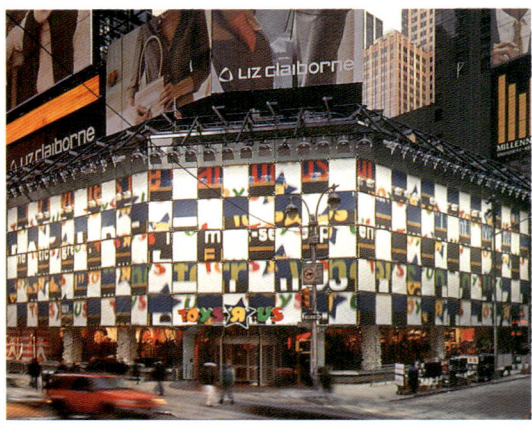

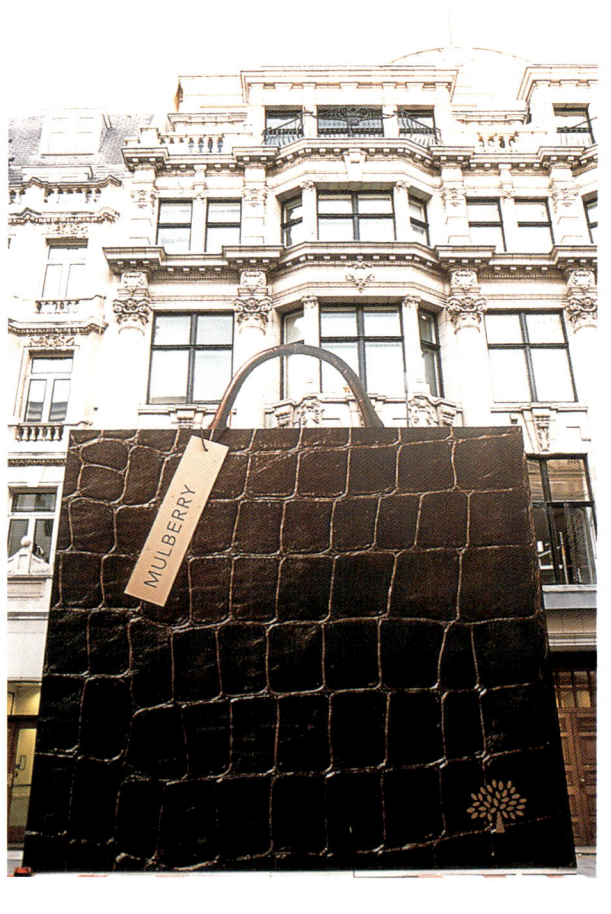

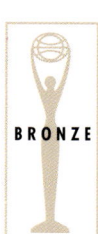

CATEGORY
Environmental Design

ADVERTISER/PRODUCT
Mulberry Bond Street (Flagship)/
Handbag Hoarding

DESIGN COMPANY
Four IV, London

MANUFACTURER
Photobition

CREATIVE DIRECTOR
Andy Bone, Kim Hartley

ART DIRECTOR
Kim Hartley

DESIGNER
Paul Skerm, Kim Hartley

PROJECT MANAGER
Louise Barnard

BRONZE

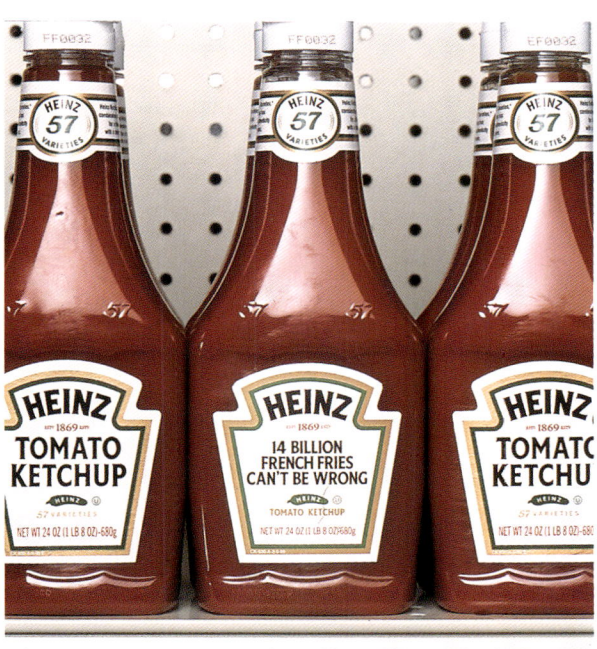

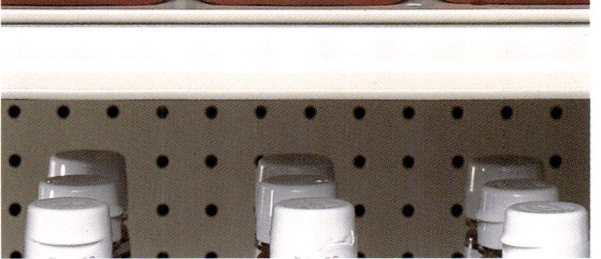

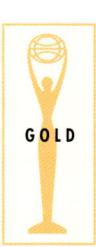

CATEGORY
Package Design

ADVERTISER/PRODUCT
Heinz—14 Billion

ADVERTISING AGENCY
Leo Burnett USA, Chicago

MANUFACTURER
Heinz, Pittsburgh

CREATIVE DIRECTOR
Dave Reger, Mike Straznickas

COPYWRITER
Dave Reger, Jim Bosilijevac

ART DIRECTOR
Mike Straznickas, Kevin Butler

GOLD

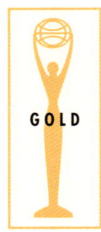

CATEGORY
Package Design

ADVERTISER/PRODUCT
Heinz—Quiet; Mustard; Thank You

ADVERTISING AGENCY
Leo Burnett USA, Chicago

MANUFACTURER
Heinz, Pittsburgh

CREATIVE DIRECTOR
Dave Reger, Mike Straznickas

COPYWRITER
Dave Reger, Jim Bosilijevac

ART DIRECTOR
Mike Straznickas, Kevin Butler

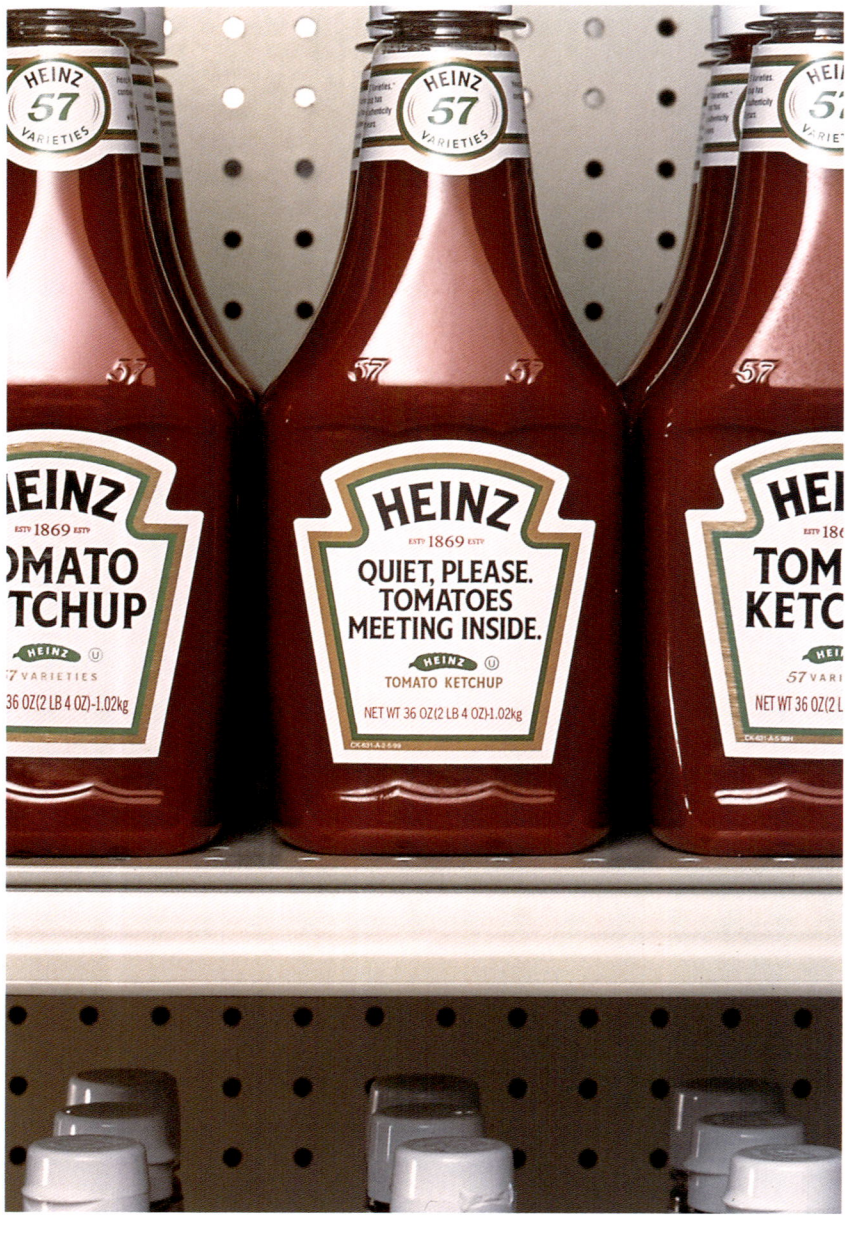

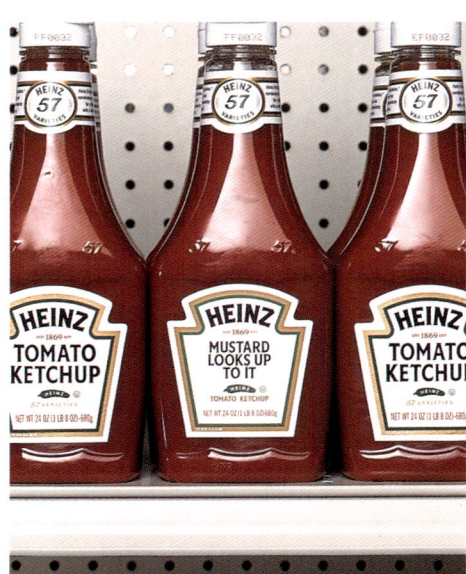

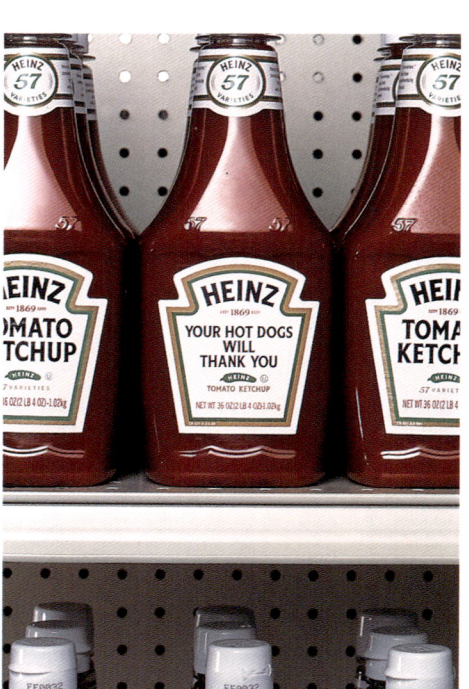

CATEGORY
Package Design

ADVERTISER/PRODUCT
Caban

DESIGN COMPANY
Blok Design, Toronto

CREATIVE DIRECTOR
Vanessa Eckstein

ART DIRECTOR
Vanessa Eckstein

DESIGNER
Vanessa Eckstein, Frances Chen,
Stephanie Yung

PHOTOGRAPHER
Richard Pierce

**DIRECTOR, INDUSTRIAL STORE
GRAPHIC DESIGN**
Alison Phillips

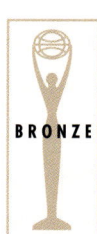

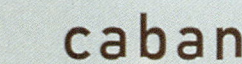

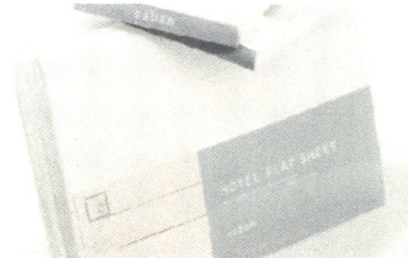

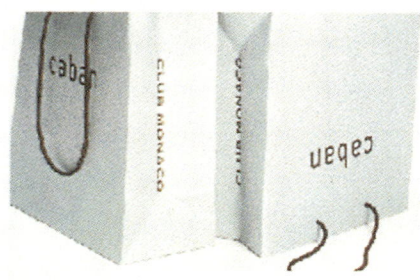

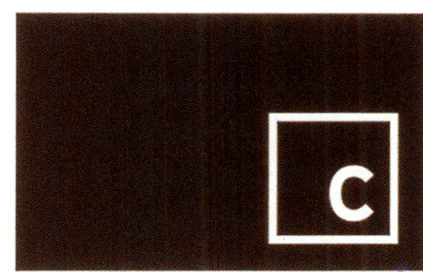

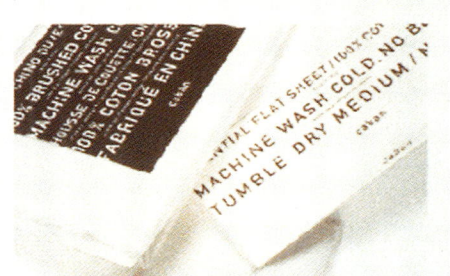

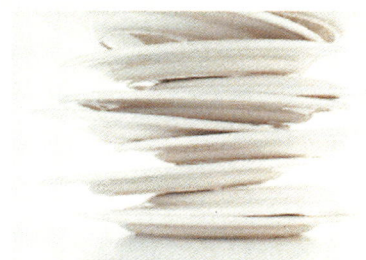

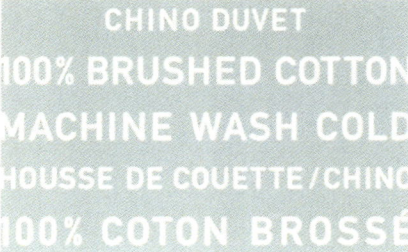

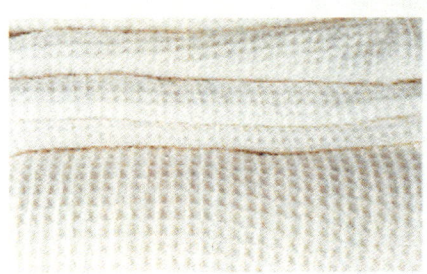

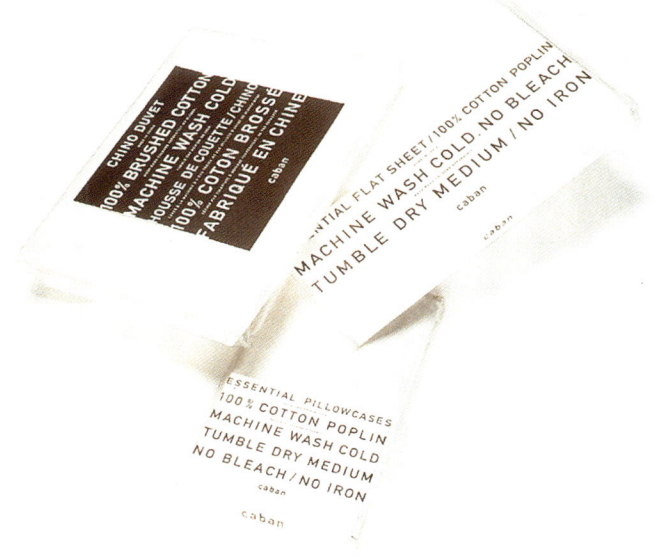

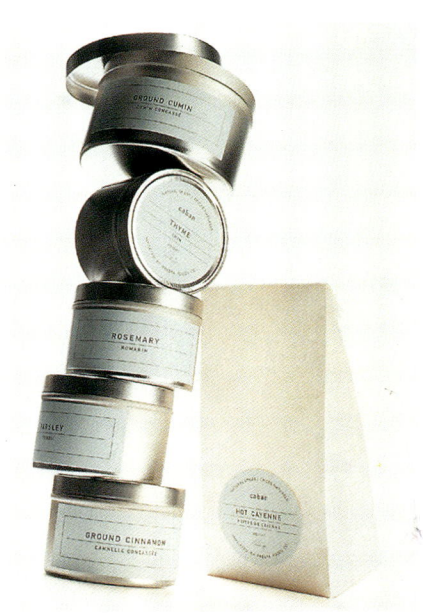

163

DESIGN

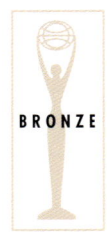

BRONZE

CATEGORY
Package Design

ADVERTISER/PRODUCT
Buddy Beer

ADVERTISING AGENCY
The Bearded Lady/Tribal DDB,
Stockholm

COPYWRITER
Johan Sandberg

ART DIRECTOR
Johan Sandberg

PRODUCTION MANAGER
Charlotte Lusiak

ILLUSTRATOR
Mats Johansson

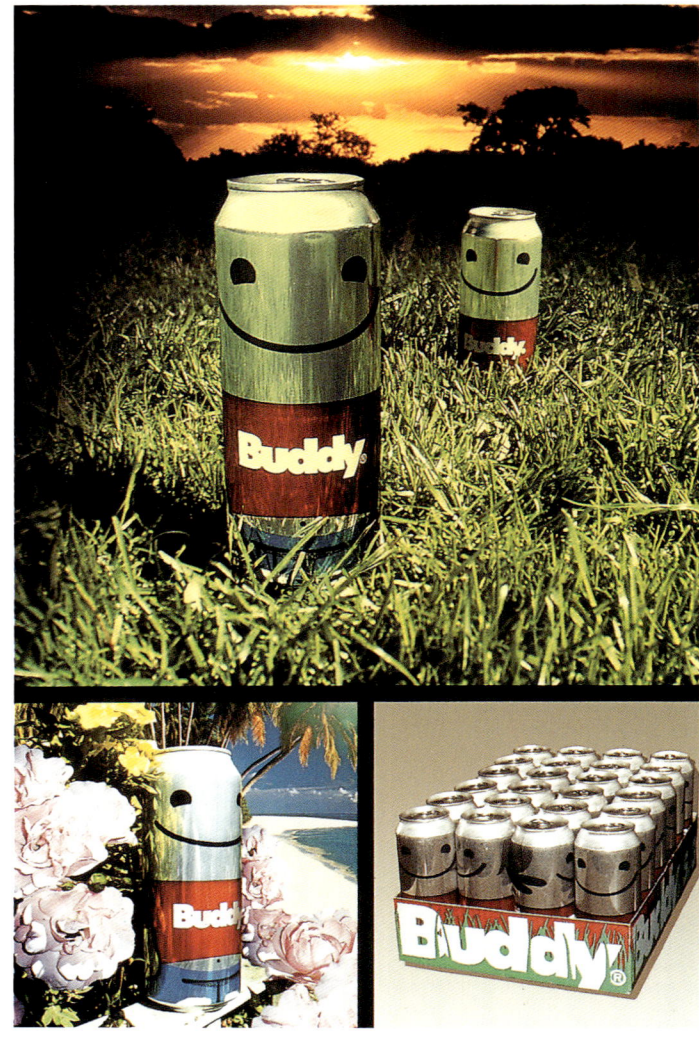

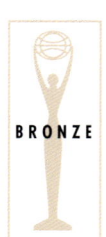

BRONZE

CATEGORY
Package Design

ADVERTISER/PRODUCT
Brewerkz India Pale Ale

ADVERTISING AGENCY
Saatchi & Saatchi, Singapore

PHOTOGRAPHY STUDIO
Alex Kai Keong Studios, Singapore

ACCOUNT EXECUTIVE
Eleanor Sia

CREATIVE DIRECTOR
Trefor Thomas

COPYWRITER
Rafiq Lehmann

ART DIRECTOR
Michelle Tranter

PRODUCTION MANAGER
Esther Yue, Keith Yeng

PHOTOGRAPHER
Alex Kai Keong

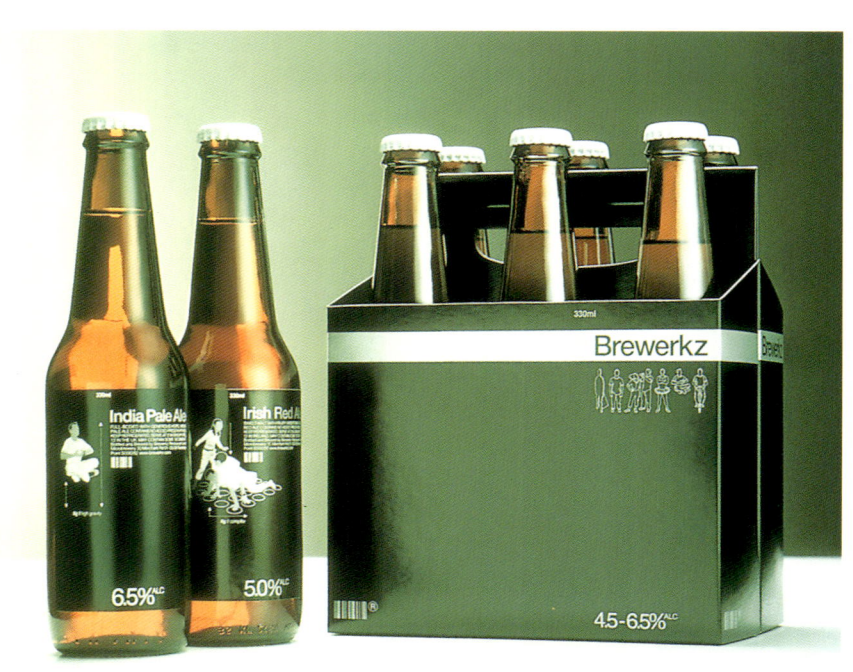

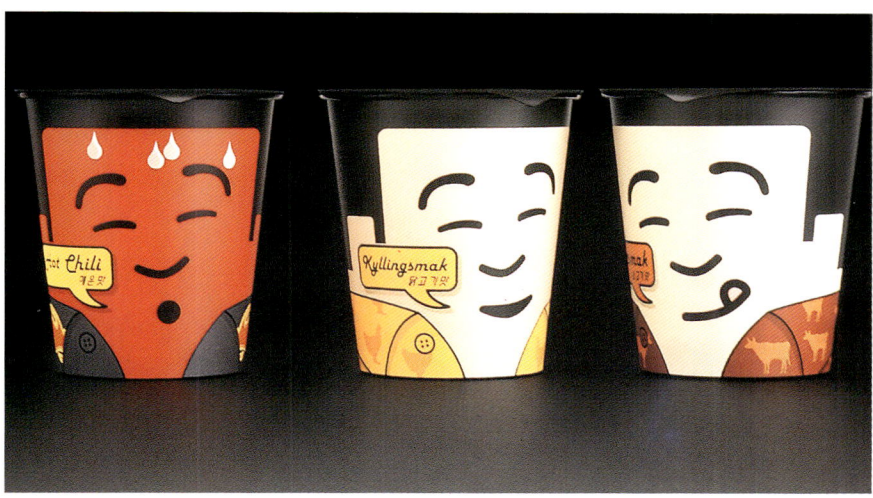

CATEGORY
Package Design

ADVERTISER/PRODUCT
Mr. Lee

DESIGN COMPANY
Design Bridge, London

ACCOUNT EXECUTIVE
Robyn Stevenson

CREATIVE DIRECTOR
Steve Elliott

ART DIRECTOR
Ian Burren

DESIGNER
Ian Burren

ILLUSTRATOR
Ian Burren

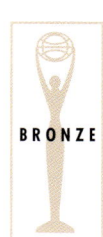

BRONZE

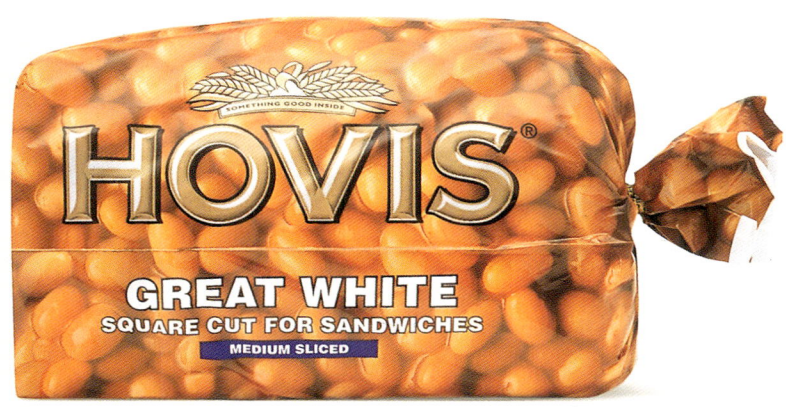

CATEGORY
Package Design

ADVERTISER/PRODUCT
Hovis Bakery

ADVERTISING AGENCY
Williams Murray Hamm, London

DESIGN COMPANY
Williams Murray Hamm, London

MANUFACTURER
British Barkery, London

ACCOUNT EXECUTIVE
Kellie Chapple

CREATIVE DIRECTOR
Garrick Hamm

ART DIRECTOR
Stewart Devlin

DESIGNER
Stewart Devlin

PHOTOGRAPHER
Jess Koppel

HOME ECONOMIST
Lyn Rutherford

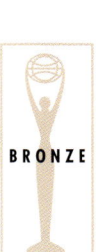

BRONZE

DESIGN

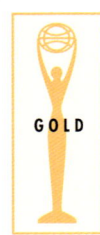

GOLD

CATEGORY
Point of Purchase

ADVERTISER/PRODUCT
Guinness

ADVERTISING AGENCY
BBDO, New York

**CHIEF CREATIVE OFFICER,
CHAIRMAN**
Ted Sann

CREATIVE DIRECTOR
Gerry Graf

ART DIRECTOR
Frank Anselmo, Jason Atienza

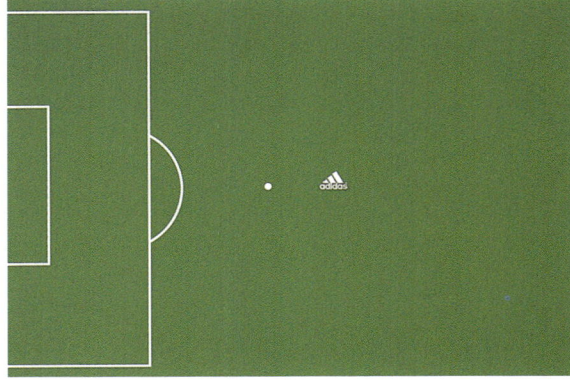

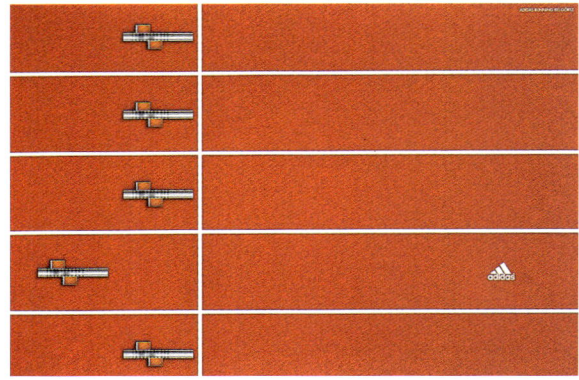

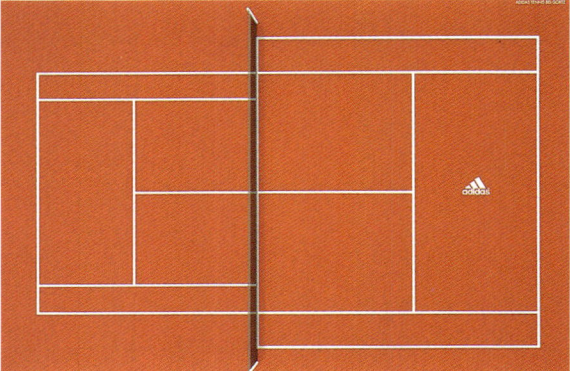

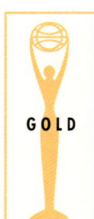

GOLD

CATEGORY
Point of Purchase

ADVERTISER/PRODUCT
Ludwig Görtz

ADVERTISING AGENCY
Springer & Jacoby, Hamburg

ACCOUNT EXECUTIVE
Niklas Frings-Rupp

CREATIVE DIRECTOR
Antje Hedde, Florian Grimm,
Amir Kassaei

COPYWRITER
Gerrit Zinke

ART DIRECTOR
Gerrit Zinke

PHOTOGRAPHER
Gerrit Zinke

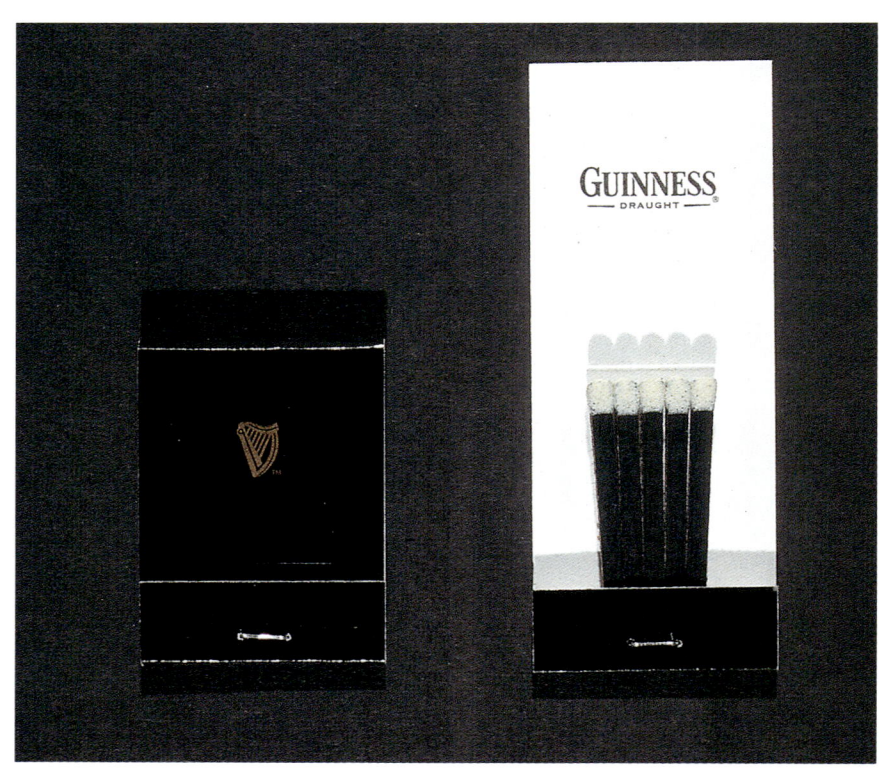

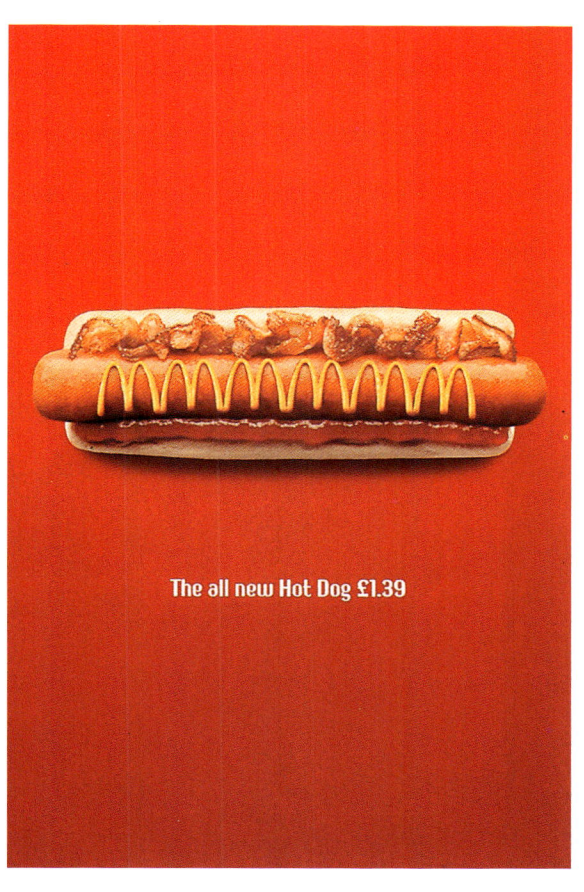

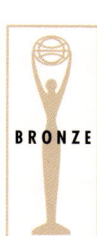

CATEGORY
Point of Purchase

ADVERTISER/PRODUCT
McDonald's/Hot Dog

ADVERTISING AGENCY
Leo Burnett, London

ACCOUNT EXECUTIVE
John Hawkes

EXECUTIVE CREATIVE DIRECTOR
Mark Tutssel, Nick Bell

COPYWRITER
Nick Bell

ART DIRECTOR
Mark Tutssel

PRODUCTION MANAGER
Colin Easton

PHOTOGRAPHER
Andy Roberts

TYPOGRAPHER
Mark Cakebread

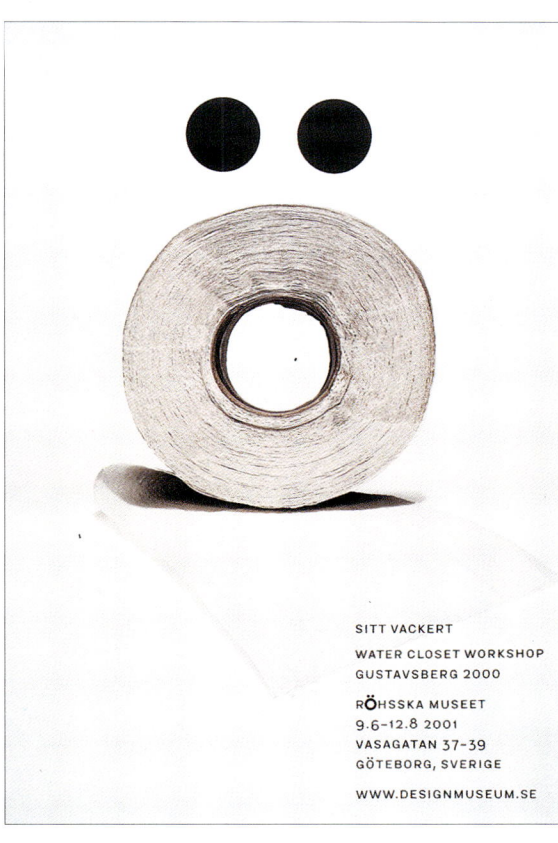

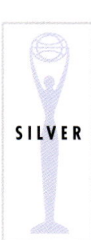

CATEGORY
Posters

ADVERTISER/PRODUCT
Sit Beautiful!/
Watercloset Workshop

ADVERTISING AGENCY
Happy Forsman & Bodenfors,
Gothenburg

MANUFACTURER
Röhsska Museet, Gothenburg

ACCOUNT EXECUTIVE
Yngve Nygren

ART DIRECTOR
Andreas Kittel

PRODUCTION MANAGER
Malin Berggren

PHOTOGRAPHER
Jesper Sundelin

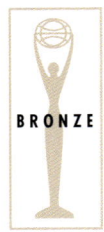

BRONZE

CATEGORY
Posters

ADVERTISER/PRODUCT
Björn Dahlström Exhibition w/
Book

ADVERTISING AGENCY
Happy Forsman & Bodenfors,
Gothenburg

MANUFACTURER
Röhsska Museet, Gothenburg

ACCOUNT EXECUTIVE
Yngve Nygren

COPYWRITER
Ingrid Sommar, Ulf Beckman

ART DIRECTOR
Andreas Kittel

PRODUCTION MANAGER
Malin Berggren

PHOTOGRAPHER
Åke E son Lindman, Jonas Linell,
Mathias Pettersson, Björn Keller,
Lasse Kärkkäinen, Joakim Bergström

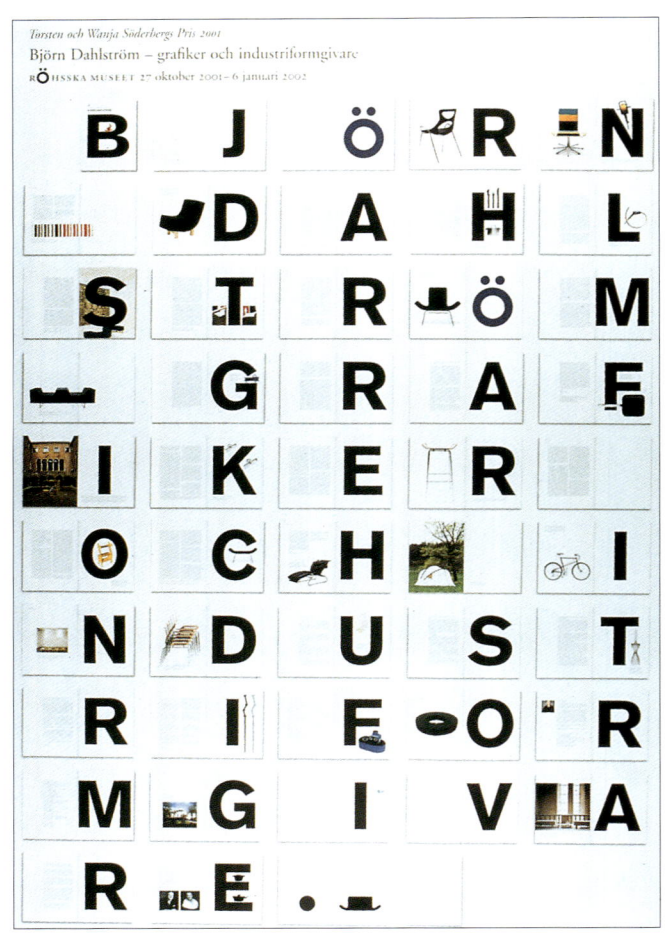

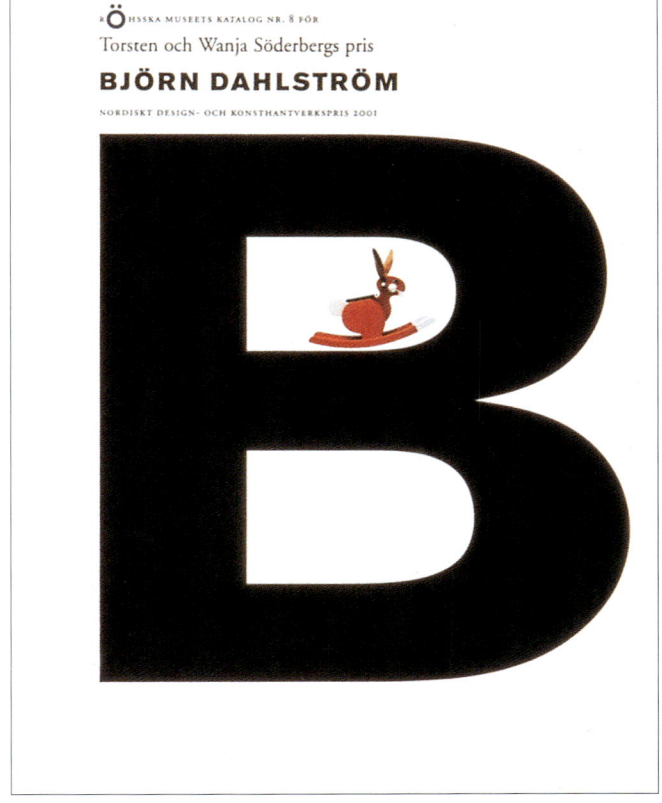

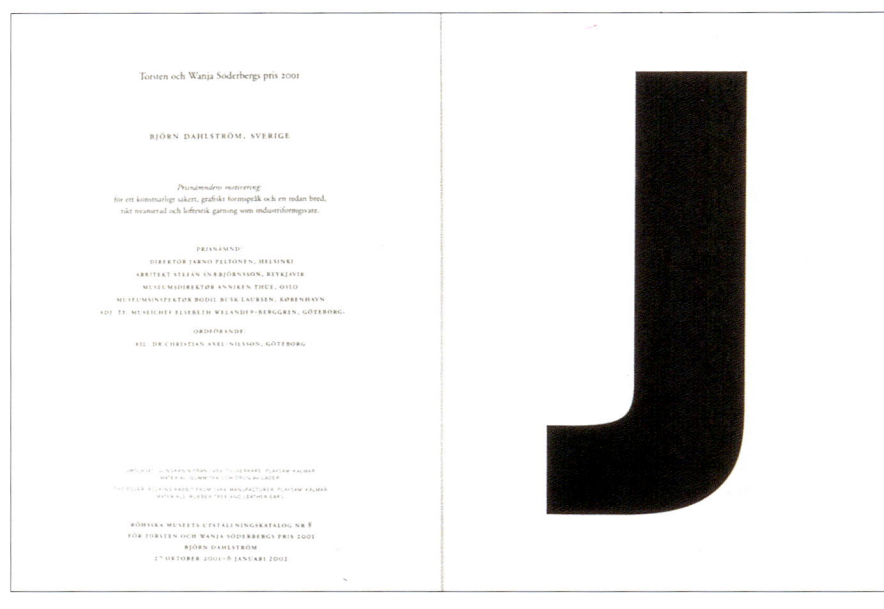

RÖHSKA MUSEET

FÖRORD

Röhska museet har utsett den svenske industridesignern, möbelformgivaren och grafikern Björn Dahlström som mottagare av Torsten och Wanja Söderbergs pris år 2001.

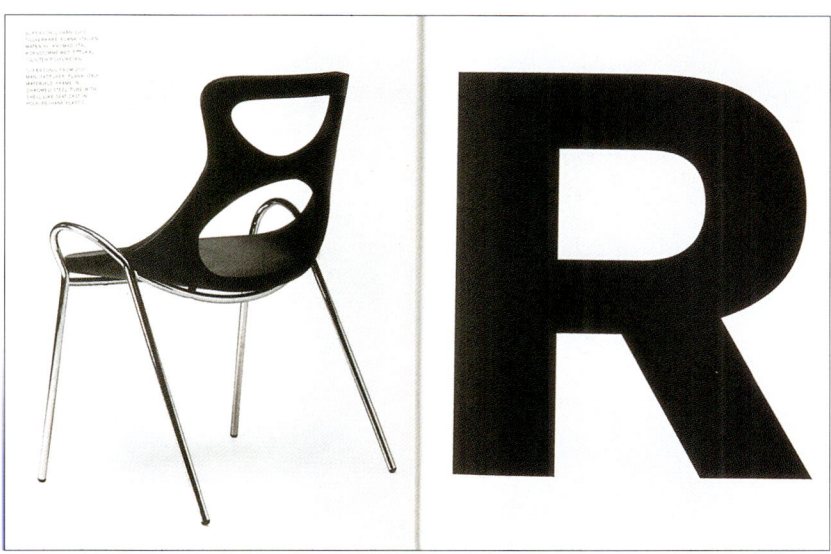

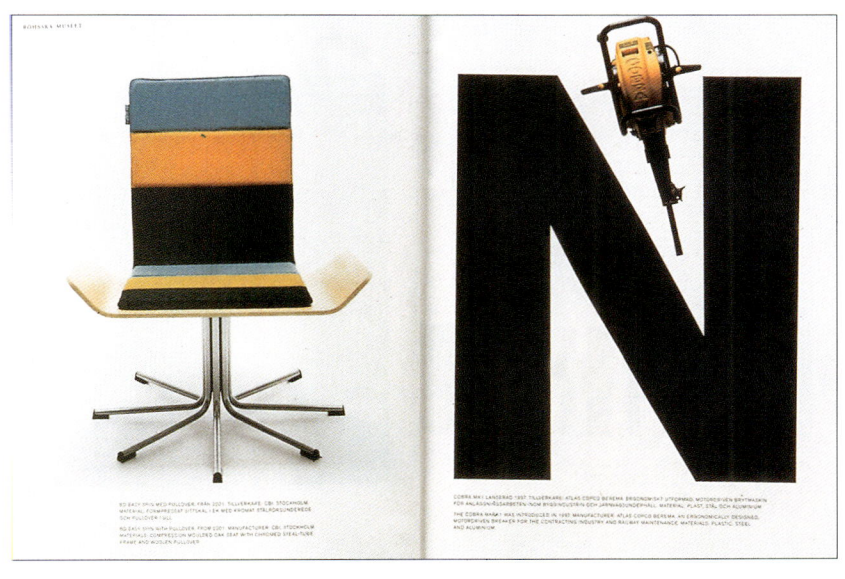

DESIGN

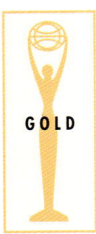

GOLD

CATEGORY
Self-Promotion

ADVERTISER/PRODUCT
White Architects/White-Book

ADVERTISING AGENCY
Happy Forsman & Bodenfors,
Gothenburg

MANUFACTURER
White Arkitekter, Gothenburg

CREATIVE DIRECTOR
Anders Kornestedt

COPYWRITER
Katja Grillner, Fredrik Nilsson

ART DIRECTOR
Lisa Careborg

PRODUCTION MANAGER
Malin Berggren

PHOTOGRAPHER
Mikael Olsson

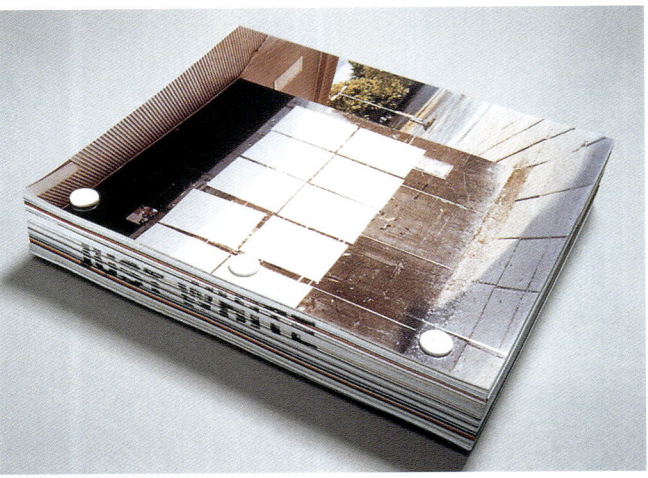

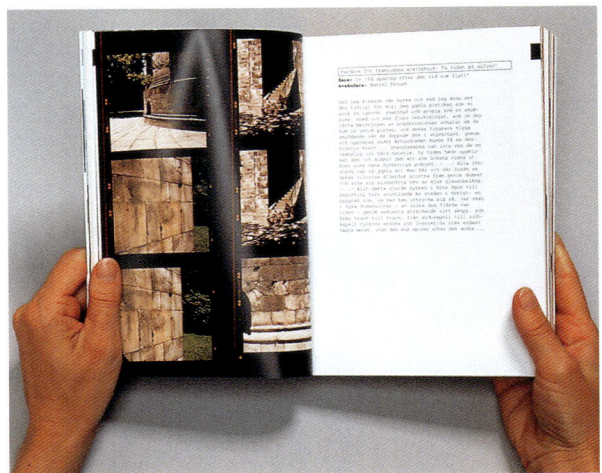

White Architects, the largest architectural firm in Sweden, celebrating its
fiftieth anniversary.

SILVER

CATEGORY
Self-Promotion

ADVERTISER/PRODUCT
Trill Birdfood/Invitation to the Blind

ADVERTISING AGENCY
D'Arcy, Hamburg

DESIGN COMPANY
D'Arcy Bianca Colussi, Hamburg

ACCOUNT EXECUTIVE
Sandra Öllering, Dr. Jens Ade

CREATIVE DIRECTOR
Deborah Hanusa, André Klein,
Veronika Claßen

COPYWRITER
André Klein

ART DIRECTOR
Deborah Hanusa

DESIGNER
Deborah Hanusa

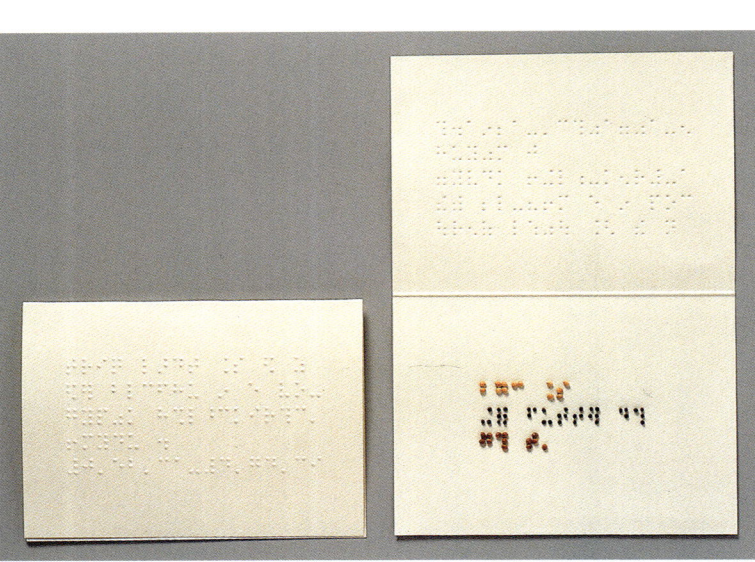

Trill Birdfood mailed out Braille invitations for a tour of a bird park
to blind members of society. The inside of the invitation included
birdseed arranged in Braille to read: "It would be a good idea to
bring this along."

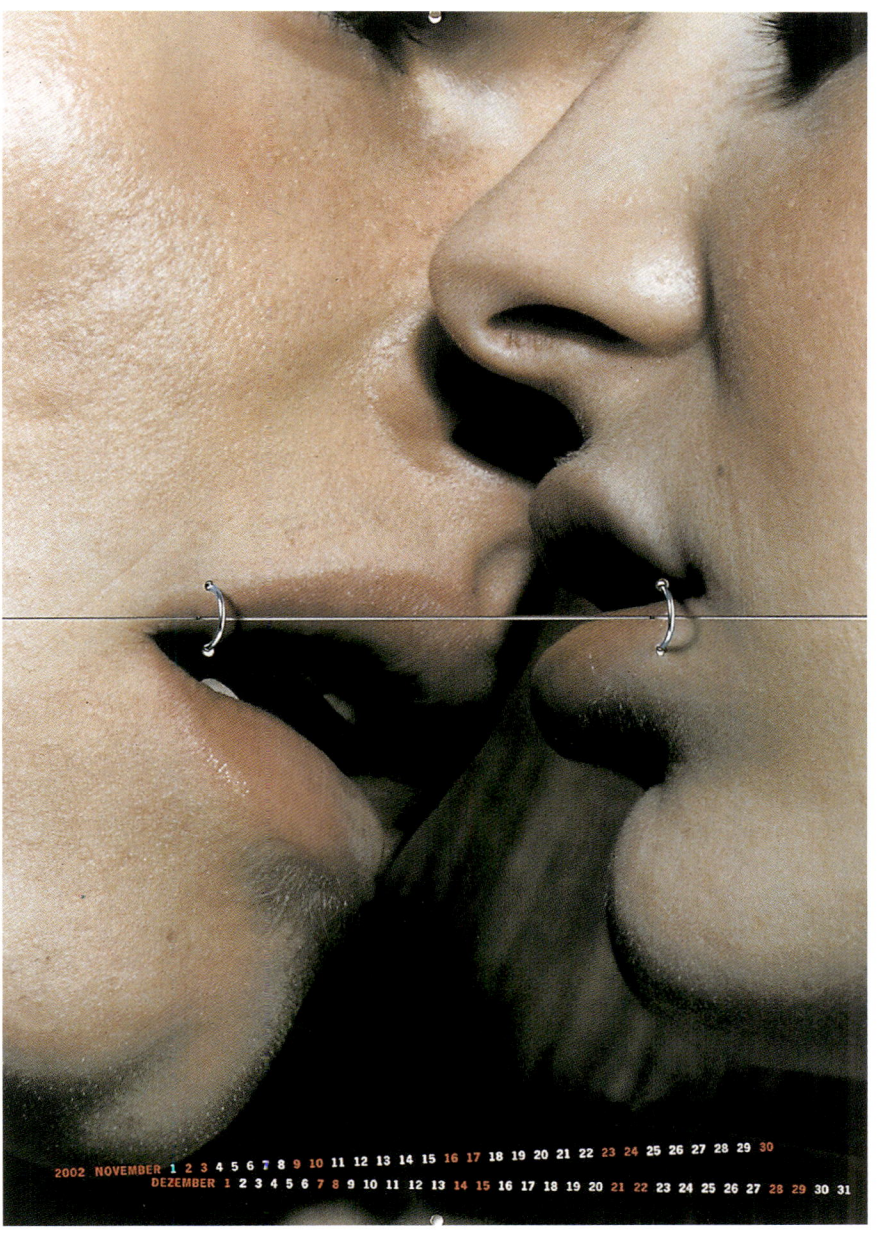

CATEGORY
Self-Promotion

ADVERTISER/PRODUCT
Endless Pain—Tattoo and Piercing
Company

ADVERTISING AGENCY
Weigertpirouzwolf, Hamburg

CREATIVE DIRECTOR
Michael Reissinger, Kay Eichner

COPYWRITER
Kay Eichner

ART DIRECTOR
Barbara Schirmer

DESIGNER
Barbara Schirmer

PHOTOGRAPHER
Hans Starck

BRONZE

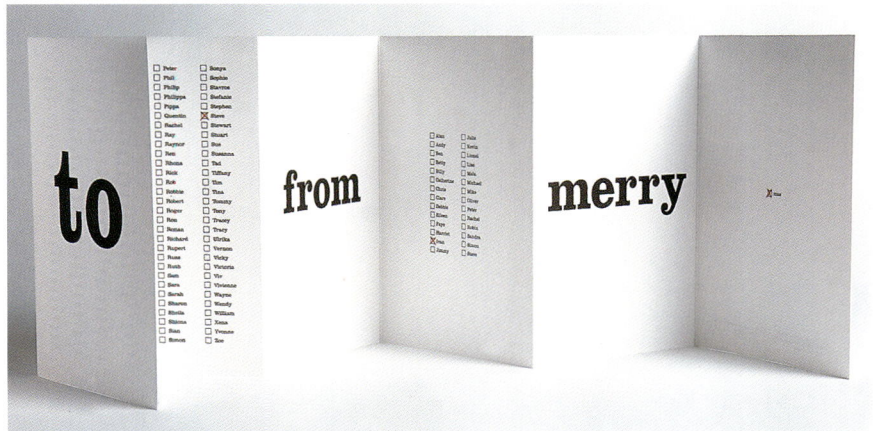

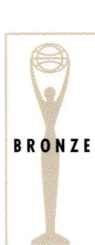

CATEGORY
Self-Promotion

ADVERTISER/PRODUCT
Chase Creative Christmas Card

DESIGN COMPANY
The Chase, Manchester

CREATIVE DIRECTOR
Ben Casey

DESIGNER
Steve Royle, Harriet Devoy

BRONZE

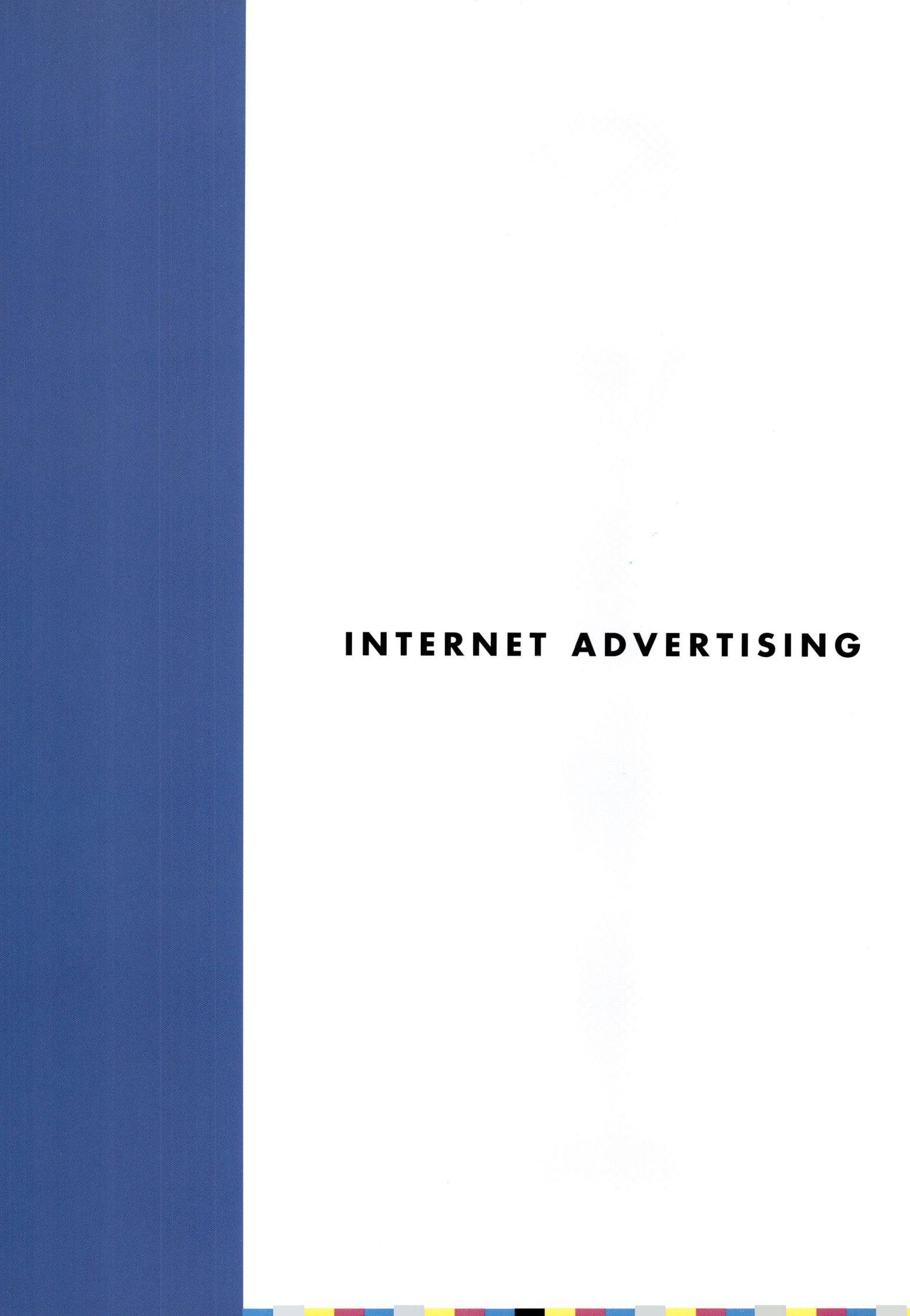

INTERNET ADVERTISING

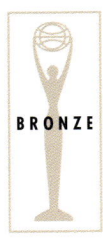

CATEGORY
Banner Ads 15K and Under

ADVERTISER/PRODUCT
Hewlett-Packard

NAME OF SITE
HP Invent Banner Campaign

ADVERTISING AGENCY
Goodby, Silverstein & Partners,
San Francisco

ACCOUNT EXECUTIVE
Christina Blosser

CREATIVE DIRECTOR
Steve Simpson

COPYWRITER
Will Elliott, John Matejczyk

ART DIRECTOR
Jeff Benjamin, Rick Casteel

DESIGN DIRECTOR
Keith Anderson

EXECUTIVE PRODUCER
Danaa Zellers

MOLECULE COMPOSER
Freestyle Interactive, San Francisco

COLOR
Orange Design

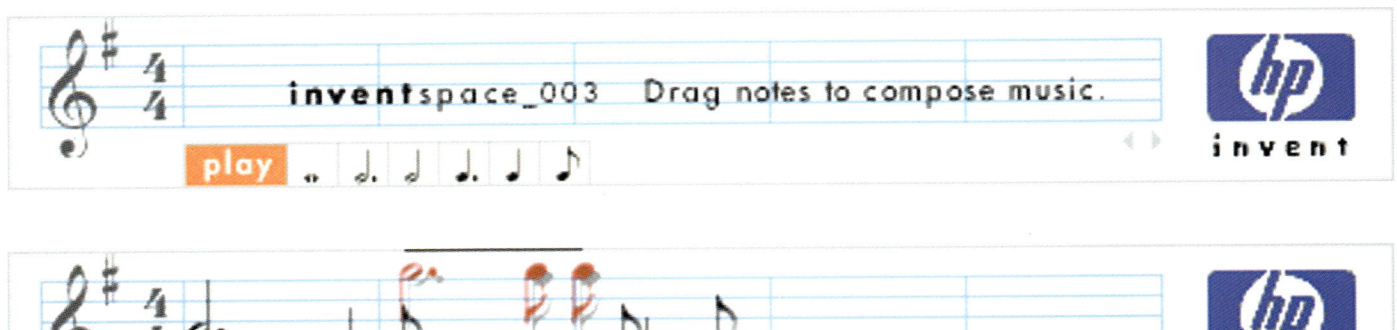

Who knew being an inventor was this much fun? These Rich Media banners invite users into the labs of HP Inventors, allowing them to do their own inventing while interacting with the HP brand. Three separate banner choices allow the user to create molecules, colors, and music.

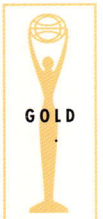

CATEGORY
Brand Building

ADVERTISER/PRODUCT
Nike

NAME OF SITE
Nike Freestyle

ADVERTISING AGENCY
Framfab, Copenhagen

ACCOUNT EXECUTIVE
Bettina Sherain

CREATIVE DIRECTOR
Lars Bastholm

COPYWRITER
Jamie McPhee

ART DIRECTOR
Rasmus Frandsen

DESIGNER
Rasmus Michelsen, Tue Wesnes

PROGRAMMER
Thomas Weiss

PRODUCTION MANAGER
Anne-Sofie Hahn-Pedersen

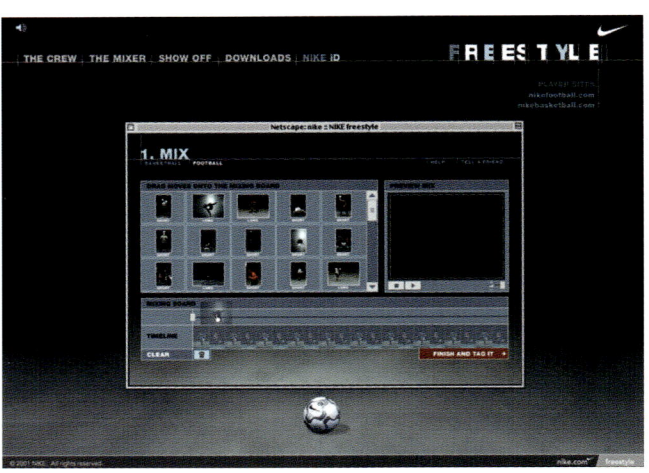

Giving respect to the true players, Nike Freestyle celebrates the creativity and style that athletes bring to their own game. To bring it to life online, the site's aim is to give users the opportunity to create, personalize, and participate. It's improvisational, innovative, and totally original. In other words, freestyle.

CATEGORY
Brand Building

ADVERTISER/PRODUCT
Vodafone

NAME OF SITE
Vodafone Microsite

WWW DEVELOPER
Paregos, Skelleftea

ADVERTISING AGENCY
Wieden + Kennedy, Amsterdam

ACCOUNT EXECUTIVE
Jared Gossler

CREATIVE DIRECTOR
Anita Lozinska

COPYWRITER
Ned McNeilage, Jenna Hall

ART DIRECTOR/DESIGNER
Anita Lozinska, Marius Gronwald

PROGRAMMER
Paregos

PRODUCER
Katie Raye, Guido van der Meersche

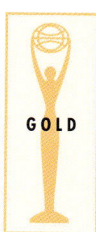

GOLD

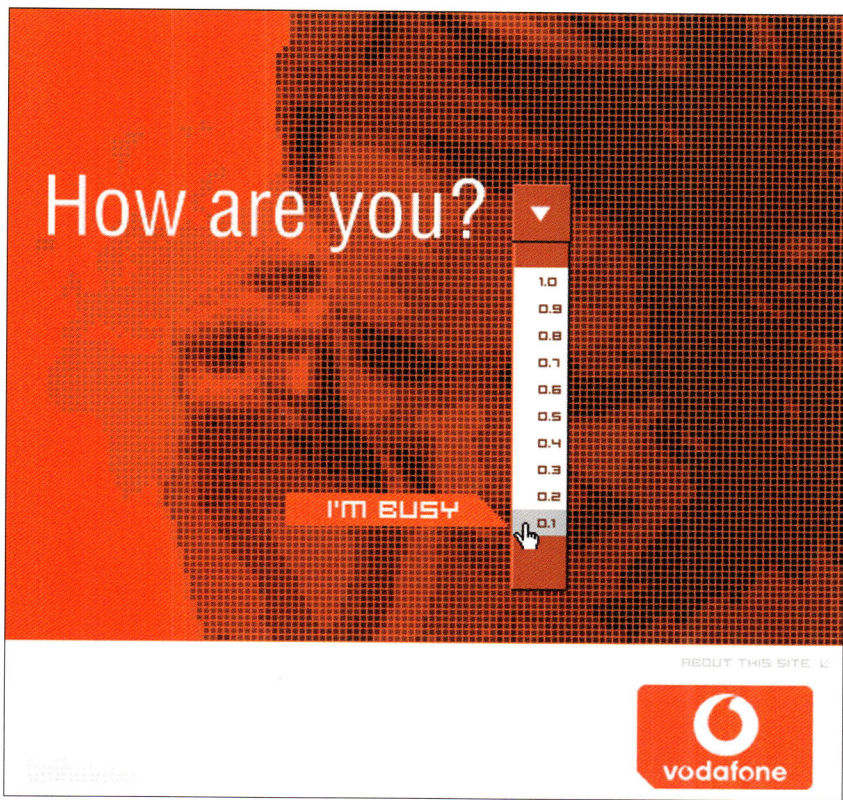

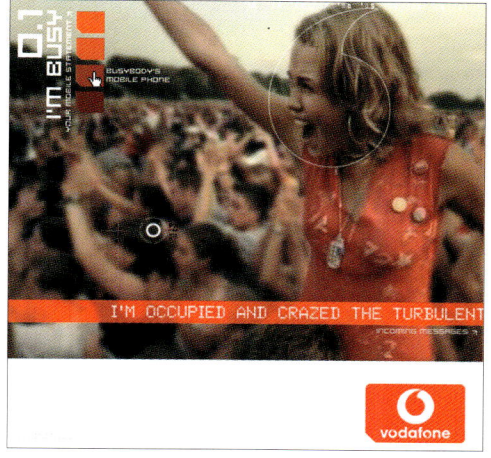

At the heart of the Vodafone brand is an understanding of the human need for communication. People want to connect with others and share how they're feeling whenever they need to, no matter where they are. The global launch of the Vodafone advertising campaign shared this idea with the public by using the simple line, "How are you?"—and asking visitors to respond. From the Vodafone perspective, online communities aren't formed by geography or nationality but, instead, around common interests and experiences. It's about connecting with others, and with giving people immediate contact to a like-minded community.

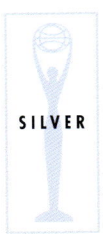

CATEGORY
Brand Building

ADVERTISER/PRODUCT
Habitat

NAME OF SITE
Habitat Web site

WWW DEVELOPER
Digit, London

ADVERTISING AGENCY
Digit, London

ACCOUNT EXECUTIVE
Claire Dimeloe

CREATIVE DIRECTOR
Daljit Singh

ART DIRECTOR
Brad Smith

DESIGNER
Chris Barnes, Matt Rice, Jon Sijan,
Adam Williams, Kevin Helas,
Thomas Poeser, Mikkel Askjaer

PROGRAMMER
Orlando Mathias

PRODUCTION MANAGER
Claire Dimeloe

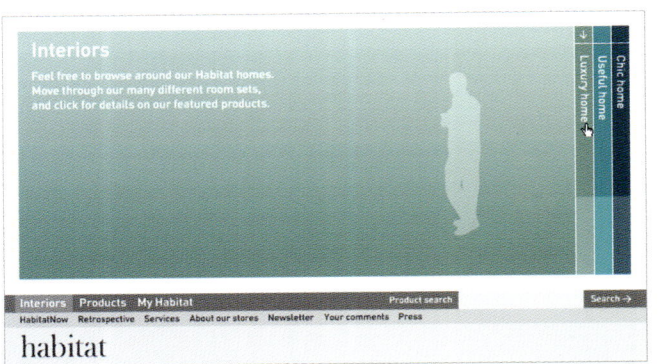
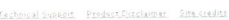
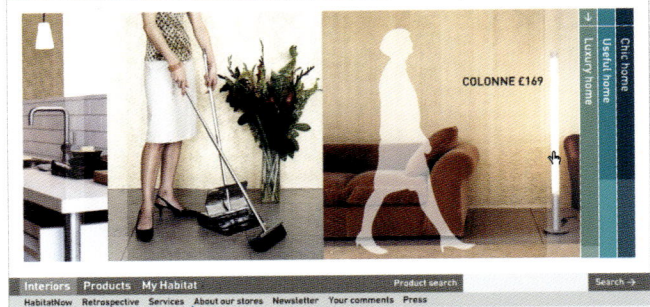

The Habitat site—which features furnishings and accessories for the home—was created with the concept that "Form IS Function," by employing simple, effective navigation for the visitor. The site was produced with the flexibility to embrace almost bimonthly seasonal product changes, and also with the knowledge that customers would benefit from seeing how Habitat products would look in their own homes and what size they are in relation to each other; hence an editable background and scaling tools.

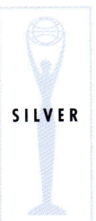

CATEGORY
Brand Building

ADVERTISER/PRODUCT
Lorgans, The Retro Store

NAME OF SITE
Lorgans, The Retro Store

WWW DEVELOPER
Kinetic, Singapore

ADVERTISING AGENCY
Kinetic, Singpore

ACCOUNT EXECUTIVE
Carolyn Teo

CREATIVE DIRECTOR
Kinetic

COPYWRITER
Lorgans

ART DIRECTOR/DESIGNER
Sean Lam, Benjy Choo

PROGRAMMER
Benjy Choo

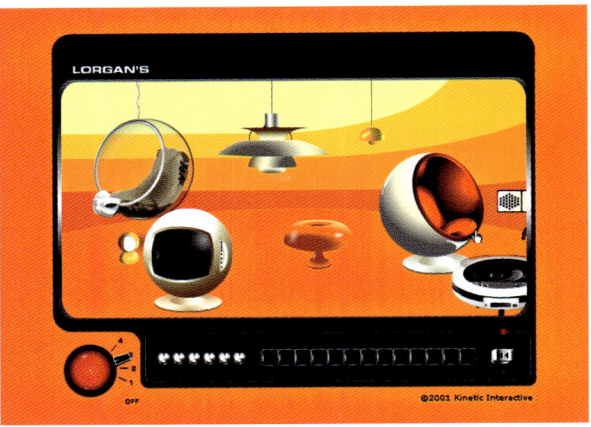
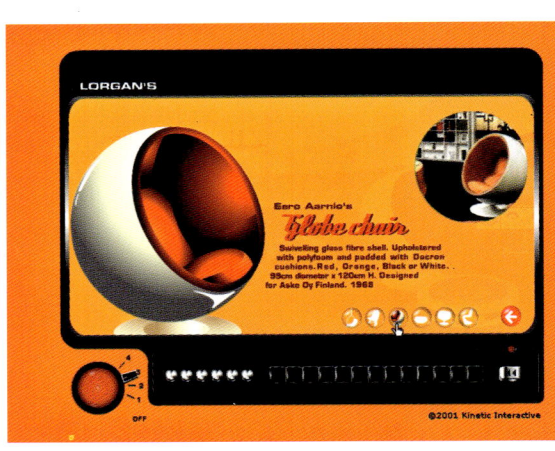

Lorgan's is a specialty store dealing in retro furnishings. The objective of the site is to educate and interest the public in retro furniture as well as to entice them to visit the actual physical store.

CATEGORY Brand Building	**ADVERTISING AGENCY** Framfab, Copenhagen	**COPYWRITER** Jamie McPhee	**PROGRAMMER** Thomas Weiss
ADVERTISER/PRODUCT Nike Retail	**ACCOUNT EXECUTIVE** Bettina Sherain	**ART DIRECTOR** Lars Cortsen	**PRODUCTION MANAGER** Anne-Sofie Hahn-Pedersen
NAME OF SITE Nike Women	**CREATIVE DIRECTOR** Lars Bastholm	**DESIGNER** Robert Thomsen	

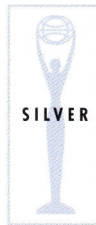

SILVER

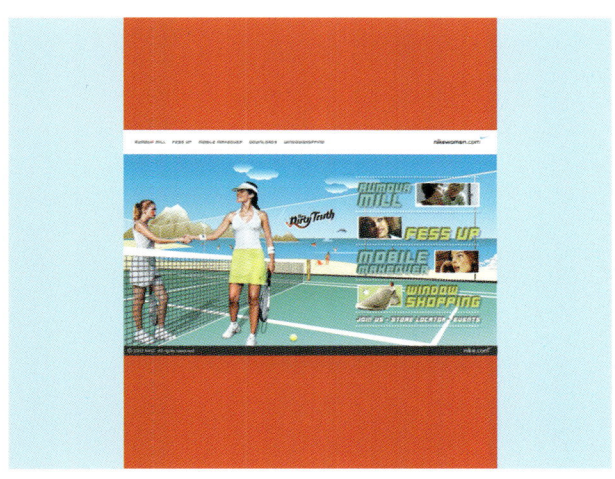

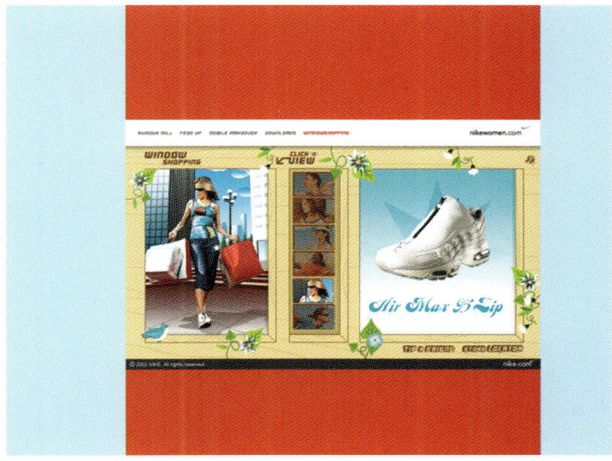

All about attitude, nikewomen.com celebrates "The Dirty Truth"—getting real and telling it like it is. It's a look into the secret habits, routines, and quirks that all women share but never actually talk about.

CATEGORY Brand Building	**WWW DEVELOPER** pixShift, Stockholm	**CREATIVE DIRECTOR** Marten Ivert	**PROGRAMMER** Oskar Sundberg
ADVERTISER/PRODUCT Absolut	**ADVERTISING AGENCY** Springtime, Stockholm	**COPYWRITER** Staffan Wilsson	**PRODUCER** Magnus Walsten
NAME OF SITE Absolut Perfection	**ACCOUNT EXECUTIVE** Ola Spanner, Otto Giesenfeld	**ART DIRECTOR** Tomas Forsberg	

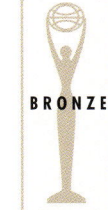

BRONZE

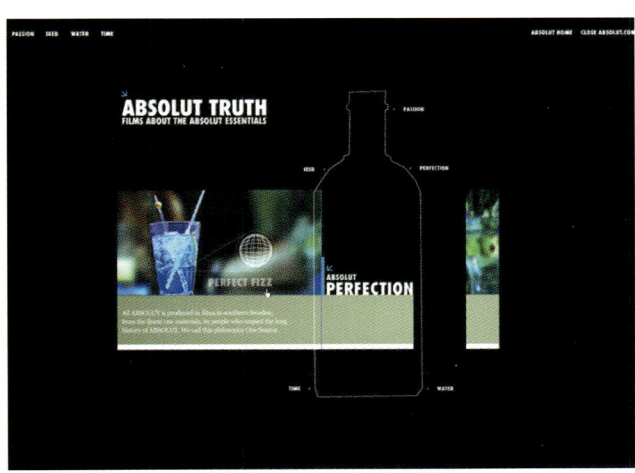

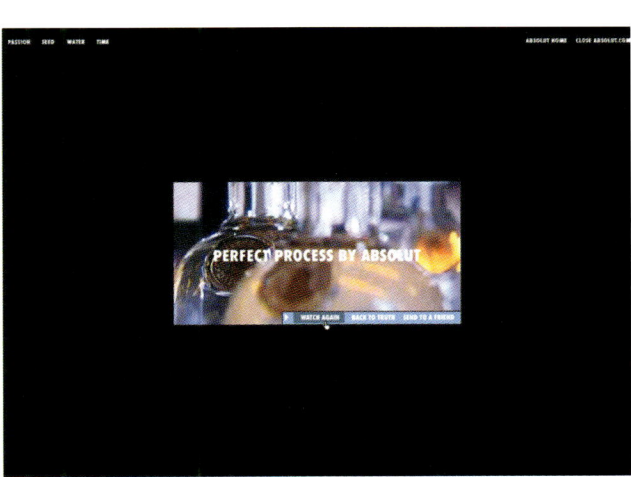

Absolut Truth, featured on the Absolut Vodka brand site, highlights various quality aspects of Absolut through a series of short films. "Absolut Perfection," a short film about the process behind every bottle of Absolut, is the fifth release in this series. In approximately ninety seconds, the visitor is taken on a backward journey all the way from a cocktail glass in a downtown bar, past the distillery, back to the very beginning of the process—all the while reaffirming the brand's smart, stylish, and witty identity.

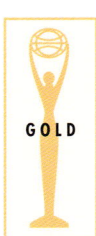

GOLD

CATEGORY
Consumer-Targeted Site

ADVERTISER/PRODUCT
BMW Films

NAME OF SITE
BMW Films Campaign

ADVERTISING AGENCY
Fallon, Minneapolis

ACCOUNT EXECUTIVE
Ginny Grossman, Cori vanBrunt,
Marit Iverson, Lisa Lavigne,
Bryan Chang

CREATIVE DIRECTOR
David Lubars, Bruce Bildsten

COPYWRITER
Andrew Kevin Walker, Joe Sweet,
Wong Kar Wei, Guy Ritchie,
Alejandro Gonzalez Iñarritu,
David Carter, Guillermo Arriaga

ART DIRECTOR
David Carter, Martin Whis,
Joe Sweet, Tom Riddle

PRODUCTION COMPANY
Anonymous Content, Los Angeles

EDITING COMPANY
Spot Welders, Los Angeles;
Jettone, Hong Kong;
Nomad Editing, Santa Monica;
Z Films, Mexico City;
Good Edit, New York;
Assembly Line, Minneapolis

MUSIC COMPANY
Hi-Fi Productions, New York;
Universal Music Mexico, Mexico
City; Elements, Santa Monica

SOUND DESIGN COMPANY
Mit Out Sound, Sausalito;
Z Films, Mexico City

EXECUTIVE PRODUCER
David Fincher

PRODUCER
Robyn Boardman, Aristides McGarry,
Rob Van de Weteringe Buys,
Tapas Blank

DIRECTOR
John Frankenheimer,
Wong Kar Wei, Guy Ritchie,
Alejandro Gonzalez Iñarritu, Ang Lee

DIRECTOR OF PHOTOGRAPHY
Newton Thomas Sigel,
Harris Savides, Frederick Elmes,
Chris Soos, Bob Richardson

SOUND DESIGNER
Ren Klyce

DIRECTOR OF SUB-STORY
Ben Younger

DESIGNER
Mark Sandau, Brooke Posard

PROJECT MANAGER
Jennifer Bremer, Jobim Hume,
Valerie Threatt

MUTIMEDIA DEVELOPER
Mark Sandau, Christian Erickson,
Chris Wiggins, Chris Stocksmith,
Laurie Brown

DEVELOPER
George Hilal, Marc Gowland,
Josh Hagen, Chris Wiggins

TECHNICAL LEAD
Matt Heinrichs

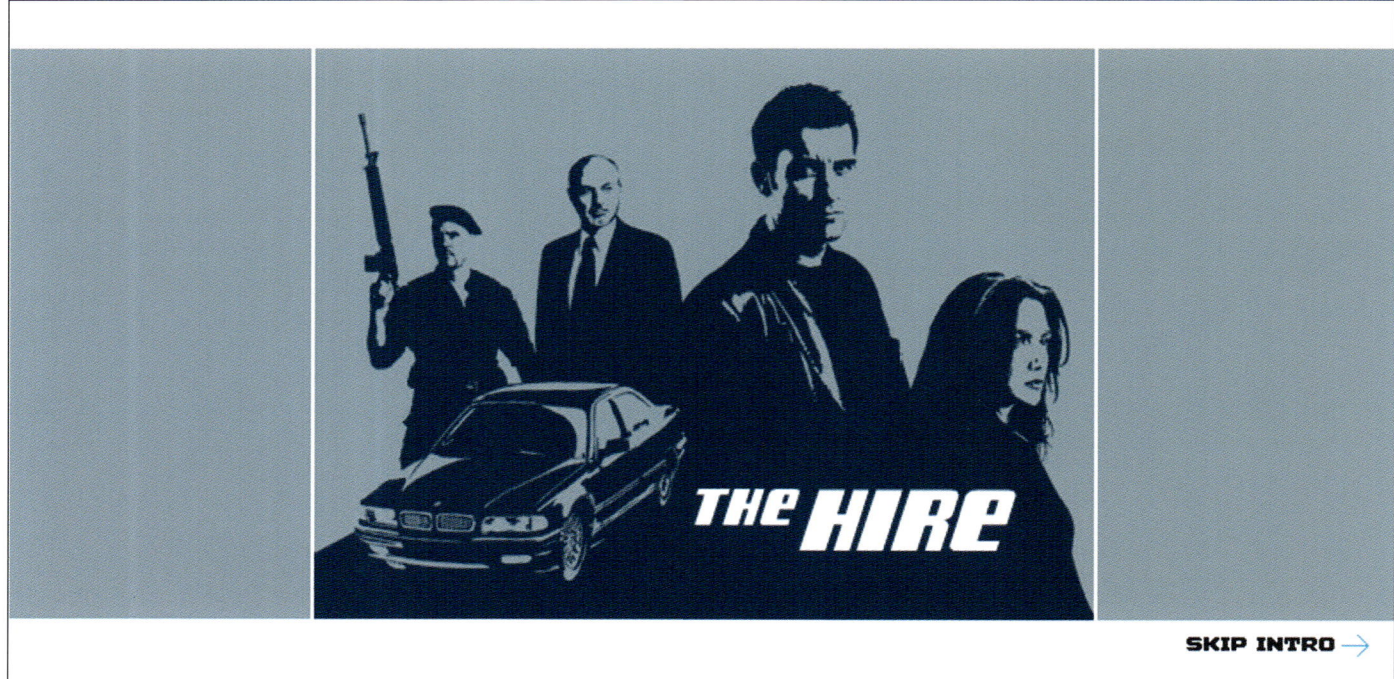

It began as an advertising brief, but advertising wasn't the answer. Traditional commercials could not impart what BMWs could really do, plus BMW customers increasingly were not watching television. They had, however, embraced the Internet in astounding numbers. The new idea was to create something so entertaining and so rewarding that people would actually seek it out. The question then became: Why not create an interactive experience more akin to home theater? What resulted was BMW Films, a series of shorts directed by and starring A-list cinema talent. Each film revolved around a central character called The Driver, the world's best when it came to transporting people out of dangerous situations. The Driver's character traits—youthfulness, integrity, passion, willingness to take risks—reflected on both the brand and the audience. Each film featured The Driver using a BMW to complete his missions, showcasing BMW's true performance.

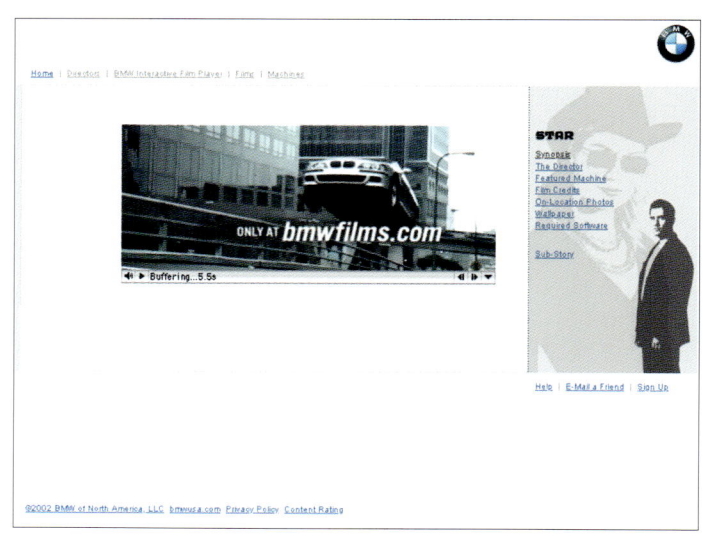

CATEGORY
Consumer-Targeted Site

ADVERTISER/PRODUCT
Ice Age

NAME OF SITE
Ice Age Film Site

WWW DEVELOPER
Genex, Los Angeles

CREATIVE DIRECTOR
Taj Tedrow

COPYWRITER
Taj Tedrow, Eric Perez

ART DIRECTOR
Eric Perez

PROGRAMMER
Jimmy Chen, Mike Kellogg,
Noah Gedrich

PRODUCTION MANAGER
Patrick Ellis

CLIENT
20th Century Fox

DIRECTOR, NEW MEDIA
Liz Jones

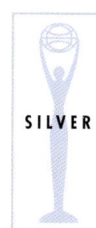

SILVER

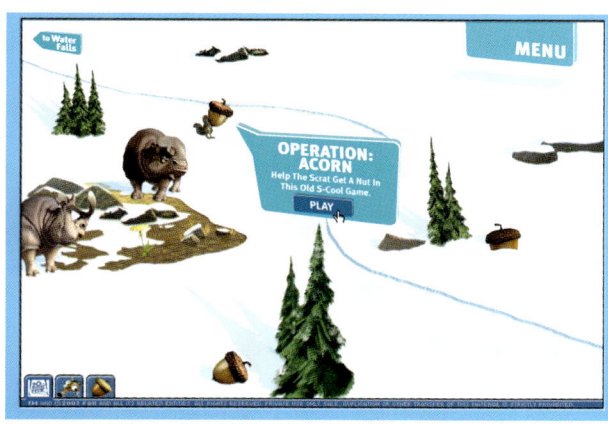
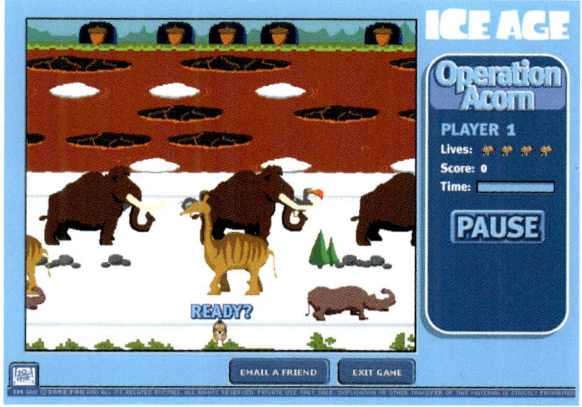

Twentieth Century Fox wanted to create an exciting online destination for their animated feature, *Ice Age*. The idea was to engage and educate audiences, leveraging the Web to introduce various prehistoric characters from the film. Genex's solution was to produce an interactive and entertaining environment that reflected the film's playful spirit.

CATEGORY
Consumer-Targeted Site

ADVERTISER/PRODUCT
The Royal Tenenbaums Movie Web Site

NAME OF SITE
The Royal Tenenbaums

WWW DEVELOPER
65 Media, West Hollywood

ADVERTISING AGENCY
Buena Vista Pictures Marketing,
Burbank

ACCOUNT EXECUTIVE
Deanna McDaniel, VP, Internet

CREATIVE DIRECTOR
Albin Reif, T. Reif

ART DIRECTOR
Fernando Ramirez

PRODUCER
Lance Porter, Susan Lambert

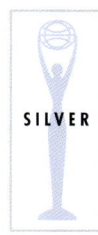

SILVER

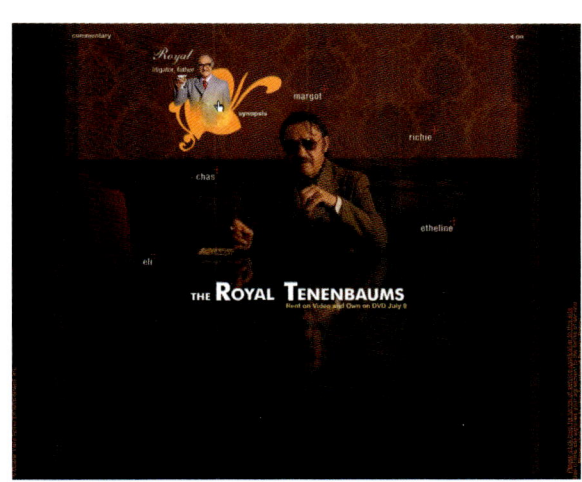
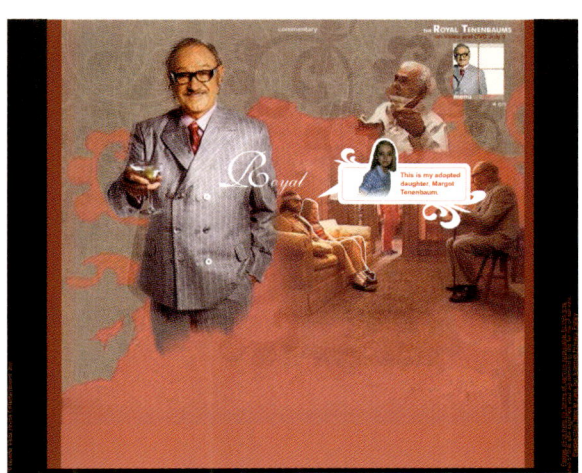

The Royal Tenenbaums' site is as eccentric, rich, and offbeat as Wes Anderson's quirky Tenenbaums and their extended family. The primary navigation page is built around the site's connecting element, the flawed hero Royal Tenenbaum. Links to each of his estranged genius children, his wife Etheline, and their neighbor Eli, swirl around his image at the head of the table. Layers of detail, bits of added commentary, and intuitive navigation encourage users to explore and interact in an extremely functional fashion with an extremely dysfunctional family.

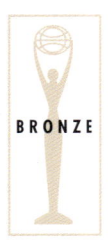

BRONZE

CATEGORY Consumer-Targeted Site	**WWW DEVELOPER** Kinetic Singapore, Singapore	**CREATIVE DIRECTOR** Kinetic Singapore	**PRODUCTION MANAGER** Benjy Choo, Sean Lam
ADVERTISER/PRODUCT Lorgan's The Retro Store	**ADVERTISING AGENCY** Kinetic, Singapore	**COPYWRITER/ART DIRECTOR** Benjy Choo, Sean Lam	
NAME OF SITE Lorgan's The Retro Store	**ACCOUNT EXECUTIVE** Carolyn Teo	**DESIGNER/PROGRAMMER** Benjy Choo, Sean Lam	

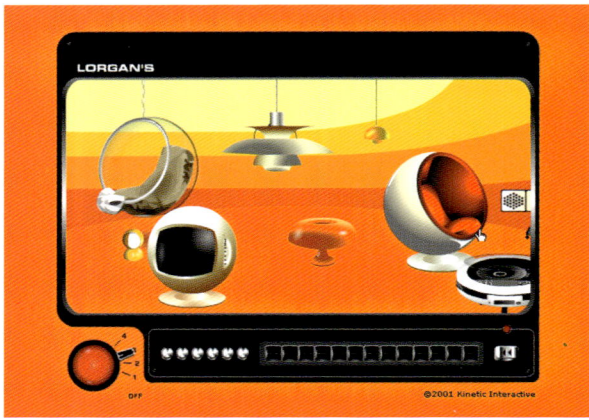
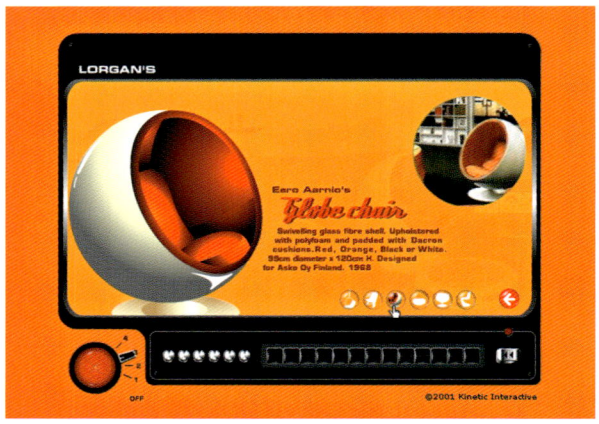

Lorgan's is a specialty store dealing in retro furnishings. The objective of the site is to educate and interest the public in retro furniture as well as to entice them to visit the actual physical store.

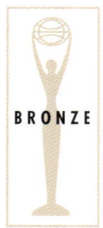

BRONZE

CATEGORY Consumer-Targeted Site	**ADVERTISING AGENCY** Abel & Baker, Stockholm	**ART DIRECTOR** Martin Cedergren, Ted Persson	**PRODUCTION MANAGER** Fredrik Heghammar
ADVERTISER/PRODUCT MTV Nordic	**ACCOUNT EXECUTIVE** Måns Ulvestam	**DESIGNER** Viktor Larsson, Arvid Tappert	**PROJECT MANAGER** Viktoria Wallner
NAME OF SITE MTV Karaoke Challenge	**COPYWRITER** Kristoffer Triumf, Magnus Larsson	**PROGRAMMER** Tony Sajdak, Tim Sajdak, Peter Karlsson	**CONCEPT** Tony Sajdak, Martin Cedergren

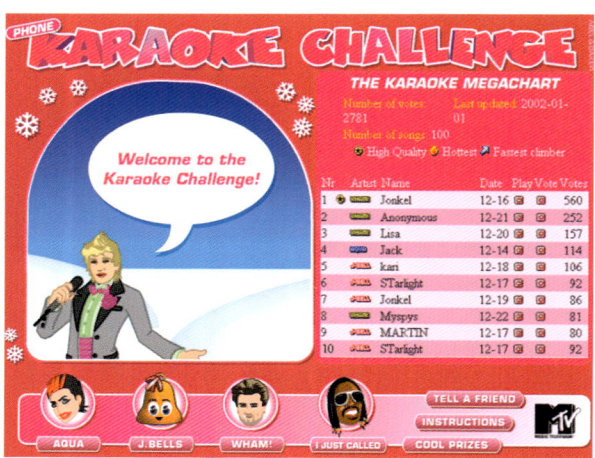
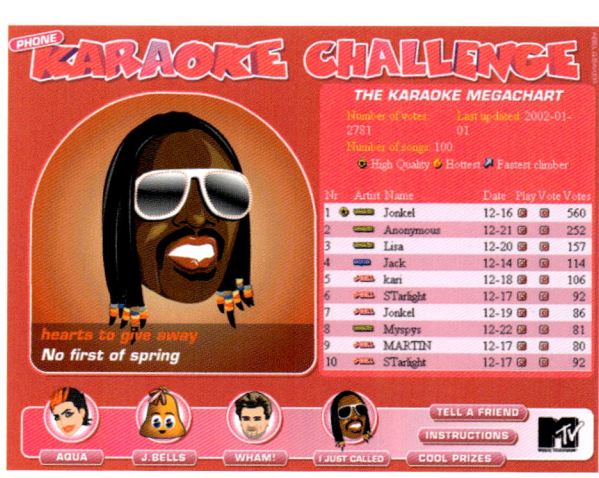

The MTV Karaoke Challenge brings karaoke to the Internet, with the invention of a karaoke machine that enables the visitors to sing to their favorite tunes and send them to their friends. The process: A mobile phone is turned into a microphone and the computer into a karaoke machine.

CATEGORY
Consumer-Targeted Site

ADVERTISER/PRODUCT
Habitat

NAME OF SITE
Habitat Web Site

WWW DEVELOPER
Digit, London

ADVERTISING AGENCY
Digit, London

ACCOUNT EXECUTIVE
Claire Dimeloe

CREATIVE DIRECTOR
Daljit Singh

ART DIRECTOR
Brad Smith

DESIGNER
Chris Barnes, Matt Rice, Jon Shaw,
Adam Williams, Kevin Helas

PROGRAMMER
Orlando Dimeloe, Thomas Poeser,
Mikkel Askjaer

PRODUCTION MANAGER
Claire Dimeloe

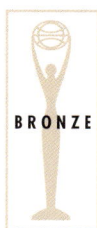

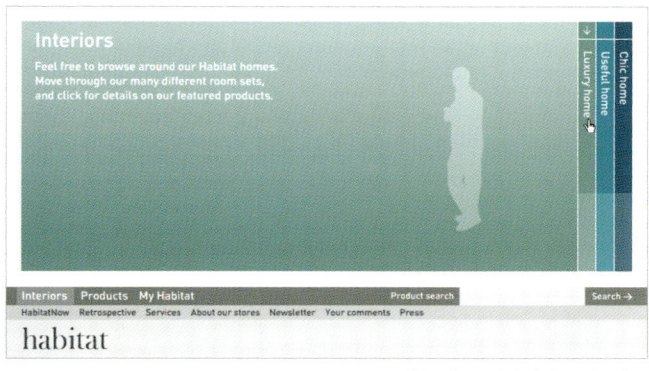

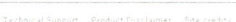

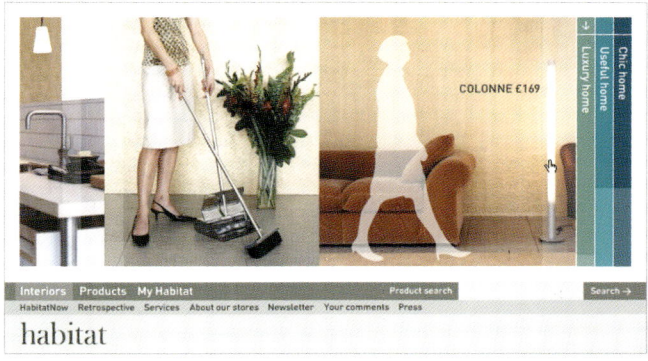

The Habitat site—which features furnishings and accessories for the home—was created with the concept that "Form IS Function," by employing simple, effective navigation for the visitor. The site was produced with the flexibility to embrace almost bimonthly seasonal product changes, and also with the knowledge that customers would benefit from seeing how Habitat products would look in their own homes and what size they are in relation to each other; hence, an editable background and scaling tools.

CATEGORY
Direct Response

ADVERTISER/PRODUCT
American Cancer Society

NAME OF SITE
Breast Exam

ADVERTISING AGENCY
Contacto Marketing & Comm,
Coral Gables

CREATIVE DIRECTOR/COPYWRITER
Yoel Henriquez

ART DIRECTOR
Lou Lozada

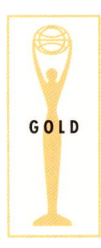

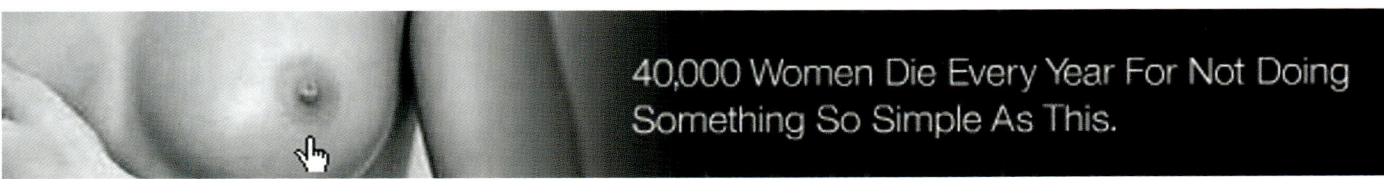

This banner was employed as a simple and powerful way to illustrate to all women how easily they can do something about breast cancer prevention. The question was, what good is it going to do anyone to simply laminate some black type on a white banner asking if you've checked your breasts today? The graphical content took a humorous approach to a serious subject. And by inviting the navigator to interact with the message, the viewer is engaged and the message is ultimately understood in a more powerful way: Show me, don't tell me.

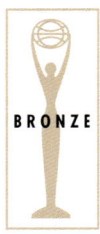

CATEGORY
Fresh Approach

ADVERTISER/PRODUCT
Volvo

NAME OF SITE
Volvo Museum

WWW DEVELOPER
OgilvyOne, Singapore

ADVERTISING AGENCY
OgilvyOne, Singapore

ACCOUNT EXECUTIVE
Dian Ali, Daphne Goh

CREATIVE DIRECTOR
Graham Kelly

COPYWRITER
Mak Kye Li, Tan Kim Lee, Graham Kelly

ART DIRECTOR
Dominic Goldman, Shane Pooley

DESIGNER
Dominic Goldman

PROGRAMMER
Chandra Barathi, Dominic Goldman

PRODUCTION MANAGER
Yow Pin Fern

MUSIC
Ben James Galvin

CLIENT
Yvonne Tey

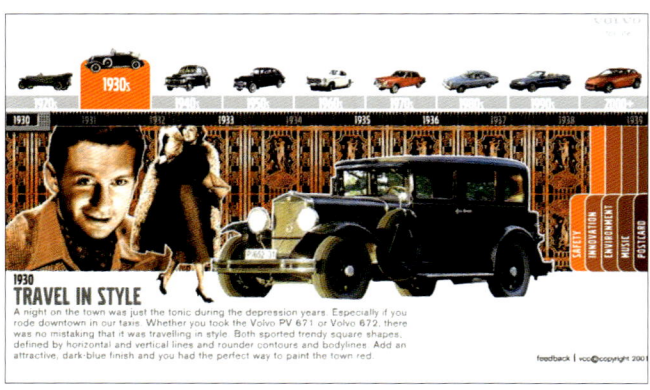

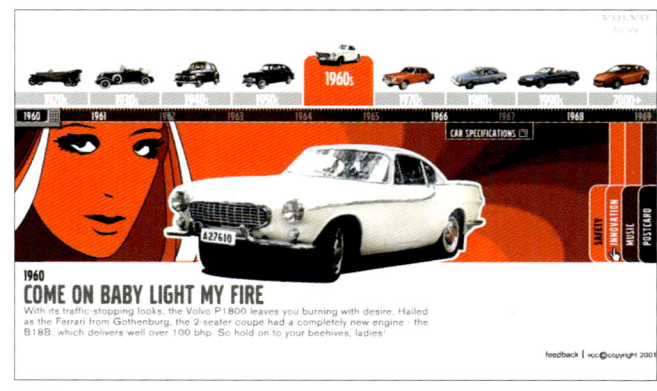

To deepen Volvo owners' relationships with the brand as well as to attract potential buyers, Volvo's rich heritage was drawn upon as the focal point of this site. This was achieved by demonstrating how Volvo has historically remained true to its key values of safety, innovation, and environmental awareness. These values are specifically highlighted in each era. However, rather than merely listing them alongside shots of cars, the information was put into the context of its particular time period with the use of the sights and sounds from its respective decade.

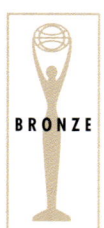

CATEGORY
Fresh Approach

ADVERTISER/PRODUCT
Hewlett-Packard

NAME OF SITE
HP Invent Banner Campaign

ADVERTISING AGENCY
Goodby, Silverstein & Partners, San Francisco

ACCOUNT EXECUTIVE
Christina Blosser

CREATIVE DIRECTOR
Steve Simpson

COPYWRITER
Will Elliott, John Matejczyk

ART DIRECTOR
Jeff Benjamin, Rick Casteel

DESIGN DIRECTOR
Keith Anderson

EXECUTIVE PRODUCER
Donaa Zellers Production Company

MOLECULE COMPOSER
Freestyle Interactive, San Francisco

COLOR
Orange Design

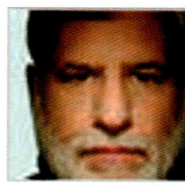

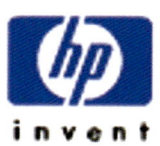

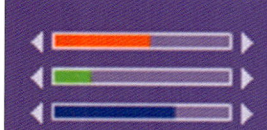

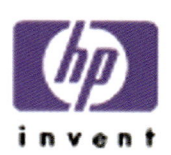

Who knew being an inventor was this much fun? These Rich Media banners invite users into the labs of HP inventors, allowing them to do their own inventing while interacting with the HP brand. Three separate banner choices allow the user to create molecules, colors, and music.

CATEGORY
Internet Rich Media Advertising

ADVERTISER/PRODUCT
BMW

NAME OF SITE
The Hire: BMW Films Banners

ADVERTISING AGENCY
Fallon, Minneapolis

ACCOUNT EXECUTIVE
Joe Lagodinski

COPYWRITER
Chuck Carlson, Allon Tatarka

DESIGNER
Brooke Posard, Craig Duffney

PRODUCTION ARTIST
Joel Herrmann

MULTIMEDIA DEVELOPER
Laurie Brown, Chris Stocksmith

PROJECT MANAGER
Laura Fischer

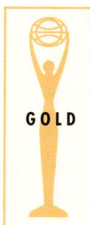

GOLD

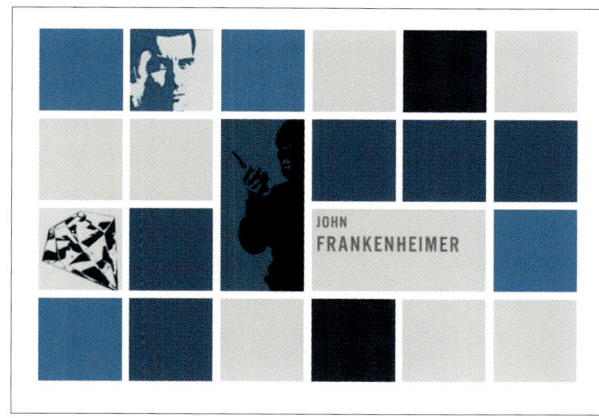

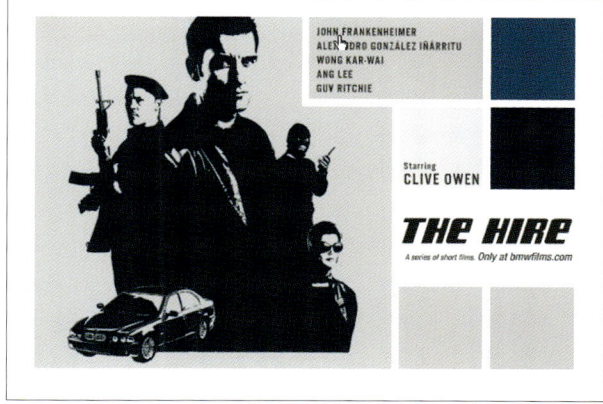

The BMW Films online advertising campaign was designed to pique the curiosity of consumers and, ultimately, drive traffic to bmwfilms.com. Promoting well-known and respected A-level directors assisted in enticing viewers to click the banners and view the short films that comprised BMW's "The Hire" campaign.

CATEGORY
Internet Rich Media Advertising

ADVERTISER/PRODUCT
Telewest Blueyonder Workwise

NAME OF SITE
I.T. Rage

WWW DEVELOPER
BloodPartnership, London

ADVERTISING AGENCY
BloodPartnership, London in association with Heresy, London

ACCOUNT EXECUTIVE
Nicola Wilson (Heresy)

CREATIVE DIRECTOR
Jeremy Garner

COPYWRITER
Jeremy Garner, Paul Knott

ART DIRECTOR/DESIGNER
Simon Lovejoy (BloodPartnership)

PROGRAMMER
Simon Lovejoy (BloodPartnership)

PRODUCER
Andy Taylor, Rick Kiesewetter, Nicola Wilson (Heresy)

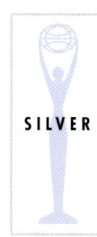

SILVER

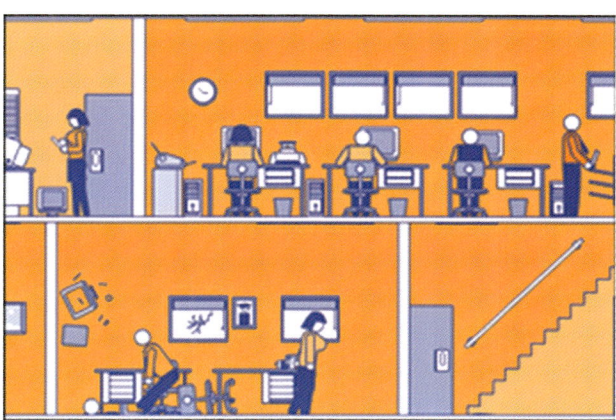

Blueyonder Workwise is an IT support service aimed at small to medium-size businesses. The audience is reached through an empathetic approach by the employment of an animated movie intro featuring an office worker going insane, smashing every computer he can lay his hands on. Who has not entertained this fantasy from time to time, out of sheer frustration with technology's inevitable glitches?

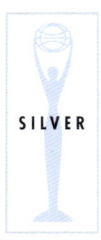

CATEGORY
Internet Rich Media Advertising

ADVERTISER/PRODUCT
Absolut Vodka

NAME OF SITE
Absolut Director

WWW DEVELOPER
Submarine/Zendo, New York

ADVERTISING AGENCY
TBWA\Chiat\Day, New York

ACCOUNT EXECUTIVE
Kim Wykjstrom

CREATIVE DIRECTOR
Dan Braun, Joseph Mazzefaro

ART DIRECTOR
Kirk Gibbons, Mike French

DESIGNER
Mike French

PROGRAMMER
Marc Blanchard, Jason Muscat

PRODUCTION MANAGER
Dan Braun, Josh Braun,
Rolanda Chu

EXECUTIVE PRODUCER
Dan Braun, Josh Braun, Pete Callaro

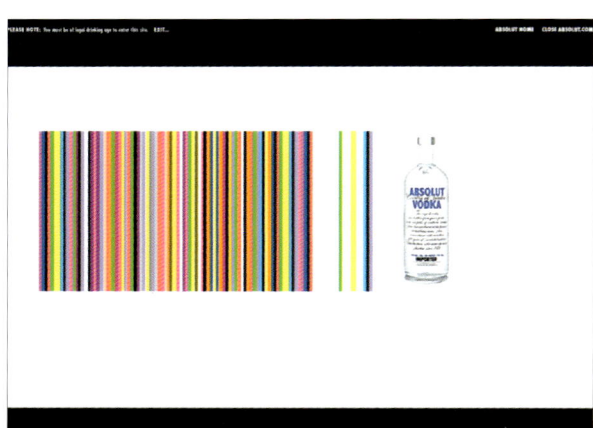
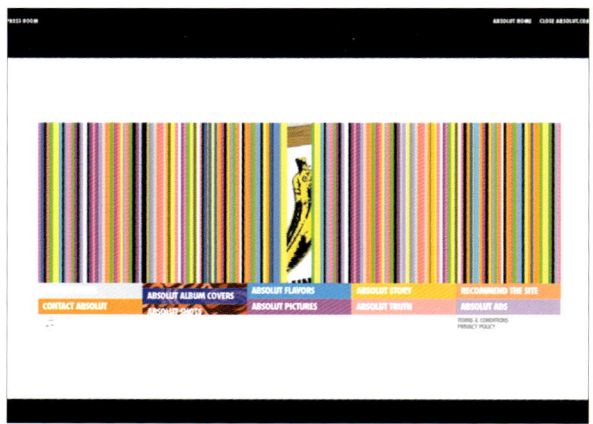

The Absolut Director site was based on the movie *What's Up, Tiger Lily*, where writer/director Woody Allen stripped the dialogue from an Asian spy film and rescripted it. The interactivity in Absolut Director requires active participation by the user. The basic idea was that anyone can be a director—choosing music, picking characters, changing shots, and, most importantly, creating dialogue. To demonstrate the functionality of the tools, director Spike Lee created his own film, which was completely produced on the Absolut Director site. Absolut Director is one of very few sites on the Internet where one can truly create and distribute a short film from scratch.

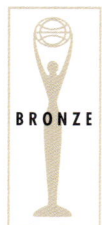

CATEGORY
Internet Rich Media Advertising

ADVERTISER/PRODUCT
Phil Brown

NAME OF SITE
Director: Phil Brown

WWW DEVELOPER
dZinenmOtion.com, Vancouver

ADVERTISING AGENCY
dZinenmOtion.com, Vancouver

**CREATIVE DIRECTOR/
ART DIRECTOR/DESIGNER/
PROGRAMMER**
Rose Pietrovito

COPYWRITER
Phil Brown

MUSIC TRACK
Gavin Froome

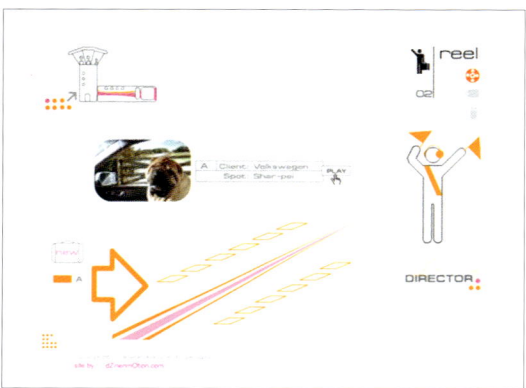
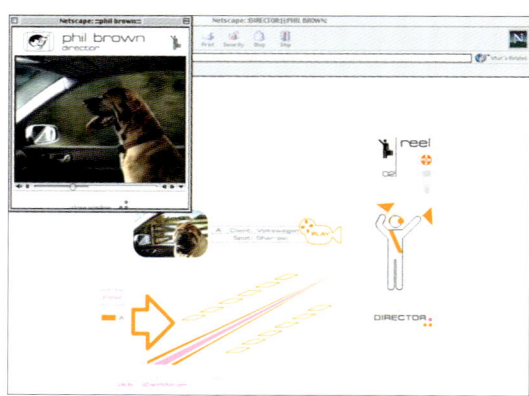

An online environment for users to get a sense of director Phil Brown's personality and to view his commercial work. The interface is clean and light, augmented with quirky elements to compliment the style of Brown's output.

CATEGORY
Internet Rich Media Advertising

ADVERTISER/PRODUCT
Hewlett-Packard

NAME OF SITE
HP Invent Banner Campaign

ADVERTISING AGENCY
Goodby, Silverstein & Partners,
San Francisco

ACCOUNT EXECUTIVE
Chrina Blosser

CREATIVE DIRECTOR
Steve Simpson

COPYWRITER
Will Elliott, John Matejczyk

ART DIRECTOR
Jeff Benjamin, Rick Casteel

DESIGN DIRECTOR
Keith Anderson

EXECUTIVE PRODUCER
Danaa Zellers

PRODUCTION COMPANY
Molecule

MOLECULE COMPOSER
Freestyle Interactive, San Francisco

COLOR
Orange Design

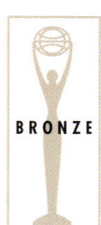

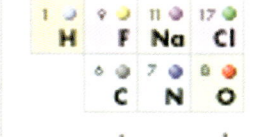 Drag atoms to create molecule.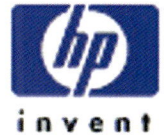

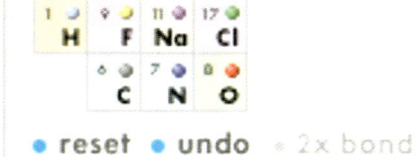 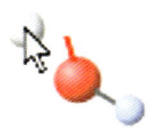 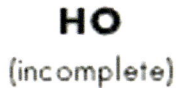
HO
(incomplete)
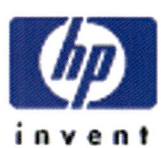

Who knew being an inventor was this much fun? These Rich Media banners invite users into the labs of HP inventors, allowing them to do their own inventing while interacting with the HP brand. Three separate banner choices allow the user to create molecules, colors, and music.

CATEGORY
Self-Promotion

ADVERTISER/PRODUCT
Phil Brown

NAME OF SITE
Director: Phil Brown

WWW DEVELOPER
dZinenmOtion.com, Vancouver

ADVERTISING AGENCY
dZinenmOtion.com, Vancouver

CREATIVE DIRECTOR
Rose Pietrovito

COPYWRITER
Phil Brown

ART DIRECTOR
Rose Pietrovito

DESIGNER
Rose Pietrovito

PROGRAMMER
Rose Pietrovito

MUSIC TRACK
Gavin Froome

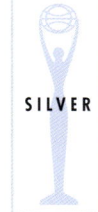

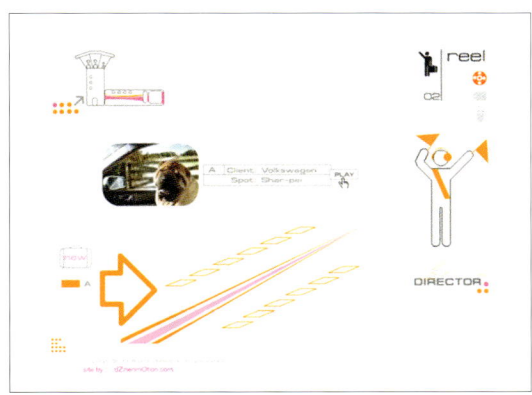 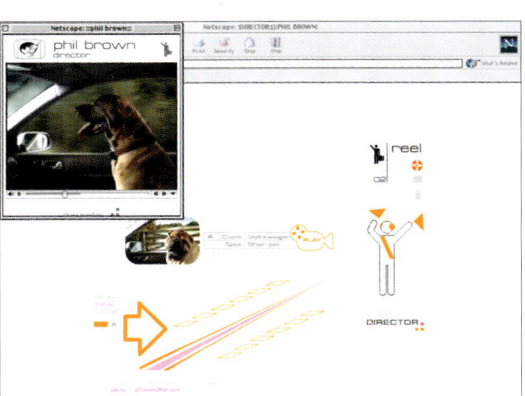

An online environment for users to get a sense of director Phil Brown's personality and to view his commercial work. The interface is clean and light, augmented with quirky elements to compliment the style of Brown's output.

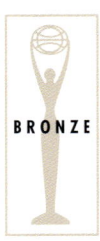

BRONZE

CATEGORY
Self-Promotion

ADVERTISER/PRODUCT
Ralf Wengenmayr Web Site

NAME OF SITE
Ralf Wengenmayr

ADVERTISING AGENCY
Scholz & Volkmer Intermediales
Design, Wiesbaden

PROJECT HEAD
Michael Volkmer

PROJECT MANAGER
Natascha Becker

CREATIVE DIRECTOR
Michael Volkmer

ART DIRECTOR
Heike Brockmann

PROGRAMMER
Peter Reichard, Samuel Ruckstuhl

SCREEN DESIGN
Melanie Lenz, Elke Grober

FLASH COMPOSING
Samuel Ruckstuhl

CLIENT
Ralf Wengenmayr

The objective of this site is to present film composer Ralf Wengenmayr's broad musical abilities, and the projects he has realized to
date. The site is clearly divided into two sections: Music and Information. The main focus lies within the music chapter, specifically in re-
gard to Wengenmayr's compositions. Pictures and information about
the films he has composed for are shown on-screen, giving the visitor
the feeling of actually being at the cinema. The information section
contains personal data relating to the artist and his various projects.

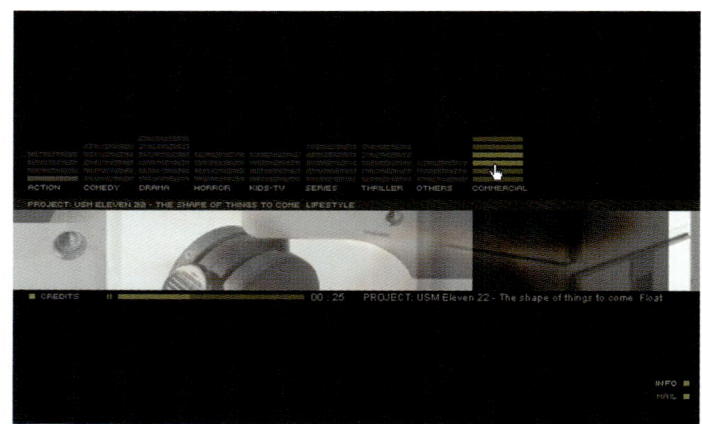

CATEGORY
Self-Promotion

ADVERTISER/PRODUCT
Herraiz Soto & Co. Interactive
Advertising Agency

NAME OF SITE
Haute Cuisine Publicitaire

WWW DEVELOPER
Heraiz Soto & Co., Madrid &
Barcelona
,

ADVERTISING AGENCY
Herraiz Soto & Co., Madrid &
Barcelona

ACCOUNT EXECUTIVE
Sandra Cerezo

ACCOUNT DIRECTOR
Marcel.lí Zuazua

CREATIVE DIRECTOR
Ángel Herraiz, Rafa Soto

COPYWRITER
Rafa Soto, Jesús Diaz

ART DIRECTOR
Ángel Herraiz, Sergi Mula,
Andreu Colomer

PHOTOGRAPHER
Óscar Álvarado

FLASH DESIGNER
Sergi Mula, Andreu Colomer,
Priscila Loba, Sebas Moranta

FLASH PROGRAMMER
Javier Alvarez, Carles Sanz,
Jaume Presas

APPLICATION PROGRAMMER
Javier Alvarez, Carles Sanz,
Jaume Presas

HTML PRODUCER
Priscila Loba, Jaume Presas

WEB PRODUCER
Susana Castillión

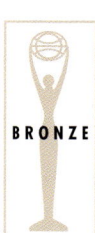

BRONZE

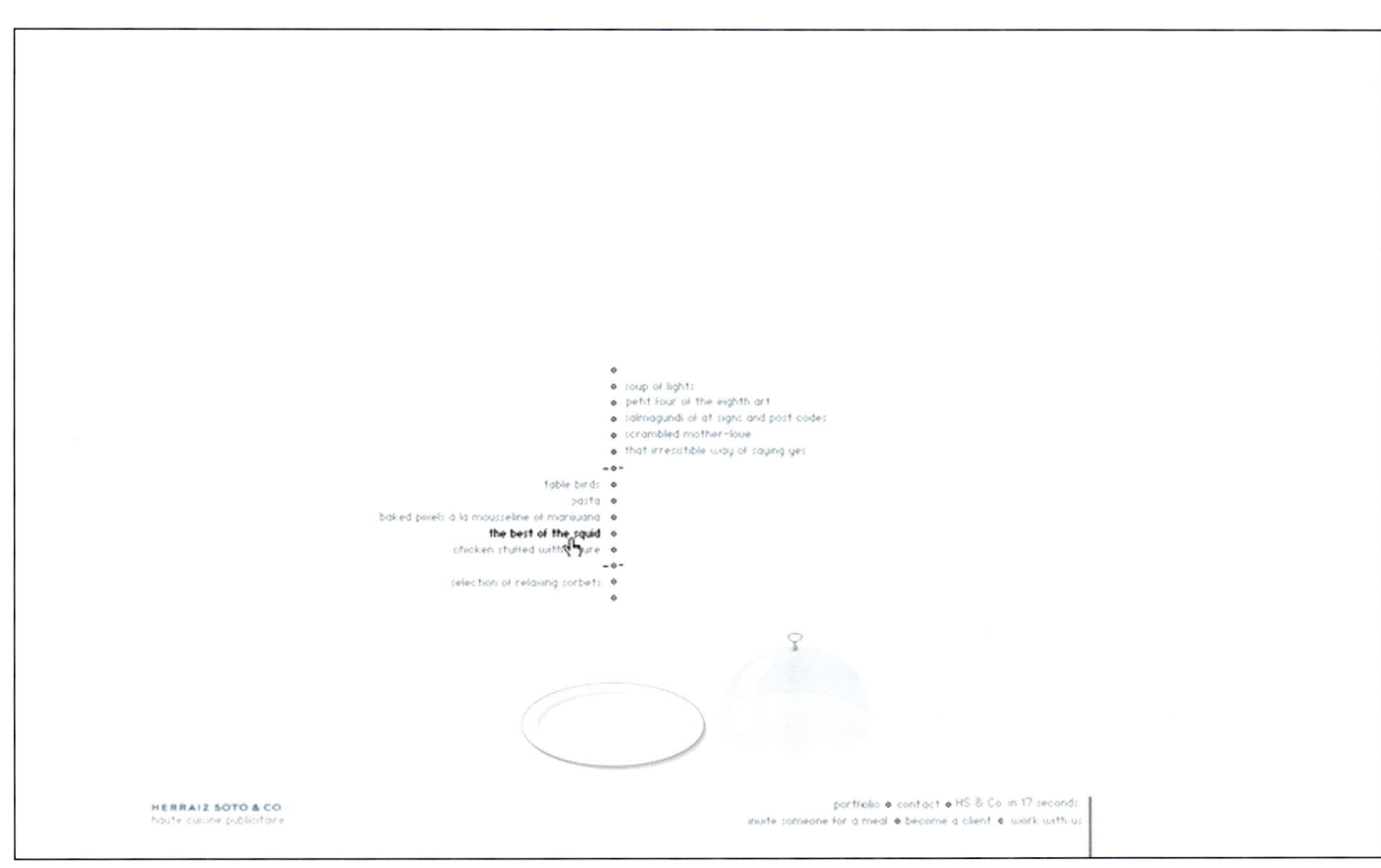

Like food, interactivity can transmit sensations. How good, bad, strong, offensive, fashionable, or reactionary these sensations might be depends on the kitchen. The "kitchen" at advertising agency Herraiz Soto and Co. is convinced that the best communication is that which is daring, imparts new values, and sets itself apart from the rest. The company's official site explores these beliefs.

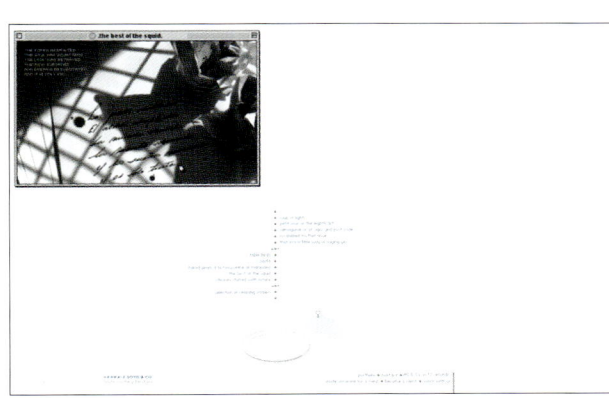

PRINT

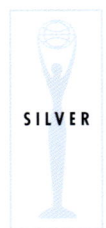

SILVER

CATEGORY
Automotive

ADVERTISER/PRODUCT
Land Transport Safety Authority

TITLE
Auto Trader Wrecks

ADVERTISING AGENCY
Clemenger BBDO, Wellington

ACCOUNT EXECUTIVE
Vicky Upton

CREATIVE DIRECTOR
Philip Andrew

COPYWRITER
Jamie Hichcock

ART DIRECTOR
Josh Lancaster

PRODUCTION MANAGER
Scott McMillan

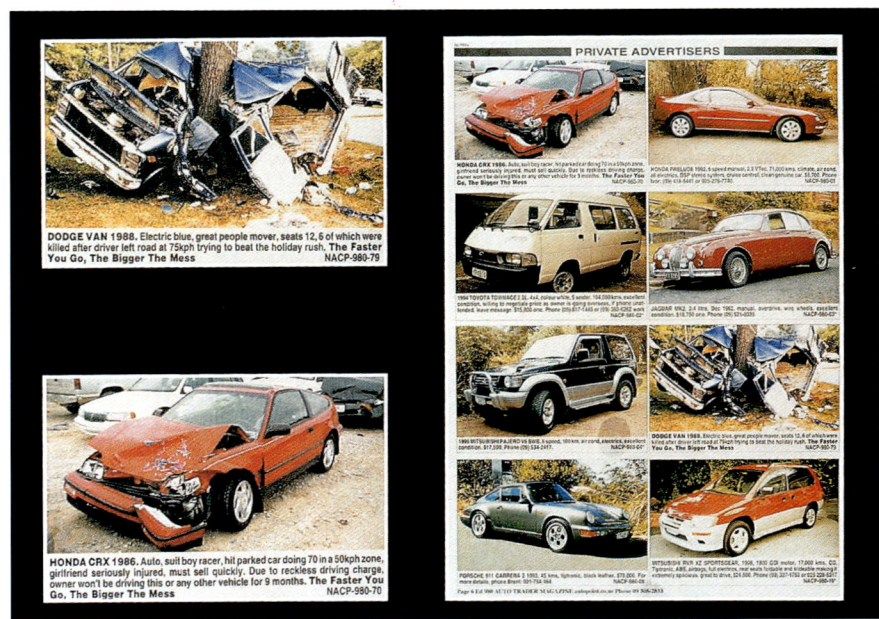

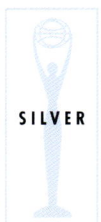

SILVER

CATEGORY
Automotive

ADVERTISER/PRODUCT
Jeep

TITLE
Climbing

ADVERTISING AGENCY
Giovanni, FCB, São Paulo

ACCOUNT EXECUTIVE
Marcelo Malachias, Luciano Olmo

CREATIVE DIRECTOR
Valdir Bianchi, Ricardo Chester

COPYWRITER
Olavo Tokutake

ART DIRECTOR
Marcos Medeiros

PRODUCTION MANAGER
Alexandre Oliveira

PHOTOGRAPHER
Fabio Ribeiro, Eduardo Girau

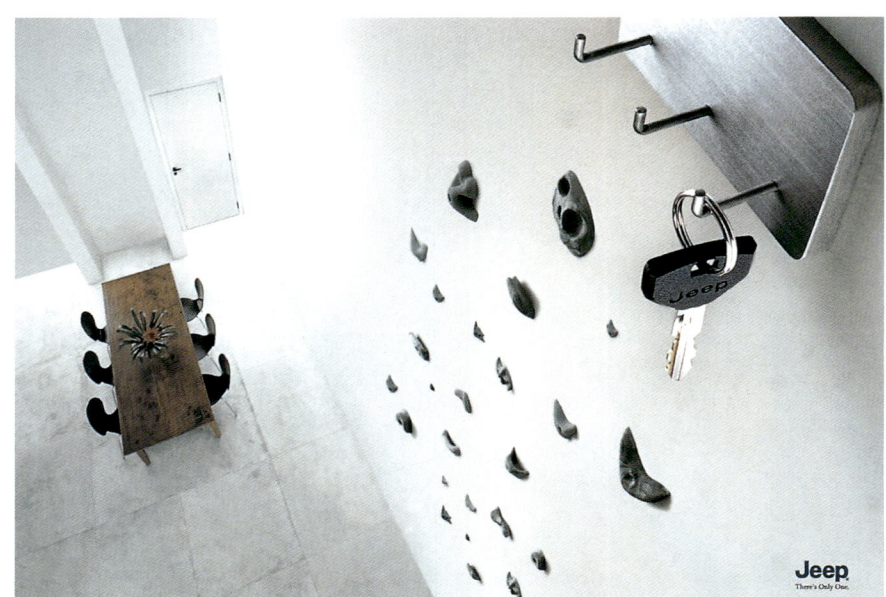

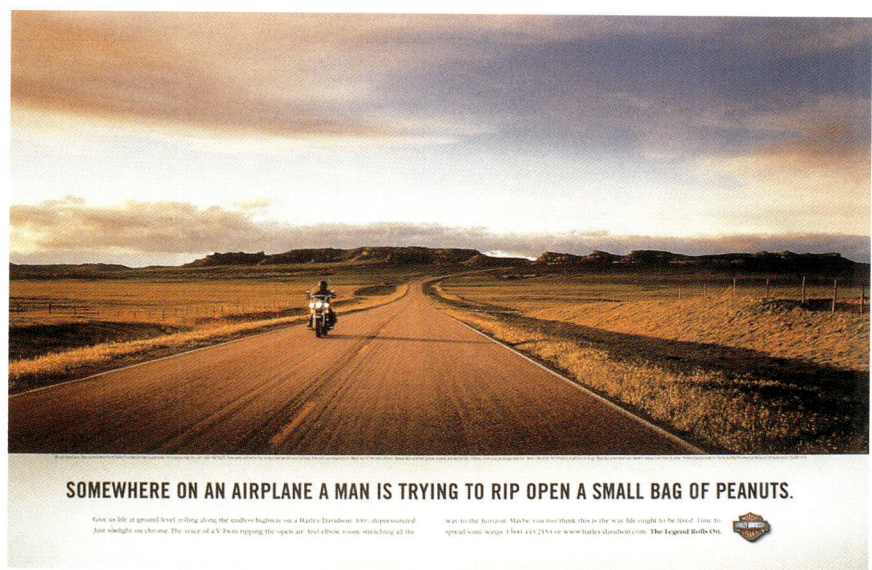

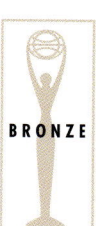

CATEGORY
Automotive

ADVERTISER/PRODUCT
Harley-Davidson Motorcycles

TITLE
Somewhere on an Airplane

ADVERTISING AGENCY
Carmichael Lynch, Minneapolis

ACCOUNT EXECUTIVE
Lisa Bickel, Joe King

CREATIVE DIRECTOR
Jim Nelson

COPYWRITER
Jim Nelson, Sheldon Clay

ART DIRECTOR
Jason Smith

PRODUCTION MANAGER
Brenda Clemons

PHOTOGRAPHER
Chris Wimpey

ART PRODUCER
Bonnie Butler

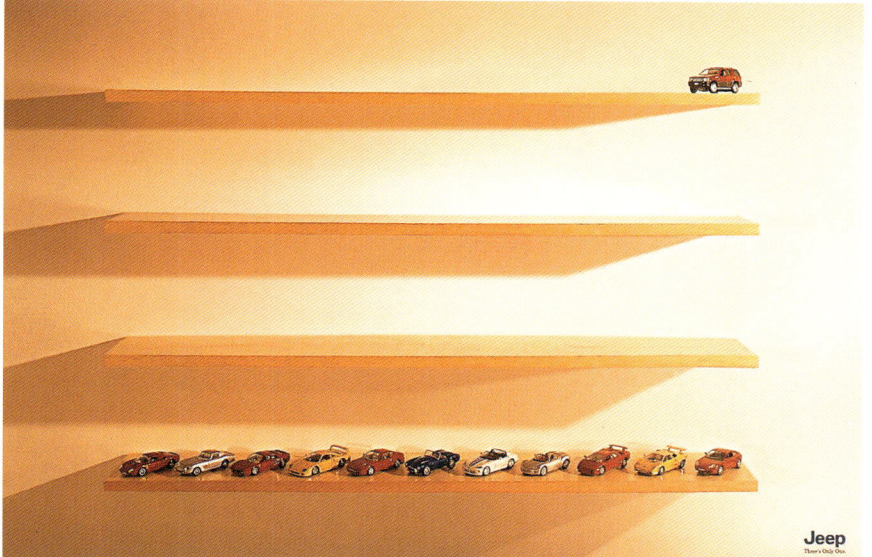

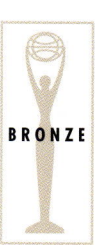

CATEGORY
Automotive

ADVERTISER/PRODUCT
Jeep

TITLE
Shelf

ADVERTISING AGENCY
Giovanni, FCB, São Paulo

ACCOUNT EXECUTIVE
Luciano Olmo

CREATIVE DIRECTOR
Valdir Bianchi, Ricardo Chester

COPYWRITER
Lorine Solomonescu

ART DIRECTOR
Bob Kincey

PRODUCTION MANAGER
Alexandre Oliveira

PHOTOGRAPHER
Danny Yin

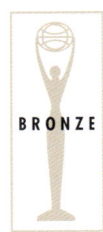

CATEGORY
Automotive

ADVERTISER/PRODUCT
Land Rover

TITLE
And Over

ADVERTISING AGENCY
D'Adda Lorenzini Vigorelli BBDO,
Milan

ACCOUNT EXECUTIVE
Luca Bernasconi

CREATIVE DIRECTOR
Pino Rozzi, Roberto Battaglia

COPYWRITER
Vicky Gitto

ART DIRECTOR
Roberto Battaglia

PHOTOGRAPHER
Pier Pado Ferrari

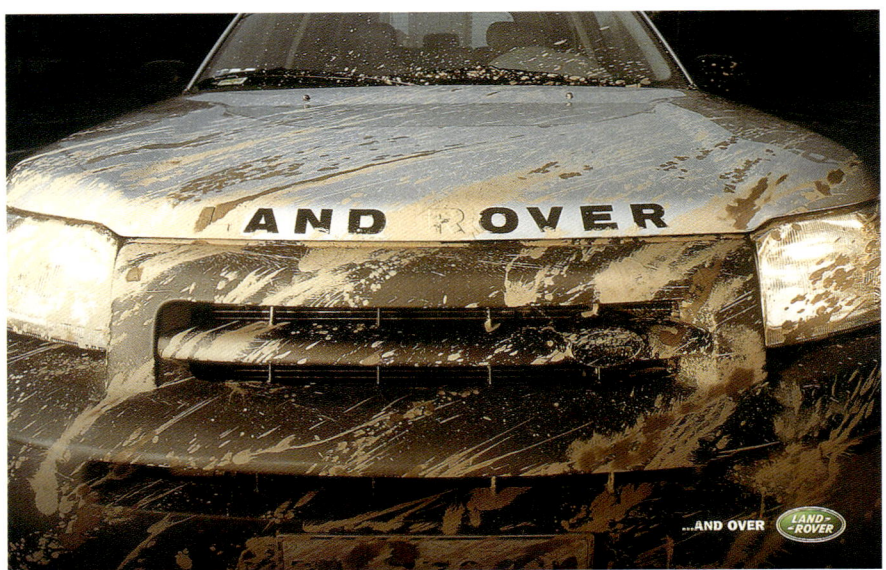

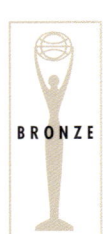

CATEGORY
Automotive

ADVERTISER/PRODUCT
Harley-Davidson Motorcycles

TITLE
Grandpa

ADVERTISING AGENCY
Giovanni, FCB, São Paulo

ACCOUNT EXECUTIVE
Mercelo Malachias, Fabio Madia

CREATIVE DIRECTOR
Valdir Bianchi, Ricardo Chester

COPYWRITER
David Romanetto

ART DIRECTOR
Marcos Medeiros

PRODUCTION MANAGER
Alexandre Oliveira

PHOTOGRAPHER
Client's File

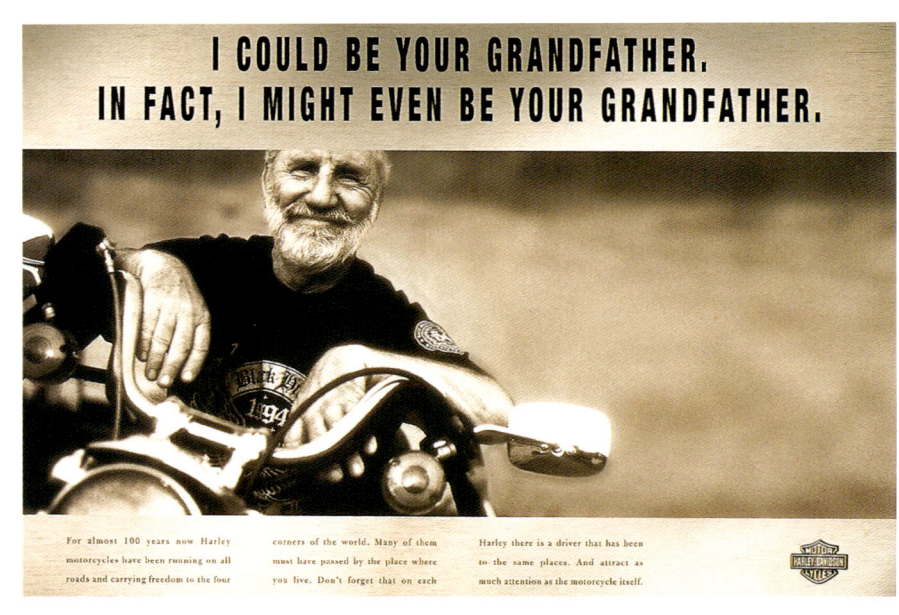

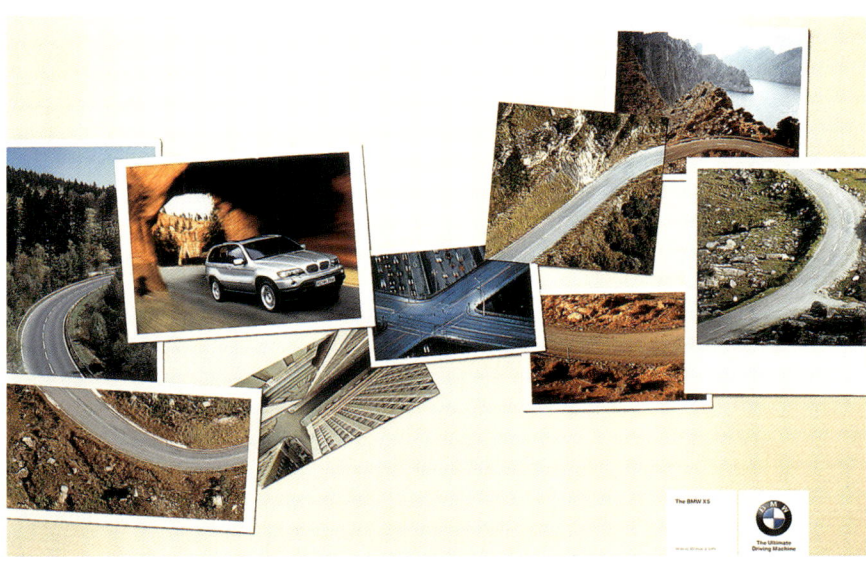

CATEGORY
Automotive

ADVERTISER/PRODUCT
BMW

TITLE
Rally Course X5 Series

ADVERTISING AGENCY
Jung von Matt/Alster, Hamburg

ACCOUNT EXECUTIVE
Christine Doss

CREATIVE DIRECTOR
Burkhart von Scheven,
Bernhard Lukas

COPYWRITER
Bjoern Lockstein

ART DIRECTOR
Mirjam Heinemann,
Timm Hanebeck

PHOTOGRAPHER
Peer Oliver Brecht, Ebo Fraterman,
Christopher Thomas

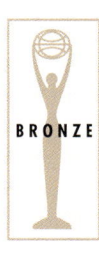

BRONZE

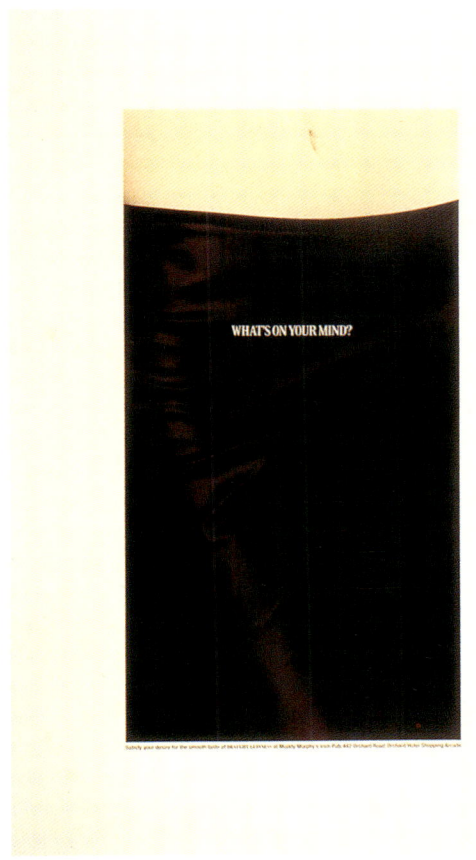

CATEGORY
Beverages/Alcoholic

ADVERTISER/PRODUCT
Guinness

TITLE
Navel

ADVERTISING AGENCY
Ogilvy & Mather, Singapore

CREATIVE DIRECTOR
Andy Greenaway

COPYWRITER
Andy Greenaway

ART DIRECTOR
Craig Smith

PHOTOGRAPHER
Roy Zhang

TYPOGRAPHER
Alfred Wee

GOLD

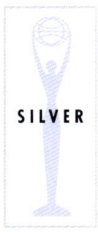

SILVER

CATEGORY
Beverages/Nonalcoholic

ADVERTISER/PRODUCT
Red Bull

TITLE
Body

ADVERTISING AGENCY
Leo Burnett, Singapore

PHOTOGRAPHY STUDIO
Studio 121, Singapore

ACCOUNT EXECUTIVE
Arthur Chung, Merwin Chew

CREATIVE DIRECTOR
Alex Shipley, Tay Guan Hin

COPYWRITER
Alex Shipley

ART DIRECTOR
Sachin Ambekar

PRODUCTION MANAGER
Dennis Gan, Victor Lee

DESIGN & ILLUSTRATION
Phenomenon, Singapore

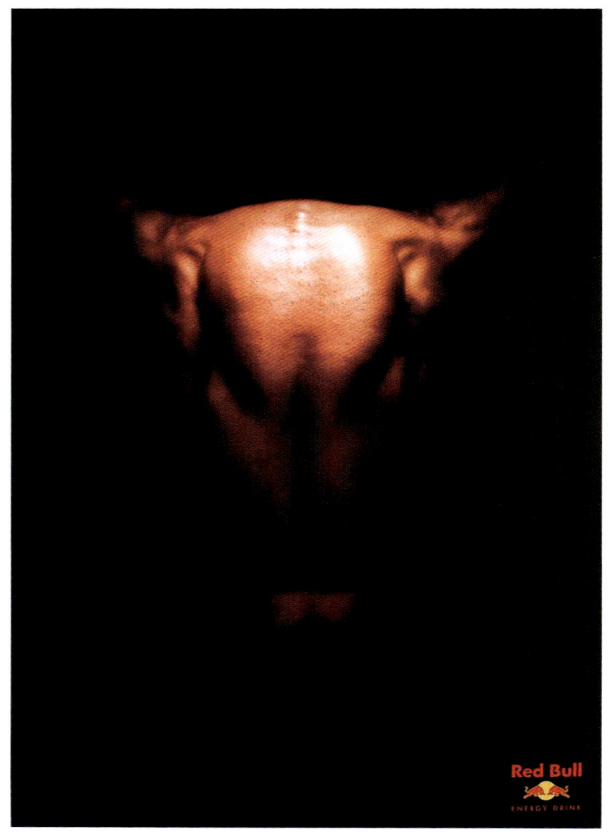

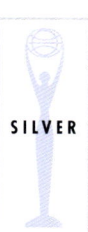

SILVER

CATEGORY
Beverages/Nonalcoholic

ADVERTISER/PRODUCT
Pepsi Light

TITLE
Woman

ADVERTISING AGENCY
AlmapBBDO, São Paulo

ACCOUNT EXECUTIVE
Ricardo Taunay

CREATIVE DIRECTOR
Marcello Serpa, Eugênio Mohallem

ART DIRECTOR
Cesar Finamori

PRODUCTION MANAGER
José Roberto Bezerra

PHOTOGRAPHER
Manolo Moran

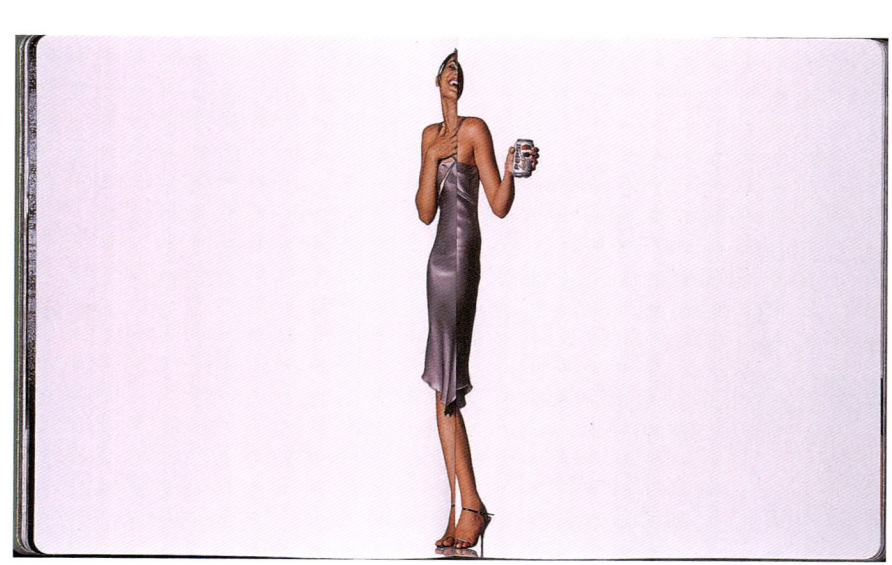

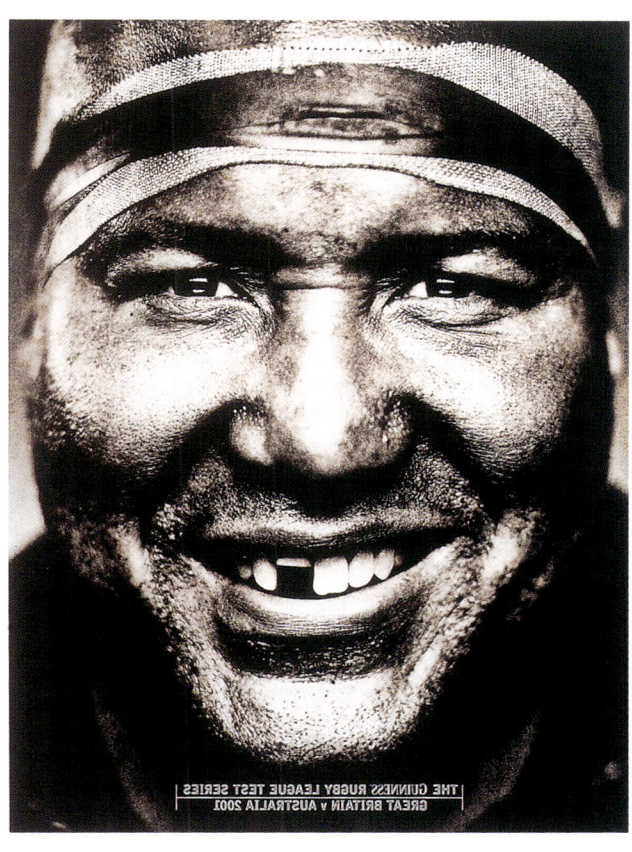

CATEGORY
Entertainment Promotion

ADVERTISER/PRODUCT
Guinness Rugby League Test Series

TITLE
Smile

ADVERTISING AGENCY
Abbott Mead Vickers BBDO, London

ACCOUNT EXECUTIVE
Cecile Beaufils, Steven Rileu

CREATIVE DIRECTOR
Peter Souter, Tony Cox

COPYWRITER
Richard Morgan

ART DIRECTOR
Simon Langley

PRODUCTION MANAGER
Andy Smith

PHOTOGRAPHER
Robert Wilson

TYPOGRAPHER
Mark Elwood

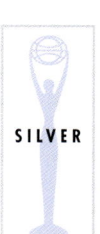

SILVER

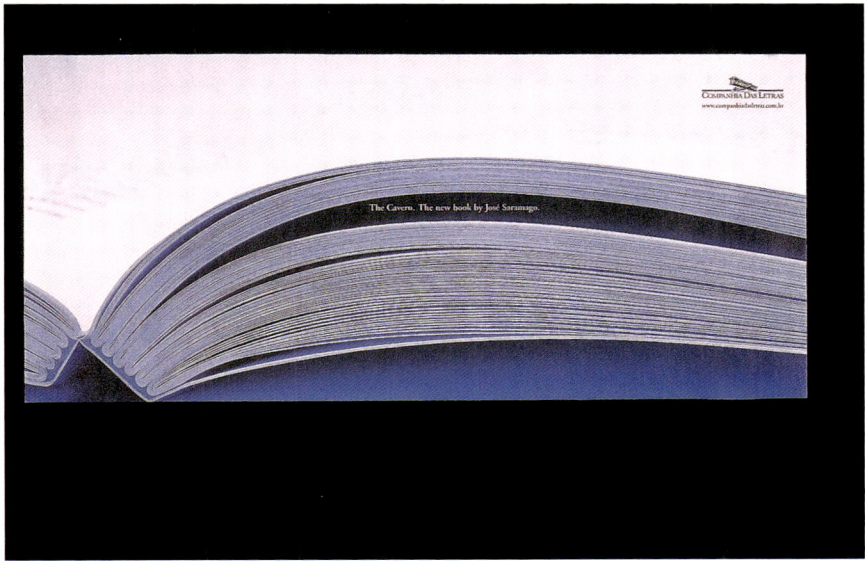

CATEGORY
Entertainment Promotion

ADVERTISER/PRODUCT
Companhia das Letras

TITLE
The Cavern
The New Book by Jose Saramago

ADVERTISING AGENCY
AlmapBBDO, São Paulo

ACCOUNT EXECUTIVE
Izabella Villaça

CREATIVE DIRECTOR
Marcello Serpa, Eugênio Mohallem

COPYWRITER
Dulcidio Caldeira

ART DIRECTOR
Renato Fernandez

PRODUCTION MANAGER
José Roberto Bezerra

PHOTOGRAPHER
Rafael Assef

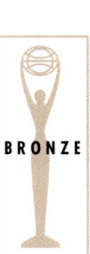

BRONZE

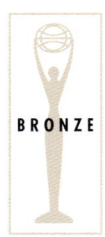

BRONZE

CATEGORY
Entertainment Promotion

ADVERTISER/PRODUCT
MASP São Paulo Museum of Art—
Freud's Life Exhibition

TITLE
Freud at MASP. The life of Freud at
the São Paulo Museum of Art

ADVERTISING AGENCY
DM9 DDB, São Paulo

ACCOUNT EXECUTIVE
Vlademir Silva

CREATIVE DIRECTOR
Erh Ray, Jader Rossetto,
Pedro Cappeletti

COPYWRITER
Marcelo Reis

ART DIRECTOR
Roberto Fernandez

PHOTOGRAPHER
Rafael Costa

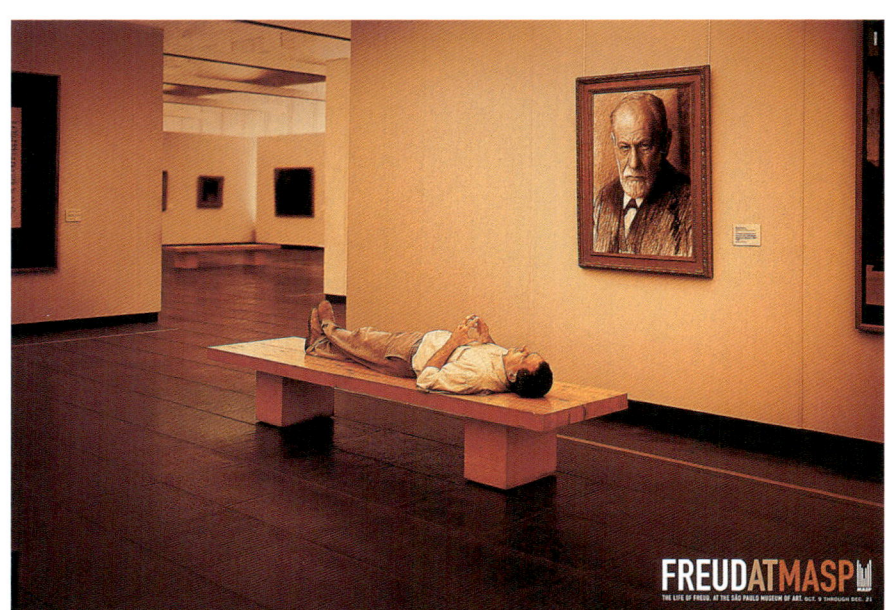

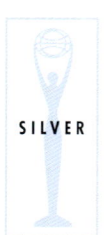

SILVER

CATEGORY
Home Entertainment

ADVERTISER/PRODUCT
PlayStation

TITLE
Thumb

ADVERTISING AGENCY
TBWA Hunt Lascaris, Johannesburg

ACCOUNT EXECUTIVE
Bridget Booms

CREATIVE DIRECTOR
Frances Luckin, Sandra de Witt

COPYWRITER
Benjamin Abramowitz

ART DIRECTOR
Gareth Lessing

PRODUCTION MANAGER
Tony Finney

PHOTOGRAPHER
Clive Stewart

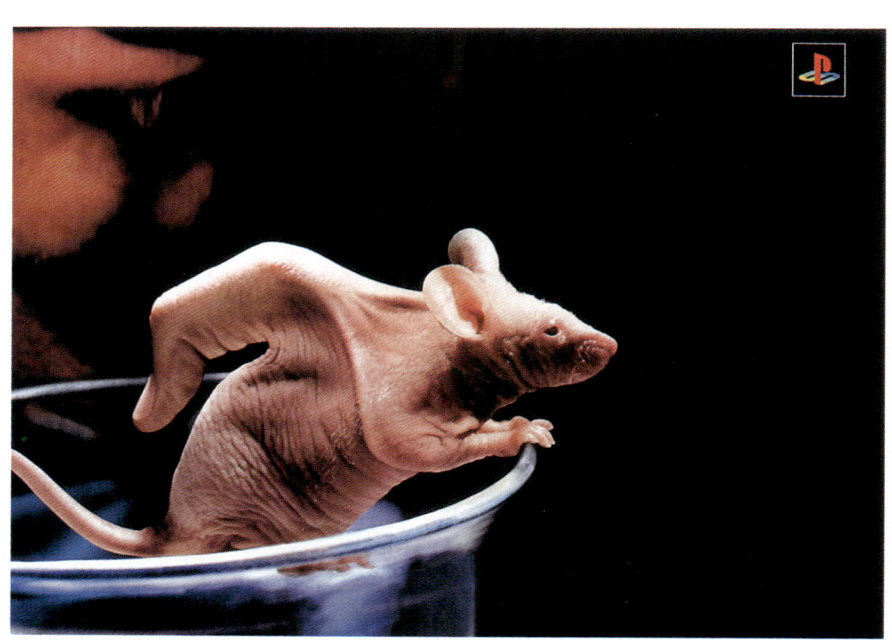

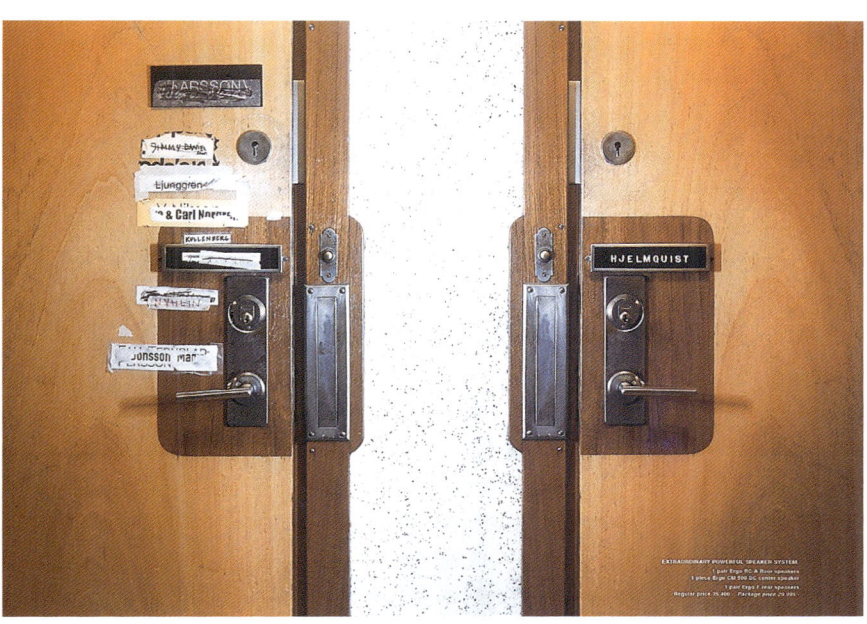

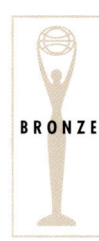

CATEGORY
Home Entertainment

ADVERTISER/PRODUCT
Paus

TITLE
Neighbours

ADVERTISING AGENCY
Åkestam, Holst, Stockholm

CREATIVE DIRECTOR
Kenneth Adenskog

COPYWRITER
Andreas Ullenius, Johan Landin

ART DIRECTOR
Andreas Ullenius, Johan Landin

PHOTOGRAPHER
Thomas Klementsson

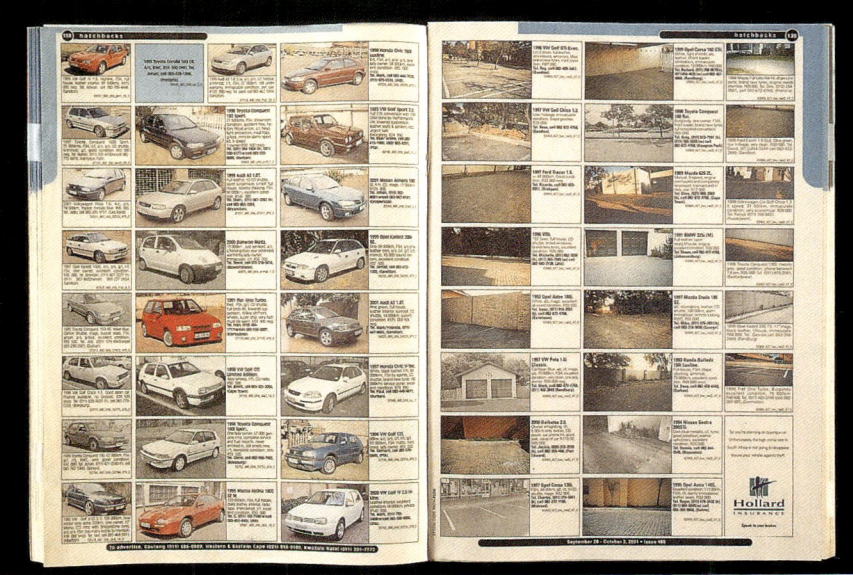

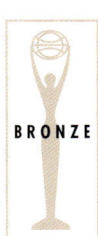

CATEGORY
Insurance

ADVERTISER/PRODUCT
Hollard Insurance

TITLE
Stolen

ADVERTISING AGENCY
Net#work BBDO, Johannesburg

ACCOUNT EXECUTIVE
Mabel

CREATIVE DIRECTOR
Mike Schalit

COPYWRITER
Mike Elmann Brown

ART DIRECTOR
Tom Cullinan

PRODUCTION MANAGER
Clinton Mitri

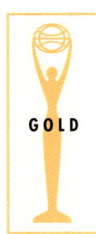

GOLD

CATEGORY
Media Promotion

ADVERTISER/PRODUCT
Campaign Brief Asia

TITLE
Marc

ADVERTISING AGENCY
Saatchi & Saatchi, Hong Kong

ACCOUNT EXECUTIVE
Laurie Kwong

CREATIVE DIRECTOR
Craig Davis

COPYWRITER
Renee Lim

ART DIRECTOR
Maurice Wee

PRODUCTION MANAGER
Ferris Tse

PHOTOGRAPHER
Stanley Wong

ILLUSTRATION/RETOUCHING
Edward Loh
(Phenomenon Singapore)

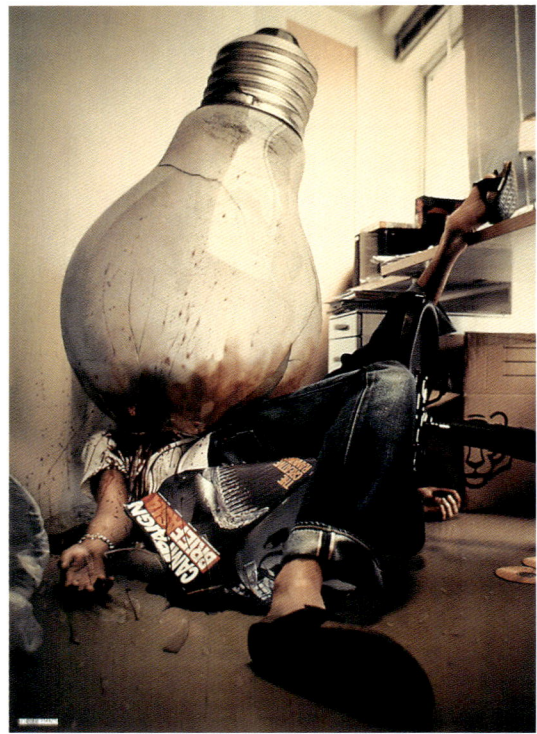

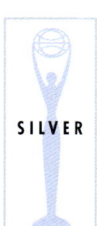

SILVER

CATEGORY
Media Promotion

ADVERTISER/PRODUCT
Saturday Star

TITLE
Soap

ADVERTISING AGENCY
TBWA Hunt Lascaris, Johannesburg

ACCOUNT EXECUTIVE
Mariana O'Kelly

CREATIVE DIRECTOR
Sandra de Witt

COPYWRITER
Mariana O'Kelly, Frances Luckin

ART DIRECTOR
Mariana O'Kelly, Frances Luckin

PRODUCTION MANAGER
Sherrol Doyle-Swallow

PHOTOGRAPHER
Jakob Doman

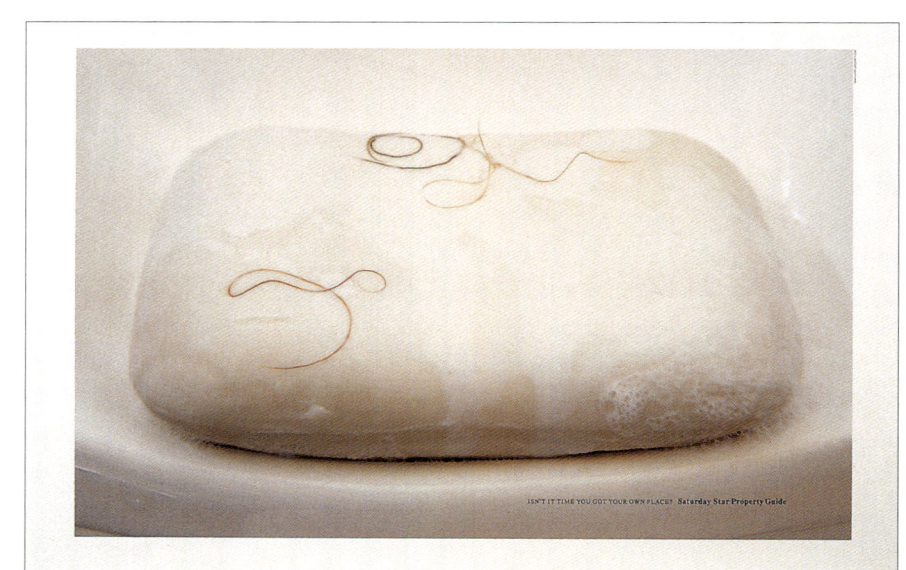

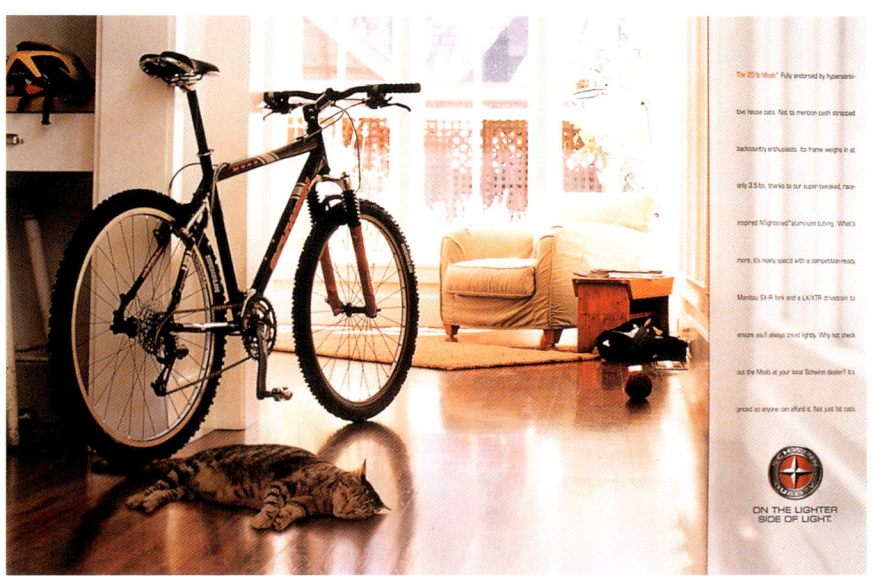

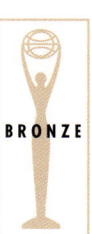

CATEGORY
Recreational Items

ADVERTISER/PRODUCT
Schwinn Bicycle and Fitness

TITLE
Lighter Side/Cat

ADVERTISING AGENCY
Crispin Porter Bogusky, Miami

ACCOUNT EXECUTIVE
Laura Bowles

CREATIVE DIRECTOR
Alex Bogusky

COPYWRITER
Rob Strasberg

ART DIRECTOR
Tony Calcao

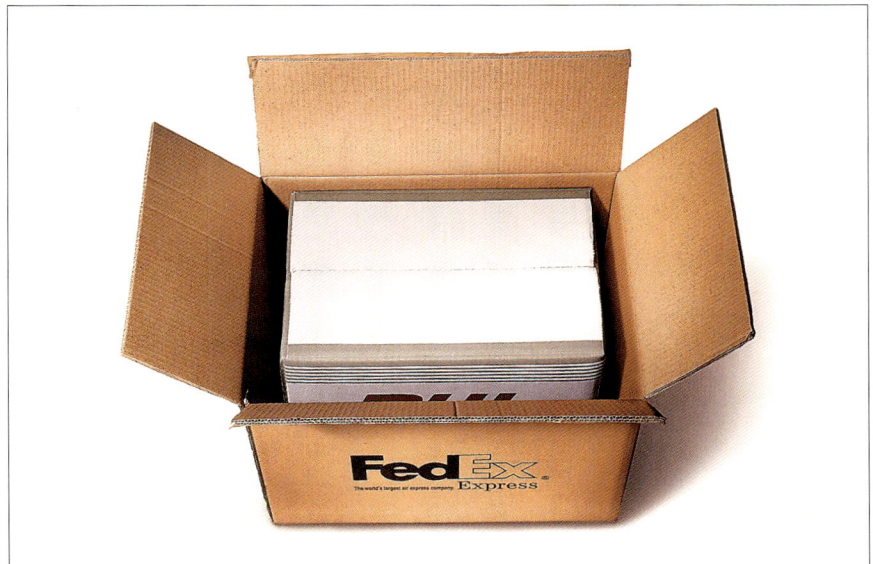

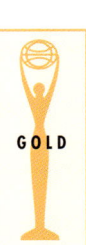

CATEGORY
Retail Services

ADVERTISER/PRODUCT
FedEx

TITLE
Box

ADVERTISING AGENCY
BBDO, Bangkok

PHOTOGRAPHY STUDIO
Remix Studio, Bangkok

ACCOUNT EXECUTIVE
Peter Wilken, Arto Hampartsournian

CREATIVE DIRECTOR
Suthisak Sucharittanonta

COPYWRITER
Kitti Chaiyaporn, David Guerrero

ART DIRECTOR
Thirasak Thanapatanakul, Suthisak
Sucharittanonta

PHOTOGRAPHER
Anuchai Secharunputong

199

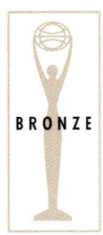

CATEGORY
Toiletries/Pharmaceuticals

ADVERTISER/PRODUCT
Kotex/Kimberly-Clark Corportation

TITLE
Thin

ADVERTISING AGENCY
Ogilvy & Mather, Hong Kong

ACCOUNT EXECUTIVE
Amy Poon, Christina Chan

CREATIVE DIRECTOR
Gary Tranter, Matt Cullen

COPYWRITER
Simon Handford

ART DIRECTOR
Annie Wong, Karen Lai

PRODUCTION MANAGER
Joann Wong

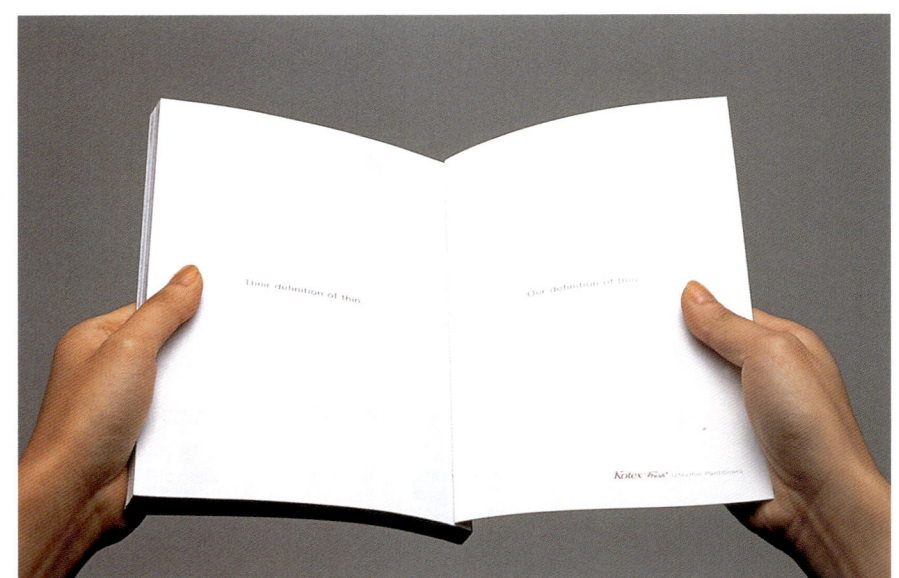

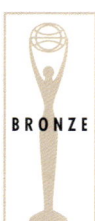

CATEGORY
Toiletries/Pharmaceuticals

ADVERTISER/PRODUCT
Pampers

TITLE
Dry Grass

ADVERTISING AGENCY
Saatchi & Saatchi, Bangkok

PHOTOGRAPHY STUDIO
Chamni's Eye Studio, Bangkok

ACCOUNT EXECUTIVE
Oranat Asanasen

CREATIVE DIRECTOR
Jureeporn Thaidumrong

COPYWRITER
Panusard Tanashindawong

ART DIRECTOR
Ketchai Parponsilp,
Jon Chalermwong

PRODUCTION MANAGER
Sushada Sudchaidee

PHOTOGRAPHER
Niphon Baiyen

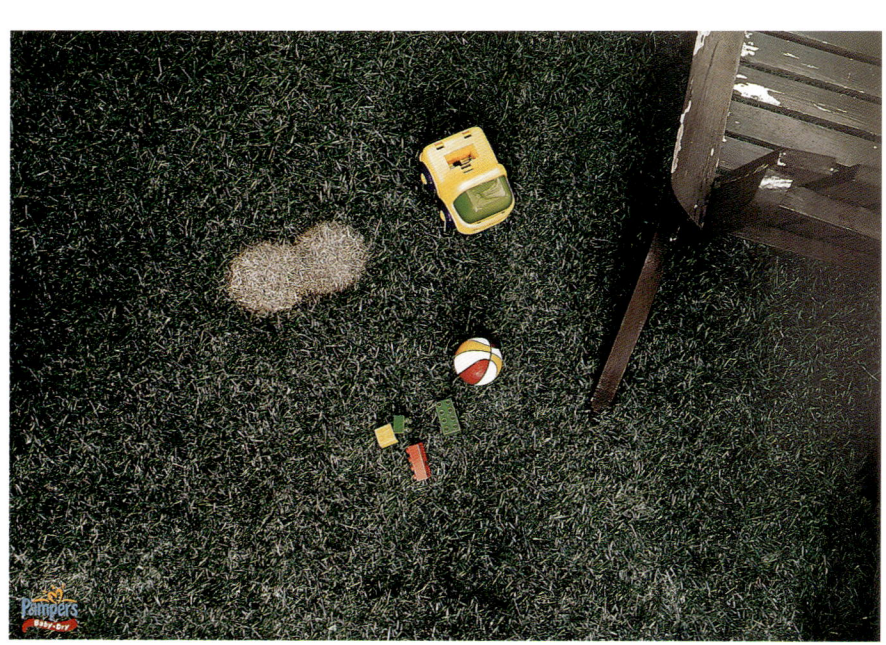

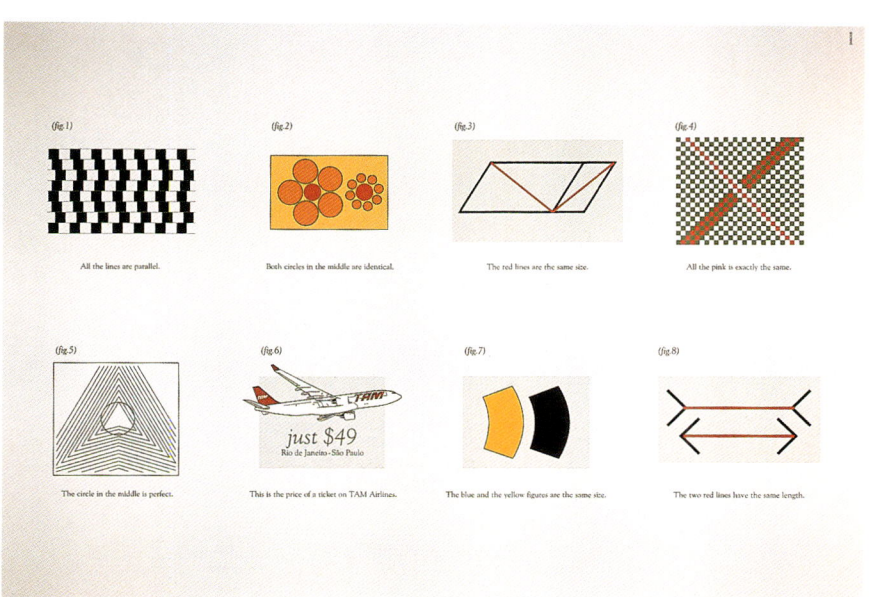

SILVER

CATEGORY
Travel/Tourism

ADVERTISER/PRODUCT
TAM Airlines

TITLE
Pictograms

ADVERTISING AGENCY
DM9 DDB, São Paulo

ACCOUNT EXECUTIVE
Marcio Santoro

CREATIVE DIRECTOR
Erh Ray, Jader Rossetto,
Pedro Cappeletti

COPYWRITER
Flávio Casarotti

ART DIRECTOR
Roberto Fernandez

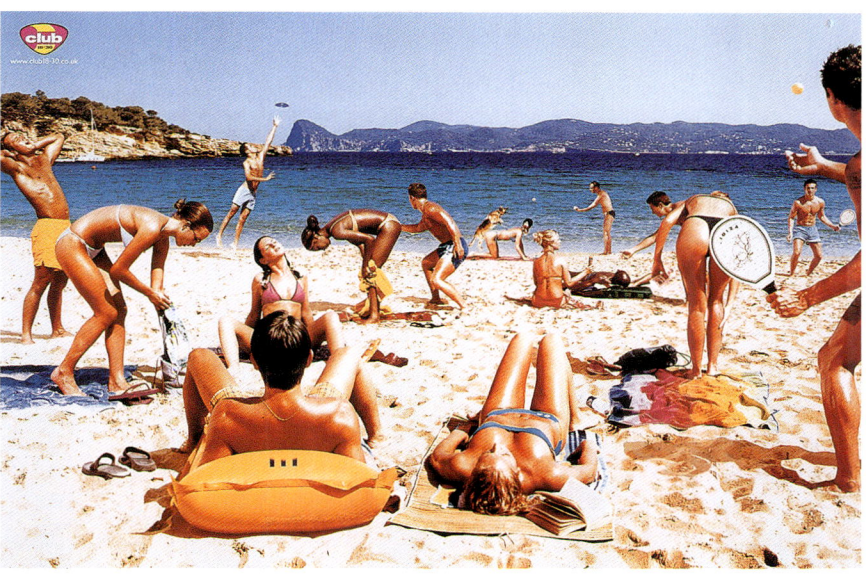

SILVER

CATEGORY
Travel/Tourism

ADVERTISER/PRODUCT
Club 18–30/Package Holidays

TITLE
Beach

ADVERTISING AGENCY
Saatchi & Saatchi, London

PHOTOGRAPHY STUDIO
Actis, London

ACCOUNT EXECUTIVE
James Griffiths, Jamie Maker

CREATIVE DIRECTOR
David Droga

COPYWRITER
Mike Sutherland

ART DIRECTOR
Antony Nelson

PRODUCTION MANAGER
Rob McLean

PHOTOGRAPHER
Trevor Ray Hart

TYPOGRAPHY
Scott Silvey

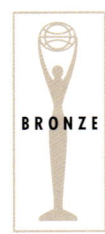

BRONZE

CATEGORY
Travel/Tourism

ADVERTISER/PRODUCT
Club 18–30/Package Holidays

TITLE
Pool

ADVERTISING AGENCY
Saatchi & Saatchi, London

PHOTOGRAPHY STUDIO
Actis, London

ACCOUNT EXECUTIVE
James Griffiths, Jamie Maker

CREATIVE DIRECTOR
David Droga

COPYWRITER
Mike Sutherland

ART DIRECTOR
Antony Nelson

PRODUCTION MANAGER
Rob McLean

PHOTOGRAPHER
Trevor Ray Hart

TYPOGRAPHY
Scott Silvey

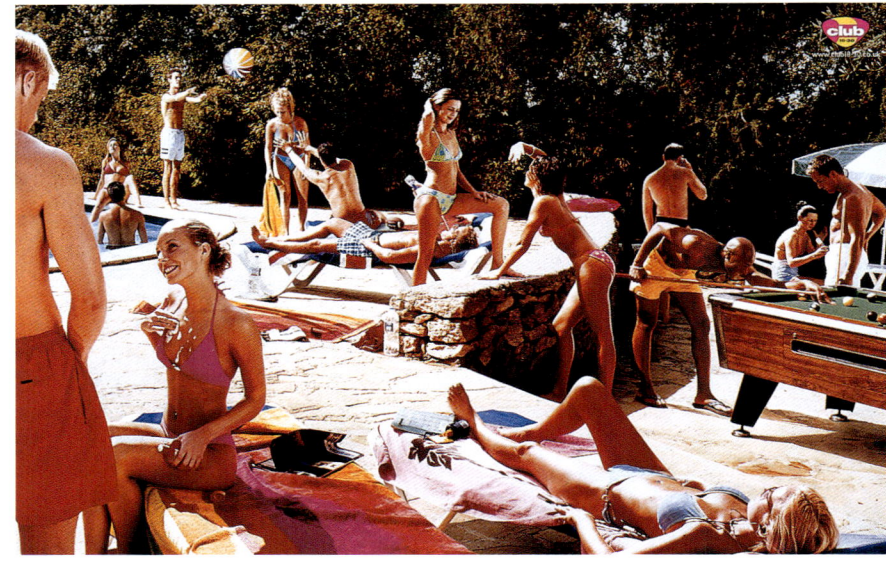

CATEGORY
Campaign

ADVERTISER/PRODUCT
Guinness

TITLE
Torso

TITLE
Navel

TITLE
Back

ADVERTISING AGENCY
Ogilvy & Mather, Singapore

ACCOUNT EXECUTIVE
David Mayo

CREATIVE DIRECTOR
Andy Greenaway

COPYWRITER
Andy Greenaway

ART DIRECTOR
Craig Smith

PHOTOGRAPHER
Roy Zhang

ILLUSTRATOR
Yau Digital

TYPOGRAPHER
Alfred Wee

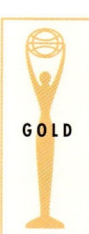

GOLD

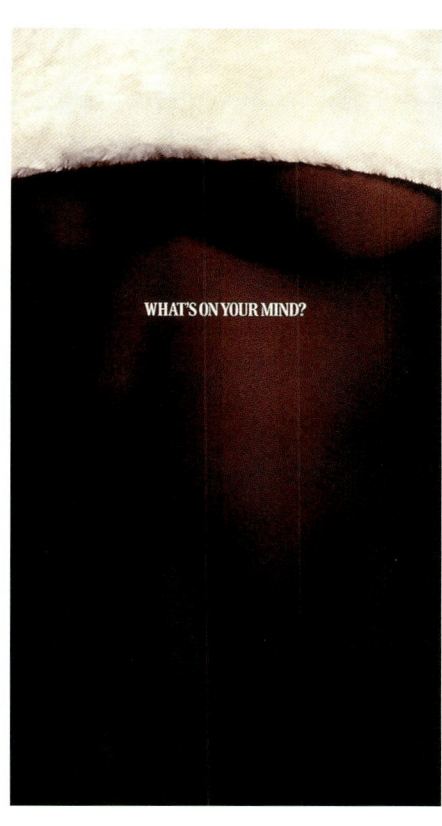

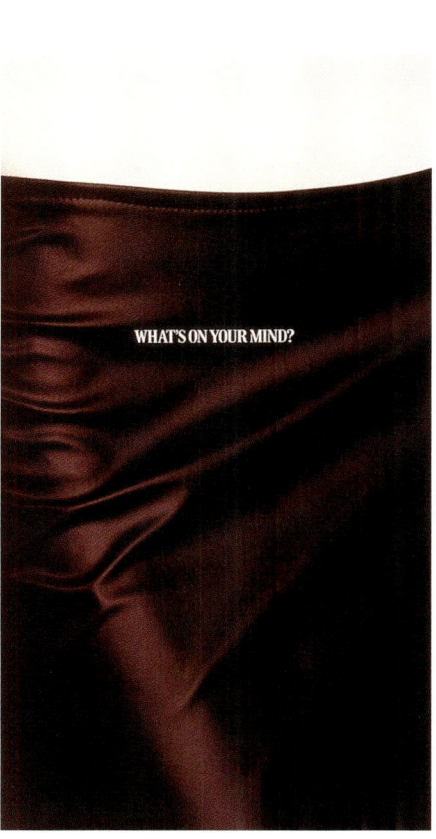

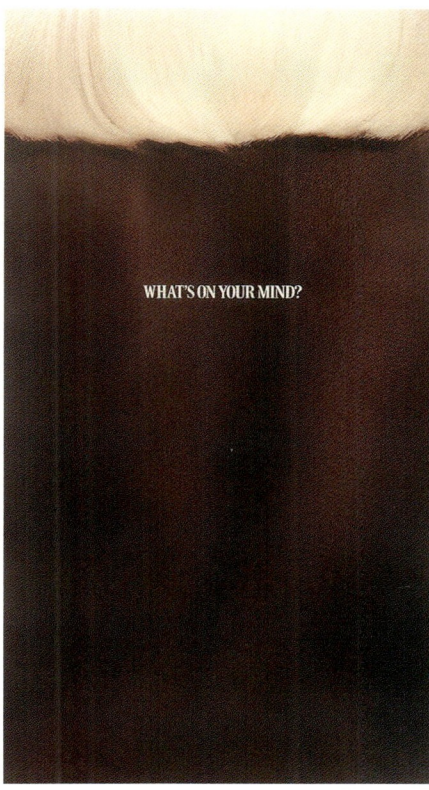

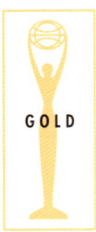

GOLD

CATEGORY
Campaign

ADVERTISER/PRODUCT
Harvey Nichols Winter Sale

TITLE
Neck

TITLE
Stomach

TITLE
Shin

ADVERTISING AGENCY
BMP DDB, London

COPYWRITER
Adam Tucker

ART DIRECTOR
Justin Tindall

PHOTOGRAPHER
Ben Stockley

TYPOGRAPHER
Kevin Clarke

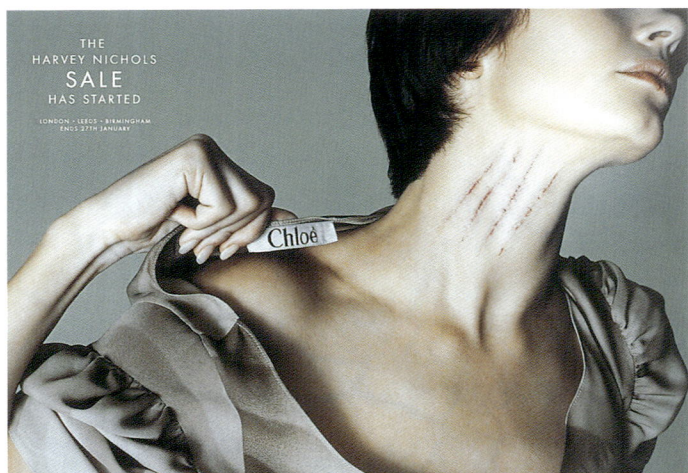

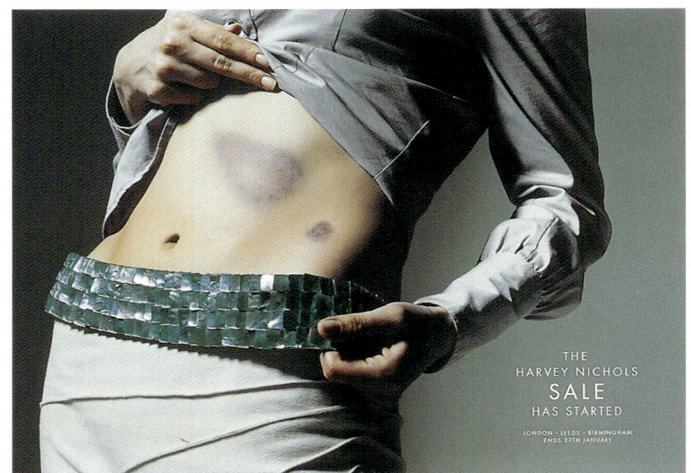

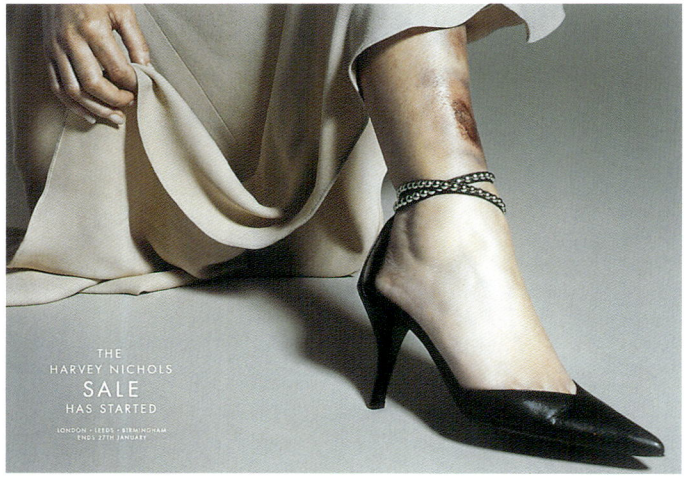

CATEGORY
Campaign

ADVERTISER/PRODUCT
Campaign Brief Asia

TITLE
Cecilia

TITLE
Marc

TITLE
Antoni

ADVERTISING AGENCY
Saatchi & Saatchi, Hong Kong

ACCOUNT EXECUTIVE
Laurie Kwong

CREATIVE DIRECTOR
Craig Davis

COPYWRITER
Renee Lim

ART DIRECTOR
Maurice Wee

PRODUCTION MANAGER
Ferris Tse

PHOTOGRAPHER
Stanley Wong

ILLUSTRATION/RETOUCHING
Edward Loh
(Phenomenon Singapore)

SILVER

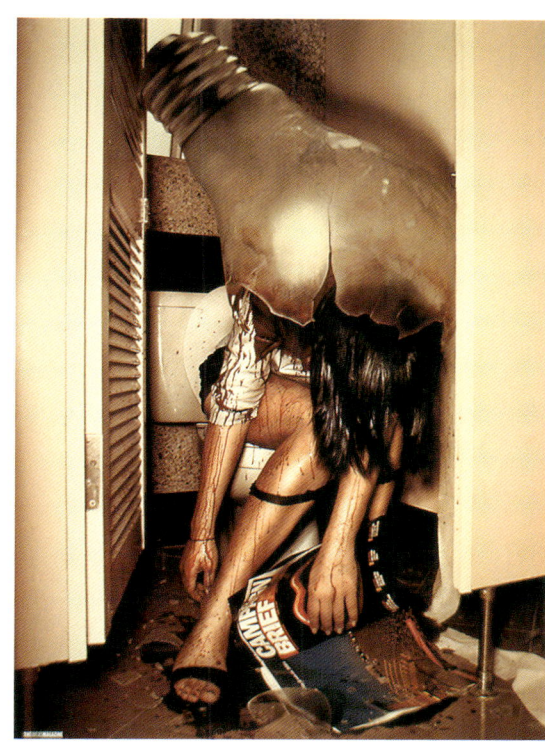

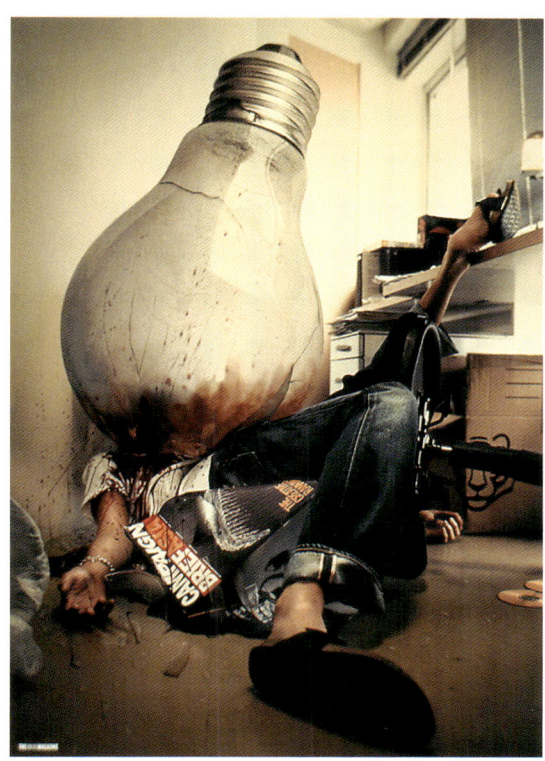

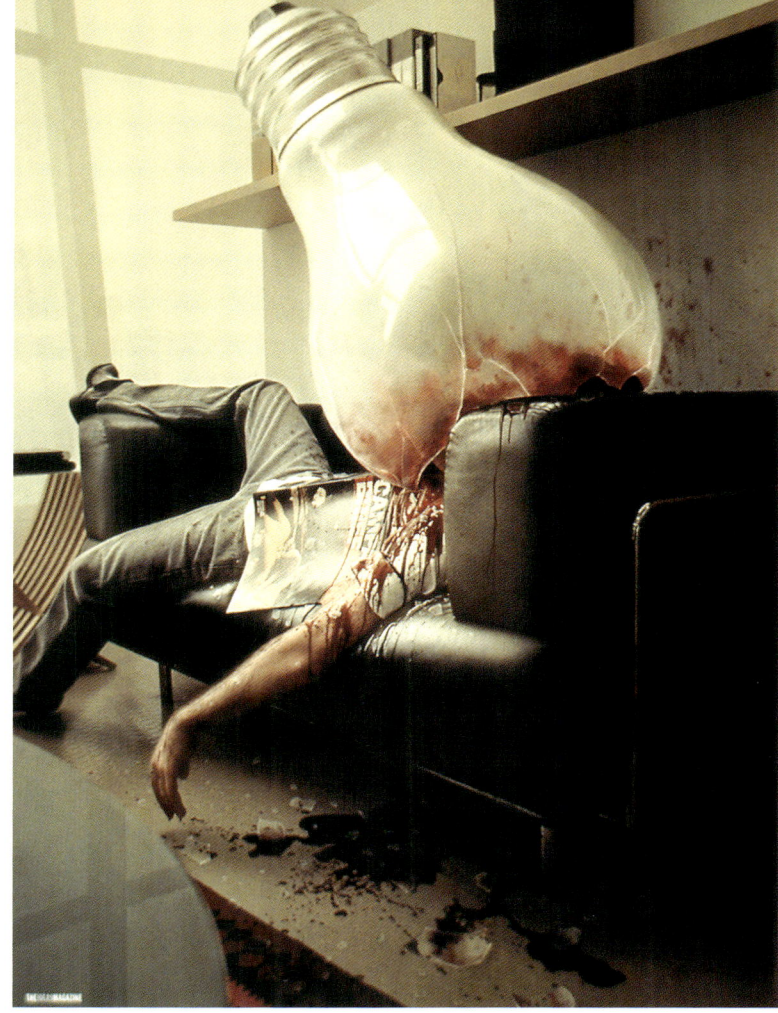

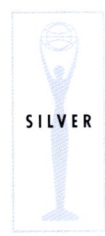

SILVER

CATEGORY Campaign	**TITLE** Pool	**PHOTOGRAPHY STUDIO** Actis, London	**COPYWRITER** Mike Sutherland
ADVERTISER/PRODUCT Club 18–30/Package Holidays	**TITLE** Bar	**ACCOUNT EXECUTIVE** James Griffiths, Jamie Maker	**ART DIRECTOR** Antony Nelson
TITLE Beach	**ADVERTISING AGENCY** Saatchi & Saatchi, London	**CREATIVE DIRECTOR** David Droga	**TYPOGRAPHY** Scott Silvey

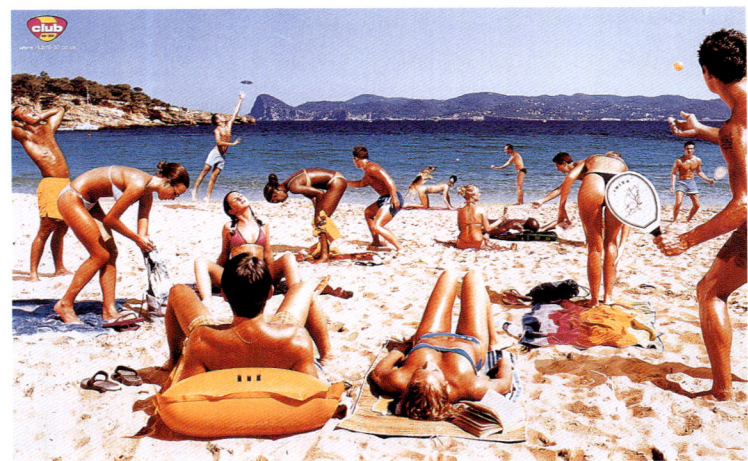

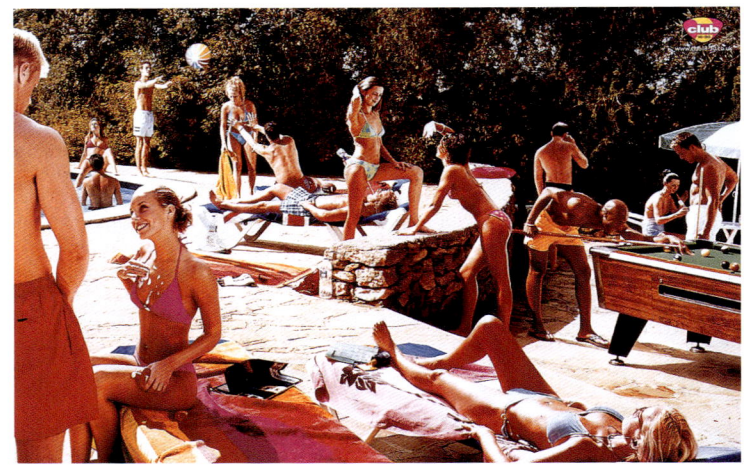

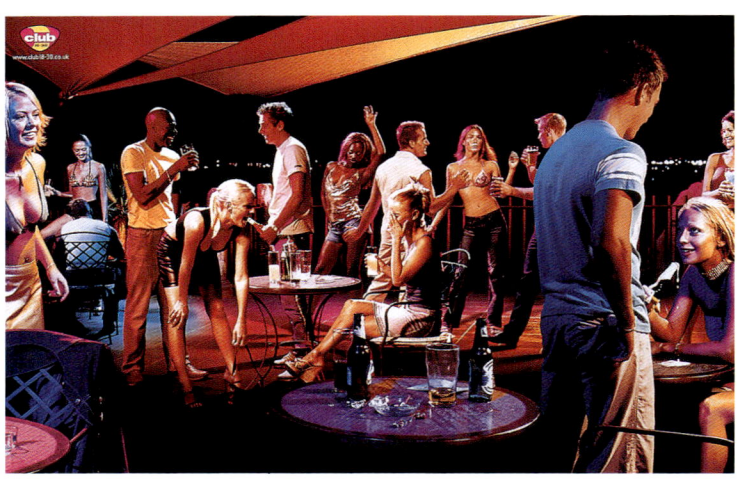

CATEGORY
Campaign

ADVERTISER/PRODUCT
International

TITLE
Burning Buildings

TITLE
Zip

TITLE
Extreme Sport

TITLE
Everything

TITLE
The Strong

TITLE
Maneuver

ADVERTISING AGENCY
Fallon, Minneapolis

ACCOUNT EXECUTIVE
Greg Brinker

CREATIVE DIRECTOR
Bob Moore

COPYWRITER
Franklin Tipton, Dean Buckhorn

ART DIRECTOR
Dan Bryant

PHOTOGRAPHER
R. J. Muna

PRINT MANAGER
Paul Morita

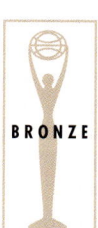

BRONZE

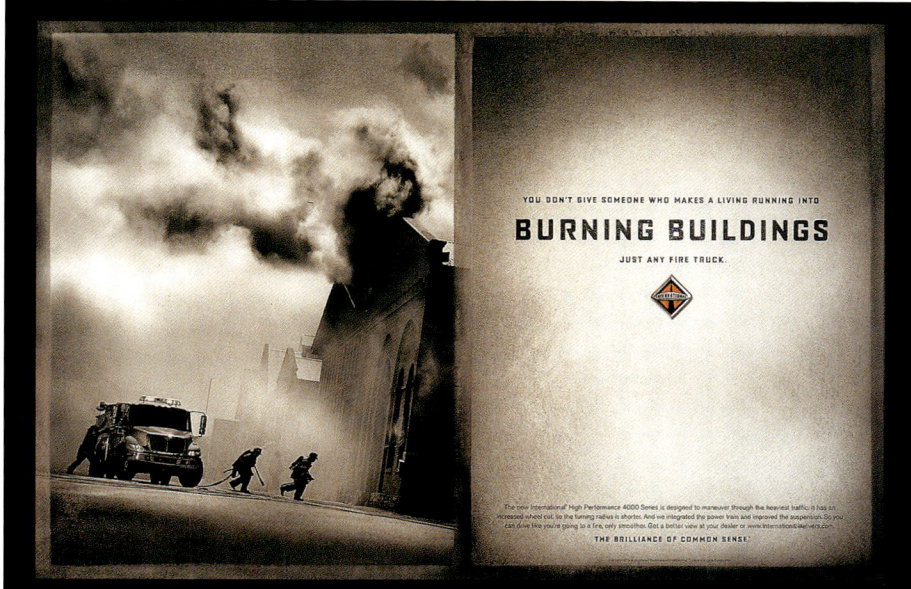

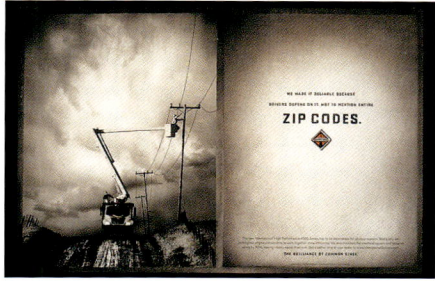

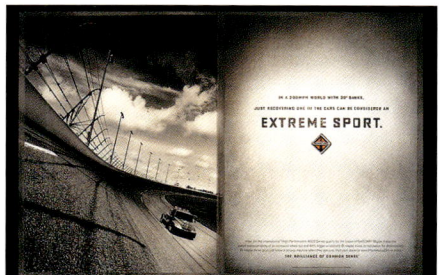

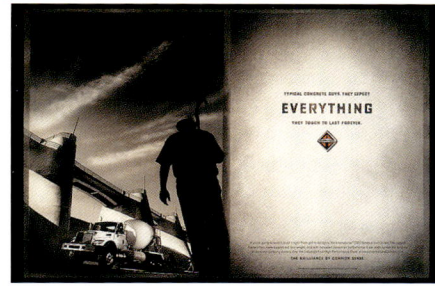

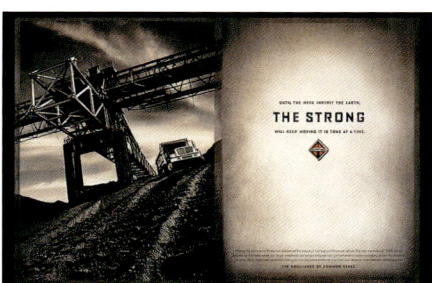

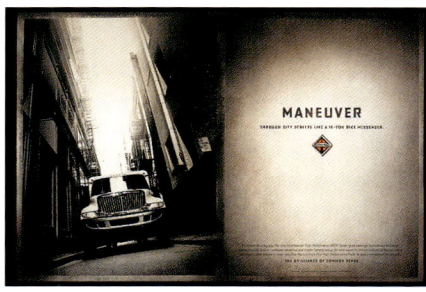

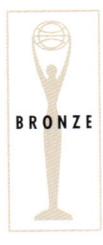

BRONZE

CATEGORY Campaign	**TITLE** The Museums' Night (Holbein)	**PHOTOGRAPHY STUDIO** Archiv	**ART DIRECTOR** Alexander Heil
ADVERTISER/PRODUCT Museums of Frankfurt	**TITLE** The Museums' Night (Passavant)	**ACCOUNT EXECUTIVE** Roland Stauber	**ART BUYING** Christina Hufgard
TITLE The Museums' Night (Goethe)	**ADVERTISING AGENCY** Ogilvy & Mather, Frankfurt	**COPYWRITER** Cora Walker	

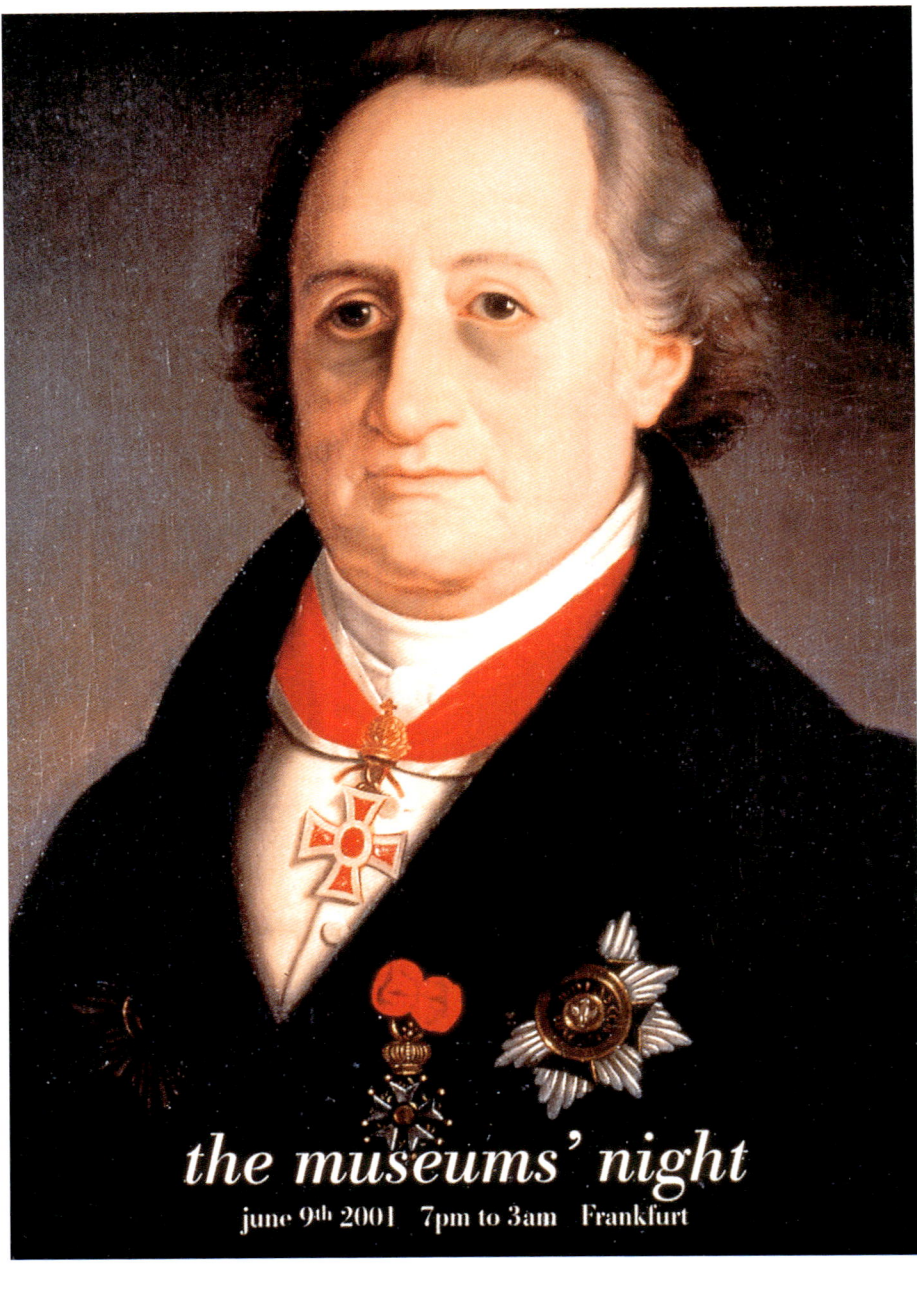

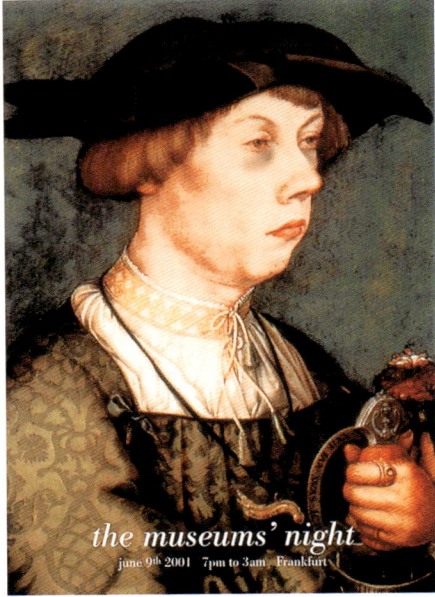

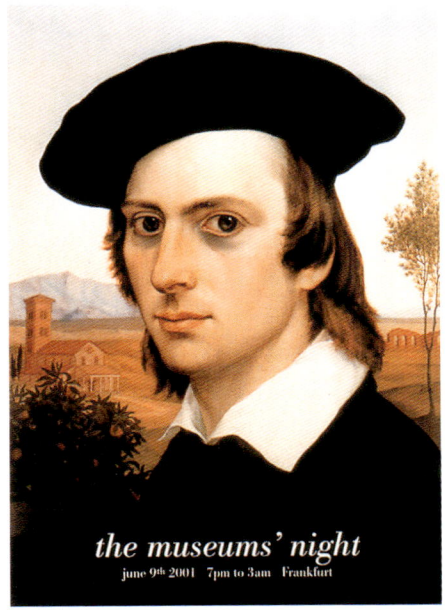

CATEGORY
Campaign

TITLE
Equalizer

CREATIVE DIRECTOR
Zak Mrouch, Paul Lavoie

PRODUCER
Beth Mackinnon

ADVERTISER/PRODUCT
Milestone/Flow 93.5

TITLE
Reggae

COPYWRITER
Christina Yu

ILLUSTRATOR
Christian Borstlap, Christina Yu

TITLE
Afro

ADVERTISING AGENCY
Taxi, Toronto

ART DIRECTOR
Christina Yu, Lance Martin

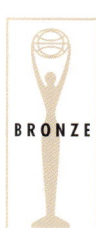

BRONZE

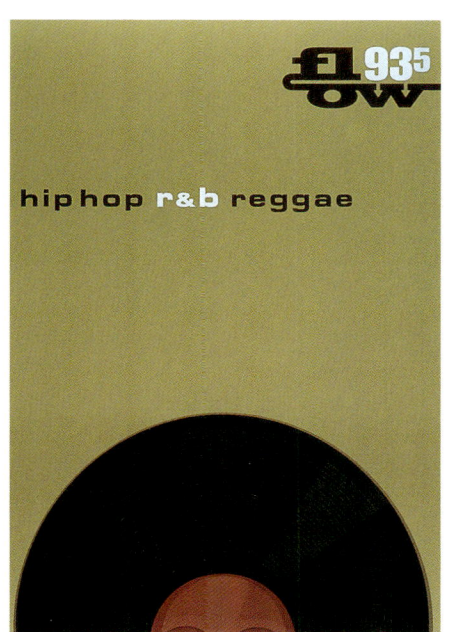

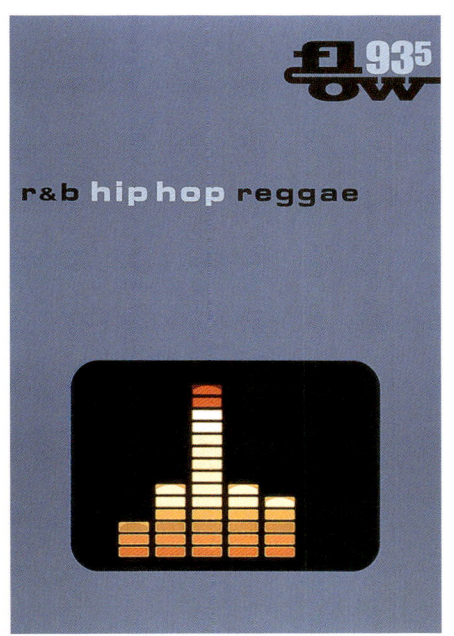

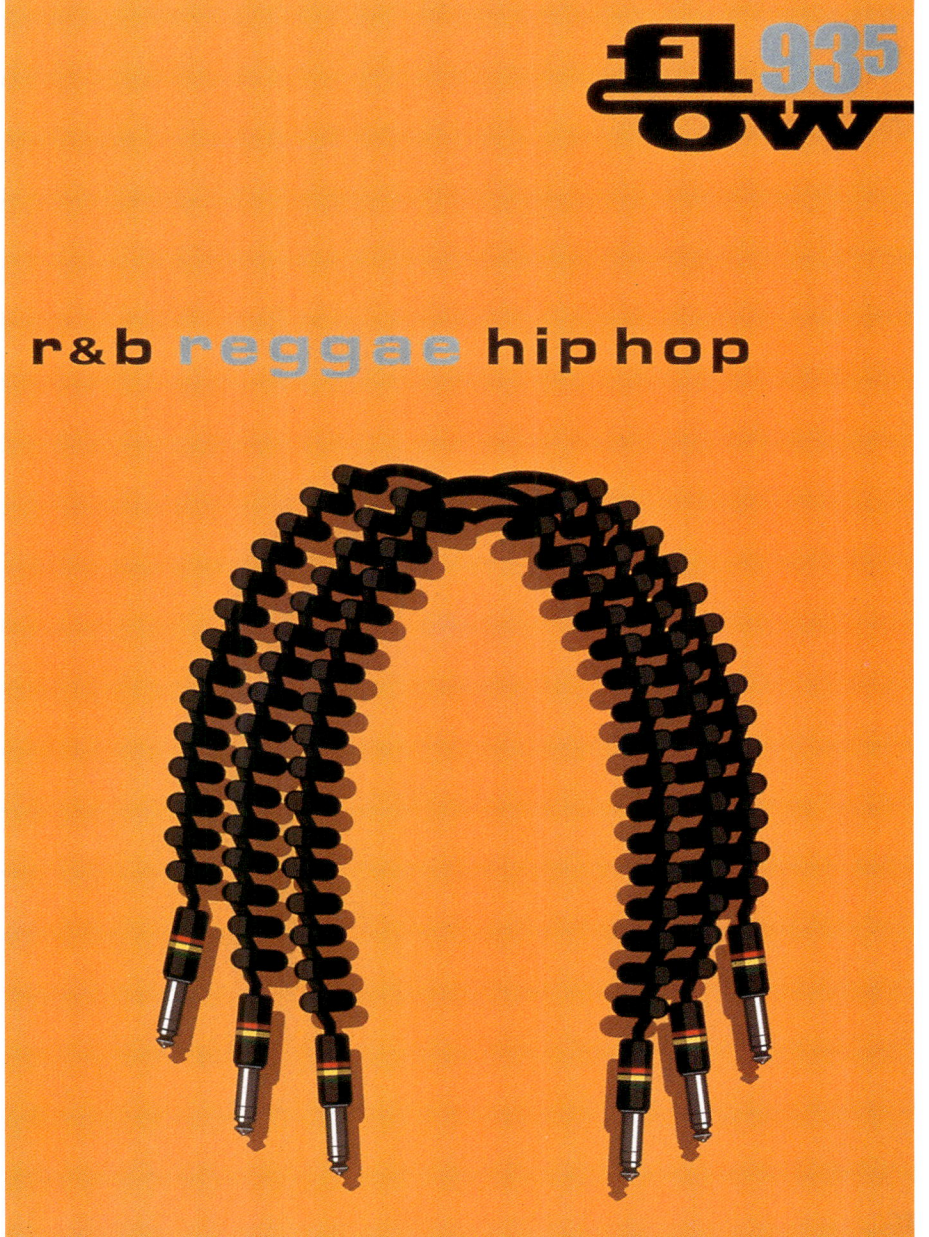

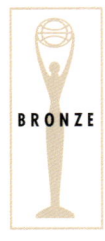

BRONZE

CATEGORY	**TITLE**	**PHOTOGRAPHY STUDIO**	**ART DIRECTOR**
Campaign	Lever Hockey	Westside Studios, Toronto	Alan Madill
ADVERTISER/PRODUCT	**TITLE**	**CREATIVE DIRECTOR**	**PHOTOGRAPHER**
Covenant House	Hockey Net	Zak Mroueh, Paul Lavoie	Frank Hoedl
TITLE	**ADVERTISING AGENCY**	**COPYWRITER**	**PRODUCER**
Computer	Taxi, Toronto	Terry Drummond	Connie Gorsline

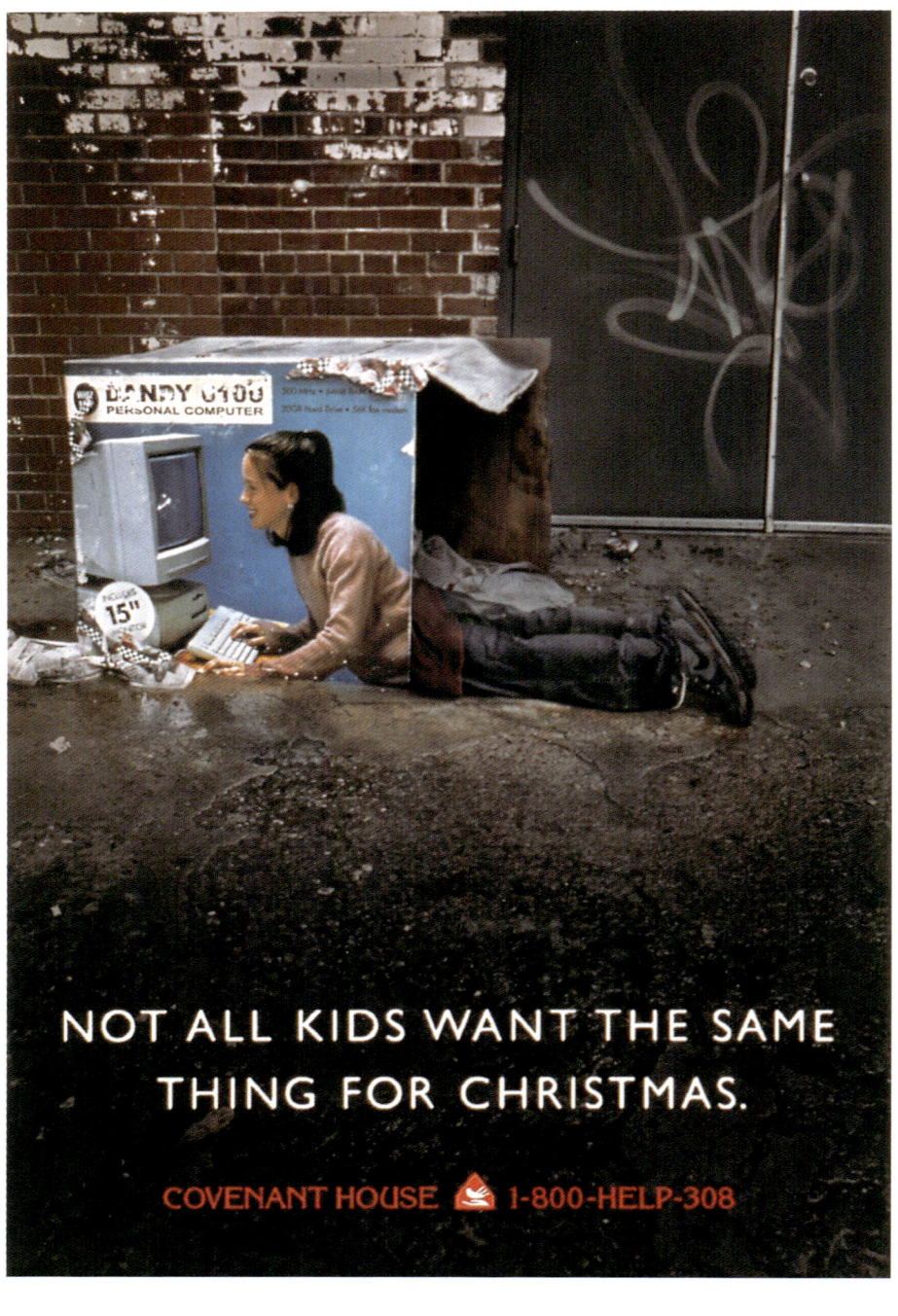

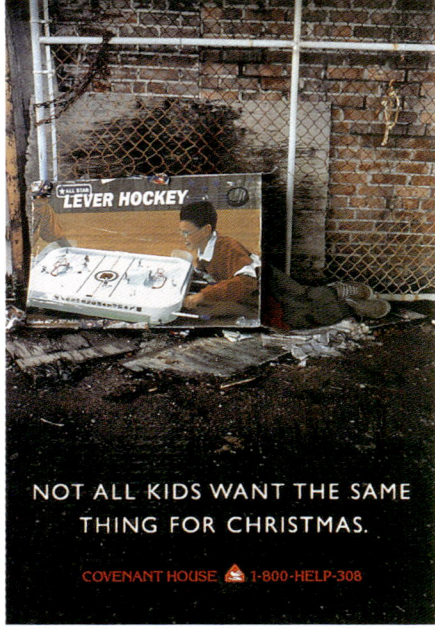

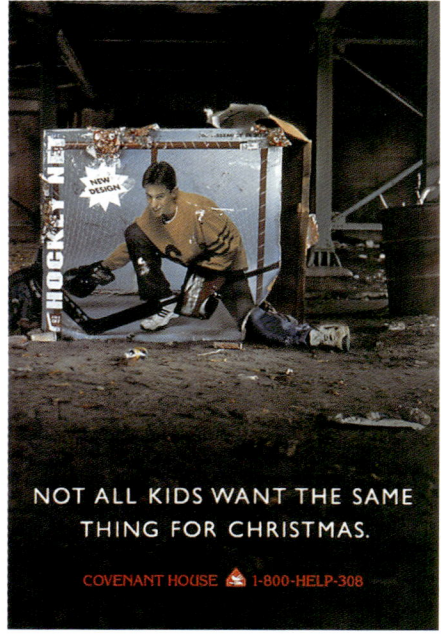

CATEGORY
Campaign

ADVERTISER/PRODUCT
Loterj State Lottery/Scratch Ticket

TITLE
Scratched/Bus

TITLE
Scratched/Bike

TITLE
Scratched/Train

ADVERTISING AGENCY
Giovanni, FCB, Rio de Janeiro

PHOTOGRAPHY STUDIO
Platinum, Rio de Janeiro

ACCOUNT EXECUTIVE
Gustavo Oliveira

CREATIVE DIRECTOR
Adilson Xavier, Cristina Amorim

COPYWRITER
André Lima

ART DIRECTOR
Cláudio Gatão

PRODUCTION MANAGER
Paulo Moraes

ILLUSTRATION
Platinum, Rio de Janerio

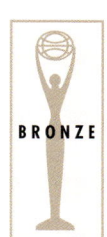

BRONZE

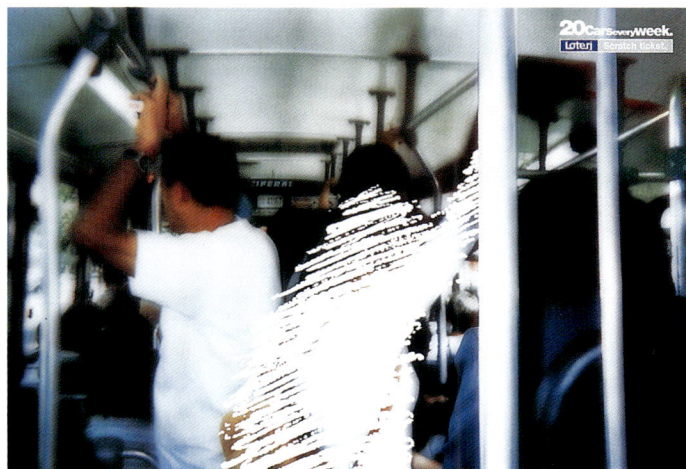

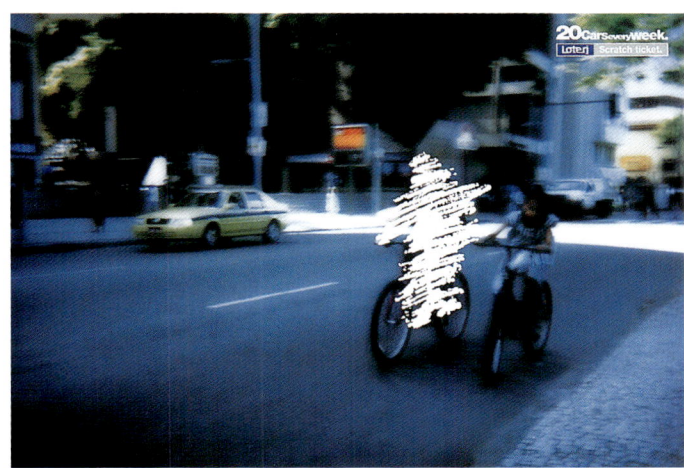

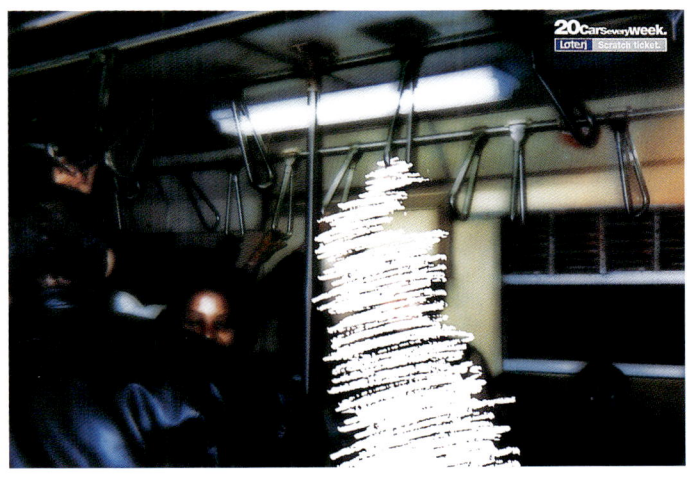

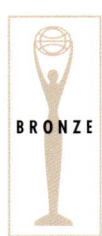

BRONZE

CATEGORY
Campaign

ADVERTISER/PRODUCT
Changi Prison

TITLE
Grandparents

TITLE
Radio Deadman

TITLE
Skeleton Men

ADVERTISING AGENCY
Ogilvy & Mather Singapore,
Singapore

ACCOUNT EXECUTIVE
David Mayo

CREATIVE DIRECTOR
Craig Smith, Andy Greenaway

COPYWRITER
Steve Hough, Gregory Yeo

ART DIRECTOR
Gregory Yeo, Steve Hough

PHOTOGRAPHER
Museum Archive

TYPOGRAPHER
Greogry Yeo, Steve Hough

ILLUSTRATOR
Alice

DREAMIMAGING
Gary Choo

PROCOLOR
Lay Ling

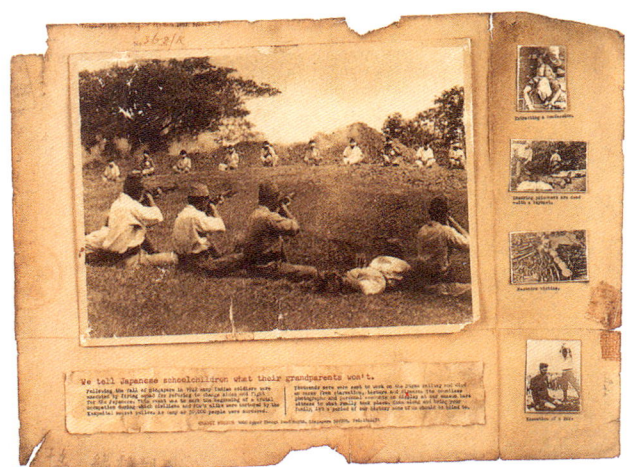

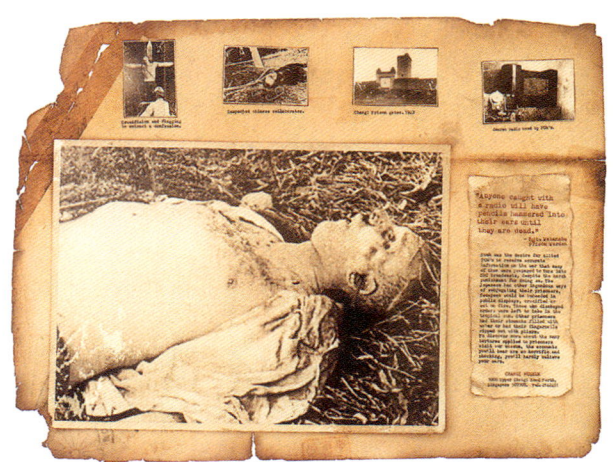

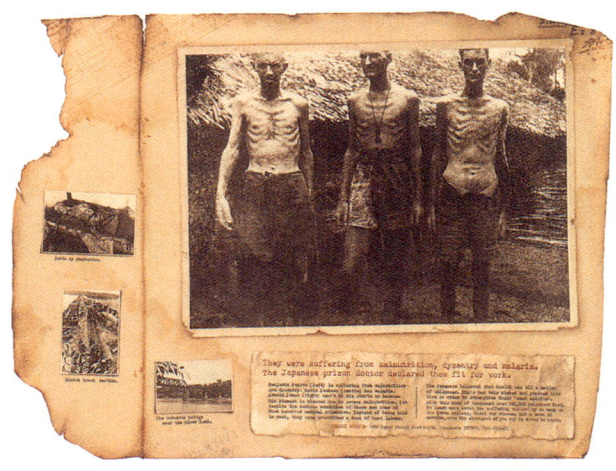

CATEGORY
Campaign

ADVERTISER/PRODUCT
Engelhard Arzneimittel
(Pellit Insektenabwehrspray)

TITLE
The Insectivores—Mr.

TITLE
The Insectivores—Mrs.

ADVERTISING AGENCY
Scholz & Friends, Berlin

ACCOUNT EXECUTIVE
Matthias Eichler,
Sandra Rueschenschmidt, Uli Geiger

CREATIVE DIRECTOR
Eric Urmetzer, Stephan Ganser

COPYWRITER
Oliver Handlos

ART DIRECTOR
Raphael Puettmann

PHOTOGRAPHER
Wilbert Weigend

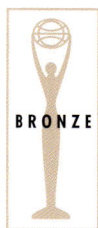

BRONZE

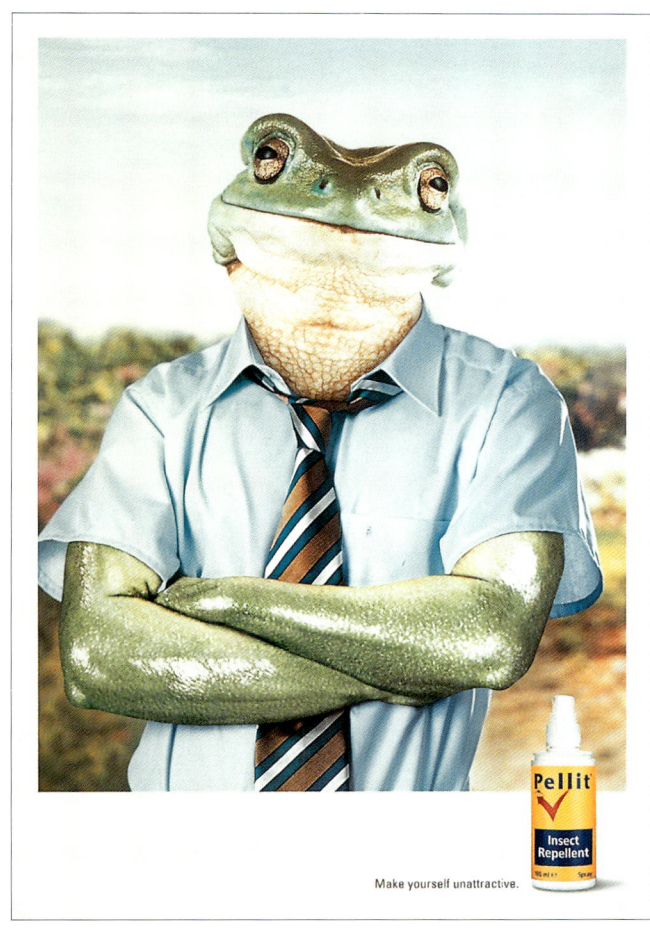

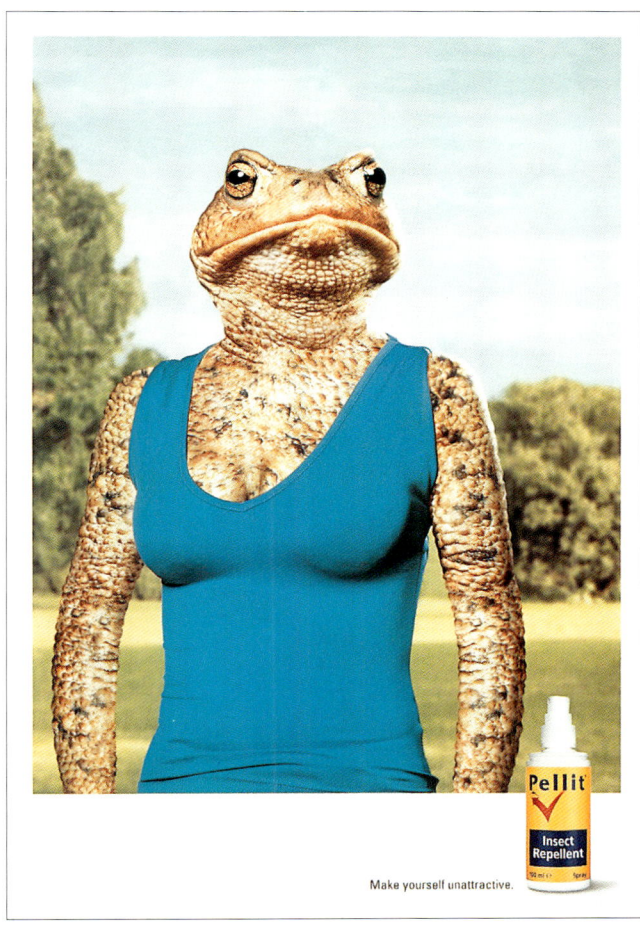

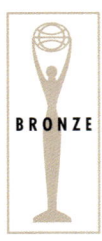

BRONZE

CATEGORY
Campaign

ADVERTISER/PRODUCT
Frankfurter Allgemeine Zeitung—
There Is Always a Clever Mind
Behind It

TITLE
Ferdinand Piech

TITLE
Reinhold Messner

TITLE
Wim Wenders

TITLE
Randolf Rodenstock

TITLE
Gerhard Richter

ADVERTISING AGENCY
Scholz & Friends, Berlin

ACCOUNT EXECUTIVE
Katrin Seegers, Marie Toya Gaillard

CREATIVE DIRECTOR
Sebastian Turner

ART DIRECTOR
Julia Schmidt

PHOTOGRAPHER
Alfred Seiland

POST PRODUCTION
Hans-Juergen Gaeltzner

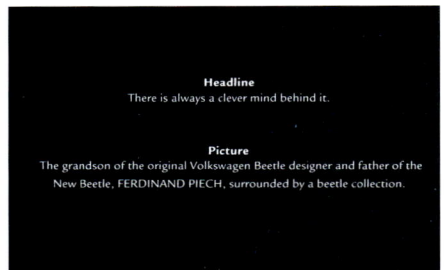

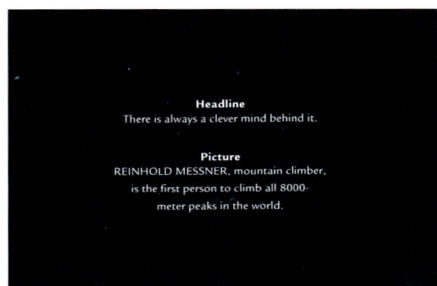

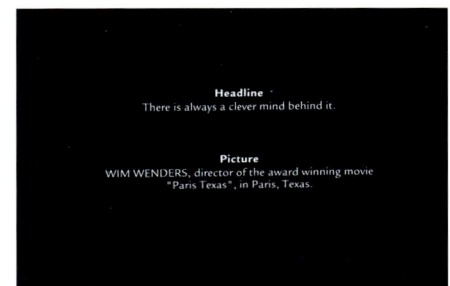

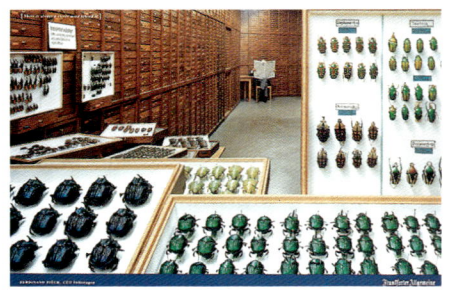

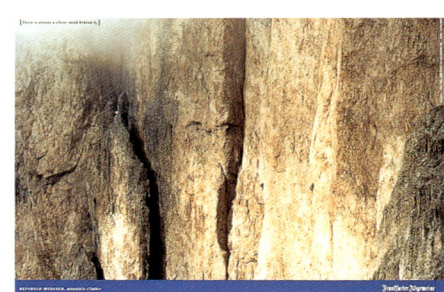

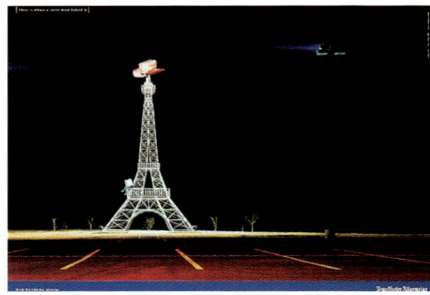

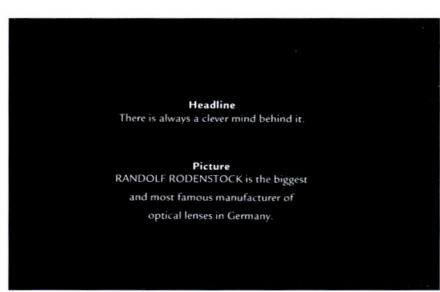

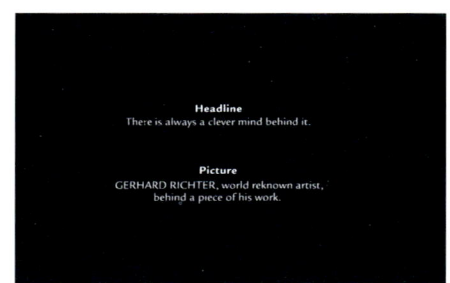

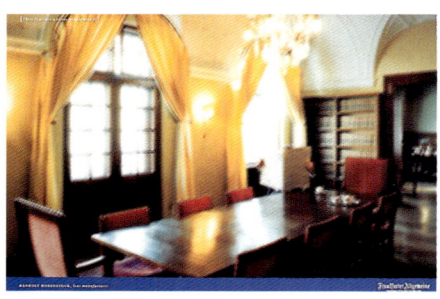

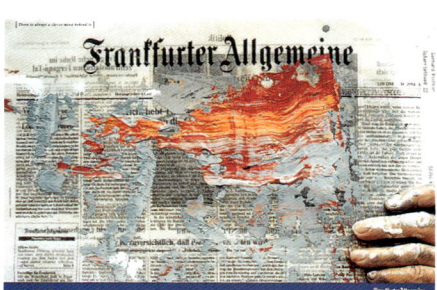

CATEGORY
Direct Marketing—Collateral

ADVERTISER/PRODUCT
SK-II Repair C

TITLE
Memo Pad

ADVERTISING AGENCY
Leo Burnett, Hong Kong

ACCOUNT EXECUTIVE
May Ng, Kara Yang

CREATIVE DIRECTOR
Connie Lo, Ray Lam

COPYWRITER
Connie Lo, Ray Lam

ART DIRECTOR
Ray Lam, Matthew Cheng,
Clara Sue

PRODUCTION MANAGER
Gary Ng

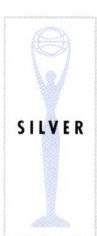

SILVER

SK II Skin Repair Spray—Make Lines Disappear

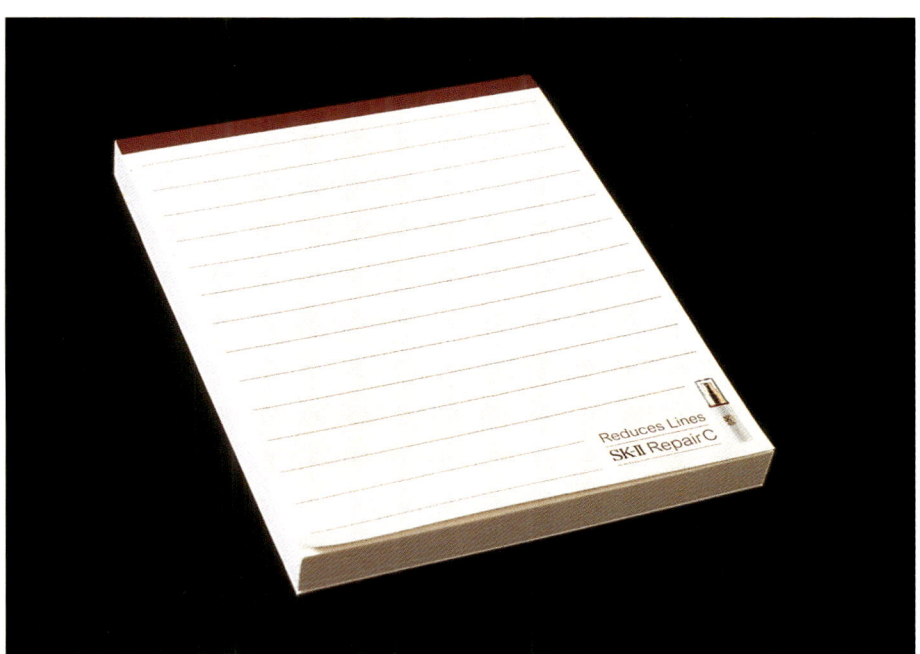

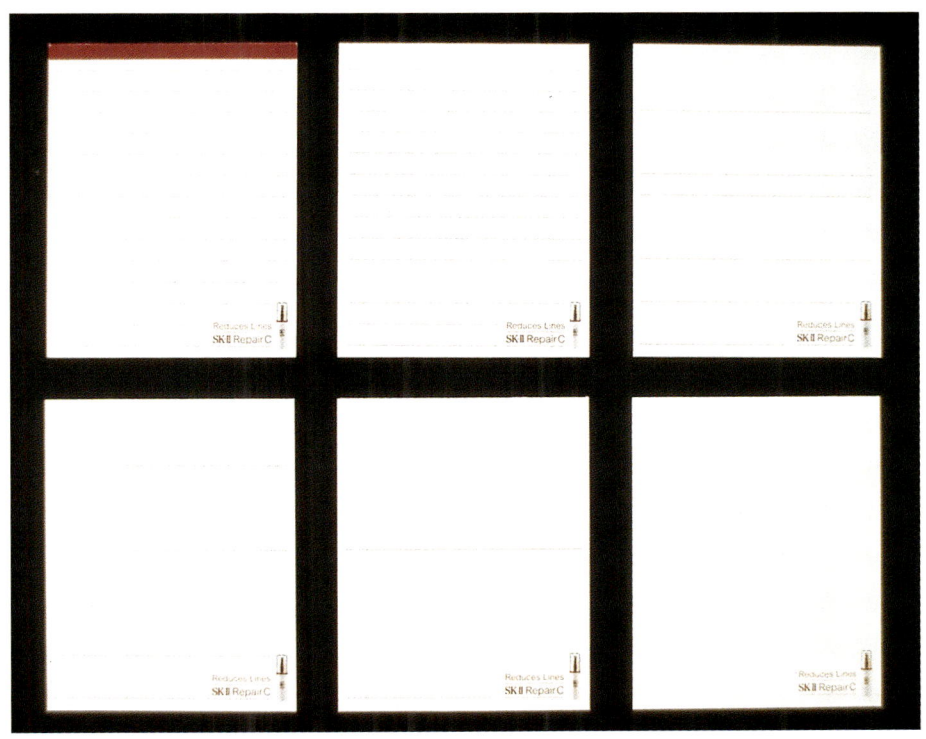

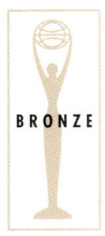

BRONZE

CATEGORY
Direct Marketing—Collateral

ADVERTISER/PRODUCT
Gothenburg Homeless Shelter

TITLE
John's Bedset

ADVERTISING AGENCY
ANR.BBDO, Gothenburg

ACCOUNT EXECUTIVE
Charlotta Warnhammer,
Joakim Brinkenberg

CREATIVE DIRECTOR
Christer Allansson

COPYWRITER
Jonas Peterson

ART DIRECTOR
Martin Lannering

PRODUCTION MANAGER
Anneli Kjellander

PHOTOGRAPHER
Magnus Eklöf

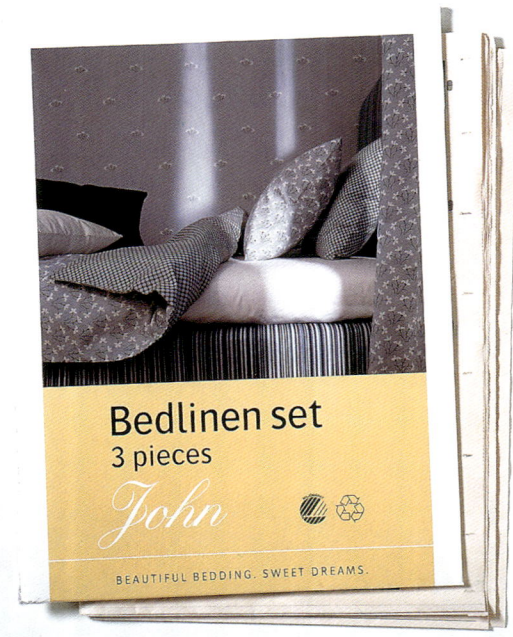

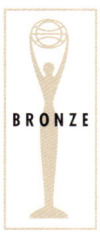

BRONZE

CATEGORY
Direct Marketing—Collateral

ADVERTISER/PRODUCT
Sea Shepherd Conservation Society

TITLE
Friends, Family, Couple

ADVERTISING AGENCY
Saatchi & Saatchi, Singapore

PHOTOGRAPHY STUDIO
Shutterbug, Singapore

CREATIVE DIRECTOR
Sion Scott Wilson

COPYWRITER
Jagdish Ramakrishnan

ART DIRECTOR
Simon Cox

PRODUCTION MANAGER
Esther Yue, Keith Yeng

PHOTOGRAPHER
Hon

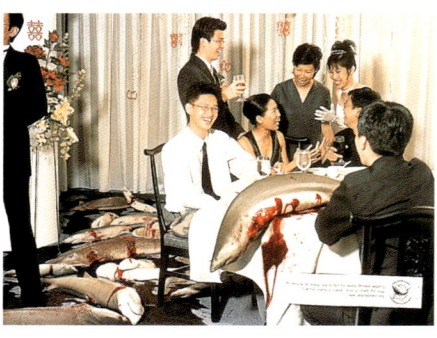
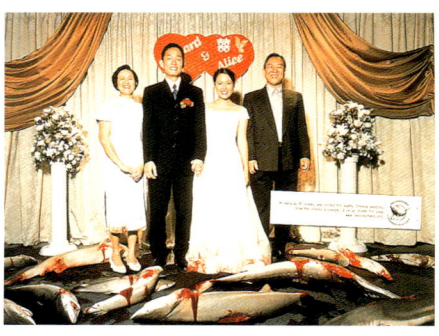
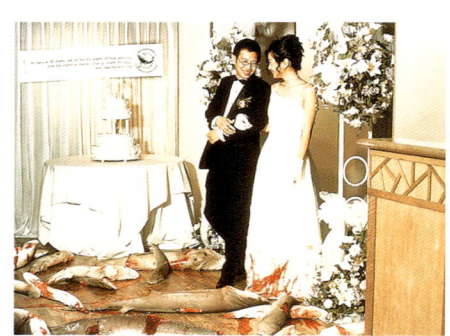

CATEGORY
Trade— Product

ADVERTISER/PRODUCT
Mercedes-Benz Atego

TITLE
The Flamingo

ADVERTISING AGENCY
Scholz & Friends, Berlin

ACCOUNT EXECUTIVE
Stephanie Wurst, Thomas Caprano,
Susanne Hirsch

CREATIVE DIRECTOR
Martin Pross

COPYWRITER
Peter Quester, Matthais Schmidt

ART DIRECTOR
Willbert Weigend

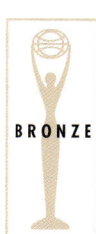

BRONZE

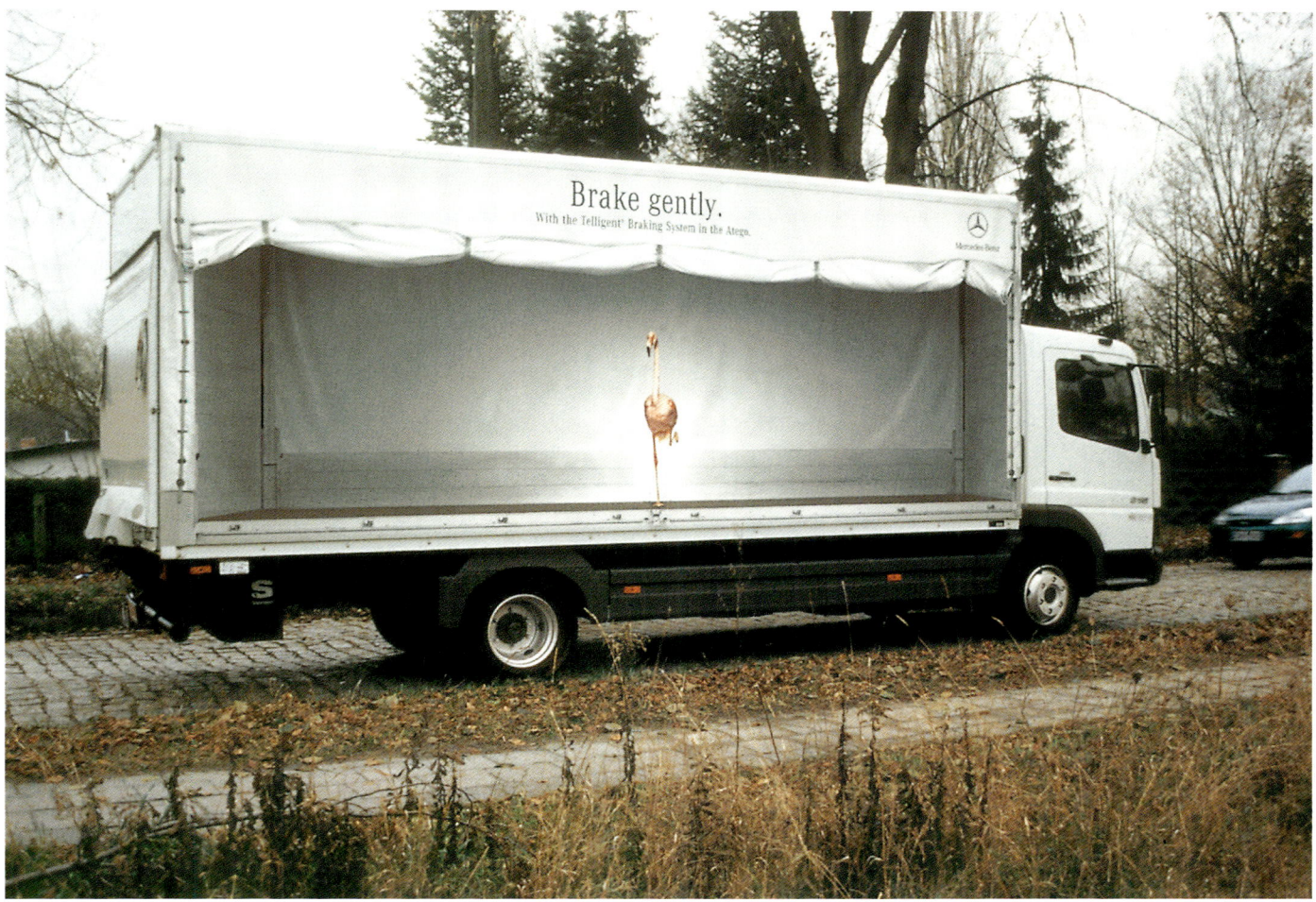

POSTER & BILLBOARD

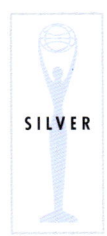

SILVER

CATEGORY
Automotive

ADVERTISER/PRODUCT
Honda Motorcycles

TITLE
Everyone's Born Dreaming
of a Honda

ADVERTISING AGENCY
DM9 DDB, São Paulo

ACCOUNT EXECUTIVE
Ana Paula Grassman

CREATIVE DIRECTOR
Erh Ray, Jader Rossetto,
Pedro Cappeletti

COPYWRITER
Flávio Gasarotti, Fabio Victoria

ART DIRECTOR
Erh Ray, Roberto Fernandez

PHOTOGRAPHER
Alexandre Catan

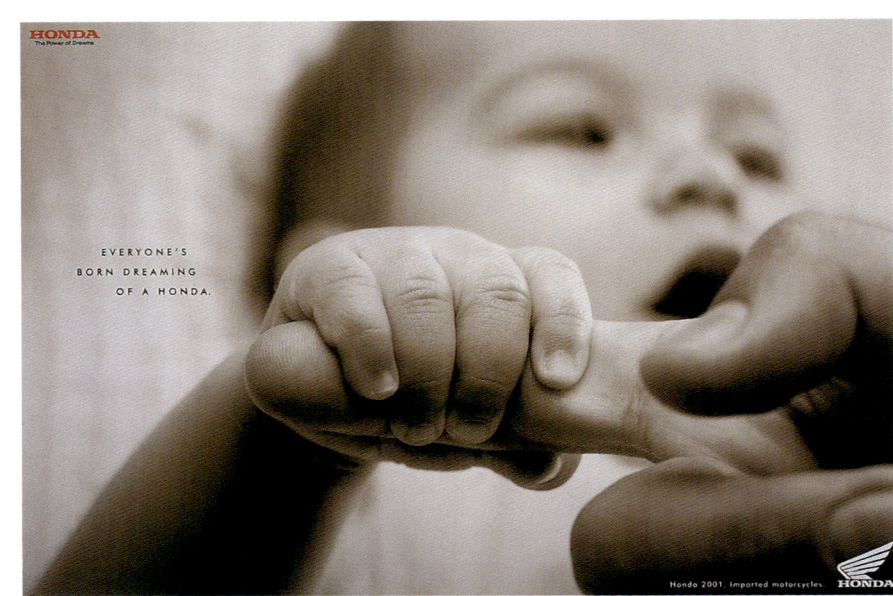

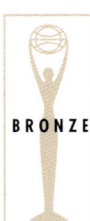

BRONZE

CATEGORY
Automotive

ADVERTISER/PRODUCT
Jeep

TITLE
Weekend Plan

ADVERTISING AGENCY
BBDO/Dongbang, Seoul

CREATIVE DIRECTOR
Dong-Su Yi

COPYWRITER
Hoon Yeo

ART DIRECTOR
Choi-Hee Kang

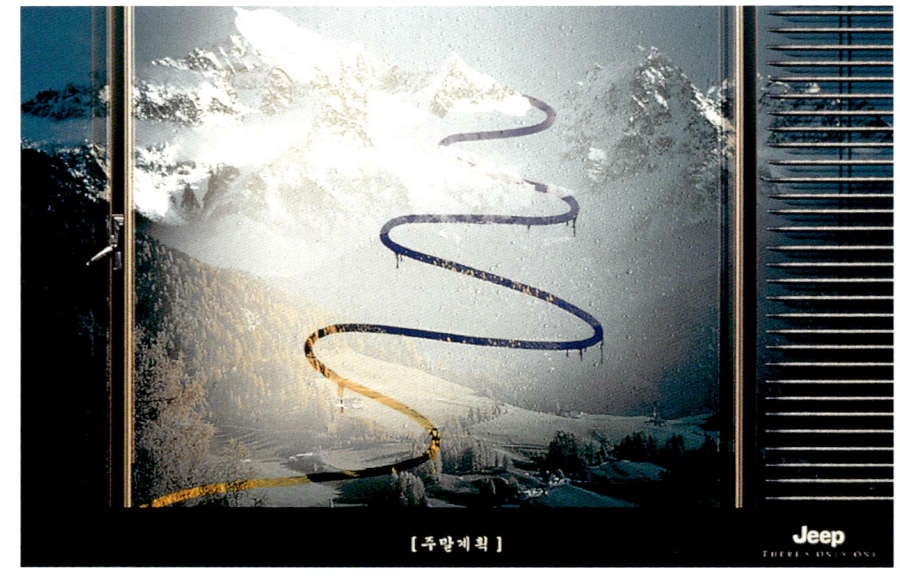

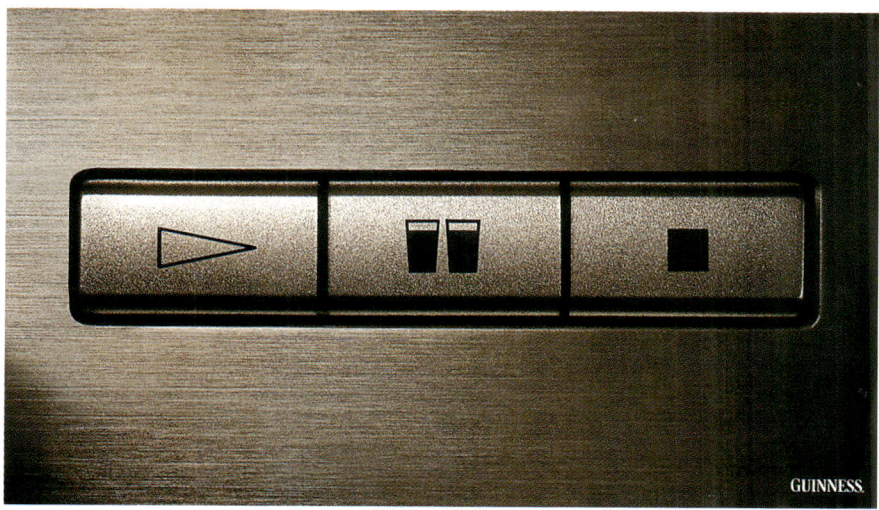

CATEGORY
Beverages/Alcoholic

ADVERTISER/PRODUCT
Guinness Stout

TITLE
Pause

ADVERTISING AGENCY
Ogilvy & Mather Malaysia,
Kuala Lumpur

PHOTOGRAPHY STUDIO
Barney Studio, Kuala Lumpur

CREATIVE DIRECTOR
Sonal Dabral

COPYWRITER
Paul Lim

ART DIRECTOR
Gavin Simpson

PRODUCTION MANAGER
Derrick Chong

PHOTOGRAPHER
Thomas

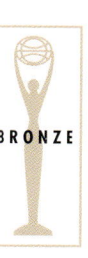

BRONZE

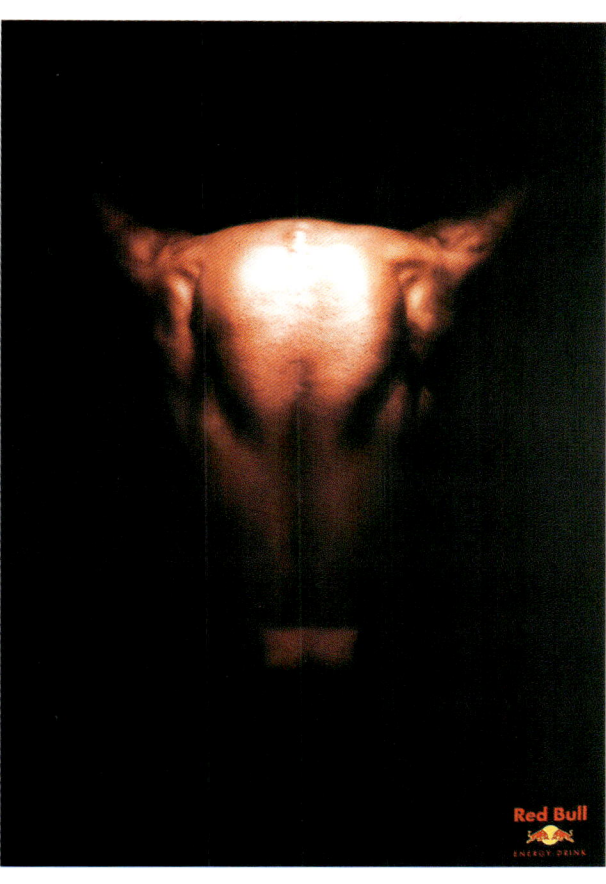

CATEGORY
Beverages/Nonalcoholic

ADVERTISER/PRODUCT
Red Bull

TITLE
Body

ADVERTISING AGENCY
Leo Burnett Singapore

PHOTOGRAPHY STUDIO
Studio 121, Singapore

ACCOUNT EXECUTIVE
Arthur Chung, Merwin Chew

CREATIVE DIRECTOR
Alex Shipley, Tay Guan Hin

COPYWRITER
Alex Shipley

ART DIRECTOR
Sachin Ambekar

PRODUCTION MANAGER
Dennis Gan, Victor Lee

DESIGN & ILLUSTRATION
Phenomenon, Singapore

SILVER

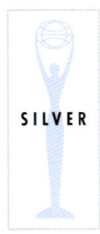

SILVER

CATEGORY
Entertainment Promotion

ADVERTISER/PRODUCT
Atom Films

TITLE
Popcorn

ADVERTISING AGENCY
Crispin Porter & Bogusky, Miami

CREATIVE DIRECTOR
Alex Bogusky

COPYWRITER
Ari Mekin

ART DIRECTOR
Amee Shah

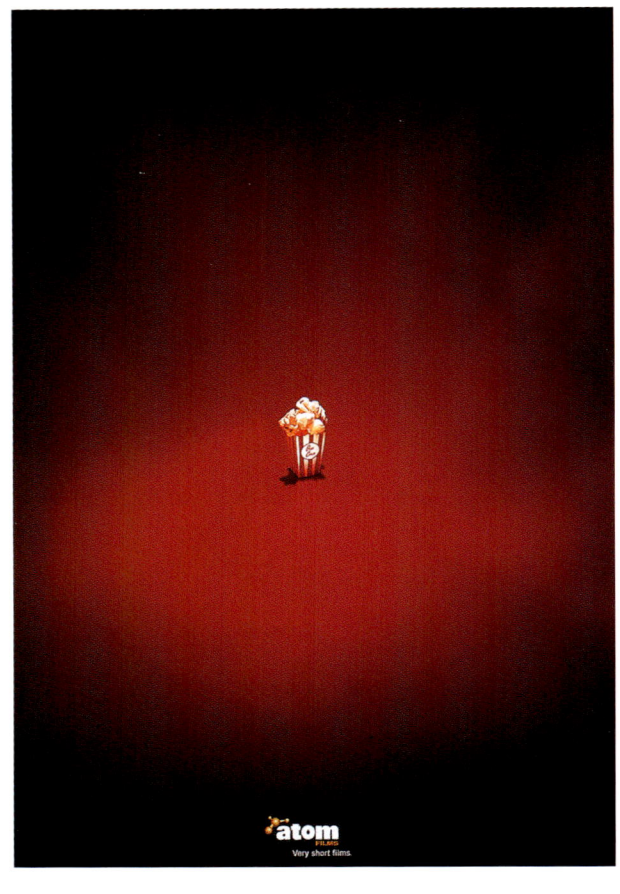

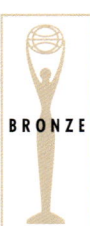

BRONZE

CATEGORY
Entertainment Promotion

ADVERTISER/PRODUCT
Auckland Theatre Company

TITLE
Vagina Monologues

ADVERTISING AGENCY
Saatchi & Saatchi New Zealand,
Auckland

ACCOUNT EXECUTIVE
Jillian Stanton

CREATIVE DIRECTOR
Andrew Tinning

ART DIRECTOR
Andy Blood, Andrew Tinning

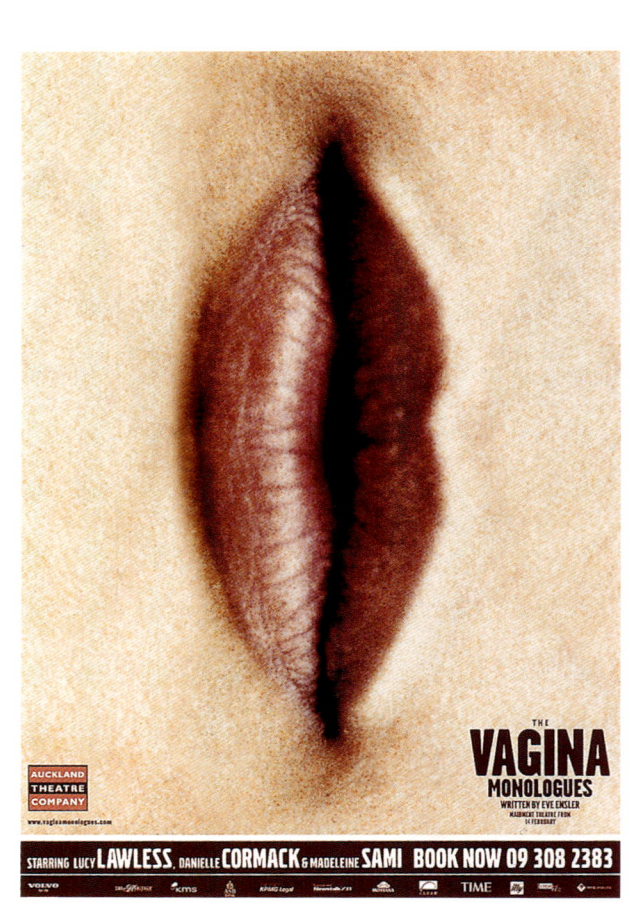

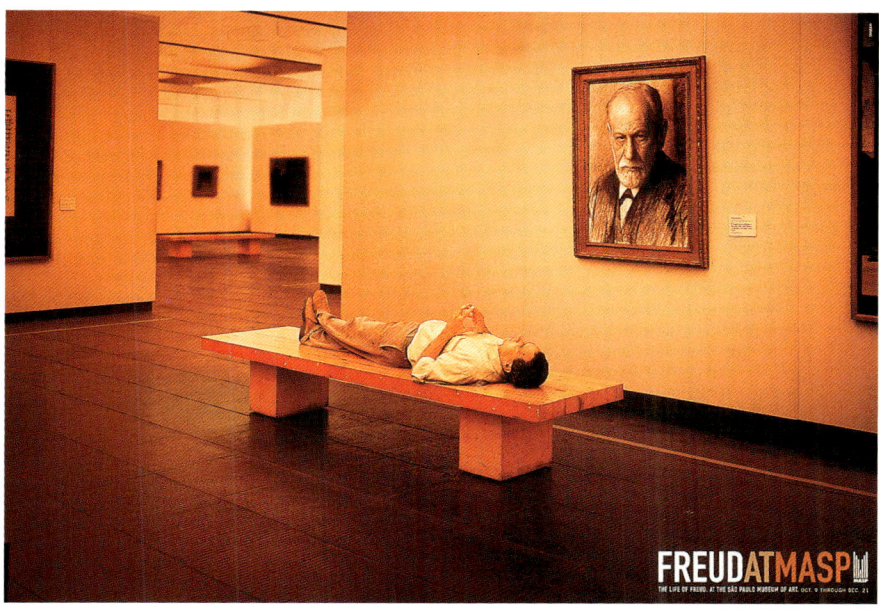

CATEGORY
Entertainment Promotion

ADVERTISER/PRODUCT
MASP São Paulo Museum of Art—
Freud's Life Exhibition

TITLE
The Life of Freud at the São Paulo
Museum of Art

ADVERTISING AGENCY
DM9 DDB, São Paulo

ACCOUNT EXECUTIVE
Vlademir Silva

CREATIVE DIRECTOR
Erh Ray, Jader Rossetto,
Pedro Cappeletti

COPYWRITER
Marcelo Reis

ART DIRECTOR
Roberto Fernandez

PHOTOGRAPHER
Rafael Costa

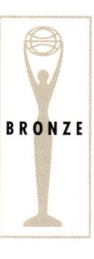
BRONZE

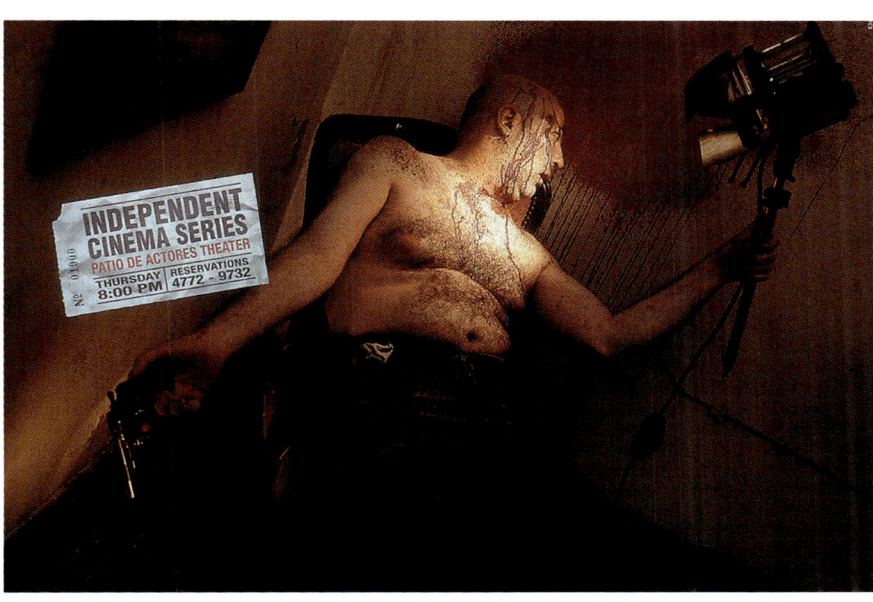

CATEGORY
Entertainment Promotion

ADVERTISER/PRODUCT
Patio de Actores Theatre

TITLE
Independent Cinema Series

ADVERTISING AGENCY
Barés, Buenos Aires

PHOTOGRAPHY STUDIO
Fabris Foto, Buenos Aires

ACCOUNT EXECUTIVE
Alfredo Barés

CREATIVE DIRECTOR
Alfredo Barés

COPYWRITER
Marcos Calandreli

ART DIRECTOR
Marcelo Saavedra, Diego Pellegrini,
Alfredo Barés

PRODUCTION MANAGER
Guido Urrutia

PHOTOGRAPHER
Fredy Fabris

BRONZE

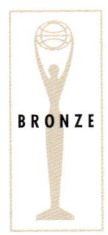

BRONZE

CATEGORY
Foods

ADVERTISER/PRODUCT
NutraSweet

TITLE
Jeans

ADVERTISING AGENCY
Del Campo Nazca Saatchi &
Saatchi, Buenos Aires

PHOTOGRAPHY STUDIO
Fredy Fabris, Buenos Aires

ACCOUNT EXECUTIVE
Roberto Fernández Monján

CREATIVE DIRECTOR
Pablo del Campo

COPYWRITER
Pablo Batlle

ART DIRECTOR
Hernán Jáuregui,
Iñaqui González del Solar

PRODUCTION MANAGER
Cosme Argerich

PHOTOGRAPHER
Fredy Fabris

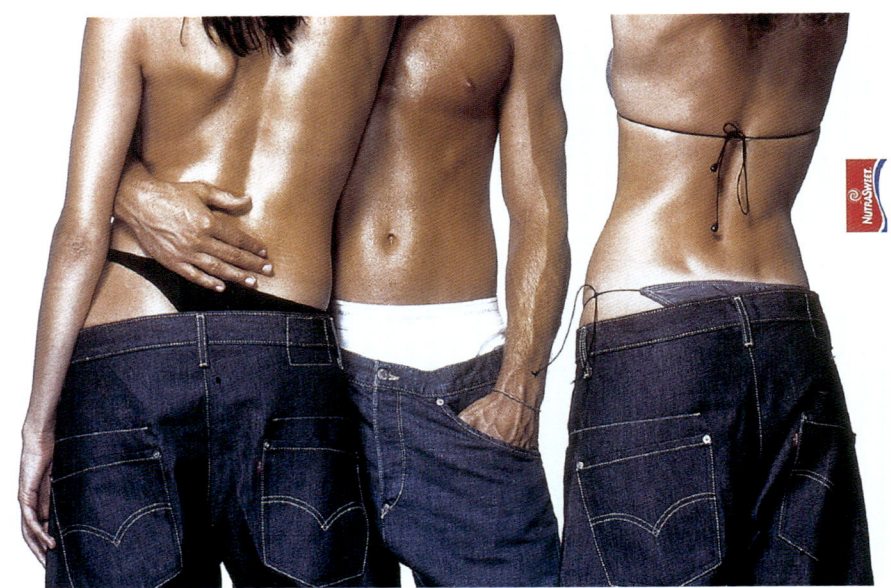

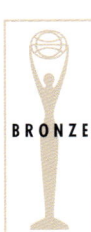

BRONZE

CATEGORY
Media Promotion

ADVERTISER/PRODUCT
Class 95 FM

TITLE
Weeping Guitar

ADVERTISING AGENCY
DYR, Singapore

PHOTOGRAPHY STUDIO
Shutterbug

ACCOUNT EXECUTIVE
Arthur Sung

CREATIVE DIRECTOR
Patrick Low, Mark Fong

COPYWRITER
Mark Fong

ART DIRECTOR
Toh Han Ming, Patrick Low

PRODUCTION MANAGER
Jean Abideen

PHOTOGRAPHER
Hon

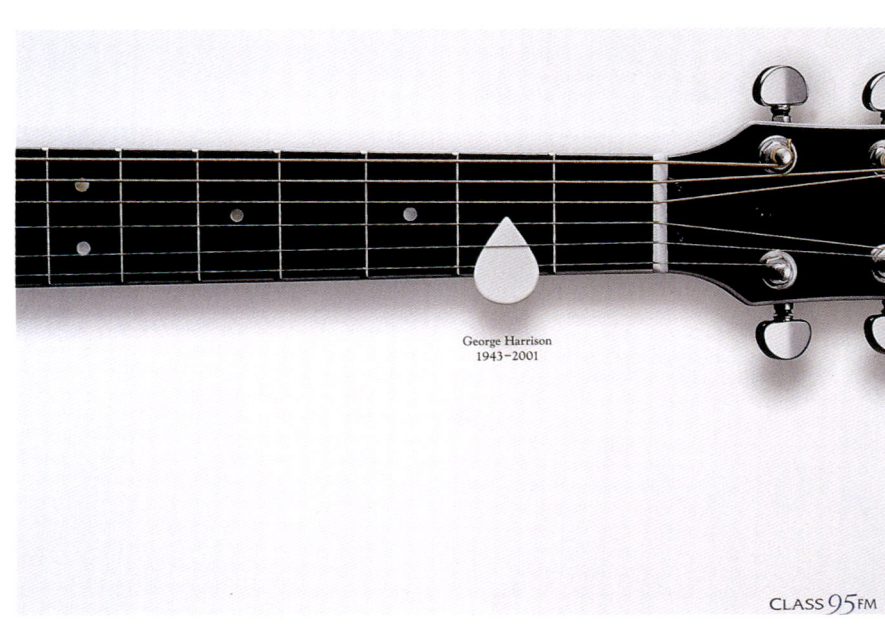

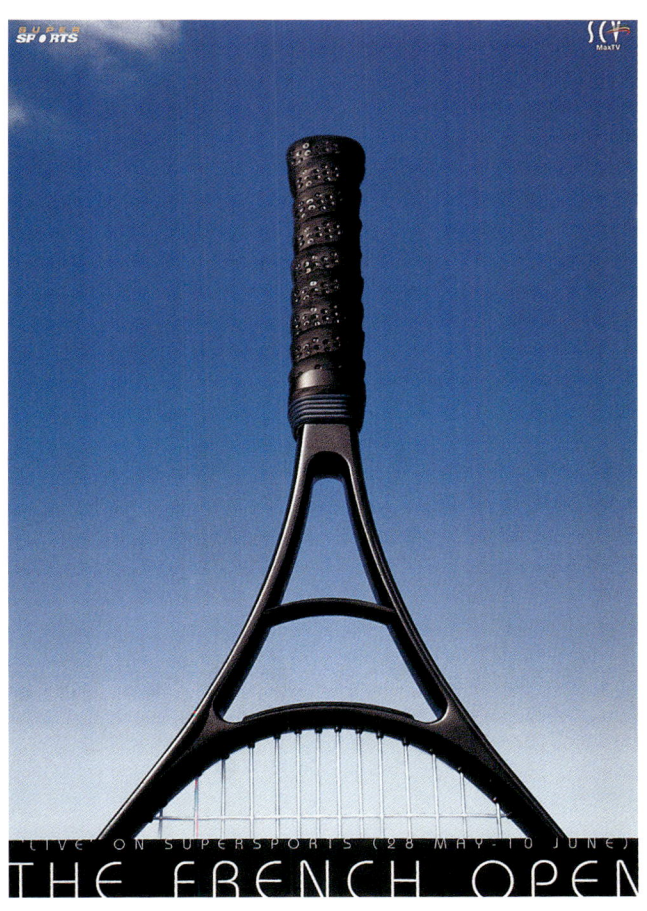

CATEGORY
Media Promotion

ADVERTISER/PRODUCT
Singapore Cable Vision

TITLE
French Open

ADVERTISING AGENCY
DYR, Singapore

PHOTOGRAPHY STUDIO
Shutterbug

ACCOUNT EXECUTIVE
Hoong Yun Peng

CREATIVE DIRECTOR
Patrick Low, Mark Fong

COPYWRITER
Mark Fong

ART DIRECTOR
Patrick Low

PRODUCTION MANAGER
Jean Abideen

PHOTOGRAPHER
Hon

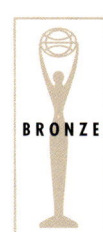
BRONZE

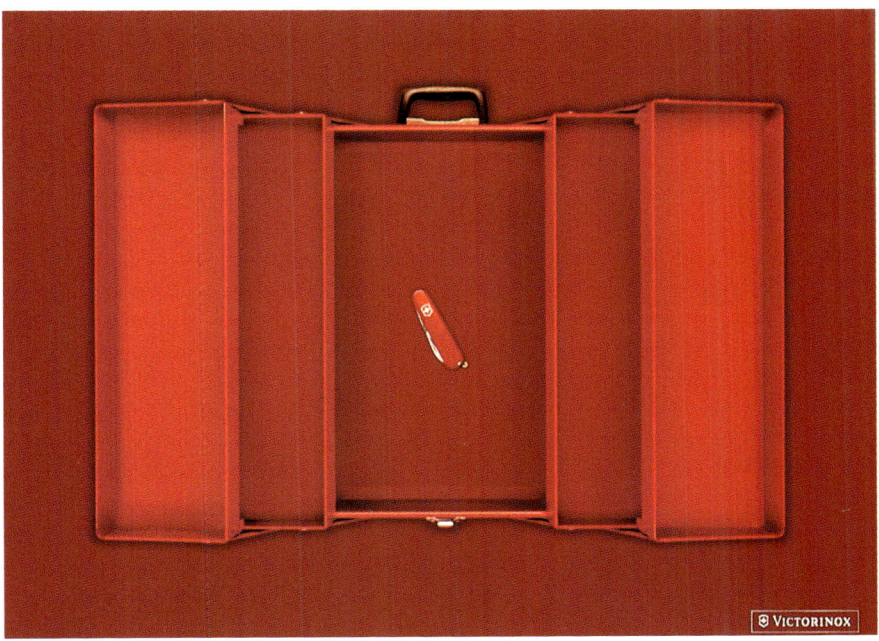

CATEGORY
Personal Items

ADVERTISER/PRODUCT
Victorinox Swiss Army Knife

TITLE
Tool Box

ADVERTISING AGENCY
Saatchi & Saatchi, Guangzhou

PHOTOGRAPHY STUDIO
Joe Lee, Hong Kong

ACCOUNT EXECUTIVE
Chris Leung

CREATIVE DIRECTOR
Roger Wong

COPYWRITER
Roger Wong

ART DIRECTOR
Roger Wong, Dan Fang

PRODUCTION MANAGER
Paul Lau, Wendy Zhou

PHOTOGRAPHER
Joe Lee

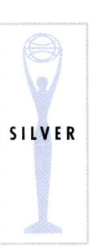
SILVER

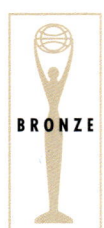

CATEGORY
Public Service

ADVERTISER/PRODUCT
Cancer Patients Aid Association

TITLE
Cowboy

ADVERTISING AGENCY
Ogilvy & Mather, Mumbai

PHOTOGRAPHY STUDIO
Shilvasa, Mumbai

CREATIVE DIRECTOR
Piyush Pandey

COPYWRITER
Piyush Pandey

ART DIRECTOR
Rajiv Rao

PHOTOGRAPHER
Suresh Natarajan

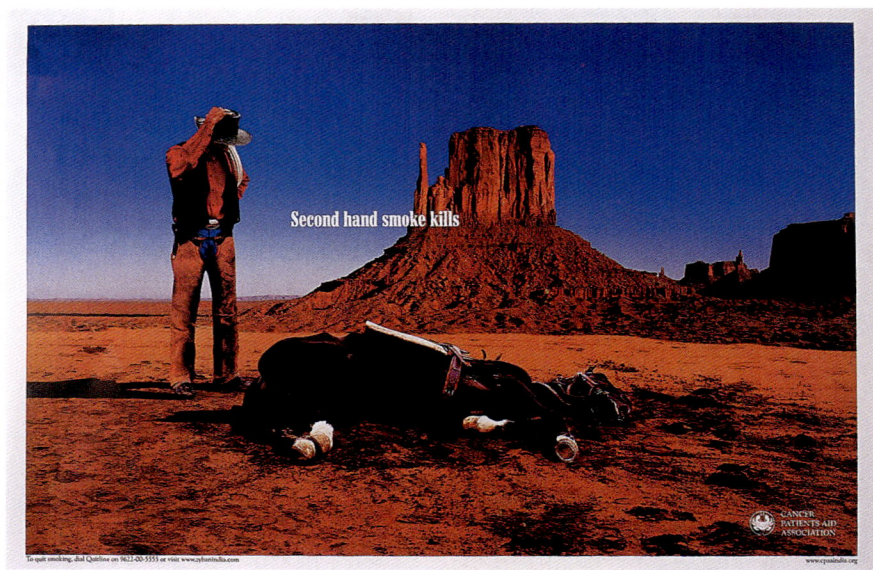

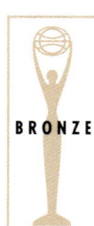

CATEGORY
Recreational Items

ADVERTISER/PRODUCT
Matchbox Miniatures

TITLE
Old Jeans

ADVERTISING AGENCY
Ogilvy, Mexico City

PHOTOGRAPHY STUDIO
Bizzarristudio, Mexico City

ACCOUNT EXECUTIVE
Adriana Veytia

CREATIVE DIRECTOR
Carlos Tornell

COPYWRITER
Holguer Ortiz

ART DIRECTOR
Marcos Reyes

PRODUCTION MANAGER
Karina Arvizu

PHOTOGRAPHER
Flavio Bizzarri

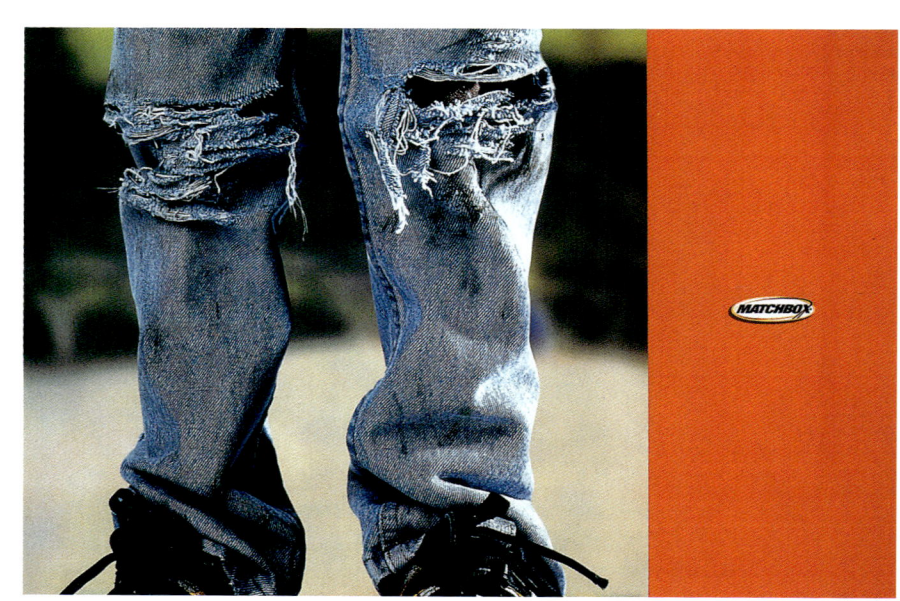

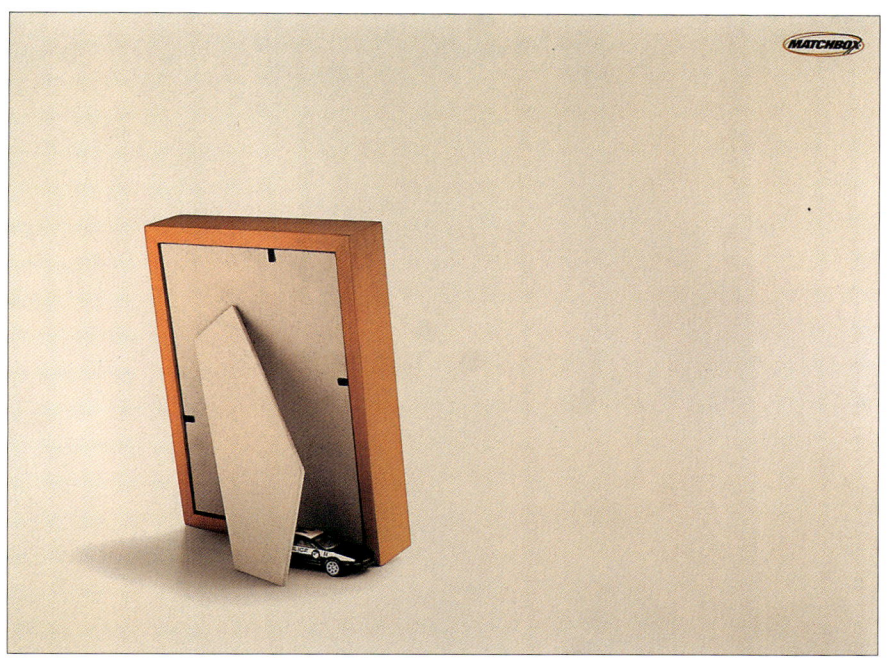

CATEGORY
Recreational Items

ADVERTISER/PRODUCT
Mattel

TITLE
Police

ADVERTISING AGENCY
Ogilvy & Mather Malaysia,
Kuala Lumpur

PHOTOGRAPHY STUDIO
Iklan Foto Lim, Kuala Lumpur

CREATIVE DIRECTOR
Sonal Dabral

COPYWRITER
Paul Lim

ART DIRECTOR
Gavin Simpson

PRODUCTION MANAGER
Derrick Chong

PHOTOGRAPHER
Fai

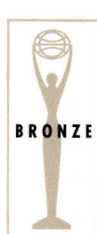

BRONZE

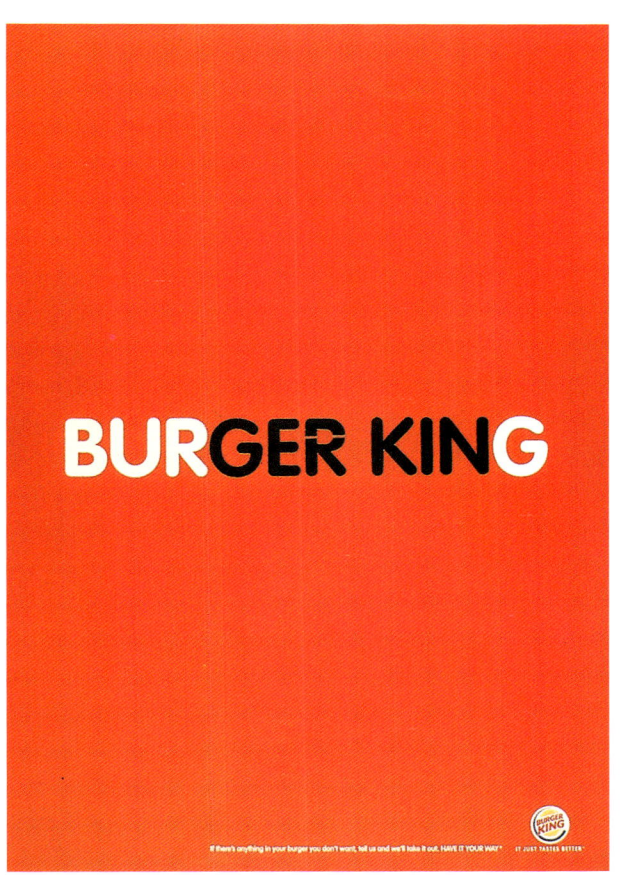

CATEGORY
Retail Food

ADVERTISER/PRODUCT
Burger King

TITLE
Gerkin

ADVERTISING AGENCY
Saatchi & Saatchi, Singapore

ACCOUNT EXECUTIVE
Jimmy Lim

CREATIVE DIRECTOR
Sion Scott-Wilson

COPYWRITER
Sion Scott-Wilson

ART DIRECTOR
Simon Cox

PRODUCTION MANAGER
Esther Yue, Joanny Wong

ILLUSTRATOR
Weng Foong

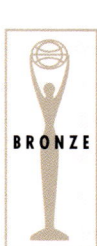

BRONZE

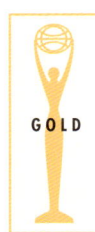

GOLD

CATEGORY
Retail Services

ADVERTISER/PRODUCT
FedEx

TITLE
Box

ADVERTISING AGENCY
BBDO, Bangkok

PHOTOGRAPHY STUDIO
Remix Studio, Bangkok

ACCOUNT EXECUTIVE
Peter Wilken, Arto Hampartsournian

CREATIVE DIRECTOR
Suthisak Sucharittanonta

COPYWRITER
Kitti Chaiyaporn, David Guerrero

ART DIRECTOR
Thirasak Thanapatanakul,
Suthisak Sucharittanonta

PHOTOGRAPHER
Anuchai Secharunputong

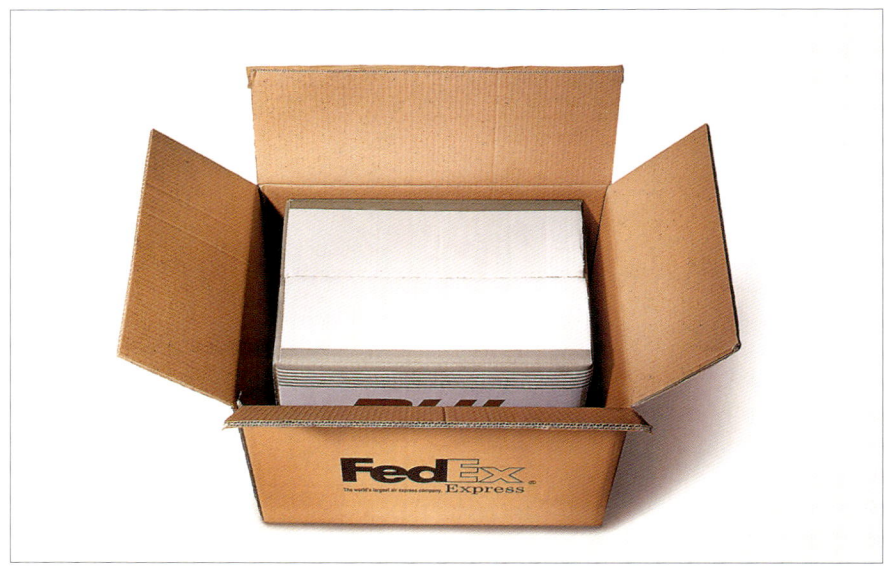

CATEGORY
Campaign

ADVERTISER/PRODUCT
Guinness

TITLE
Torso

TITLE
Navel

TITLE
Bottom

ADVERTISING AGENCY
Ogilvy & Mather, Singapore

ACCOUNT EXECUTIVE
David Mayo

CREATIVE DIRECTOR
Andy Greenaway

COPYWRITER
Andy Greenaway

ART DIRECTOR
Craig Smith

PHOTOGRAPHER
Roy Zhang

TYPOGRAPHER
Alfred Wee

ILLUSTRATOR
Yau Digital

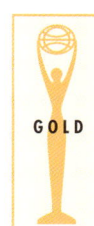

GOLD

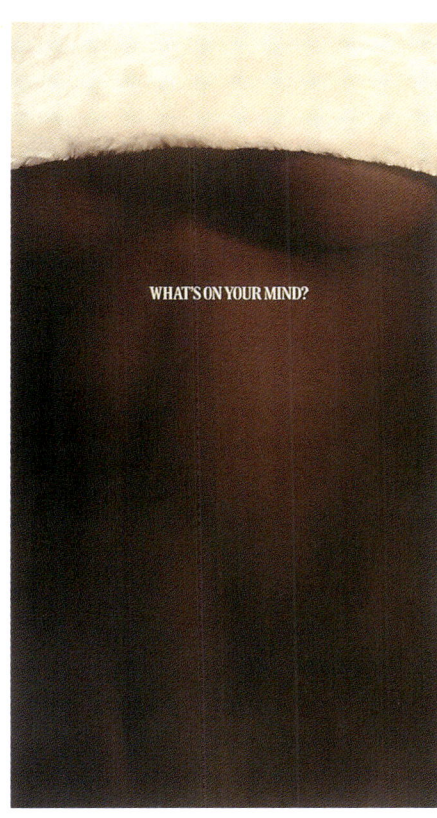

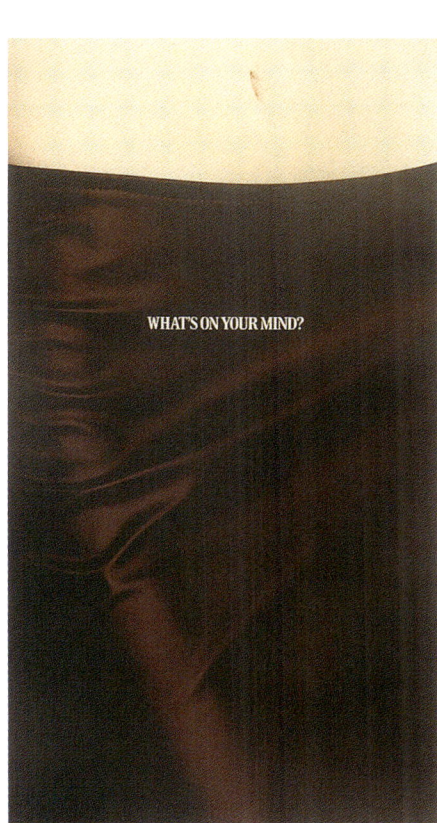

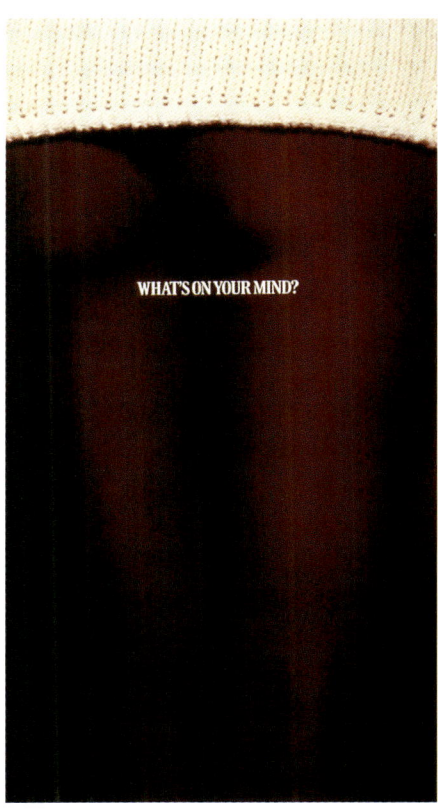

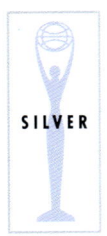

SILVER

CATEGORY Campaign	**TITLE** T-shirt	**CREATIVE DIRECTOR** Bettina Olf, Timm Weber	**ART BUYER** Anna Fauth, Anja Heineking
ADVERTISER/PRODUCT UNICEF/Child Labour	**ADVERTISING AGENCY** Springer & Jacoby, Hamburg	**COPYWRITER** Sven Keitel	
TITLE Jeans	**PHOTOGRAPHY STUDIO** Jan Burwick	**ART DIRECTOR** Claudia Tödt	
TITLE Tennis Shoe	**ACCOUNT EXECUTIVE** Niklas Frings-Rupp, Sophie Schweyer	**DESIGNER & ILLUSTRATION** Arne Weitkämper	

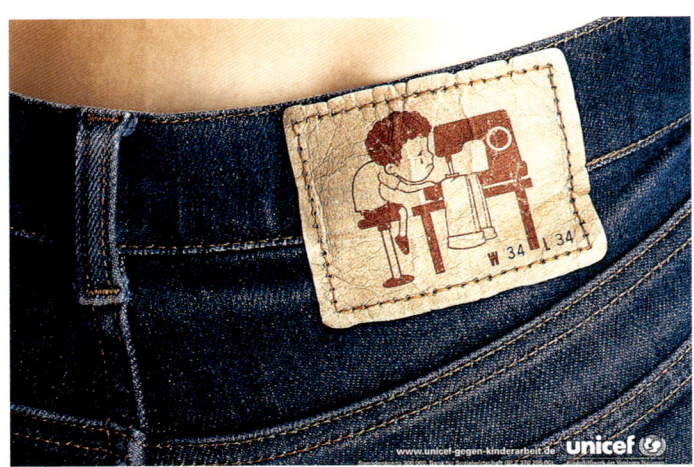

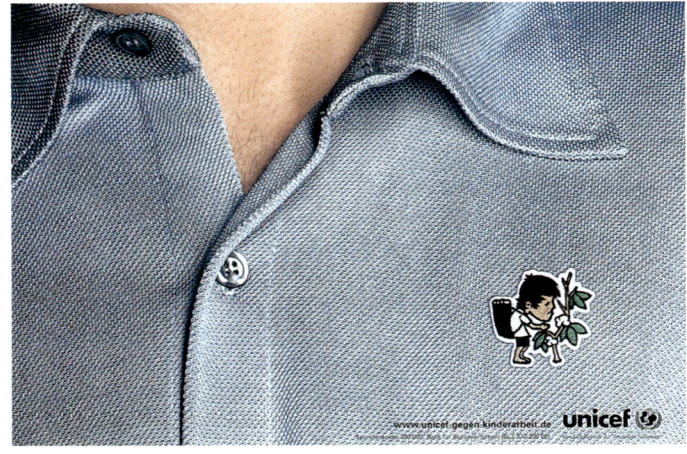

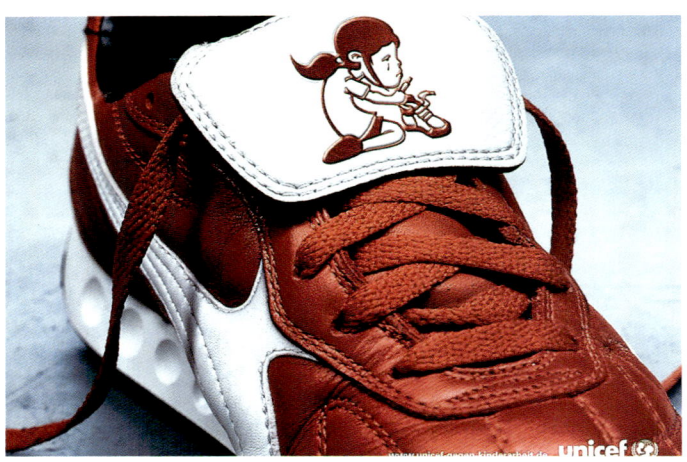

CATEGORY
Campaign

ADVERTISER/PRODUCT
Ludwig Görtz AG/Adidas

TITLE
Running

TITLE
Soccer

TITLE
Tennis

ADVERTISING AGENCY
Springer & Jacoby, Hamburg

ACCOUNT EXECUTIVE
Niklas Frings-Rupp

CREATIVE DIRECTOR
Florian Grimm, Antje Hedde,
Amir Kassaei

COPYWRITER
Gerrit Zinke

ART DIRECTOR
Gerrit Zinke

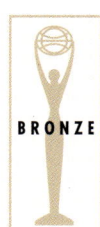

BRONZE

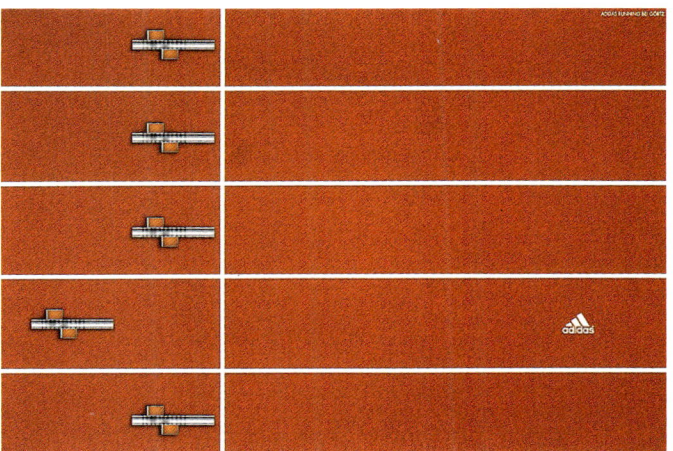

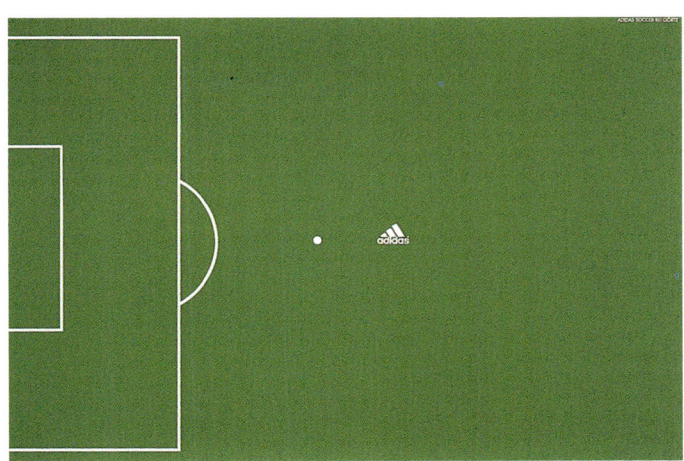

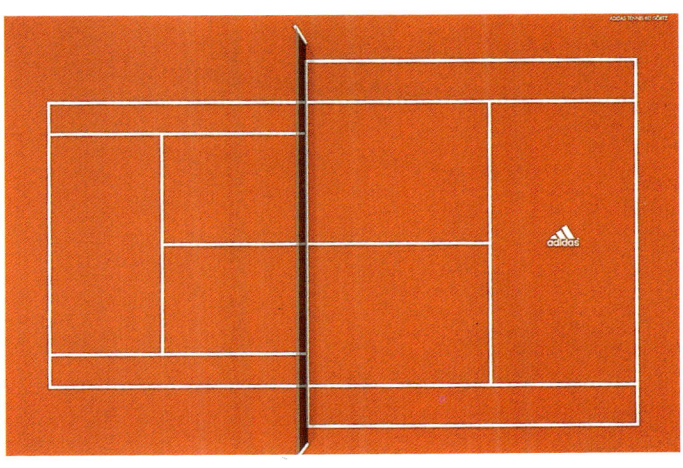

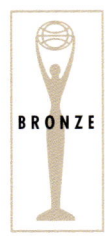

BRONZE

CATEGORY	**TITLE**	**ACCOUNT EXECUTIVE**	**ART DIRECTOR**
Campaign	Bent	Louise Garaway	Alfred Wee
ADVERTISER/PRODUCT	**TITLE**	**CREATIVE DIRECTOR**	**PHOTOGRAPHER**
Panadol Extra	Twisted	Andy Greenaway	Roy Zhang
TITLE	**ADVERTISING AGENCY**	**COPYWRITER**	**ILLUSTRATOR**
Crushed	Ogilvy & Mather, Singapore	Tham Yin May	Yau Digital

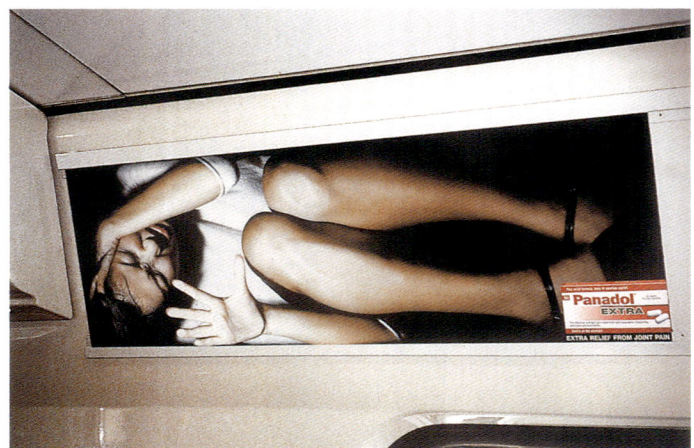

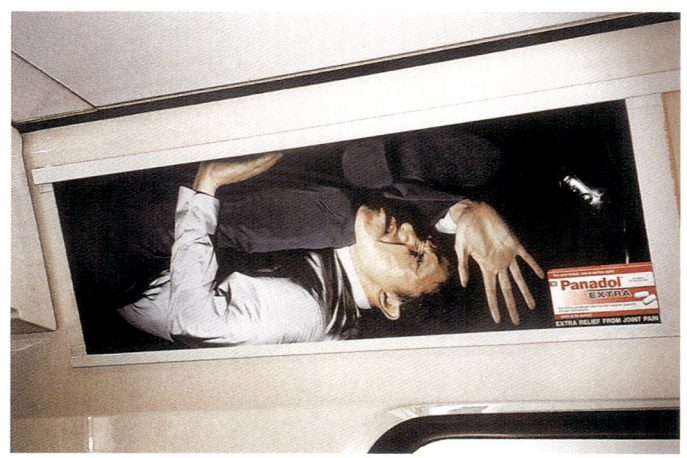

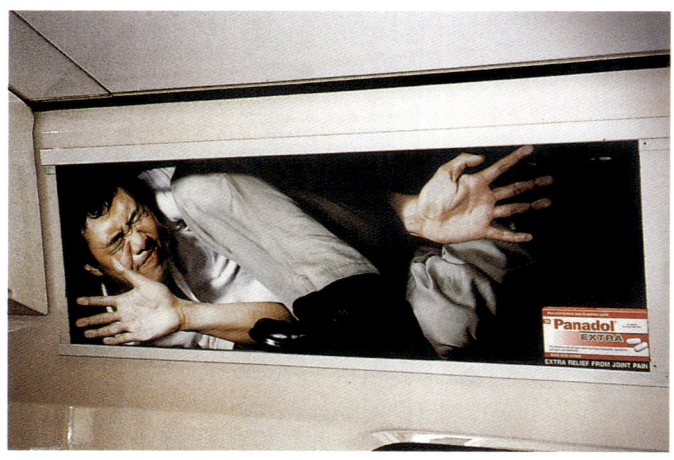

CATEGORY
Campaign

ADVERTISER/PRODUCT
Matchbox

TITLE
Serpentine

TITLE
Sink

TITLE
Bannister

ADVERTISING AGENCY
Ogilvy & Mather, Frankfurt

ACCOUNT EXECUTIVE
Peter Bodensohn, Angela Müller

CREATIVE DIRECTOR
Simon Oppmann, Peter Römmelt

COPYWRITER
Olga Potempa

ART DIRECTOR
Jürgen Schanz, Simon Oppmann

PHOTOGRAPHER
Joachim Bacherl

ART BUYING
Christina Hufgard, Nathalie Schultz

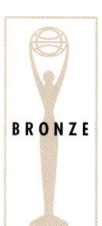

BRONZE

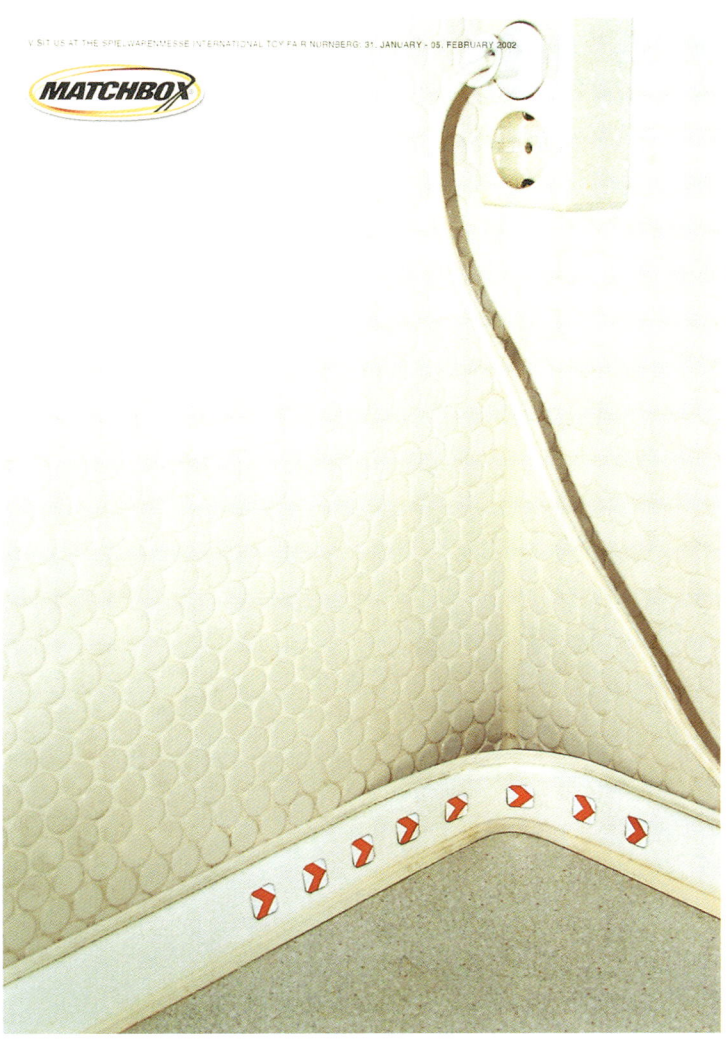

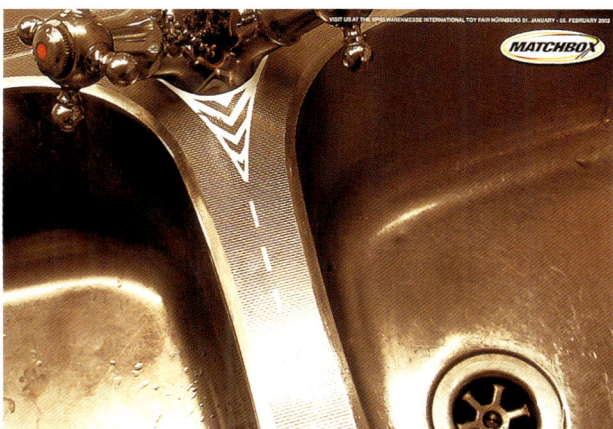

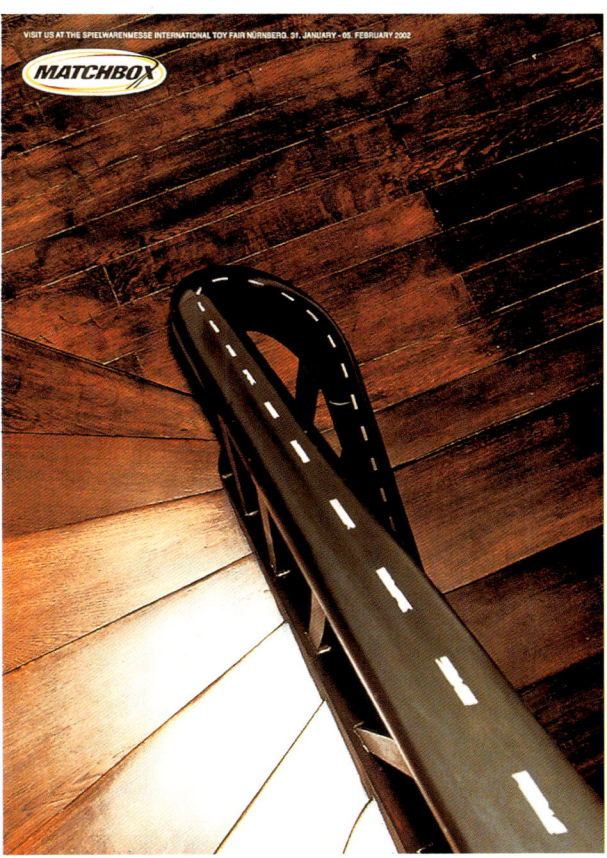

233

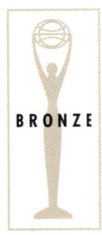

BRONZE

CATEGORY
Campaign

ADVERTISER/PRODUCT
Hasbro Singapore/Monopoly

TITLE
Boot

TITLE
Hat

TITLE
Car

ADVERTISING AGENCY
DDB, Singapore

PHOTOGRAPHY STUDIO
Szeling Pictures, Singapore

ACCOUNT EXECUTIVE
Wendy Ong

CREATIVE DIRECTOR
Tim Evill

COPYWRITER
James Lim

ART DIRECTOR
Scott Lambert

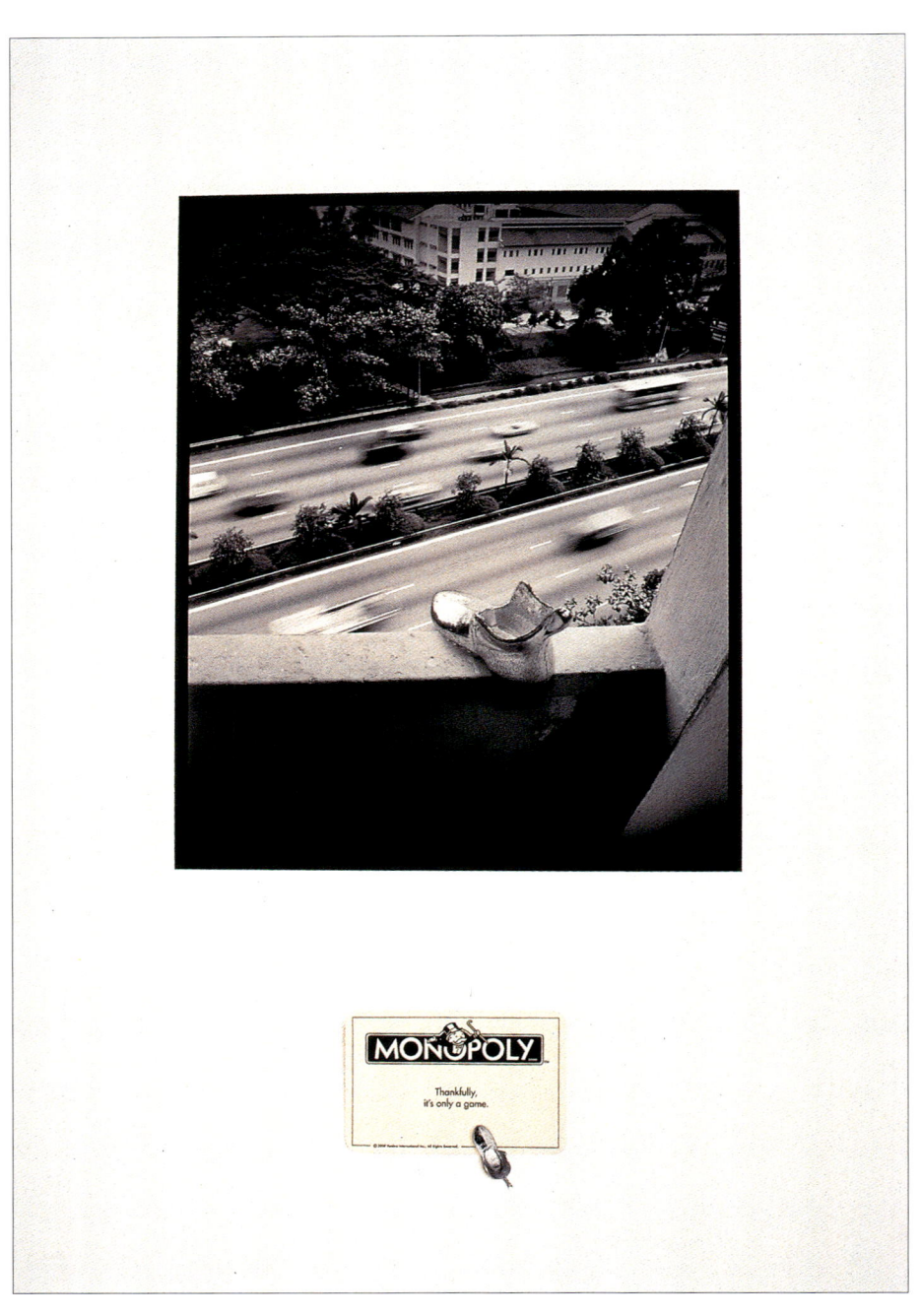

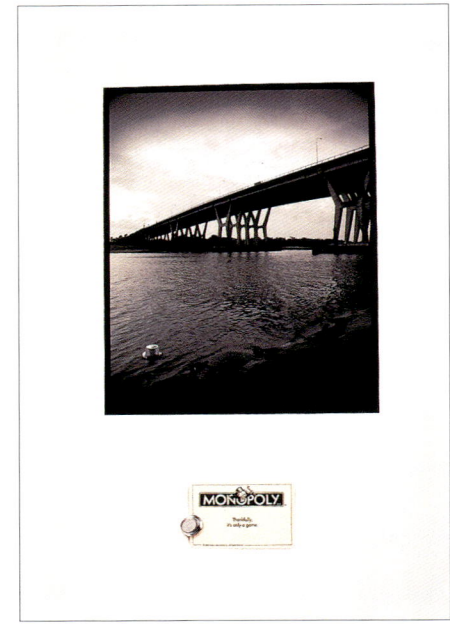

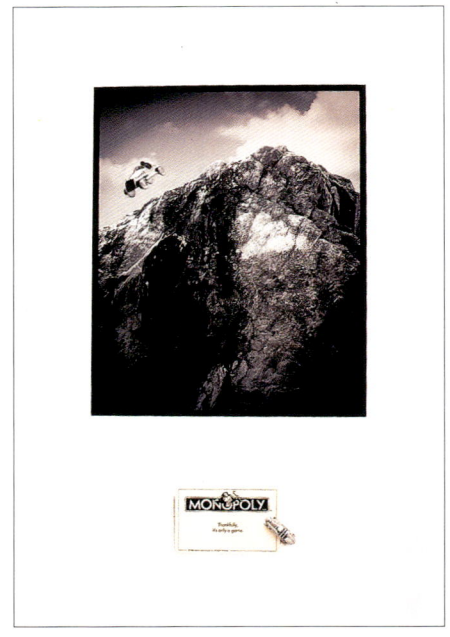

CATEGORY
Beverages/Alcoholic

ADVERTISER/PRODUCT
Guinness Rugby League Test Series

TITLE
Smile (Crop)

ADVERTISING AGENCY
Abbott Mead Vickers BBDO,
London

ACCOUNT EXECUTIVE
Cecile Beaufils, Steven Riley

CREATIVE DIRECTOR
Peter Souter, Tony Cox

COPYWRITER
Richard Morgan

ART DIRECTOR
Simon Langley

PRODUCTION MANAGER
Andy Smith

PHOTOGRAPHER
Robert Wilson

TYPOGRAPHER
Mark Elwood

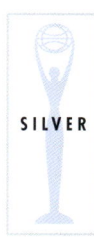

SILVER

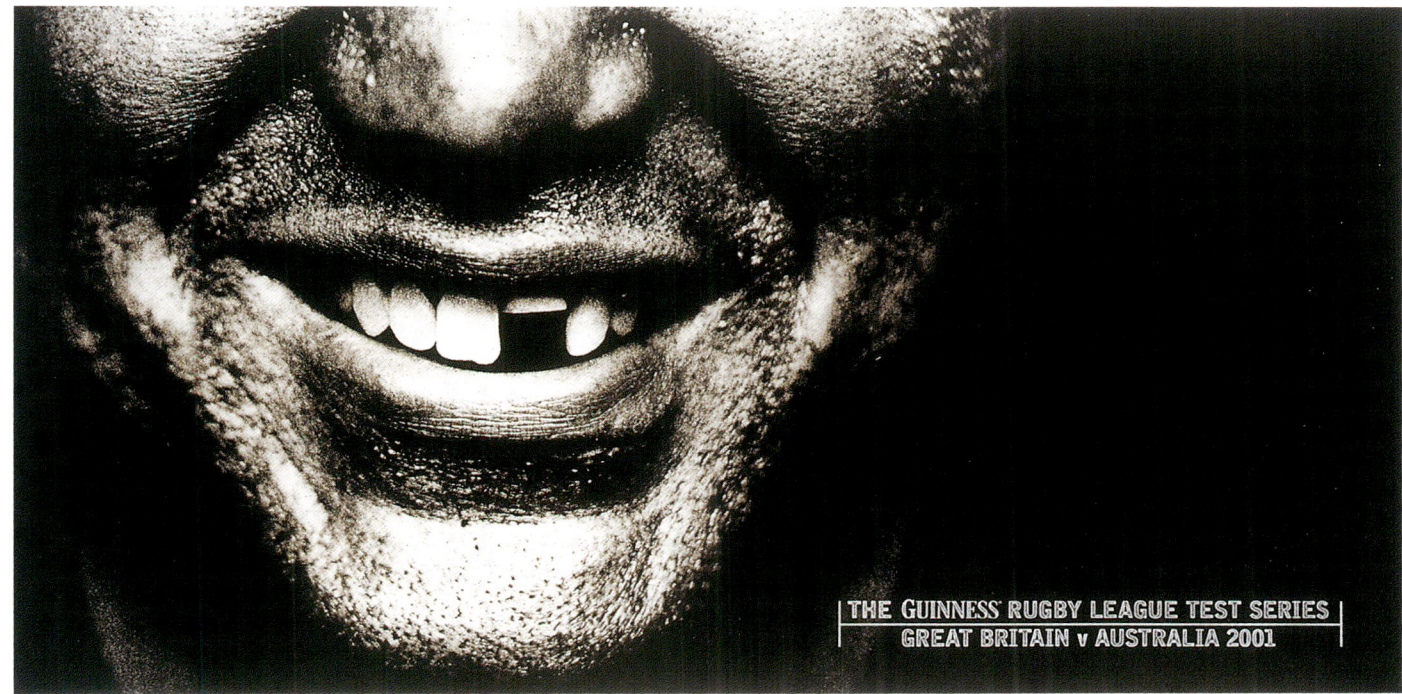

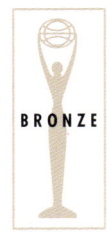

CATEGORY
Entertainment Promotion

ADVERTISER/PRODUCT
SKY Television

TITLE
Perfect Storm

ADVERTISING AGENCY
DDB NZ, Auckland

ACCOUNT EXECUTIVE
Rose Thompson

CREATIVE DIRECTOR
Jeneal Rohrback

COPYWRITER
Richard Loseby, Mike Babich

ART DIRECTOR
Martin Hermans, Wendy Lawn

PRODUCTION MANAGER
Nick Conetta

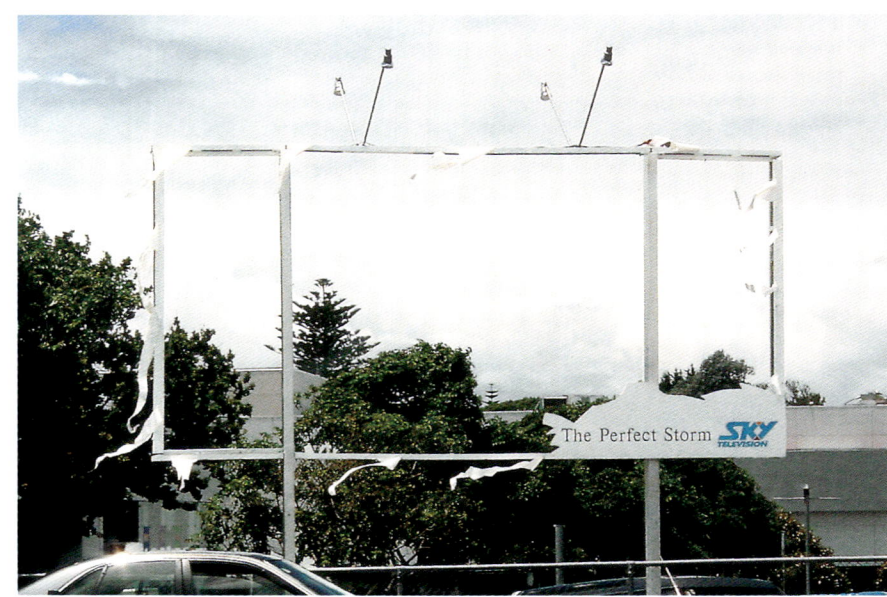

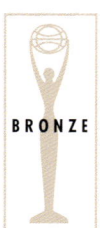

CATEGORY
Entertainment Promotion

ADVERTISER/PRODUCT
Washington State Lottery

TITLE
Cubicles

ADVERTISING AGENCY
Publicis in the West, Seattle

PHOTOGRAPHY STUDIO
Bob Peterson, Seattle

ACCOUNT EXECUTIVE
Kristin Mackay

CREATIVE DIRECTOR
Kevin Kehoe

ART DIRECTOR
George Boutilier

PRODUCTION MANAGER
Pete Anderson

PHOTOGRAPHER
Bob Peterson

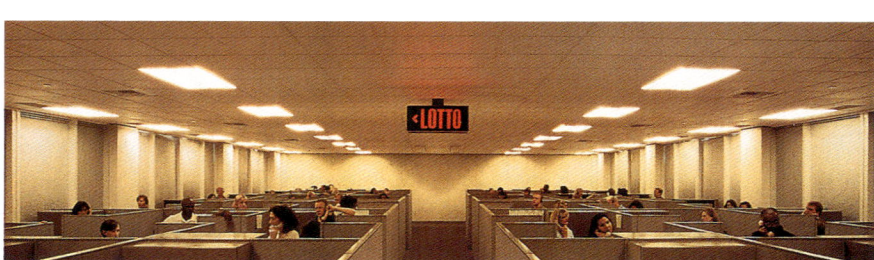

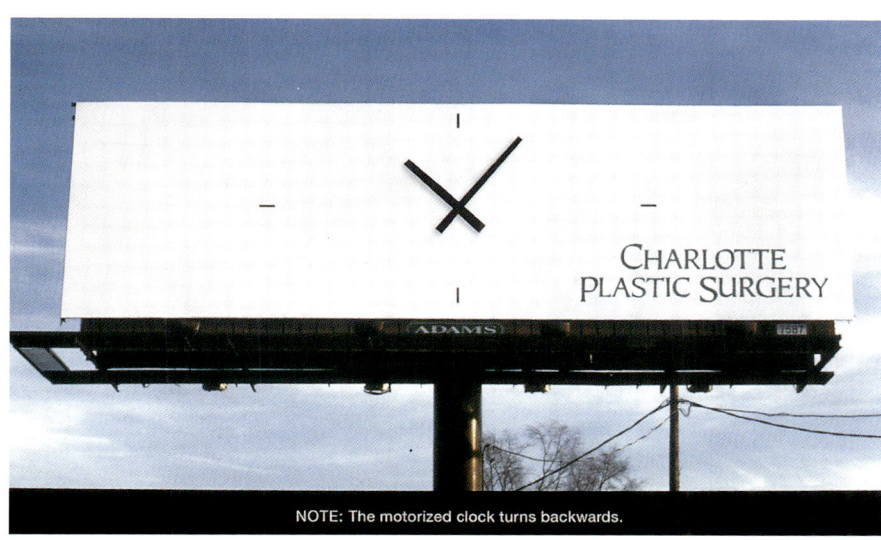

NOTE: The motorized clock turns backwards.

CATEGORY
Health Care Services

ADVERTISER/PRODUCT
Charlotte Plastic Surgery

TITLE
The Hands of Time

ADVERTISING AGENCY
Boone/Oakley, Charlotte

ACCOUNT EXECUTIVE
Taylor Busby

CREATIVE DIRECTOR
David Oakley, John Boone

COPYWRITER
Miguel Fernandez

ART DIRECTOR
Phil Mimaki

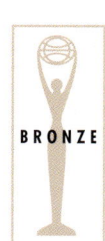

BRONZE

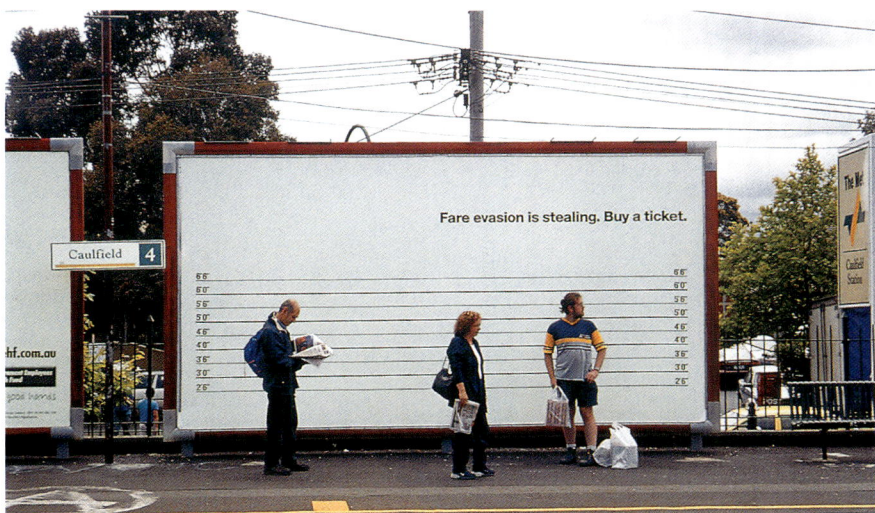

CATEGORY
Travel/Tourism

ADVERTISER/PRODUCT
Fare Evasion

TITLE
Line Up

ADVERTISING AGENCY
M&C Saatchi, Melbourne

ACCOUNT EXECUTIVE
Jodie Rochetich, Alicia Cox

CREATIVE DIRECTOR
Paul Taylor

COPYWRITER
Rohan Lancaster

ART DIRECTOR
Darren Pitt

PRODUCTION MANAGER
Pat Vitetta

HEAD OF ART
Tony Banks

TYPOGRAPHER
Jason Kilgour

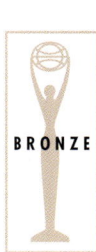

BRONZE

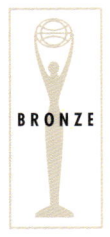

CATEGORY
Campaign

ADVERTISER/PRODUCT
Shire Skin Cancer Clinic

TITLE
Eric

TITLE
Lifesaver

TITLE
Burnadette

ADVERTISING AGENCY
Colenso BBDO, Auckland

CREATIVE DIRECTOR
Mike O'Sullivan

COPYWRITER
Leo Premutico, Guy Rooke

ART DIRECTOR
Leo Premutico, Guy Rooke

ILLUSTRATOR
Guy Hastings, Antonella Mascioli

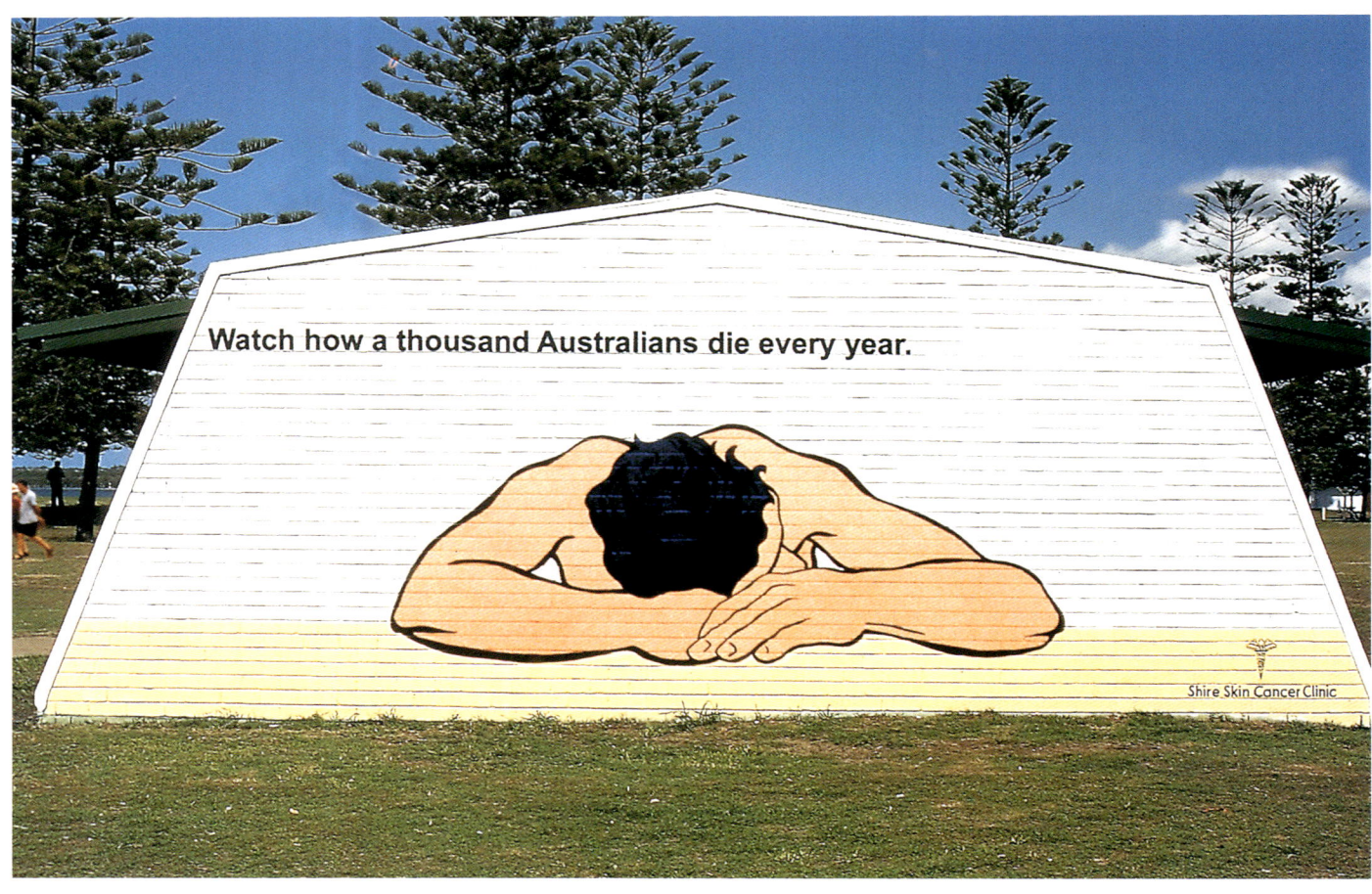

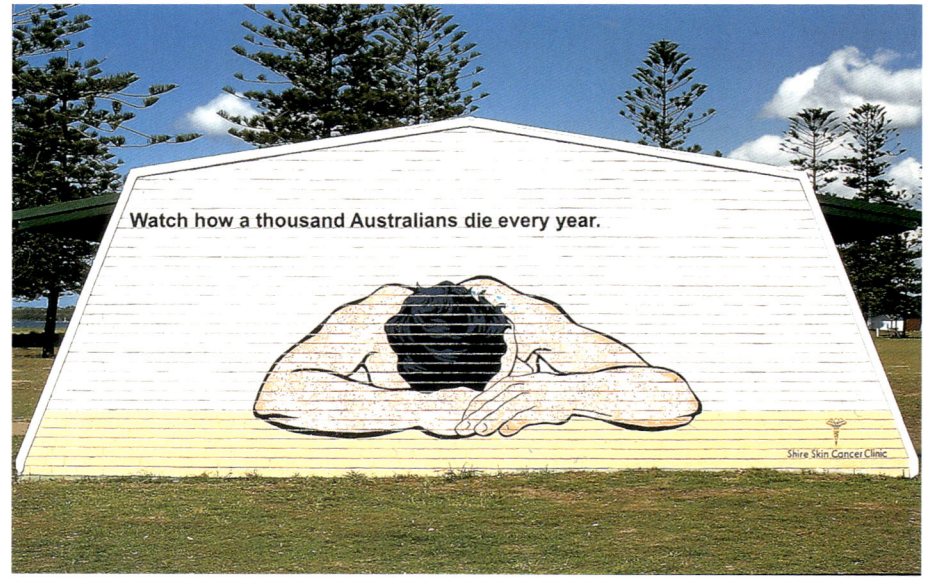

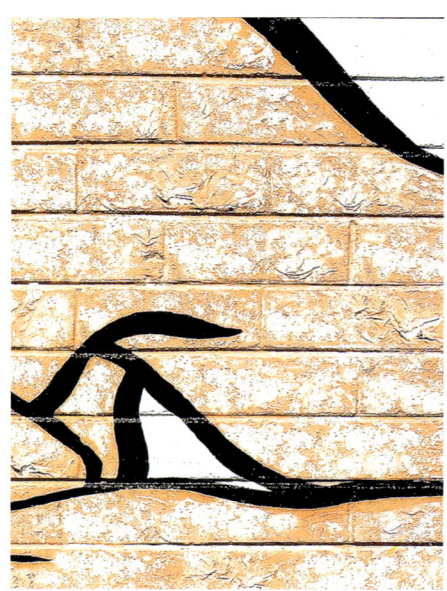

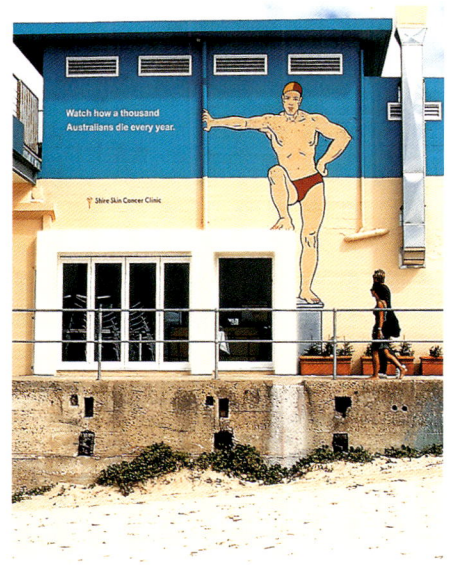

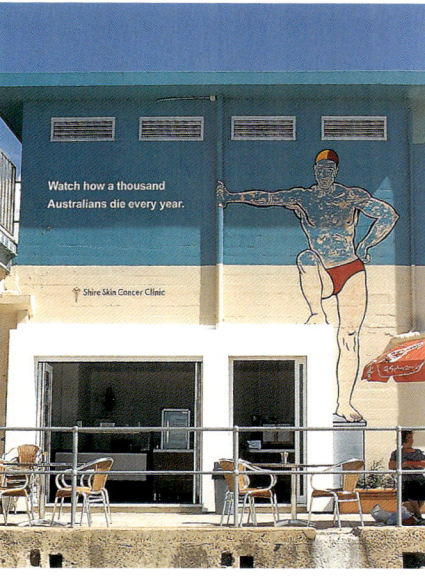

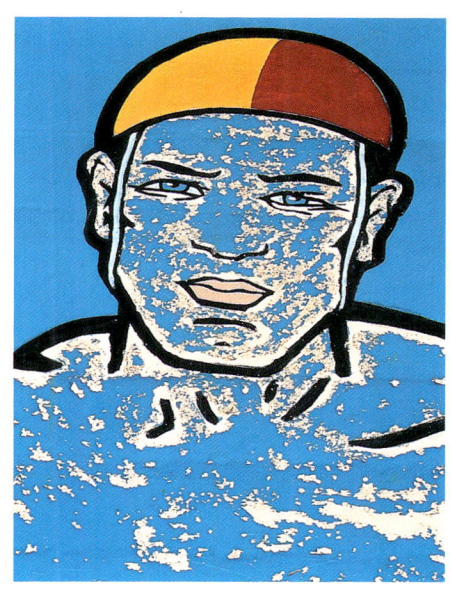

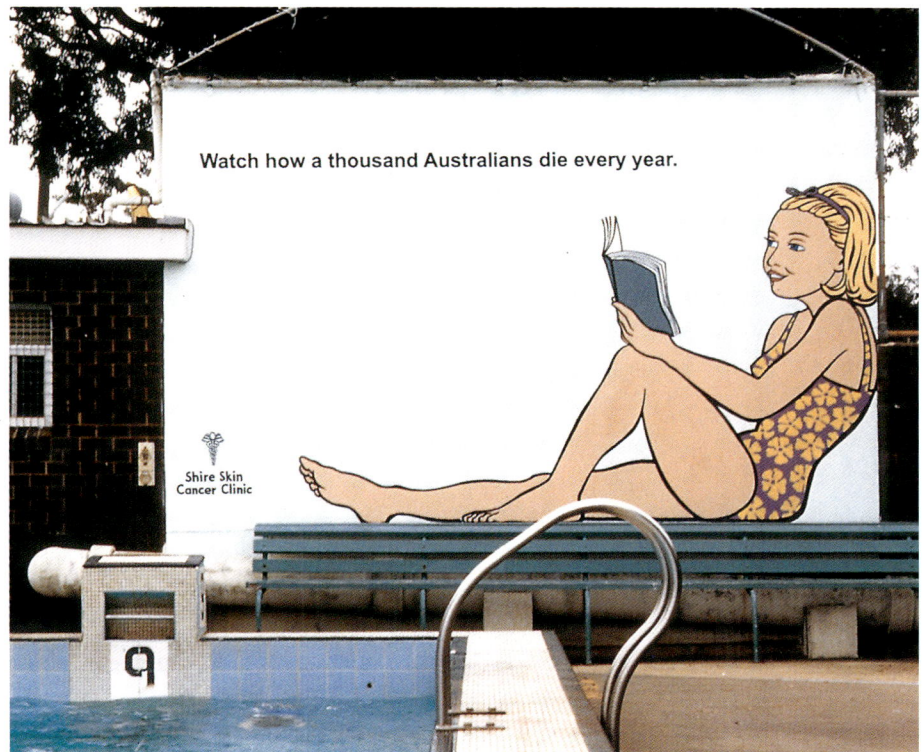

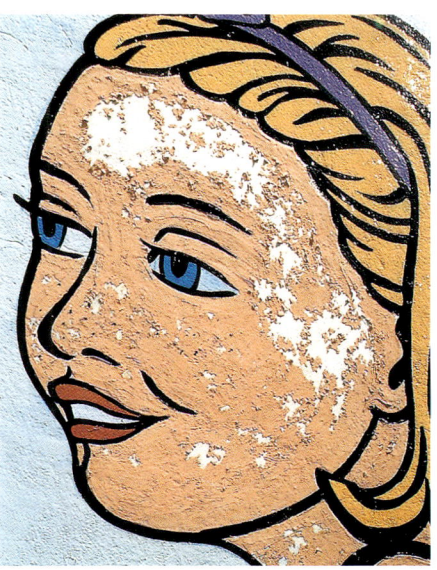

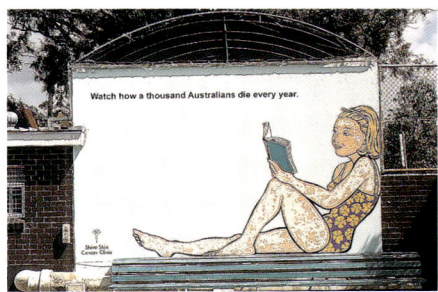

INNOVATIVE MEDIA

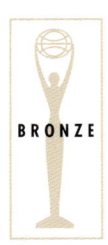

BRONZE

CATEGORY
Apparel/Fashion

ADVERTISER/PRODUCT
Nike—Bill Bowerman

TITLE
Bowerman Race Day

ADVERTISING AGENCY
The Jupiter Drawing Room
(South Africa)

ACCOUNT EXECUTIVE
Chiquita King

CREATIVE DIRECTOR
Graham Warsop

COPYWRITER
Bernard Hunter, Graham Warsop

ART DIRECTOR
Michael Bond

PRODUCTION MANAGER
Hilary Simpson

JUDGES NOTE

How best to communicate the story of Bill Bowerman to the running fraternity?

We chose a captive audience - runners in the 56km Two Oceans Marathon - and placed the following posters, in sequence, approximately 2km apart, along the route.

In a questionnaire completed after the race, many competitors not only recalled the Bowerman Story, but actually claimed they looked forward to reading the story along the way.

(8 slides to follow)

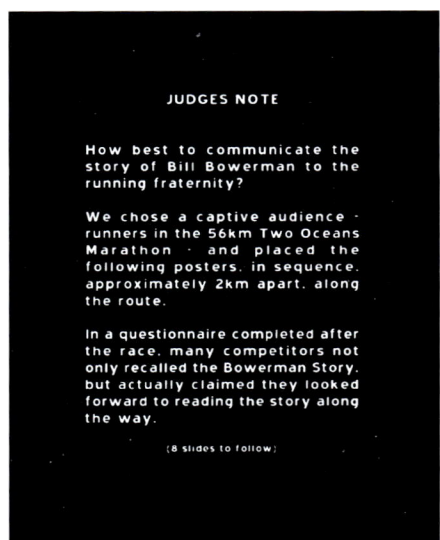

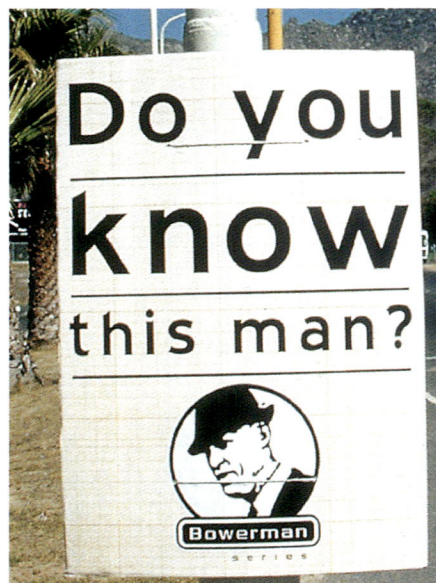

How best to communicate the story of Nike shoe inventor Bill Bowerman to the running fraternity? A captive audience was chosen—runners in the 56 km Two Oceans Marathon—and placed the following posters, in sequence, approximately 2 kilometers apart, along the route. In a questionnaire completed after the race, many competitors not only recalled the Bowerman story, but actually claimed they looked forward to reading the story along the way.

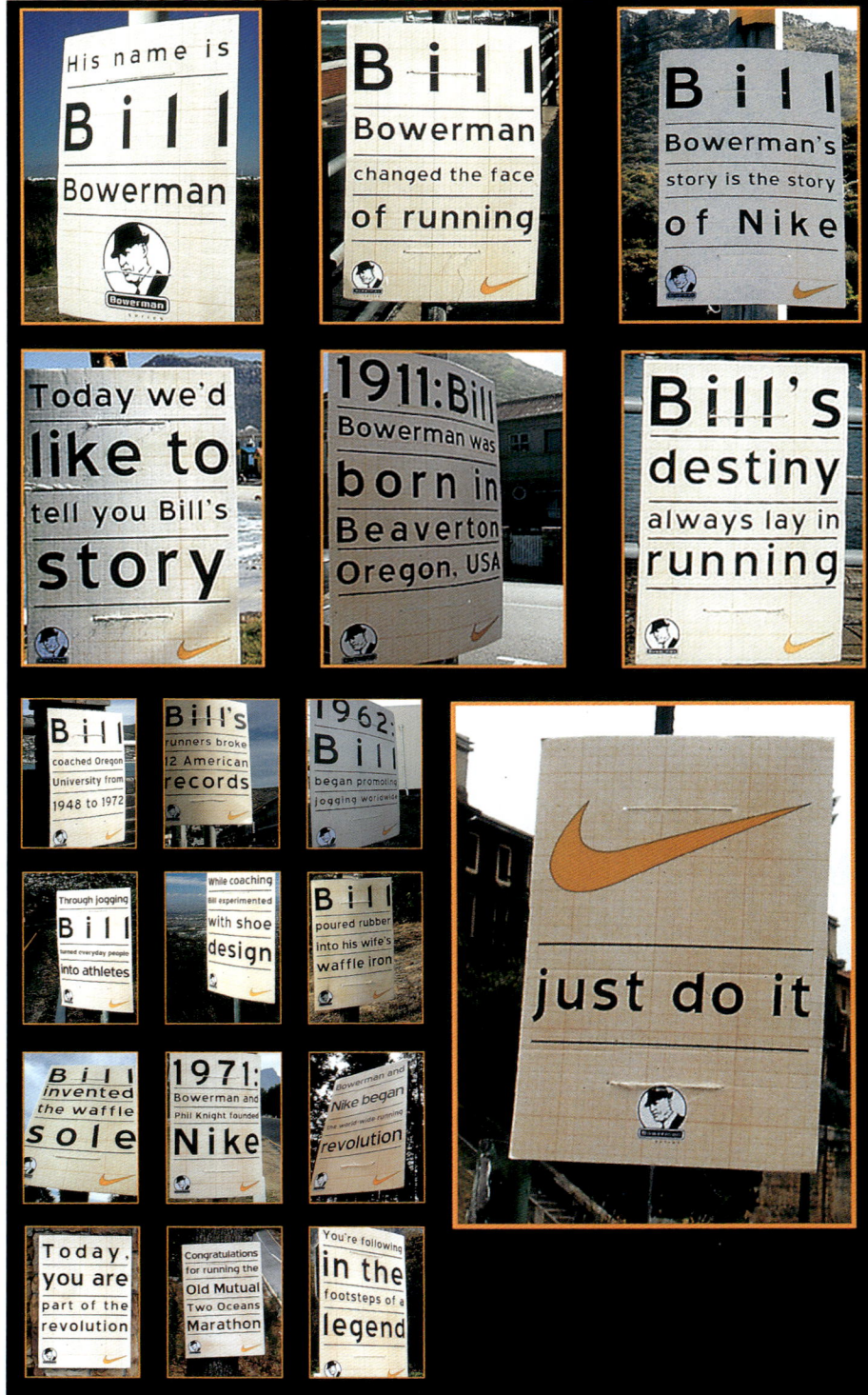

CATEGORY
Automotive Products

ADVERTISER/PRODUCT
Mercedes-Benz Sprinter

TITLE
Forget the Clutch Pedal

ADVERTISING AGENCY
Scholz & Friends, Berlin

ACCOUNT EXECUTIVE
Stefanie Wurst, Christina Kloss,
Holger Gerecke

CREATIVE DIRECTOR
Martin Pross, Matthias Schmidt

COPYWRITER
Peter Quester

ART DIRECTOR
Sandra Schilling

PHOTOGRAPHER
Nina Mallmann

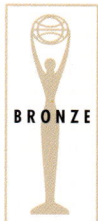

BRONZE

Mercedes-Benz introduced its new 6-gear automatic Sprinter van with a car-sticker demonstrating its benefit: Relax and forget the clutch pedal.

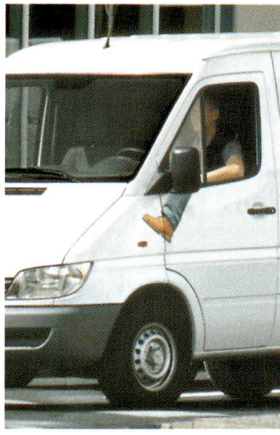

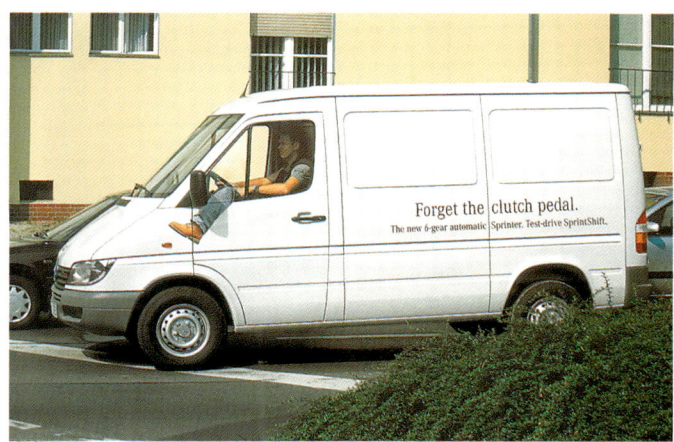

CATEGORY
Entertainment Promotion

ADVERTISER/PRODUCT
The Power of Amazement

TITLE
The Power of Amazement

ADVERTISING AGENCY
Jung von Matt, Vienna

CREATIVE DIRECTOR
Andreas Putz

COPYWRITER
Alexander Rabl

ART DIRECTOR
Peter Kaimer, Stephanie Lackner

PRODUCTION MANAGER
Verena Rottmar

PHOTOGRAPHER
Peter Kaimer, Stephanie Lackner

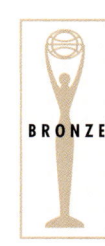

BRONZE

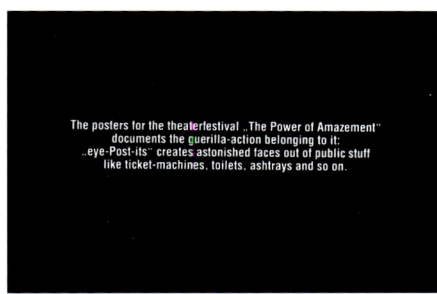

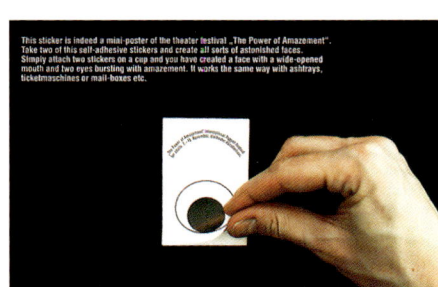

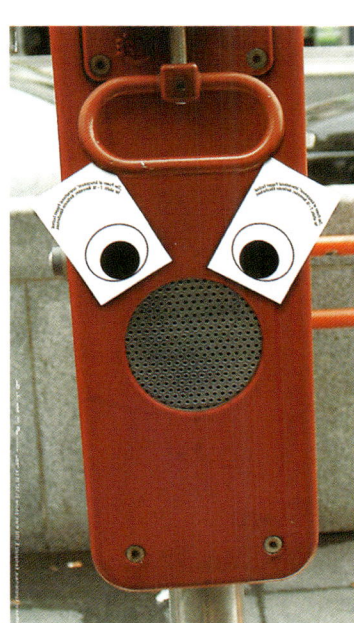

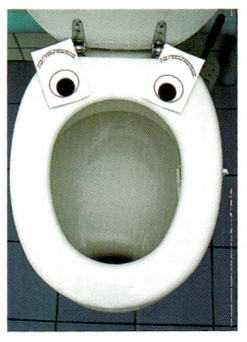

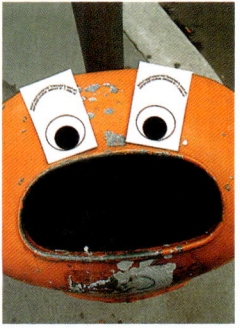

A low-budget theater festival wanted maximum PR and attention with its campaign. This year's festival, entitled "The Power of Amazement," was to be reflected in the campaign itself. An eye and eyebrow were painted onto small adhesive labels, which were then distributed throughout the city. As a result, people were creating their own "faces of amazement" in a wide variety of different places: toilets, wastebaskets, ticket machines, cups, etc., suddenly appeared like wide open mouths and eyes—the look of a face when astonished and amazed, which is the ultimate aim of the theater festival.

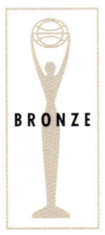

BRONZE

CATEGORY
Foods

ADVERTISER/PRODUCT
Kellogg's Special K

TITLE
Sizes

ADVERTISING AGENCY
Leo Burnett Colombiana, Bogota

ACCOUNT EXECUTIVE
Ines Elvira Posada

CREATIVE DIRECTOR
Maria Angelica Palacio

COPYWRITER
Vivian Varela

ART DIRECTOR
Tito Chamorro

Size rings were placed on clothes racks in women's wear stores, where clothes are hanging and separated by size: L (large), M (medium), and S (for Special K)—which is the most desired size, as attained by Special K consumers.

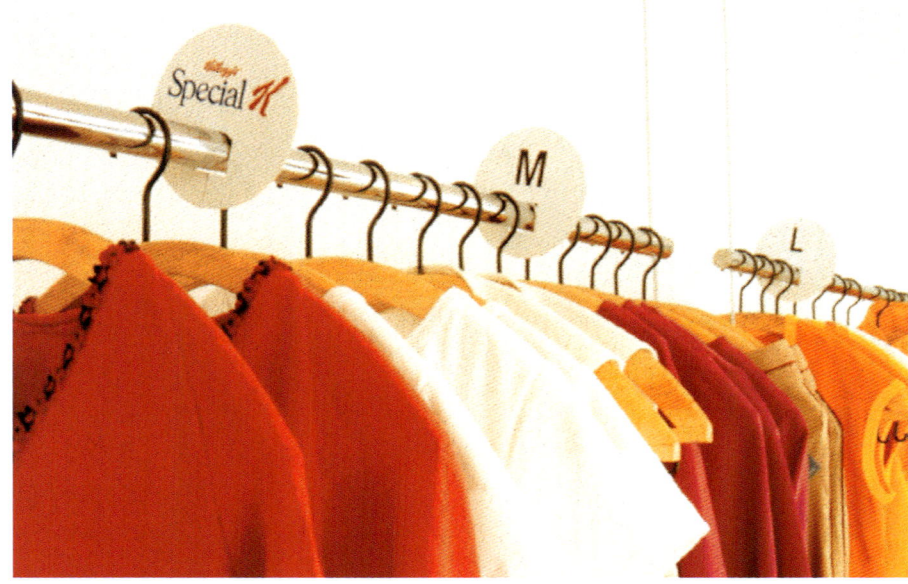

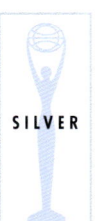

SILVER

CATEGORY
Media Promotion

ADVERTISER/PRODUCT
The Economist

TITLE
Doors

ADVERTISING AGENCY
Ogilvy One Worldwide, Manila

ACCOUNT EXECUTIVE
Elly Puyat

CREATIVE DIRECTOR
Peachy Todino Pacquing

COPYWRITER
Rosene Santos

ART DIRECTOR
Dorky Mallare

PRODUCTION MANAGER
Jun Jamolangue

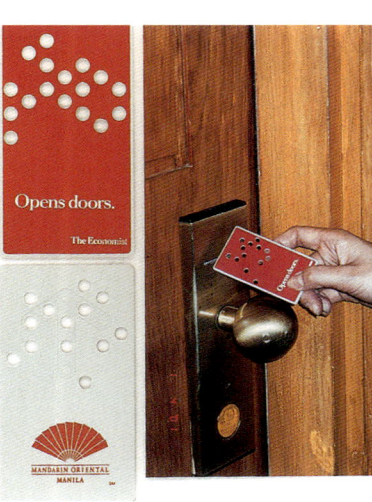

In order to increase awareness of *The Economist* brand among resident and visiting business executives in Manila, a presence was required at airports and hotels. This resulted in advertising on various materials, such as valet tickets, newspaper bags, and key cards. The key cards were given to the hotel guests—in the heart of the business district—when they checked in. A line that can be interpreted two ways—literal and what *The Economist* brand is all about—"Opens doors"—was employed.

CATEGORY
Public Service

ADVERTISER/PRODUCT
Coalition for Gun Control

TITLE
Gun Sight Stunt

ADVERTISING AGENCY
Saatchi & Saatchi, Sydney

ACCOUNT EXECUTIVE
Tim Bullock

COPYWRITER
Jay Furby

ART DIRECTOR
Jay Furby

PRODUCTION MANAGER
Scott Mackenzie

STUNT COORDINATOR
Barry Disco

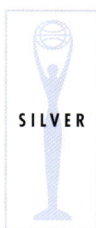

SILVER

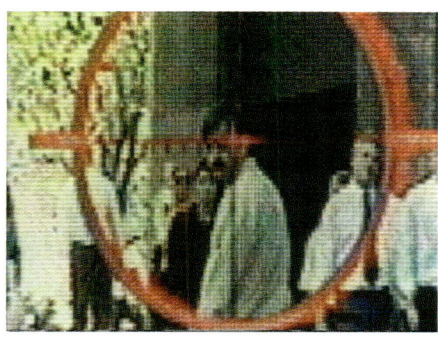 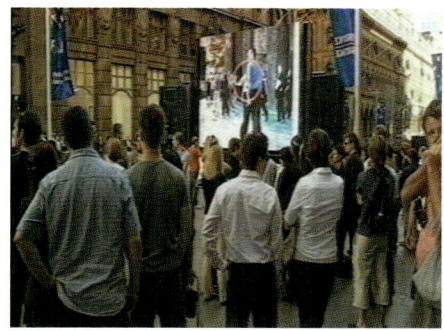 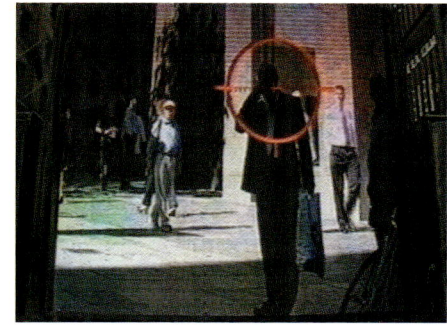

Busy unsuspecting pedestrians (in Sydney, Australia) were confronted with footage of themselves featured on an interactive 9 × 5-meter video billboard. A gun site crosshair graphic moved across the screen, hovering over individuals and giving them the unnerving sense that a gun was being pointed at them. Captions appeared on the screen reading: "Last year, 24,000 Americans didn't expect to be shot dead either. Help us ban semiautomatic handguns. Coalition for Gun Control."

CATEGORY
Retail Food

ADVERTISER/PRODUCT
Kingyo Sushi & Don

TITLE
Escalator

ADVERTISING AGENCY
10AM Communications, Singapore

PHOTOGRAPHY STUDIO
T2 Studios, Singapore

ACCOUNT EXECUTIVE
Ally Lim

CREATIVE DIRECTOR
Lim Sau Hoong, Terrence Tan

COPYWRITER
Vanessa Goh

ART DIRECTOR
Ng Swee Ling

PRODUCTION MANAGER
Jason Sia

PHOTOGRAPHER
T2 Studios

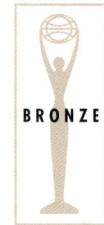

BRONZE

To draw shoppers to a "conveyor belt" sushi bar, this concept was re-created on a shopping mall escalator handrail, which led directly to the level where the restaurant was located.

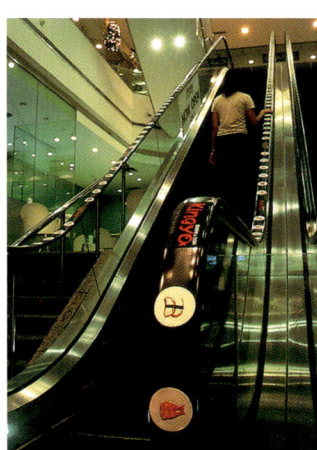 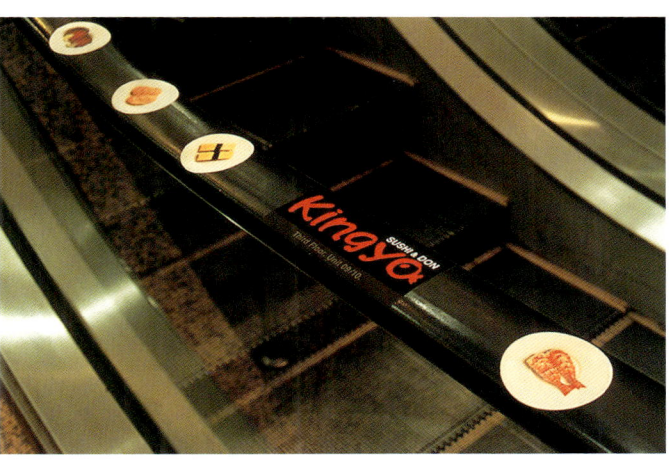

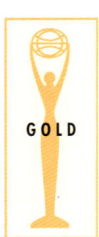

GOLD

CATEGORY
Campaign

ADVERTISER/PRODUCT
BMW of North America

TITLE
Ambush

TITLE
Star

TITLE
Powder Keg

TITLE
The Follow

TITLE
The Hire

ADVERTISING AGENCY
Fallon, Minneapolis

ACCOUNT EXECUTIVE
Ginny Grossman

CREATIVE DIRECTOR
David Lubars, Bruce Bildsten

COPYWRITER
Andrew Kevin Walker, Joe Sweet,
Wong Kar Wei, Guy Ritchie,
Alejandro Gonzalez Iñarritu,
David Carter, Guillermo Arriaga

ART DIRECTOR
David Carter, Martin Whis,
Joe Sweet, Tom Riddle

PRODUCTION COMPANY
Anonymous Content, Los Angeles

EDITING COMPANY
Spot Welders, Los Angeles; Jettone,
Hong Kong; Nomad Editing,
Santa Monica; Z Films, Mexico City

MUSIC COMPANY
Hi-Fi Productions, New York;
Universal Music Mexico,
Mexico City

SOUND DESIGN COMPANY
Mit Out Sound, Sausalito; Nomad
Editing, Santa Monica; Z Films,
Mexico City

SOUND DESIGNER
Ren Klyce

PRODUCER
Robyn Boardman, Aristides McGarry,
Rob Van de Weteringe Buys,
Tapas Blank

DIRECTOR
John Frankenheimer,
Wong Kar Wei, Guy Ritchie,
Alejandro Gonzalez Iñarritu

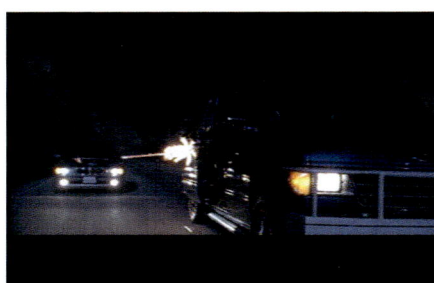

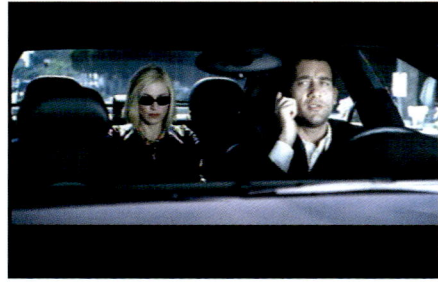

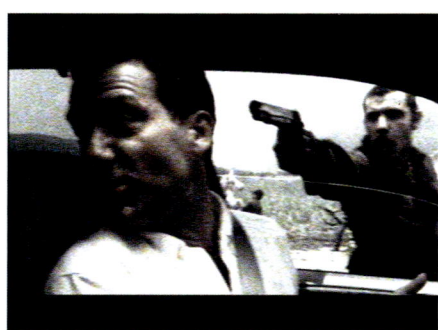

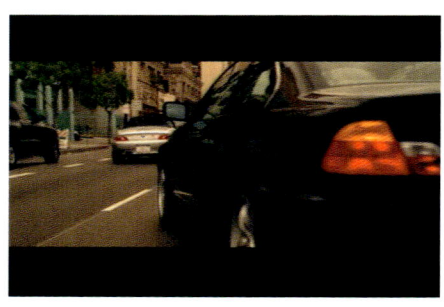

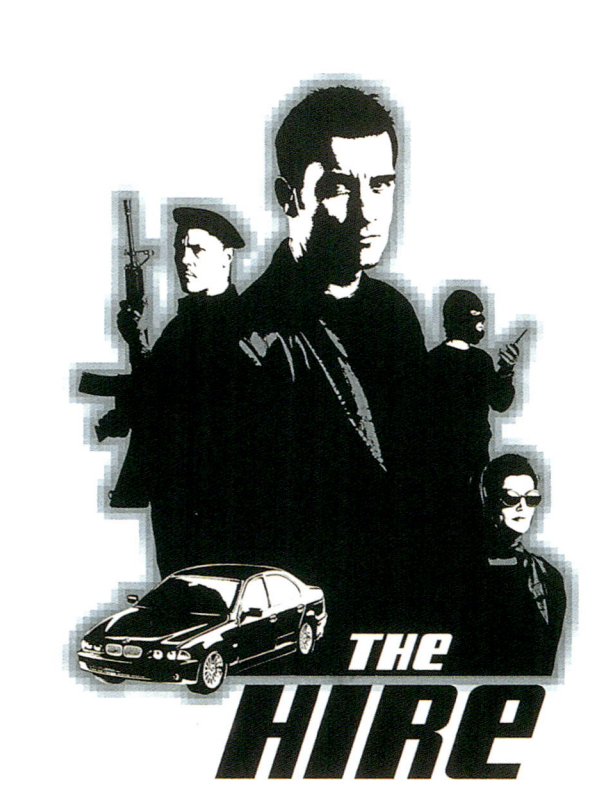

It began as an advertising brief, but advertising wasn't the answer. Traditional commercials could not impart what BMWs could really do, plus BMW customers increasingly were not watching television. They had, however, embraced the Internet in astounding numbers. The new idea was to create something so entertaining and so rewarding that people would actually seek it out. The question then became: Why not create an interactive experience more akin to home theater? What resulted was BMW Films, a series of shorts directed by and starring A-list cinema talent. Each film revolved around a central character called The Driver, the world's best when it came to transporting people out of dangerous situations. The Driver's character traits—youthfulness, integrity, passion, willingness to take risks—reflected on both the brand and the audience. Each film featured The Driver using a BMW to complete his missions, showcasing BMW's true performance.

CATEGORY
Campaign

ADVERTISER/PRODUCT
Amnistia Internacional/Campaign
against Torture

TITLE
Lat Sami Khamphoui

TITLE
Adrien Wayi

TITLE
Amal Faroua

ADVERTISING AGENCY
Contrapunto, Madrid

ACCOUNT EXECUTIVE
Angel Guirao

CREATIVE DIRECTOR
Antonio Montero,
Carlos Sanz de Andino

COPYWRITER
Félix del Valle

ART DIRECTOR
Carlos Jorge

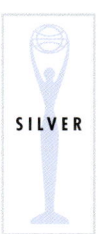

SILVER

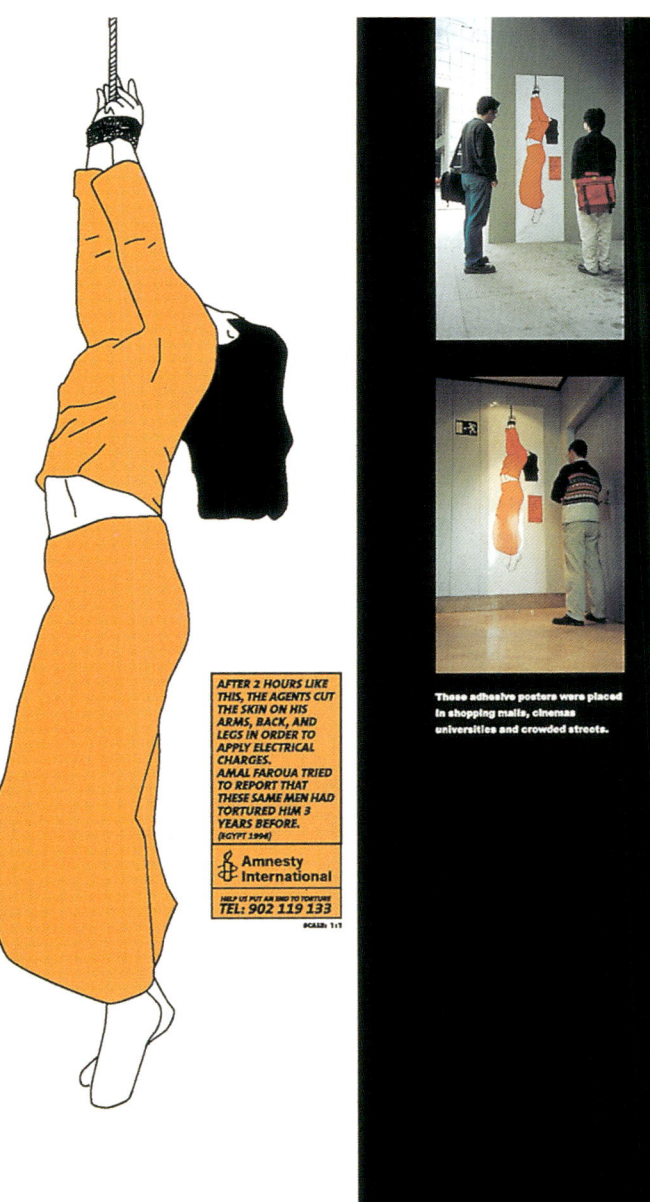

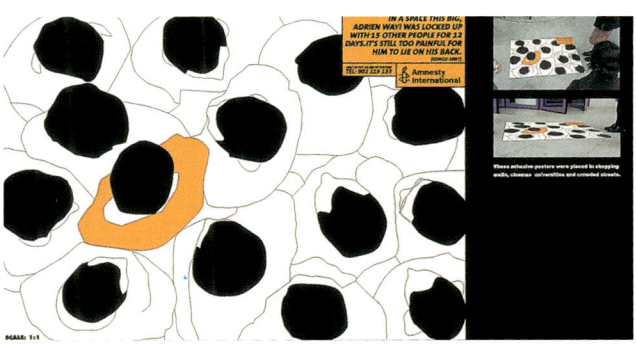

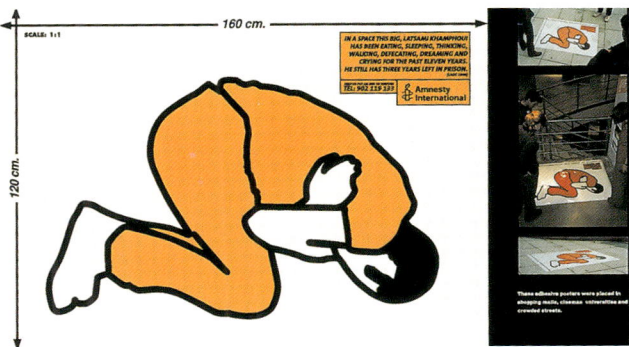

A campaign by Amnesty International consisting of adhesive posters
placed in streets, universities, and commercial centers. Some were
adhered to floors, others to walls. The silhouettes that appear in these
posters are lifesize, used in order for the public to imagine the horror
of the real-life inhumane treatment that so many continue to suffer.

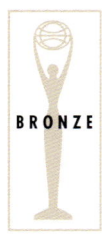

BRONZE

CATEGORY
Campaign

ADVERTISER/PRODUCT
Göteborgs-Posten (Morning Paper)

TITLE
Hospital Bed

TITLE
Greenhouse Effect

TITLE
Hens

ADVERTISING AGENCY
Forsman & Bodenfors, Gothenburg

ACCOUNT EXECUTIVE
Alison Arnold

COPYWRITER
Björn Engström

ART DIRECTOR
Staffan Forsman, Staffan Håkanson

PHOTOGRAPHER
Peter Boström

ACCOUNT DIRECTOR
Hans Andersson

CLIENT
Göteborgs-Posten (Morning Paper)

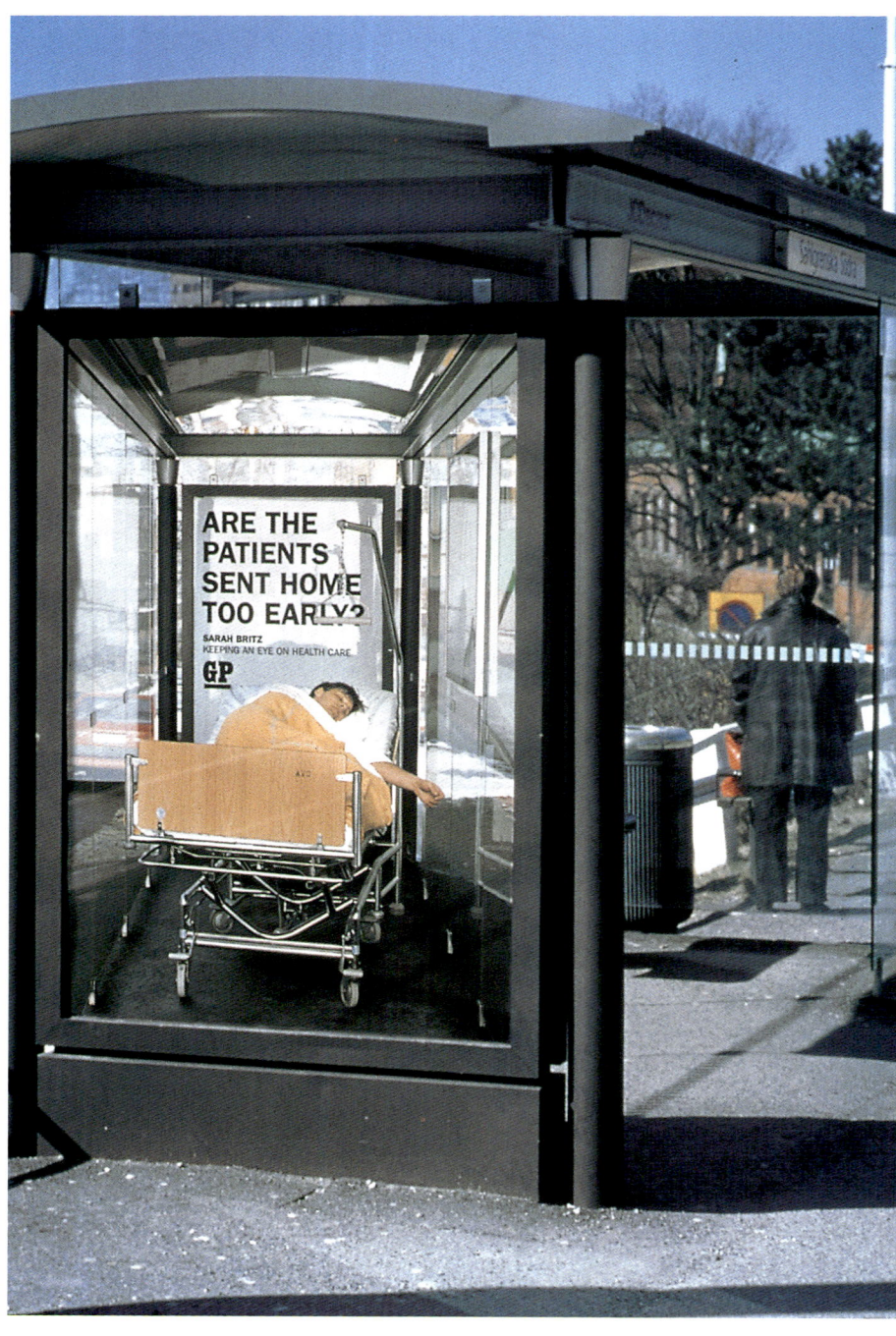

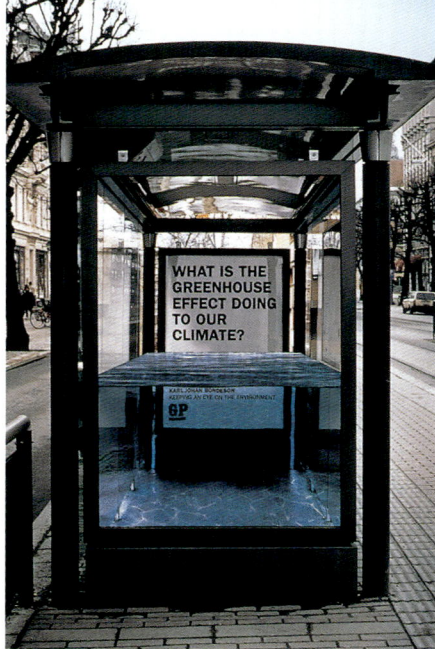

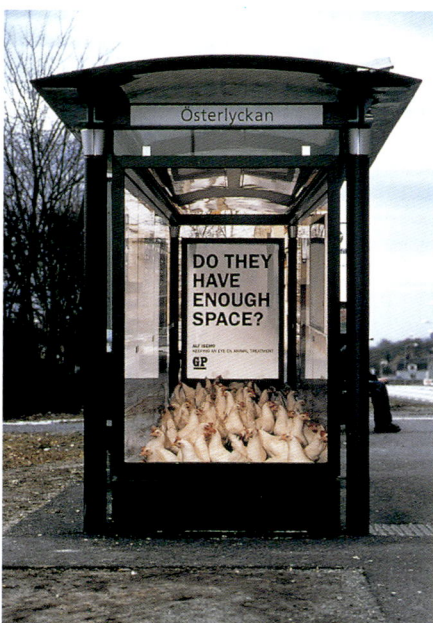

A promotion for *The Gothenburg Post* newspaper. The idea of the campaign was to highlight interesting examples of the type of editorial feature stories written by key journalists working for the paper.

For this outdoor campaign, the actual installations, such as bus shelters, were used as central components of the creative executions.

CATEGORY
Campaign

ADVERTISER/PRODUCT
Torture Museum Praha

TITLE
Grass

TITLE
Dustbin

TITLE
Steal

TITLE
Graffiti

TITLE
Drink and Drive

ADVERTISING AGENCY
Leo Burnett, Prague

PHOTOGRAPHY STUDIO
Leo Burnett, Prague

ACCOUNT EXECUTIVE
Robert Penazka

CREATIVE DIRECTOR
Basil Mina, Paolo Grippa

COPYWRITER
Steve Porcaro

ART DIRECTOR
Paolo Grippa, David Cuchinello

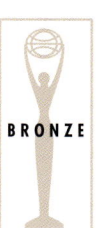

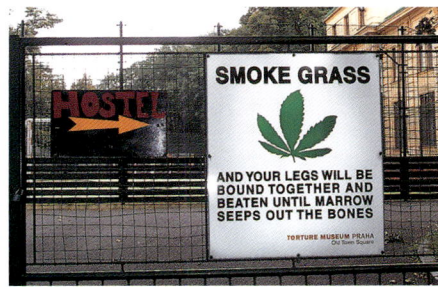

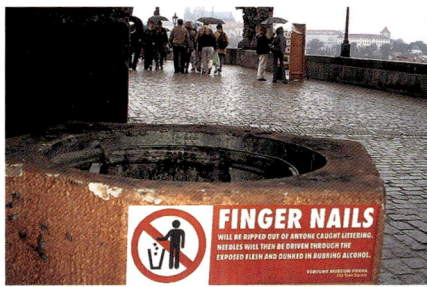

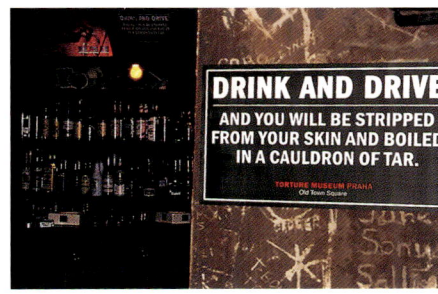

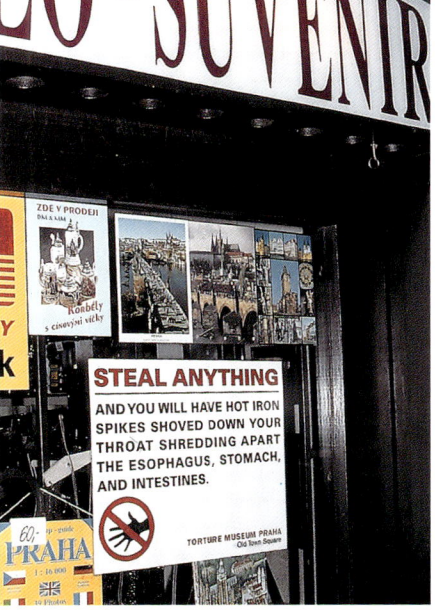

In order too get tourists through the doors of the Torture Museum, signs were placed tactically around popular sites: On dustbins in the town square, the windows of souvenir shops, back-packer hostels, tourist bars, etc. As a result, traffic increased significantly.

STUDENT

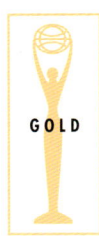

GOLD

CATEGORY
Student

ADVERTISER/PRODUCT
FedEx

TITLE
Faster Than You Think

SCHOOL
Academy of Art College,
San Francisco

COPYWRITER
Kittitat Larppitakpong

ART DIRECTOR
Kittitat Larppitakpong

PRODUCER
Keith E. Bowden

DIRECTOR
Keith E. Bowden

VISUAL: On a downtown street, a man stops and puts his package into a FedEx box. As he is walking off his cell phone rings and he answers.

MAN: Hello…You got the package? I just sent the package.

SUPER: FedEx. Faster Than You Think.

VISUAL: The man sticks his head into the FedEx box.

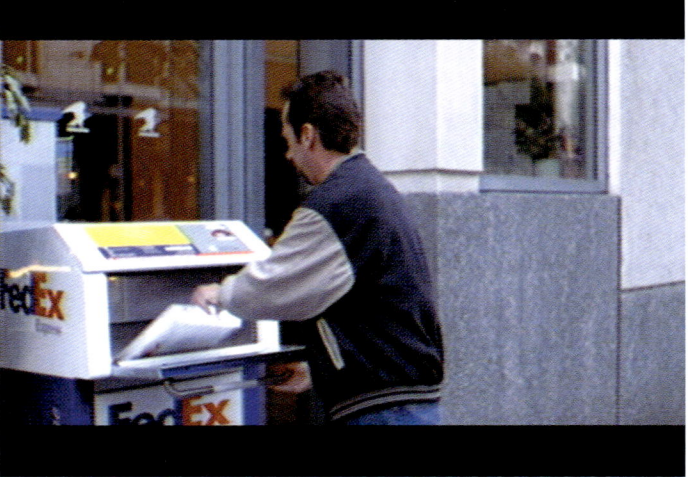

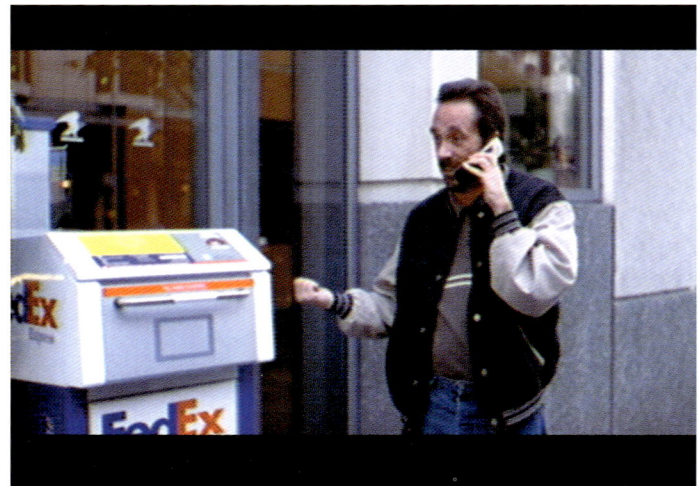

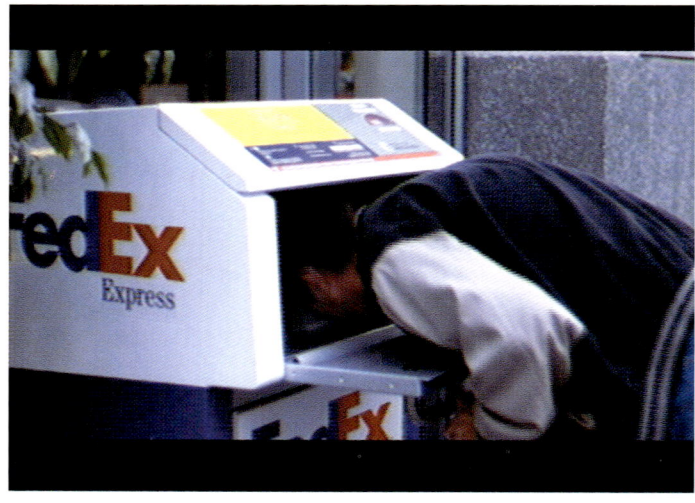

CATEGORY
Student

ADVERTISER/PRODUCT
Adopt-a-Pet

TITLE
Companionship

SCHOOL
Art Center College of Design, Pasedena

CREATIVE DIRECTOR
Richard Hartman, Ken Saba, Vee Vitanza

COPYWRITER
Richard Hartman, Ken Saba

ART DIRECTOR
Jeff Wang

PRODUCER
Jerry Magana

DIRECTOR
Vee Vitanza

ASSISTANT PRODUCER
Kirsten Hanna

EDITOR
Vee Vitanza

SOUND DESIGNER
Alex Rembrandt

CINEMATOGRAPHER
Jonah Torreano

ANIMATOR
Rubina Chabra

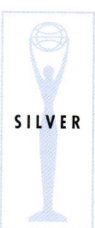

SILVER

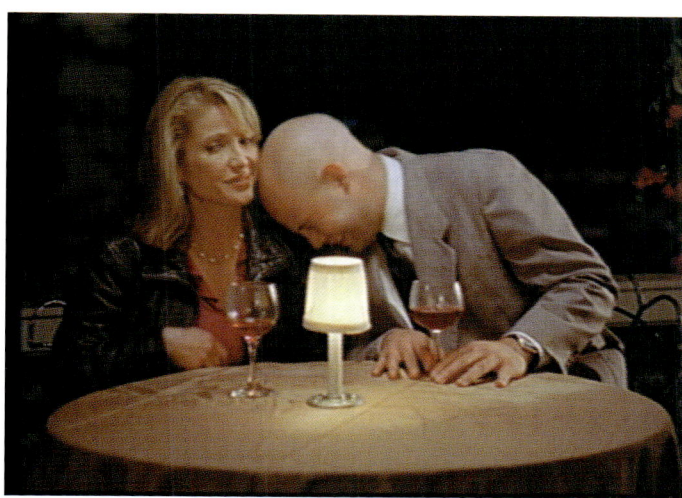

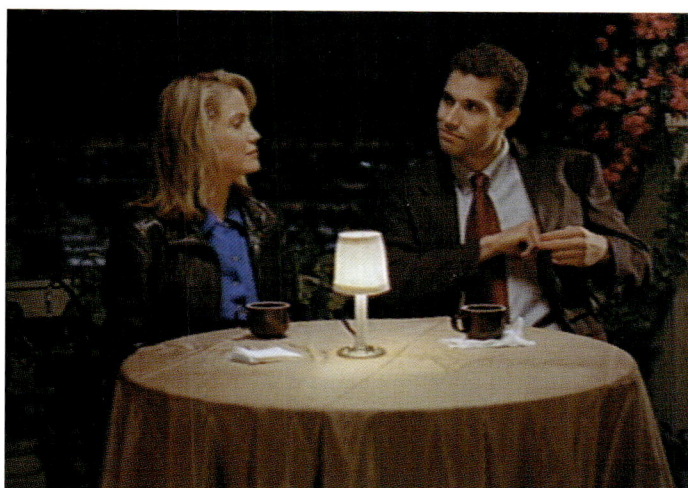

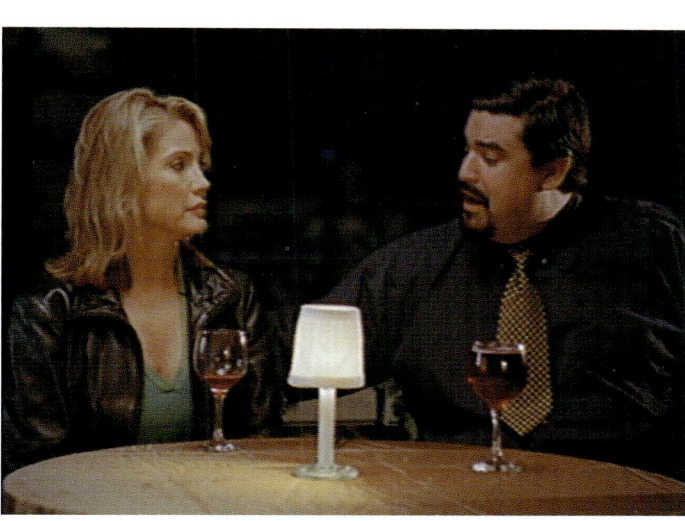

SUPER: Be careful what you wish for.

VISUAL: Sara and Berry are having a romantic dinner on a restaurant terrace. Berry shows Sara photographs of his mother.

BERRY: That's mom dressed up like a cowboy.

SARA: You still live with your mother?

BERRY: Oh yeah. I don't know what I'd do without her.

VISUAL: Sara looks anguished.

SUPER: If at first you don't succeed.

VISUAL: Sara is now on a date with Jay at the same restaurant. Jay bursts into tears and cries on Sara's shoulder. He is upset about his previous girlfriend. With some reluctance, Sara comforts Jay. Again, she looks quite upset.

SUPER: Never give up.

VISUAL: Sara is on a third date at the same restaurant; this time with Perry.

PERRY: It's an $80,000 automobile.

VISUAL: Sara looks disinterested and unimpressed.

PERRY (obnoxiously, to waiter): Hey, you!

VISUAL: Sara is upset by Perry's rudeness and the fact that he has just shouted in her ear.

SUPER: It could be worse.

VISUAL: A fourth dinner at the same restaurant; now with Louis: He should be looking at Sara's face but, instead, is staring at her chest.

LOUIS: You've got a wicked rack. Are those real?

VISUAL: Sara frowns.

SUPER: On the other hand. Adopt-a-Pet, Better Companionship.

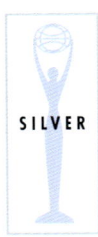

CATEGORY
Student

ADVERTISER/PRODUCT
Playboy.com

TITLE
Boardroom

TITLE
Porn Surfer

TITLE
Couple

SCHOOL
Art Center College of Design, Pasadena

COPYWRITER
Nicolas Hill

PRODUCER
Robert Hanson

DIRECTOR
Nicolas Hill

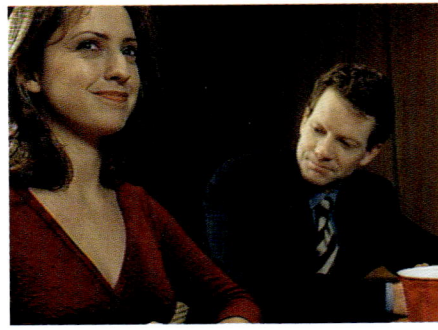 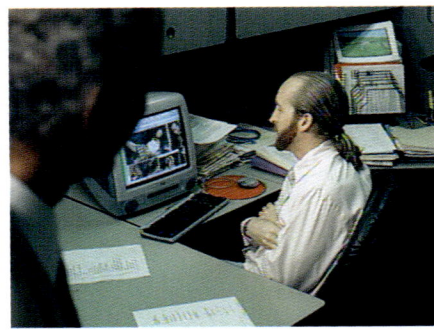 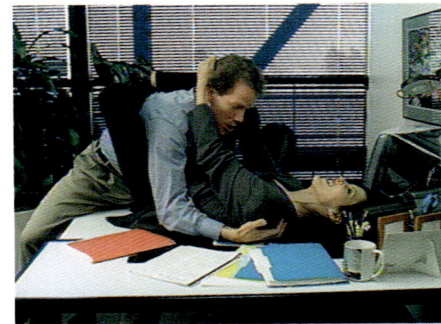

VISUAL: A group of business people is meeting around a conference table. One man is standing and making a presentation.

MAN 1: As you all know, I've been working diligently on this, so if you'll bear with me, I'd like to present a detailed analysis of…Lisa's firm breasts.

VISUAL: Everyone turns toward Lisa, who blushes slightly.

MAN 1: They're a tremendous asset to our corporation. They're firm, they're round, and the nipples stick up ever so slightly.

VISUAL: People are listening except for one man, Matthews, who is ignoring the speaker and concentrating on paperwork. The boss notices that Matthews is not paying attention.

MAN 1: They're not the largest nipples. They're not Canadian bacon nipples.

BOSS: Excuse me. Matthews! Put that away and listen. This is an important presentation.

VISUAL: Mathews closes his notebook.

BOSS: Thank you.

MAN 1: Thank you, sir. They definitely make a statement.

SUPER: Playboy.com logo.

VISUAL: In an office, the boss is walking past a row of cubicles. He stops at one where a man, Johnson, is working on a purchase order at his computer.

BOSS (annoyed): Johnson!

VISUAL: Quickly, Johnson switches his computer screen to some pictures of a partially nude woman. The boss smiles, nods his head in approval, and continues on his way.

VO: A perfect world.

SUPER: Playboy.com logo

VISUAL: A woman enters an office and closes the door.

WOMAN: We're all alone.

VISUAL: A man at his desk smiles and winks.

WOMAN: Do you have the sales reports from the Denver office?

VISUAL: The man holds up the sales reports.

WOMAN: Great, let's see.

VISUAL: She looks at the reports.

WOMAN: Are these the final figures?

MAN: This is a draft, but the numbers will be very close.

WOMAN: Okay. I need you to…

VISUAL: They are interrupted by the boss, who bursts into the office and sees them concentrating on the reports.

BOSS: What the hell do you think you're doing?

VISUAL: Quickly, the man and woman lay across the desk and embrace. She wraps her legs around him as he kisses her neck.

WOMAN: You bad little boy.

VISUAL: The boss smiles and leaves the office. The couple continues their passionate encounter.

VO: A perfect world.

SUPER: Playboy.com logo.

CLIO AWARDS

THE 43RD ANNUAL AWARDS COMPETITION

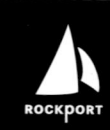

© 2003 by the Clio Awards
220 Fifth Avenue, Suite 1500
New York, NY 10001

Distributed by

Rockport Publishers, Inc.
33 Commercial Street
Gloucester, Massachusetts 01930-5089

Telephone: (978) 282-9590
Fax: (978) 283-2742
www.rockpub.com

ISBN 1-56496-965-7

10 9 8 7 6 5 4 3 2 1

Layout and Production: *tabula rasa* graphic design
Cover Design: MATTER

Printed in China

CLIO INTERNATIONAL REPRESENTATIVES

ARGENTINA
Carlos Acosta
Reporte Publicidad
Buenos Aires

AUSTRALIA
Kim Shaw
Campaign Brief
Subiaco

AUSTRIA
Chrigel Ott
Creative Club of Austria
Vienna

BELGIUM
Siglinda Paquay
Creative Club of Belgium
Brussels

BRAZIL
Enrique Lipszyc
Escola Panamericana de Arte
São Paulo

CANADA
Mike Lewis
The Advertising & Design
Club of Canada
Toronto

CHINA
Margaret Wong
The Association of Accredited
Advertising Agents of Hong Kong
Hong Kong

Mao Li Feng
ASTDC/Clio China
Shanghai

COLOMBIA
Christian Toro
Toro Fischer America
Bogota

COSTA RICA
Dennis Aguiluz Milla
ASCAP (Asociacion Costaricense de
Agencias de Publicidad)
San Jose

CZECH REPUBLIC
Jiri Mikes
ARA (Asociace Reklamnich Agentur)
Prague

DENMARK
Carl Gyllenhoff
Art & Copy
Espergaerde

ECUADOR
Jose Antonio Moreno
AEAP (Asociacion Equatoriana
de Agencias de Publicidad)
Quito

EL SALVADOR
Arturo Hirlemann
ANAES (National Association
of Advertisers)
San Salvador

FINLAND
Sinikka Virkkunen
Finnish Association of
Advertising Agencies
Helsinki

FRANCE
Anne Saint-Dreux
Maison de la Pub
Paris

GERMANY
Werner Bitz
GWA Service
Frankfurt/Main

GREECE
Maro Cambouris
EDEE (Hellenic Advertising
Agencies Association)
Athens

GUATEMELA
Luisa Maria Mata Arias
Corporacion Mariposa S.A.
Guatemala City

HUNGARY
Gabor Ergi
MaRS (Magyarorszagi
Rehlamugynoksegek Szovelsege)
Budapest

INDIA
Bipin Pandit
The Advertising Club of Bombay
Mumbai

INDONESIA
J. Daniel Rembeth
Cakram Magazine
Jakarta

ITALY
Milka Pogliani
Art Directors Club Italiano
Milan

JAPAN
Kenji Kashima
AJCC (All Japan Commercial
Confederation)
Tokyo

KOREA
Won Seok Hee
Korea Commercial Film Maker's Union
Seoul

MALAYSIA
J. Matthews
Macomm Management Services
Petalying Jaya

MEXICO
Antonio Delius
El Publicista
Mexico City

NEW ZEALAND
Lynne Clifton
CAANZ (Communication Agencies
Association of New Zealand)
Auckland

NORWAY
Sol M. Olving
Reklamebyråforeningen
Oslo

PHILIPPINES
Oli Laperal
R.S. Video & Film Production
Manilla

POLAND
Leslaw Wilk
Crackfilm Agency
Kraków

PORTUGAL
Rui Cupido
Meios Publicidade/Work Media
Lisbon

SINGAPORE
Florence Oh
Association of Accredited Advertising
Agents of Singapore
Mandarin Singapore

SWEDEN
Anna Serner
The Advertising Association of Sweden
Stockholm

SWITZERLAND
Walter Merz
Association of Swiss Advertising
Agencies BSW/USC
Zurich

TAIWAN
Helen Wang
Brain Magazine
Taipei

THAILAND
Niwat Wongprompreeda
The Advertising Association of Thailand
Bangkok

TURKEY
Arsun Akün
Reklamcilar Dernegi
Istanbul

URUGUAY
Carlos Ricagni
McCann-Erickson
Montevideo

VENEZUELA
Raul Lotitto
Grupo Editorial Producto
Caracas

CREDITS

CLIO STAFF

ANDREW JAFFE
Executive Director

TONY GULISANO
Managing Director

KATHY BAKER
General Manager, Chicago

LOU ISIDORA
General Manager, New York

JOEL GOODMAN
Project Manager/Judging Director

WAYNE YOUKHANA
Video Editor/Producer

BARBARA DASILVA SANT'ANA
Project Coordinator

XOCHITL GONZALEZ
Director of Special Events

JOHN MACDONALD
Systems Analyst/Programmer

PUBLIC RELATIONS

DEF P.R. INC.
New York

MALISSA PIAZZA
Director of Public Relations,
Clio Awards

NORMA ROMEO
Partner

LEGAL COUNCIL

JOHN M. ANDERSON, ESQ.
Heller Ehrman White & McAuliffe
San Francisco & New York

DESIGN FIRM

tabula rasa grapic design
Arlington, Massachusetts

ROCKPORT PUBLISHERS
Gloucester, Massachusetts

CATEGORY
Student

ADVERTISER/PRODUCT
Lucky Brand Dungarees

TITLE
Mortician

SCHOOL
Art Center College of Design, Pasadena

COPYWRITER
Patrick O'Rourke

ART DIRECTOR
Patrick O'Rourke

DIRECTOR
Michael Chaves

DIRECTOR OF PHOTOGRAPHY
Florian Stadler

EDITOR
Justin Amore

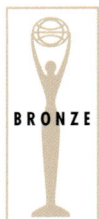

BRONZE

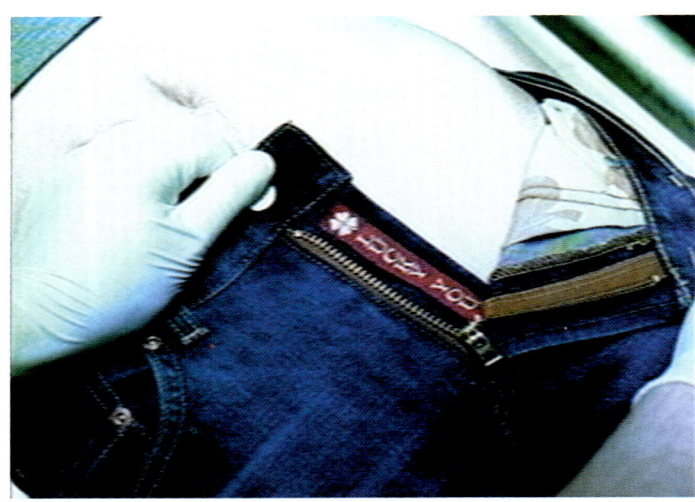

VISUAL: A mortician is methodically preparing his tools for the next embalming—a young woman. He unzips the fly of her jeans and is caught off guard by a tag on the inside of the fly: "Lucky You." The mortician looks at the jeans for a moment, then at the woman, and then around the empty morgue.

SUPER: Get Lucky. Lucky Brand Dungarees.

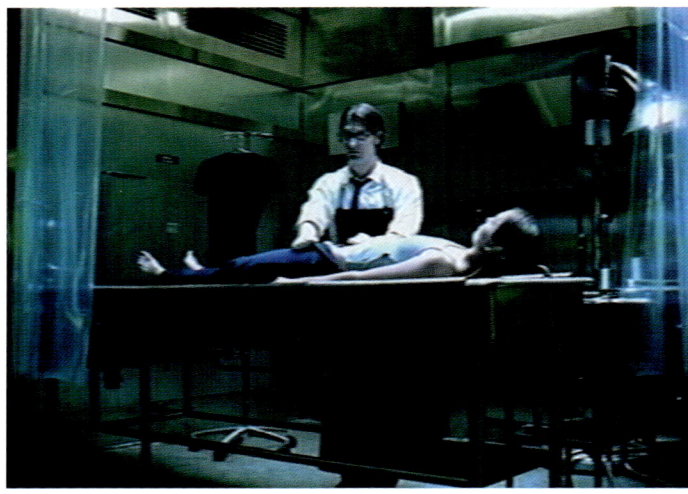

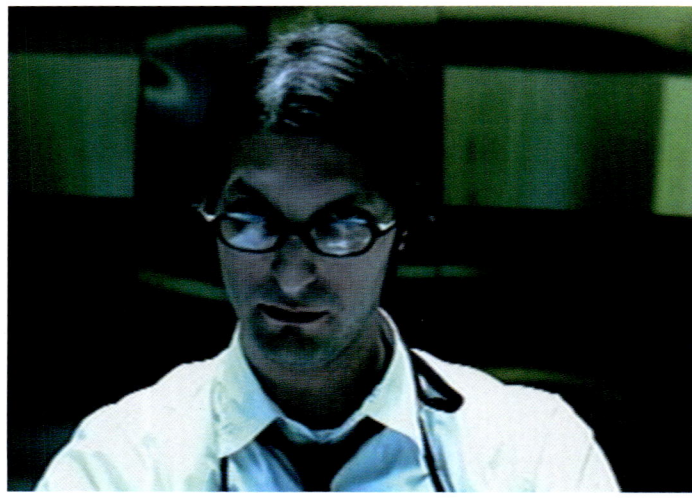

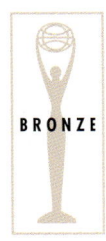

CATEGORY
Student

ADVERTISER/PRODUCT
Marvel Comics

TITLE
Halftime

SCHOOL
Art Center College of Design,
Pasadena

COPYWRITER
Patrick O'Rourke

ART DIRECTOR
Patrick O'Rourke

DIRECTOR
Michael Chaves

DIRECTOR OF PHOTOGRAPHY
Florian Stadler

EDITOR
Justin Amore

VISUAL: A crowded bathroom, during halftime, at a sporting event. A young man is waiting impatiently for his turn. He steps up to the toilet and begins to urinate. From above his head a stream of urine pours forth. Befuddled, he looks up.

SUPER: The Amazing Spider-Man.

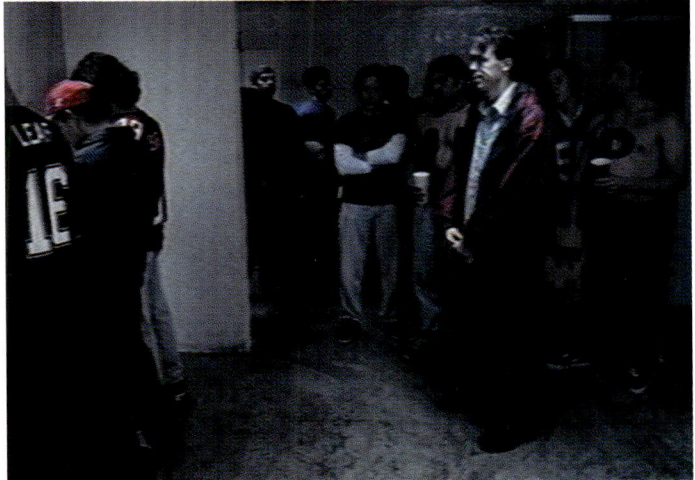

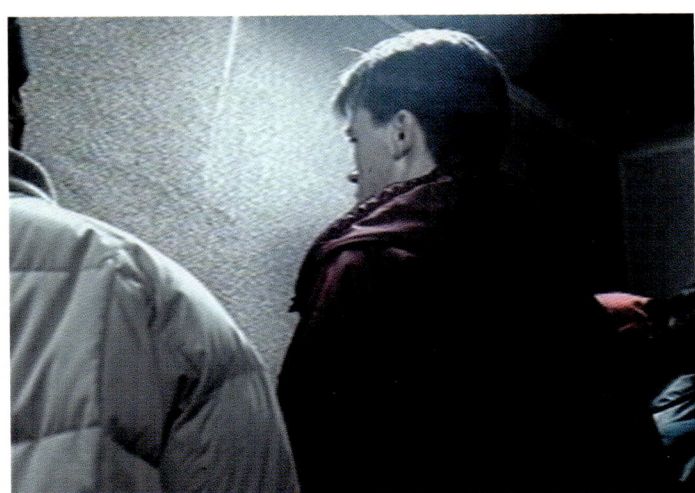

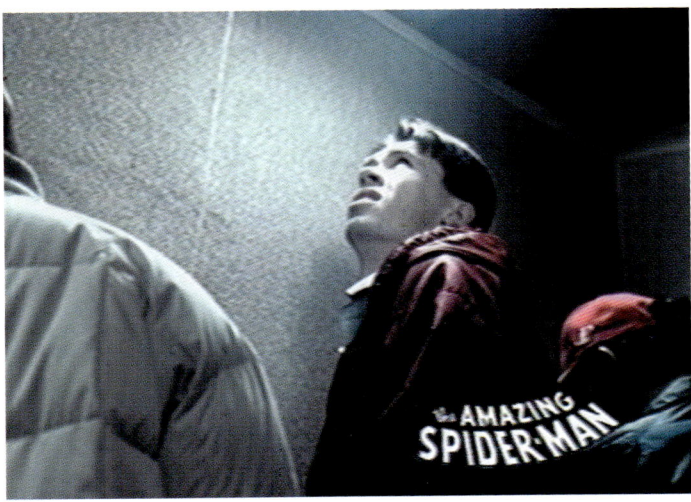

CATEGORY
Student

ADVERTISER/PRODUCT
KSAN 107.7 FM/The Bone

TITLE
Society Pays the Price

TITLE
Tragically Alive

TITLE
The Horror of Human Cloning

SCHOOL
Academy of Art College,
San Francisco

COPYWRITER
Allan Manaysay

ART DIRECTOR
Allan Manaysay

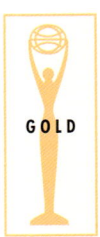

GOLD

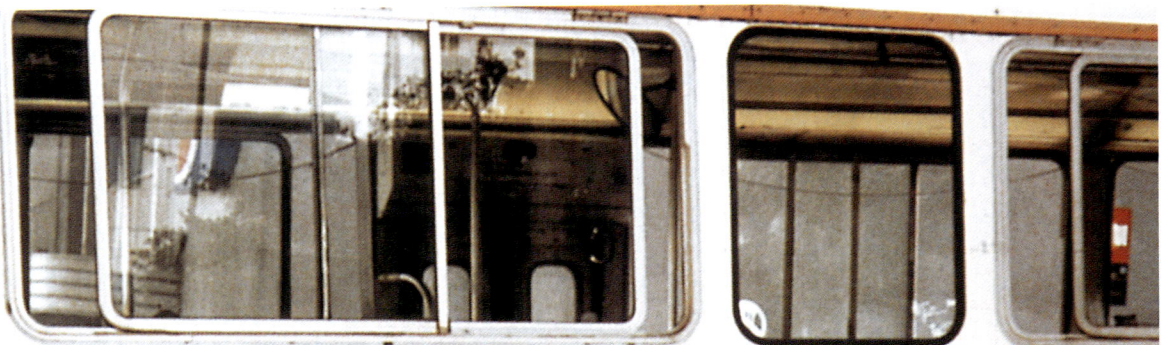

The Backstreet Boys, 'N Sync, and 98°.
When pregnant women don't smoke, society pays the price.

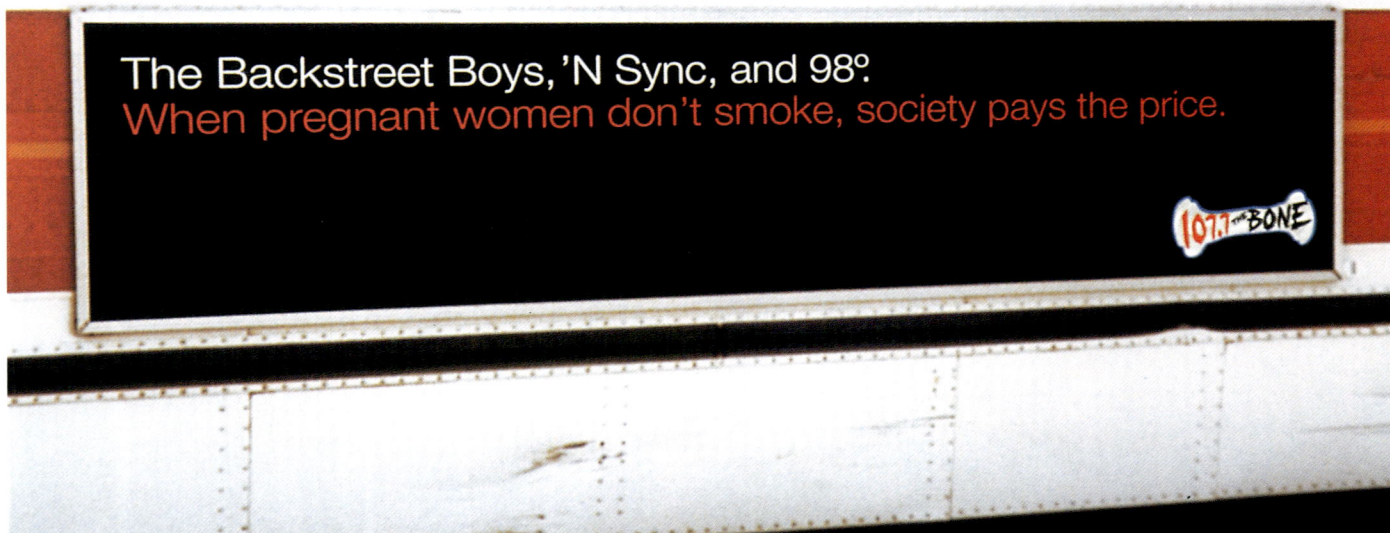

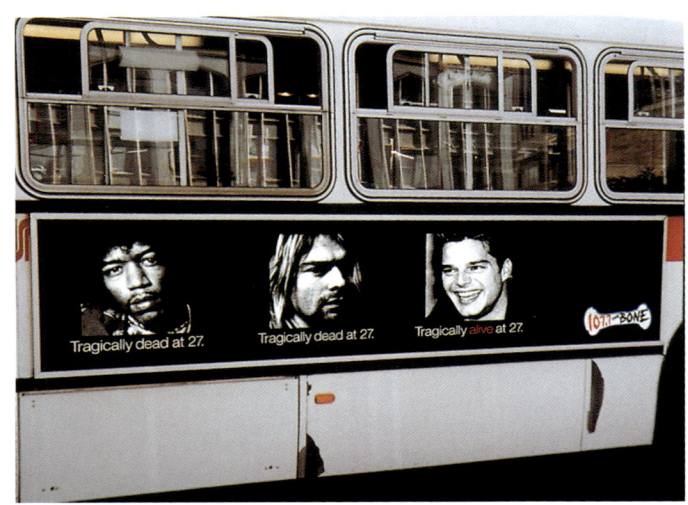

Tragically dead at 27. Tragically dead at 27. Tragically alive at 27.

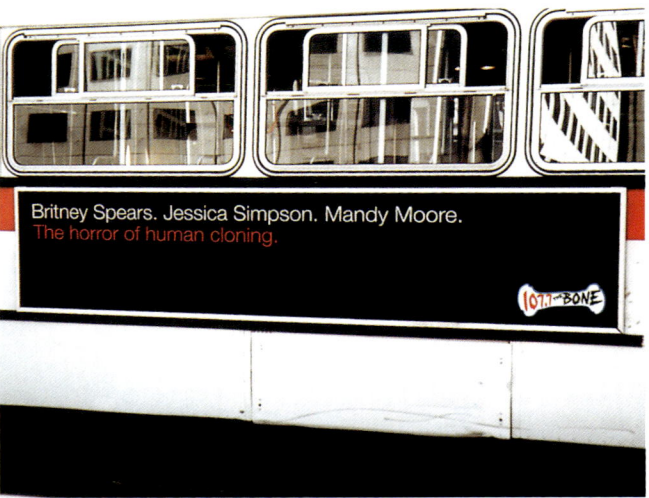

Britney Spears. Jessica Simpson. Mandy Moore.
The horror of human cloning.

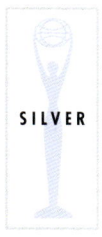

SILVER

CATEGORY Student	**TITLE** Partaking	**COPYWRITER** Adam Kanzer
ADVERTISER/PRODUCT Shakespeare in the Park	**TITLE** Unwanted Vessels	**ART DIRECTOR** Kamal Collins, Mark Infusino
TITLE Tis Your Duty	**SCHOOL** Miami Ad School, Miami Beach	**PHOTOGRAPHER** Scott Cirlin

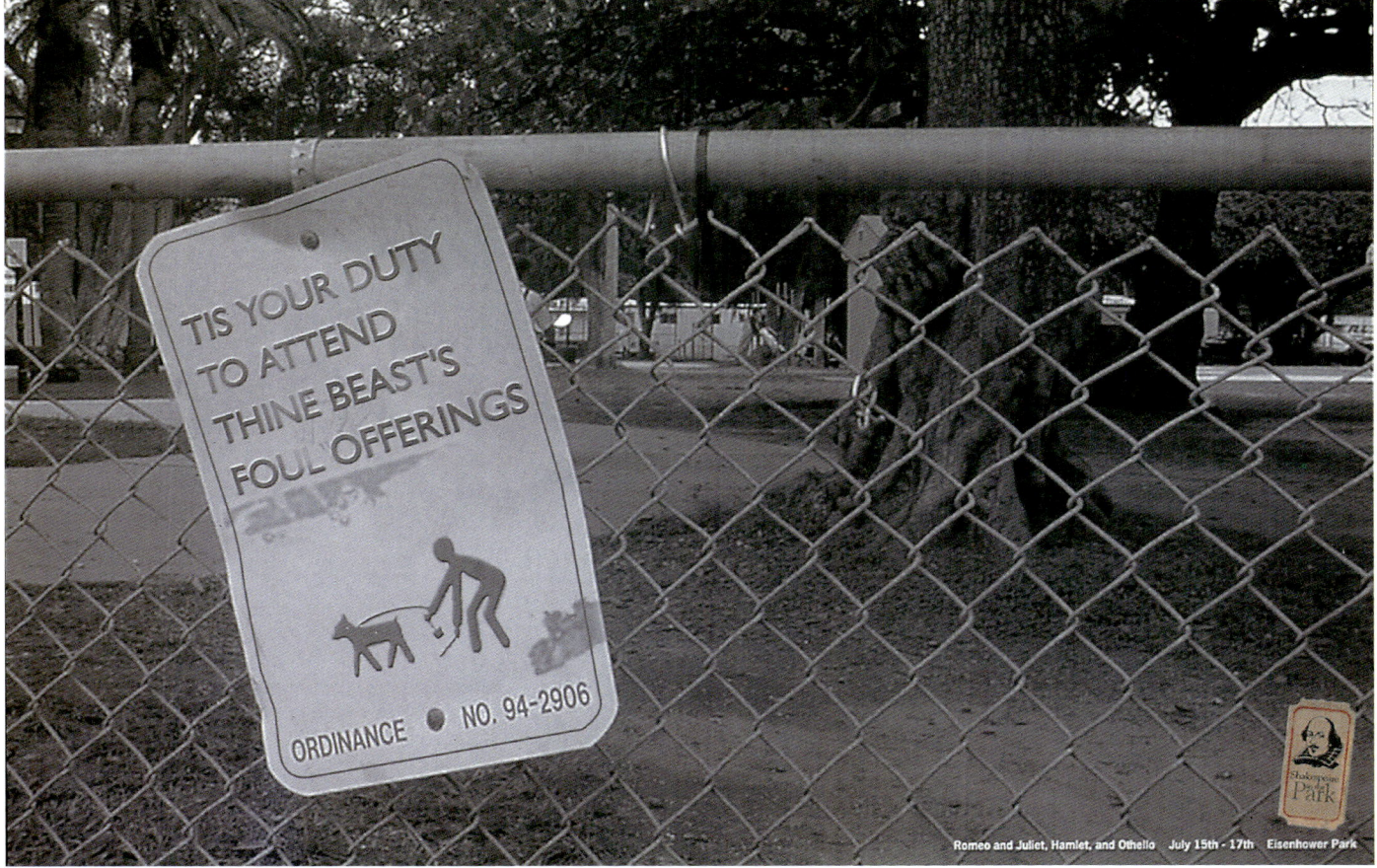

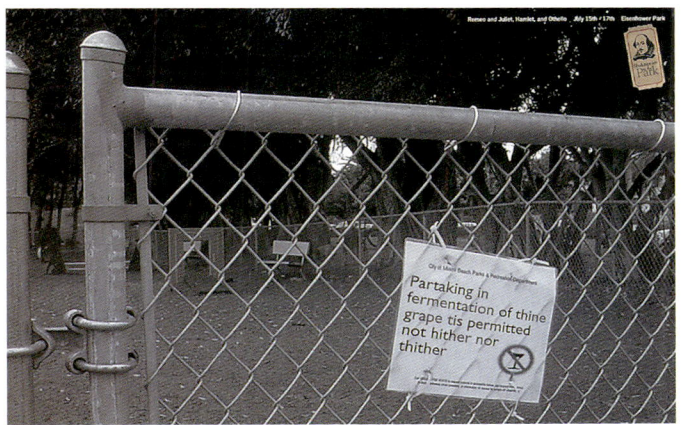

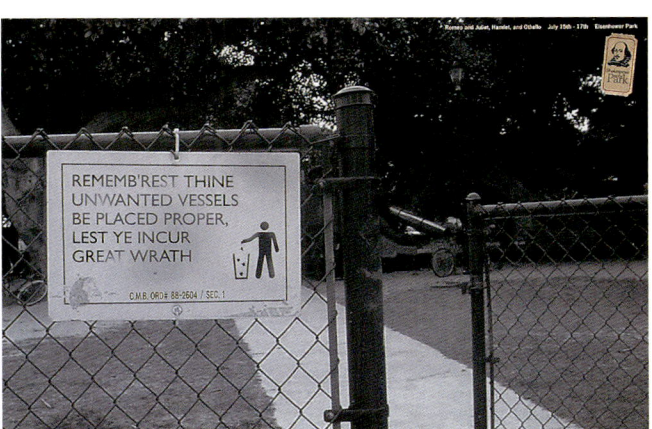

CATEGORY
Student

ADVERTISER/PRODUCT
Tide

TITLE
NBA

TITLE
Nautica

TITLE
Timberland

SCHOOL
School of Visual Arts, New York

COPYWRITER
Shareif Ziyadat

ART DIRECTOR
Naoki Ga

INSTRUCTOR
Sal Devito

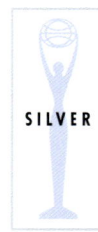

SILVER

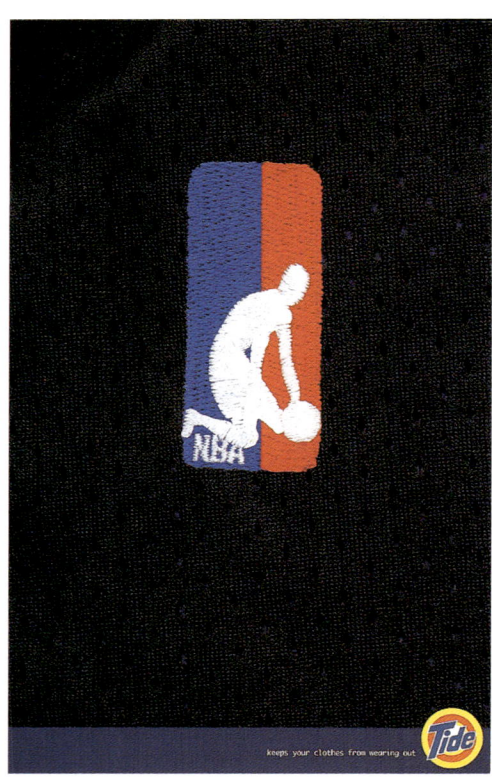

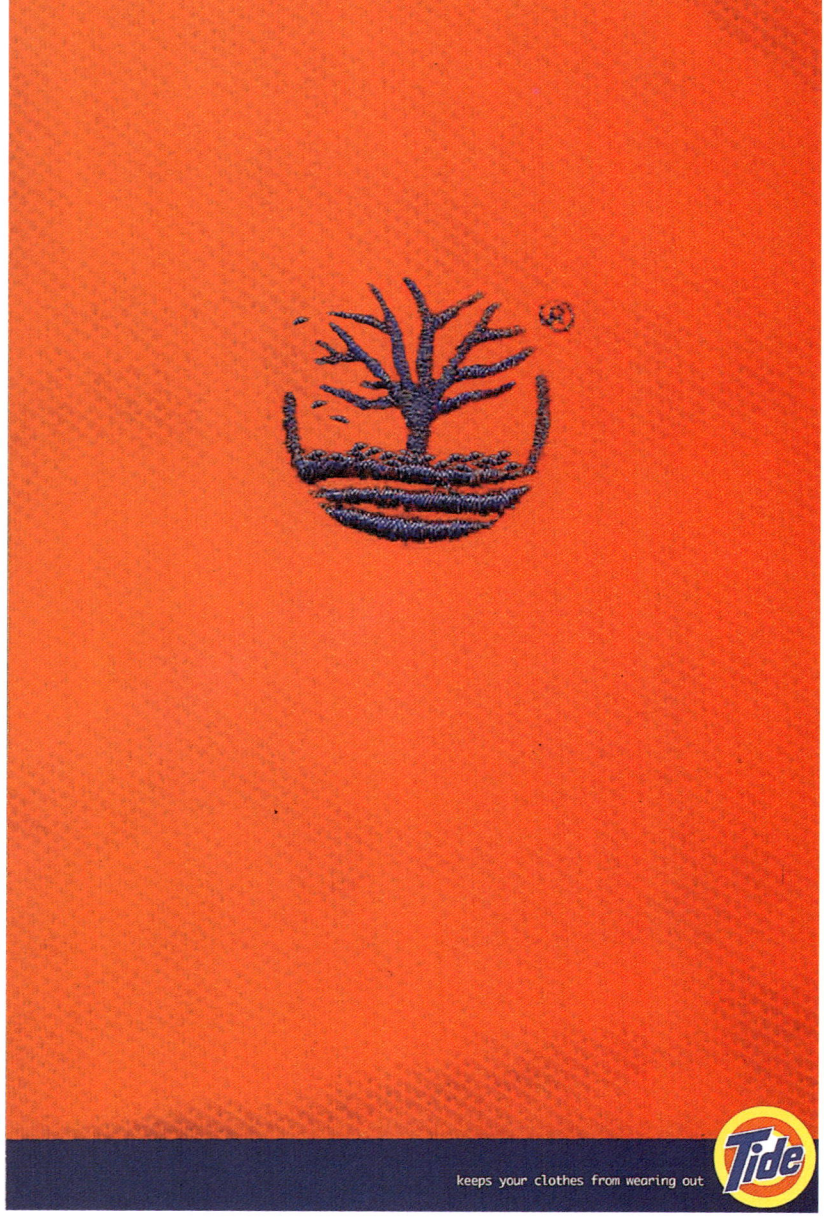

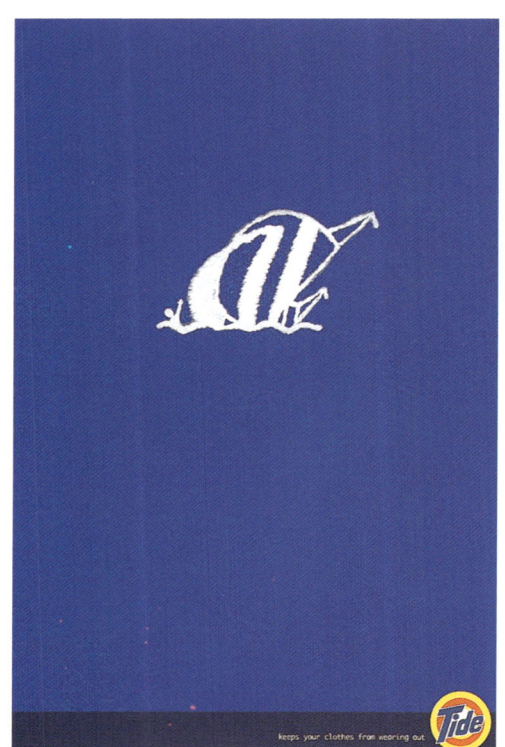

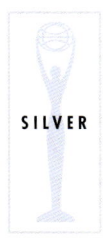

SILVER

CATEGORY
Student

ADVERTISER/PRODUCT
The Bible

TITLE
2000 Years before the Sopranos

TITLE
John 20:27

TITLE
Genesis 19

SCHOOL
The Book Shop, Los Angeles

COPYWRITER
Leslie Goodbar

ART DIRECTOR
Joseph Kaiser

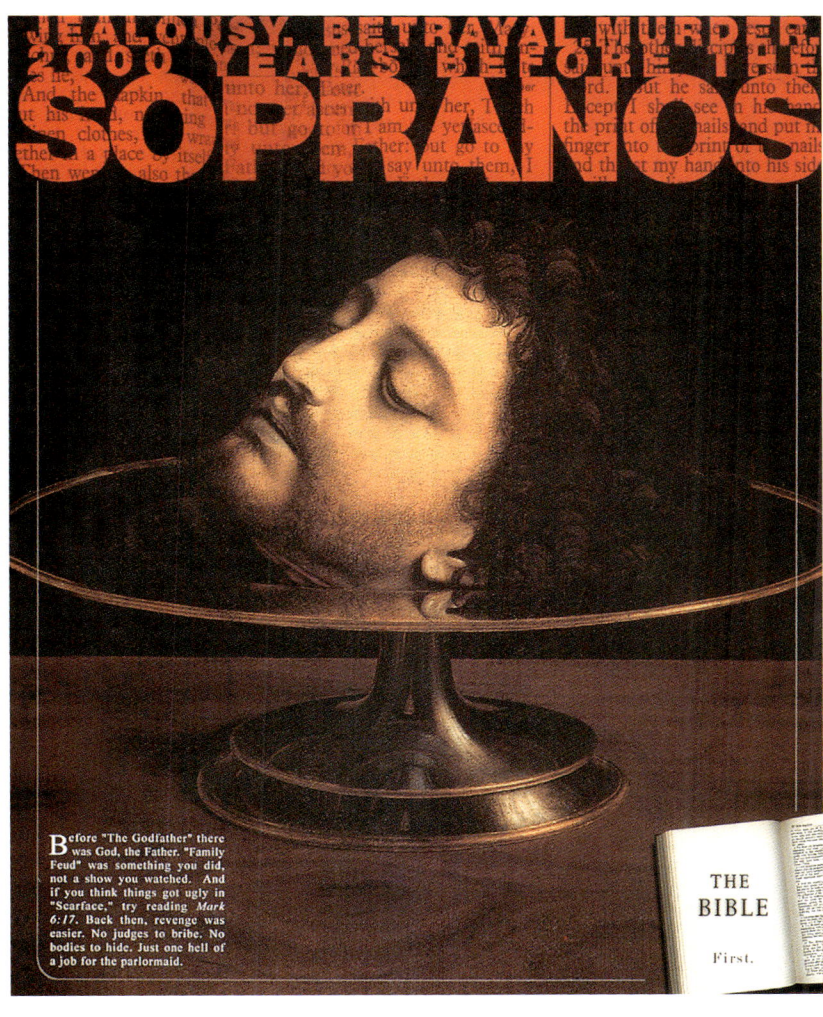

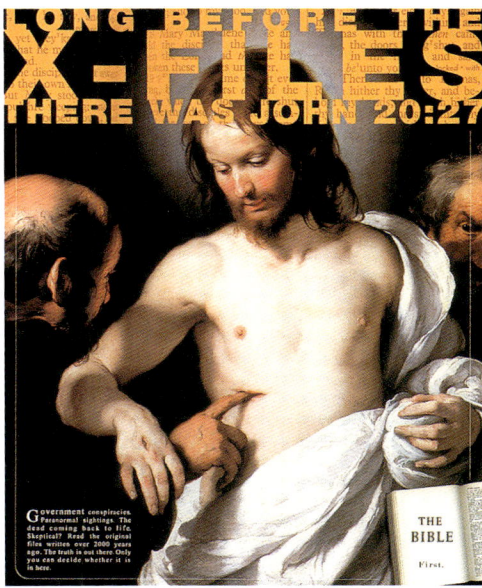

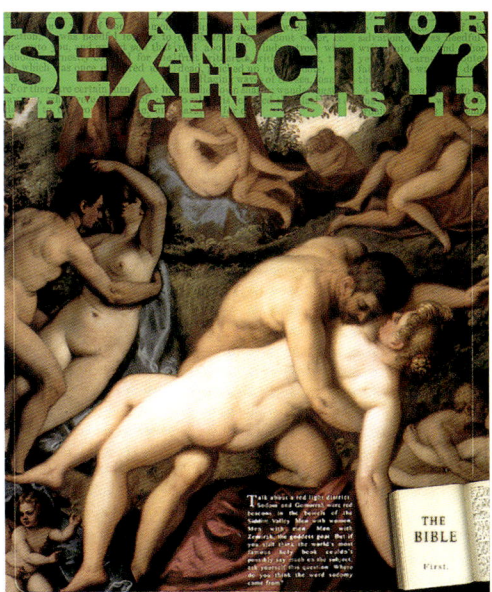

CATEGORY
Student

ADVERTISER/PRODUCT
Post-it

TITLE
Get Batteries

SCHOOL
The Book Shop, Los Angeles

COPYWRITER
Joseph Kaiser

ART DIRECTOR
Joseph Kaiser

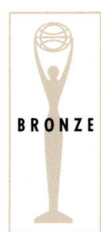

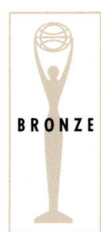

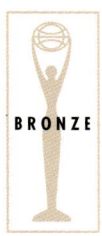

CATEGORY
Student

ADVERTISER/PRODUCT
Guitar Center

TITLE
Kiss

TITLE
Oompa

TITLE
Quartet

SCHOOL
Academy of Art College,
San Francisco

COPYWRITER
David Ciano

ART DIRECTOR
Nicoletta Nelson, Christian Osmers

PHOTOGRAPHER
Jon Branscombe

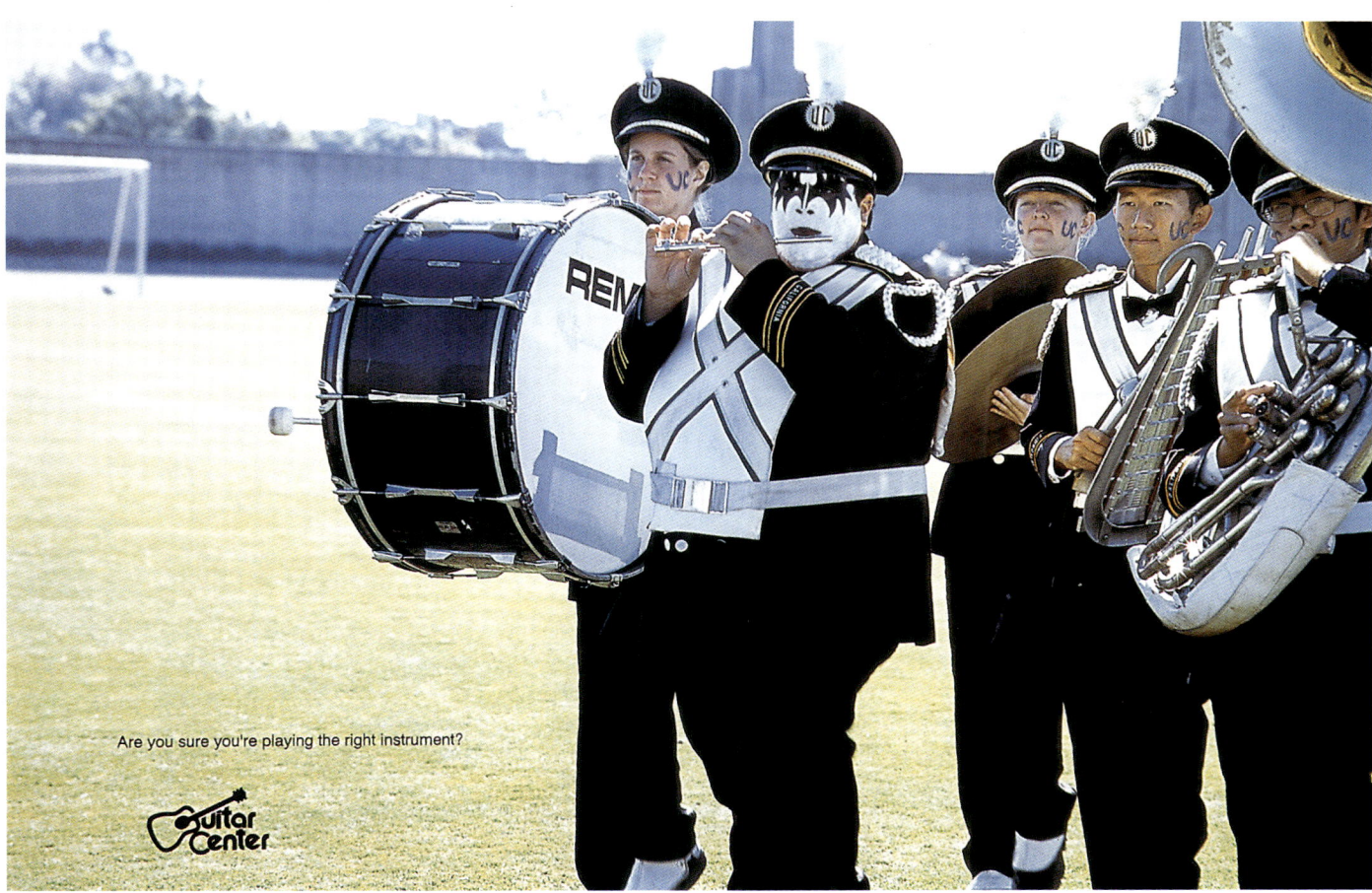

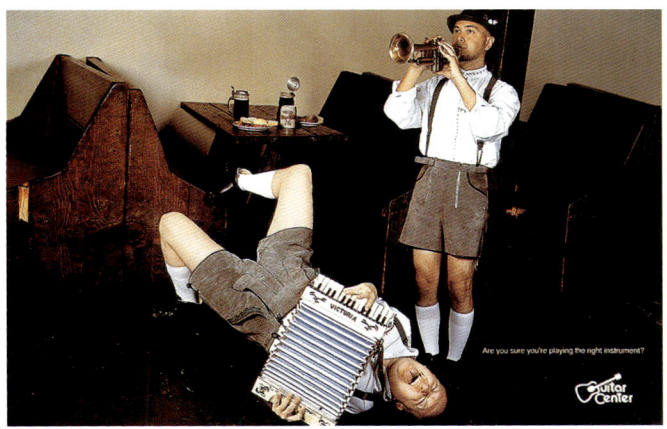

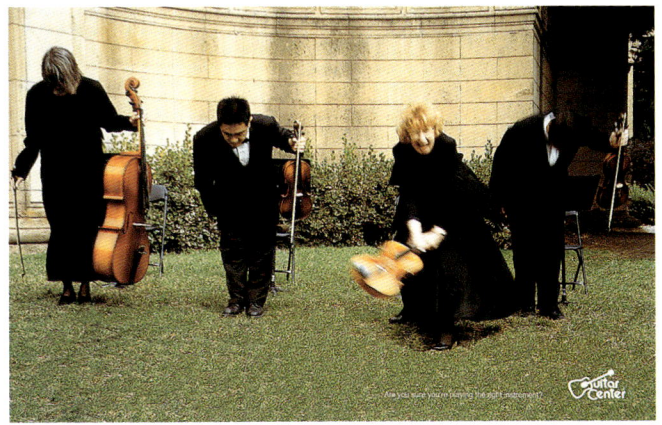

CATEGORY
Student

ADVERTISER/PRODUCT
Discovery Channel

TITLE
Hitler/Chaplin

TITLE
Natives/Earrings

TITLE
Pope/E.R.

SCHOOL
VCU Adcenter, Richmond

COPYWRITER
David Fredette, Mark Svartz

ART DIRECTOR
Jon Bunning

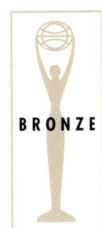

BRONZE

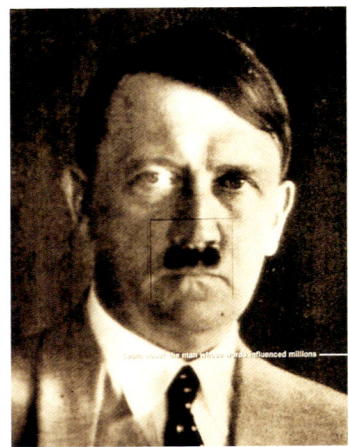
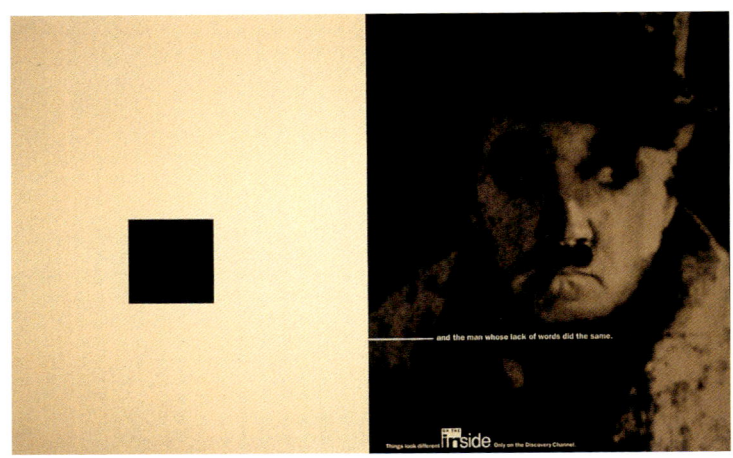

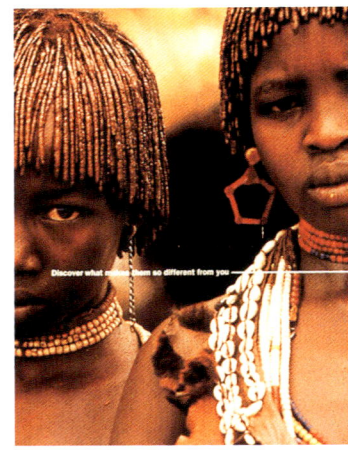
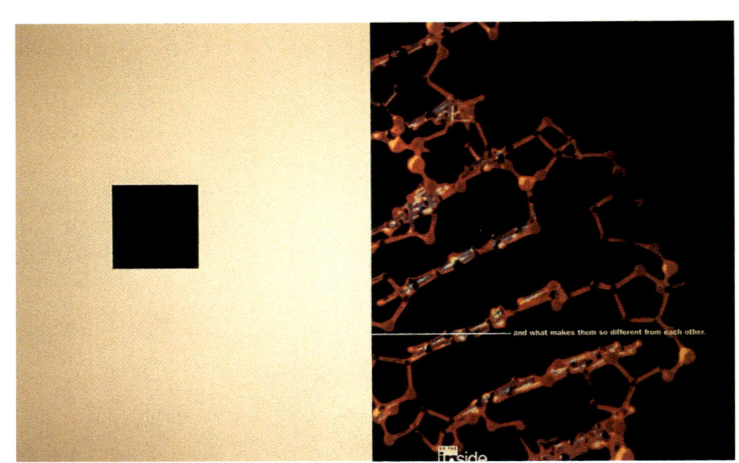

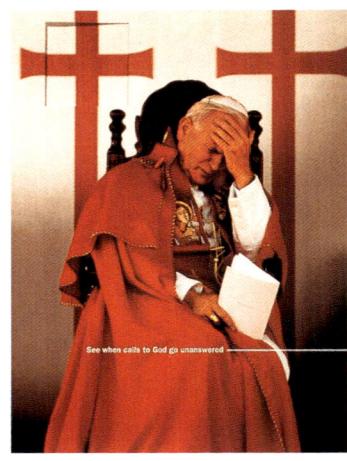
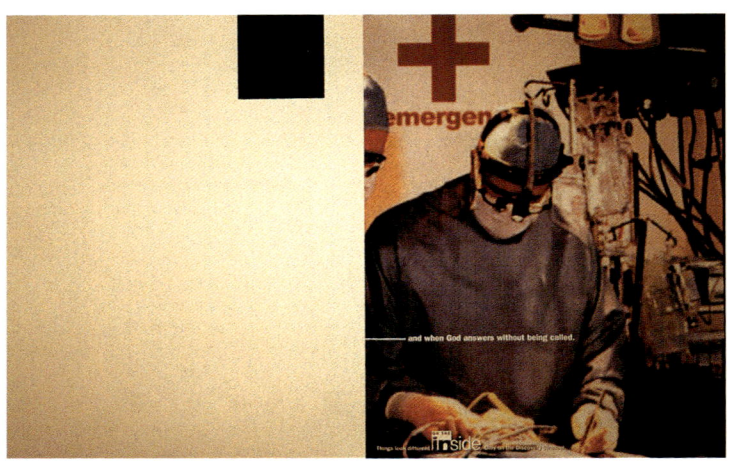

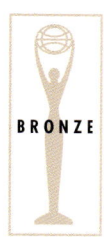

BRONZE

CATEGORY Student	**TITLE** Downhill	**COPYWRITER** Jon Yasgur
ADVERTISER/PRODUCT Baby Jogger	**TITLE** Cheetah	**ART DIRECTOR** Jay F. Miller
TITLE Wind	**SCHOOL** Brainco, The Minneapolis School of Advertising, Minneapolis	**PHOTOGRAPHER** Jay F. Miller, Jon Yasgur

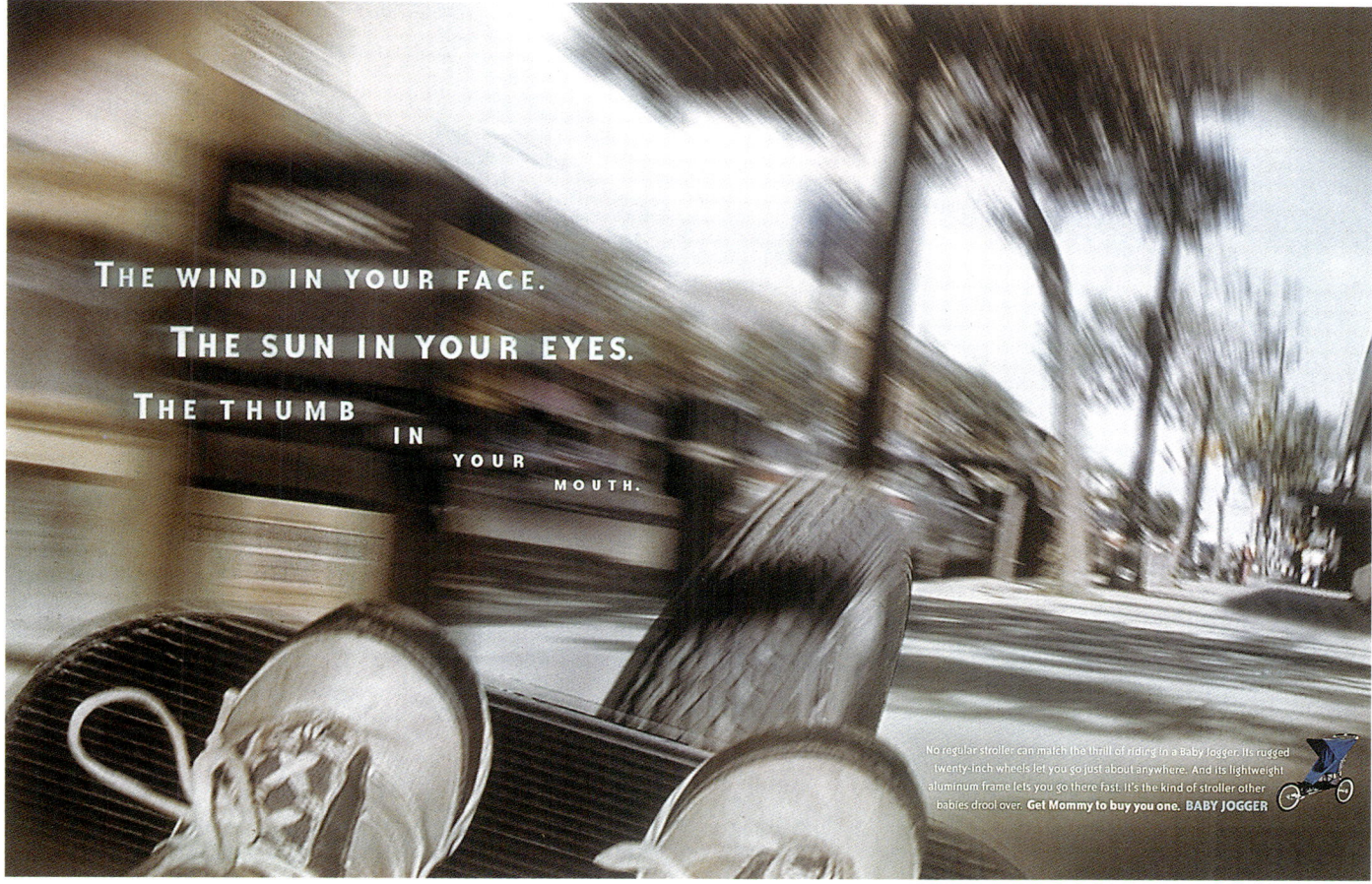

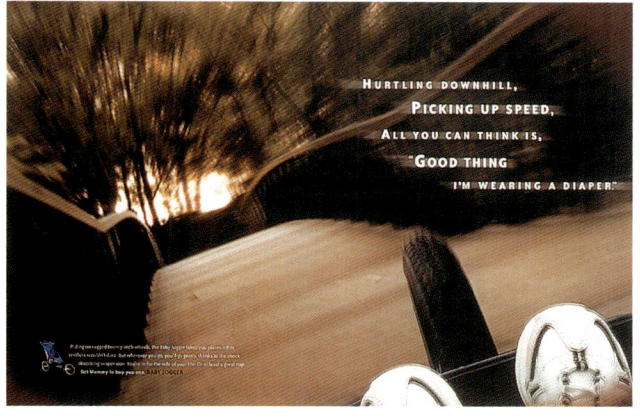

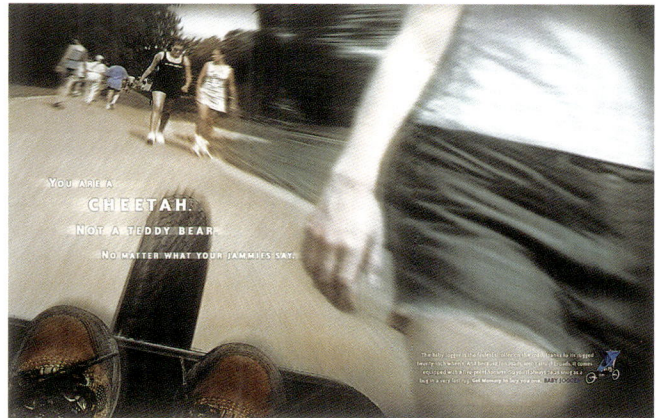

CATEGORY
Student

ADVERTISER/PRODUCT
G-Shock Watches

TITLE
Scar

TITLE
Burn

TITLE
Cast

SCHOOL
Academy of Art College,
San Francisco

COPYWRITER
Hijiri Kameyama

ART DIRECTOR
Hijiri Kameyama

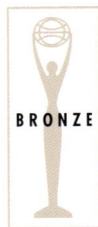

BRONZE

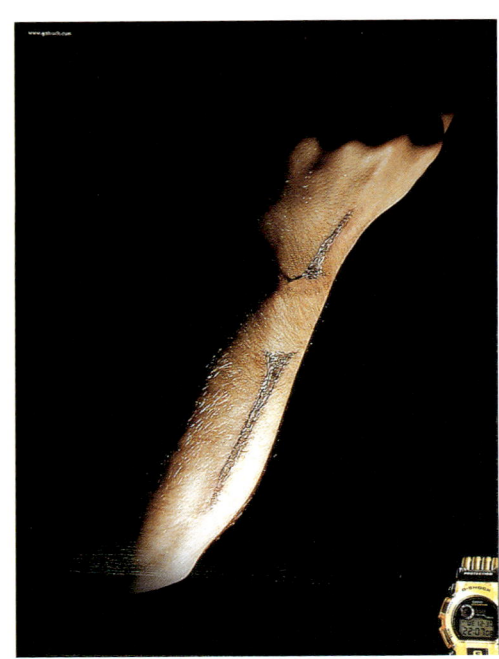

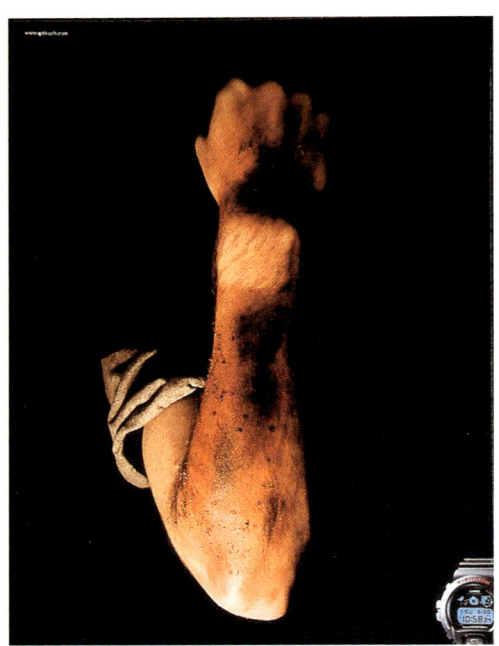

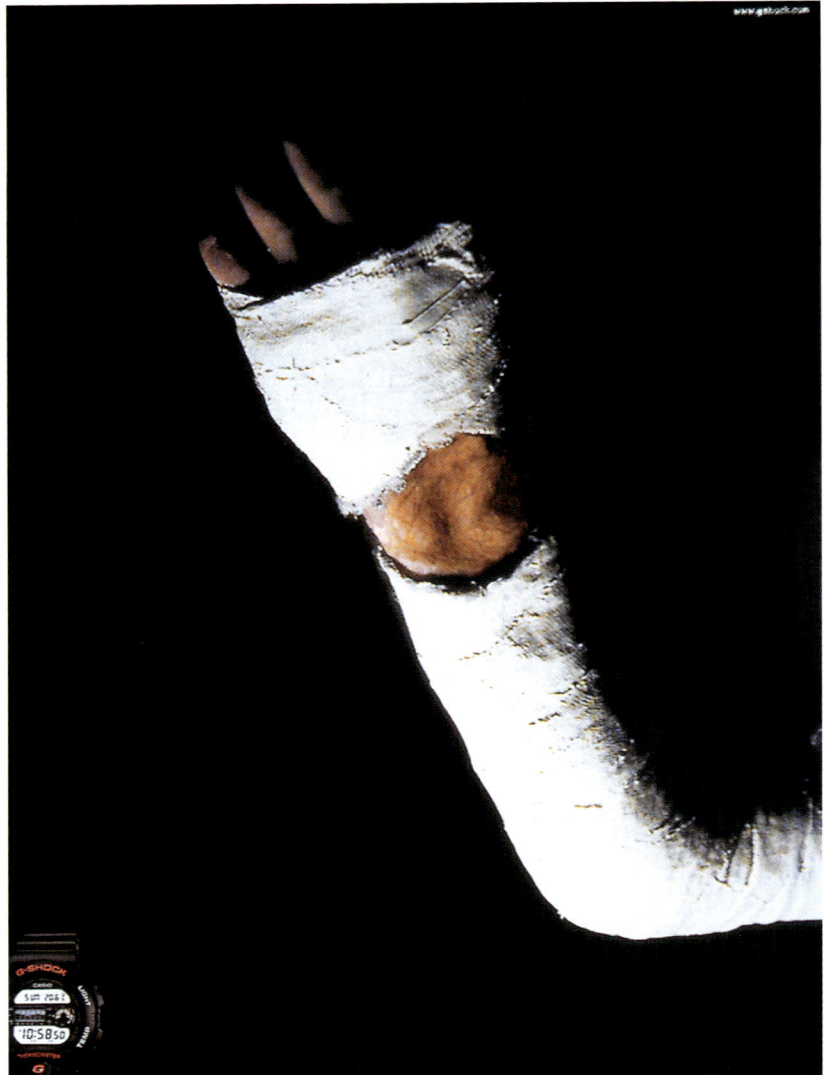

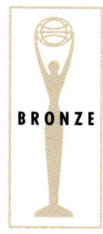

BRONZE

CATEGORY
Student

ADVERTISER/PRODUCT
Bow Wow Pet Products

SCHOOL
Academy of Art College,
San Francisco

STUDENT
Nitta Chinalai

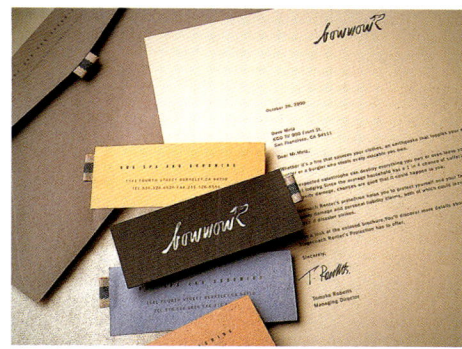

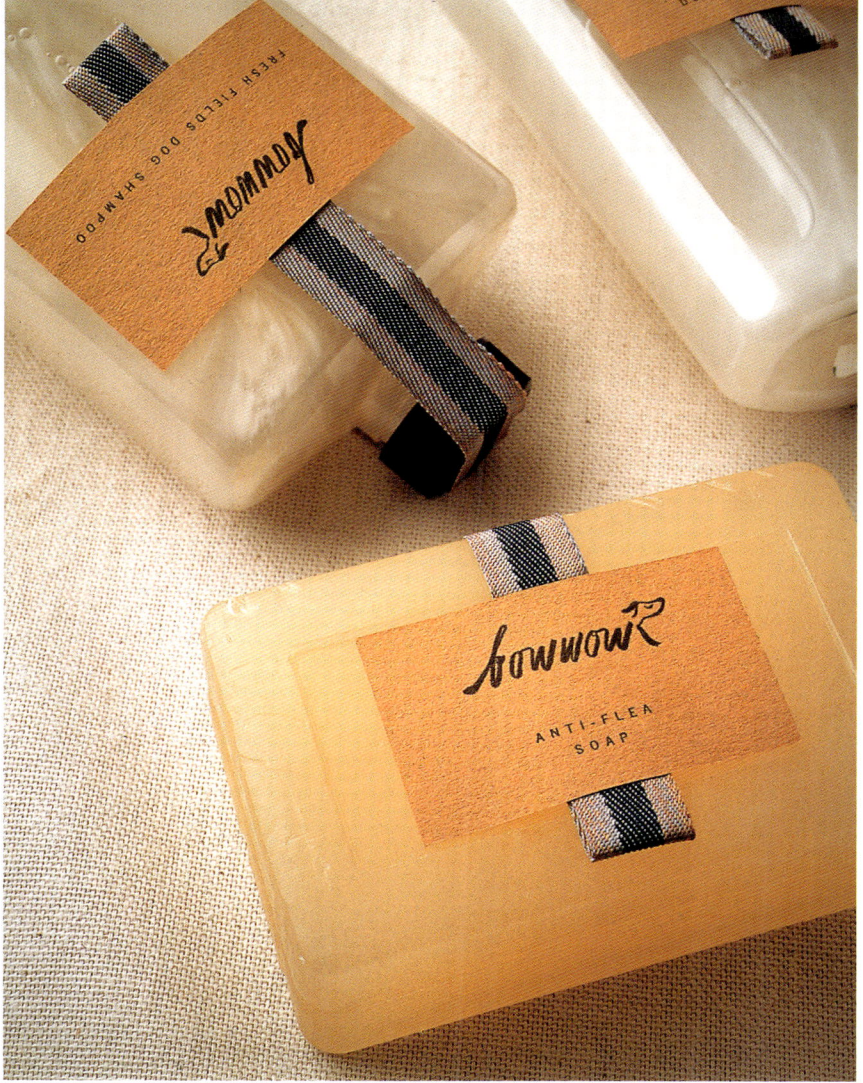

CATEGORY
Student

ADVERTISER/PRODUCT
Sound of the City: Luba Lukova

SCHOOL
The Cooper Union for the
Advancement of Science & Art,
Astoria

STUDENT
Kathryn Cho

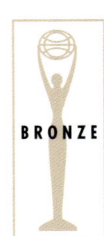

BRONZE

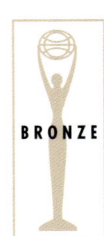

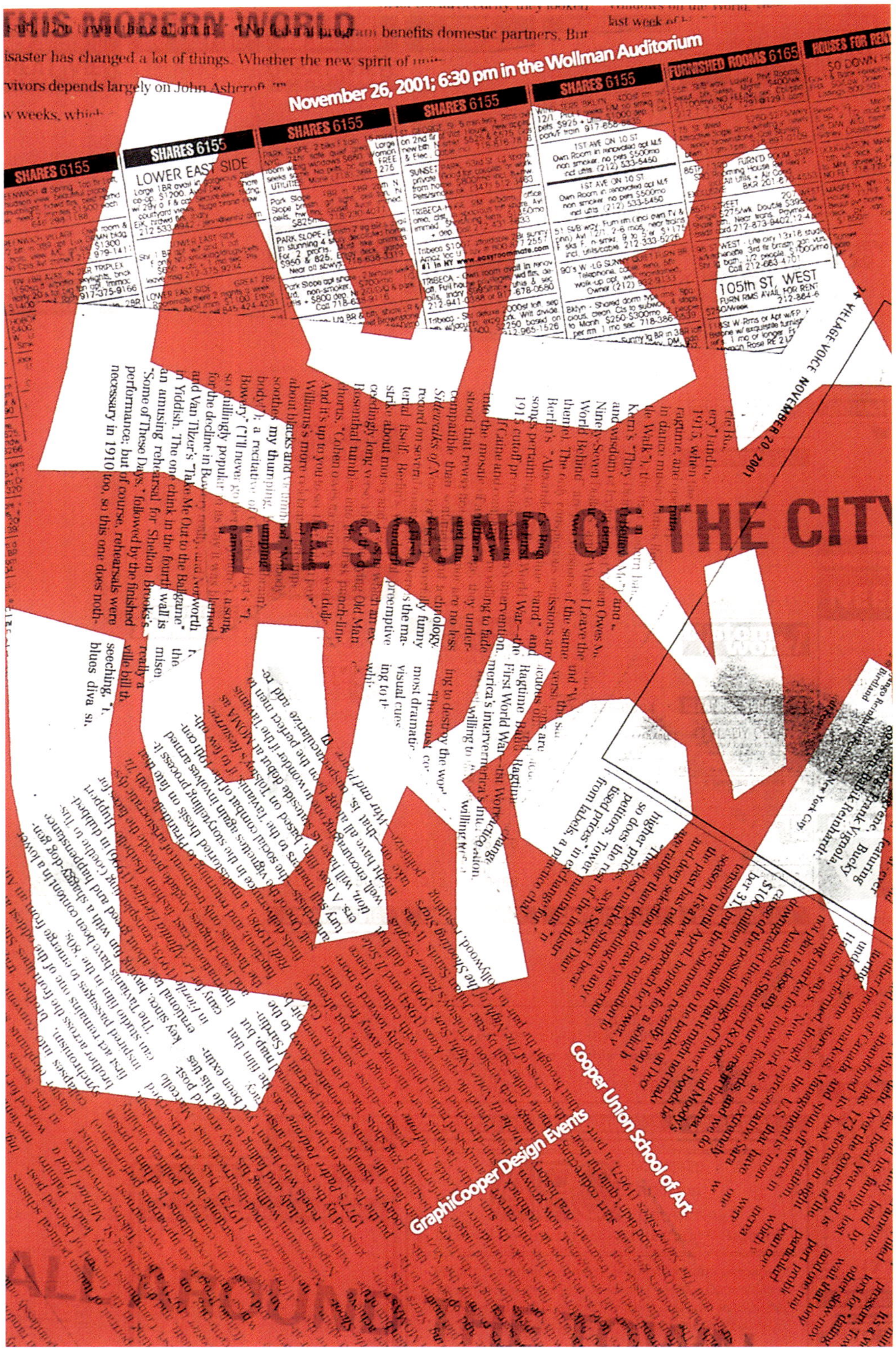

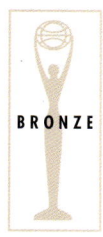

BRONZE

CATEGORY
Student

ADVERTISER/PRODUCT
Simplicity Calendar—Time to Fit

SCHOOL
Academy of Art College,
San Francisco

STUDENT
Naureen Ono

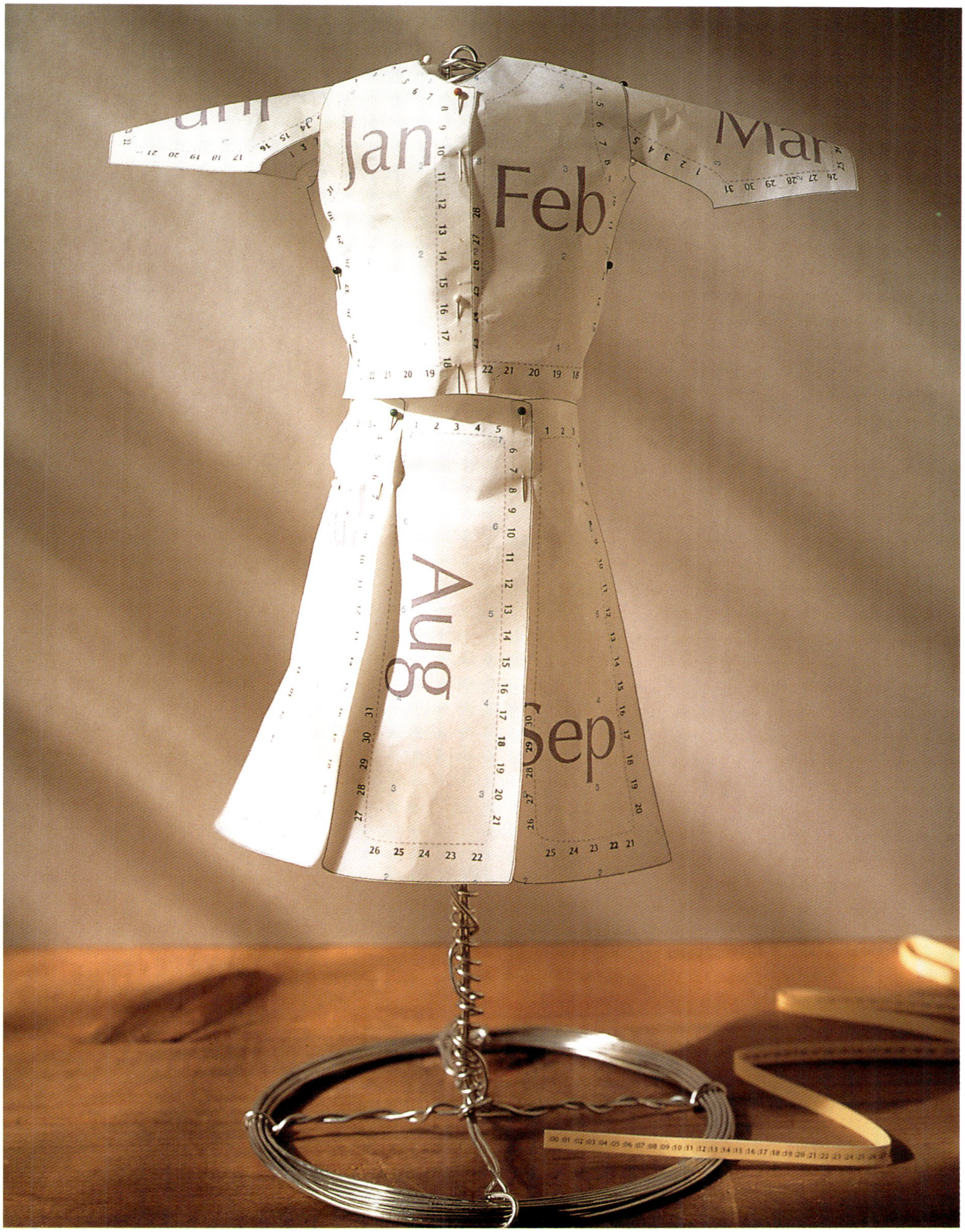

CATEGORY
Student

ADVERTISER/PRODUCT
Travel Guide Hamburg

SCHOOL
University of Applied Sciences/
Department of Design, Hamburg

ART DIRECTOR
Stan Skolnik

DESIGNER
Stan Skolnik

PHOTOGRAPHER
Stan Skolnik

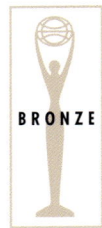

BRONZE

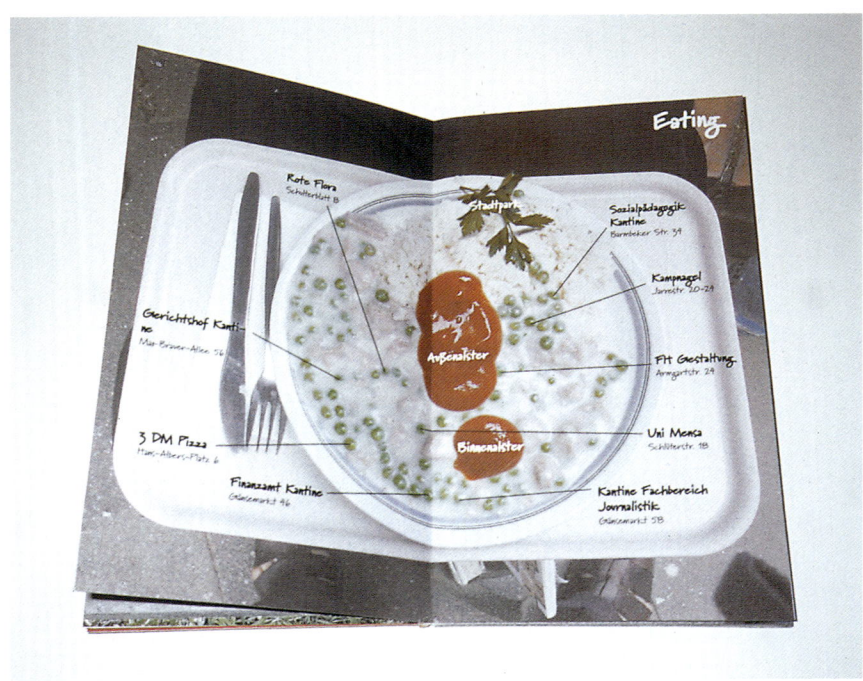

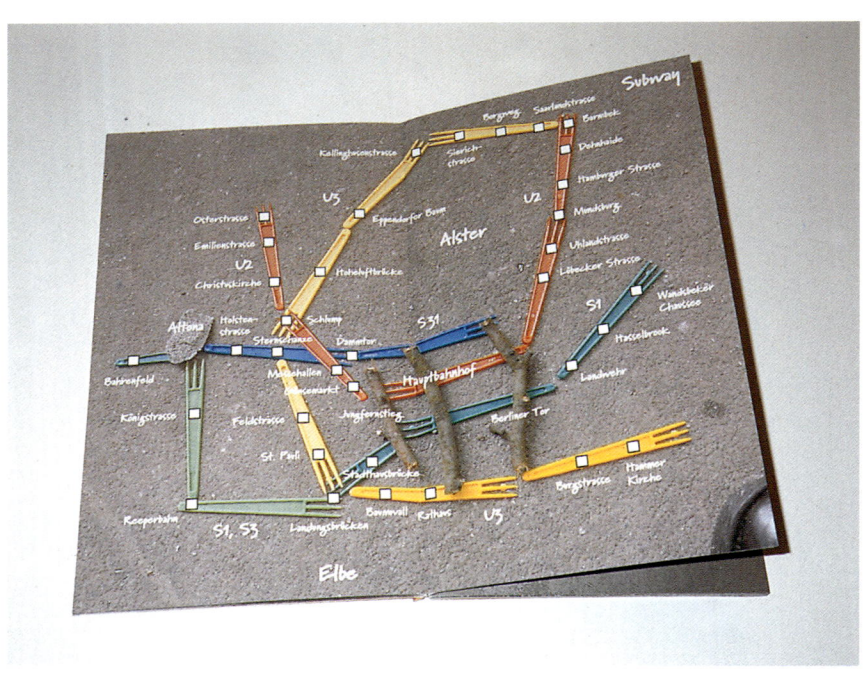